Shortlisted for the Samuel Johnson Prize for Non-Fiction; the Duff Cooper Prize; and the Marsh Biography Award

'It is a wonderful story, and Simon Sebag Montefiore tells it with joyful verve ... He has a firm grasp of the politics at the Russian court and of the diplomatic context, which is not easy, since the centre of gravity of this story shifts between St Petersburg, Vienna, Berlin and Istanbul. He is very good on the relationship between Potemkin and Catherine. His explanation of the day-to-day mechanics of the unusual ménage is light-handed, movingly told and psychologically credible'
Adam Zamoyski, *The Times*

'If you want a good racy historical read, *Catherine the Great and Potemkin* certainly provides it' Antonia Fraser, *Daily Mail*, Books of the Year

'*Catherine the Great and Potemkin* opened up a whole world ... to me'
Alain de Botton, *Sunday Telegraph*, Books of the Year

'This wonderful history book'
Jeremy Paxman, *Start the Week*, BBC Radio Four

'This well researched and highly ambitious biography has succeeded triumphantly ... Sebag Montefiore also provides a remarkably good panorama of the period' Antony Beevor, *Sunday Times*

'Exhaustive and beautifully written ... Montefiore vividly brings to life his supporting cast of envious conspirators, aristocratic mistresses, dandies, diplomats and adventurers' Christopher Hudson, *Daily Mail*

'With a dazzling mastery of detail, and enough literary flair to engage the non-specialist, Simon Sebag Montefiore brings out the highly unusual mixture of qualities required to succeed in Russia's debauched, ruthless court' *Economist*

'This book is a conspicuous achievement. The author's researches have been extensive and his command of his subject exemplary. His writing has the quality of a vivid soap-opera of the highest class, more than equal to his subject. He brings out Potemkin's personality perfectly ... Potemkin is depicted in this work as the giant he undoubtedly was, and the biog........ .... ed place in history

D1102638

'Splendidly written ... Clearly what fascinates Sebag Montefiore is [Potemkin] himself – his personality, his achievements, his lifelong relationship with his sovereign/lover – and that fascination shines through every page of this book. Although more than 500 pages long, it could easily have been double the length, so enjoyable is it to read. Obviously, it was enjoyable to write as well'

Anne Applebaum, *Sunday Telegraph*

'With great industry and huge enthusiasm [Montefiore] has combed the archives to give us a detailed account of a gigantic but, until now, almost forgotten figure. The writing is fluent, the sympathy obvious'

Nigel Jones, *Sunday Express*

'One of the greatest love stories of modern history . . . The contradictions in Potemkin's character are beautifully brought out in this magnificent biography' Petronella Wyatt, *Independent*

'With this lavish biography [Montefiore] has announced himself as a historian who deserves to be taken seriously'

Victor Sebestyen, *Evening Standard*

'This splendid biography, as sprawling, magnificent and exotic as its subject, provides for the first time in English a fully researched, accurate and immensely readable history of this extraordinary man'

Nikolai Tolstoy, *Literary Review*

'Magnificent . . . Montefiore's passionate and committed revisionism on behalf of his hero is just one of a host of excellent things about this book. Massively researched in Russian archives, it is a work of fine scholarship . . . This is a superb biography and it is hard to see how it can ever be superseded' Frank McLynn, *Financial Times*

'Exhilarating . . . In describing Potemkin's career, Sebag Montefiore succeeds admirably in capturing its scale and ambition'

Stella Tillyard, *Mail on Sunday*

'This gripping and richly researched biography . . . makes it easy to see why novelists are often seduced away from fiction to write biography – where, just sometimes, implausible reality exceeds plausible fantasy many times over' Peter Nasmyth, *Times Literary Supplement*

'A wonderful book . . . as magnificent as its subject. For two centuries, this roaring giant of a man has been either ignored or misrepresented. Now Simon Sebag Montefiore has written a book that captures the iridescent spirit of Russia's greatest adventurer'   Amanda Foreman

'An example of how to make a page-turner out of the most profound scholarship'   *New Statesman*

'Impeccably researched, beautifully written and handsomely presented, it takes us at an unslackening pace through the colourful life of one of the most legendary of all Russians, a war hero, consummate politician, visionary and lover of Catherine the Great'   Simon Heffer, *Daily Mail*

'This is a most Russian of loves, narrated with a blend of exuberance and knowledge appropriate to its restless and irresistible subject'
Hywel Williams, *The Oldie*

'This irresistible biography is history from above. To write this stupendous, engaging tour de force, the first biography of Potemkin in any language since 1891, Montefiore has devoted many hours in the archives of Moscow and Petersburg and covered thousands of miles of the former Russian empire'   Philip Mansel, *Spectator*

'Sebag Montefiore is effortlessly readable and compelling. This is history as it should be written'   Brian Morton, *Sunday Herald*

'This book . . . written with great verve . . . is based on a wealth of sources . . . Montefiore's narrative breathes new life into them. Montefiore makes the reader appreciate the genius and forgive the absurdity'
Professor Lindsey Hughes, *Rossica magazine*

Simon Sebag Montefiore is a prizewinning historian whose bestselling books have been published in over forty languages. *Catherine the Great and Potemkin* was shortlisted for the Samuel Johnson Prize; *Stalin: The Court of the Red Tsar* won the History Book of the Year Prize at the British Book Awards; *Young Stalin* won the Costa Biography Prize, *LA Times* Biography Prize and Le Grand Prix de Biographie; *Jerusalem: The Biography* was a number one bestseller. His latest book is *The Romanovs, 1613–1918*. Montefiore is the also author of the acclaimed novels *Sashenka* and *One Night in Winter*. He read history at Cambridge University where he received his PhD, and now lives in London with his wife, the novelist Santa Montefiore, and their two children.

www.simonsebagmontefiore.com
@simonmontefiore

By Simon Sebag Montefiore

Catherine the Great and Potemkin
Stalin: The Court of the Red Tsar
Young Stalin
Jerusalem: The Biography
The Romanovs

Fiction
Sashenka
One Night in Winter

CATHERINE THE GREAT & POTEMKIN

The Imperial Love Affair

SIMON SEBAG MONTEFIORE

WEIDENFELD & NICOLSON

To Santa

A W&N PAPERBACK

First published in Great Britain in 2000
by Weidenfeld & Nicolson
as *Prince of Princes: The Life of Potemkin*

This paperback edition published in 2001
by Phoenix Press
as *Potemkin: Prince of Princes*

Reissued 2007 and 2011
by Phoenix

Reissued in 2016 by Weidenfeld & Nicolson
an imprint of Orion Books Ltd,
Carmelite House, 50 Victoria Embankment,
London EC4Y 0DZ

An Hachette UK company

1 3 5 7 9 10 8 6 4 2

Copyright © Simon Sebag Montefiore 2000, 2016

A CIP catalogue record for this book
is available from the British Library.

ISBN 978 1 780 22834 1

Typeset by Input Data Services Ltd, Bridgwater, Somerset

Printed and bound in Great Britain by

The Orion Publishing Group's policy is to use papers that
are natural, renewable and recyclable products and
made from wood grown in sustainable forests. The logging
and manufacturing processes are expected to conform to
the environmental regulations of the country of origin.

www.orionbooks.co.uk

CONTENTS

ILLUSTRATIONS

Credits for the illustration sections.

Serenissimus Prince Grigory Potemkin, by Johann Baptist von Lampi (1751–1830), Hermitage, St Petersburg, photo by N. Y. Bolotina

Catherine the Great in 1762 by Vigilius Ericksen (1722–1782), Musée des Beaux-Arts, Chartres, France, Lauros-Giraudon/Bridgeman Art Library

Countess Alexandra Branicka by R. Brompton, Alupka Palace Museum, Ukraine, photo by the author

Portrait of Paul I, 1796–7 by Stepan Semeonovich Shukin (1762–1828), Hermitage, St Petersburg, Russia/Bridgeman Art Library

Potemkin's Palaces*

Portrait of Catherine II the Great in a Travelling Costume, 1787 (oil on canvas) by Mikhail Shibanov (fl. 1783–89), State Russian Museum, St Petersburg, Russia/Bridgeman Art Library

Portrait of Field Marshal Potemkin, 1787 by Alexander Roslin, courtesy of the West Wycombe Collection of Sir Edward Dashwood, photo by Sir Edward Dashwood

Potemkin's signature

Catherine the Great, 1793 by Johann Baptist von Lampi (1751–1830), Hermitage, St Petersburg, Russia/Bridgeman Art Library

Portrait of Prince Potemkin-Tavrichesky by Johann Baptist von Lampi (attrib.) (1751–1830), Suvorov Museum, St Petersburg

The roadside memorials marking Potemkin's death, photo by author

The board announcing Potemkin's death, photo by author

The trapdoor in St Catherine's church in Kherson, Ukraine, leading to Potemkin's tomb, photo by author

Potemkin's coffin, St Catherine's, Kherson, Ukraine, photo by author

The ruined church in Potemkin's home village of Chizhova, Russia, photo author's collection

Potemkin in Chevalier-Garde uniform, collection of V. S. Lopatin

*Potemkin's Palaces: Taurida, photo by author; Anichkov, author's collection; Ostrovky, author's collection; Bablovo, photo by author; Ekaterinoslav, photo by author; Nikolaev, Nikolaev State History Museum, photo by author; Kherson, Kherson State History Museum, photo by author

PREFACE TO THE NEW EDITION

For two centuries Catherine the Great and Potemkin were relegated to the lascivious and romantic, even shady, alleyways of history, mocked as power-mad, sex-mad or farcically inept. More recently, they have been rehabilitated as statesmen, and now again, in the twenty-first century, they find themselves at the centre of the crossroads where history meets current events.

Without cameras or eye-witnesses, it is impossible for historians to know what really happened behind the doors of bedrooms and cabinet rooms – unless the protagonists wrote frank letters. Catherine and Potemkin wrote thousands of such letters on love and power; we know how they spoke and thought, and the exceptional intensity of their passion. We know more about them than we do about many politicians today in the digital age. 'Can one love anybody else after having known you?' wrote Catherine. 'There's not a man in the world that equals you . . . Oh Monsieur Potemkin! What trick have you played to unbalance a mind that was once one of the best in Europe?' Their outrageously libertine lifestyle and exuberant political triumphs certainly titillated Western critics of Russian success and excess – 'This is Potemkin,' wrote Byron, 'a great thing in days when homicide and harlotry made great' – while the British newspapers propagated stories of Catherine's nymphomania and Potemkin's false villages. But those who really knew Catherine and Potemkin regarded them as utterly singular, brilliant, ambitious and complementary in their talents: 'no wonder they love each other,' wrote one, 'they're exactly the same.' Catherine was probably the greatest female leader of modern times. The Prince de Ligne thought Potemkin 'the most extraordinary man I ever met . . . Genius, genius and more genius.' Together, they saw themselves as patriotic statesmen serving Russia – crown, nation and state. They were supreme politicians and thoughtful visionaries who trusted and admired each other because they were also personal partners.

Yet they were the ultimate realists too. Potemkin defined the politician's art thus: 'to improve on events.' And they did more than that. Their mission was to expand the empire into the southern regions of Ukraine they dubbed 'New Russia'. They annexed swathes of this territory (1774, 1775 and 1791) and Crimea (1783), where they founded Russia's Black Sea navy and the new naval base Sebastopol. They built many new cities including Odessa, as well as advancing into the Caucasus, establishing a protectorate over Georgia (1783). Their aspirations reached into the Middle East, where Catherine backed local Arab strongmen in the Ottoman provinces in today's Syria–Lebanon and temporarily occupied Beirut in 1772–4. In the 1780s they planned invasions of Iran (then Persia) and, to support the Armenians, thrusts into present-day Turkey and Iraq, both part of the Ottoman empire. The colossal achievements of Catherine and Potemkin in the south are equivalent to those of Peter of Great in the north. They altered the balance of power in Europe, making Russia an empire with new Near Eastern and Mediterranean interests. Their colonization of New Russia and annexation of Crimea changed Russia's political centre of gravity and her vision of herself as an imperial power. It is a perspective that survived the fall of the Romanov dynasty.

After the mayhem of 1917 and the civil war, Lenin and Stalin shrewdly managed to keep together most of the Romanovs' empire (losing only Poland, Finland and the Baltics) by creating the façade of a voluntary Soviet Union of fifteen republics. Stalin had little time for Catherine and Potemkin's louche extravagance, preferring severe, macho role models such as Peter the Great, but he admired them as politicians: 'the genius of Catherine,' he said, 'lay in her choice of Prince Potemkin . . . to govern the state.' However, when the USSR collapsed in 1991, Russia lost all the republics, including the most important, Ukraine.

When this book was first published in 2000, just as that dynamic and ruthless ex-KGB officer Vladimir Putin was elected president, I was surprised to find the apparatchiks of his new regime were keen to read and discuss it – even to the extent of organizing surreal secret meetings with this English historian to talk about statesmen dead for two hundred years. Putin and his henchmen regarded the fall of the USSR and loss of empire as one of the greatest catastrophes of the twentieth century; the Kremlin looked to Catherine and Potemkin as unlikely heroes, regarding their achievements in the Caucasus, Crimea and Ukraine as talismanic and essential to Russia's status as a Great Power.

Catherine and Potemkin had long been neglected by Soviet history as too decadent, aristocratic and feminine. When I started to research this book in Russian archives in the mid-1990s, some of their papers had not even been studied since the reign of Nicholas II. Now they are once again in fashion, inspirations to a new regime that combines imperial nostalgia with nationalistic ambition: the early twenty-first-century Kremlin has fused the gilded majesty of the Romanov empire with the grim glory of a Stalinist superpower in a peculiar modern hybrid.

The new leaders, often trained in the elite KGB, have no interest in Catherine and Potemkin's culture, enlightenment and humanity, which have little in common with their intolerant authoritarianism. But they *are* interested in their autocratic and imperial legacy, particularly in the south. The eighteenth-century couple and the new masters of the Kremlin share a belief in the prestige and discipline of the state; the essential facility of autocracy to govern unruly Russia; a vision of the exceptionalist mission of Russian civilization in the world; and the idea that Russia cannot be a Great Power without Ukraine and Crimea. Pushkin understood what Potemkin had achieved for Catherine and Russia: 'The glory of a name dear to his empress and his motherland . . . touched by the hand of history, he won us the Black Sea.' Potemkin's conquests, new cities and fleet are part of what makes this imperial couple important two hundred years after their deaths.

In 2008, President Putin went to war against Georgia to reassert Russian hegemony there. In February 2014, he challenged American and European Union advances into independent Ukraine using unmarked Russian military units, the mysterious 'green men', to occupy and successfully annex Crimea – Russia's first territorial recovery since the disastrous disintegration of the Soviet Union. Crimea had been part of the Russian Federation in Soviet times until Stalin, just before his death, decided to award it to Ukraine on an imperial whim: his successors transferred it in 1954. But it retained its military, imperial and mystical significance to Russia.

This lush peninsula had been the place where Vladimir the Great, Grand Prince of Kiev converted to Christianity in 988, an event cited by Potemkin in his letter to Catherine urging the immediate annexation of Crimea in 1783. In 2014, Putin declared, 'Crimea is as sacred to Russia as Jerusalem's Temple Mount is to Judaism and Islam.' After this success, Moscow launched a secret war to undermine independent Ukraine and detach the eastern part of the country: 'New Russia' was widely used to describe it, echoing Catherine and Potemkin. This opportunistic war – costing thousands of innocent lives, fought secretly by unmarked Russian army units and publicly by nationalistic freebooters – was probably launched to confirm and stimulate the archaic if popular conviction that a Russia that dominates Ukraine is still a great Russia.

In 2015, Russia reasserted its traditional interest in the Middle East, backing a long-time client regime in Syria with military force, a policy that echoed the path first tentatively followed by Catherine in Ottoman Syria, though pursued more powerfully by Tsar Nicholas I and then the Soviets during the Cold War. But in a one-man regime, these were the policies of President Putin, and their success and ultimate outcome all depend on his survival and the nature of his successors.

Catherine and Potemkin remain perhaps the most enlightened and humane rulers Russia has ever enjoyed – though the bar is not set particularly high. Brilliant and imaginative, tolerant and magnanimous, passionate and eccentric, extravagant and epicurean, industrious and ambitious, they were very different characters from today's rulers, the grim children of the Soviet Union. Yet, strangely, in the twenty-first century, they are more relevant than ever.

Simon Sebag Montefiore
September 2015

ACKNOWLEDGEMENTS

Over several years and thousands of miles, I have been helped by many people, from the peasant couple who keep bees on the site of Potemkin's birthplace near Smolensk to professors, archivists and curators from Petersburg, Moscow and Paris to Warsaw, Odessa and Iasi in Rumania.

I owe my greatest debts to three remarkable scholars. The inspiration for this book came from Isabel de Madariaga, Professor Emeritus of Slavonic Studies at the University of London and the doyen of Catherinian history in theWest. Her seminal work *Russia in the Age of Catherine the Great* changed the study of Catherine. She also appreciated the remarkable character of Potemkin and his relationship with the Empress, and declared that he needed a biographer. She has helped with ideas, suggestions and advice throughout the project. Above all, I must thank her for editing and correcting this book during sessions which she conducted with the amused authority and intellectual rigour of the Empress herself, whom she resembles in many ways. It was always I who was exhausted at the end of these sessions, not she. I lay any wisdom in this work at her feet; the follies are mine alone. I am glad that I was able to lay a wreath on her behalf on Potemkin's neglected grave in Kherson.

I must also thank Alexander B. Kamenskii, Professor of Early & Early-Modern Russian History at Moscow's Russian State University for the Humanities, and respected authority on Catherine, without whose wisdom, charm and practical help, this could not have been written. I am deeply grateful to V. S. Lopatin, whose knowledge of the archives is without parallel and who was so generous with that knowledge: Lopatin and his wife Natasha have been so hospitable during Muscovite stays. He too has read the book and given me the benefit of his comments.

I must also thank Professor J. T. Alexander for answering my questions and Professor Evgeny Anisimov, who was so helpful during my time in Petersburg. The advice of George F. Jewsbury on Potemkin's military performance was most enlightening. Thanks to Professor Derek Beales, who helped greatly with Josephist matters, especially the mystery of the Circassian slavegirls. I should mention that he and Professor Tim Blanning, both of Sidney Sussex, Cambridge, were the supervisors whose compelling teaching of Enlightened Despotism, while I was an under-graduate, laid the foundations for this book. I want to stress my debt too to three recent works that I have used widely – Lopatin's *Ekaterina i Potemkin Lichnaya Perepiska*, the aforementioned book by Isabel de Madariaga, and J. T. Alexander's *Catherine the Great*.

I would like the thank the following without whom this could not have been written: His Royal Highness the Prince of Wales, for his kind help in connection with his work for the restoration of St Petersburg and the Pushkin Bicentenary. Sergei Degtiarev-Foster, that champion of Russian history who made many things possible from Moscow to Odessa, and Ion Florescu who made the Rumanian-Moldovian expedition such a success. Thanks also to Lord Rothschild, Professor Mikhail Piotrovsky and Geraldine Norman, chairman, president and director of Hermitage Development Trust, who are creating the permanent exhibition of Catherine the Great's treasures, including the famous Lampi portrait of Potemkin, at Somerset House in London.

I owe a debt to Lord Brabourne for reading the entire book and, for reading parts of it, to Dr Amanda Foreman, Flora Fraser, and especially to Andrew Roberts for his detailed advice and encouragement. William Hanham read the sections on art, Professor John Klier read the Jewish sections, and Adam Zamoyski read those on Poland.

In Moscow, I thank the Directors and staff of the RGADA and RGVIA archives; Natasha Bolotina, with her special knowledge on Potemkin, her mother Svetlana Romanovna, Igor Fedyukin, Dmitri Feldman, and Julia Tourchaninova and Ernst Goussinski, Professors of Education, all helped immensely. Galina Moiseenko, one of the brightest scholars of the History Department of the Russian State Humanities University, was excellent at selecting and finding documents and her historical analysis and precision were flawless.

Thanks to the following. In St Petersburg, I thank my friend Professor Zoia Belyakova, who made everything possible, and Dr Sergei Kuznetzov, Head of Historical Research of the Stroganov Palace Department of the State Russian Museum, and the staff of the RGIA. I am grateful to Professor Mikhail Piotrovsky, Director of the State Hermitage Museum (again), to Vladimir Gesev, Director of the Russian State Museum of the Mikhailovsky Palace; Liudmilla Kurenkova, Assistant to the Director of the Russian State Museum, A. N. Gusanov of the Pavlovsk Palace State Museum; Dr Elena V. Karpova, Head of the XVIII–early XXth Century Sculpture Department of the State Russian Museum, Maria P. Garnova of the Hermitage's Western Europe Department, and G. Komelova, also of the Hermitage. Ina Lokotnikova showed me the Anichkov Palace and L. I. Diyachenko was kind enough to give me a private tour, using her exhaustive knowledge, of the Taurida Palace. Thanks to Leonid Bogdanov for taking the cover-photograph of Potemkin.

In Smolensk: Anastasia Tikhonova, Researcher for the Smolensk Historical Museum, Elena Samolubova, and Vladimir Golitchev, Deputy Head of the Smolensk Regional Department of Education, responsible for Science. In Chizhova, the schoolteacher and expert on local folklore, Victor Zheludov and fellow staff at the school in Petrishchevo, the village nearest to Chizhova, with thanks for the Potemkin feast they kindly laid on.

For the south Ukrainian journey, I thank Vitaly Sergeychik of the UKMAR shipping company and Misha Sherokov. In Odessa: Natalia Kotova, Professor Semyon J. Apartov, Professor of International Studies, Odessa State University. At the Odessa Regional Museum of History – Leonila A. Leschinskaya, Director, Vera V. Solodova, Vice-Director, and, especially, to the knowledgeable, charming master of the archives themselves, Adolf Nikolaevich Malikh, chief of the Felikieteriya section, who helped me so much. The Director of the Odessa Museum of Merchant Fleet of the Ukraine, Peter P. Klishevsky and the photographer there, Sergei D. Bereninich. In Ochakov: the Mayor, Yury M. Ishenko. In Kherson: Father Anatoly of St Catherine's Church. At Dniepropetrovsk: Olga Pitsik, and the staffs of the museums in Nikolaev and Simpferopol; Anastas Victorevich of the Sabastopol Naval Museum. But above all, at the Alupka Palace, Anna Abramovna Galitchenko, author of *Alupka A Palace inside a Park*, proved a font of knowledge.

In Rumania, thanks to Professor Razvan Magureanu, Professor of Electrical Engineering at the Polytechnic University of Bucharest, and Ioan Vorobet who drove us to Iasi, guarded us and made it possible to enter Moldova. In Iasi: Professor Fanica Ungureanu, authority on the Golia Monastery, and Alexander Ungureanu, Professor of Geography at Iasi University, without whose help I would never have found the site of Potemkin's death. In Warsaw, Poland: Peter Martyn and Arkadiusz Bautz-Bentkowski and the AGAD staff. In Paris: the staff of AAE in the Quai d'Orsay. Karen Blank researched and translated German texts. Imanol Galfarsoro translated the Miranda diary from Spanish. In Telavi, Georgia: Levan Gachechiladze, who introduced me to Lida Potemkina.

In Britain, I have many to thank for things great and small: my agent Georgina Capel, the Chairman of Orion, Anthony Cheetham, the Publisher of Weidenfeld & Nicolson, Ion Trewin, and Lord and Lady

Weidenfeld. Thanks to John Gilkes for creating the maps. Great thanks are owed to Peter James, my legendary editor, for applying his wisdom to this book. The staff of the British Library, British Museum, the Public Records Office, the London Library, the Library of the School of Eastern European and Slavonic Studies, the Cornwall and Winchester Records Offices and the Antony Estate. I thank my father, Dr Stephen Sebag Montefiore MD, for his diagnosis of Potemkin's illnesses and singular psychology, and my mother, April Sebag Montefiore, for her insights into Potemkin's personal relationships. I have a special thank you for Galina Oleksiuk, my Russian teacher, without whose lessons this book could not have been written. I would also like to thank the following for their help or kind answers to my questions: Neal Ascherson, Vadim Benyatov, James Blount, Alain de Botton, Dr John Casey, the Honourable L. H. L. (Tim) Cohen, Professor Anthony Cross, Sir Edward Dashwood, Ingelborga Dapkunaite, Baron Robert Dimsdale, Professor Christopher Duffy, Lisa Fine, Princess Katya Golitsyn, Prince Emmanuel Golitsyn, David Henshaw, Professor Lindsey Hughes, Tania Illingworth, Anna Joukovskaya, Paul and Safinaz Jones, Dmitri Khankin, Professor Roderick E. McGrew, Giles MacDonogh, Noel Malcolm, the Earl of Malmesbury, Neil McKendrick the Master of Gonville & Caius College, Cambridge, Dr Philip Mansel, Sergei Alexandrovich Medvedev, Charles and Patty Palmer-Tomkinson, Dr Monro Price, Anna Reid, Kenneth Rose, the Honourable Olga Polizzi, Hywel Williams, Andre Zaluski. The credit for their gems of knowledge belongs to them; the blame for any mistakes rests entirely on me.

Last but not least, I must thank my wife, Santa, for enduring our ménage-à-trois with Prince Potemkin for so long.

NOTES

Dates are given in the Old Style Julian Calendar used in Russia which was eleven days earlier than the New Style Gregorian used in the West. In some cases both dates are given.

Money: 1 rouble contained 100 kopecks. Approximately 4 roubles = £1 Sterling = 24 French Livres in the 1780s. At that time, an English gentleman could live on £300 a year, a Russian officer on 1,000 roubles.

Distances and measurements: 1 verst equalled 0.663 miles or 1.06 km. 1 desyatina equalled 2.7 acres.

Names and proper names: I have used the most recognizable form of most names, which means that absolute consistency is impossible in this area – so I apologize in advance to those offended by my decisions. The subject of this book is 'Potemkin', even though in Russian the pronunciation is closer to 'Patiomkin'. I have used the Russian form of names except in cases where the name is already well known in its English form; for example, the Tsarevich Pavel Petrovich is usually called Grand Duke Paul; Semyon Romanovich Vorontsov is Simon Vorontsov; the Empress is Catherine, not Ekaterina. I usually spell Peter and other first names in the English form, instead of Piotr and so on. I have used the Russian feminized form of names such as Dashkova instead of Dashkov. In Polish names, such as Branicki, I have left the name in its more polonized form, pronounced 'Branitsky'. Thus, in the feminine, I have used the Russian for Skavronskaya but the Polish for Branicka. Once someone is known by a suffix or title, I try to use it, so that A. G. Orlov is Orlov-Chesmensky once he had received this surname.

DEATH ON THE STEPPES

'Prince of Princes'
Jeremy Bentham on Prince Potemkin

Whose bed – the earth: whose roof – the azure
Whose halls the wilderness round?
Are you not fame and pleasure's offspring
Oh splendid prince of Crimea?
Have you not from the heights of honors
Been suddenly midst empty steppes downed?
Gavrili Derzhavin, *The Waterfall*

Shortly before noon on 5 October 1791, the slow cavalcade of carriages, attended by liveried footmen and a squadron of Cossacks in the uniform of the Black Sea Host, stopped halfway down a dirt track on a desolate hillside in the midst of the Bessarabian steppe. It was a strange place for the procession of a great man to rest: there was no tavern in sight, not even a peasant's hovel. The big sleeping carriage, pulled by eight horses, halted first. The others – there were probably four in all – slowed down and stopped alongside the first on the grass as the footmen and cavalry escort ran to see what was happening. The passengers threw open their carriage doors. When they heard the despair in their master's voice, they hurried towards his carriage.

'That's enough!' said Prince Potemkin. 'That's enough! There is no point in going on now.' Inside the sleeping carriage, there were three harassed doctors and a slim countess with high cheekbones and auburn hair, all crowded round the Prince. He was sweating and groaning. The doctors summoned the Cossacks to move their massive patient. 'Take me out of the carriage ...' Potemkin ordered. Everyone jumped when he commanded, and he had commanded virtually everything in Russia for a long time. Cossacks and generals gathered round the open door and slowly, gently began to bear out the stricken giant.

The Countess accompanied him out of the carriage, holding his hand, dabbing his hot brow as tears streamed down her face with its small retroussé nose and full mouth. A couple of Moldavian peasants who tended cattle on the nearby steppe ambled over to watch. His bare feet came first, then his legs and his half-open dressing gown – though this vision in itself was not unusual. Potemkin notoriously greeted empresses and ambassadors in bare feet and open dressing gowns. But now it was different. He still had the leonine Slavic handsomeness, the thick head of hair, once regarded as the finest in the Empire, and the sensual Grecian profile that had won him the nickname 'Alcibiades" as a young man. However, his hair was now flecked with grey and hung over his feverish forehead. He was still gigantic in stature and breadth. Everything about him was exaggerated, colossal and original, but his life of reckless indulgence and relentless ambition had bloated his body and aged his face. Like a Cyclops he had only one eye; the other was blind and damaged, giving him the appearance of a pirate. His chest was broad and hairy. Always a force of nature, he now resembled nothing so much as a magnificent animal reduced to this twitching, shivering pile of flesh.

The apparition on this wild steppe was His Most Serene Highness Prince of the Holy Roman Empire, Grigory Alexandrovich Potemkin, probably husband of the Empress of Russia, Catherine the Great, and certainly the love of her life, the best friend of the woman, the co-ruler of her Empire and the partner in her dreams. He was Prince of Taurida, Field-Marshal, Commander-in-Chief of the Russian Army, Grand Hetman of the Black Sea and Ekaterinoslav Cossacks, Grand Admiral of the Black Sea and Caspian Fleets, President of the College of War, viceroy of the south, and possibly the next King of Poland, or of some other principality of his own making.

The Prince, or Serenissimus, as he was known across the Russian Empire, had ruled with Catherine II for nearly two decades. They had known each other for thirty years and had shared each other's lives for almost twenty. Beyond that, the Prince defied, and still defies, all categorization. Catherine noticed him as a witty young man and summoned him to be her lover at a time of crisis. When their affair ended, he remained her friend, partner and minister and became her co-Tsar. She always feared, respected and loved him – but their relationship was stormy. She called him her 'Colossus', and her 'tiger', her 'idol', 'hero', the 'greatest eccentric'.[2] This was the 'genius'[3] who hugely increased her Empire, created Russia's Black Sea Fleet, conquered the Crimea, won the Second Turkish War and founded famed cities such as Sebastopol and Odessa. Russia had not possessed an imperial statesman of such success in both dreams and deeds since Peter the Great.

Serenissimus made his own policies – sometimes inspired, sometimes quixotic – and constructed his own world. While his power depended on his partnership with Catherine, he thought and behaved like one of the sovereign powers of Europe. Potemkin dazzled its Cabinets and

Courts with his titanic achievements, erudite knowledge and exquisite taste, while simultaneously scandalizing them with his arrogance and debauchery, indolence and luxury. While hating him for his power and inconsistency, even his enemies acclaimed his intelligence and creativity.

Now this barefoot Prince half staggered – and was half carried by his Cossacks – across the grass. This was a remote and spectacular spot, not even on the main road between Jassy, in today's Rumania, and Kishnev, in today's Republic of Moldova. In those days, this was the territory of the Ottoman Sultan, conquered by Potemkin. Even today it is hard to find, but in 200 years it has hardly changed.[4] The spot where they laid Potemkin was a little plateau beside a steep stone lane whence one could see far in every direction. The countryside to the right was a rolling green valley rising in a multitude of green, bushy mounds into the distance, covered in the now almost vanished high grass of the steppes. To the left, forested hills fell away into the mist. Straight ahead, Potemkin's entourage would have seen the lane go down and then rise up a higher hill covered in dark trees and thick bushes, disappearing down the valley. Potemkin, who loved to drive his carriage at night through the rain,[5] had called a stop in a place of the wildest and most beautiful natural drama.[6]

His entourage could only have added to it. The confection of the exotic and the civilized in Potemkin's companions that day reflected his contradictions: 'Prince Potemkin is the emblem of the immense Russian Empire,' wrote the Prince de Ligne, who knew him well, 'he too is composed of deserts and gold-mines.'[7] His Court – for he was almost royal, though Catherine teasingly called it his 'basse-cour', halfway between a royal court and a farmyard[8] – emerged on to the steppe.

Many of his attendants were already weeping. The Countess, the only woman present, wore the long-sleeved flowing Russian robes favoured by her friend the Empress, but her stockings and shoes were the finest of French fashion, ordered from Paris by Serenissimus himself. Her travelling jewellery was made up of priceless diamonds from Potemkin's unrivalled collection. Then there were generals and counts in tailcoats and uniforms with sashes and medals and tricorn hats that would not have been remarkable at Horse-Guards in London or any eighteenth-century court, but there was also a sprinkling of Cossack atamans, Oriental princelings, Moldavian boyars, renegade Ottoman pashas, servants, clerks, common soldiers – and the bishops, rabbis, fakirs and mullahs whose company Potemkin most enjoyed. Nothing relaxed him as much as a discussion on Byzantine theology, the customs of some

Eastern tribe such as the Bashkirs, or Palladian architecture, Dutch painting, Italian music, English Gardens...

The bishops sported the flowing robes of Orthodoxy, the rabbis the tangled ringlets of Judaism, the Ottoman renegades the turbans, pantaloons and slippers of the Sublime Porte. The Moldavians, Orthodox subjects of the Ottoman Sultan, wore bejewelled kaftans and high hats encircled with fur and encrusted with rubies, the ordinary Russian soldiers the 'Potemkin' hats, coats, soft boots and buckskin trousers designed for their ease by the Prince himself. Lastly the Cossacks, most of them Boat Cossacks known as Zaporogians, had fierce moustaches and shaven heads except for a tuft on top leading down the back in a long ponytail, like characters from *Last of the Mohicans*, and brandished short curved daggers, engraved pistols and their special long lances. They watched sadly, for Potemkin adored the Cossacks.

The woman was Potemkin's shrewd and haughty niece, Countess Alexandra Branicka, aged thirty-seven and a formidable political force in her own right. Potemkin's love affairs with the Empress and a brazen parade of noblewomen and courtesans had shocked even French courtiers who remembered Louis XV's Versailles. Had he really made all five of his legendarily beautiful nieces into his mistresses? Did he love Countess Branicka the most of all?

The Countess ordered them to place a rich Persian rug on the grass. Then she let them lower Prince Potemkin gently on to it. 'I want to die in the field,' he said as they settled him there. He had spent the previous fifteen years travelling as fast across Russia's vastness as any man in the eighteenth century: 'a trail of sparks marks his swift journey', wrote the poet Gavrili Derzhavin in his ode to Potemkin, *The Waterfall*. So, appropriately for a man of perpetual movement, who barely lived in his innumerable palaces, Serenissimus added that he did not want to die in a carriage.[9] He wanted to sleep out on the steppe.

That morning, Potemkin asked his beloved Cossacks to build him a makeshift tent of their lances, covered with blankets and furs. It was a characteristically Potemkinian idea, as if the purity of a little Cossack camp would cure him of all his suffering.

The anxious doctors, a Frenchman and two Russians, gathered round the prone Prince and the attentive Countess, but there was little they could do. Catherine and Potemkin thought doctors made better players at the card table than healers at the bedside. The Empress joked that her Scottish doctor finished off most of his patients with his habitual panacea for every ailment – a weakening barrage of emetics and bleedings. The doctors were afraid that they would be blamed if the Prince perished, because accusations of poisoning were frequently whispered at the Russian Court. Yet the eccentric Potemkin had been a thoroughly unco-operative patient, opening all the windows, having eau-de-Cologne poured on his head, consuming whole salted geese from Hamburg with gallons of wine – and now setting off on this tormented journey across the steppes.

The Prince was dressed in a rich silk dressing gown, lined with fur, sent to him days earlier by the Empress all the way from distant St Petersburg, almost two thousand versts. Its inside pockets bulged with bundles of the Empress's secret letters in which she consulted her partner, gossiped with her friend and decided the policies of her Empire. She destroyed most of his letters, but we are grateful that he romantically kept many of hers in that sentimental pocket next to his heart.

Twenty years of these letters reveal an equal and amazingly successful partnership of two statesmen and lovers that was startling in its mod-ernity, touching in its ordinary intimacy and impressive in its statecraft. Their love affair and political alliance was unequalled in history by Antony and Cleopatra, Louis XVI and Marie-Antoinette, Napoleon and Josephine, because it was as remarkable for its achievements as for its romance, as endearing for its humanity as for its power. Like everything to do with Potemkin, his life with Catherine was crisscrossed with mys-teries: were they secretly married? Did they conceive a child together? Did they really share power? Is it true that they agreed to remain partners while indulging themselves with a string of other lovers? Did Potemkin pimp for the Empress, procuring her young favourites, and did she help him seduce his nieces and turn the Imperial Palace into his own family harem?

As his illness ebbed and flowed, his travels were pursued by Catherine's caring, wifely notes, as she sent dressing gowns and fur coats for him to wear, scolded him for eating too much or not taking his medicines, begged him to rest and recover, and prayed to God not to take her beloved. He wept as he read them.

At this very moment, the Empress's couriers were galloping in two directions across Russia, changing their exhausted horses at imperial posthouses. They came from St Petersburg, bearing Catherine's latest letter to the Prince, and from here in Moldavia they bore his latest to her. It had been so for a long time – and they were always longing to receive the freshest news of the other. But now the letters were sadder.

'My dear friend, Prince Grigory Alexandrovich,' she wrote on 3 October, 'I received your letters of the 25th and 27th today a few hours ago and I confess that I am extremely worried by them ... I pray God that He gives health back to you soon.' She was not worried when she wrote this, because it usually took ten days for letters to reach the capital from the south, though it could be done in seven, hell for leather.[10] Ten days before, Potemkin appeared to have recovered – hence Catherine's calmness. But a few days earlier on 30 September, before his health seemed to improve, her letters were almost frantic. 'My worry about your sickness knows no bounds,' she had written. 'For Christ's sake, if necessary, take whatever the doctors think might ease your condition. I beg God to give you your energy and health back as soon as possible. Goodbye my friend ... I'm sending you a fur coat ...'[11] This was just sound and fury – for, while the coat was sent on earlier, neither of the letters reached him in time.

Somewhere in the 2,000 versts that separated the two of them, the couriers must have crossed paths. Catherine would not have been so optimistic if she had read Potemkin's letter, written on 4 October, the day before, as he set out. 'Matushka [Little Mother] Most Merciful Lady,' he dictated to his secretary, 'I have no energy left to suffer my torments. The only escape is to leave this town and I have ordered them to carry me to Nikolaev. I do not know what will become of me. Most faithful and grateful subject.' This was written in the secretary's hand but pathetically, at the bottom of the letter, Potemkin scrawled in a weak, angular and jumping hand: 'The only escape is to leave.'[12] It was unsigned.

The last batch of Catherine's letters to reach him had arrived the day before in the pouch of Potemkin's fastest courier, Brigadier Bauer, the devoted adjutant whom he often sent galloping to Paris to bring back silk stockings, to Astrakhan for sterlet soup, to Petersburg for oysters, to Moscow to bring back a dancer or a chessplayer, to Milan for a sheet of music, a virtuoso violinist or a wagon of perfumes. So often and so far had Bauer travelled on Potemkin's whim that he jokingly requested this for his epitaph: 'Cy git Bauer sous ce rocher, Fouette, cocher!'[13]*

As they gathered round him on the steppe, the officials and courtiers would have reflected on the implications of this scene for Europe, for their Empress, for the unfinished war with the Turks, for the possibilities of action against revolutionary France and defiant Poland. Potemkin's armies and fleets had conquered huge tracts of Ottoman territory around the Black Sea and in today's Rumania: now the Sultan's Grand Vizier hoped to negotiate a peace with him. The Courts of Europe – from the port-sodden young First Lord of the Treasury, William Pitt, in London,

---

* 'Here lies Bauer under this stone, Coachman, drive on!'

who had failed to halt Potemkin's war, to the hypochondriacal old Chancellor, Prince Wenzel von Kaunitz, in Vienna – carefully followed Potemkin's illness.

His schemes could change the map of the Continent. Potemkin juggled crowns like a clown in a circus. Would this mercurial visionary make himself a king? Or was he more powerful as he was – consort of the Empress of all the Russias? If he was crowned, would it be as king of Dàcia, in modern Rumania, or King of Poland, where his sprawling estates already made him a feudal magnate? Would he save Poland, or partition it? Even as he lay on the steppe, Polish potentates were gathering secretly to await his mysterious orders.

These questions would be answered by the outcome of this desperate rush from the fever-stricken city of Jassy to the new town of Nikolaev, inland from the Black Sea, to which the sick man wished to be borne. Nikolaev was his last city. He had founded many, like the hero whose achievements he had emulated, Peter the Great. Potemkin designed each city, treating it lovingly like a cherished mistress or a treasured work of art. Nikolaev (now in Ukraine) was a naval and military base, on the cool banks of the Bug, where he had built himself a Moldavian–Turkish-style palace, low by the river, cooled by a steady breeze that would ease his fever.[14] This was a long journey for a dying man.

The convoy had left the day before. The party spent the night in a village *en route* and set off at 8 a.m. After five versts, Potemkin was so uncomfortable that they transferred him to the sleeping carriage. He still managed to sit up.[15] After five more versts, they had stopped right here.[16]

The Countess cradled his head: at least she was there, for the two best friends in his life were women. One was this favourite niece; the other, of course, was the Empress herself, fretting a thousand miles away, waiting for news. On the steppe, Potemkin was shaking, sweating and moaning, undergoing agonizing convulsions. 'I am burning,' he said. 'I'm on fire!' Countess Branicka, known as 'Sashenka' to Catherine and Potemkin, urged him to be calm, but 'he answered that the light grew dark in his eyes, he could not see any more and was able only to understand voices.' The blindness was a symptom of falling blood pressure, common in the dying. Ravaged by malarial fever, probable liver failure and pneumonia, after years of compulsive overwork, frantic travel, nervous tension and unbridled hedonism, his powerful metabolism was finally collapsing. The Prince asked the doctors: 'What can you cure me with now?' Dr Sanovsky answered that 'he had to put his hopes only in

God'. He handed a travelling icon to Potemkin, who embraced both the mischievous scepticism of the French Enlightenment and the superstitious piety of the Russian peasantry. Potemkin was strong enough to take it. He kissed it.

An old Cossack, watching nearby, noticed that the Prince was slipping away and said so respectfully, with the sensitivity to death found among frontiersmen who live close to nature. Potemkin removed his hands from the icon. Branicka held them in hers. Then she embraced him.[17] At the supreme moment, he naturally thought of his beloved Catherine and murmured: 'Forgive me, merciful Mother–Sovereign'.[18] Then Potemkin died.[19] He was fifty-two.

The circle froze around the body in that shocked silence that must always mark the passing of a great man. Countess Sashenka gently placed his head on a pillow, then raised her hands to her face and fell back in a dead faint. Some wept loudly; some knelt to pray, raising their hands to the heavens; some hugged and consoled each other; the doctors stared at the patient they had failed to save; others just peered at his face with its single open eye. To the left and right, groups of Moldavian boyars or merchants sat watching while a Cossack tried to control a rearing horse, which perhaps sensed how 'the earthly globe was shaken' by this 'untimely, sudden passing!'.[20] The soldiers and Cossacks, veterans of Potemkin's wars, were sobbing, one and all. They had not even had time to finish building their master's tent.

So died one of Europe's most famous statesmen. Contemporaries, while admitting his contrasts and eccentricities, rated him highly. All visitors to Russia had wished to meet this force of nature. He was always – by pure power of personality – the centre of attention: 'When absent, he alone was the subject of conversation; when present he engaged every eye'.[21] When they did meet him, no one was disappointed. Jeremy Bentham, the English philosopher who stayed on his estates, called him 'Prince of Princes'.[22]

The Prince de Ligne, who knew all the titans of his time, from Frederick the Great to Napoleon, best described Potemkin as 'the most extraordinary man I ever met . . . dull in the midst of pleasure; unhappy for being too lucky; surfeited with everything, easily disgusted, morose, inconstant, a profound philosopher, an able minister, a sublime politician or like a child of ten years old . . . What is the secret of his magic? Genius, genius and still more genius; natural abilities, an excellent memory, much elevation of soul; malice without the design of injuring, artifice without craft . . . the art of conquering every heart in his good moments, much generosity . . . refined taste – and a consummate knowledge of mankind.'[23] The Comte de Ségur, who knew Napoleon and George Washington, said that 'of all the personalities, the one that struck me the most, and which was the most important for me to know well, was the famous Prince Potemkin. His entire personality was the most original because of an inconceivable mixture of grandeur and pettiness, laziness and activity, ambition and insouciance. Such a man would have been remarkable by his originality anywhere.' Lewis Littlepage, an American visitor, wrote that the 'astonishing' Serenissimus was more powerful in Russia than Cardinal Wolsey, Count-Duke of Olivares and Cardinal Richelieu had ever been in their native kingdoms.[24]

Alexander Pushkin, who was born eight years after this death on the Bessarabian steppe, was fascinated by Potemkin, interviewed his ageing nieces about him and recorded their stories: the Prince, he often said, 'was touched by the hand of history'. In their flamboyance and quint-essential Russianness, the two complemented each other.[25] Twenty years later, Lord Byron was still writing about the man he called 'the spoiled child of the night.'[26]

Russian tradition dictated that the dead man's eyes must be closed and coins placed on them. The orbs of the great should be sealed with gold pieces. Potemkin was 'richer than some kings' but, like many of the very rich, he never carried any money. None of the magnates in his entourage had any either. There must have been an awkward moment of searching pockets, tapping jackets, summoning valets: nothing. So someone called over to the soldiers.

The grizzled Cossack who had observed Potemkin's death throes produced a five-kopeck piece. So the Prince had his eye closed with a humble copper coin. The incongruity of the death passed immediately into legend. Perhaps it was the same old Cossack who now stepped back and muttered: 'Lived on gold; died on grass.'

This *bon mot* entered the mythology of princesses and common soldiers: a few years later, the painter Elisabeth Vigée Lebrun asked a gnarled princess in St Petersburg about Potemkin's death: 'Alas, my darling, this great Prince, who had so many diamonds and such gold, died on the grass!', replied the dowager, as if he had had the bad taste to expire on one of her lawns.[27] During the Napoleonic Wars, the Russian army marched singing songs of Potemkin's death 'on the steppe lying on a raincoat'.[28] The poet Derzhavin saw the romance in the death of this unbounded man in the natural wilderness, 'like mist upon a cross-roads'.[29] Two observers at different ends of the Empire – Count Fyodor Rostopchin (famous as the man who, in 1812, burned Moscow) in nearby Jassy, and the Swedish envoy, Count Curt Stedingk, in faraway

Petersburg[30] – reacted with exactly the same words: 'His death was as extraordinary as his life.'[31]

The Empress had to be told at once. Sashenka Branicka could have told her – she was already reporting to Catherine on the Prince's health – but she was too distraught. So an adjutant was sent galloping ahead to inform Potemkin's devoted and indefatigable secretary Vasily Popov.

There was one last, almost ritual, moment. As the melancholy convoy began to retrace its footsteps back to Jassy, someone must have wanted to mark the spot where the Prince died so that they could build a monument to recall his glory. There were no rocks. Branches would blow away. It was then that the Ataman (Cossack General) Pavel Golavaty, who had known Potemkin for thirty years, commandeered the Zaporogian lance of one of his horsemen. Before he joined the rearguard of the procession, he rode to the little plateau and plunged the lance into the ground at the very spot.[32] A Cossack lance to mark the place of Potemkin was as characteristic as the arrow that Robin Hood was supposed to have used to select his grave.

Meanwhile, Popov received the news and, at once, wrote to the Empress: 'We have been struck a blow! Most Merciful Sovereign, Most Serene Prince Grigory Alexandrovich is no more among the living.'[33] Popov despatched the letter with a trusted young officer who was ordered not to rest until he had delivered the terrible news.

Seven days later, at 6 p.m. on 12 October,[34] this courier, dressed respectfully in black – and the dust of the road – delivered Popov's letter to the Winter Palace. The Empress fainted away. Her courtiers thought she had suffered a stroke. Her doctors were called to bleed her. 'Tears and desperation' is how Alexander Khrapovitsky, Catherine's private secretary, described her shock. 'At eight, they let blood, at ten she went to bed.'[35] She was in a state of collapse: even her grandchildren were not admitted. 'It was not the lover she regretted,' wrote a Swiss imperial tutor, who understood their relationship. 'It was the friend.'[36] She could not sleep. At 2 a.m., she rose again to write to her loyal and fussy confidant, the *philosophe* Friedrich Melchior Grimm: 'A terrible death-blow has just fallen on my head. At six in the afternoon, a messenger brought the tragic news that my pupil, my friend, almost my idol, Prince Potemkin of Taurida, has died in Moldavia after about a month's illness. You cannot imagine how broken I am . . .'[37]

In many ways, the Empress never recovered. The golden age of her reign died with him. But so did his reputation: Catherine told Grimm on that tragic sleepless night, scribbling by candlelight in her Winter

Palace apartments, that Potemkin's achievements had always confounded the jealous 'babblers'. But if his enemies could not defeat him in life, they have succeeded in death. He was barely cold before a vicious legend grew up around his outlandish character that was to obscure his achievements for 200 years.

Catherine would be amazed and appalled to discover that today her 'idol' and 'statesman' is best known for a calumny and a film. He is remembered for the historical libel of the 'Potemkin Villages', while he really built cities, and for the film *Battleship Potemkin*, the story of the mutinous sailors who heralded the revolutions that, long after his death, destroyed the Russia he loved. So the Potemkin legend was created by Russia's national enemies, jealous courtiers and Catherine's unstable successor, Paul I, who avenged himself, not just on the reputation, but even the bones, of his mother's lover. In the nineteenth century, the Romanovs, who presided over a rigid militaristic bureaucracy with its own Victorian primness, fed off the glories of Catherine but were embarrassed by her private life, especially by the role of the 'demi-Tsar' Potemkin.[38] Their Soviet successors shared their scruples while expanding their lies (though it has recently emerged that Stalin,* that avid student of history, privately admired Potemkin). Even the most distinguished Western historians still treat him more as a debauched clown and sexual athlete than historical statesman.† All these strands came together to ensure that the Prince has not received his rightful place in history. Catherine the Great, ignorant of the calumnies to come, mourned her friend, lover, soldier, statesman and probably husband for the remaining years of her life.

On 12 January 1792, Vasily Popov, the Prince's factotum, arrived back in St Petersburg with a special mission. He carried Potemkin's most cherished treasures – Catherine's secret letters of love and state. They remained tied up in bundles. Some of them were – and still are – stained by the dying Potemkin's tears as he read, and re-read them, in the

* 'What was the genius of Catherine the Great?' asked Stalin during a famous discussion about history with his favourite henchman, Andrei Zhdanov, in the summer of 1934. Stalin answered his own question thus: 'Her greatness lay in her choice of Prince Potemkin and other such talented lovers and officials to govern the State.' This author discovered this story during the research for his book, 'Stalin: the Court of the Red Tsar': he interviewed Yury Zhdanov, son of Andrei and later the dictator's son-in-law, now in his eighties, who, as a boy, witnessed the scene.
† Writing in 1994, for example, one highly respected Professor of History at Cambridge University evaluates Potemkin's political and military abilities, with the amusing but completely unjustifiable claim that he 'lacked self-confidence anywhere outside the bedroom.'

knowledge that he would never set eyes on Catherine again.

The Empress received Popov. He handed over the letters. She dismissed everyone except Popov and locked the door. Then the two of them wept together.[39] It was almost thirty years since she first met Potemkin on the very day she seized power and became Empress of all the Russias.

Part One

POTEMKIN AND CATHERINE
1739–1762

1

THE PROVINCIAL BOY

*I would rather hear that you had been killed than that you had
brought shame on yourself.*
(The advice of a Smolensk nobleman to his son, joining the army.)
L. N. Engelhardt, *Memoirs*

'When I grow up,' the young Potemkin is said to have boasted, 'I shall
be either a statesman or an archbishop.' His schoolfriends probably
mocked his dreams, for he was born into the ranks of respectable provincial gentry without the benefits of either name or fortune. His godfather, who understood him better, liked to mutter that the boy would
either 'rise to great honour – or lose his head'.[1] The only way to rise
swiftly to such eminence in the Russia of that time was through the
favour of the monarch – and by the time he had reached the age of
twenty-two this obscure provincial had contrived to meet two reigning
empresses.

Grigory Alexandrovich Potemkin was born on 30 September 1739* in
the small village of Chizhova, not far from the old fortress city of Holy
Smolensk. The Potemkins owned the modest estate and its 430 male
serfs. The family were far from rich, but they were hardly poor either.
However, they made up for their middling status by behaviour that was
strange even by the standards of the wilder borderlands of the Russian
Empire. They were a numerous clan of Polish descent and, like all
nobility, they had concocted a dubious genealogy. The more minor the
nobility, the more grandiose this tended to be, so the Potemkins claimed
they were descended from Telesin, the prince of an Italian tribe which
threatened Rome in about 100 BC, and from Istok, a Dalmatian prince
of the eleventh century AD. After centuries of unexplained obscurity,
these royal Italian–Dalmatians reappeared around Smolensk bearing the
distinctly unLatinate name 'Potemkin' or the polonized 'Potempski'.

The family proved adept at navigating the choppy seas between the

* The date of his birth is, like everything else about him, mysterious because there is
much confusion about the age that he went to live in Moscow and that he was put down
for the Guards. There is an argument for saying he was born in 1742, the date given by
his nephew Samoilov. The dates and military records contradict each other without
creating a particularly interesting debate. This date is the most likely.

tsars of Muscovy and the kings of Poland, receiving estates around Smolensk from both. The family patriarch was Hans-Tarasy (supposedly a version of Telesin) Potemkin, who had two sons, Ivan and Illarion, from whom the two branches of the family were descended.[2] Grigory came from Illarion's junior line. Both sides boasted middle-ranking officers and courtiers. From the time of Potemkin's great-grandfather, the family exclusively served Muscovy, which was gradually recovering these traditional Kievan lands from the Commonwealth of Poland–Lithuania.

The Potemkins became pillars of the intermarried cousinhood of Smolensk nobility, which possessed its own unique Polish identity. While Russian nobility was called the *dvoryanstvo*, the Smolensk nobles still called themselves *szlachta*, like their brethren in Poland. Smolensk today appears deeply embedded in Russia, but when Potemkin was born it was still on the borderlands. The Russian Empire in 1739 already stretched eastwards from Smolensk across Siberia to the Chinese border, and from the Baltic in the north towards the foothills of the Caucasus in the south – but it had not yet grasped its golden prize, the Black Sea. Smolensk had been conquered by Peter the Great's father, Tsar Alexei, as recently as 1654 and before then it had been part of Poland. The local nobility remained culturally Polish, so Tsar Alexei confirmed their privileges, permitted the Smolensk Regiment to elect its officers (though they were not allowed to keep their Polish links) and decreed that the next generation had to marry Russian, not Polish, girls. Potemkin's father may have worn the baggy pantaloons and long tunic of the Polish nobleman and spoken some Polish at home, though he would have worn the more Germanic uniform of the Russian army officer outside. So Potemkin was brought up in a semi-Polish environment and inherited much closer links to Poland than most Russian nobles. This connection assumed importance later: he acquired Polish naturalization, toyed with Poland's throne and sometimes seemed to believe he was Polish.[3]

Potemkin's only famous forebear (though a scion of Ivan's line) was Peter Ivanovich Potemkin, a talented military commander and later ambassador of Tsar Alexei and his successor, Tsar Fyodor, father and brother of Peter the Great. This earlier Potemkin could best be described as a one-man trans-European diplomatic incident.

In 1667, this local Governor and *okolnichy* (a senior court rank) was sent as Russia's first ambassador to Spain and France and then later, in 1680, as special envoy to many European capitals. Ambassador Potemkin went to almost any lengths to ensure that the prestige of his master was protected in a world that still regarded the Muscovite Tsar as a barbarian.

The Russians in their turn were xenophobic and disdained the unOrthodox Westerners as not much better than Turks. At a time when all monarchs were highly sensitive about titles and etiquette, the Russians felt they had to be doubly so.

In Madrid, the bearded and heavily robed Ambassador demanded that the Spanish King uncover his head each time the Tsar's name was mentioned. When the King replaced his hat, Peter Potemkin demanded an explanation. There were rows when the Spaniards queried the Tsar's titles and then even more when they were listed in the wrong order. On the way back to Paris, he argued again over titles, almost came to blows with customs officials, refused to pay duty on his jewel-encrusted icons or diamond-studded Muscovite robes, grumbled about over-charging and called them 'dirty infidel' and 'cursed dog'. Louis XIV wished to appease this nascent European power and apologized personally for these misunderstandings.

The Ambassador's second Parisian mission was equally badtempered, but he then sailed to London, where he was received by Charles II. This was apparently the sole audience in his diplomatic career that did not end in farce. When he visited Copenhagen and found the Danish King ill in bed, Peter Potemkin called for a couch to be placed alongside and lay down on it so that the Ambassador of the Tsar could negotiate on terms of supine royal equality. On his return, Tsar Fyodor was dead and Potemkin was severely reprimanded for his over-zealous antics by the Regent Sophia.* This curmudgeonly nature seemed to run in both lines of the family.[4]

Grigory Potemkin's father, Alexander Vasilievich Potemkin, was one of those oafish military eccentrics who must have made life in eighteenth-century provincial garrisons both tedious and colourful. This early Russian prototype of Colonel Blimp was almost insane, permanently indignant and recklessly impulsive. Young Alexander served in Peter the Great's army throughout the Great Northern War, and fought at the decisive Battle of Poltava in 1709, at which Peter defeated the Swedish invader, Charles XII, and thereby safeguarded his new city St Petersburg and Russia's access to the Baltic. He then fought at the siege of Riga, helped capture four Swedish frigates, was decorated and later wounded in the left side.

* When Grigory Potemkin, who was to prove even more shocking to Western sensibilities, rose to greatness in St Petersburg, it was felt he required a famous ancestor. A portrait of the foul-tempered, xenophobic and pedantic Ambassador of the era of the Sun King and the Merry Monarch was found, possibly a present from the English Embassy, and placed in Catherine the Great's Hermitage.

After the war, the veteran had to serve as a military bureaucrat conducting tiresome population censuses in the distant provinces of Kazan and Astrakhan and commanding small garrisons. We do not know many details of his character or career, but we do know that when he demanded to retire because of his aching wounds he was called before a board of the War College and according to custom was stripping off his uniform to show his scars when he spotted that one of the board had served under him as an NCO. He immediately put on his clothes and pointed at this man: 'What? *HE* would examine *ME*? I will *NOT* tolerate that. Better remain in the service no matter how bad my wounds!' He then stormed out to serve another two boring years. He finally retired as an ailing lieutenant-colonel in 1739, the year his son was born.[5]

Old Alexander Potemkin already had a reputation as a domestic tyrant. His first wife was still alive when the veteran spotted Daria Skouratova, probably on the Bolshoia Skouratova estate that was near Chizhova. Born Daria Vasilievna Kondyreva, she was, at twenty, already the widow of Skouratov, its deceased proprietor. Colonel Potemkin married her at once. Neither of these ageing husbands was an appetizing prospect for a young girl, but Skouratov's family would have been glad to find her a new home.

The Colonel's young wife now received a most unfortunate shock. It was only when she was pregnant with her first child, a daughter named Martha Elena, that she discovered that Colonel Potemkin was still married to his first wife, who lived in the village. Presumably the whole village was only too aware of the Colonel's secret, and Daria must have felt she had been made to look a fool in front of her own serfs. Bigamy then was as contrary to the edicts of Church and state as it is now, but places like Chizhova were so remote, the records so chaotic, and the power of men over women so dominant that stories of bigamous provincial gentry were quite common. At roughly the same time, General Abraham Hannibal, Pushkin's Abyssinian grandfather, was remarrying bigamously while torturing his first wife in a dungeon until she agreed to enter a monastery, and one of his sons repeated his performance.[6] Torture was usually unnecessary to persuade Russian wives to enter monasteries, thereby releasing the husbands to marry again. Daria visited the first wife and tearfully persuaded her to take holy orders, finally making her own bigamous marriage legitimate.

We can glean enough about this marriage to say that it was profoundly unhappy: Alexander Potemkin kept his wife almost perpetually pregnant. She had five daughters and one son – Grigory was her third child. Yet the splenetic taskmaster was also manically jealous. As jealousy often precipitates the very thing it most fears, the young wife was not short of admirers. We are told by one source that, around the time of Grigory's birth, Colonel Potemkin was extremely suspicious of his visiting cousin, who was to be Grigory's godfather, the worldly Grigory Matveevich Kizlovsky, a senior civil servant from Moscow. Presumably the boy was named after Kizlovsky – but was he his natural father? We simply do not know: Potemkin inherited some of his father's manic, often morose character. He also loved Kizlovsky like a father after the Colonel's death. One simply has to confront the prosaic fact that, even in the adulterous eighteenth century, children were occasionally the offspring of their official fathers.

We know far more about Potemkin's mother than about his father because she lived to see Grigory become the first man of the Empire. Daria was good-looking, capable and intelligent. A much later portrait shows an old lady in a bonnet with a tough, weary but shrewd face, a bold lumpy nose and sharp chin. Her features are cruder than her son's, though he was supposed to resemble her. When she discovered she was pregnant for the third time in 1739, the augurs were good. Locals in Chizhova still claim that she had a dream that she saw the sun detach itself from the sky to fall right on her belly – and at that point she woke up. The village soothsayer, Agraphina, interpreted this as the prospect of a son. But the Colonel still found a way to ruin her happiness.[7] When her time was near, Daria waited to give birth in the village *banya* or bathhouse, attended probably by her serf-maids. Her husband, according to the story still told by the locals, sat up all night drinking strong home-made berry wines. The serfs waited up too – they wanted an heir after two daughters. When Grigory was delivered, the church bells rang. The serfs danced and drank until dawn.[8] The place of his birth was fitting, since the *banya* in the Winter Palace was one day to be the frequent venue for his trysts with Catherine the Great.

Daria's children were born into a house with a shadow hanging over it – paternal paranoia. Her marriage must have lost whatever meagre romance it ever had when she discovered her husband's bigamy. His accusations of infidelity must have made it worse: he was so jealous that, when their daughters married, he banned the sons-in-law from kissing Daria's hand in case the impression of male lips on soft skin led inexorably to sin. After the birth of his heir, the Colonel was visited by, among others coming to congratulate him, his cousin Sergei Potemkin, who informed him that Grigory was not his son. Sergei's motives in delivering this news were scarcely philanthropic: he wanted his family to inherit the estates. The old soldier flew into a rage, and petitioned to annul the marriage and declare Grigory a bastard. Daria, imagining the monastery gates closing on her, summoned the worldly, sensible godfather Kizlovsky. He hurried from Moscow and persuaded the half-senile husband to drop the divorce petition. So Gregory's mother and father were stuck with each other.[9]

Grigory Potemkin's immediate world for his first six or so years was to be his father's village. Chizhova stood on the River Chivo, a stream that cut a small, steep, muddy gully through the broad flat lands. It was several hours' journey from Smolensk, whence Moscow was a further 350 versts. St Petersburg was 837 versts away. In summer, it could be baking hot there, but its flatness meant that the winters were cruel, the winds biting. The countryside was beautiful, rich and green. It was and still is a wild, open land and a refreshing and exciting place for a child.

In many ways, this village was a microcosm of Russian society: there were two essential facts of Russian statehood at that time. The first was the Empire's perpetual, elemental instinct to expand its borders in every possible direction: Chizhova stood on its restless western borderland. The second was the dichotomy of nobility and serfdom. Potemkin's home village was divided into these two halves, which it is still possible to see, even though the village scarcely exists today.

On a slight rise above the stream, Potemkin's first home was a modest, one-storey wooden manorhouse, with a handsome façade. It could not have been in greater contrast to the houses of rich magnates higher up the social scale. For example, later in the century, Count Kirill Razumovsky's estate, further to the south in the Ukraine, 'resembled more a little town than a country house ... with 40 or 50 outhouses ... his guard, a numerous train of retainers, and a large band of musicians'.[10] In Chizhova, the only outhouse around the manor was probably the bathhouse where Grigory was born, which would have stood right above the stream and its well. This *banya* was an integral part of Russian life. Country folk of both sexes bathed together,* which was very shocking to a visiting French schoolmaster since 'persons of all ages and both sexes use them together and the habit of seeing everything unveiled from an early age deadens the senses'.[11] For Russians, the *banya* was a cosy, sociable and relaxing extension of the home.

---

* This continued right up to 1917. When Rasputin's enemies grumbled to Nicholas II about his bathing with his female devotees, the last Tsar retorted that this was a usual habit of the common people.

Apart from the problems of his parents' marriage, this was probably a happy, if unsophisticated, environment to grow up in. We have one account of a boy of the lower nobility growing up in Smolensk Province: though born thirty years later, Lev Nikolaevich Engelhardt was Potemkin's kinsman, who recorded the probably unchanged life in a nearby village. He was allowed to run around in a peasant shirt and bare feet: 'Physically my education resembled the system outlined by Rousseau – the Noble Savage. But I know that my grandmother was not only ignorant of that work but had a very uncertain acquaintance with Russian grammar itself.'[12] Another memoirist, also related to Potemkin, recalled: 'The richest local landowner possessed only 1,000 souls,' and 'he had . . . one set of silver spoons which he set out before the more important guests, leaving the others to manage with spoons of pewter'.[13]

Grigory or Grisha, as he was known, was the heir to the village and he was, apart from his old father, the only man in a family of women – five sisters and his mother. He was presumably the centre of attention and this family atmosphere must have set the tone for his character, because he was to remain the cynosure of all eyes for the rest of his life. Throughout his career, he described himself as 'Fortune's spoilt child'. He had to stand out and dominate. The household of women made him absolutely relaxed in female company. In manhood, his closest friends were women – and his career depended on his handling of one in particular. This rough household enlivened by the bustle of female petticoats could not last. Most of his sisters soon married respectably into the cousinhood of Smolensk gentry (except for Nadezhda, who died at nineteen). In particular, the marriages of Elena Marfa to Vasily Engelhardt and Maria to Nikolai Samoilov were to produce nieces and nephews who were to play important roles in Potemkin's life.[14]

Service to the state was the sole profession of a Russian noble. Born into the military household of an officer who had served with Peter at Poltava, Grisha would have been brought up to understand that his duty and his path to success could be found only in serving the Empire. His father's exploits were probably the hinterland of the boy's imagination. The honour of a uniform was everything in Russia, particularly for the provincial gentry. In 1721, Peter the Great had laid down a Table of Ranks to establish the hierarchy within the military, civil and court services. Any man who reached the fourteenth military or the eighth civil rank was automatically raised to hereditary nobility – *dvoryanstvo* – but Peter also imposed compulsory life service on all noblemen. By the time of Potemkin's birth, the nobility had whittled down this humiliating obligation, but service remained the path to fortune. Potemkin showed an interest in the priesthood. He was descended from a seventeenth-century archimandrite and his father sent him to an ecclesiastical school in Smolensk. But he was always destined for the colours.[15]

Right beneath the house, beside the stream, was the well, still named after Catherine today. Legend says Potemkin brought the Empress there to show her his birthplace. It is likely that as a child he himself drew water from it, for the lives of middling gentry were better than those of their well-off serfs but not much. Potemkin was probably farmed out at birth to a serf wet-nurse in the village, but, whether literally or not, this prototype of the 'Noble Savage' was raised on the milk of the Russian countryside. He would have been brought up as much by serf women as by his mother and sisters; the music he heard would have been the soulful laments that the serfs sang at night and at festival time. The dances he knew would have been the boisterous and graceful peasant gigs far more than the cotillions danced at the balls of local landowners. He would have known the village soothsayer as well as the priest. He was just as at home beside the warm, smelly hearths of the peasant houses – steamy with *kasha*, the buckwheat porridge, *shchi*, the spicy cabbage broth, and *kvass*, the yellow sour beer they drank alongside vodka and berry wine – as he was in the manor. Tradition tells us the boy lived simply. He played with the priest's children, grazed horses with them and gathered hay with the serfs.[16]

Chizhova's little Orthodox Church of Our Lady stood (and its ruined successor building remains) on the serfs' side of the village: Potemkin spent much of his time there. The serfs themselves were devout: each, 'besides the consecrated amulet round his neck from baptism, carries a little figure of his ... patron saint, stamped on copper. Soldiers and peasants often take it out of their pockets, spit on it and rub it ... then place it opposite to them and, on a sudden, prostrate themselves ...'.[17] When a peasant entered a house, it was usual for him to demand where 'the God' was and then cross himself before the icon.

Potemkin grew up with a peasant's mixture of piety and superstition: he was baptized at the village church. Many landowners could afford a foreign tutor for their children, preferably French or German – or sometimes an aged Swedish prisoner-of-war, captured in the Great Northern War, like the poor landowning family in Pushkin's novella, *The Captain's Daughter*. But the Potemkins did not even have this. It is said that the local priest, Semen Karzev, and sexton, Timofei Kras-nopevzev, taught him alphabet and prayers, which were to spark a lifelong fascination with religion. Grisha learned to sing and to love music, another feature of his adult life: Prince Potemkin was never without his orchestra and a pile of new orchestral scores. There was a legend that, decades later, one of these village sages visited St Petersburg and, hearing that his pupil was now the most important man at Court, called on the Prince, who received him warmly and found him a job as curator of the Bronze Horseman, Falconet's statue of Peter the Great.[18]

The 430 male serfs and their families lived around the church on the other side of the village. Serfs, or 'souls' as they were called, were valued according to the number of males. The wealth of a nobleman was measured not in cash or acres but in souls. Out of a population of nineteen million, there were about 50,000 male nobles and 7.8 million serfs. Half of these were manorial peasants, owned by the individual nobles or the imperial family, while the other half were state peasants owned by the state itself. Only noblemen could legally own serfs, yet a mere one per cent of the nobles owned more than a thousand souls. The households of great noblemen, who might own hundreds of thousands of serfs, were to reach a luxurious and picturesque climax in Catherine's reign when they owned serf orchestras and serf painters of exquisite icons and portraits: Count Sheremetev, the wealthiest serfowner in Russia, owned a serf theatre with a repertoire of forty operas. Prince Yusupov's ballet was to boast hundreds of serf ballerinas. Count Ska-vronsky (a kinsman of Catherine I who married one of Potemkin's nieces) was so obsessed with music that he banned his serfs from speaking: they had to sing in recitative.[19] These cases were rare: 82 per cent of nobles were as poor as church mice, owning fewer than a hundred souls. The Potemkins were middling – part of 15 per cent who owned between 101 and 500.[20]

Chizhova's serfs were the absolute possessions of Colonel Potemkin. Contemporary French writers used the word 'esclaves' – slaves – to describe them. They had much in common with the black slaves of the New World, except that they were the same race as their masters. There was irony in serfdom, for while the serfs in Russia at the time of Potemkin's birth were chattels at the bottom of the pyramid of society, they were also the basic resource of the state's and the nobles' power. They formed the Russian infantry when the state raised an army by forced *levées*. Landowners despatched the selected unfortunates for a lifetime of service. The serfs paid the taxes that the Russian emperors used to finance their armies. Yet they were also the heart of a nobleman's wealth. Emperor and nobility competed to control them – and squeeze as much out of them as possible.

Souls were usually inherited, but they could also be granted to favourites by grateful emperors or bought as a result of advertisements in newspapers like today's used cars. For example, in 1760, Prince Mikhail Shcherbatov, later a critic of Potemkin's morals, sold three girls to another nobleman for three roubles. Yet the masters often took pride in their paternalist care for their serfs. 'The very circumstance of their persons being property ensures them the indulgence of their masters.'[21] Count Kirill Razumovsky's household contained over 300 domestic servants, all serfs of course (except the French chef and probably a French or German tutor for his sons), including a master of ceremonies, a chief *valet de chambre*, two dwarfs, four hairdressers, two coffee-servers and so on. 'Uncle,' said his niece, 'it seems to me you have a lot of servants you could well do without.' 'Quite so,' replied Razumovsky, 'but they could not do without me.'[22]

Sometimes the serfs loved their masters: when the Grand Chamberlain Count Shuvalov was obliged to sell an estate 300 versts from Petersburg, he was awakened one morning by a rumpus in his courtyard in the capital. A crowd of his serfs, who had travelled all the way from the countryside, were gathered there. 'We were very content under your authority and do not wish to lose so good a master,' they declared. 'So with each of us paying . . . we have come to bring you the sum you need to buy back the estate.' The Count embraced his serfs like children.[23] When the master approached, an Englishman noted, the serfs bowed almost to the ground; when an empress visited remote areas, a French diplomat recorded that they made obeisance on their knees.[24] A landowner's serfs were his labour force, bank balance, sometimes his harem and completely his responsibility. Yet he always lived with the fear that they might arise and murder him in his manorhouse. Peasant risings were common.

Most owners were relatively humane to their serfs, but only a tiny minority could conceive that slavery was not the serf's natural state. If serfs fled, masters could recover them by force. Serf-hunters earned bounties for this grim chore. Even the most rational landowners regularly punished their serfs, often using the knout, the thick Russian leather whip, but they were certainly not permitted to execute them. 'Punishments ought to be inflicted on peasants, servants and all others in consideration of their offence with switches,' wrote Prince Shcherbatov in his instructions to his stewards in 1758. 'Proceed cautiously so as not to commit murder or maim. So therefore do not beat on the head or legs or arms with a club. But when such a punishment occurs that calls for a club, then order him to bend down and beat on the back, or better lash with switches on the back and lower down for the punishment will be more painful, but the peasant will not be maimed.'

The system allowed plenty of scope for abuse. Catherine in her *Memoirs* recalled that most households in Moscow contained 'iron collars, chains and other instruments of torture for those who commit the slightest infraction'. The bedchamber of one old noblewoman, for example, contained 'a sort of dark cage in which she kept a slave who dressed her hair; the chief motive ... was the wish of the old baggage to conceal from the world that she wore false hair ...'.[25]

The absolute power of the landowner over serfs sometimes concealed Bluebeardish tortures: the worst of these were perpetrated by a female landowner, though perhaps it was only because she was a woman that anyone complained. Certainly the authorities covered up for her for a long time and this was not in some distant province, but in Moscow itself. Daria Nikolaevna Saltykova, aged twenty-five and known as 'the maneater' – *liudoed* – was a monstress who took a sadistic pleasure in torturing hundreds of her serfs, beating them with logs and rolling pins. She killed 138 female serfs, supposedly concentrating on their genitals. When she was finally arrested early in Catherine's reign, the Empress, who depended on noble support, had to punish the maneater carefully. She could not be executed, because the Empress Elisabeth had abolished the death penalty in 1754 (except for treason), so Saltykova was chained to the scaffold in Moscow for one hour with a placard round her neck reading 'torturer and murderer'. The whole town turned out to look at her: serial killers were rare at that time. The maneater was then confined for life in a subterranean prison–monastery. Her cruelty was the exception, not the rule.[26]

This was Grisha Potemkin's world and the essence of life in the Russian countryside. He never lost the habits of Chizhova. One can imagine him running through hay-strewn pastures with the serf children, chewing on a turnip or a radish – as he was to do later in life in the apartments of the Empress. It was not surprising that, in the refined Voltairean Court of St Petersburg, he was always regarded as a quintessential child of Russia's soil.

In 1746, this idyll ended when his father died aged seventy-four. The six-year-old Grisha Potemkin inherited the village and its serfs, but it was a paltry inheritance. His mother, widowed for the second time at forty-two, with six children to rear, could not make ends meet in Chizhova. The adult Grigory would behave with the heedless extravagance of those who remember financial straits – but it was never grinding poverty. He later granted the village to his sister Elena and her husband

Vasily Engelhardt. They built a mansion on the site of the wooden manorhouse and an exquisite church on the serf side of the village to the glory of Serenissimus, the family's famous son.[27]

Daria Potemkina was ambitious. Grigory was not going to make a career in that remote hamlet, buried like a needle in the sprawling haystack of Russia. She did not have connections in the new capital, St Petersburg, but she did in the old. Soon the family were on the road to Moscow.*

Grisha Potemkin's first glimpse of the old capital would have been its steeples. Deep in the midst of the Russian Empire, Moscow was the fulcrum of everything opposed to St Petersburg, Peter the Great's new capital. If the Venice of the North was a window on to Europe, Moscow was a trapdoor into the recesses of Russia's ancient and xenophobic traditions. Its grim and solemn Russian grandeur alarmed narrow-minded Westerners: 'What is particularly gaudy and ugly at Moscow are the steeples,' wrote an Englishwoman arriving there, 'square lumps of different coloured bricks and gilt spire ... they make a very Gothic appearance.' Indeed, though it was built around the forbidding medieval fortress, the Kremlin, and the bright onion-domes of St Basil's, all its twisting, cramped and dark alleys and courtyards were as obscure as the superstitions of old Orthodoxy. Westerners thought it barely resembled a Western city at all. 'I cannot say Moscow gives me any idea other than of a large village or many villages joined.' Another visitor, looking at the noble châteaux and the thatched cottages, thought the city seemed to have been 'rolled together on coasters'.[28]

Potemkin's godfather (and possibly natural father) Kizlovsky, retired President of the Kamer-Collegium, the Moscow officer of the ministry in charge of the Court (Petrine ministries were called *Collegia* or Colleges), took the family under his protection and helped Daria, whether his mistress or just his protégé, move into a small house on Nikitskaya Street. Grisha Potemkin was enrolled in the gymnasium school attached to the university with Kizlovsky's own son, Sergei.

Potemkin's intelligence was recognized early; he had a brilliant ear for

---

* Today, there is little on the Potemkin side of the village except Catherine's Well and the hut of two octogenarian peasants who subsist on bees. On the serf's side, there is just the ruins of the church. In Communist times, the villagers say, the commissars kept cattle in 'Potemkin's church' but all the cattle sickened and died. The villagers are still digging for an Aladdin's Cave which they call 'Potemkin's Gold'. But all they have found are the bodies of eighteenth-century women, probably Potemkin's sisters, in the graveyard.

languages, so he soon excelled at Greek, Latin, Russian, German and French as well as passing Polish, and it was said later that he could understand Italian and English. His first fascination was Orthodoxy: even as a child, he would discuss the liturgy with the Bishop of the Greek convent, Dorofei. The priest of the Church of St Nikolai encouraged his knowledge of church ceremonies. Grisha's remarkable memory, which would be noted later, enabled him to learn long tracts of Greek liturgy by heart. Judging by his knowledge and memory as an adult, he found learning perhaps too easy and concentration tedious. He bored quickly and feared no one: he was already well known for his epigrams and his mimicry of his teachers. Yet he somehow befriended the high-ranking clergyman Ambrosius Zertis-Kamensky, later Archbishop of Moscow.[29]

The boy used to help at the altar, but even then he was either immersed in Byzantine theology or bursting to commit some outrageous act of mischief. When Grisha appeared before his godfather's guests dressed in the vestments of a Georgian priest, Kizlovsky said: 'One day you will really shame me because I was unable to educate you as a nobleman.' Potemkin already believed he was different from others: he would be a great man. All manner of his predictions of his own future eminence are recorded: 'If I'm a general, I'll command soldiers; if a bishop, it will be priests.' And he promised his mother that when he was rich and famous he would destroy the dilapidated houses where she lived and build a cathedral.* The happy memories of this time remained with him for the rest of his life.[30]

In 1750, the eleven-year-old travelled to Smolensk, escorted probably by his godfather, to register for his military service. The first time a boy dressed up in his uniform and felt the weight of a sabre, the creak of boots, the stiff grip of a tunic, the proud trappings of service, remained a joyful memory for every child–soldier of the *dvoryantsvo*. Noble children were enrolled at absurdly young ages, sometimes as young as five, serving as supernumerary soldiers, to get round Peter's compulsory life service. When they actually became soldiers in their late teens they would technically have served for over ten years and already be officers. Parents signed their sons into the best regiments, the Guards, just as English noblemen used to be 'put down for Eton'. In Smolensk, Grisha testified to the Heraldic Office about his family's service and nobility, recounting his *soi-disant* Roman descent, and his connection to Tsar Alexei's

---

* He did endow the round Nikitskaya Church (Little Nikitskaya) and it was rebuilt by his heirs. But he was still planning the big project when he died. Historians who believe he married Catherine II in Moscow point to this church as the venue for the wedding.

irascible Ambassador. The provincial office confusingly recorded his age as seven but, since children usually registered at eleven, it is probably a bureaucratic slip. Five years later, in February 1755, he returned for his second inspection and was put down for the Horse-Guards, one of the five elite Guards regiments.[31] The teenager returned to his studies.

He then enrolled at Moscow University, where he appeared near the top of his classes in Greek and ecclesiastical history.[32] He was to keep some of his friends from there for the rest of his life. The students wore uniforms – a green coat with red cuffs. The university itself had only just been founded. Potemkin's contemporary Denis von Vizin, in his *Frank Confession of my Affairs and Thoughts*, recounted how he and his brother were among the first students. Like Potemkin, they were the children of the poor gentry who could not afford private tutors. This new university was chaotic. 'We studied without any order ...', he recalled, due to 'the teachers' negligence and hard drinking ...'.[33] Von Vizin claimed that the teaching of foreign languages was either abysmal or non-existent. Potemkin's records were lost in the fire of 1812, but he certainly learned a lot, possibly through his clerical friends.

This pedogogic debauchery did not matter because Potemkin, who later in life was said to have read nothing, was addicted to reading. When he visited relations in the countryside, he spent his whole time in the library and even fell asleep under the billiard table, grasping a book.[34] Another time, Potemkin asked one of his friends, Ermil Kostrov, to lend him ten books. When Potemkin gave them back, Kostrov did not believe he could have read so much in so short a time. Potemkin replied he had read them from cover to cover: 'If you do not believe me, examine them!', he said. Kostrov was convinced. When another student named Afonin lent Potemkin the newly published *Natural Philosophy* by Buffon, Potemkin returned it a day later and amazed Afonin with his absolute recall of its every detail.[35]

Now Potemkin caught the eye of another powerful patron. In 1757, Grisha's virtuosity at Greek and theology won him the university's Gold Medal, and this impressed one of the magnates of the Imperial Court in Petersburg. Ivan Ivanovich Shuvalov, the erudite and cultured founder and Curator of Moscow University, was young, round-faced and gentle with sweet pixie-like features – but he was also unusually modest considering his position. Shuvalov was the lover of the Empress Elisabeth, who was eighteen years his senior, and one of her closest advisers. That June, Shuvalov ordered the university to select its twelve best pupils and send them to St Petersburg. Potemkin and eleven others were despatched to the capital, where they were met by Shuvalov himself and conveyed to the Winter Palace to be presented to the Empress of all the Russias. This was Potemkin's first visit to Petersburg.

Even Moscow must have seemed a backwater compared to St Petersburg. On the marshy banks and islands of the estuary of the River Neva, Peter the Great had founded his 'paradise' in 1703 on territory that still belonged to Sweden. When he had finally defeated Charles VII at Poltava his first reaction was that St Petersburg was safe at last. It became the official capital in 1712. Thousands of serfs died driving the piles and draining the water on this vast building site as the Tsar forced the project ahead. Now it was already a beautiful city of about 100,000 inhabitants, with elegant palaces lining the embankments: on the northern side stood the Peter and Paul Fortress and the red-brick palace that had belonged to Peter's favourite, Prince Menshikov. Almost opposite these buildings stood the Winter Palace, the Admiralty and more aristocratic mansions. Its boulevards were astonishingly wide, as if built for giants, but their Germanic straightness was alien to the Russian soul, quite the opposite of the twisting lanes of Moscow. The buildings were grandiose, but all were half finished, like so much in Russia.

'It's a cheerful fine looking city with streets extremely wide and long,' wrote an English visitor. 'Not only the town but the manner of living is upon too large a scale. The nobles seem to vie with each other in extravagances of every sort.' Everything was a study of contrasts. Inside the palaces, 'the homes are decorated with the most sumptuous furniture from every country but you pass into a drawing room where the floor is of the finest inlaid woods through a staircase of coarseness, stinking with dirt.'[36] Even its palaces and dances could not completely conceal the nature of the Empire it ruled: 'On the one hand there are the elegant fashions, gorgeous dresses, sumptuous repasts, splendid fêtes and theatres equal to those that adorn Paris and London,' observed a French diplomat, 'on the other there are merchants in Asiatic costume, domestics and peasants in sheepskins and wearing long beards, fur-bonnets, gloves without fingers and hatchets hanging from their leather belts.'[37]

The Empress's new Winter Palace was not yet finished, but it was magnificent nonetheless – one room would be gilded, painted, hung with chandeliers and filled with courtiers, the next would be draughty, leaky, almost open to the elements and strewn with masons' tools. Shuvalov led the twelve prize-winning students into the reception rooms where Elisabeth received foreign envoys. There, Potemkin and his fellow scholars were presented to the Empress.

Elisabeth, then nearly fifty and in the seventeenth year of her reign, was a big-boned Amazonian blonde with blue eyes. 'It was impossible on seeing her for the first time not to be struck by her beauty,' Catherine the Great remembered. 'She was a large woman who in spite of being very stout was not in the least disfigured by her size.'[38] Elisabeth, like her sixteenth-century English namesake, was raised in the glorious shadow of a dominant royal father and then spent her youth in the risky limbo between the throne and the dungeon. This honed her natural political instincts – but there end the similarities with Gloriana. She was impulsive, generous and frivolous, but also shrewd, vindictive and ruthless – truly Peter the Great's daughter. This Elisabethan Court was dominated by the exuberance and vanity of the Empress, whose appetites for elaborate fêtes and expensive clothes were prodigious. She never wore the same clothes twice. She changed her dresses twice a day and female courtiers copied her. When she died, her successor found a wardrobe in the Summer Palace filled with 15,000 dresses. At Court, French plays were still a rare and foreign innovation: the usual entertainment was the Empress's so-called transvestite balls where everyone was ordered to dress as the opposite sex: this led to all sorts of horseplay with the men in 'whale-boned petticoats' and the women looking like 'scrubby little boys' – especially the old ones. There was a reason for this: 'the only woman who looked really fine, and completely a man, was the Empress herself. As she was tall and powerful, male attire suited her. She had the handsomest leg I have ever seen on any man . . .'[39]

Even the purported fun at this Elisabethan Court was permeated by the struggle for political influence and fear of imperial caprice: when the Empress could not get powder out of her hair and had to shave her head to remove it, she ordered all the ladies at court to shave theirs too. 'The ladies obeyed in tears.' When she was jealous of other beauties, she cut the ribbons of one with scissors and the curls of another two. She actually issued orders to ensure that no other woman emulated her *coiffeur de jour*. As she lost her looks, she alternated between Orthodox devotions and the frantic application of cosmetics.[40] Politics was a risky game, even for fashionable noblewomen. Early in her reign, Elisabeth ordered that a pretty courtier named Countess Natalia Lopukhina have her tongue cut out just for vaguely chattering about a plot – yet this was the soft-hearted woman who also abolished the death penalty.

She combined her Orthodox piety with hearty promiscuity. Elisabeth's love affairs were legion and uninhibited, much more so than Catherine's: they varied from French doctors and Cossack choristers to that rich reservoir of local virility, the Guards. Her great love, nicknamed

'The Night Emperor', was a young Ukrainian half-Cossack, whom she first noticed singing in the choir: his name was Alexei Razum, which was soon dignified into Razumovsky. He and his younger brother Kirill, a teenage shepherd, were rewarded with riches and raised to count, one of the new Germanic titles imported by Peter the Great. In 1749, Elisabeth took a new lover, Ivan Shuvalov, aged twenty-two, so another family were raised to the diamond-studded status of magnates.

By the time young Potemkin visited Petersburg, many of these magnates were the scions of a newly coined Petrine and Elisabethan aristocracy – there was no better advertisement for the benefits of life at Court. 'Orderlies, choristers, scullery boys in noble kitchens', as Pushkin put it, were raised on merit or just favour to the height of wealth and aristocracy.[41] These new men served in the higher echelons of Court and military alongside the old untitled Muscovite nobles and the princely clans, who were the descendants of ruling houses: the Princes Golitsyn, for example, were descended from Grand Duke Gedemin of Lithuania, the Princes Dolgoruky from Rurik.

This was Potemkin's introduction to a world of empresses and favourites that he was ultimately to dominate. Elisabeth's father, Peter I (the Great), had celebrated his conquest of the Baltic by declaring himself *imperator* or emperor in 1721 in addition to the traditional title of tsar, which itself derived from the Roman *Caesar*. But Peter had also ensured a century of instability by decreeing that Russian rulers could choose their own heirs without consulting the opinion of anyone else: this has been called 'the apotheosis of autocratic rule'. Russia was not to have a law of succession until the reign of Paul I. Since Peter had tortured his own son and heir – the Tsarevich (Tsar's son) Alexei – to death in 1718 and his other male sons had died, he was succeeded in 1725 by his lowborn widow as Empress Catherine I in her own right, backed by the Guards Regiments and a camarilla of his closest cronies. Catherine was the first of a line of female or child rulers, the symptom of a grievous lack of adult male heirs.

In this 'era of palace revolutions', emperors were raised to the purple by combinations of Court factions, noble magnates and the Guards Regiments, which were stationed in St Petersburg. On Catherine I's death in 1727, Peter's grandson, the son of the murdered Alexei, ruled as Peter II for a mere two years. On his death,* the Russian Court offered

---

* The young Emperor, who moved the Court back to Moscow, died in the suburban Palace which today contains the War College archives (RGVIA), where most of Potemkin's papers are stored.

the throne to Peter's niece Anna of Courland, who ruled, with her hated German favourite Ernst Biron, until 1740. Then a baby, Ivan VI, acceded to the throne, which was controlled by his mother, Anna Leopoldovna, the Duchess of Brunswick, as regent. The Russians did not appreciate children, German or female rulers. All three was too much to bear.

On 25 November 1741, after a series of palace coups during the reign of the infant Ivan VI, the Grand Duchess Elisabeth, aged thirty-one, seized the Russian Empire with just 308 Guardsmen – and consigned the child–Emperor to a cell in the fortress of Schlüsselburg. The mixture of palace intrigue and praetorian coup set the tone for Russian politics for the century. Foreigners were confused by this – especially in the century of Enlightenment when politics and law were being obsessively analysed: wits could only decide that the Russian throne was neither elective nor hereditary – it was occupative. The Russian constitution, to paraphrase Madame de Staël, *was* the character of the Emperor. The personality of the Autocrat *was* the government. And the government, as the Marquis de Custine put it, was 'an absolute monarchy tempered by assassination'.[42]

This rule of women created a peculiar Russian version of the Court favourite. Shuvalov, Potemkin's patron, was the Empress's latest. A favourite was a trusted associate or lover, often of humble origins, favoured by a monarch out of personal choice instead of noble birth. Not all aspired to power. Some were happy merely to become rich courtiers. But in Russia the empresses needed them because only men could command armies. They were ideally placed to become minister–favourites[43] who ran the country for their mistresses.*

When Shuvalov, still only thirty-two, presented the eighteen-year-old Grisha Potemkin to the now bloated and ailing Empress, he drew attention to his knowledge of Greek and theology. The Empress ordered Potemkin to be promoted to Guards corporal as a reward, even though so far he had done no soldiering whatsoever. She probably presented the boys with a trinket – a glass goblet engraved with her silhouette – as a prize.†

*

---

* Favourites had developed by the seventeenth century into the minister–favourites such as Olivares in Spain and Richelieu and Mazarin in France, who were not the King's lovers but able politicians chosen to run the increasingly heavy bureaucracies. When Louis XIV chose to rule himself on the death of Mazarin in 1661, the fashion ended. But Russia's female rulers, beginning with Catherine I in 1725, reinvented it.

† In the Smolensk Local History Museum, there is just such a glass goblet which is said to have belonged to Potemkin. The story goes that when Catherine the Great passed through Smolensk she drank a toast from it.

The Court must have turned Potemkin's head because when he returned to Moscow he no longer concentrated on his studies. Perhaps the drunkenness and indolence of the professors infected the students. In 1760, the linguist, who had won the Gold Medal and presentation to the Empress, was expelled for 'laziness and non-attendance of lessons'. Years later, when he was already a prince, Potemkin visited Moscow University and met the Professor Barsov who had expelled him. The Prince asked the Professor if he remembered their earlier encounter. 'Your Highness deserved it,' replied Barsov. The Prince characteristically enjoyed the reply, embraced the aged Professor, and became his patron.[44]

Potemkin's expulsion appeared to be something of a disaster. His godfather and mother felt that obscure young men like Grisha could not afford to be so lazy. Fortunately, he was already enrolled in the Guards, but he did not even have the money for the trip to St Petersburg, a sure sign that his family either disapproved or had cut him off. He drifted apart from his mother: indeed they hardly saw each other later in life. The Empress Catherine II later made her a lady-in-waiting and she was proud of her son – but openly disapproved of his love life. So this was not just a process of leaving home. He was leaving on his own. He borrowed 500 roubles, a considerable sum, from his friend Ambrosius Zertis-Kamensky, now Bishop of Mojaisk. Potemkin often said he meant to return it with interest, but the Bishop was to be savagely murdered later in this story before Potemkin rose to power. He never repaid it.

The life of a young Guardsman was idle, decadent and exceedingly expensive, but there was no surer path to greatness. Potemkin's timing was opportune – Russia was fighting the Seven Years War against Prussia, while in Petersburg Empress Elisabeth was dying. The Guards were already seething with intrigue.

On arrival in St Petersburg, Potemkin reported for duty at the Headquarters of his Horse-Guards Regiment, which comprised a little village of barracks, houses and stables built round a quadrangle by the Neva river near the Smolny Convent. The Regiment had its own church, hospital, bathhouse and prison. There was a meadow behind it for feeding horses and holding parades. The oldest Guards Regiments – such as the Preobrazhensky and the Semyonovsky – were founded by Peter the Great first as play regiments but then as his loyal forces in the vicious struggle against the corps of state musketeers, the Streltsy. His successors added others. In 1730, Empress Anna founded Potemkin's regiment, the Garde-à-Cheval – the Horse-Guards.[45]

Guards officers were quite unable to withstand 'the seductions of the metropolis'.[46] When these teenage playboys were not carousing, they fought a sometimes fatal guerrilla war through the balls and backstreets with the Noble Cadet Corps that was based in the Menshikov Palace.[47] So many young bloods were ruined by debts, or exhausted by endless whoring in the Metshchansky district or by games of whist or faro, that more ascetic parents preferred their boys to join an ordinary regiment, like the father in *The Captain's Daughter* who exclaims, 'Petrusha is not going to Petersburg. What would he learn, serving in Petersburg? To be a spendthrift and a rake? No, let him be a soldier and not a fop in the Guards!'[48]

Potemkin soon became known to the raciest daredevils among the Guards. At twenty-two, he was tall – well over six foot – broad and highly attractive to women. Potemkin 'had the advantage of having the finest head of hair in all Russia'. His looks and talents were so striking that he was nicknamed 'Alcibiades', a superlative compliment in a neo-Classical age.* Educated people at that time studied Plutarch and Thucydides, so the character of the Athenian statesman was familiar – intelligent, cultured, sensuous, inconsistent, debauched and flamboyant. Plutarch raved about the 'brilliance' of Alcibiades' 'physical beauty'.[49] Potemkin immediately attracted attention as a wit – he was an outstanding mimic, a gift that was to carry him far beyond the realm of comedians.[50] It was soon to win the admiration of the most glamorous ruffians in the Guards – the Orlovs – and they in turn would draw him into the intrigues of the imperial family.

The Guards protected the imperial palaces, and it was this that gave them their political significance.[51] Being in the capital and close to the Court, 'the officers have more opportunity to be known,' a Prussian diplomat observed.[52] They had the run of the city, 'admitted to the games, dances, soirées and theatrical performances of Court into the interior of that sanctuary'.[53] Their duties at the palaces gave them a detailed but irreverent acquaintance with magnates and courtiers – and a sense of personal involvement in the rivalries of the imperial family itself.

During the months that Empress Elisabeth was suspended between life and death, groups of Guardsmen became increasingly embroiled in plans to change the succession to exclude the hated Grand Duke Peter and replace him with his popular wife, Grand Duchess Catherine. Guarding the imperial palaces, Potemkin now had the chance to observe

---

* Alcibiades was famously bisexual – his lovers included Socrates – but there was *never* any suggestion that Potemkin emulated his sexual tastes. The other eighteenth-century figure known as Alcibiades was a favourite of King Gustavus III of Sweden and later friend of Tsar Alexander – Count Armfeld was 'l'Alcibiade du Nord'.

the romantic figure of Grand Duchess Catherine, who would soon rule in her own right as Catherine II. She was never beautiful, but she possessed qualities far superior to that ephemeral glaze: the indefinable magic of imperial dignity combined with sexual attractiveness, natural gaiety and an all-conquering charm that touched everyone who met her. The best description of Catherine at this age was written a few years earlier by Stanislas Poniatowski, her Polish lover:

> She had reached that time in life when any woman to whom beauty had been granted will be at her best. She had black hair, a radiant complexion and a high colour, large prominent and expressive blue eyes, long dark eyelashes, a pointed nose, a kissable mouth ... slender figure, tall rather than small; she moved quickly yet with great nobility and had an agreeable voice and a gay good-tempered laugh.

Potemkin had not met her yet – but just about the time of his arrival in Petersburg she began to cultivate the Guards, who ardently admired her and hated her husband, the Heir. So it was that the provincial boy from Chizhova found himself perfectly placed to join the conspiracy that would place her on the throne – and bring the two of them together. Catherine herself overheard one general declare the gallant sentiments that young Potemkin would soon share: 'There goes a woman for whose sake an honest man would gladly suffer several lashes of the knout.'[54]

2

THE GUARDSMAN AND
THE GRAND DUCHESS:
CATHERINE'S COUP

Heaven knows how it is that my wife becomes pregnant.
Grand Duke Peter, in Catherine the Great, *Memoirs*

The future Catherine II, known as the Great, was not a Russian at all, but she had lived at Elisabeth's Court since she was fourteen and she had made every effort to behave, in her words, 'so the Russians should love me'. Few yet realized that this Grand Duchess aged thirty-two was a gifted politician, far-sighted statesman and consummate actress, with a burning ambition to rule the Russian Empire, a role for which she was admirably qualified.

She was born Princess Sophia of Zerbst-Anhalt on 21 April/2 May 1729 in Stettin. Her dreary destiny as the daughter of a minor German princely house was changed in January 1744 when the Empress Elisabeth scoured the Holy Roman Empire, that dating agency for kings, to find a girl to marry her newly appointed Heir, Karl-Peter-Ulrich, Duke of Holstein, her nephew and therefore a grandson of Peter the Great. He had just been proclaimed Grand Duke Peter Fyodorovich of Russia and required an heir to safeguard Elisabeth's throne. For a variety of reasons – political, dynastic and personal – the Empress settled on Sophia, who converted to Orthodoxy as Ekaterina Alexevna – Catherine – and then married Peter on 21 August 1745, wearing modest dress and unpowdered hair. Observers remarked on her excellent Russian and cool composure.

Catherine realized swiftly that Peter was not suited to be either her husband or the tsar of Russia. She noted ominously that he was 'very childish', lacking in 'judgement' and 'not enamoured of the nation over which he was destined to reign'. It was not to be a happy or romantic marriage. On the contrary, it was a tribute to Catherine's character that she survived it in such an advantageous way.

Peter was already afraid of the Russian Court and perhaps sensed that he was out of his depth. Despite being the grandson of Peter the Great, ruling Duke of Holstein and, at one moment, the heir of Russia and

Sweden, Peter had had an ill-starred life. When he was a boy, his late father had handed him over to the pedantic and cruel marshal of the Holstein Court, who starved him, beat him and made him kneel for hours on dried peas. He grew up into a teenage paradomaniac obsessed with drilling dolls and later soldiers. Alternately starved of affection and spoilt with sycophancy, Peter developed into a confused, pitiful creature who loathed Russia. Once ensconced at the Russian Court, he clung desperately on to his belief in all things German – particularly Prussian. He despised the Russian religion, preferring Lutheranism; he disdained the Russian army, avidly hero-worshipping Frederick the Great.[1] He could not help but display his worrying lack of sense and sensitivity, so Catherine resolved on this plan: '(1) to please the Grand Duke, (2) to please the Empress, (3) to please the nation'. Gradually the third became more important than the first.

Peter's already unprepossessing features had been scarred by smallpox soon after Catherine's arrival. She now found him 'hideous' – though his hurtful behaviour was worse.[2] On the night of her wedding, no one came to join her, a humiliation for any bride.[3] During the peripatetic seasonal migrations of the Court from Petersburg's Summer to Winter Palaces, from Peterhof on the Gulf of Finland and Tsarskoe Selo inland, south to Moscow and westwards to Livonia, she consoled herself by reading the classics of the Enlightenment – for the rest of her life she always had a book to hand – and by energetic riding. She had designed a special saddle so that she could pretend to ride sidesaddle for the Empress and then switch once she was on her own. Though far from our own age of psychology, when one reads her *Memoirs* one has the distinct impression that the era of *sensibilité* perfectly understood the sexual implications of this frantic exercise.[4]

Catherine was sensuous and flirtatious, though possibly unawakened, but she found herself stranded in a sterile, unconsummated marriage to a repulsive and childish man while being surrounded by a treacherous Court filled with the most handsome and sophisticated young men in Russia. Several now fell in love with her, including Kirill Razumovsky, brother of the Empress's favourite, and Zakhar Chernyshev, her future minister. She was watched at all times. The pressure became awkwardly specific: she had to be faithful and she had to conceive a child. Faced with this life, Catherine became addicted to games of chance, especially faro – the lot of many unhappy and privileged women in that time.

By the early 1750s, the marriage had deteriorated from awkwardness to misery. Catherine had every reason to ruin the reputation of Peter, but she also showed pity and kindness towards him until his behaviour began to threaten her very existence. Yet in this aspect her accounts of his backwardness and rudeness are not exaggerated: the marriage had still not been consummated. Peter may have had a physical malformation like that of Louis XVI. Certainly he was an inhibited and ignorant late developer.[5] The details of the marriage would chill any female heart: Catherine lay alone in bed while her puny husband played with dolls and toy soldiers and sometimes scratched away at a violin beside her; he kept his dogs in her room and made her stand guard for hours with a musket.[6]

Most of her flirtations came to nothing, but Serge Saltykov, then twenty-six and a scion of old Muscovite nobility, was different: he was 'handsome as the dawn' according to Catherine, but, reading between the lines, he was something of a cheap ladies' man. She fell for him. He was probably her first lover. Amazingly, steps were now taken at the highest level to make sure this was indeed the case – the Empress required an heir no matter who was the father.[7]

After one miscarriage, Catherine found herself pregnant again. The moment the child was born on 20 September 1754, the heir, named Paul Petrovich, was taken away by the Empress. Catherine was left in tears, 'cruelly abandoned' for hours in her sweaty and soiled linen: 'nobody worried about me'.[8] She comforted herself by reading Montesquieu's *Esprit des lois* and Tacitus' *Annals*. Saltykov was sent away.

Who was the father of the future Emperor Paul I, from whom the rest of the Romanov dynasty, down to Nicholas II, were descended? Was it Saltykov or Peter? Catherine's claim that the marriage was never consummated may or may not be true: she had every reason to belittle Peter and she later considered disinheriting Paul. He grew up to be ugly and pug-nosed while Saltykov, nicknamed 'le beau Serge', was admired for his looks. But then Catherine slyly noted the ugliness of Saltykov's brother. Most likely, Saltykov was the natural father.

It was possible to feel some pity for Peter, who was so unqualified for the venomous subtleties of Court intrigues, but it was impossible to like this vainglorious, drunken bully. One day Catherine found an immense rat hanging in Peter's rooms. When she asked him what it was doing there, he replied that the rodent had been convicted of a crime and deserved the highest penalty according to military law. Its 'crime' had been to climb over Peter's cardboard fortress and eat two sentinels made of starch. Another time he broke down in front of Catherine and told her he knew that Russia would be the ruin of him.[9]

Catherine's *Memoirs* claim that it was only when his wilful foolishness endangered her and Paul that this innocent young mother began to consider the future. She implies that her ultimate accession to the throne was almost preordained. This was far from true – Catherine plotted to usurp the throne with an ever changing cast of conspirators throughout the 1750s, from Elisabeth's Chancellor to the English envoy. As Elisabeth's health began to fail and Peter took to drink, as Europe edged closer to the Seven Years War and the strings of Russian politics tightened, she had every intention of surviving – and on top.

Yet her domestic life was freer, now she had delivered an heir. She began to enjoy the pleasures of being an attractive woman in a Court fragrant with amorous intrigue, as she herself explained:

> I have just said I was attractive. Consequently one half of the road to temptation was already covered and it is only human in such situations that one should not stop halfway. For to tempt and be tempted are closely allied ... Perhaps escape is the only solution but there are situations when escape is impossible for how can one escape ... in the atmosphere of a Court? ... and if you do not run away, nothing is more difficult ... than to avoid something that fundamentally attracts you.[10]

In 1755, at a ball at Oranienbaum, the Grand Duke's country palace near Peterhof, Catherine met Stanislas Poniatowski, aged twenty-three, the Polish secretary to the new English envoy.[11] It happened that Poniatowski was the representative of Poland's powerful pro-Russian party, based around his uncles, the Czartoryski brothers, and their cousinhood, hence known as the 'Familia'. But he was also the young ideal of the cultured Enlightened man of the world, with a streak of romantic, melancholic idealism. The pair fell in love.[12] It was her first true love affair in which her feelings were passionately reciprocated.

A series of skirmishes between the British and the French in the upper Ohio river now set off the events that would lead to the Seven Years War, a global conflagration that extended from the Rhine to the Ganges, from Montreal to Berlin. The starting point of the Russian involvement was Elisabeth's hatred of Prussia's new power and of Frederick the Great, whose jokes about her carnality infuriated her. In this huge diplomatic dance, the other powers suddenly changed partners in a dramatic switch that ended the 'Old System' of alliances and became known as the 'Diplomatic Revolution'. When the music stopped in August 1756, Russia, allied with Austria and France, went to war against Prussia, which was financed by English subsidies (though Russia was not at war with England). Russian armies invaded East Prussia in 1757. The war poisoned

Court politics and ruined Catherine's love affair with Poniatowski, who was obviously in the English camp and ultimately had to leave. Catherine was pregnant with Poniatowski's child – Anna Petrovna was born in December 1757 and again purloined and raised by Elisabeth herself.[13]

Catherine now entered the most dangerous crisis of her life as Grand Duchess. After a victory over Prussia on 19/30 August 1757 at the Battle of Gross-Jägersdorf, Field-Marshal Apraxin, with whom Catherine was friendly, heard that the Empress Elisabeth had fallen ill. He let the Prussians retreat in good order and withdrew his own armies, probably believing the Empress was about to die and Peter III would make peace with his hero, Frederick the Great. The Empress did not die and, like all tyrants, she was extremely sensitive about her mortality. In wartime, such thoughts were treasonable. The pro-English party was destroyed and Catherine found herself under grave suspicion, especially after her terrified husband denounced her. The Grand Duchess was alone and in real danger. She burned her papers, waited – and then played her hand with cool, masterly skill.[14]

Catherine provoked a showdown: on 13 April 1758, as she recounted in her *Memoirs*, she demanded to go home to her mother, exploiting Elisabeth's fondness for her and growing disgust for her nephew. The Empress decided to interrogate Catherine personally. In a scene of Byzantine drama, Catherine argued her case to the Empress while Peter grunted denunciations. She used charm, wide-eyed indignation and her usual display of loving gratitude to disarm the Empress. When they parted, Elisabeth whispered: 'I have many more things to say to you . . .'.[15] Catherine knew she had won and was especially cheered to hear from a maid that Elisabeth was repelled by Peter: 'My nephew is a monster.'[16] When the dust settled, Catherine and Peter managed to coexist quite cordially. Peter had taken a famously plain mistress named Elisabeth Vorontsova, the Chancellor's niece, and so he tolerated Catherine's liaison with Poniatowski, who had returned for a while. Finally, the Pole, who still loved Catherine, had to leave and she was alone again.

Two years later, Catherine noticed Grigory Orlov, a lieutenant of the Izmailovsky Guards who, after distinguishing himself by taking three wounds from the Prussians at the Battle of Zorndorf, had returned to Petersburg charged with guarding a noble Prussian prisoner-of-war, Count Schwerin. Peter, who worshipped all things Prussian, flaunted his friendship with Schwerin. This was probably how Catherine came to know Orlov, though legend claims she first admired him on guard duty from her window.

Grigory Grigorevich Orlov was handsome, tall and blessed, wrote an

English diplomat, with 'every advantage of figure, countenance and manner'.[17] Orlov came of a race of giants* – all five brothers were equally gargantuan.[18] His face was said to be angelic, but he was also the sort of cheerful bluff soldier everyone loved – 'he was a simple and straight-forward man without pretensions, affable, popular, good-humoured and honest. He never did an unkindness to anyone'[19] – and was immensely strong.[20] When Orlov visited London fifteen years later, Horace Walpole caught something of his over-sized charm: 'Orlov the Great or rather the Big is here ... he dances gigantic dances and makes gigantic love.'[21]†

Orlov was the son of a provincial governor and not of wealthy higher nobility. He was descended from a Streltsy officer who was sentenced to beheading by Peter the Great. When it was his turn to die, Orlov's grandfather stepped up to the reeking block and kicked the head of the man before him out of the way. The Tsar was so impressed with his swagger that he pardoned him. Orlov was not particularly clever – 'very handsome', wrote the French envoy Breteuil to his Minister Choiseul in Paris, 'but ... very stupid'. On his return in 1759, Orlov was appointed adjutant to Count Peter Shuvalov, Grand Master of Ordnance, the cousin of Potemkin's university patron. Orlov soon managed to seduce Shuvalov's mistress, Princess Elena Kurakina. It was Orlov's luck that Shuvalov died before he could avenge himself.

Early in 1761, Catherine and Orlov fell in love. After the slightly precious sincerity of Poniatowski, Grigory Orlov provided physical vigour, bearlike kindness and, more importantly, the political muscle that would soon be needed. As early as 1749, Catherine had been able to offer her husband the support of those Guards officers who were devoted to her. Now she received the support of the Orlov brothers and their merry band. The most impressive in terms of ability and ruthlessness was Grigory's brother Alexei. He closely resembled Grigory, except that he was scar-faced and of 'brute force and no heart', the qualities that made the Orlovs such an effective force in 1761.[22]

Orlov and his fellow Guardsmen discussed various daring plans to

---

* Potemkin too was described by foreigners as a giant. The best specimens were bound to join the Guards, but the physique of Russian men seems to have been undergoing a blossoming in this period, to judge by the comments of visitors: 'The Russian peasant is a fine, stout, straight, well-looking man,' gushed Lady Craven as she travelled the Empire.

† His strength was no legend – as witnessed by Baroness Dimsdale in 1781 when the Empress Catherine's carriage on the fairground Flying Mountain, an early version of the 'big dipper', flew off its wooden groove: Orlov, 'a remarkably strong man, stood behind the carriage and with his foot guided it in its proper direction'.

raise Catherine to the throne in late 1761 – though probably in the vaguest terms. The precise order of events is obscure but it was also around this time that young Potemkin first came into contact with the Orlovs. One source recalled that it was Potemkin's reputation as a wit that attracted the attention of Grigory Orlov, though they shared other interests too – both were known as successful seducers and daring gamblers. They never became friends exactly, but Potemkin now moved in the same galaxy.[23]

Catherine needed such allies. In the last months of Elisabeth's life, she was under no illusions about Grand Duke Peter, who talked openly of divorcing Catherine, marrying his mistress Vorontsova and reversing Russia's alliances to save his hero Frederick of Prussia. Peter was a danger to her, her son, her country – and himself. She saw her choices starkly:

> *Primo* – to share His Highness's fate, whatever it might be; *Secundo* – to be exposed at any moment to anything he might undertake for, or against, me; *Tertio* – to take a route independent of any such eventuality … it was a matter of either perishing with (or because of) him, or else saving myself, the children, and perhaps the State, from the wreckage …

Just at the moment that Elisabeth began her terminal decline and Catherine needed to be ready to save herself 'from the wreckage' and lead a possible coup, the Grand Duchess discovered that she was pregnant by Grigory Orlov. She carefully concealed her belly, but, politically, she was *hors de combat*.

At 4 p.m. on the afternoon of 25 December 1761, the Empress Elisabeth, now fifty, had become so weak that she no longer had the strength to vomit blood. She just lay writhing on her bed, her breathing slow and rasping, her limbs swollen like balloons, half filled with fluid, in the imperial apartments of the unfinished, baroque Winter Palace in St Petersburg. The courtiers, bristling with hope and fear of what her death would bring them, were gathered around her. The death of a ruling monarch was even more public than a royal birth: it was a formal occasion with its own etiquette, because the demise of the Empress was the passing of sacred power. The pungence of sweat, vomit, faeces and urine must have overwhelmed the sweetness of candles, the perfume of the ladies and the vodka breath of the men. Elisabeth's personal priest was praying, but she no longer recited with him.[24]

The succession of the spindly, pockmarked Grand Duke Peter, now thirty-four and ever more uncomfortable with Russian culture and people, was accepted, though hardly with jubilance. There was already an undercurrent of anxiety about Peter and hope about Catherine. Many of the magnates knew the Heir was patently ill-suited to his new role. They had to make the appropriate calculations for their careers and families, but the key to survival was always silence, patience and vigilance.

Outside the Palace, the Guards stood sentry duty in the freezing cold, tensely observing the transfer of power, proudly aware of their own role in raising and breaking tsars. The will to act existed especially among the daredevils around the Orlovs, who included Potemkin. However, Catherine's relationship with Orlov, and especially the tightly guarded secret that she was six months pregnant, was known only to the inner circle. It was hard enough for private individuals to conceal pregnancy, yet alone imperial princesses. Catherine managed it even in the crowded sickroom of a dying empress.

Elisabeth's two veteran favourites, the genial, athletic Alexei Razumovsky, the Cossack choirboy-turned-Count, and the aesthetic, round-faced Ivan Shuvalov, Potemkin's university patron, still only thirty-four, attended her fondly – and anxiously. Prince Nikita Trubetskoi, the bull-like Procurator-General of the Senate, watched on behalf of the older Russian nobility. The Heir, Grand Duke Peter, was nowhere to be seen. He was drinking with his German cronies outside the sickroom, with the lack of dignity and tact that would make him hated. But his wife Catherine, who half hated and half loved the Empress, was ostentatiously beside the deathbed and had been there, sleeplessly and tearfully, for two nights.

Catherine was a picture of solicitous affection for her dying aunt and Empress. Who, admiring her lachrymose sincerity, would have guessed that a few years earlier she had mischievously quoted Poniatowski about the Empress thus: 'Oh, this log! She simply exhausts our patience! Would that she die sooner!' The Shuvalovs, the latest of a succession of intriguers, had already approached Catherine about altering the succession in favour of her and her infant son, Grand Duke Paul – but to no avail. All those intriguers had fallen or departed. Catherine alone survived, closer and closer to the throne.[25]

The Empress became still. The gawky Grand Duke was summoned, as Elisabeth was about to die. He came at once. As soon as she died, the courtiers fell to their knees before Peter III. He left swiftly, heading straight for the Council to take control. According to Catherine, he ordered her to remain beside the body until she heard from him.[26] Elisabeth's ladies had already begun bustling around the body, tidying up the detritus of death, drying the sweat on her neck and brow, rouging her cheeks, closing those bright-blue eyes for the last time.

Everyone was weeping – for Elisabeth had been loved despite her frivolities and cruelties. She had done much to restore Russia to its position as a great European power, the way her father had left his Empire. Razumovsky rushed to his room to mourn. Ivan Shuvalov was overcome with 'hypochondriacal thoughts' and felt helpless. The sturdy Procurator-General threw open the doors into the anteroom and announced, with tears rolling down his old face, 'Her Imperial Majesty has fallen asleep in God. God save Our Most Gracious Sovereign the Emperor Peter III.' There was a murmur as they hailed the new reign – but the Court was filled with 'moans and weeping'.[27] Outside, the Guards on duty 'looked gloomy and dejected. The men all spoke at once but in a low voice ... That day [thus] wore an almost sinister aspect with grief painted on every face.'[28]

At 7 p.m., Senators, generals and courtiers swore allegiance to Peter III. A thanksgiving 'Te Deum' was sung. While the Metropolitan of Novgorod solemnly lectured the new Emperor, Peter III was beyond himself with glee and did not conceal it, behaving outrageously and 'playing the fool'.[29] Later the 150 leading nobles of the Empire gathered for a feast in the gallery to toast the new era, three rooms from the chamber where the imperial cadaver lay. The weeping Catherine, who was both a woman of *sensibilité* and a cool-hearted political player, acted her part. She mourned the Empress and went to sit beside the body three days afterwards. By then, the overheated rooms must have been thoroughly rank.[30]

In Prussia, Russian troops had just taken the fortress of Kolberg and were occupying East Prussia, while in Silesia another corps was advancing with units of Russia's Austrian allies. The destruction of Frederick the Great was imminent. The road to Berlin was open. Only a miracle could save him – and the death of Elisabeth was just that. Peter ordered an immediate halt and opened peace talks with an astonished, relieved King of Prussia. Frederick was willing to offer East Prussia to Russia, but even this was not necessary.* Instead, Peter prepared to start his own private war against Denmark, to win back Schleswig for his German Duchy of Holstein.

At Elisabeth's funeral on 25 January 1762, Emperor Peter III, in high

* This was the Miracle of the House of Brandenburg that so inspired Hitler and Goebbels in 1945 in the Berlin bunker when the death of President Roosevelt was supposed to split the Allies. Frederick exulted that 'The Messalina of the North is dead' and acclaimed Peter III's 'truly German heart.'

spirits, invented a game to make the day pass more quickly: he loitered behind the hearse, let it advance for thirty feet and then ran after it to catch up, dragging the elderly courtiers, who had to hold his black train, along behind him. 'Criticism of the Emperor's outrageous behaviour spread rapidly.'

His critics naturally looked to his wife. In the very hour of Elisabeth's death, Catherine received a message from Prince Kirill Dashkov of the Guards which said: 'You have only to give the order and we will enthrone you.' Dashkov was another of a circle of Guardsmen including heroes of the Seven Years War like the Orlov brothers. The pregnant Catherine discouraged treason. What is remarkable about her eventual coup was not that it was successful, because so much of a conspiracy depends on chance, but that it was already fully formed six months earlier. Catherine somehow managed to prevent it blossoming before she had recovered from her confinement.

It was the new Emperor himself who unconsciously decided both the timing and the intensity of the conspiracy. In his reign of barely six months, Peter contrived to alienate virtually all the major forces of Russian political society. Yet his measures were far from barbarous, though often imprudent. On 21 February 1762, for example, he abolished the feared Secret Chancellery – though its organs survived and were concealed as the Secret Expedition under the aegis of the Senate. Three days earlier, the Emperor had promulgated his manifesto on the freedom of the nobility, which liberated the nobles from Peter the Great's compulsory service.

These measures should have won him some popularity, but his other actions seemed deliberately designed to alienate Russia's most powerful interests. The army was the most important: during the Seven Years War, it had defeated Frederick the Great, raided Berlin and brought Prussia's awesome military machine to the very edge of destruction. Now Peter III not only made peace with Prussia but also arranged to lend Frederick the corps that had originally aided the Austrians. And it got worse: on 24 May, Peter issued his ultimatum to Denmark, on behalf of Holstein, that was calculated to lead to a war, quite unconnected to Russian interests. He decided to command his armies in person.

Peter mocked the Guards as 'Janissaries' – the Turkish infantrymen who enthroned and deposed Ottoman sultans – and decided to disband parts of them.[31] This redoubled the Guards' conspiracies against him. Sergeant-Major Potemkin himself, who already vaguely knew the Orlovs, now demanded to join the plot. This is how it happened. One of the Orlov set, a captain in the Preobrazhensky Guards, invited a university friend of Potemkin's, Dmitri Babarykin, to 'enter their society'. Babarykin refused – he disapproved of their 'wild life' and Grigory Orlov's affair with Catherine. But he confided his distaste to his university friend. Potemkin 'on the spot' demanded that Babarykin introduce him to the Preobrazhensky captain. He immediately joined the conspiracy.[32] In his first recorded political act, this Potemkin rings true – shrewd, brave, ambitious and acting on the emotional impulse that was to be his trademark. For a young provincial, it was truly a stimulating moment to be a Guardsman.

Meanwhile Peter promoted his Holsteiner family to major positions. His uncle (and Catherine's) Georg-Ludwig of Holstein-Gottorp was appointed member of the Council, colonel-in-chief of the Horse-Guards, and field-marshal. This Georg-Ludwig had once flirted with a teenage Catherine before she left for Russia. By coincidence, when he arrived from Holstein on 21 March, Prince Georg-Ludwig was assigned Sergeant-Major Potemkin as his orderly.[33] Potemkin was not shy in pushing himself forward: this position ensured that, as the regime unravelled, he was well placed to keep the conspiracy informed. His immaculate horsemanship was noted by Prince Georg-Ludwig, who had him promoted to Guards full sergeant. Another Holstein prince was named governor-general of St Petersburg and commander of all Russian troops around the Baltic.

Lastly the Empress Elisabeth had agreed to secularize much of the lands of the Orthodox Church, but early in his reign, on 21 March, Peter issued a *ukaz*, an imperial decree, to seize the property.[34] His buffoonery and disrespect at Elisabeth's funeral had displayed contempt for Orthodoxy – as well as a lack of manners. All these actions outraged the army, alarmed the Guards, insulted the pious, and wasted the victories of the Seven Years War.

Such was the anger in Petersburg that Frederick the Great, who most benefited from Peter's follies, was afraid that the Emperor would be overthrown if he left Russia to command the Danish expedition.[35] To anger the army was foolish, to upset the Church was silly, to outrage the Guards was simply idiotic, and to arouse all three was probably suicidal. But the plot, suspended at Elisabeth's death because of Catherine's pregnancy, could not stir until it had a leader. As Peter himself was aware, there were three possible claimants to the throne. In his unfortunate and clumsy way, the Tsar was probably planning to remove them from the succession, one by one – but he was too slow.

*

On 10 April 1762, Catherine gave birth to a son by Grigory Orlov, named Alexei Grigorevich Bobrinsky, her third child. Even four months into Peter's reign only a small circle of Guardsmen were aware of Catherine's relationship with Orlov – her friend Princess Ekaterina Dashkova, a player in the coup and wife of one of her Guards supporters, did not know. Peter certainly acted as if *he* was in the dark. This gives us a clue to how the conspiracies remained undiscovered. No one was informing him. He was unable to use the secret powers that autocrats require.[36]

Catherine had recovered from her confinement by early May, but she still hesitated. The drunken Emperor boasted ever more loudly that he would divorce her and marry his mistress, Elisabeth Vorontsova. This concentrated Catherine's mind. She confirms to Poniatowski in her letter of 2 August 1762 that the coup had been mooted for six months. Now it became real.[37]

Peter's 'rightful' successor was not his wife but his son Grand Duke Paul, now aged six: many of the conspirators joined the coup believing that he would be acclaimed emperor with his mother as a figurehead regent. There were rumours that Peter wanted to force Saltykov to admit that he was Paul's real father so that he could dispense with Catherine and start a new dynasty with Vorontsova.

It is easy to forget that there was another emperor in Russia: Ivan VI, buried alive in the bowels of Schlüsselburg, east of Petersburg on the shore of Lake Ladoga, since being overthrown by Elisabeth as a baby in 1741, was now over twenty. Peter went to inspect this forgotten Tsar in his damp dungeon and discovered he was mentally retarded – though his answers sound relatively intelligent. 'Who are you?' asked Emperor Peter. 'I am the Emperor,' came the reply. When Peter asked how he was so sure, the prisoner said he knew it from the Virgin and the angels. Peter gave him a dressing gown. Ivan put it on in transports of delight, running round the dungeon like 'a savage in his first clothes'. Needless to say, Peter was relieved that at least one of his possible nemeses could never rule.[38]

Peter himself transformed the plot from a few groups of daredevil Guardsmen into a deadly coalition against him. On 21 May, he announced he would leave Petersburg to lead his armies in person against Denmark. While he made arrangements for his armies to begin the march west, he himself left the capital for his favourite summer palace at Oranienbaum near Peterhof, whence he would set off for war. Many soldiers did not wish to embark on this unpopular expedition.

A couple of weeks earlier, Peter had managed to light the fuse of his own destruction: at the end of April, the Emperor held a banquet to celebrate the peace with Prussia. Peter was drunk as usual. He proposed a toast to the imperial family, thinking of himself and his Holstein uncles. Catherine did not stand. Peter noticed and shouted at her, demanding to know why she had neither risen nor quaffed. When she reasonably replied that she was a member of the family too, the Emperor shrieked, 'Dura!' – 'Fool!' – down the table. Courtiers and diplomats went silent. Catherine blushed and burst into tears but regained her composure.

That night, Peter supposedly ordered his Adjutant to arrest Catherine so that she could be packed off to a monastery – or worse. The Adjutant rushed to Prince Georg-Ludwig of Holstein, who grasped the folly of such an act. Peter's uncle, whom Potemkin served as orderly, persuaded him to cancel the order.

Catherine's personal and political existence as well as the lives of her children were specifically threatened. She had little choice but to protect herself. During the next three weeks, the Orlovs and their subalterns, including Potemkin, canvassed feverishly to raise the Guards.[39]

The plan was to arrest Peter as he left Oranienbaum for his foolish war against Denmark and imprison him in the fortified tomb of Schlüsselburg with the simpleton–Tsar, Ivan VI. According to Catherine, thirty or forty officers and about 10,000 men were ready.[40] Three vital conspirators came together but, until the last few days, they barely knew of each other's involvement. Catherine was the only link. So, comically, each of the three believed that it was they – and only they – who had placed Catherine on the throne.

Orlov and his Guardsmen, including Potemkin, were the muscle and the organizers of the coup. There were officers in each regiment. Potemkin's job was to prepare the Horse-Guards.[41] But the other two groups were necessary not merely for the coup to succeed but to maintain the reign of Catherine II afterwards.

Ekaterina Dashkova, née Vorontsova, was certain that she alone had made the coup possible. This slim, gamine nineteen-year-old, married to one of Catherine's supporters in the Guards, thought of herself as Machiavelli in petticoats. She was a useful conduit to the high aristocracy: the Empress Elisabeth and Grand Duke Peter stood as godparents at her christening. She personified the tiny, interbred world of Court because she was not only the niece of both Peter III's Chancellor, Mikhail Vorontsov, and Grand Duke Paul's Governor, Nikita Panin, later Catherine's Foreign Minister, but also the sister of the Emperor's 'ugly, stupid' mistress.[42] She was appalled by her sister's taste in emperors. Dashkova demonstrates how family ties did not always decide political loyalties: the Vorontsovs were in power, yet this Vorontsova was conspiring to overthrow them. 'Politics was a subject that interested me from my earliest years,' she writes in her immodest and deluded *Memoirs* that, with Catherine's own writings, are the best accounts of those days.[43]

Nikita Ivanovich Panin, Dashkova's uncle, was the third key conspirator: as the Ober-Hofmeister or Governor of the Grand Duke Paul, he controlled a crucial pawn. Thus Catherine needed Panin's support. When Peter III considered declaring Paul illegitimate, he threatened Panin's powerbase as his Ober-Hofmeister. Panin, aged forty-two, lazy, plump and very shrewd, was far from being an industrious public servant: one has the sense of something almost eunuch-like in his swollen, smooth-skinned insouciance. According to Princess Dashkova, Panin was 'a pale valetudinarian ... studious only of ease, having passed all his life in courts, extremely precise in his dress, wearing a stately wig with three well-powdered ties dangling down his back, he gave one the pasteboard idea of an old courtier from the reign of Louis XIV'.[44] However, Panin did not believe in the unbridled tyranny of the tsars, particularly in the light of Peter III's 'most dissolute debauchery of drunkenness'.[45] Like many of the educated higher nobility, Panin hoped to create an aristocratic oligarchy on Peter's overthrow. He was the righteous opponent of favouritism but his family's rise stemmed from imperial whim.* In the 1750s, the Empress Elisabeth had shown interest in Nikita Panin and there may have been a short affair before the ruling favourite, Ivan Shuvalov, had him despatched on a diplomatic mission to Sweden. When Panin returned in 1760, he was untainted by the poison of Elisabethan politics and acceptable to all factions.[46] So both Catherine and Panin wished to overthrow Peter, but there was a worrying difference in the details: Catherine wanted to rule herself, while Panin, Dashkova and others believed that Grand Duke Paul should become emperor.[47] 'A youthful and female conspirator', writes Princess Dashkova, 'was not likely all at once to gain the confidence of a cautious politician like Monsieur Panin,' but this uneasy cabal of differing interests now came together.

On 12 June, Peter left Petersburg for Oranienbaum. Just eight versts away in Peterhof, Catherine waited in her summer villa, Mon Plaisir.

On 27 June, the conspiracy was suddenly thrown into disarray when Captain Passek, one of the plotters in the Guards, was denounced and

---

* The Panin fortunes were founded on marriage to the niece of Peter the Great's favourite Prince Alexander Menshikov, who had started life as a pie-seller.

arrested. Peter III would not remain unaware of the plot for long. Though nobles were rarely tortured, the threat was there. Passek would surely sing.

The Orlovs, Dashkova and Panin came together for the first and last time in a panic-stricken meeting, while Potemkin and other plotters awaited their instructions. The tough Orlovs, according to Dashkova, were distraught, but 'to quieten apprehensions ... as well as to show that I did not personally shrink from the danger, I desired them to repeat an assurance to their soldiers, as coming direct from me, that I had daily account from the Empress ... and they should be tranquil'. Since a mistake could cost these men their lives, the bragging of this bumptious teenage Princess can hardly have been reassuring.[48]

On her side, the little Princess was not impressed with the coarse Orlovs, who were too vulgar and arrogant for her taste. She told Alexei Orlov, the main organizer of the coup and known as 'Le Balafre' – 'Scarface' – to ride to Mon Plaisir at once. However, Grigory Orlov vacillated over whether to fetch Catherine that night or wait until the next day. Dashkova claimed she decided for them: 'I did not attempt to suppress the rage I felt against these brothers ... to hesitate on the directions I had given Alexei Orlov. "You've lost time already," I said. "As to your fears of alarming the Empress, rather let her be conveyed to St Petersburg in a fainting fit than expose her to the risk ... of sharing with us the scaffold. Tell your brother to ride full speed without a moment's delay ..." '[49]

Catherine's lover finally agreed. The plotters in Petersburg were ordered to rouse the Guards in rebellion. In the middle of the night, Alexei Orlov set off in a travelling carriage to fetch Catherine from Mon Plaisir, accompanied by a handful of Guardsmen who either rode on the running-boards or followed in another carriage: Sergeant Potemkin was among them.

At 6 a.m. the next morning, they arrived outside Mon Plaisir. While Potemkin waited around the carriage with postillions on the box, horses at the ready, whips raised, Alexei Orlov hurried into the special extension built onto the pavilion and burst into Catherine's bedroom, waking his brother's mistress.

'All is ready for the proclamation,' said Alexei Orlov. 'You must get up. Passek has been arrested.' Catherine did not need to hear any more. She dressed swiftly in plain black. The coup would succeed today – or never. If it failed, they would all mount the scaffold.[50]

Alexei Orlov helped Catherine into his carriage, threw his cloak over her and ordered the postillions to drive the eighteen kilometres back to Petersburg at top speed. As the carriage pulled away, Potemkin and another officer, Vasily Bibikov, leaped on to its shafts to guard their precious cargo. There has always been some doubt as to where Potemkin was during these hours, but this story, cited here for the first time, was recorded by the Englishman Reginald Pole Carew, who later knew Potemkin well and probably heard it from the horse's mouth.[51]

Catherine was still wearing her lace nightcap. They met a carriage coming from the capital. By a fortunate coincidence, it turned out to contain her French hairdresser, Michel, who jumped into her carriage and did her hair on the way to the revolution, though it was still unpowdered when she arrived. Nearer the capital, they met Grigory Orlov's small carriage hurtling along the other way. Catherine, with Alexei and the hairdresser, swapped conveyances. Potemkin may have swapped too. The carriages headed directly to the barracks of the Izmailovsky Guards, where they found 'twelve men and a drummer'. From such small beginnings are empires taken. 'The soldiers', Catherine recounted breathlessly, 'rushed to kiss my hands, my feet, the hem of my dress, calling me their saviour. Two ... brought a priest with a crucifix and started to take the oath.' Their Colonel – and Catherine's former admirer – Count Kirill Razumovsky, Hetman of the Ukraine, kissed hands on bended knee.

Catherine mounted the carriage again and, led by the priest and the soldiers, set off towards the Semyonovsky Guards barracks. 'They came to meet us shouting Vivat!' She embarked on a canvassing perambulation which grew into a triumphant procession. But not all the Guards officers supported the coup: Dashkova's brother and nephew of Peter III's Chancellor, Simon Romanovich Vorontsov, resisted and was arrested. Just as Catherine was between the Anichkov Palace and the Kazan Cathedral, Sergeant Potemkin reappeared at the head of his Horse-Guards. The men hailed their Empress with frenzied enthusiasm. She may already have known his name as one of the coup's organizers because she later praised Lieutenant Khitrovo and 'a subaltern of seventeen named Potemkin' for their 'discernment, courage and action' that day – though the Horse-Guards officers also supported the coup. In fact, Potemkin was twenty-three.[52]

The imperial convoy, swelled with thousands of Guardsmen, headed for the Winter Palace, where the Senate and Synod assembled to put out her already printed Manifesto and take the oath. Panin arrived at the Palace with her son, Grand Duke Paul, still wearing his nightshirt and cotton cap. Crowds milled outside as the news spread. Catherine appeared at a window and the mob howled its approval. Meanwhile the doors of the Palace were open and its corridors, like a ball deluged by gate-crashers, were jammed with soldiers, priests, ambassadors and townspeople, all come to take the oath to the new Sovereign – or just gawp at the revolution.

Princess Dashkova arrived soon after Panin and the Grand Duke: 'I ordered my maid to bring me a gala dress and hastily set off for the Winter Palace ...'. The appearance of an over-excited teenage princess dressed to the nines caused more drama: first she could not get in and then, when she was recognized, the crowd was so dense that she could not push through. Finally, the slim girl was passed overhead by the soldiers, hand to hand, like a doll. With 'one shout of approbation', they 'acknowledged me as their common friend'. All this was enough to turn anyone's head and it certainly turned hers. 'At length, my head giddy, my robe tattered ... I rushed into Her Majesty's presence.'[53]

The Empress and the Princess embraced but, while the coup had already seized Petersburg, the advantage remained with Peter: his armies in nearby Livonia, primed for the Danish war, could easily crush the Guards. Then there was the fortress of Kronstadt, still under his control, which commanded the sea approaches to St Petersburg itself. Catherine, advised by Panin, the Orlovs and other senior officials such as Count Kyrill Razumovsky, sent Admiral Talyzin to win over Kronstadt.

The Emperor himself now had to be seized. The Empress ordered the Guards to prepare to march on Peterhof. Perhaps remembering how fine the Empress Elisabeth had looked in men's clothes, Catherine demanded a Guardsman's uniform. The soldiers eagerly shed the hated Prussian uniforms that Peter had made them wear and replaced them with their old tunics. If her men were tearing off their old clothes, so would Catherine. 'She borrowed one suit from Captain Talyzin [cousin of the Admiral],' wrote Dashkova, 'and I procured another from Lieutenant Pushkin, two young officers of our respective sizes ... of the ancient costume of the Preobrazhensky Guards.'[54]

While Catherine received her supporters in the Winter Palace, Peter arrived, as arranged, at Peterhof to celebrate the Feast of St Peter and St Paul with Catherine. Mon Plaisir was deserted. Catherine's gala dress, abandoned on her bed, was an almost ghostly auspice – for she had changed her clothes in every sense. Peter III saw it and collapsed: he wept, drank and dithered.

The only one of his courtiers not to lose his head was the octogenarian Field-Marshal Count Burhard von Münnich, a German veteran of the palace revolutions of 1740/1, recently recalled from exile. Münnich proposed an immediate march on St Petersburg in the spirit of his grand-father – but this was no Peter the Great. The Tsar sent emissaries into Petersburg to negotiate or arrest Catherine, but each one defected to her: Chancellor Mikhail Vorontsov, who had ridden on the boards of Elisabeth's sleigh during *her* coup twenty years earlier, volunteered to go but joined Catherine at once, falling to his knees. Already dejected and confused, Peter's dwindling entourage trundled sadly back the eight versts to Oranienbaum. The grizzled Münnich finally persuaded the Emperor that he should seize the fortress of Kronstadt to control the capital. Emissaries were sent ahead. When Peter's schooner arrived at Oranienbaum at about 10 p.m. on this white silvery night, he was drunk and had to be helped aboard by his mistress, Elisabeth Vorontsova, and the old Field-Marshal. Three hours later, he appeared off Kronstadt.

Münnich called to the Kronstadt watch that the Emperor was before them, but they shouted back: 'There is no longer an Emperor.' They declared that they only recognised Catherine II. It was too late: Admiral Talyzin had reached Kronstadt just in time. Peter lost all control of himself and events. He fainted in his cabin. On his return to Oran-ienbaum, the broken, tipsy Emperor, who had always foreseen this destiny, just wanted to abdicate and live in Holstein. He decided to negotiate.

In Petersburg, Catherine massed her Guards outside the Winter Palace. It was at this exhilarating and unforgettable moment that Pot-emkin contrived to meet his new Empress for the first time.[55]

3

FIRST MEETING: THE
EMPRESS'S RECKLESS SUITOR

The Horse-Guards came, in such a frenzy of joy as I have never
seen, weeping and shouting that the country was free at last.
Catherine the Great to Stanislas Poniatowski, 2 August 1762

Of all the sovereigns of Europe, I believe the Empress of Russia
is the richest in diamonds. She has a kind of passion for them;
perhaps she has no other weaknesses...
Sir George Macartney on Catherine the Great

The newly acclaimed Catherine II, dressed raffishly in a borrowed green
uniform of a captain of the Preobrazhensky Guards, appeared at the
door of the Winter Palace on the night of 28 June 1762, accompanied by
her entourage, and holding a naked sabre in her bare hands. In the blue
incandescence of St Petersburg's 'white nights', she walked down the
outside steps into the crowded square and towards her thoroughbred
grey stallion, who was named Brilliant. She swung into the saddle with
the ease of a practised horsewoman – her years of frantic exercise had
not been wasted.

The Guards, 12,000 who had rallied to her revolution, were massed
around her in the square, ready to set off on 'The March to Peterhof' to
overthrow Peter III. All of them must have peered at the thirty-three-
year-old woman in her prime, with her long auburn hair, her bright-
blue eyes, her black eyelashes, so at home in the Guardsman's uniform,
at the moment of the crucial drama of her life. Among them, Potemkin,
on horseback in his Horse-Guards uniform, eagerly awaited any opportunity to distinguish himself.

The soldiers stiffened to attention with the Guards' well-drilled
pageantry – but the square was far from silent. It more resembled the
bustling chaos of an encampment than the polished stiffness of a parade.
The night resounded with clattering hooves, neighing horses, clinking
spurs and swords, fluttering banners, the coughing, muttering and whis-
pering of thousands of men. Many of the troops had been waiting there
since the night before in a carnival atmosphere. Some of them were
drunk – the taverns had been looted. The streets were littered with

discarded Prussian-style uniforms, like the morning after a fancy-dress party. None of this mattered because every man knew he was changing history: they peered at the enchanting vision of this young woman they were making empress and the excitement of it must have touched all of them.

Catherine took Brilliant's reins and was handed her sword, but she realized that she had forgotten to attach a *dragonne*, or sword-knot, to the sabre. She must have looked around for one because her hesitation was noticed by a sharp-eyed Guardsman who was to understand her better, more instinctively, than anyone else. He instantly galloped over to her across the square, tore the *dragonne* off his own sword and handed it to her with a bow. She thanked him. She would have noticed his almost giant stature, that splendid head of auburn-brown hair and the long sensitive face with the cleft chin, the looks that had won him the nick-name 'Alcibiades'. Grigory Potemkin could not have brought himself to her attention in a more daring way, at a more memorable occasion, but he had a talent for seizing the moment.

Princess Dashkova, also dressed dashingly in a Guardsman's uniform, mounted her horse just behind the Empress. There was a distinct element of masquerade in this 'petticoat revolution'. Now it was time to move in order to strike at dawn: Peter III was still at large and still emperor in name at Oranienbaum, a night's march away. Yet Alcibiades was still beside the Empress.

Catherine took the *dragonne* from Potemkin, fixed it to her sword and urged Brilliant forward. Potemkin spurred his mount back to join his men, but his horse had been trained in the Horse-Guards to ride, knee to knee, in squadron formation for the charge. The beast stubbornly refused to return, so that for several minutes, as the fate of the Empire revolved around this little scene, Potemkin struggled to master his obstinate horse and was forced to talk to the new Empress. 'This made her laugh . . . she noticed his looks . . . she talked to him. Thus', Potemkin himself told a friend when he was Catherine's co-ruler, he was 'thrown into the career of honour, wealth and power – all thanks to a fresh horse'.[1]

All accounts agree on the way he met Catherine but differ on the detail: was it the *dragonne* or the upright plumage for a hat, a *sultane*?[2] What mattered for the superstitious Potemkin was the way the horse would not leave the imperial side, as if the beast sensed their joint destiny: this 'happy chance', he called it.[3] But it was not chance that had made him gallop up to offer his *dragonne*. Knowing Potemkin's artifice, love of play-acting and fine horsemanship, it is quite possible that it was not the horse that delayed his return to the ranks. Either way, it now obeyed its rider and galloped back to his place.

The long column of men, marching around two mounted women in male uniforms, set out into the light night. Military bands played; the men sang marching songs. Sometimes they whistled and shouted: 'Long live our little mother Catherine!'

At 3 a.m., Catherine's column stopped at Krasni-Kabak to rest. She lay down on a narrow, straw bed beside Dashkova, but she did not sleep. The Orlovs pushed ahead with their vanguard. The main body set off again two hours later and were met by the Vice-Chancellor, Prince A. M. Golitsyn, with another offer from Peter. But there was nothing to negotiate except unconditional abdication. The Vice-Chancellor took the oath to Catherine.

Soon the news arrived that Alexei Orlov had taken peaceful possession of the two summer estates, Oranienbaum and Peterhof. At 10 a.m., Peterhof received Catherine as sovereign empress: it was only twenty-four hours since she had left in her lace nightcap. Her lover Grigory Orlov, accompanied by Potemkin, was already at nearby Oranienbaum forcing Peter to sign the unconditional abdication.[4] When the name was on the paper, Grigory Orlov brought it back to the Empress. Potemkin remained behind to guard this husk of an emperor.[5] A disgusted Frederick the Great, for whom it might be said that Peter III had sacrificed his Empire, remarked that the Emperor 'let himself be driven from the throne as a child is sent to bed'.[6]

The ex-Emperor was guided into his carriage accompanied by his mistress and two aides. The carriage was surrounded by a guard. Potemkin was among them. The milling troops taunted the convoy with hurrahs of 'Long live the Empress Catherine the Second.'[7] At Peterhof, Peter handed over his sword, his ribbon of St Andrew and his Pre-obrazhensky Guards uniform. He was taken to a room he knew well, where Panin visited him: the ex-Tsar fell to his knees and begged not to be separated from his mistress. When this was refused, an exhausted, weeping Peter asked if he could take his fiddle, his negro Narcissus and his dog Mopsy. 'I consider it one of the great misfortunes of my life that I had to see Peter at that moment,' Panin remembered later, 'the greatest misfortune of my life.'[8]

Before he could be taken to his permanent home at Schlüsselburg, a closed Berline carriage with guards on the running-boards, commanded by Alexei Orlov, transferred the ex-Emperor to his estate at Ropsha (about nineteen miles inland). Potemkin is not mentioned among this guard, but he was there days later, so he was probably present. Catherine granted her husband his fiddle, blackamoor – and dog.[9] She never saw Peter again.

A few days later, Princess Dashkova entered Catherine's cabinet and was 'astonished' to see Grigory Orlov 'stretched at full length on a sofa' going through the state papers. 'I asked what he was about. "The Empress has ordered that I open them," he replied.' The new regime was in power.[10]

Catherine II arrived back in the jubilant capital on 30 June. Now she had won, she had to pay for her victory. Potemkin was among the beneficiaries specified by the Empress herself: no doubt she remembered the sword-knot. The cost was over a million roubles in a total annual budget of only sixteen million. Her supporters received generous rewards for their roles in the coup: St Petersburg's garrison were given half a year's salary – a total of 225,890 roubles. Grigory Orlov was promised 50,000 roubles; Panin and Razumovsky got pensions of 5,000 roubles. On 9 August, Grigory and Alexei Orlov, Ekaterina Dashkova and the seventeen leading plotters received either 800 souls or 24,000 roubles each.

Grigory Potemkin was among the eleven junior players who received 600 souls or 18,000 roubles.[11] He appeared on other lists in Catherine's own handwriting: in one, the Horse-Guards commanders presented their report, suggesting that Potemkin be promoted to cornet. Catherine in her own hand wrote, 'has to be lieutenant', so he was promoted to second lieutenant,[12] and she promised him another 10,000 roubles. Catherine left Chancellor Vorontsov in his job, but Nikita Panin became her chief minister. Panin's coterie wanted a regency for Paul, steered by aristocratic oligarchy, but the Orlovs and their Guards protected Catherine's absolute power, which was their sole reason for being in government at all.[13] However, the Orlovs had a further plan: the marriage of Grigory Orlov to the Empress. There was a not insurmountable obstacle to this: Catherine was already married.

Peter III, Narcissus and Mopsy remained at Ropsha, guarded by Alexei Orlov and his 300 men, Potemkin among them. Orlov kept Catherine abreast of this awkward situation in a series of hearty, informal yet macabre letters. He mentioned Potemkin by name in these notes, another sign that Catherine was acquainted with him, albeit vaguely. But he concentrated on mocking Peter as the 'freak'. One senses a tightening garotte in Orlov's sinister jokes, as if he was seeking Catherine's approval for his deed before he undertook it.[14]

She cannot have been surprised to learn around 5 July that Peter had been murdered. The details remain as murky as the deed. All we know is that Alexei Orlov and his myrmidons played their roles and that the ex-Emperor was throttled.[15]

The death served everyone's ends. Ex-emperors were always living liabilities for their successors in a country plagued by pretenders. Even dead, they could rise again. Peter III's mere existence undermined Catherine's usurpation. He also threatened the Orlovs' plans. There was no mistake in his murder. Was Potemkin involved? Since he was to be accused of every imaginable sin in his subsequent career, it is significant that the murder of Peter is never mentioned in connection with him, and this can only mean that he played no part in it. But he was at Ropsha.

Catherine shed bitter tears – for her reputation, not for Peter: 'My glory is spoilt, Posterity will never forgive me.' Dashkova was shocked but was also thinking about herself. 'It is a death too sudden, Madame, for your glory and mine.'[16] Catherine appreciated the benefits of the deed. No one was punished. Indeed Alexei Orlov was to play a prominent role for the next thirty years. But it made Catherine notorious in Europe as an adulterous regicide and matricide.

The Emperor's body lay in state in a plain coffin at the Alexander Nevsky Convent for two days in a blue Holstein uniform without any decorations. A cravat covered its bruised throat and a hat was placed low over its face to hide the blackening caused by strangulation.[17]

Catherine recovered her composure and issued a much mocked statement blaming Peter's death on 'a haemorrhoidal colic'.[18] This absurd if necessary diagnosis was to become a euphemism in Europe for political murder. When Catherine later invited the *philosophe* d'Alembert to visit her, he joked to Voltaire that he did not dare since he was prone to piles, obviously a very dangerous condition in Russia.[19]

The tsars of Russia were traditionally crowned in Moscow, the old Orthodox capital. Peter III, with his contempt for his adopted land, had not bothered to be crowned at all. Catherine, the usurper, was not about to make the same mistake. On the contrary, a usurper must follow the rituals of legitimacy down to the smallest detail, whatever the cost. Catherine ordered a lavish, traditional coronation to be arranged as soon as possible.

On 4 August, the very day he was promoted to second lieutenant on the personal order of the Empress, Potemkin was among three squadrons of Horse-Guards who departed for Moscow to attend the coronation. His mother and family still lived there to welcome the homecoming of the prodigal, for he had left as a scapegrace and now returned to guard an empress at her coronation. On the 27th, Grand Duke Paul, aged eight, the sole legitimate pillar of the new regime, accompanied by his Governor Panin with twenty-seven carriages and 257 horses, left the capital, followed by Grigory Orlov. The Empress left five days later with an entourage of twenty-three courtiers, sixty-three carriages and 395 horses. The Empress and the Tsarevich entered Moscow, city of cupolas and towers and old Russia, on Friday, 13 September. She always hated Moscow, where she felt disliked and where she had once fallen gravely ill. Now her prejudice was proved right when little Paul contracted fever, which just held off for the actual ceremony.

On Sunday, 22 September, in the Assumption Cathedral at the heart of the Kremlin, the Empress was crowned 'the most serene and all-powerful Princess and lady Catherine the Second, Empress and Autocrat of all the Russias' before fifty-five Orthodox dignitaries standing in a semi-circle. Like Elisabeth before her, she deliberately placed her own crown on her head to emphasize that her legitimacy derived from herself, then took the sceptre in her right hand and the orb in her left, and the congregation fell to its knees. The choir sang. Cannons fired. The Archbishop of Novgorod anointed her. She took communion.

Catherine returned to her palace in a golden carriage, guarded by the unmounted Horse-Guards including Potemkin, while gold coins were tossed to the crowds. When she had passed, the people fell to their knees. Later, when it was time for the coronation honours to be announced, the new regime began to take shape: Grigory Orlov was named adjutant-general, and the five brothers, with Nikita Panin, were raised to counts of the Russian Empire. Second Lieutenant Potemkin, who was there on duty at the palace, once again appeared in these lists: he received a silver table set and another 400 souls in the Moscow region. On 30 November, he was appointed *Kammerjunker*, or gentleman of the bedchamber, with permission to remain in the Guards[20] while other new *Kammerjunker*s left the army and became courtiers.[21]

There was now a tiring week of balls, ceremonies and receptions, but the Grand Duke Paul's fever worsened: if he died, there could be no worse omen for Catherine's reign. Since Catherine had claimed power partly to protect Paul from Peter III, his death would also remove much of her justification for ruling. It was clear that his claim to the throne was superior to hers. One emperor had already suffered from murderous piles; the death of his son would taint Catherine, already a regicide, with more sacred royal blood. The crisis reached its height during the first two weeks of October with the Tsarevich in delirium, but afterwards he began to improve. This did not help the tense atmosphere. Catherine's regime had survived to her coronation, but already there were plots and counter-plots. In the barracks, Guardsmen who had made one emperor now thought they could make others. At Court, the Orlovs wanted their Grigory to marry Catherine, while Panin and the magnates wished to curb imperial powers and govern in Paul's name.

In the year or so since he had arrived at Horse-Guards from Moscow, Potemkin had advanced from an expelled student to serving the Empress as gentleman of the bedchamber, doubling his souls and being promoted two ranks. Now, back in Petersburg, the Orlovs told the Empress about the funniest man in the Guards, Lieutenant Potemkin, who was an outrageous mimic. Catherine, who knew the name and the face from the coup, replied that she would like to hear this wit. So the Orlovs summoned Potemkin to amuse the Empress. He must have thought his moment had come. The self-declared 'spoilt child of fortune', always swinging between despair and exultation, possessed an absolute belief in his own destiny, that he could achieve anything, beyond the limits of ordinary men. Now he had his chance.

Grigory Orlov recommended his imitation of one particular noble-man. Potemkin could render the man's peculiar voice and mannerisms perfectly. Soon after the coronation, the Guardsman was formally presented for the first time and Catherine requested this particular act. Potemkin replied that he was quite unable to do any mimicry at all – but his voice was different and it sent a chill through the whole room. Everyone sat up straight or looked studiously at the floor. The voice was absolutely and unmistakably perfect. The accent was slightly German and the intonation was exquisitely accurate. Potemkin was imitating the Empress herself. The older courtiers must have presumed that this youngster's career was to finish before it had started. The Orlovs must have waited nonchalantly to see how she would take this impertinence. Everyone concentrated on the boldly handsome, somewhat mannish face and high, clever forehead of their Tsarina. She started to laugh uproariously, so everyone else laughed too and agreed that Potemkin's imitation was brilliant. Once again, his gamble had paid off.

It was then that the Empress looked properly at Second Lieutenant and Gentleman of the Bedchamber Potemkin and admired the striking looks of this 'real Alcibiades'. Being a woman, she at once noticed his flowing and silky head of brown-auburn hair – 'the best *chevelure* in all Russia'. She turned to Grigory Orlov and complained that it was more beautiful than hers: 'I'll never forgive you for having introduced me to this man,' she joked. 'It was you who wanted to present him but you'll repent.' Orlov would indeed regret it. These stories are told by people who knew Potemkin at this time – a cousin and a fellow Guardsman. Even if they owe as much to hindsight as history, they ring true.[22]

In the eleven-and-a-half years between the coup and the beginning of their love affair, the Empress was watching Potemkin and preparing him for something. There was nothing inevitable in 1762 about his rise to almost supreme power, but the more she saw of him, the more fascinating she found his infinite originality. They were somehow converging on each other, running on apparently parallel lines that became closer and closer. At twenty-three, Potemkin flaunted his mimicry and intelligence to the Empress. She soon realized that there was much more to him than a gorgeous *chevelure*: he was a Greek scholar and an expert in theology and the cultures of Russia's native peoples. But he appears scantily in the history of those years and always swathed in legend: while we sketch the daily life of Empress and Court, we catch glimpses of Potemkin, stepping out of the crowd of courtiers to engage in repartee with Catherine – and then disappearing again. He made sure these fleeting appearances were memorable.

Lieutenant Potemkin had fallen in love with the Empress and he did not seem to mind who knew it. He was unafraid of the Orlovs or anyone else in the bearpit of Catherine's unstable Court. This is the world he now entered, playing only for the highest stakes. The reign of Catherine II appears to us as long, glorious and stable – but this is with hindsight. At the time, the illicit regime of a female usurper and regicide seemed to the foreign ambassadors in St Petersburg to be ill-starred and destined to last only a short time. Potemkin, who had been in the capital for little over a year, had much to learn about both the Empress and the magnates of the Court.

'My position is such that I have to observe the greatest caution,' Catherine wrote to Poniatowksi, her ex-lover, who was threatening to visit her, on 30 June. 'The least soldier of the Guard thinks when he sees me: "That is the work of my hands." ' Poniatowski was still in love with Catherine – he always would be – and now he longed to reclaim the Grand Duchess he had been forced to leave. Catherine's reply leaves us in no doubt about the atmosphere in Petersburg nor about her irritation with Poniatowski's naive passion: 'Since I have to speak plainly, and you have resolved to ignore what I have been telling you for six months, the fact is that, if you come here, you are likely to get us both slaughtered.'[23]

While she was busy creating the magnificent Court she believed she needed, she was simultaneously struggling behind the scenes to find stability amid so many intrigues. Almost at once, she was deluged with revelations of conspiracies against her, even among the Guardsmen who had just placed her on the throne. Catherine's secret police, inherited from Peter III, was the Secret Expedition of the Senate, run throughout her reign by Stepan Sheshkovsky, the feared 'knout-wielder', under the Procurator-General. The Empress tried to reduce the use of the torture, especially after the suspect had already confessed, but it is impossible to know how far she succeeded: it is likely that the further from Petersburg, the more torture was liberally applied. Whipping and beating were more usual than real torture. The Secret Expedition was tiny – around only forty employees, a far cry from the legions employed by the NKVD or KGB of Soviet times – but there was little privacy: courtiers and foreigners were effectively watched by their own servants and guards while civil servants would not hesitate to inform on malcontents.[24] Catherine sometimes ordered political opponents to be watched and she was always ready to receive Sheshkovsky. There was no such thing as a police state in the eighteenth century, but, whatever her noble sentiments, the Secret Expedition was always ready to observe, arrest and interrogate – and they were particularly busy in these early years.

There were two other candidates for the throne with a better claim than hers: Ivan VI, the simpleton of Schlüsselburg, and Paul, her own son. The first conspirators, on behalf of Ivan, were uncovered in October 1762 during her coronation in Moscow: two Guardsmen of the Izmailovsky Regiment, Guriev and Khrushchev. They were tortured and beaten with sticks, with Catherine's permission, but their 'plot' was really little more than inebriated boasting.

Catherine never lost her nerve: she balanced the different factions at Court while simultaneously strengthening her security and shamelessly bribing the Guards with lavish gifts. Each side in this factional struggle had its own dangerous agenda. Catherine made it clear at once that, like Peter the Great before her and following the example of the hero of the day, Frederick the Great, she would be her own Chancellor. She ran Russia through a strong secretariat which became the true government of the Empire. Within two years, she found Prince Alexander Alexeiovich Viazemsky, aged thirty-four, the tireless if unloved administrator with bug eyes and ruddy face, who would run the internal affairs of Russia for almost thirty years from the Senate as her Procurator-General, a role which combined the modern jobs of Finance, Justice and Interior Ministers.

Nikita Panin became her senior minister. That believer in aristocratic restraint of absolutist whim proposed an imperial council which would be appointed by the Empress but which she could not dismiss. Panin's ideal was a threat both to Catherine and to the 'upstarts' in the Guards who had placed her on the throne.[25] Panin's guardianship of Paul, widely regarded as the rightful Emperor, made him the natural advocate of a handover to the boy as soon as he was of age. He openly despised the rule of 'capricious favourites'.[26] So the five Orlovs were his enemies. During the next twelve years, both factions tried to use Potemkin's growing imperial friendship in their struggle for supremacy.

Catherine distracted Panin from his schemes by confining him to foreign policy as 'senior member' of the College of Foreign Affairs – Foreign Minister – but she never forgot that Panin had wanted to place Paul, not her, on the throne in 1762. It was safer for this reptilian schemer to be the serpent inside her house. They needed each other: she thought Panin was 'the most skilful, intelligent and zealous person at my Court', but she did not particularly like him.[27]

Beneath these two main factions, the court of the new Empress was a labyrinth of families and factions. Catherine appointed her admirer from the 1750s, Zakhar Chernyshev, to run the College of War, while his brother Ivan was made head of the navy: the Chernyshevs initially remained neutral between the Panins and Orlovs. But members of the big families often supported different factions as we saw with Princess Dashkova and the Vorontsovs.[28] Even she soon overreached herself by claiming to exercise power she did not possess.[29] 'This celebrated conspirator who boasted of having given away a crown ... became a laughingstock to all Russians.'[30] Dashkova, like the Elisabethan magnates Chancellor Vorontsov and Ivan Shuvalov, would 'travel abroad', the euphemism for a gentle exile in the spa-resorts of Europe.

Catherine's Court became a kaleidoscope of perpetually shifting and competing factions that were groups of individuals linked by friendship, family, greed, love or shared views of the vaguest sort. The two basic shibboleths remained whether a courtier supported a Prussian or Austrian alliance, and whether he or she was closer to the Empress or the Heir. All was dominated by the simplest self-interest – 'Thy enemy's enemy is my friend.'

The new regime's first foreign-policy success was the placing of the crown of Poland on the head of Catherine's last lover. Within days of the coup, on 2 August 1762, Catherine wrote to earnest Stanislas Poniatowski: 'I am sending Count Keyserling to Poland immediately to make you king after the death of the present one,' Augustus III.

This has often been presented as an imperial caprice to thank

Poniatowski for his amorous services. But that tautological institution, the Serene Commonwealth of Poland, was not a frivolous matter. Poland was in every way unique in Europe, but it was an infuriating state of absurd contradictions: it was really not one country, but two states – the Kingdom of Poland and the Grand Duchy of Lithuania; it had one parliament, the Sejm, but parallel governments; its kings were elected and almost powerless; when they appointed some officials, they could not dismiss them; its nobility, the *szlachta*, were almost omnipotent. Sejms were elected by the entire *szlachta*, which, since it included almost 10 per cent of the population, made Poland more democratic than England. One vote was enough to annul the proceedings of an entire Sejm – the famous *liberum veto* – which made the poorest delegate more powerful than the King. There was only one way around this: nobles could form a Confederation, a temporary alternative Sejm that would exist only until it had achieved its aims. Then it would disband. But really Poland was ruled by its magnates, 'kinglets' who owned estates as large as some countries and possessed their own armies. The Poles were extremely proud of their strange constitution, which kept this massive land in a humiliating chaos that they regarded as golden, unbridled freedom.

Choosing Polish kings was one of the favourite diplomatic sports of the eighteenth century. The contestants in this diplomatic joust were Russia, Prussia, Austria and France. Versailles had three traditional allies in the East, the Ottoman Empire, Sweden and Poland. But ever since 1716, when Peter the Great had guaranteed the flawed constitution of Poland, Russia's policy was to dominate the Commonwealth by maintaining its absurd constitution, placing weak kings in Warsaw, encouraging the power of the magnates – and having a Russian army ever ready on the border. Catherine's sole interest in all this was to preserve the Petrine protectorate over Poland. Poniatowski was the ideal figurehead for this because through his pro-Russian Czartoryski uncles, the 'Familia', backed by Russian guns and English money, Catherine could continue to control Poland.

Poniatowski began to dream of becoming king and then marrying Catherine, hence, as his biographer writes, he could combine the two great desires of his life.[31] 'If I desired the throne,' he pleaded to her, 'it was because I saw you on it.' When told that this was impossible, he beseeched her: 'Don't make me king, but bring me back to your side.'[32] This gallant if whining idealism did not auger well for his future relationship with the female paragon of *raison d'état*. Since the usual contestants in this game of king-making were exhausted after the Seven

Years War, Catherine and Panin were able to pull it off. Catherine won Frederick the Great's backing because Prussia had been ruined by the Seven Years War and was so isolated that this alliance with Russia, signed on 31 March/11 April 1764, was his only hope. On 26 August/6 September the Election Sejm, surrounded by Russian troops, elected Poniatowski king of Poland. He adopted the name Stanislas-Augustus.

The Prussian alliance – and the Polish protectorate – were meant to form the pillars of Panin's much vaunted 'Northern System', in which the northern powers, including Denmark, Sweden and hopefully England, would restrain the 'Catholic Bloc' – the Bourbons of France and Spain, and the Habsburgs of Austria.[33]

Now that Poniatowski was a king, would Catherine marry Grigory Orlov? There was a precedent of sorts. The Empress Elisabeth was rumoured to have married her Cossack chorister Alexei Razumovsky. He now lived in retirement in Moscow.

An old courtier called at Alexei Razumovsky's Elisabethan Baroque palace and found him reading the Bible. The visitor was Chancellor Mikhail Vorontsov, performing his last political role before 'travelling abroad'. He came to offer Razumovsky the rank of imperial highness. This was a polite way of asking if he had secretly married the Empress Elisabeth. Catherine and the Orlovs wished to know: was there a marriage certificate? Razumovsky must have smiled at this. He closed his Bible and produced a box of ebony, gold and pearl. He opened it to reveal an old scroll sealed with the imperial eagle . . .

Catherine had to tread carefully. She absolutely understood the dangers of raising the Orlovs too high. If she married Orlov, she would threaten Grand Duke Paul's claim to the throne, and possibly his life, as well as outraging the magnates and the army. But she loved Orlov. She owed the Orlovs her throne. She had borne Grigory a son.* This was an age when the imperial public and private lives were indissoluble. All through her life, Catherine longed for a family: her parents were dead; her aunt had terrorized her and taken away her son; the interests of her son were a living threat to her reign if not her life; even Anna, her daughter with Poniatowski, had died young. Her position was extraordinary, yet she yearned for an almost bourgeois home with Grigory

---

* This was the child with whom she was pregnant at Elisabeth's death – Alexei Grigorevich Bobrinsky, 1762–1813. Though he was never officially recognized, Catherine saw to his upbringing. He led a debauched life in Paris with the Empress paying his debts, before returning home and later travelling again. Paul I finally recognized him as a half-brother and made him a count.

Orlov, whom she regarded as her partner for life. So she let the question ride – and probably allowed the Orlovs to send this envoy to ask Razumovsky whether the precedent existed.

Yet the brothers were not the most subtle of operators. At one small party, Grigory boasted with gangsterish swagger that, if he wished, he could overthrow Catherine in a month. Kirill Razumovsky, the good-natured brother of Alexei, replied quick as a flash: 'Could be; but, my friend, instead of waiting a month, we would have hanged you in two weeks.'[34] The guffaws were hearty – but chilling. When Catherine hinted at an Orlov marriage, Panin supposedly replied: 'The Empress can do what she wishes but Madame Orlov will never be Empress of Russia.'[35]

This vacillation was not a safe policy. In May 1763, while Catherine was on a pilgrimage from Moscow to Rostov-on-Don, she was given a shock that put paid to Orlov's project. Gentleman of the Bedchamber Fyodor Khitrovo, who with Potemkin had raised the Horse-Guards for Catherine, was arrested. Under interrogation, he admitted planning to kill the Orlovs to stop the marriage and marry Catherine to Ivan VI's brother. This was no ordinary officer muttering over his vodka but a player in the inner circle of Catherine's conspiracy. Did Panin or Catherine herself create this decisive *nyet* to Orlov ambitions? If so, it served its purpose.

This brings us back to the question asked of Alexei Razumovsky, who toyed with the scroll in the bejewelled box until Chancellor Vorontsov held out his hand. Razumovsky tossed it into the fire. 'No, there is no proof,' he said. 'Tell that to our gracious Sovereign.'[36] The story is mythical, but it appears in some histories that Razumovsky thus stymied Catherine's wish to marry Orlov. In fact, Catherine was fond of both Razumovskys – two genial charmers and old friends of about twenty years. There probably was no marriage certificate. The burning of the scroll sounds like the droll Cossack's joke. But, if the question was asked, it is most likely that Alexei Razumovsky gave the answer that Catherine wanted in order to avoid having to marry Orlov. If she needed to ask the question, she did not want an answer.[37]

Just as she celebrated success in Poland, Catherine faced another challenge from the simpleton known as 'Nameless Prisoner Number One', the Emperor in the tower. On 20 June 1764, the Empress left the capital on a progress through her Baltic provinces. On 5 July a tormented young officer, Vasily Mirovich, with dreams of restoring his family's fortunes, launched a bid to liberate Ivan VI from the bowels of Schlüsselburg and make him emperor. Poor Mirovich did not know that Catherine had reconfirmed Peter III's orders that, if anyone tried to free Prisoner Number One, he had to be killed instantly. Meanwhile Mirovich, whose regiment was stationed at Schlüsselburg, was trying to discover the identity of the mysterious prisoner without a name who was held so carefully in the fortress.

On 4 July, Mirovich, who had lost his most trusted co-conspirator in a drowning accident, wrote a manifesto proclaiming the accession of Emperor Ivan VI. Given the atmosphere of instability after the regicide of Peter III and the superstitious reverence Russians held for their tsars, he managed to recruit a few men. At 2 a.m. Mirovich seized control of the gates, overpowered the commandant and headed for Ivan's cell. Shooting broke out between the rebels and Ivan's guards and then abruptly ceased. When he rushed into the cell, he found the ex-Emperor's body still bleeding from a handful of stab wounds. Mirovich understood immediately, kissed the body and surrendered.

Catherine continued with her trip for one more day but then returned, fearing that the conspiracy might have been wider. Under interrogation, it turned out that Mirovich was not the centre of a spider's web, just a loner. After a trial in September, he was sentenced to death. Six soldiers were variously sentenced to run the gauntlet of 1,000 men ten or twelve times (which would probably prove fatal) – and then face exile if they survived. Mirovich was beheaded on 15 September 1764.

The murder of two emperors shocked Europe: the *philosophes*, who were already enjoying a flattering correspondence with the Empress and regarded her as one of their own, had to bend over backwards to overcome their scruples: 'I agree with you that our philosophy does not want to boast of too many pupils like her. But what can one do? One must love one's friends with all their faults,' wrote d'Alembert to Voltaire. The latter wittily coined a new euphemism for murdering two tsars: 'These are family matters,' said the sage of Ferney, 'which do not concern me.'[38]

Being Catherine, she did not relax. She knew that it was not enough merely to rule. Her Court was the mirror which would reflect her successes to the world. She knew that she herself had to be its finest ornament.

'I never saw in my life a person whose port, manner and behaviour answered so strongly to the idea I had formed of her,' wrote the English envoy Sir George Macartney. 'Though in her 37th year of her age, she may still be called beautiful. Those who knew her younger say they never remembered her so lovely as at present and I very readily believe it.'[39] The Prince de Ligne, looking back from 1780, thought, 'She had been more handsome than pretty. The majesty of her forehead was tempered by the eyes and agreeable smile.'[40] The perspicacious Scottish professor William Richardson, author of *Anecdotes of the Russian Empire*, wrote, 'The Russian Empress is above average height, gracious and well proportioned but well covered, has pretty colouring but seeks to embellish it with rouge, like all women in this country. Her mouth is well-shaped with fine teeth; her blue eyes have a scrutinizing expression. The whole is such that it would be insulting to say she had a masculine look but it would not be doing her justice to say she was entirely feminine.' The celebrated lover Giacomo Casanova, who met Catherine and knew something about women, captured the workings of her charm: 'Of medium stature, but well built and with a majestic bearing, the Sovereign had the art of making herself loved by all those whom she believed were curious to know her. Though not beautiful, she was sure to please by her sweetness, affability and her intelligence, of which she made very good use to appear to have no pretensions.'[41]

In conversation, she was 'not witty herself'[42] but she made up for it by being quick and well informed. Macartney thought 'her conversation is brilliant, perhaps too brilliant for she loves to shine in conversation'. Casanova revealed her need to appear effortlessly clever: when he encountered her out walking, he talked about the Greek calendar and she said little, but when they met again, she was fully informed on the subject. 'I felt certain that she had studied the subject on purpose to dazzle.'[43]

She possessed the gift of tact: when she was discussing her reforms with some deputies from Novgorod, the Governor explained that 'these gentlemen are not rich'. Catherine shot back: 'I demand your pardon, Mr Governor. They *are* rich in zeal.' This charming response brought tears to their eyes and pleased them more than money.[44]

When she was at work, she dressed sensibly in a long Russian-style dress with hanging sleeves, but when at play or display, 'her dress is never gaudy, always rich . . . she appears to great advantage in regimentals and is fond of appearing in them'.[45] When she entered a room, she always made 'three bows *à la Russe* . . .' to the right, left and middle.[46] She understood that appearances mattered, so she followed Orthodox rituals to the letter in public, despite Casanova noticing that she barely paid attention in church.

She was indeed a woman who took infinite pains to be a great empress and she had a Germanic attitude to wasting time: 'waste as little time as possible', she said. 'Time belongs, not to me, but to the Empire.'[47] One part of her genius was choosing talented men and getting the best out of them: 'Catherine had the rare ability to choose the right people,' wrote

Count Alexander Ribeaupierre, who knew her and her top officials. 'History has justified her choices.'[48] Once they had been selected, she managed her men so adroitly that each of them 'began to think [what she proposed] was his own idea and tried to fulfil it with zeal'.[49] She was careful not to humiliate her servants: 'My policy is to praise aloud and scold in a low voice.'[50] Indeed many of her sayings are so simple and shrewd that they could be collected as a modern management guide.

In theory, the absolute power of the tsars received blind obedience in an empire without law – but Catherine knew it was different in practice, as Peter III and later her son Paul I never learned. 'It is not as easy as you think [to see your will fulfilled] . . .', she explained to Potemkin's secretary, Popov. 'In the first place my orders would not be carried out unless they were the kind of orders which could be carried out . . . I take advice, I consult . . . and when I am already convinced in advance of general approval, I issue my orders and have the pleasure of observing what you call blind obedience. And that is the foundation of unlimited power.'[51]

She was polite and generous to her courtiers, kind and considerate to her servants, but there were sinister sides to her thorough enjoyment of power: she relished the secret powers of her state, reading the police reports, then chilling her victims like any dictator by letting them know that they were being watched. Years later, the young French volunteer Comte de Damas, alone in his room watching some troops parade past the window on their way to fight the Swedes, muttered, 'If the King of Sweden were to see those soldiers . . . he'd make peace.' Two days later, when he was paying his court to the Empress, 'she put her lips close to my ear and said, "So you think if the King of Sweden were to inspect my Guards, he'd make peace?" And she began to laugh.'[52]

Her charm did not fool everyone: there was some truth in the barbs of the priggish Prince Shcherbatov, who served at Court, when he described this 'considerable beauty, clever, affable', who 'loves glory and is assiduous in pursuit of it'. She was 'full of ostentation . . . infinitely selfish'. He claimed: 'True friendship has never resided in her heart and she is ready to betray her best friend . . . her rule is to cajole a man as long as he is needed and then in her own phrase "to throw away a squeezed-out lemon".'[53] This was not exactly so, but power always came first. Potemkin was the one exception who proved the rule.

As a gentleman of the bedchamber, Potemkin now spent much of his time around the imperial palaces performing his duties, which included standing behind her chair at meals to serve her and her guests. This meant that he saw the Empress frequently in public, getting to know the routine of her life. She took an interest in him – and he began to take a reckless interest in her that was not necessarily fitting for such a junior courtier.

Part Two

CLOSER
1762–1774

4

CYCLOPS

Nature has made Grigory Orlov a Russian peasant and he will
remain thus until the end.
Durand de Distroff

When the Empress and the Second Lieutenant of the Horse-Guards
encountered each other in the hundreds of corridors of the Winter
Palace, Potemkin would fall to his knees, take her hand and declare he
was passionately in love with her. There was nothing unusual about
them meeting one another in such a way, because Potemkin was a
gentleman of the bedchamber. Any courtier might literally have bumped
into his Sovereign somewhere in the Palace – they saw her every day.
Indeed, even members of the public could enter the Palace, if they were
decently dressed and not wearing livery. However, Potemkin's conduct –
kissing Catherine's hands on bended knee and declaring his love – was
rash, not to say careless. It can only have been saved from awkwardness
by his exuberant charm – and her flirtatious acquiescence.

There were probably several young officers at Court who believed
themselves in love with her – and many others who would have pretended to be for the sake of their careers. A long list of suitors, including
Zakhar Chernyshev and Kirill Razumovsky, had fallen in love with Catherine over the years and accepted her gentle rebuttals. But Potemkin
refused to accept either the conventions of the courtier or the dominance
of the Orlovs. He went further than anyone else. Most courtiers were
wary of the brothers who had murdered an emperor. Potemkin flaunted
his courage. Long before he was in power, he disdained the hierarchies
of court. He teased the secret police chief. Magnates treated Sheshkovsky
circumspectly but Potemkin is said to have laughed at the knout-wielder,
asking: 'How many people are you knout-beating today?'[1]

He could not have behaved like this before the Orlovs without some
encouragement from the Empress. She could easily have stopped him if
she had wished. But she did not. This was unfair of her for there could
be no prospect of Catherine accepting Potemkin as a lover in 1763/4.
She owed her throne to the Orlovs. Potemkin was still too young. So
Catherine could not have taken him seriously. She was in love with

Grigory Orlov and, as she later told Potemkin, she was a creature of habit and loyalty. She regarded the dashing but not particularly talented Orlov as her permanent companion and 'would have remained for ever, had he not been the first to tire'.[2] Nonetheless she seemed to recognize that she enjoyed a special empathy with Potemkin. So did the Gentleman of the Bedchamber who contrived to meet her as much as he could during the routine of her days.

Catherine arose daily at 7 a.m., but, if she woke earlier, she lit her own stove so as not to wake her servants. She then worked until eleven on her own with her ministers or her cabinet secretaries, sometimes giving audiences at 9 a.m. She wrote furiously in her own hand – she herself called it 'graphomania' – to a wide variety of correspondents, from Voltaire and Diderot to the Germans Dr Zimmerman, Madame Bielke and later Baron Grimm. Her letters were warm, outspoken and lively, laced with her slightly ponderous sense of humour.[3] This was the age of letter-writing: men and women of the world took a pride in the style and the content of their letters. If they were from a great man in an interesting situation – a Prince de Ligne or a Catherine the Great or a Voltaire – they were copied and read out in the salons of Europe like a cross between the despatches of a distinguished journalist and the spin of an advertising agency.[4] Catherine liked writing, and not just letters. She loved drafting decrees – *ukase* – and instructions in her own hand. In the middle 1760s, she was already writing her General Instruction for the Great Commission she was to call in 1767 to codify existing laws. She copied out large portions of the books she had studied since adolescence, especially Beccaria and Montesquieu. She called this her 'legislomania'.

At 11 a.m. she did her toilette and admitted those whom she knew best into her bedroom, such as the Orlovs. They might then go for a walk – if it was summer, she loved to stroll in the Summer Palace gardens where members of the public could approach her. When Panin arranged for Casanova to meet her,[5] she was accompanied only by Grigory Orlov and two ladies-in-waiting. She dined at 1 p.m. At 2.30 p.m. she returned to her apartments, where she read until six, the 'lover's hour', at which time she entertained Orlov.

If there was a Court evening, she then dressed and went out. Dress at Court was a long coat for men *à la Française* and for ladies a gown with long sleeves and a short train and whalebone bodice. Partly because it suited Russian wealth and flamboyance and partly because it was a court that needed to advertise its legitimacy, both men and women competed to wear diamonds on anything where they could be attached – buttons, buckles, scabbards, epaulettes and often three rows on the borders of hats. Both sexes wore the ribbons and sashes of the five orders of Russian chivalry: Catherine herself liked to wear the ribbon of St Andrew – red edged with silver studded with diamonds – and St George over one shoulder with the collars of St Alexander Nevsky, St Catherine and St Vladimir and two stars – St Andrew and St George – on her left breast.[6] Catherine inherited the lavishness of dress from the Elisabethan Court. She enjoyed splendour, appreciated its political uses and she was certainly not remotely economical, but she never approached Elisabeth's sartorial extravagance, later toning down the magnificence. She understood that too much glitter undermines the very power it is meant to illustrate.

While the Guards patrolled outside the palaces, the Sovereign's own apartments were guarded by an elite force, founded by Catherine in 1764 and made up of nobles – the sixty men of the Chevaliers-Gardes – who wore blue coats faced with red covered in silver lace. Everything from bandolier to carbine was furnished in silver, even their boots. On their heads they wore silver helmets with high plumes. The Russian eagle was embroidered on their backs and adorned the silver plates of armour on arms, knees and breast, fastened by silver cords and silver chains.[7]

On Sunday evenings there was a court; on Mondays a French comedy; on Thursdays, there was usually a French tragedy and then a ballet; on Fridays or Saturdays there was often a fancy-dress masquerade at the Palace. Five thousand guests attended these vast and semi-public fêtes. Catherine and her Court displayed their magnificence to the foreign ambassadors and to each other. What better guide to such an evening than Casanova? 'The ball went on for sixty hours ... Everywhere I see joy, freedom and the great profusion of candles ...'. He heard a fellow masked guest say: 'There's the Empress ... you will see Grigory Orlov in a moment; he has orders to follow her at a distance ...'. Guests pretended not to recognize her. 'Everyone recognized him because of his great stature and the way he always kept his head bent forward.' Casanova the international freeloader ate as much as he could, watched a *contredance* quadrille executed perfectly in the French style and then, naturally being who he was, met an ex-mistress (now kept by the Polish Ambassador) whose delights he rediscovered. By this point, he had long since lost sight of the Empress.[8]

Catherine enjoyed dressing up and being masked. On one occasion, disguised as an officer in her pink domino (loose cloak) and regimentals, she recorded some of her slightly erotic conversations with guests who genuinely did not recognize her. One princess thought her a handsome man and danced with her. Catherine whispered, 'What a happy man I am,' and they flirted. Catherine kissed her hand; she blushed. 'Please say who you are,' asked the girl. 'I am yours,' replied Catherine, but she would not identify herself.[9]

Catherine seldom ate much in the evening and virtually always retired by 10.30 p.m., accompanied by Grigory Orlov. She liked to be asleep by eleven.[10] Her disciplined routine formed the public world of Court, but Potemkin's wit had won him access to its private world. This brought him closer to the vigilant, violent Orlovs, but it also gave him the chance to let the Empress know how passionately he felt. Potemkin would pay dearly for his recklessness.

In the early evenings, Catherine invited an inner circle of about eighteen to her apartments and later to the extension of the Winter Palace that she called her Little Hermitage. Her habitués included Countess Bruce, that attractive fixer whom Catherine trusted in the most private matters; the Master of Horse, Lev Naryshkin, whom she called her 'born clown',[11] the epitome of the rich and frivolous Russian nobleman; the Orlovs of course – and, increasingly, among others, Potemkin.

The Russian Court was much less stiff and formal than many in Western Europe, including that of George III. Even when Catherine received ministers who were not part of her private coterie, they sat and worked together, not like British Prime Ministers, who had to stand in George III's presence unless he granted them the rare privilege of sitting. In Catherine's Little Hermitage, this casualness went even further. Catherine played cards – whist or faro usually – until around 10 p.m. Guardsmen like Orlov and Potemkin were instantly at home, since they had spent much of their youth sitting at the green baize tables. They also took part in word and paper games, charades and even singsongs.

Grigory Orlov was the master of the salon: Catherine gave her lover the rooms above her own in the Winter Palace so that he could descend the green staircase without being announced. While Catherine took a prim view of risqué jokes in her inner circle, she was open in her displays of affection with Orlov. A visiting Englishman later recorded, 'they did not forbear their caresses for his presence'.[12] Orlov adored music and his good humour set the tone of these evenings, when the Empress herself almost became one of a circle of friends. 'After dinner,' the Court Journal recorded on one evening, 'Her Imperial Majesty graciously returned to her inner apartments, and the gentlemen in the card room themselves sang songs, to the accompaniment of various wines; then the Court singers and servants ... and, on the orders of Count G. G. Orlov, the NCOs and soldiers of the guard at Tsarskoe Selo, sang gay songs in another room.'[13]

The Orlovs had achieved their ambitions – up to a point. While the marriage was now a dead letter, Orlov was the Empress's constant companion, which in itself gave him influence. But it was certainly she who ran the government. There was a fault in the design of the Orlovs as a political force: the brains, the brawn and the charm were not united in one man but were distributed with admirable fairness among the five brothers. Alexei Orlov, Le Balafre, had the ruthlessness; Fyodor the culture and political savvy; while Grigory, who needed all of the above, possessed only handsomeness, a wonderful nature and solid good sense.

Diplomats claimed Orlov, 'having grown up in alehouses and places of ill-repute, ... led a life of a reprobate though he was kind and good-hearted'. It was said that 'all his good qualities' were 'overshadowed by a licentiousness' that 'turned the Royal Court into a den of debauchery. There was hardly a single maiden at Court ... not subjected to his importunings,'[14] alleged Prince Shcherbatov, the self-appointed moral conscience of the Russian aristocracy.[15] 'The favourite', wrote the British envoy, Sir Thomas Gunning, 'is dissipated ...' and kept low company. As the 1760s went on, Catherine either ignored his infidelities like a worldly wife or did not know of them. Orlov however was not as simple as foreign diplomats claimed, but nor was he an intellectual or a statesman: he corresponded with Voltaire and Rousseau but probably to please Catherine and because it was expected of a cultured grandee of that time.

Catherine never overpromoted Orlov, who was to have only two big jobs: straight after the coup, he was appointed to head the Special Administration for Foreigners and Immigrants in charge of attracting colonists to the empty regions of the approaches to the Black Sea and the marches of the northern Caucasus. There he performed energetically and laid some of the foundations for Potemkin's later success. In 1765, she appointed him Grand Master of Ordnance, head of the artillery, though it is significant that she felt the need to consult Panin, who advised her to scale down the powers of that position before giving it to him. Orlov never mastered the details of artillery and 'seemed to know less about them than a schoolboy', according to the French diplomat Durand, who met him at military exercises. Later he rose heroically to the challenge of fighting the Moscow Plague.[16]

Orlov swaggered around in Catherine's wake, but he did not exert himself in exercising power and was never allowed the political independence she later delegated to Potemkin. While physically intimate with the Empress, Orlov was semi-detached from actual government.

Potemkin was in a hurry to display his insolent cleverness before the Empress, whose informality gave him plenty of scope to do so. On one occasion, he carelessly wandered up to the salon where Grigory Orlov was playing cards with the Empress. He leaned on the card table and started looking at Orlov's cards. Orlov whispered that he should leave, but Catherine intervened. 'Leave him alone,' she said. 'He's not interrupting us.'[17]

If the Orlovs decided to get rid of Potemkin, it was Nikita Panin who intervened at this 'dangerous time' to save him from whatever the Orlovs were planning.[18] Late in the summer of 1762, Potemkin was given his first – and last – foreign assignment: to travel to Stockholm to inform Count Ivan Osterman, the Russian Ambassador to Sweden, of the change of regime.[19] The Russian Court traditionally treated Sweden as a cooling area for overheated lovers. (Panin himself and Catherine's first lover Serge Saltykov had been despatched there for similar reasons.) From the patchy evidence that we have of his early career, it seems that the irrepressible Potemkin had learned nothing from this shot across his bows and kept playing the fool in front of the Orlovs until he had to be taught a lesson.

On his return, Catherine remained as interested as ever in this original young friend. Potemkin, whom she later called her 'pupil', benefited from this generosity of spirit. On duty as gentleman of the bedchamber, he was sitting opposite the Empress at table when she asked him a question in French. He replied in Russian. When a courtier told him off for such rudeness, Potemkin exclaimed: 'On the contrary, I think a subject should answer in the language in which he can best express his thoughts – and I've been studying Russian for twenty-two years.'[20] This was typical of his flirtatious impertinence but also of his defiance of the Gallomania of many courtiers. There is a legend that Catherine suggested he improve his French and arranged for him to be taught by a defrocked French priest named Chevalier de Vivarais, who had served under Dupleix at Pondicherry in India during the Seven Years War. This seedy mountebank was no chevalier and travelled with a 'wife' called Vaumale de Fages who apparently made a pleasurable contribution to Potemkin's French lessons. The name has a courtesan's ring to it: doubtless she was a most patient teacher. Vivarais was the first of a long line of sophisticated crooks whose company Potemkin enjoyed. As for French, it became his second language.[21]

Catherine charted a special government career for her young protégé. She knew his religious interests well enough to appoint Potemkin assistant to the Procurator of the Holy Synod, the council created by Peter the Great to run the Orthodox Church. The Procurator was administrator and judge in all matters religious – the equivalent of the Procurator-General in secular matters. The Empress cared enough about him to draft his instructions herself. Entitled 'Instruction to our Gentleman of the Monarch's Bedchamber Grigory Potemkin', and dated 4 September 1763, her first letter to him, which shows the maternal tone she favoured with younger men, reads:

> From the *ukase* given about you to the Holy Synod: though you know well why you have been appointed to this place, we are ordering the following for the best fulfilment of your duty ... 1. For better understanding of the affairs run from this place ... 2. it will be useful for you to make it a rule to come to the Synod when they are not sitting ... 3. To know the agenda in advance ... 4. You will have to listen with diligent attention...

Point six decreed that, in the event of the Procurator-General's illness, 'you will have to report to us all business and write our orders down in the Synod. In a word, you will have to learn all things which will lighten the course of business and help you to understand it better.'[22] Potemkin's first period in the Synod was short, possibly because of his problems with the Orlovs, but we know from Decree 146 of the Synod's records that he attended the Synod on a day-to-day basis during September.[23] He was on the rise.

While paying court to the Empress and beginning his political career, Potemkin did not restrict himself. Alcibiades won himself a reputation as a lover. There was no reason why he should be loyal to Catherine while Orlov was in possession of the field. Potemkin's stalwart but uninspiring nephew, Alexander Samoilov, recorded his uncle as paying 'special attention' to a 'certain well-born young girl' who 'was not indifferent towards him'. Infuriatingly he added: 'whose name I will not reveal'.[24] Some historians believe this was Catherine's confidante Countess Bruce, who was to gain notoriety as the supposed 'éprouveuse'[25] who 'tried out' Catherine's lovers. Countess Bruce unselfishly did all she could to help Potemkin with Catherine: in that worldly court, there was no better foundation for a political alliance than an amorous friendship. Certainly Countess Bruce always found it hard to resist a young man. But the Countess was already thirty-five, like Catherine – hardly the 'girl', who remains mysterious.[26]

Whoever it was, Catherine let Potemkin continue his melodramatic role as her *cavalier servente*. Was he really in love with Catherine? There is no need to over-analyse his motives: it is impossible in matters of love to separate the individual from the position. He was ambitious and was devoted to Catherine – the Empress and the woman. Then he suddenly disappeared.

Legend has it that sometime that year Grigory and Alexei Orlov invited Potemkin for a game of billiards. When he arrived, the Orlovs turned on him and beat him up horribly. Potemkin's left eye was damaged. The wound became infected. Potemkin allowed a village quack – one Erofeich – to bind it up, but the peasant remedy he applied only made it worse. The wound turned septic and Potemkin lost his eye.[27]

Potemkin's declarations to Catherine and the fight with the Orlovs are both part of the Potemkin mythology: there are other accounts that he lost the eye playing tennis and then went to the quack, whose ointment burned it. But it is hard to imagine Potemkin on a tennis court. The fight story was widely believed, because Potemkin *was* overstepping the limits of prudence by courting Catherine, but it is unlikely that it really happened because Grigory Orlov always behaved decently to his young rival.

This was his first setback – however it occurred. In two years he had gone from arriving poor and obscure from Moscow to being the indulged protégé of the Empress of all the Russias herself. But he had peaked far too early. Losing the sight in his eye was tragic, but ironically his withdrawal from Court made strategic sense. This was the first of many occasions when Potemkin used timely withdrawals to concentrate the mind of the Empress.

Potemkin no longer visited Court. He saw no one, studied religion, grew a long beard and considered taking the tonsure of a monk. He was always prone to religious contemplation and mysticism. This true son of the Orthodox Church often retired to monasteries to pray. While there was always play-acting in his antics, his contemporaries, who attacked him whenever possible, never doubted that he was genuinely tempted by a life of prayer. Nor did they doubt his ascetic and very Russian disgust with the pursuit of worldly success, particularly his own.[28] But the crisis was much more serious than that. Some of Potemkin's charm derived from the wild giddiness of his mood swings, the symptom of a manic personality that explains much of his strange behaviour. He collapsed into a depression. His confidence was shattered. The breakdown was so serious that some accounts even claim that he put his eye out himself 'to free it from the blemish which it derived from the accident'.[29]

There was vanity in his disappearance too: his blind eye was certainly half closed – but not lost.* He was ashamed of it and probably believed that the Empress would now be disgusted by him. Potemkin's over-sensitivity was one of his most winning qualities. Even as a famous statesman, he almost always refused to pose for portraits because he felt disfigured. He convinced himself that his career was over. Certainly his opponents revelled in his ruined looks: the Orlovs nicknamed him after the one-eyed giants of Homer's *Odyssey*. 'Alcibiades', they said, had become the 'Cyclops'.

Potemkin was gone for eighteen lost months. The Empress sometimes asked the Orlovs about him. It is said she even cancelled some of her little gatherings, she so missed his mimicry. She sent him messages through anonymous ladyfriends. Catherine later told Potemkin that Countess Bruce always informed her that he still loved her.[30] Finally, according to Samoilov, the Empress sent this message through the go-between: 'It is a great pity that a person of such rare merits is lost from society, the Motherland and those who value him and are sincerely well disposed to him.'[31] This must have raised his hopes. When Catherine drove by his retreat, she is said to have ordered Grigory Orlov to summon Potemkin back to Court. The honourable and frank Orlov always showed respect for Potemkin to the Empress. Besides he probably believed that, with Potemkin's looks ruined and his confidence broken, he was no longer a threat.[32]

Suffering can foster toughness, patience and depth. One senses that the one-eyed Potemkin who returned to Court was a different man from the Alcibiadean colt who left it. Eighteen months after losing his eye, Potemkin still sported a piratical bandage round his head, which suggests the contradictions of shyness and showmanship that were both part of his personality. Catherine welcomed him back to Court. He reappeared in his old position at the Synod; and when Catherine celebrated the third anniversary of the coup by presenting silver services to her thirty-three leading supporters, Potemkin was remembered near the bottom of the list, far below grandees like Kirill Razumovsky, Panin and Orlov.

* This did not stop one diplomat claiming he had 'procured a glass eye in Paris'.

The latter was firmly and permanently at her side, but she had obviously not forgotten her reckless suitor.[33]

So the Orlovs devised a more agreeable way to remove him. One legend tells how Grigory Orlov suggested to the Empress that Kirill Razumovsky's daughter, Elisabeth, would be a most advantageous match for the Guardsman from Smolensk and Catherine did not object.[34] There is no evidence of this courtship but we know that Potemkin later helped the girl – and always got on well with her father who 'received him like a son.'

Indeed the Count's kindness to young Potemkin was typical of the lack of snobbery of this Cossack ex-shepherd who was one of the most likeable of Catherine's magnates. It was said Razumovsky had been a peasant at sixteen and a Field-Marshal at twenty-two, which was almost true.* Whenever his sons, who grew up to be proud Russian aristocrats, were embarrassed by his humble Cossack beginnings, he used to shout for his valet: 'Here, bring me the peasant's rags in which I came to St Petersburg. I want to recall the happy time when I drove my cattle crying, "Tsop! Tsop!" '[35] He lived in fabulous state – he was said to have introduced champagne to Russia. Potemkin, who certainly enjoyed the sparkling stories (and probably the sparkling wine) of this cheerful raconteur, became obsessed by the Cossacks: did the enthusiasm of a lifetime start over the ex-Hetman's champagne at the Razumovsky Palace? The real reason there would be no marriage was that Potemkin still loved Catherine and that she held out some sort of glorious hope for the future.[36] Catherine 'has at times had eyes for others', wrote the British envoy, the Earl of Buckinghamshire, 'particularly for an amiable and accomplished man, who is not undeserving of her affection; he has good advisers and is not without some chance of success.'[37] The 'accomplishment' makes him sound like Potemkin and his 'good advisers' could not be any better placed than Countess Bruce.

In 1767, he received a job that again showed how Catherine was specially creating tasks that suited his interests. After a short tenure at the Synod, she had given him duties as an army paymaster and responsibilities for the manufacturing of daytime army uniforms. Now Catherine was embarking on the most daring political experiment of

* Brother of the Empress Elisabeth's favourite, he was appointed Hetman of the Ukraine in his early twenties. This meant that he was the governor of the nominally semi-independent Cossack borderlands throughout Elisabeth's reign. Razumovsky backed Catherine's coup, then requested that she make the Hetmanate hereditary in his family. She refused, abolished the Hetmanate, replacing it with a College of Little Russia, and made him a field-marshal instead.

her life: the Legislative Commission. Potemkin, who had evidently showed off his knowledge of Oriental cultures, was appointed one of three 'Guardians of Exotic Peoples'[38] alongside the Procurator-General Prince Viazemsky and one of Catherine's secretaries, Olsufiev. The Empress was gently introducing Potemkin to the most important officials in the realm. Nothing was ever a coincidence with Catherine II.

The Legislative Commission was an elected body of about 500 delegates from an impressively broad range (for its day) of representatives of the nobility, townspeople, state peasants and non-Russian peoples. They converged that year on Moscow bearing the instructions of their electors. There were fifty-four non-Russians – from Tartars to Baskirs, Yakuts to Kalmyks. Since Viazemsky and Olsufiev had weightier tasks, they were Potemkin's responsibility.

Potemkin went on ahead of the Empress to Moscow with two squadrons of Horse-Guards to help oversee the arrival of the delegates. Catherine herself followed in February, setting off from Moscow on a cruise down the Volga as far as Kazan and Simbirsk, with a suite of over 1,500 courtiers, including two Orlovs and two Chernyshevs, and foreign ambassadors – a voyage designed to show that Catherine was feeling the pulse of her Empire. She then returned to Moscow to open the Commission.

Catherine may have considered abolishing or reforming serfdom, according to the tenets of the Enlightenment, but she was far from wanting to overturn the Russian political order. Serfdom was one of the strongest links between the throne and the nobility: she would break it at her peril. The 500 or more articles of her Great Instruction, which she wrote out herself, were a digest of a lifetime of reading Montesquieu, Beccaria and the *Encyclopaedia*. The Commission's aim was the codification of existing laws – but even that was a risky encroachment on her own autocracy. Far from a revolutionary, she was a believer in Russian absolutism. Indeed most of the *philosophes* themselves, those enemies of superstition, were not democrats, just advocates of reason, law and order imposed from above. Catherine was sincere, but there was an element of window-dressing, for it showed her confidence and Russia's stability. But it turned out to be a very long-winded advertisement.

At 10 a.m. on Sunday, 30 July 1767, Catherine, in a coach drawn by eight horses and followed by sixteen carriages of courtiers, was escorted from Moscow's Golovin Palace to the Kremlin by Grigory Orlov and a squadron of Horse-Guards, probably including Potemkin. Grand Duke Paul followed. At the Cathedral of the Assumption, she dismounted for a service of blessing. She was followed by the Procurator-General

Viazemsky and all the delegates – Russians and exotics – who marched behind, two by two, like the passengers on Noah's Ark. The non-Christian delegates waited outside the church. Then all walked in the same order to the Great Kremlin Palace to be received by their Empress in imperial mantle and crown, standing before the throne, accompanied by Grand Duke Paul, courtiers and bishops. On her right were displayed copies of her Great Instruction. The next morning in the Kremlin's Faceted Palace, the Empress's Instruction was read and the Commission opened in a ceremony based on the English opening of Parliament, with its similar speech from the throne.[39]

Potemkin escorted the Empress when she attended some of the Commission's sessions. He would have read the Instruction: his vast library later contained every work Catherine used – Montesquieu's *Esprit des lois*, all thirty-five volumes of Diderot's *Encyclopaedia* (in French) and tomes of Voltaire. But he did not take the floor.[40] The Commission itself did not succeed in codifying the laws, but instead became a talking shop. It did succeed in collecting useful information for Catherine's future legislation. The Commission also coined the sobriquet 'Catherine the Great', which she refused. Her stay reminded Catherine how much she disliked Moscow so she returned to Petersburg, where she re-convened the Commission in February 1768. The coming of war finally gave her the excuse to end its ponderous deliberations.[41]

On 22 September 1768 Potemkin was promoted from *Kammerjunker* to receive the ceremonial key of a *Kamerherr* – chamberlain[42] of the Court. Unusually he was still to remain in the military, where he was promoted to captain of Horse-Guards. Then, two months later, he was removed from the army and attached to the Court full time on Catherine's specific orders. For once, Potemkin did not want to be at Court at all. On 25 September 1768, the Ottoman Empire declared war on Russia. Potemkin saw his chance.

5

THE WAR HERO

Attacked and out-numbered by the enemy, he was the hero of
the victory...

Field-Marshal Count Peter Rumiantsev-Zadunaisky on General
Potemkin during the First Russo–Turkish War

'Your Majesty, The exceptional devotion of Your Majesty for the
common good has made our Motherland dear to us,' wrote Potemkin
to the Empress on 24 May 1769. The chivalry in this first surviving letter
is framed to state his personal passion for her as explicitly as possible.

It is the duty of the subject to demand obedience to Your wishes from
everyone. For my part, I have carried out my duties just as Your Majesty
wishes.

I have recognized the fine deeds that Your Majesty has done for our
Motherland, I have tried to understand your laws and be a good citizen.
However, your mercy towards my person fills me with zeal for the
person of Your Majesty. The only way I can express my gratitude to
Your Majesty is to shed my blood for Your glory. This war provides an
excellent opportunity for this and I cannot live in idleness.

Allow me now, Merciful Sovereign, to appeal at Your Majesty's feet
and request Your Majesty to send me to Prince Prozorovsky's corps in
the Army at the front in whatever rank Your Majesty wishes but without
inscribing me in the list of military service for ever, but just for the
duration of the war.

I, Merciful Sovereign, have tried to be qualified for Your service; I
am especially inclined to cavalry which, I'm not afraid to say, I know
in every detail. As regards the military art, I learned the main rule by
heart: the best way to achieve great success is fervent service to the
Sovereign and scorn for one's life ... You can see my zeal ... You'll
never regret your choice.

Subject slave of Your Imperial Majesty,
Grigory Potemkin.[1]

The war was indeed the best way for Potemkin to break out of the
frustrating routine of the Court and distinguish himself. But it was also

to provoke the crises that made the Empress need him. The leaving of Catherine was, paradoxically, to bring him much closer to her.

The First Russo–Turkish War began when Russian Cossacks pursued the rebels of the Confederacy of Bar, a group of Poles opposed to King Stanislas-Augustus and Russian influence in Poland, over the Polish border into the small Tartar town of Balta on what was technically Turkish territory. There the Cossacks massacred Jews and Tartars. France encouraged the Sublime Porte – the Ottoman Government, already threatened by the recent extension of Russian power over Poland – to issue an ultimatum demanding that Russia withdraw from the Commonwealth altogether. The Turks arrested the Russian envoy to Istanbul, Alexei Obreskov, and locked him in the fortress of the Seven Towers, where Suleiman the Magnificent had kept his treasure but which was now a high-class prison, the Turkish Bastille. This was the traditional Ottoman way of declaring war.

Catherine reacted by creating a Council of State, containing her leading advisers, from Panin, Grigory Orlov and Kirill Razumovsky to two Golitsyn cousins and the two Chernyshev brothers, to help co-ordinate the war and act as a policy sounding-board. She also gave Potemkin what he wanted. 'Our Chamberlain Potemkin must be appointed to the army,' Catherine ordered her War Minister, Zakhar Chernyshev.[2] Potemkin headed straight for the army. Within a few days, as a major-general of the cavalry – the military rank equivalent to Court chamberlain – he was reporting to Major-General Prince Alexander Prozorovsky at the small Polish town of Bar.

The Russian army, nominally 80,000 strong, was ordered to win control of the Dniester river, the strategic waterway that stretched from the Black Sea into southern Poland. Access to, and control of, the Black Sea was Russia's ultimate objective. By fighting down the Dniester, Russian troops hoped to arrive on those shores. Russian forces were divided into two: Potemkin served in the First Army under General Prince Alexander Golitsyn aiming for the fortress of Khotin. The Second under General Peter Alexandrovich Rumiantsev was ordered to defend the southern borders. If all went well in the first campaign, they would fight their way round the Black Sea coast, down the Pruth to the great Danube. If they could cross the Danube into the Turkish provinces of Bulgaria, they could threaten the Sublime Porte in its own capital, Constantinople.

The Empress was wildly overconfident. 'My soldiers are off to fight the Turks as if they were going to a wedding!', she boasted to Voltaire.[3] But war is never a wedding – especially not for Russia's peasant–soldiers. Potemkin himself, whose sole experience of war was the swagger of the Guards life in Petersburg, arrived in the harsh and chaotic world of the real Russian army.

The life of a Russian conscript was so short that it often ended before he had even reached his camp. When they left home for their lifelong service (Potemkin later reduced it to twenty-five years), their families tragically wished them goodbye with laments and dirges as if they were already dead. The recruits were then marched away in columns, sometimes chained together. They endured a grim, brutal trauma, torn away from their villages and families. A modern historian rightly says this experience had most in common with the trans-Atlantic passage of negro slaves. Many died on thousand-verst marches, or arrived so weak at their destination that they soon perished: the Comte de Langeron, a Frenchman in Russian service later that century, estimated that 50 per cent of these recruits died. He graphically described the sadistic regime of beatings and discipline that was designed to keep these serf–soldiers from rebelling against their serfmaster–officers – though it may have been no worse than the cruelty of the Prussian army or the Royal Navy. Like the negro slaves, the Russian soldiers consoled themselves in their own colourful, sacred and warm culture: they earned only 7 roubles 50 kopecks a year (a premier-major's salary was 300 roubles), while Potemkin, for example, hardly a rich man, had received 18,000 roubles just for his part in the coup. So they shared everything in the soldiers' commune – the *artel* – that became their village, church, family, club, kitchen and bank, all rolled into one.[4] They sang their rich repertoire of songs 'for five or six hours at a stretch without the slightest break'[5] (and were later to sing many about Potemkin).

The Russian conscript was already regarded as 'the finest soldier in the world', wrote Langeron. 'He combines all the qualities which go to make a good soldier and hero. He is as abstemious as the Spaniard, as enduring as a Bohemian, as full of national pride as an Englishman and as susceptible to impulse and inspiration as French, Walloons, or Hungarians.'[6] Frederick the Great was impressed and terrified by Russian courage and endurance during the Seven Years War and coined a word to describe their maniacal ursine savagery – 'les oursomanes'.[7] Potemkin served in the cavalry, which had earned its own reputation for bloody bravery, especially since it fought beside Russia's ferocious irregular light cavalry, the Cossacks.

The Russian army was unique in Europe because, until the American and French Revolutions, armies drilled and fought for kings but not for ideas or nations. Most armies were made up of many nationalities – mercenaries, unwilling recruits and riffraff – who served a flag, not a country. But the Russian army was filled with Russian peasants who were recruited in mass *levées* from the roughly seven million souls available. This was seen as the reason for their almost mindless bravery.[8]

The officers, either Russian landowners addicted to gambling and debauch, or German, or later, French soldiers of fortune, were notoriously cruel: General Mikhail Kamensky, an extreme example, actually bit his soldiers. But they were also extraordinarily brave.[9] The characteristics of their peasant *chair du cannon* – brutality, discipline, self-sufficiency, endurance, patriotism and stoicism in the face of appalling suffering – made the Russian army a formidable fighting force. 'The Turks are tumbling like ninepins,' went the Russian saying; 'but, through the grace of God, our men stand firm, though headless.'[10]

Some contemporaries believed that war in the eighteenth century had become less bloody. Certainly, the dynasties of Europe, Habsburgs and Bourbons, at least pretended to fight according to the rules of aristocratic etiquette. But, for the Russians, wars against the Turks were different. After the centuries in which the Moslem Tartars, and then Turks, had threatened Orthodox Russia, the Russian peasant regarded this as a crusade. Havoc – the medieval giving of no quarter – was the order of battle.

Potemkin had only just arrived in Bar when the phoney war, giving both the unprepared Turks and Russians time to amass their forces, ended abruptly. On 16 June 1769, some 12,000 Tartar horsemen, under the command of the Crimean Khan, the Sultan's ally, who were raiding the Russian Ukraine, crossed the Dniester and attacked Potemkin's camp. Even then, the Tartars, armed with lassos and bows and arrows, were a vision from another age but they were the only Turkish forces ready for war. The Tartar Khan, Kirim Giray, a direct descendant of Genghis Khan, was an aggressive and fearless cavalry commander. He was accompanied by Baron de Tott, a French officer seconded to Istanbul to improve the Turkish forces. He has left his account of this medieval expedition – the last of its kind. Five hundred years after Genghis Khan, the Crimean Tartars, the descendants of those Mongol hordes, were still Europe's finest horsemen. As they swept out of the Crimea through the Ukraine and towards the Russian troops still stationed in southern Poland, they must have looked and sounded as terrifying as their Mongol ancestors. Yet, like most of the irregular cavalry, they were undisciplined and usually too distracted by booty to be much strategic use. But the raid bought the Turks time to build up their armies, which were said to be 600,000 strong.

In his first battle, Potemkin engaged these wild Tartar and Turkish horsemen and repulsed them. He acquitted himself well, for 'Chamberlain Potemkin' appears in the list of those who distinguished themselves. This was the beginning of Potemkin's run of success. On 19 June, he fought again in the Battle of Kamenets and took part in further skirmishing, helping General Golitsyn take Kamenets.[11] In St Petersburg Catherine celebrated these minor engagements with a 'Te Deum' on Sunday, 19 July, but the vacillating Golitsyn faltered before Khotin. Furious and impatient, in August the Empress recalled him. There are hints that Potemkin, via the Orlovs, played some part in the intrigue that dispensed with Golitsyn.[12] But, if he was laughably slow, Golitsyn was at least lucky. He was opposed by a Grand Vizier, Mehmed Emin, who was happier reading Islamic poetry than slicing off heads. So Catherine was embarrassed when, before her orders had arrived at the front, Golitsyn pulled himself together and crossed the Dniester.

Major-General Potemkin and his cavalry was now in action virtually every day: he distinguished himself again on 30 June and repulsed Turkish attacks on 2 and 6 July. When Golitsyn finally recrossed the Dniester, Potemkin served at the taking of Khotin. He fought heroically with his cavalry on 14 August at the Battle of Prashkovsky and then helped defeat the Moldavanzi-Pasha on the 29th. 'I am immediately recommending the courage and skill shown in battle by Major-General Potemkin,' wrote Golitsyn, 'because until that time our cavalry has never acted with such discipline and courage as it did under the command of the Major-General.'[13] Potemkin was becoming a war hero.

This praise must have been welcome to Catherine back in the capital. It was far from welcome at the Sublime Porte, where Sultan Mustafa III recalled his Grand Vizier: Emin-Pasha may have lost his mind at the front but, in Ottoman tradition, he lost his head as soon as he got home. These victories were too late for Golitsyn, however, who was consoled with a field-marshal's baton. The Foreign Minister's brother, General Peter Ivanovich Panin, assumed command of the Bender army, so that, in September, the First Army was taken over by Peter Rumiantsev. Thus began the command of one of the most glorious generals in the history of Russia, who became Potemkin's patron – and then his rival.

The new commander could not have been more different from the twenty-nine-year-old Major-General on his staff. Yet Potemkin respected him immensely. Aged forty-three, Rumiantsev was a tall, thin,

fastidious soldier with a biting dry wit – and he was Countess Bruce's
brother. Like his hero Frederick the Great, he 'loved and respected no
one in the world', but was 'the most brilliant of all Russian generals,
endowed with outstanding gifts'.[14] Again like his hero, Rumiantsev was
a severe disciplinarian yet a wonderful conversationalist. 'I've passed
days with him *tête-à-tête*,' enthused Langeron, 'and never felt a moment's
boredom.'[15] He amassed a fortune and lived in 'ancient feudal magnificence', always displaying the most refined manners of a *seigneur*. This
is unsurprising since he was a living specimen of Petrine history: he was
probably Peter the Great's natural son.*

The general had learned his craft fighting Prussia in the Seven Years
War, during which even Frederick admired his skill. Catherine appreciated his talent but never quite trusted him and appointed him President
of the Little Russian College, a position worthy of his status, but safely
distant from Court. He remained unimpressed by Catherine, liked the
Russian army's Prussianized uniforms and wigs, believed in Prussian
military discipline – and worked to improve on the Prussian tactics of
the Seven Years War. He tended to prefer Germans to Russians.[16]

Rumiantsev was a father to his soldiers but a general to his sons. When
one visited him after finishing his studies, he asked, 'Who are you?' 'Your
son,' replied the boy. 'Yes, how pleasant. You have grown,' snapped the
general. The son asked if he could find a position there and if he could
stay. 'Certainly,' said his father, 'you must surely know some officer or
other in the camp who can help you out.'[17]

Potemkin was always keen to have things both ways – access to the
commander and the chance to find glory in the field; chamberlain at
Court, general at the front. He wrote to Rumiantsev about 'the two
things on which my service is founded ... devotion to my Sovereign and
desire for approval from my highly respected commander'.[18] Rumiantsev
appreciated his intelligence but also must have known of his acquaintance with the Empress. His demands were granted. As the war entered
its second year, Catherine was frustrated by the slowness of Russian
success. War in the eighteenth century was seasonal: in the Russian

---

* Rumiantsev's mother was born in 1699 and lived to be eighty-nine. The grandest lady-
in-waiting at Court had known the Duke of Marlborough and Louis XIV, remembered
Versailles and the day St Petersburg was founded. She liked to boast until her dying day
that she was Peter the Great's last mistress. The dates certainly fitted: the boy was named
Peter after the Tsar. His official father, yet another Russian giant, was a provincial boy
who became a Count, a General-en-Chef and one of Peter the Great's hard men: he was
the ruffian sent to pursue Peter's fugitive son, the Tsarevich Alexei, to Austria and bring
him back to be tortured to death by his father.

winter, armies hibernated like hedgehogs. Battle with the main Ottoman armies – and the fall of Bender – had to wait for the spring.

As soon as it was possible, Rumiantsev reassembled his army in several manoeuvrable corps and advanced down the Dniester. Even in freezing January, Potemkin, now sent by Rumiantsev to serve with the corps of General Schtofel'n, was involved in skirmishes, driving off the attacks of Abdul-Pasha. On 4 February, Potemkin helped capture Jurja in a series of daring cavalry raids, defeating 12,000 enemy troops, capturing two cannons and a handful of banners. It was still bitterly cold but he 'did not spare himself'.[19] At the end of the month, when Rumiantsev's report was read out at the Council before the Empress, he mentioned 'the fervent feats of Major-General Potemkin', who 'asked me to send him to the corps of Lieutenant-General von Schtofel'n where, as soon as was possible, he distinguished himself both by his courage and by martial skill.'[20] The commander recommended Potemkin should be decorated and he received his first medal, the Order of St Anna.

As the Russians marched south after the Turkish army, Potemkin, according to Rumiantsev's later report, 'protected the left bank with the troops entrusted to him and repulsed the enemy attacks against him'. On 17 June, the main army forded the Pruth to attack the 22,000 Turks and 50,000 Tartars encamped on the other bank. Meanwhile Major-General Potemkin and the reserves crossed the river three miles downstream and ambushed the Turkish rear. The camp disintegrated; the Turks fled.[21]

Just three days later, Rumiantsev advanced towards a Turkish army of 80,000, comfortably encamped where the River Larga joined the Pruth, while they awaited the arrival of the Grand Vizier and his main army.[22]

Forming up into their squares, on 7 July 1770, Rumiantsev, Potemkin and the Russians stormed the Turkish camp, braced for the wild Turkish charges. This was Potemkin's first glimpse of an Ottoman army. It was an immense and impressive, noisy vision of silken tents and rickety carts, green banners and swishing horsetails (those Ottoman symbols of power) – sprawling, messy, alive with women and camp-followers and exotic uniforms, as much like a bazaar as an army. The Ottoman Empire was not yet the giant and flabby weakling it was to become in the next century. It was still capable of raising huge forces from its distant pashaliks, from the plains of Mesopotamia and the hills of Anatolia to the Barbary ports and the Balkans: all sent their cannon-fodder when the Sultan raised the banner of the Prophet.

'The Turks, who pass for blockheads in the art of war, carry it out with a kind of method,' explained the Prince de Ligne later. The method was to amass teeming armies roughly in a pyramidal formation and then throw them upon the Russians forces in waves of charging cavalry and whooping infantry. Their Janissaries had once formed the most feared infantry in Europe. They were gradually degenerating into a rich and arrogant Praetorian Guard more interested in their trading posts and palace coups than fighting, but they were still proud of their prowess and Islamic fervour: they wore bonnets of red and gold with white shirts, billowing pantaloons and yellow boots and bore scimitars, javelins, muskets.

The best of the Ottoman cavalry were the Tartars and the Spahis, the feudal Turkish horsemen, who leaped on and off their horses to fire their muskets. They wore breastplates embedded with jewels or just bright waistcoats with pantaloons, often leaving their arms bare while bearing curved and engraved sabres, daggers, lances and gem-encrusted pistols. They were so indisciplined that they fought only when they were ready and often mutinied: it was quite common for Janissaries to steal horses and gallop off the battlefield, strike their officers or sell the army's food for private profit. The mass of the Ottoman armies were unpaid irregulars recruited by Anatolian feudal lords, who were expected to live by plunder. Despite the efforts of French advisers like Baron de Tott, their artillery was way behind that of the Russians and their muskets were outdated. If their marksmanship was admirable, their firing rate was slow.

They wasted much energy in obsolete display. When all was ready, this martial rabble of hundreds of thousands worked themselves up into a fever of religious outrage fuelled with drops of opium.[23] 'They advance', Potemkin later reminisced to the Comte de Ségur, 'like an overflowing torrent.' He claimed their pyramidal formation was arranged in order of decreasing courage – the 'bravest warriors, intoxicated with opium', headed its apex while its base was formed of 'nothing but' cowards. The charge, recalled Ligne, was accompanied by 'frightful howlings, the cries of Allah Allah'. It took a disciplined infantryman to hold his ground. Any captured Russian was instantly beheaded with a cry of 'Neboisse!' or 'Be not afraid!' – and the heads brandished on the end of pikes. Their religious fever 'increased in proportion to the danger'.

The Russians solved the problem of the momentum of the Turkish charge by using the square, which could withstand any shrieking onslaught. The Turk was both the 'most dangerous, and most con-temptible, enemy in the world', wrote Ligne later, 'dangerous, if they are suffered to attack; contemptible, if we are beforehand with them'. The Spahis or Tartars, 'humming around us like wasps', could envelop the Russian squares, 'curveting, leaping, caracoling, displaying their horse-manship and performing their riding-house croups' until they exhausted themselves. Then Rumiantsev's squares, drilled with Prussian precision, protected by their Cossacks and Hussars, and linked together by Jaegers, light, sharpshooting infantry, advanced. Once broken, the Turks either fled like rabbits or fought to the death. 'Dreadful slaughter', said Potemkin, was the usual result. 'The instinct of the Turks renders them dextrous and capable of all kinds of warlike employments ... but they never go beyond the first idea, they are incapable of a second. When their moment of good sense ... is over, they partake of the madman or the child.'[24]

This was what happened when Rumiantsev's squares stormed the Turkish camp at the Battle of Larga, shrugging off the Turkish charges with stoical endurance and blasts of artillery. Seventy-two thousand Turks and Tartars were forced to evacuate their fortifications and flee. Potemkin, attached to Prince Nikolai Repnin's corps, commanded the advance guard that attacked the camp of the Crimean Khan and was, according to Rumiantsev, 'among the first to attack and capture its fortification'. Potemkin was again decorated, this time with the Order of St George, Third Class: he wrote to thank the Empress.[25]

The new Grand Vizier now advanced with the main Turkish army to prevent the union of the two Russian armies of Rumiantsev and Panin. He crossed the Danube and marched up the Pruth to meet the fleeing troops from the Battle of Larga. On 21 July 1770, only slightly to the south of Larga, Rumiantsev marched his 25,000 troops towards the 150,000 men of the Grand Vizier's massed Turkish army, which had camped behind triple fortifications near Lake Kagul. Despite the numerical inequality, he decided to attack. Using the lessons and confidence provided by Larga, he formed five squares facing the main Turkish positions. Potemkin and his cavalry defended the army's transport against 'the attacks of numerous Tartar hordes and prevented them from ... attacking the army's rear'. As he gave Potemkin this duty, Rumiantsev is supposed to have told him: 'Grigory Alexandrovich, bring us our provisions, balanced on the top of your sabre.'[26]

The Turks, who had learned nothing from Larga, were completely surprised, fought savagely for the whole day but were finally routed in scenes of desperate carnage, leaving 138 guns, 2,000 prisoners, and 20,000 dead on the field. Rumiantsev brilliantly exploited his victory by pushing down towards the lower Danube: on 26 July Potemkin helped Repnin take the fortress of Izmail, then that of Kilia on 10 August. General Panin stormed Bender on 16 September, and Rumiantsev finally closed his campaign with the taking of Brailov on 10 November.[27] There was one more magnificent piece of news.

Catherine had sent the Russian Baltic Fleet, proud creation of Peter the Great, across the North Sea, through the English Channel and the Straits of Gibraltar all the way to hit the Turkish rear in the eastern Mediterranean. Its admiral was Count Alexei Orlov, who had never been to sea, but its real lights were two Scottish officers, John Elphinstone and Samuel Greig. Despite Peter the Great's brave attempts to inspire sea-legs in Russian ploughmen, only the Livonians or Estonians took to the ocean. There were few Russian officers and most of them were lamentable. When Elphinstone grumbled, Catherine replied: 'The ignorance of the Russians is due to youth; that of the Turks to decrepitude.'[28] England helped the Russian expedition: London did not yet regard the Turk as a natural ally or the 'Bear' as a natural enemy. The 'Eastern Question' had not yet been asked. On the contrary, France was England's enemy, Turkey a French ally. By the time the leaky Russian fleet reached England, 800 sailors were ill. These seasick Russian peasants must have been an incongruously pathetic sight as they re-rigged, watered and recovered in Hull and Portsmouth.

After gathering at their base, Leghorn (Livorno) in Tuscany, Orlov's fleet finally reached Ottoman waters. It failed to raise a rebellion among the tricky Greeks and Montenegrins and then indecisively engaged the Turkish fleet off Chios. The Turks withdrew to the deceptive safety of Chesme harbour. Samuel Greig arranged a fiery lullaby for the sleeping Turks. Overnight on 25/26 June, his fireships floated into the harbour of Chesme. This 'ingenious ambuscade' turned the harbour into an inferno. 'Encumbered with ships, powder and artillery,' Chesme, wrote Baron de Tott, watching from the Turkish side, 'soon became a volcano that engulfed the whole naval force of the Turks'.[29] Eleven thousand Turks perished. Alexei Orlov boasted to Catherine that the water of Chesme was stained incarnadine, and the victorious Empress passed this macabre and distinctly unEnlightened vision on to an excited Voltaire.[30] It was the most disastrous day for Turkish arms since the Battle of Lepanto.

When news of Chesme reached St Petersburg, so soon after the glories of Kagul, the Russian capital exploded with joy. There were 'Te Deums' and rewards for every sailor in the fleet inscribed simply: 'I was there.' Catherine rewarded Rumiantsev for Kagul with his field-marshal's baton and the construction of an obelisk in her park at Tsarskoe Selo, while Alexei Orlov got the title of Chesmensky ('of Chesme'). It was the greatest array of Russian triumphs since Poltava. Catherine was riding high – especially in Europe: Voltaire actually jumped up and down on his sickbed at Ferney and sang at the thought of so many dead infidels.[31]

Potemkin had covered himself in glory in this year of Russian victories and decided to capitalize on his new success. When operations ceased in November 1770, he asked Rumiantsev for leave to go to St Petersburg. Had someone raised his hopes that Catherine would receive him with open arms? Afterwards, Potemkin's enemies claimed that Rumiantsev was relieved to be rid of him. But he actually admired Potemkin's brains and military record, and approved this trip, charging him to protect the interests of himself and his army. His letters to his protégé were as paternal as Potemkin's to him were filial.

Potemkin returned to Petersburg with the prestige of a war hero and Rumiantsev's enthusiastic recommendations: 'This officer of great ability can make far-sighted observations about the land which has been the theatre of war, which deserve your Majesty's attention and respect and, because of this, I'm entrusting him with all the events that have to be reported to Her Majesty.'[32]

The Empress, in an exultant mood after Kagul and Chesme, welcomed him warmly: we know from the Court Journal that he was invited to dine with Catherine eleven times during his short stay.[33] Legend says there was a private audience at which Potemkin could not resist more dramatics on bended knee. He and Catherine agreed to correspond, apparently through her librarian Petrov and trusted Chamberlain Ivan Perfilevich Yelagin – useful allies around the Empress. We know little of what happened behind closed doors but one senses that they felt the stirrings of something that both knew could become serious.* Whether the private state of Catherine's relationship with Grigory Orlov himself was already shaky, Count Alexei Orlov-Chesmensky had increased the family credit at Court. Potemkin was too early to displace Grigory Orlov, but the trip was not wasted.[34]

Grigory Orlov certainly noticed Potemkin's welcome and made sure he returned to the army. Potemkin went back late in February, bearing a letter from Orlov to Rumiantsev in which the favourite recommended Potemkin and asked his commander to be his 'tutor and guide'. This was

* Catherine, in one of the undated love letters usually placed at the official start of their affair in 1774, tells Potemkin that a nameless courtier, perhaps an Orlov ally, has warned her about her behaviour with him and asked permission to send him back to the army, to which she agrees.

a benign way for Orlov to remind his younger rival of his place, but also a sign that he had become much more important on that trip to Petersburg. He was marked.[35]

Within weeks, the fighting had started again. But, compared to the feats of the year before, 1771 was to be a disappointment in the theatre of Moldavia and Wallachia, today's Rumania, where Potemkin served. When the Turks sensibly refused to endure any more of Rumiantsev's battles, the Field-Marshal spent the year attacking Turkish positions on the lower Danube, pushing into Wallachia. Potemkin did well: given the task of holding the Kraovsky region, he 'not only repulsed the enemy ... but struck at him too. He was the first to head across the Danube.' On 5 May, he pulled off a minor coup when he attacked the small town of Zimbry on the other side of the Danube, ravaged it, burned enemy provisions and stole the ships of their flotilla, which he brought back to the Russian side of the river. On 17 May, Potemkin defeated and pursued 4,000 Turks near the Ol'ta river – 'a glorious and famous feat', according to Rumiantsev, 'achieved only thanks to Potemkin's skill and courage'. The Turks attacked him on 27 May but were defeated and driven off. He joined up with Repnin again, and together they drove off a powerful Turkish corps under a *seraskier* (Turkish equivalent of a field-marshal) on 10 June and then took[36] Bucharest.

Some time after this fighting advance, Potemkin was struck down by a dangerous fever, which was endemic in the summer months in these Danubian principalities. It was so serious that 'only his strong constitution allowed him to recover because he would not accept any help from doctors', wrote Samoilov. Instead, the prone general put himself in the hands of two Zaporogian Cossacks, whom he charged to take care of him and spray him with cooling water. He had always been interested in the exotic peoples of the Empire – hence his position at the Legislative Commission – but this is our first hint of his special friendship with the Cossacks. He studied the culture of his Cossacks and admired their freedom and *joie de vivre*. They nicknamed him 'Gritsko Nechosa', or 'Grey Wig', after the peruke he sometimes wore, and invited him to become an honorary Cossack. A few months later, on 15 April 1772, he wrote to their Hetman to ask for admittance into this martial order. Entered into the lists of the Zaporogian Host in May that year, he wrote to the Hetman: 'I am delighted.'[37]

Potemkin had recovered by the time the army crossed the Danube and made a thrust towards the key Turkish fortress of Silistria, which commanded a stretch of the Danube. It was here that Potemkin won the undying hostility of Count Simon Romanovich Vorontsov, a young scion of the family that had reached its peak under Peter III. Born in 1744, the cultured Vorontsov, son of a notoriously corrupt provincial governor (nicknamed Big Pocket), nephew of Peter III's Chancellor, had been arrested during the coup for supporting Peter III, but he later made a name for himself as the first officer in to the Turkish trenches at Kagul. Like all Vorontsovs, this pudding-faced Anglophile had a marked appreciation of his own credentials but was rightly regarded by Catherine and Potemkin as politically unreliable and spent most of his career in honourable exile as Ambassador to London. Now, outside Silistria, he had to face the indignity of having his Grenadiers rescued from 12,000 Turkish cavalry by a reluctant Potemkin.

Six days later, Potemkin was in turn saved by Vorontsov: 'not only did we cover him, but we chased those Turks into town', using three batteries of artillery, and killing 'lots'. Vorontsov, writing in 1796, cited both fights as evidence of his own virtuosity and Potemkin's incompetence. Both found it intolerable to be saved by the other. The malice was perfectly symmetrical.[38]

Silistria did not fall, the army reforded the Danube and there ended Rumiantsev's tepid campaign. The real action that June was the successful invasion of the weakened Khanate of the Crimea – its army was away on the Danube, facing Rumiantsev – by the Second Army, now commanded by Prince Vasily Dolgoruky.

Catherine was learning that glory was not as quick or cheap as she hoped. The bottomless maw of the army demanded more and more recruits. The harvests were bad. Soldiers' pay was in arrears. Fever ravaged the army while rashes of bubonic plague broke out across the Ottoman Empire. The Russians feared it would spread through the southern armies. It was time to talk peace with the Ottomans before they forgot Chesme and Kagul. Then, in September 1771, terrible news arrived from Moscow.

The plague descended with ghastly intensity on the old capital. In August, the toll was reaching 400 to 500 deaths a day. It was not long before order in the city evaporated. The nobles fled; officials panicked; the Governor abandoned his post; and Moscow became a surreal charnel house, scattered with rotting cadavers, stinking bonfires of flesh and rumours of miracles, curses and conspiracies. In the abandoned city, the streets were patrolled by desperate crowds of peasants and workers who increasingly placed their hopes in a miracle-working icon.[39]

The last effective authority, Bishop Ambrosius, ordered the icon to be

removed to reduce the risk of infection among the crowds who flocked
to invoke its miraculous powers. The mob rioted and tore the Bishop to
pieces. This was the same Bishop Ambrosius who had lent Potemkin the
money to make the trip to St Petersburg. As Russia suffered the strain
of the huge cost of war, the mob took control. There was a real danger
that the plague might unleash something even worse – a peasant uprising
in the countryside. The death toll kept rising.

Grigory Orlov, restless since Catherine gave him no chance to prove
himself, offered to travel to Moscow and sort out the situation. On 21
September 1771, he set off. By the time he arrived, 21,000 people were
dying every month. Orlov displayed common sense, competence, energy
and humanity. He worked tirelessly. Just showing his cherubic countenance and lofty figure around the city reassured the people. He burned
3,000 old houses where the infection could linger, disinfected 6,000
more, founded orphanages, reopened the public baths closed in the
quarantine, and spent over 95,000 roubles distributing food and clothing. His Herculean efforts restored order in this Augean Stable. When
he departed on 22 November, deathrates were falling – probably thanks
to the cold, but the state was once again in control of Moscow. He
reached Petersburg on 4 December to popular acclaim. Catherine built
one of her arches in his honour in her Tsarskoe Selo park, which was
dotted with monuments to her triumphs. She even struck a commemorative medal. It seemed that the Orlovs, that race of heroes, as
Voltaire called them, were secure.[40]

When the Turkish talks began the next year, Catherine gave Grigory
Orlov the enormous responsibility of negotiating peace. Catherine saw
him off in a costume she had given him, embroidered and diamond-
studded on every seam. The sight of him inspired her again. 'Count
Orlov', she gushed to Madame Bielke, 'is the handsomest man of his
generation.'[41]

As Orlov left St Petersburg, was Potemkin arriving there to help Catherine with her latest crisis? His precise activities during these months
are mysterious. But, some time during the truce with Turks, he certainly
visited St Petersburg again.

Orlov's departure for the south precipitated another plot against the
Empress which also helped Potemkin. Between thirty and a hundred
non-commissioned officers in the Preobrazhensky Guards mutinied.
They believed Orlov was travelling to 'the army to persuade them to
swear allegiance to him' and make himself 'Prince of Moldavia and
Emperor'. Their mission was Catherine's ever present nightmare: to

overthrow her and enthrone her son Paul as emperor. The plot was foiled but, as Paul approached his majority, Catherine was understandably nervous.[42] The Swedish diplomat Ribbing wrote to his Court in July that Catherine had withdrawn to an estate in Finland, to decide what measures to take, accompanied by Kirill Razumovsky, Ivan Chernyshev, Lev Naryshkin – and Potemkin.[43] The first names required no explanation – she had trusted them for almost twenty years. But the presence of Potemkin, still only thirty-one, is unexpected. It is his first mention as a close adviser of the Empress. Even if the Swede was mistaken, it still suggests that Potemkin was in Petersburg and already much closer to Catherine than anyone realized.

There are more hints that he was already privately advising her, if not making love to her, much earlier than previously thought. When she summoned him in late 1773, she told him that he was '*already* [author's italics] very close to our heart'.[44] In February 1774, she told him that she regretted not starting their relationship 'a year and a half ago'[45] – in other words, in 1772. It was now she started to fall for him.

Then, two months later, when Grigory Orlov opened talks with the Turks in Fokshany in faraway Moldavia, Potemkin, according to Samoilov,[46] was at the talks, behaving in the manner for which he would later become famous. As Orlov negotiated, Potemkin supposedly spent the hours lazing on a sofa in his dressing gown, plunged in thought. This sounds just like him. It was natural that he and his troops would be in the area along with the rest of the army. Rumiantsev was there of course. Potemkin was presumably in his entourage, but he must have had Catherine's blessing to lounge in the midst of an international peace conference, chaired by the suspicious Orlov. Did Catherine send Potemkin to watch Orlov? Why else would Orlov have tolerated him?

The real story is why Orlov himself was there at all: he had neither diplomatic experience nor the temperament for the job. It emerged that Catherine had her own private reasons to remove him from St Petersburg, yet would she really have risked the peace conference merely to get him out of the capital? Admittedly he was assisted by the experienced Obreskov, the Russian Ambassador to the Sublime Porte, recently freed from the Seven Towers. But Orlov was scarcely suited to the tortuous horse-trading that the Turks regarded as good manners.

Then he argued with Rumiantsev. Orlov wanted to start the war again; Rumiantsev, who knew that recruits were few, disease rampant and money short, did not. The Field-Marshal's fastidious intelligence gave him the acuteness of an ice-pick. This must have riled the easygoing giant, who was far out of his depth. Finally, he lost his temper in mid-session and, to the astonishment of the Turkish plenipotentiaries, threatened to hang Rumiantsev himself. The Turks, who still regarded themselves as the receptacles of all that was elegant and civilized, no doubt shook their heads at these manifestations of Slavic barbarism. But the issues at risk there were extremely complicated and becoming more so by the day. Catherine was determined that the Turks should agree to the independence of the Crimea from Turkish sovereignty. The Crimea, suspended from the continent like a diamond from a belly dancer's navel, dominated the Black Sea. The Turks claimed it as their 'pure and immaculate virgin' – the Sultan's lake. Catherine's proposal would remove Turkey from direct control of the northern coast of the Black Sea, except for its fortresses, and bring Russia one step closer to Peter the Great's foiled dream of controlling its power and commerce.

Meanwhile Prussia and Austria were becoming restless at the Russian successes: acquisitive, ruthless Frederick the Great was jealous that his Russian ally might gain too much Ottoman territory. Austria, hostile to Prussia and Russia, secretly negotiated a defensive treaty with the Turks. Prussia wanted some compensation for being a loyal ally to Russia; Austria wanted a reward for being a thoroughly disloyal one to Turkey. Whatever they said, Russia and Prussia both looked longingly at the helpless chaos of Poland. Austria's Empress–Queen, Maria Theresa, balked at this thievery – yet, as Frederick the Great put it, 'she wept, but she took'. Picturesque, feeble and self-destructive Poland was like an unlocked bank from which these imperial brigands could steal what they wished to pay for their expensive wars, satisfy their greed and ease their jealousy of each other. Austria, Prussia and Russia negotiated the First Partition of Poland, leaving Catherine free to enforce her demands on Turkey.

Just when the Polish partition was all but agreed, Sweden, Turkey's traditional ally, stepped in to spoil the party. Over the years, Russia had spent millions of roubles on bribes to ensure that Sweden remain a limited monarchy, split between the French and Russian parties. But in August 1772 its new young King, Gustavus III, restored absolutism in a coup. He encouraged the Turks to fight on. So, back in Fokshany, Orlov became tired of the Turks' intransigence over his demand for Crimean independence. Whether it was the complexity of the diplomacy, the minutiae of Turkish etiquette or the presence of Potemkin, yawning in his dressing gown on the sofa, Orlov now delivered an ultimatum to the Turks that ruined the conference. The Turks walked out.

Orlov had other things on his mind: the Court was in crisis. Suddenly on 23 August, without awaiting orders, he abandoned the conference and headed for Petersburg as fast as his horses would carry him. Potemkin, if he still lay on the sofa as Orlov galloped away, would have been even deeper in thought than usual.

Grigory Orlov was stopped at the gates of St Petersburg at the express order of the Empress. He was ordered, for reasons of quarantine, to proceed to his nearby estate of Gatchina.

Just a few days before, on 30 August, a good-looking ensign in the Horse-Guards, Alexander Vassilchikov, aged twenty-eight, was formally appointed adjutant-general to the Empress and moved into a Winter Palace apartment. Courtiers knew that they had been lovers for a month. After being introduced to Vassilchikov, at the behest of Nikita Panin, Catherine had watched him closely. At Tsarskoe Selo, when he escorted her carriage, she presented him with a gold snuff-box engraved 'For the good bearing of the bodyguards', an unusual reward for sentry duty. On 1 August, he was appointed gentleman of the bedchamber.[47]

When Catherine heard that Grigory Orlov was on his way from Fokshany, she was alarmed but also furious, because his abandonment of the already tottering talks exposed her love life to the gaze of the cabinets of Europe. Indeed the foreign ambassadors were confused: they had presumed Orlov was Catherine's partner for life. They were used to the balance between Panins and Orlovs, now allied to the Chernyshev brothers. No one knew the political effects of the arrival of Vassilchikov, except that the Orlovs were in decline and the Panins were in the ascendant.

Orlov and Catherine had drifted apart for a couple of years: we do not know exactly why. She was now forty and he thirty-eight: perhaps they both longed for younger partners. He had never really shared her intellectual interests. Politically she trusted him and they had been through much together: they shared a son. But Orlov had his intellectual limits – Diderot, who later met him in Paris, thought he was like 'a boiler always boiling but never cooking anything'. Perhaps Potemkin's company made Orlov's uncomplicated solidity less attractive to Catherine. Yet it is a mystery why she did not choose Potemkin to replace him. Perhaps after years of repaying her debt to Orlov and his family, she was not yet ready for Potemkin's dominant and eccentric character. Later, she regretted not summoning him at once.

On the very day that Orlov departed for the south, she later told Potemkin, somebody revealed to her the extent of his infidelities. It was then Catherine admitted that Orlov 'would have remained for ever, had he not been the first to tire'. This is usually taken at face value but she must at least have suspected his peccadilloes for years. His omnivorous sexual appetites were common knowledge among the ambassadors. 'Anything is good enough for him,' Durand claimed. 'He loves like he eats – he is as happy with a Kalmyk or a Finnish girl as with the prettiest girl at Court. That's the sort of oaf he is.' Whatever the real reason, the Empress decided she 'could no longer trust him'.[48]

Catherine negotiated a full settlement with Orlov with a generosity that was to be her lodestar in love: he received an annual pension of 150,000 roubles, 100,000 roubles to set up his household, and the neo-Classical Marble Palace, then under construction, 10,000 serfs, all sorts of other treasures and privileges – and two silver services, one for ordinary use and one for special occasions.[49] In 1763, the Holy Roman Emperor Francis, Maria Theresa's consort, had granted him the title prince of the Holy Roman Empire. The title prince, or *kniaz* in Russian, existed in Russia only among the descendants of ancient royal houses.* If eighteenth-century tsars wished to raise someone to prince, they requested the Holy Roman Emperor to create him an imperial prince. Now Catherine allowed her ex-lover to use his title.

In May 1773, Prince Orlov returned to court and resumed his official positions, though Vassilchikov remained favourite – and Potemkin was left, impatiently suspended in limbo.[50]

It must have been a disappointed Potemkin who returned to the war. At least Catherine promoted him to lieutenant-general on 21 April 1773. The old establishment was envious. 'The promotion of Potemkin is for me a pill I cannot swallow', wrote Simon Vorontsov to his brother.[51] 'When he was a lieutenant of the Guards, I was already a colonel and he has certainly served less than me ...'.[52] Vorontsov decided to resign the moment the campaign was over. There is a feeling of exhaustion and reluctance about this frustrating, bad-tempered campaign, even among the veterans of Rumiantsev's victories. There was another attempt to negotiate, this time in Bucharest. But the moment had passed.

Once again, Rumiantsev's tired army, now down to just 35,000 men, struck across the Danube at the obstinate fortress of Silistria. Potemkin 'was the first to open the campaign in the severe winter with his march to the Danube', reported the Field-Marshal, 'and the organizing of a series of raids across to the other bank of the river with his reserve corps. When the army approached the Danube crossing and when the enemy

* Peter the Great did make his favourite Prince Menshikov, but that was an exception. After 1796, Emperor Paul and his successors began to create princes themselves so promiscuously that they ultimately caused an inflationary glut in the prestige of that title.

in great numbers of people and artillery consolidated on the opposite bank on the Gurabalsky hills to prevent our passage', Potemkin, continued Rumiantsev, 'was the first to get across the river on the boats and to land his forces against the enemy'. The new Lieutenant-General captured the Ottoman camp on 7 June. But Potemkin was already marked as a coming man: a fellow general, Prince Yuri Dolgoruky, another of that ubiquitous clan, claimed that 'timid' Potemkin 'never kept order' during the river crossings and was respected by Rumiantsev only because of his 'connections at Court'. Yet Dologoruky's memoirs are notoriously untrustworthy. The demanding Rumiantsev – and his fellow officers – admired and liked Potemkin – and valued him highly during this campaign.[53]

Silistria's 'very strong' garrison made a powerful sortie against Potemkin. On 12 June, not far from Silistria, he repelled another attack, according to Rumiantsev, taking the enemy artillery. Rumiantsev's forces approached the familiar walls of Silistria. On 18 June, Lieutenant-General Potemkin, 'in command of the advance corps, overcame all the biggest difficulties and dangers, driving the enemy away from the fortifications before the town'. On 7 July, he defeated a Turkish corps of 7,000 cavalry. Even in the arms of Vassilchikov, indeed especially in his worthy but dull company, Catherine did not forget Potemkin: when she told Voltaire that June about the strike across the Danube, she mentioned Potemkin's name for the first time. She was missing him.[54]

As summer turned to autumn, Potemkin supervised the building of batteries of artillery on the island opposite Silistria. The weather was deteriorating; the Turks showed every sign that they were not going to give up Silistria. 'Tormented by the severity of the weather and the sallies of the enemy', Potemkin 'carried out all the necessary actions to bombard the town, causing fear and damage'.[55] When the Russians did penetrate the walls, the Turks fought street by street, house by house. Rumiantsev withdrew. The weather was now freezing. Potemkin's batteries went back to bombarding the fortress.

At this tense and uncomfortable moment, an imperial courier arrived in Rumianstev's camp with a letter for Potemkin. Dated 4 December, it speaks for itself:

Sir! Lieutenant-General and Chevalier, you are probably so absorbed by gazing at Silistria that you have no time to read letters and though I do not as yet know whether your bombardment was successful, I am sure that every one of your deeds is done out of zeal for me personally and out of service for our beloved Motherland.

But, since on my part I am most anxious to preserve fervent, brave, clever and talented individuals, I beg you to keep out of danger. When you read this letter, you may well ask yourself why I have written it. To this, I reply: I've written this letter so that you should have confirmation of my way of thinking about you, because I have always been your most benevolent,
Catherine.[56]

In the filthy, freezing and dangerous discomfort of his benighted camp beneath Silistria, this letter must have seemed like a communication from Mount Olympus, and that is what it was. It does not read like a passionate love letter written in a hurry. On the contrary, it is an arch, cautious and carefully drafted declaration that says much and yet nothing. It did not invite Potemkin to the capital, but it is obviously a summons, if not what is popularly known as a 'come-on'. One suspects he already knew Catherine's 'way of thinking' about him – that she was already in love with the man who had loved her for over a decade. They were already corresponding – hence Catherine implied that Potemkin had not bothered to answer all her letters. His moody insouciance in ignoring imperial letters must have made him all the more attractive, given the sycophantic reverence which surrounded Catherine. The excited Potemkin understood this as the long-awaited invitation to Petersburg.

Moreover, Catherine's fear for Potemkin's life was not misplaced. Rumiantsev now had to extract his army from its messy operations at Silistria and get it safely across the Danube. Potemkin was given the honour of the most dangerous role in this operation: 'When the main part recrossed back over the river,' remembered Rumiantsev, 'he was the last to do so because he covered our forces on the enemy's bank.'[57] Nonetheless, it would probably be an understatement to say Potemkin was in a hurry to reach the capital.

Potemkin's critics, such as Simon Vorontsov and Yuri Dolgoruky, mostly writing after his death when it was fashionable to denounce him, claimed he was an incompetent and a coward.[58] Yet, as we have seen, Field-Marshals Golitsyn and Rumiantsev acclaimed his exploits well before he rose to power, and other officers wrote to their friends about his daring, right up until Silistria. Rumiantsev's report described Potemkin as 'one of those military commanders who extolled the glory … of Russian arms by courage and skill'. What is the truth?

Rumiantsev's complimentary report to Catherine was written after Potemkin's rise in 1775 and was therefore bound to exaggerate his achievements – but Rumiantsev was not the sort of man to lie. So Potemkin performed heroically in the Turkish War and made his name.

As soon as the army was in winter quarters, he dashed for St Petersburg. His impatience was noticed, suspected and analysed by the many observers of Court intrigues, who asked one another – 'Why so hastily?'[59]

6

THE HAPPIEST MAN ALIVE

Thy lovely eyes captivated me yet I trembled to say I loved.
G. A. Potemkin to Catherine II, February/March 1774

This clever fellow is as amusing as the very devil.
Catherine II on G. A. Potemkin

So much changed the moment Grigory Alexandrovich
[Potemkin] arrived!
Countess Ekaterina Rumiantseva to Count Peter Rumiantsev,
20 March 1774

Lieutenant-General Grigory Potemkin arrived in St Petersburg some time in January 1774 and strode exuberantly into a Court in turmoil, no doubt expecting to be invited into Catherine's bed and government. If so, he was to be disappointed.

The general moved into a cottage in the courtyard of his brother-in-law Nikolai Samoilov's house[1] and then went to present himself to the Empress. Did she tell him of the disasters and intrigues that swirled around her? Did she beg him to be patient? Potemkin was so enervated with anticipation that he found patience difficult. Ever since he was a child, he had believed he was destined to command and, ever since he joined the Guards, he had been in love with the Empress. He appeared to be all impulse and passion, yet he had learned to wait a little. He appeared frequently at Court and made Catherine laugh. The courtiers knew that Potemkin was suddenly ascending. One day, he was going upstairs at the Winter Palace when he passed a descending Prince Orlov. 'Any news?', Potemkin asked Orlov. 'No,' Prince Orlov replied, 'except that I am on the way down and you're on the way up.' But nothing happened – at least not in public. The days passed into weeks. The wait was excruciating for someone of Potemkin's nature. Catherine was in a complicated and sensitive situation, personally and politically, so she moved slowly and cautiously. Vassilchikov remained her official lover – he still lived in his Palace apartments and he presumably shared her bed. However, Vassilchikov was a disappointing companion for Catherine, who found him corrosively dull. Boredom bred unhappiness, then contempt. 'His caresses only made me cry,' she told Potemkin afterwards.[2]

Potemkin became more and more impatient: she had sent him encouraging letters and summoned him. He had come as fast as he could. He had waited for this moment for twelve devoted years. She knew how clever and capable he was: why not let him help her? She had admitted she had feelings for him as he had for her. Why not throw out Vassilchikov?

Still nothing happened. He confronted her about the meaning of the summons. She replied something like: '*Calme-toi.* I am going to think about what you have said and wait until I tell you my decision.'[3] Perhaps she wanted him to master the intricacies of her political situation first, perhaps she was teasing him, hoping that their relationship would grow when the moment was right. No one believed in the benefits of careful preparation like Catherine. Most likely, she simply wanted him to force the issue, for she needed his fearless confidence as much as his brains and love. Potemkin learned fast enough why Catherine needed him now: he would have known much of it already. But when he was briefed by the Empress and his friends, he must have realized she was embroiled in her gravest crisis – politically, militarily, romantically – since the day she came to power. It had started, just a few months earlier, in the land of the Yaik Cossacks.

On 17 September 1773, a charismatic Don Cossack appeared before an enthused crowd of Cossacks, Kalmyks and Tartars near Yaiksk, the headquarters of the Yaik Cossacks, thousands of versts south-east of Moscow in another world from Petersburg, and declared that he was the Emperor Peter III, who had not been murdered, but was there to lead them against the evil Catherine. He called her 'the German, the Devil's daughter'. The *soi-disant* 'Emperor' was really Emelian Pugachev, a lean, swarthy army deserter with a black goatee beard and brown hair. He did not even look like Peter III. But that did not matter because no one in those remote parts would have recognized the real thing: Pugachev, born around 1740 (almost the same age as Potemkin), had fought in the Seven Years War and at the siege of Bender. He had grievances against the Government, had been arrested and had escaped.

He promised all things to all men – he was the 'sweet-tongued, merciful, soft-hearted Russian Tsar'. He had already displayed the 'Tsar's marks' on his body to convince these simple angry people that he bore the stigmata they expected of their anointed ruler. He promised them 'lands, waters, woods, dwellings, grasses, rivers, fishes, bread . . .', and anything else he could possibly conjure.

This exceedingly generous political manifesto proved irresistible to many of those who listened to him – but especially to the Yaik Cossacks.

The Cossacks were martial communities or Hosts of freemen, outcasts, escaped criminals, runaway serfs, religious dissidents, deserters, bandits of mixed Tartar and Slavic blood who had fled to the frontiers to form armed bands on horseback, living by plunder and rapine, and raising horses. Each Host – the Don, the Yaik, the Zaporogian and their Polish and Siberian brothers – developed its own culture, but they were generally organized as primitive frontier democracies who elected a hetman or ataman in times of war.

For centuries, they played the middle ground, allying with Poland, Lithuania or Sweden against Muscovy, with Russia against the Crimean khans or Ottoman sultans. In the eighteenth century, they remained as likely to rob Russians as Turks but were useful to Russia as border guards and light cavalry. However, the tension between the Russian state and the Cossacks was growing. These Cossacks were concerned with their own problems – they were worried that they were going to be incorporated into the regular army with its drilling discipline and that they would have to shave their beards. The Yaik Cossacks particularly were concerned with recent disputes about fishing rights. A mutiny had been harshly suppressed just a year earlier. But there was more: the Russo-Turkish War was now in its fifth full year and its costs in men and money fell especially on the peasantry. These people wanted to believe in their scraggly 'Peter III'.

Pugachev ignited this powderkeg. In Russia, the tradition of 'pretenderism' was still strong. In the seventeenth-century 'Time of Troubles', the 'False Dmitri' had even ruled in Moscow. In a vast primitive country where the tsars were all-powerful and all-good and the simple folk believed them to be touched by God, the image of this kind, Christ-like ruler, wandering among the people and then emerging to save them, was a powerful element of Russian folklore.* This was not as odd as it might sound: England had had its share of pretenders, such as Perkin Warbeck, who in 1490 claimed to be Richard, Duke of York, one of the murdered 'Princes in the Tower'.

Pretenderism became a historical vocation for a certain breed of mavericks, deserters, Old Believers who lived on the frontiers – outsiders who would claim to be a recently dead or overthrown Tsar. The real Tsar in question had to have ruled for a short enough time to maintain the illusion that, if evil nobles and foreigners had not overthrown him, he

---

* When Emperor Alexander I died in 1825, he was widely believed to have become a monk wandering the Russian vastness.

would have saved the common people. This made Peter III an ideal candidate. By the end of Catherine's reign, there had been twenty-four ersatz Peters, but none had the success of Pugachev.

There was one other successful impostor: the False Peter III of Montenegro, in today's Yugoslavia. At the beginning of the war in 1769, when the fleet was trying to raise Balkan Orthodoxy against the Turks, Catherine had Alexei Orlov send an envoy to the remote Balkan land of Montenegro, which was ruled by a sometime healer, possibly an Italian, named 'Stephen the Small' who had united the warlike tribes by claiming to be Peter III. The envoy, Prince Yuri Dolgoruky (later the critic of Potemkin's soldiering), was amazed to discover that this Montenegran 'Peter III', a curly-haired thirty-year-old with a high voice, a white silk tunic and a red cap, had ruled since 1766. Dolgoruky exposed the mountebank. But, unable to control Montenegro, he put him back on his throne, wearing the dignity of a Russian officer's uniform. Small Stephen ruled Montenegro for another five years until his murder. Indeed, he was one of the best rulers Montenegro ever had.[4]

The day after Pugachev declared himself emperor, his wily opportunism had won him 300 supporters, who began storming government forts. His army increased. Those so-called forts were really just villages encircled by wooden fences and filled with unreliable Cossacks, discontented peasants and a small sleepy garrison of soldiers. They were not hard to capture. Within weeks, the south-eastern borderlands were almost literally ablaze.[5]

On 5 October, 'Peter III' arrived before the local capital of Orenburg, now with an army of 3,000 and over twenty cannons, leaving the bodies of nobles and officers hanging in their fallen strongholds or outside their burning mansions, usually headless, handless and legless. Women were raped and then beaten to death; men were often hanged upside down. One corpulent officer was flayed alive and stuffed while the rebels cut out his fat and rubbed it on to their wounds. His wife was torn to pieces and his daughter was consoled by being placed in the 'Amparator's' harem, where she was later murdered by Cossacks who envied her place of favour.

On 6 November, 'Amperator Peter Fadarivich' founded a College of War at his headquarters at Berda outside Orenburg. Soon he wore a gold-embroidered kaftan and a fur hat, his chest was covered in medals and his henchmen were known as 'Count Panin' and 'Count Vorontsov'. He had secretaries writing out his manifestos in Russian,

German, French, Arabic and the Turkic languages; judges to keep order among his men; commanders to lead different armies; deserters to fire his cannons. His mounted army must have been an awesome, exotic and barbaric sight: much of it was made up of peasants, Cossacks and Turkic horsemen, armed with lances, scythes, and bows and arrows.

When the news first reached the 'Devil's daughter' back in St Petersburg in mid-October, Catherine took it for a minor Cossack mutiny and despatched General Vasily Kar with a force to suppress it. In early November, Kar was defeated by the frenzied horde, suddenly 25,000 strong, and fled back to Moscow in shame.

These initial successes gave Pugachev the prestige he needed. As his ruffians took cities, he was received by bell-ringing, icon-bearing reception committees of priests and townsfolk offering prayers to 'Peter III and the Grand Duke Paul' (not to Catherine of course).

'Pugachev was sitting in an armchair on the steps of the commandant's house,' wrote Pushkin in his story *The Captain's Daughter*, which is based on his research and conversations with witnesses. 'He was wearing a red Cossack coat trimmed with gold lace. A tall sable cap with gold tassels was set low over his flashing eyes ... The Cossack elders surrounded him ... In the square gallows were being prepared'.[6] Sometimes, sixty nobles were hanged together. It is said rewards of 100 roubles were offered for each dead nobleman and the title 'general' for ten burned mansions.

'The Emperor' would then dine in the local governor's house, often accompanied by his terrified widow and daughters; the governor himself would probably be hanging outside. The ladies would either be hanged or granted to a chieftain for his private pleasure. While he was publicly hailed as Sovereign, the Emperor's private dinners were informal Cossack feasts. After recruiting more men, commandeering cannons and stealing the local treasury, he would ride off again to the ringing of bells and the singing of prayers.[7] By early December, Pugachev was besieging the towns of Samara and Orenburg, as well as Ufa in Baskiria, with an army now approaching 30,000, swelled by all the discontented of the south – Cossacks, Tartars, Bashkirs, Kirghiz and Kalmyks.

Pugachev was already making mistakes; his marriage for example to his favourite mistress was hardly the behaviour of an emperor who, if he was really alive, was already married to a certain 'Devil's daughter' in St Petersburg. Nonetheless, as December arrived, it was suddenly clear that he was a real threat to the Russian Empire.

The timing of Catherine's letter to Potemkin was far from coincidental.

She wrote to him when she had just received news that Pugachev had routed Kar. This was no minor upheaval: the Volga region was rising under what appeared to be an organized and competent leader. Five days before lifting her pen to Potemkin, she had appointed the impressive General Alexander Bibikov, a friend of both Panin and Potemkin, to suppress the pretender. Politically, she needed someone unattached to the leading parties but linked only to her who could advise on her military matters. Personally, she missed the friend whom she now loved. It was as if all the years of their strange relationship, potentially so close yet perpetually so distant, had been preparing for this moment.

As Potemkin got ready to come to her, the rebellion was far from the only worrying challenge. There was another true pretender, much closer to home and all the more dangerous: her son. On 20 September 1772, Grand Duke Paul – the Tsarevich and the threat to her reign and therefore her life – turned eighteen, so she could not long delay recognizing his majority when he had every reason to expect to be allowed to marry, maintain his own court and play a significant political role. The first was possible, if not attractive, the second was feasible but far from convenient and the third was impossible. Catherine feared that to take Paul as any sort of co-ruler would be the first step to her own overthrow. While she considered what to do, a new plot demonstrated that Paul remained her Achilles' heel.

Catherine's difficulties had started with her dismissal of Prince Orlov a year earlier and her embrace of Vassilchikov, who was no help in matters of state – or the heart. The fall of Orlov appeared to mark the triumph of Nikita Panin, who as Paul's Governor must have anticipated an even larger slice of power. But the balance was restored by the reappearance of a cheerful Prince Orlov in May 1773, after 'travelling abroad'. He rejoined the Council in June. He must have imposed a three-line whip of his family since Petersburg now felt the formidable presence of all five Orlov brothers.

Faced with Paul's majority, Catherine searched for a grand duchess in much the same way that Elisabeth had found her. Then and now, the Empress decided that a German princess, not directly linked to either Austria or Prussia, would be most appropriate. In June, Paul expressed his interest in Princess Wilhelmina, second daughter of the Landgraf of Hesse-Darmstadt, whose family business was renting out his Hessians as mercenaries. At about the time Wilhelmina converted to Orthodoxy on 15 August, Paul received a not altogether unattractive proposition from a diplomat in the Russian service, Caspar von Saldern, a native of Paul's Duchy of Holstein. He persuaded Paul to put his name to a plan for mother and son to rule jointly like Maria Theresa and Joseph of Austria. As soon as Panin heard of this, he tried to cover up. When Catherine discovered the plot, she was so angry with Saldern she wanted 'the wretch tied neck and heels and brought straight here'.[8] He never visited Russia again.[9]

As if all this – war, filial tension, possible treason and the widespread peasant rebellion – was not enough, a literary celebrity arrived in Petersburg on 28 September 1773 and provided Catherine with a short interval of comic relief. The Empress admired his *Encyclopaedia* but it is hard to imagine a more inconvenient moment for Denis Diderot's visit. The Encyclopaedist, bearing all the ludicrous delusions of the French *philosophes*, expected to advise Catherine on the immediate reform of her entire Empire. Staying for five months in a house a few hundred yards from the Winter Palace (it is marked with a plaque near St Isaac's Cathedral), his conversations helped her through the monotony of life with Vassilchikov.

However, Diderot soon began to irritate her – though if one compares his sojourn to Voltaire's disastrous stay with Frederick the Great, it was a moderate success. Catherine naughtily claimed that he bruised her knees which he pummelled as he over-excitedly told her how to run Russia.[10] He did at least introduce her to his companion Frederich Melchior Grimm, who became her dearest correspondent for the rest of her life.

Diderot's sole achievement was probably to convince her, if Pugachev had not already done so, that abstract reform programmes had little use in Russia: 'you only work on paper ...', she told him, 'while I, poor Empress, I work on human skin.'[11] Catherine, said Diderot, had 'the soul of Caesar with the seductions of Cleopatra.'[12]

On 29 September, Paul, undermined by the Saldern Affair, married his Grand Duchess Natalia (formerly Wilhelmina), followed by ten days of celebrations. Count Panin remained Foreign Minister but he had to give up his position as Paul's Governor, losing his rooms in the palaces. He was consoled with promotion to the highest echelon of the Table of Ranks, a pension of 30,000 roubles and a gift of 9,000 souls. To pacify the Orlovs, Catherine promoted their ally Zakhar Chernyshev to field-marshal and President of the College of War. But the Saldern Affair had damaged all of them: Catherine no longer trusted Panin but was stuck with his Northern System. She no longer respected Orlov, but his clan was a pillar of her regime. She forgave him the folly of Fokshany but would not take him back as a lover. She found her own son Paul narrow-minded, bitter and uncongenial. She could never trust him in government – yet he was Heir. She was bored with Vassilchikov yet she had made him her official favourite. Catherine, surrounded by a fierce rivalry between Panins and Orlovs, had never been more alone.[13]

This risky dilemma was also harming her image in Europe. Frederick the Great, that misanthropic genius who presided over an austere all-male court, was particularly disgusted: Orlov had been recalled to all offices, he fumed, 'except that of fucking'. Frederick also sensed that the uncertainty at Court would threaten Panin and his Prussian alliance. 'It is a terrible business', declared the King of Prussia, 'when the prick and the cunt decide the interests of Europe.'[14] But by late January the freshly arrived Potemkin was deciding nothing. He could not wait any longer. He decided to force Catherine's hand.

Potemkin declared he was no longer interested in earthly glories: he was to take holy orders. He at once left Samoilov's cottage, moved into the Alexander Nevsky Monastery, founded by Peter the Great, on the outskirts of eighteenth-century Petersburg, and lived, as a monk, growing a beard, fasting, reading, praying and chanting ostentatiously. The suspense of waiting, on the verge of success, in a political and personal hothouse, was, in itself, enough to strain Potemkin's manic nature to the edge of a breakdown, which he soothed by immersing himself in Orthodox mysticism. But he was also a born politician with the appropriate thespian talents. His melodramatic retreat put public pressure on Catherine; he was almost going 'on strike', withdrawing his advice and support unless she gave him the credit for it. It has been suggested that he and the Empress arranged this together to accelerate his rise. The pair were soon to show they were quite capable of prearranged stunts, but in this case Potemkin's behaviour seems equally divided between piety, depression and artifice.[15]

His cell, more like a coenobitic political campaign headquarters, saw much coming and going between fasts. Carriages galloped through the gates and departed again; servants, courtiers and the rustling skirts of imperial ladies, particularly Countess Bruce, rushed on and off the Baroque stage of the monastery like characters in an opera, bearing notes and whispered messages.[16] First, as in every opera, there was a song. Potemkin let Catherine know that he had written one to her. It has the ring of Potemkin's passion – and also the mawkishness that is the hallmark of love songs, then and now. But as a description of his situation, it is not bad. 'As soon as I beheld thee, I thought of thee alone ... But O Heavens, what torment to love one to whom I dare not declare it! one who can never be mine! Cruel gods! Why have you given her such charms? And why did you exalt her so high? Why did you destine me to love her and her alone?'[17] Potemkin made sure Countess Bruce told the Empress how his 'unfortunate and violent passion had reduced him to despair and, in his sad situation, he deemed it prudent to fly the object of his torment since the sight alone could aggravate his sufferings which were already intolerable.'[18] He began 'to hate the world because of his love for her – and she was flattered'.[19]

Catherine replied with an oral message that went something like this: 'I cannot understand what can have reduced him to such despair since I have never declared against him. I fancied on the contrary that the affability of my reception must have given him to understand that his homage was not displeasing.'[20] It was not enough. The fasting, chanting, rustling of go-between skirts and delivery of messages continued. The holier of the monks must surely have rolled their eyes at this worldly bustle.

Catherine, by all accounts, made up her mind and despatched Countess Bruce – ironically, Rumiantsev's estranged sister – to bring Potemkin back. The Countess, in all her finery, arrived at the monastery in a Court coach. She was taken to Potemkin, who was bearded, wearing monk's habit and prostrated in a plain cell before an icon of St Catherine. In case the Countess was in any doubt about his sincerity, he continued praying and chanting for a very long time. Finally Potemkin deigned to hear her message. He then swiftly shaved, washed and dressed in uniform to re-emerge at Court.

What was Catherine feeling during this operatic interlude? During the next weeks, when they were finally lovers, she revealed to him, in this most tender and moving account, how she already loved him by the time he returned from the army:

Then came a certain hero [*bogatr*]: this hero, through his valour and demeanour, was already very close to our heart; on hearing of his arrival, people began to talk of his staying here, not knowing we had already written to him, on the quiet, asking him to do so, with the secret intention however of not acting blindly when he did come, but of trying to discover whether he really had the inclination of which Countess Bruce said that many suspected him, the inclination I wanted him to have.[21]

The Empress was at Tsarskoe Selo outside the city. Potemkin rode out there, most likely accompanied by Countess Bruce. The Court Journal tells us that Potemkin was presented on the evening of 4 February: he was ushered straight into her private apartments, where they remained alone for an hour. He is mentioned again on the 9th, when he attended a formal dinner at the Catherine Palace. They dined officially together four times in February, but we can guess that they were together much more: we have a few undated notes from Catherine to Potemkin that we can place in those days.[22] The first is addressed 'Mon ami', which suggests a growing warmth but warns him about bumping into a shocked Grand Duke, who already hated Prince Orlov for being his mother's lover.[23] In the second, written a few days later, Potemkin has been promoted to 'Mon cher ami'. Already she is using the nicknames they have made up for the courtiers: one of the Golitsyns is 'M. le Gros' – 'Fatty' – but, more importantly, she calls Potemkin 'l'esprit' – 'the wit'.[24]

They were coming closer by the hour. On the 14th, the Court returned to the Winter Palace in town. On the 15th, there was another dinner with both Vassilchikov and Potemkin among the twenty guests. One can imagine the unhappiness of poor Vassilchikov as Potemkin dominated the scene.

Potemkin and the Empress might have consummated their love affair around this time. Few of their thousands of notes are dated, but there is one that we can tentatively place around 15 February in which Catherine cancels a meeting with 'l'esprit' in the *banya*, the Russian steam-bath, mainly because 'all my ladies are there now and probably won't leave for another hour'.[25] Ordinary men and women bathed together in banyas in the eighteenth century, much to the indignation of foreigners, but empresses did not. This is the first mention of Catherine and Potemkin meeting in the *banya*, but it was to be their favourite place for rendezvous. If they were meeting in the intimate *banya* on the 15th, it is likely they were already lovers.

On the 18th, the Empress attended a Russian comedy at the House of Opera and then probably met Potemkin in her apartments. They talked or made love until one in the morning – extremely late for that disciplined Germanic princess. In a note in which one can sense their increasing intensity but also her submissiveness to him, she sweetly worries that 'I exceeded your patience ... my watch stopped and the time passed so quickly that an hour seemed like a minute.'[26]

'My darling, what nonsense you talked yesterday ...', she wrote in these early days. 'The time I spend with you is so happy. We passed four hours together, boredom vanishes and I don't want to part with you. My dear, my friend, I love you so much: you are so handsome, so clever, so jovial, so witty: when I am with you, I attach no importance to the world. I've never been so happy . . .'.[27] For the first time, we can hear the intimate laughter that must have echoed at night out of the Winter Palace *banya*. They were both sensualists – a pair of Epicureans. 'My darling friend, I fear you might be angry with me. If not, all the better. Come quickly to my bedroom and prove it.'[28]

Vassilchikov was still in residence – at least officially. Catherine and Potemkin nicknamed him 'soupe à la glace' – 'iced soup'.[29] It was now she told Potemkin that she wished they had started a year and half before instead of wasting precious time unhappily.[30] But the presence of Vassilchikov in his apartments was still upsetting Potemkin, who was always hysterically jealous. He had apparently flounced off because, in a letter a few days later, Catherine had to coax him back: 'I cannot force someone to caress . . . You know my nature and my heart, you know my good and bad qualities, I let you choose your behaviour . . . It is silly to torment yourself . . . You ruin your health for nothing.'[31]

Vassilchikov has been almost forgotten, but these days must have been agonizing for him. Catherine was ruthless with those she could not respect and one senses she was ashamed of his mediocrity. Vassilchikov realized that he could never play the role of Potemkin, whose 'standing was very different from mine. I was merely a sort of kept woman . . . I was scarcely allowed to see anyone or go out. When I asked for anything, no notice was taken whatsoever . . . When I was anxious for the Order of St Anna, I spoke about it to the Empress and found 30,000 roubles in my pocket next day in notes. I always had my mouth closed like that . . . As for Potemkin, he gets what he wants . . . he is the master.'[32]

'The master' insisted that the unfortunate bowl of 'Iced Soup' be removed from the table. Vassilchikov moved out of his apartments in the Winter Palace. They became the Council Room, because Potemkin refused to live in someone else's apartments. New rooms were decorated for him. Potemkin himself moved out of the cottage at the Samoilovs' to stay with the trusted Chamberlain Yelagin.[33]

By late February, the relationship was no longer either an amorous courtship or a sexual affair: the couple were absolutely committed. On the 27th, Potemkin was confident enough to write a letter requesting that he be appointed 'general and personal aide-de-camp to Her Majesty'. There were a handful of adjutant-generals, mostly just courtiers. But in this case the meaning would be clear. He added in what was presumably a Potemkinian joke, 'it could not offend anybody'. Both of them must have laughed at this. His arrival would offend everybody, from the Orlovs to the Panins, from Maria Theresa and Frederick the Great to George III and Louis XVI. It would change the political landscape and ultimately Russia's alliances abroad. But no matter, because he touchingly added his real feelings: 'I would be the happiest man alive . . .'.[34] The letter was handed in to Stekalov, who was in charge of requests, like any other petition. But this one was answered far more quickly.

'Lieutenant-General . . . I think your request is appropriate,' she replied the next day, taking off official language, 'in view of the services that you have rendered to me and our Motherland.' It was typical of Potemkin simply to write officially: 'he was the only one of her favourites who dared to become enamoured of her and to make the first advances', wrote Charles Masson, later Swiss mathematics tutor at Court and author of scandalous but unreliable memoirs. Catherine appreciated this courage in her reply: 'I am ordering the drawing up of your nomination to adjutant-general. I must confess to you that I am pleased that you, trusting me, decided to send your request directly to me without looking for roundabout ways.'[35] It is at this moment that Potemkin steps out of the shadows of history to become one of the most described and discussed statesmen of the century.

'A new scene has just opened,' Sir Robert Gunning, the English envoy, reported to the Earl of Suffolk, Secretary of State for the North, in London on 4 March, having just watched the new Adjutant-General at Court, 'which is likely to merit more attention than any that has presented itself since the beginning of this reign.' Since this was the age of letter-writing, everyone now wrote about Potemkin. Diplomats were agog because, as Gunning saw at once, Potemkin was abler than both Prince Orlov and Vassilchikov. It is interesting that, just a few days after appearing as official favourite, even foreigners not intimate with the Court were informing their kings that Potemkin had arrived to love the Empress *and* help her rule. 'Mr Vassilchikov the favourite whose understanding was too limited to admit of his having any influence in affairs or sharing his mistress's confidence', explained Gunning, 'is replaced by a man who bids fair for possessing them both in the most supreme degree.'[36] The Prussian Ambassador Count von Solms went further to Frederick: 'Evidently Potemkin . . . will become the most influential person in Russia. Youth, intellect and positive qualities will give him such importance . . . Soon Prince Grigory Grigorevich [Orlov] will be forgotten and Orlov's family will drop to the common standard.'[37]

Russia's chief ally was even more repulsed than he had been by the arrival of Vassilchikov two years before. Thoroughly informed by Solms,

Frederick the Great wrote to his brother Prince Henry ridiculing the newcomer's name – 'General Patukin or Tapukin' – but recognized that his rise to power 'might prove prejudicial to the well-being of our affairs'. Being Frederick, he coined a philosophical principle of misogynistic statesmanship: 'A woman is always a woman and, in feminine government, the cunt has more influence than a firm policy guided by straight reason.'[38]

The Russian courtiers observed Potemkin carefully, chronicling every move of the new favourite, even his jewellery and the decoration of his apartments. Every detail meant something that was important for them to know. Solms had already discovered that Potemkin's arrival did not trouble the Panins.[39] 'I think this new actor will play his part with great vivacity and big changes if he'll be able to consolidate his position,'[40] wrote General Peter Panin to Prince Alexander Kurakin on 7 March. Evidently, the Panins thought they could use Potemkin to obliterate the credit of the Orlovs.[41] 'The new Adjutant-General is always on duty instead of all the others,' Countess Sievers wrote to her husband, one of Catherine's senior officials. 'They say he is pleasant and modest.'[42] Potemkin was already amassing the sort of power Vassilchikov never possessed. 'If you want anything, my sweet,' Countess Rumiantseva wrote to her husband, the Field-Marshal, down with the army, 'ask Potemkin.'[43]

To her friend Grimm, Catherine paraded her exhilaration at escaping Vassilchikov and finding Potemkin: 'I have drawn away from a certain good-natured but extremely dull character, who has immediately been replaced by one of the greatest, wittiest and most original eccentrics of this iron century.'[44]

Part Three

TOGETHER
1774–1776

> The doors will be open ... I am going to bed ... Darling, I will
> do whatever you command. Shall I come to you or will you
> come to me?
>
> Catherine II to G. A. Potemkin

> This was Potemkin, a great thing in days
> When homicide and harlotry made great.
> If stars and titles could entail long praise,
> His glory might half equal his estate.
> This fellow, being six foot high, could raise
> A kind of phantasy proportionate
> In the then sovereign of the Russian people,
> Who measured men as you would do a steeple.
>
> Lord Byron, *Don Juan*, Canto VII: 37

Everything about the love of Catherine and Potemkin is exceptional. Both were extraordinary individuals in the most unique of circumstances. Yet the love affair on which they were now embarked has features that are universal, even today. Their passion was so exhausting and tumultuous that it is easy to forget that they loved one another while ruling a vast empire – at war abroad, in civil war at home. She was an empress and he a subject – both of matching 'boundless ambition' – living in a highly competitive Court where everything was seen and every glance had political consequences. They often forgot themselves in their love and moods, but neither was ever completely private: Catherine was always the Sovereign, and Potemkin, from the first day, was more than a mere favourite, a politician of the first rank.

The lovers were no longer young by the standards of their time: Potemkin was thirty-four, Catherine ten years older. But their love was all the more touching for their imperfections. In February 1774, Potemkin had long since lost his Alcibiadean perfection. Now he was a bizarre and striking sight that fascinated, appalled and attracted his contemporaries in equal measure. His stature was colossal, yet his figure was still lithe; his admired head of hair was long and unbrushed, a rich brown, almost auburn, sometimes covered by grey wigs. His head too was titanic, but almost pear-like in shape. His profile resembled the soft

lines of a dove – perhaps that is why Catherine often called him that.
The face was pale, long, thin and oddly sensitive in such a huge man –
more that of a poet than a general. The mouth was one of his best
features: his lips were full and red; his teeth strong and white, a rare asset
at that time; his chin had a dimple cleft. His right eye was green and
blue; his left one was useless, half closed, and sometimes it made him
squint. It looked strange – though Jean-Jacob Jennings, a Swedish diplomat, who met him much later, said 'the eye defect' was much less
noticeable than he had expected. Potemkin never got over his sensitivity
about it, but it gave him a certain vulnerability as well as a piratical air.
The 'defect' did make this outlandish figure seem more like a mythical
beast – Panin called him 'Le Borgne' – 'the blindman', but most followed
the Orlovs and called him 'Cyclops'.[1]

The diplomatic corps were immediately rapt: 'his figure is gigantic
and disproportioned and his countenance is far from engaging', wrote
Gunning, but:

> Potemkin appears to have a great knowledge of mankind and more of
> the discriminating faculty than his countrymen in general possess and
> as much address in intrigue and suppleness in his station as any of
> them. Though the profligacy of his manner is notorious, he is the only
> one to have formed connections with the clergy. With these quali-
> fications he may naturally flatter himself with the hopes of rising to
> that height to which his boundless ambition aspires.[2]

Solms reported, 'Potemkin is very tall, well formed but has an unpleasant
appearance because he squints,' but three days later he added that given
his 'youth and intellect ... it will be easy for General Potemkin ... to
occupy Orlov's place in the Empress's heart'.[3]

His manners varied from those of a courtier at Versailles to those of
one of his Cossack friends. This is why Catherine delighted in nick-
naming him after Cossacks, Tartars and wild animals. His contemporaries, especially Catherine, agreed that the whole picture, with its
Russian scale and its mixture of ugliness and beauty, reeked of primitive
energy, an almost animalistic sexuality, outrageous originality, driving
intellect and surprising sensitivity. He was either loved – or hated. As
one of Kirill Razumovsky's daughters asked: 'How can one pay court to
the blind beggar and why?'[4]

Catherine remained a sexually attractive, handsome and very majestic
woman in her prime. Her brow was high and strong, the blue eyes bright,
playful and coolly arrogant. Her eyelashes were black, her mouth shapely,

her nose slightly aquiline, her skin remained white and blooming, and her bearing made her appear taller than she was. She was already voluptuous, which she camouflaged by always wearing 'an ample robe with broad sleeves ... similar to ancient Muscovite costume'.[5] Everyone acclaimed her 'dignity tempered with graciousness',[6] which made her 'still beautiful, infinitely clever and knowledgeable but with romantic spirit in her loves'.[7]

Catherine and Potemkin were suddenly inseparable. When they were not together, even when they were just in their own apartments, a few yards apart, they wrote to each other manically. They were both highly articulate. Fortunately for us, words were enormously important to them. Sometimes they sent several notes a day, back and forth: they were the equivalent of telephone calls or, even more, the e-mail of the Internet. Being secret love letters that often dealt with state affairs as well, they were usually unsigned. Potemkin's handwriting, a surprisingly fine and scratchy hand for such a big man, gets progressively worse as times goes on until it is almost illegible in any language by his death. The letters are in a mixture of Russian and French, sometimes almost randomly; at other times, matters of the heart were in French, those of state in Russian. A wealth of these letters have survived, a record of a lifelong love and political partnership. Some belong in that century, but others are so modern they could have been written by a pair of lovers today. Some could have been written only by an empress and a statesman; others speak the timelessly trivial language of love. There are even complete conversations: 'Go, my dove, and be happy,' wrote Catherine to Potemkin in one letter. He departed. When he returned, Catherine received this: 'Mother, we are back, now it's time for supper.' To this she replied: 'Good God! Who might have thought you would return?'[8]

Catherine addressed her lover as 'my darling soul', 'my heart', 'sweetheart' and 'bijou'. Later she often used the traditional Russian 'batushka' or 'batinka' – or 'papa' – and endless diminutives of Grigory: 'Grisha', 'Grishenka', 'Grishenok', even 'Grishefishenka'. At the height of their love, her names for him become even more colourful: 'My golden pheasant', 'Golden cockerel', 'Dearest dove', 'Kitten', 'Little Dog', 'Tonton', 'dear little heart', 'Twin Soul', 'Little parrot', 'part-bird, part-wolf', and lots of others that combine his force with his sensitivity. If he was playing up, she ironically brought him down to size as 'Dear Sir' or 'Dear Lieutenant-General' or 'Your Excellency'. If she was giving him a new title, she liked to address him accordingly.

Potemkin virtually always addressed Catherine as 'Matushka', or 'Little

Mother', or 'Sovereign Lady' or both. In other words, he deliberately used the old Russian way of addressing a tsarina rather than calling her Katinka, as some of her later lovers did. This was due not to a lack of intimacy but rather to Potemkin's reverence for his Sovereign. For example, he made the courier who brought the Empress's notes kneel until he had written the reply, which amused Catherine with its romanticism: 'Write please, has your Master of Ceremonies brought my messenger to you today and has he knelt as he usually does?'

Potemkin always worried that the letters could be stolen. The diligent Empress burned some of *his* earlier love letters as soon as she read them. Those that survive from this period were mostly *her* letters, or *his* letters that she sent back to him with an addendum. So we have far more of hers. Later, most of his letters survived because they became state as well as personal papers. The passionate Russian treasured his in a scruffy wad, tied up with string and often secreted in his pocket, close to his heart, so that he could read and reread them. 'Grishenka, good morning,' she began a letter probably in March 1774, '. . . I am in good health and slept well . . . I am afraid you will lose my letters: someone will steal them from your pocket . . . They'll think they are banknotes and pocket them.'[9] But, luckily for us, he was still carrying them around when he died seventeen years later. They had nicknames for all the main courtiers, which sometimes are hard to interpret, and also a secret coded language possibly so that Potemkin could tell her in what way he would like to make love to her.

'My dove, good morning,' she greeted him typically. 'I wish to know whether you slept well and whether you love me as much as I love you.'[10] Sometimes they were as short as this: 'Night darling, I'm going to bed.'[11]

When the court returned to town from Tsarskoe Selo on 9 April, Potemkin moved out of Yelagin's house, where he had been living since he became the Empress's lover, into his newly decorated apartments in the Winter Palace: 'they are said to be splendid', Countess Sievers reported the next day. Potemkin was now a familiar sight around the town: 'I often see Potemkin who rushes around in a coach and six.' His fine carriage, expensive horses and speed became elements of his public image. If the Empress went out, Potemkin was usually in attendance. When Catherine went to the theatre on 28 April, 'Potemkin was in the box,' noticed Countess Sievers. Royalty, indeed sometimes the entire audience, often talked throughout the play – Louis XV irritated Voltaire with this royal habit. Here, Potemkin 'talked to the Empress all the way through the play; he enjoys her greatest confidence.'[12]

Potemkin's new rooms were directly beneath Catherine's in the Winter Palace. Both their apartments looked out on to the Palace Square and into an internal courtyard, but not on to the Neva river. When Potemkin wished to visit – which he did, unannounced, whenever he liked – he came up (as Orlov had come down) the spiral staircase, as always decorated with green carpets. Green was the colour of amorous corridors – for the staircase linking Louis XV's apartments to the boudoir of the Marquise de Pompadour was green too.

Potemkin was given apartments in all the imperial palaces, including the Summer Palace in town and Peterhof outside, but they were most often at the Catherine (or Great) Palace at Tsarskoe Selo, where Potemkin reached the imperial bedroom by crossing a corridor so chilly that their letters often warn each other against traversing this arctic tundra. 'Sorry you're sick,' she wrote. 'It is a good lesson for you: don't go barefoot on staircases. If you want to get rid of it, take a little tobacco.'[13] They rarely spent the night together (as Catherine did with some later favourites), because Potemkin liked to gamble and talk late and lie in all morning, while the Empress awoke early. She had the metabolism of a tidy German schoolmistress, though with a strong vein of sensuality; his was that of a wild frontiersman.

At Catherine's intimate evenings, Potemkin often burst in, unannounced, dishevelled in a Turkish dressing gown or some other species of wrap, usually with nothing underneath so that his hairy chest and legs were quite visible. Whatever the weather, he would be barefoot. If it was cold, he threw on a fur cloak over the top which gave him the look of a giant who could not decide if he was a brute or a dandy. In addition to all this, he liked to wear a pink bandana round his head. He was an Oriental vision far from the Voltairean tastes of the Court, which was why she called him 'bogatr', the knightly Slavic hero from the mythology of Rus. Even in the earliest days of the affair, Potemkin knew that he was different from everybody else: if summoned, he might languidly decide not to turn up. He appeared in the Empress's rooms when it suited him and never bothered to be announced, nor waited to be summoned: he lumbered in and out of her apartments like an aimless bear, sometimes the wittiest member of the party, other times silently, not even bothering to acknowledge the Empress herself.

His tastes were 'truly barbaric and Muscovite' and he liked 'nothing better than the plain food of his people, particularly Russian pastries, like *pirozki*, and raw vegetables', which he kept at his bedside.[14] When he came upstairs, he would often be nibbling apples, turnips, radishes, garlic, behaving in the Winter Palace exactly as he had as a boy wandering with serf children through Chizhova. The political significance of the Prince's choice of nibble was as natural and deliberate in its Russian rusticity as Walpole's red Norfolk apples were of his earthy Englishness.

Potemkin's uncouth behaviour shocked the usually Francophile courtiers and the fastidious ambassadors, but when he felt like it he appeared in formal or military uniform with the perfect grace and immaculate presentation of a dapper courtier. Everything with him was a battle of extremes. If he was thoughtful or brooding, as he was very often, he would bite his nails to the quick: he was to suffer terribly from hangnail for his whole life, so that the letters between the two rulers of the Empire would often be distracted from laws and wars by the state of his fingertips. 'The greatest nailbiter in the Russian Empire', was what Catherine called him. 'The Cyclops', wrote Alexander Ribeaupierre, 'has a charming habit. He bites his nails with frenzy right down to the skin.'[15] If it was not his nails, it was anything else close within reach. At the Little Hermitage, where the Empress had written out a list of rules to enforce informality, she added a special rule aimed at her Potemkin. 'You are requested to be cheerful,' went Rule Three, 'without however destroying, breaking or biting anything.'[16]

Nonetheless Potemkin took over Catherine's apartments too: he put a huge Turkish divan in her salon so he could lounge around in his dressing gown – 'Mister Tom [Catherine's English greyhound] is snoring very deeply behind me on the Turkish divan General Potemkin has introduced,'[17] Catherine told Grimm rather proudly. His effects were strewn around her neat rooms – and she admired his untamed, almost Bohemian, nonchalance: 'How much longer will you leave things in my rooms that belong to you!', she wrote to him. 'Please do not throw your handkerchiefs all over the shop in your Turkish fashion. Many thanks for your visit and I love you a lot.'[18]

It is impossible to reduce a friendship yet alone a love to its components. But, if anything, their relationship was based on laughter, sex, mutually admired intelligence, and power in an order that changed all the time. His wit had made her laugh when Orlov presented him twelve years before – and that continued throughout their lives. 'Talking of originals who make me laugh and above all of General Potemkin,' Catherine told Grimm on 19 June that year, 'who is more *à la mode* than any one else and who makes me laugh so much I could burst my sides.'[19] Their letters were pervaded as much by her guffaws as by the force of their ambition and attraction: 'Darling, what stories you told me yesterday! I can't stop laughing when I think of them. What happy times I am spending with you!'[20]

There were lots of games that involved Potemkin competing with Mister Tom to see who could unleash more disorder in the imperial apartments. Her letters to Grimm are filled with Potemkin's antics including his covering himself with Mister Tom's little rug, a most incongruous sight: 'I'm sewing a new bed-blanket for Thomas . . . that General Potemkin pretends to steal from him.'[21] Later Potemkin was to introduce a badly behaved monkey.

She was never bored with Potemkin and always bored without him: he was protean, creative and always original. When she had not seen him for a while, she grumbled: 'I'm bored to death. When will I see you again?' But, as so often happens in love affairs, the laughter and the love-making seemed to lead inexorably to each other. Her sexual happiness shines through her letters. The affair was highly sexual. She was extremely proud of his sex appeal to other women and his record of female conquests. 'I don't wonder that there are so many women attributed to you,' she wrote to him. 'It seems to me that you are not an ordinary person and you differ from everyone else in everything.'[22]

Darling I think you really thought I would not write today. I woke up at five and now it is seven, I will write . . . I have given strict orders to the whole of my body, down to the last hair to stop showing you the smallest sign of love. I have locked up my love in my heart under ten locks, it is suffocating there and I think it might explode. Think about it, you are a reasonable man, is it possible to talk more nonsense in a few lines? A river of absurdities flows from my head, I do not understand how you can bear a woman with such incoherent thoughts. Oh Monsieur Potemkin! What a trick have you played to unbalance a mind, previously thought to be one of the best in Europe. It is time, high time, for me to become reasonable. What a shame! What a sin! Catherine II to be the victim of this crazy passion . . . one more proof of your supreme power over me. Enough! Enough! I have already scribbled such sentimental metaphysics that can only make you laugh. Well, mad letter, go to that happy place where my hero dwells . . . Goodbye, *Giaour*, Muscovite, Cossack . . .[23]

This is how she felt, probably during March 1774, when she woke early, the morning after a tryst with Potemkin, who was still asleep in his apartments. The roguish names she gave him – the 'Cossack', 'giaour' (the pejorative Turkish for a non-Moslem), 'Lion of the Jungle', 'Golden

Tiger', 'Golden Cockerell' and 'Wolf' – may refer to sexual energy. She even called him 'Pugachev' of all things, presumably meaning ferocious, energetic, and unbridled like a Cossack.

In these months, they were sharing everything; their meetings seem to have been frantic sessions of laughter, love-making and political planning, one after another, because both enjoyed all three. The sex was instantly mixed with politics. 'I love you very much,' she began a letter, some time in April, 'and when you caressed me, my caress always hurries to answer you ... Don't forget to summon Pavel [P. S. Potemkin, his cousin, who was being sent to assist in suppressing Pugachev]: when he arrives, it will be necessary to do two things'[24] – and on she went on to discuss the measures against the rebellion.

Catherine was addicted to him: one night when he did not come to visit her, she actually 'got up from my bed, dressed myself and went to the library towards the doors so that I might wait for you, where I stood for two hours in the draught; and then at 11 o'clock went to bed in misery where, thanks to you, I had not slept for five nights.'[25] The vision of the Empress waiting outside Potemkin's room for two hours in her dressing gown and bonnet gives us some idea of her passion for him. There were the inevitable rumours of Potemkin's elephantine sexual equipment and this may explain the persistent myth that Catherine took a cast of his formidable member to console herself during his increasingly long absences in the south.[26] This ranks in terms of historical veracity with the other malicious smears against Catherine, but stories of Potemkin's 'glorious weapon' found their way into the homosexual mythology of St Petersburg.*

If he was busy, she respected his privacy, even though she was the Empress. One day, she could not resist visiting him in his apartments. She ventured downstairs but as she approached, 'I saw through the doorway the back of a clerk or an adjutant and I fled at top speed. I love

---

* In the late nineteenth century, the painter Constantine Somov, one of the 'Art for Art's Sake' circle of intellectuals, whose father was then Curator of the Hermitage Museum, held a tea party for his mainly homosexual friends, the poet Kuzmin, probably the ballet impresario Sergei Diaghilev, and a handful of others. Somov, according to O. Remizov, the author of *The Other Petersburg*, told them how his father, the Curator, had discovered a magnificent lifesize cast of Potemkin's member in Catherine's collection. When the others did not believe him, the men were invited into the other room where they admired, with the bated breath of true connoisseurs, 'the glorious weapon of Potemkin', cast in porcelain, which lay wrapped in cottonwool and silk in a wooden box. It was then returned to the Hermitage, where, one must add, it has never been seen again. When this author recently visited the Hermitage to find Potemkin's collection, no one knew of it. But it is a very large museum.

you all the time with all my soul.'²⁷ This also shows how carefully the Empress had to behave in front of clerks and servants in her own palaces. Catherine complained repeatedly about her love for him making her lose her reason, the governing ideal of this devotee of Voltaire and Diderot. This Enlightened ruler in the Age of Reason revelled in the swooning language of schoolgirl silliness: 'When you are with me, closing my eyes is the only way not to lose my mind; the alternative which would make me laugh for the rest of my life would be to say, "My eyes are charmed by you." ' Was she referring to his romantic song to her? 'My stupid eyes gaze at you; I become silly and unable to reason.' She dreamed about him: 'A strange thing happened to me. I have become a somnambulist' – and she recounted how she imagined meeting 'the most fascinating of men'. Then she awoke: 'now I am looking everywhere for this man of my dreams ... How I treasure him more than the whole world! ... Darling, when you meet him, give him a kiss for me.'²⁸

Downstairs in the Winter Palace on the basement floor, beneath Catherine's chapel, there was her Russian bath – the *banya* – where much of their love affair seems to have taken place.*

'My dear fellow, if you want to eat some meat, everything's ready in the bath. But I beg you not to swipe any food from there because everyone will know that we're cooking in there.'²⁹ After his promotion in the Guards in March 1774, Catherine writes:

> Good morning Mr Lieutenant-Colonel, how are you feeling after your bath? I am well and feel very jolly thanks to you. As soon as you left, do you know what we talked about? It is easy to guess, seeing how intelligent you are: about you, my darling! Good things were said about you, you were found beyond comparison. Goodbye, will you look after the regiment and the officers all day? As to me, I know what I am going to do. I will think – of whom? Of him, it is true that the thought of Grisha never leaves me ...³⁰

One day, Potemkin arrived back at the Palace. 'Dear matushka, I have just arrived but I am so frozen that I cannot even get my teeth warm,' he announced to her. 'First I want to know how you are feeling. Thank you for the three garments and I kiss your feet.' We can imagine the messengers

* Today the *banya*, like their apartments, does not exist. They were destroyed in the fire of 1837. But from the outside we can see the chapel by the golden dome and cross. Now the *banya* is the Egyptian section of the Hermitage Museum. It has the cool dampness of a bathhouse even today.

or ladies-in-waiting scampering back and forth down the miles of corridors in the Winter Palace bearing Catherine's reply: 'I rejoice that you are back, my dear. I am well. To get warm: go to the bath; it has been heated today.'[31] Later the servant brought her the news that Potemkin had finished his bath. So the Empress sent back another note: 'My beauty, my darling, whom nothing resembles, I am full of warmth and tenderness for you and you will have my protection as long as I live. You must be, I guess, even more handsome than ever after the bath.'[32]

Lovers tend to share the details of their health: Potemkin and Catherine shared theirs through their lives. '*Adieu monsieur*,' she scribbled one morning before going out, 'how did you sleep? How is your fever? It would be so nice to sit and talk.'[33] When his fever eased, she tempted him back. 'You will see a new routine,' she promised. 'At first I will receive you in my boudoir, I will make you sit down near the table and there you will be warm and so will not get a cold ... And we will start to read a book and I will let you go at half past ten ...'[34]

When he was better, it was her turn to be ill: 'I slept very well but not much; I've got a headache and pain in my chest. I don't know if I'll go out today. If I do go out, it's only because I love you more than you love me and I can prove it as 2+2=4. I will go to see you. Not every person is so clever, so handsome, so lovely as you are.'[35]

Potemkin himself was a notorious hypochondriac. But even when he was ill he was always in a state of nervous tension, so that sometimes Catherine assumed the tyrannical tone of a brisk German matron to calm him down: 'Really, it is time to settle down to the right order of things. Be quiet and let me be quiet too. I tell you sincerely that I'm most sympathetic about your illness but I will not spoil you by words of tenderness.'[36] When he really was sick: 'My beloved soul, precious and unique, I can find no words to express my love for you. Don't be upset about your diarrhoea – it will clean up the bowels well ...'[37] Bowels particularly resonate through the letters of that century.

When she herself came down with diarrhoea, she was concerned, like any woman would be, that her lover did not startle her in an undignified position. 'If you really must see me, send somebody to tell me; since six this morning I have had the most atrocious diarrhoea.' Besides she did not want to visit him down the icy Tsarskoe Selo corridor: 'I am sorry but passing through the non-heated corridor ... would only make my aches worse ... I'm sorry you're ill. Try to be quiet, my friend, that is the best cure.'[38]

*

Catherine was thrilled to have found a partner who could be an equal of sorts: 'My darling, the time I spend with you is so happy. We pass four hours, boredom vanishes and I don't want to part from you. My dearest friend, I LOVE YOU SO MUCH, you are so handsome, clever, jovial and funny; when I am with you I attach no importance to the world. I have never been so happy. Very often I want to keep my feelings from you but usually my heart just blabs out my passion.'[39] But even in these early idyllic days of this great love Potemkin was already tormented by his contradictory appetites: a childish hunger for attention and love versus a wild yearning for freedom and independence.

Catherine's solution to the first problem was to spoil Potemkin day and night with her attention, which he sucked up, for he was quite as greedy for love as she was. The Empress of all the Russias could not humble herself enough before this proud Russian: 'My dear dove, my precious friend, I must write to you to keep my promise. Please know that I love you and this shouldn't surprise anyone. For you, one would do the impossible and so I'll be either your humble maid or your lowly servant or both at once.'[40] Potemkin constantly demanded more and more attention. He wanted to know she was always thinking about him. If not, he sulked.

'I never forget you,' she reassured 'her beloved friend' after one of his moods. 'As soon as I finished listening to reports, which took three hours, I wanted to send somebody to you, especially as it was not yet ten o'clock and I was afraid of waking you up before. As you see, your anger has no foundation ... Darling I love you like my soul.'[41] If she was truly angry, she let him know it: 'Fool! I am not ordering you to do anything! Not deserving this coldness, I blame it on our deadly enemy, your spleen!'[42] She indulged his moods, finding his passion somewhat flattering, and tried to understand his torments: 'You are talking non-sense, my darling. I love you and I'll love you for ever in spite of yourself.' Even more sweetly: 'Batinka, come to see me so that I can calm you with my endless caresses.'[43] Her role is often to soothe this angry and frustrated man with her love.

Potemkin's moods were so changeable that the two played games with each other. 'Was there anything on that sheet?', she wrote, pretending not to have read one of his raging notes. 'Certainly reproaches, for Your Excellency has sulked all evening and I, brokenhearted, sought your caresses in vain ... The quarrel took place the day before yesterday when I tried in all sincerity to have it out with you about my plans that ... could be very useful to you. Last night, I confess, I deliberately did not send anyone ... But when you had not arrived by nine o'clock I sent for news of your health. Then you turned up but with a sulky face. I pretended not to notice your bad mood which ended by really upsetting you ... Wait darling, let my wounded heart heal again, tenderness will return as soon as we grant each other an audience.'[44]

Perhaps it was after this that Potemkin sent her a blank piece of paper. The Empress was hurt yet somewhat amused and she rewarded him with an almost complete encyclopaedia of his nicknames: 'This is not April Fool's Day to send me a blank sheet. Probably ... you have done it not to spoil me too much. But ... I don't guess the meaning of your silence either. Yet I am full of tenderness for you, *giaour*, Muscovite, Pugachev, golden cockerel, peacock, cat, pheasant, golden tiger, lion in the jungle.'[45]

Catherine concealed an obsessive emotional neediness – 'my cruel tenderness' – beneath her cool German temperament, which was enough to suffocate any man, let alone the impossibly restless Potemkin. Rewarded lavishly, rising fast, spoilt by the woman he loved, he was such a bundle of nerves, poetical melodrama and Slavic contrariness that he could never relax and just be happy: 'Calmness is for you a state your soul cannot bear.' He needed space to breathe. His restlessness attracted her, but she could not help finding it insulting: 'I came to wake you up and ... I see you are out. Now I understand this sleep of yours was just an excuse to get rid of me. In town, you spent hours with me ... whereas here I can only see you for short moments. *Giaour*, Cossack, Muscovite, you are always trying to avoid me! ... You can laugh about me but I do not laugh when I see you bored in my company ...'.[46] But Potemkin was as manipulative as Catherine herself. Whether it was pride or restlessness that made him avoid her, he liked to let her know it. 'I'll never come to see you if you're avoiding me,'[47] she wrote pathetically on one occasion. Potemkin's quicksilver mind was easily bored, though he never tired of Catherine's company. They had too much in common.

It was difficult for a traditional Russian like Potemkin, even one educated in the classics of the Enlightenment, to maintain an equal relationship with a woman not only more powerful but also so sexually independent. Potemkin's behaviour was selfishly indulgent but he was in a difficult situation with enormous pressures on him, politically and personally. That is why he tormented Catherine. He was obsessively jealous of other men, which was foolish given her absolute devotion to him. The role of official lover was not easy on a masterful man.

First he was jealous of Vassilchikov. Now Catherine gave him the satisfaction of negotiating the terms of departure – or pay-off for 'Iced

Soup'. 'I am handing over the question of deciding to someone far cleverer than me ... I ask you to be moderate.' Her letter gives us a fascinating glimpse into her generosity: 'I will not give him more than two villages,' she informed Potemkin. 'I have given him money four times but I don't remember how much. I think it was 60,000 ...'. Potemkin along with his ex-host Yelagin arranged a most generous deal for Vassilchikov, though it was positively meagre compared to what was given to his successors. Vassilchikov, who had already left the Winter Palace to stay with his brother, now received a fully decorated mansion, 50,000 roubles for setting up house, 5,000 roubles a year pension, villages, tableware, linen and a twenty-place silver service, no doubt including bowls for frozen soup. Poor 'kept' Vassilchikov humiliatingly had to 'bow low' and thank Potemkin – but he had reason to be grateful.[48] This was an early example of Potemkin's lack of personal or political vindictiveness. However, he remained tortured by the inherent humiliation of his own position: Catherine could dispense with him as she had dispensed with Iced Soup.

'No Grishenka,' she replied in French after a row, 'it is impossible for me to change as far as you are concerned. You must be fair to yourself: can one love anybody after having known you? I think there is not a man in the world that could equal you. All the more so since my heart is constant by nature and I will say even more: generally, I do not like change.' She was sensitive about her reputation for 'wantonness':

When you know me better you will respect me for I assure you I am respectable. I am very truthful, I love truth, I hate changes, I suffered horribly in the last two years, I burned my fingers, I will not return to that ... I am very happy. If you go on letting yourself be upset by this sort of gossip, do you know what I shall do? Lock myself up in my room and see no one but you. When necessary I could do something that extreme and I love you beyond myself.[49]

Her patience was saintly but not inexhaustible: 'If your silly bad temper has left you, kindly let me know for it seems to persist. Since I've given you no reason for such tenacious anger, it seems to me that it has gone on far too long. Unfortunately, it is only I who find it too long, for you are a cruel Tartar!'[50]

Their relationship thrived on his wild mood swings, but they were very exhausting. Somehow his appalling behaviour seemed to keep him Catherine's respect and love, even though his moods were openly manipulative. Catherine was excited by his passions and complimented by his jealousy, but, lacking restraint, he sometimes went too far. He threatened to kill any rivals for her heart. 'You ought to be ashamed of yourself,' she ticked him off. 'Why did you say that anyone who takes your place would die? It is impossible to compel the heart by threats . . . I must admit there is some tenderness in your misgivings . . . I've burned my fingers with the fool [Vassilchikov]. I feared . . . the habit of him would make me unhappy and shorten my life . . . Now you can read my heart and soul. I am opening them to you sincerely and if you don't feel it and see it, then you're unworthy of the great passion you have aroused in me.'[51]

Potemkin demanded to know everything. He claimed there had been fifteen lovers before him. This was a rare example of an empress being accused of low morals to her face. But Catherine hoped to settle his jealousies with what she called 'A sincere confession'. This is a most extraordinary document for any age. The modern feminine tone belongs in our confessional twenty-first century, the worldly and practical morals in the eighteenth. The sentiments of romance and honesty are timeless. For an empress to explain her sex life like this is without parallel. She discussed her four lovers before him – Saltykov, Poniatowski, Orlov and Vassilchikov. She regretted Saltykov and Vassilchikov. Potemkin appeared as the giant hero, the 'bogatr' that he so resembled: 'Now, Sir Hero, after this confession, may I hope that I will receive forgiveness for my sins? As you will be pleased to see, there is no question of fifteen but only a third of that figure of which the first [Saltykov] occurred unwillingly and the fourth [Vassilchikov] out of despair, which cannot be counted as indulgence; as to the other three, God is my witness, they were not due to debauchery for which I have no inclination. If in my youth I had been given a husband whom I could love, I would have remained eternally faithful to him.'

Then she confessed her version of the truth of her nature: 'The trouble is only that my heart cannot be content even for an hour without love . . .'. This was not the nymphomania that schoolboys have assigned to Catherine but an admission of her emotional neediness. The eighteenth century would have called this a statement of *sensibilité*; the nineteenth century would have seen it as a poetic declaration of romantic love; today, we can see that it is only one of part of a complex, passionate personality.

Their love for each other was absolute, yet Potemkin's turbulence and the demands of power meant that it was always stormy. Nonetheless, Catherine finished her Confession with this offer: 'If you wish to keep me for ever, show as much friendship as affection and continue to love me and to tell me the truth.'[52]

8

POWER

She is crazy about him. They may well be in love because they
are exactly the same.
Senator Ivan Yelagin to Durand de Distroff

'These two great characters were made for each other,' observed Masson.
'He first loved his Sovereign as his mistress and then cherished her
as his glory.'[1] Their similarity of ambitions and talents was both the
foundation of their love and its flaw. The great love affair of the Empress
heralded a new political era because everyone immediately appreciated
that, unlike Vassilchikov or even Grigory Orlov, Potemkin was capable
of exerting his power and would strive to do so at once. But, in early
1774, they had to be very careful at the most sensitive moment in Catherine's reign so far: Pugachev was still rampaging through the territory
north of the Caspian, south of the Urals, east of Moscow – and the
worried nobles wanted him stopped quickly. The Turks were still not
ready to negotiate and Rumiantsev's army was tired and fever-stricken.
A false move against Pugachev, a defeat by the Turks, a provocation
against the Orlovs, a slight to the Guards, a concession to the Grand
Duke – any of these could literally have cost the lovers their heads.

Just in case they were under any illusions, Alexei Orlov-Chesmensky
decided to let them know that he was carefully watching the illuminated
window of the imperial bathhouse. The Orlov brothers, who had recovered so much ground since 1772, would be the first casualties of
Potemkin's rise.

'Yes or no?', 'Le Balafre' asked the Empress with a slight laugh.

'About what?', replied the Empress.

'Is it love?', persisted Orlov-Chesmensky.

'I cannot lie,' said the Empress.

Scarface asked again: 'Yes or no?'

'Yes!', said the Empress finally.

Orlov-Chesmensky began to laugh again: 'Do you meet in the *banya*?'

'Why do you think so?'

'Because for four days we've seen the light in the window of the bath
later than usual.' Then he added: 'It was clear yesterday that you've made

an appointment later so you'd agree not to display affection, to put others off the scent. Good move.'[2] Catherine reported all this to her lover and the two revelled in it like naughty children shocking the adults. But there was always something menacing in Alexei Orlov's jokes.

Between bouts of love-making and laughter in the *banya*, Potemkin immediately began to help Catherine on both the Russo-Turkish War and the Pugachev Rebellion. These political actors often discussed how to play a scene: 'Goodbye brother,' she told him. 'Behave cleverly in public and that way, no one will know what we are really thinking.'[3] Yet she felt safe with Potemkin, who gave her the feeling that everything was possible, that all their glorious dreams were achievable and that the problems of the moment could be settled.

Catherine was already under pressure about Potemkin. In early March, unidentified but powerful courtiers, including one nicknamed 'the Alchemist' – possibly Panin or an Orlov – advised Catherine to dispense with Potemkin: 'The man you call "the Alchemist" visited . . . He tried to demonstrate to me the frenzy of yours and my actions and finished by asking if he wanted me to ask you to go back to the Army: to which I agreed. They are all of them at least trying to lecture me . . . I didn't own up but I didn't excuse myself too so they couldn't claim that I'd lied.' But the letters also show Potemkin and Catherine's unity in political matters:

> In short, I have masses of things to tell you and particularly on the subject we spoke about yesterday between noon and two o'clock; but I do not know if you are in the same mood as yesterday and I don't know either whether your words correspond always to your actions since you promised me several times you would come and you do not come . . . I am thinking about you all the time. Oh! La! La! What a long letter I have written to you. Excuse me, I always forget that you don't like it. I'll never do it again.[4]

Catherine struggled to prevent Potemkin's rise from causing a rift with the Orlovs: 'I ask you – don't do one thing: don't injure and don't try to injure Prince Orlov in my thoughts because that would be ingratitude on your part. Before your arrival there was no one who was praised and loved by him as you.'[5]

Potemkin now demanded a place in government. The most important positions were war and foreign affairs. Since he had come back as a war hero from the Danube, it was natural for him to choose the War College as his target. As early as 5 March 1774, within a week of his appointment as her adjutant-general, she channelled orders to Zakhar Chernyshev, President of the College of War, Orlov's ally, through Potemkin.[6] As ever, the Pugachev Rebellion worked to Potemkin's advantage: all governments require scapegoats for public disasters. Thus Zakhar Chernyshev, who received none of the credit for Rumiantsev's victories, bore the blame for the rampages of Pugachev, and was none too happy about it: 'Count Chernyshev is very anxious and keeps saying he will retire.'[7] Ten days after Potemkin had delivered Catherine's messages to Chernyshev, she promoted him to lieutenant-colonel of the Preobrazhensky Guards, of which she was colonel. This had been Alexei Orlov's place, so it was a sign of the highest favour – and of the eclipse of the Orlovs. And he became captain of the sixty gorgeously attired Chevaliers-Gardes who patrolled the palaces in silver helmets and breastplates and whose Hussar or Cossack squadrons escorted her carriage.

Potemkin knew that it would be madness to take on all the factions at Court, so he tried 'to be friends with everyone', wrote Countess Rumiantseva[8] – especially Nikita Panin.[9] The smug and slothful Panin looked 'more content than before' Potemkin's advent. But Count Solms did not underestimate him: 'I'm only afraid that Potemkin, who has a reputation for being sly and wicked, can benefit by Panin's kindness.'[10]

The favourite hoped, through Panin, to neutralize the other dangerous element in Catherine's Court – the pug-nosed, punctilious, Prussophile Heir Grand Duke Paul, now twenty, who longed to play a political role befitting his rank. Paul had disliked Prince Orlov, but he was to hate the new favourite even more, because he already sensed that Potemkin would forever exclude him from Court. Potemkin soon crossed him. Paul, a stickler for military discipline *à la Prusse*, bumped into the favourite when he visited his mother and grumbled about Potemkin's dress. 'My darling,' Catherine told her lover, 'the Grand Duke comes to me on Tuesdays and Fridays ... 9 to 11 o'clock ... No criticism because Count ... Andrei Razumovsky [friend of Grand Duke Paul] goes to see them in the same dress, I don't find him any worse dressed than you ...'.[11] Fortunately, Grand Duke Paul had not encountered Potemkin in one of his half-open bearskins with the pink bandanna, which was enough to alarm anyone.

Panin undertook to stroke the increasingly bitter Tsarevich towards 'clever' Potemkin's side.[12] So Potemkin was using Panin, who thought he was using Potemkin. Countess Rumiantseva told her husband that Potemkin's return had changed everything politically – and she was right.[13]

*

Potemkin was concentrating on the Pugachev Rebellion. Soon after Catherine and Potemkin had become lovers and political partners, General Alexander Bibikov, setting up his headquarters at Kazan, managed to defeat Pugachev's 9,000-strong army on 22 March, raise the sieges of Orenburg, Ufa and Yaiksk and force the impostor to abandon his 'capital' at Berda, outside Orenburg. The favourite suggested the appointment of his cousin, Pavel Sergeievich Potemkin, the son of the man who had tried to persuade his father that he was illegitimate, to head the Secret Commission in Kazan which was to find the cause of the Rebellion – the Turks and the French were the main suspects – and punish the rebels. Potemkin and Catherine ordered Zakhar Chernyshev[14] to recall Pavel Potemkin from the Turkish front. Pavel Sergeievich was a very eighteenth-century all-rounder – efficient soldier, gracious court- ier, poet and multilingual scholar, the first to translate Rousseau into Russian. When he arrived in Petersburg, Catherine immediately 'told him to join Bibikov' in Kazan.[15] Now that Bibikov was so close to throttling the false Peter III and Pavel Potemkin was on his way to handle the post-mortem, the lovers switched their minds to ending the Turkish War.

'Matushka,' Potemkin scrawled as he read through one of Catherine's drafts of the Russian peace terms, 'what do the articles underlined mean?' Underneath, the Empress replied: 'It means that they have already been added and if there is debate, they will not be insisted on ...'.[16] The moment he arrived in the Empress's counsels, he began working with her on the instructions to be given to Field-Marshal Rumiantsev. At first the courtiers presumed that Potemkin was trying to destroy his former chief. The Potemkin legend claims that throughout his life he was viciously jealous of the few others as talented as himself. This was not so. 'It was said he was unkind to Rumiantsev,' Solms told Frederick, 'but I got to know the opposite – they are friends and he defends him against reproaches.' The Field-Marshal's wife was equally surprised that 'he tries to serve you at every opportunity ... he even favours me.'[17]

A forceful jolt was required to drive the Turks to the peace table, but Rumiantsev's dwindling army needed reinforcements for his planned attack across the Danube, and the authority to make peace on the spot. In late March, Potemkin persuaded Catherine 'to empower Rumiantsev and so the war was ended', as she put it herself.[18] This meant that the traditional Ottoman delaying tactics would not work, because Rum- iantsev was given authority to make peace on the spot, within the bound- aries defined by Catherine and Potemkin, but without the need to refer back to Petersburg. The Field-Marshal was sent the new peace terms corrected by Potemkin on 10 April. By this time, the Turks had lost their appetite for talking. Ottoman decision-making, agonizingly slow at the best of times, had been delayed by the death of Sultan Mustafa III and the succession of his cautious brother Abdul-Hamid. The Turks were encouraged to keep fighting by the French and probably by the duplicitous Prussians: Frederick, while swallowing his share of the Polish Partition, was still jealous of Russian gains in the south. More than that, the Turks were also heartened by the Pugachev Rebellion. So there could be no more peace without war first. Once again, Field-Marshal Rumiantsev prepared to cross the Danube.

Potemkin's first step to power was to join the State Council, the consultative war cabinet created by Catherine in 1768. His rise is always described as quick and effortless. But, contrary to historical cliché, imperial favour did not guarantee him power. Potemkin thought he was ready for the Council. Few agreed with him. Besides, all the other members of the Council were on the First or Second of the Table of Ranks; Potemkin was still on the Third. 'What am I to do? I am not even admitted to the Council. And why not? They won't have it but I'll bring things about,' raged Potemkin, 'with an openness that astonished' the French diplomat Durand.[19] He tended to stun most diplomats he encountered with his outspoken asides. This was the first sign to the foreign ambassadors that Potemkin, after barely three months in Catherine's bed, wanted real power and was set on getting it.

While the Court was at Tsarskoe Selo for the summer, Catherine still refused to appoint him to the Council. He brought his determination and moodiness to bear. 'On Sunday, when I was sitting at the table near him and the Empress,' Durand recorded, 'I saw that not only did he not speak to her but that he did not even reply to her questions. She was beside herself and we for our part very much out of countenance. The silence was only broken by the Master of Horse [Lev Naryshkin] who never succeeded in animating the conversation. On rising from the table, the Empress retired alone and reappeared with red eyes and a troubled air.'[20] Had Potemkin got his way?

'Sweetheart,' the Empress wrote on 5 May, 'because you asked me to send you with something to the Council today, I wrote a note that must be given to Prince Viazemsky. So if you want to go, you must be ready by twelve o'clock. I'm sending you the note and the report of the Kazan Commission.'[21] This note asking Potemkin to discuss the Secret Commission created to investigate and punish the Pugachev rebels sounds casual, but it was not: Catherine was inviting Potemkin to join the Council. Potemkin ostentatiously delivered the note to Procurator-General Viazemsky and then sat down at the top table: he was never to leave it. 'In no other country', Gunning informed London the next day, 'do favourites rise so fast. To the great surprise of the Council members, General Potemkin took his place among them.'[22]

It was about this time that the Kazan Secret Commission uncovered a 'plot' to assassinate Catherine at her summer residence, Tsarskoe Selo: a captured Pugachev supporter had confessed under interrogation that assassins had been despatched. Potemkin arranged the investigation with Viazemsky: 'I think the mountain will give birth to a mouse,'[23] Catherine bravely told Potemkin. He was alarmed, but it turned out the story was probably invented under interrogation by the Commission in the south, one reason why Catherine was against the Russian habit of knouting suspects. She was too far away to prevent the Commission using torture on rebels, though she tried to get Bibikov to minimize its use.[24]

On 30 May, Potemkin was promoted to General-en-Chef and Vice-President of the College of War. It is easy for us to forget that, while this tough factional battle was going on in the councils of the Empress, Potemkin and Catherine were still enjoying the first glow of their affair. On possibly the very same day as his promotion, the Empress sent Potemkin this note in babyish love-talk: 'General loves me? Me loves General a lot.'[25] The undermined War Minister Chernyshev was 'hit so hard', reported Gunning, 'that he could not remain at his post . . .'.[26] The lame duck soon resigned to become governor of the new Belorussian provinces, taken in the First Partition of Poland. There ended the factional crisis that had started two years earlier with the fall of Prince Orlov.

Honours, responsibilities, serfs, estates and riches rained down on Potemkin: on 31 March he had been appointed Governor-General of New Russia, the huge southern provinces that bordered on the Tartar Khanate of the Crimea and the Ottoman Empire; on 21 June, he was made commander-in-chief of all irregular forces, namely his beloved Cossacks. It is hard to imagine the scale of wealth that Potemkin suddenly enjoyed. It was a world away from his upbringing in Chizhova or even his god-father's house in Moscow. A peasant soldier in the Russian infantry was paid about seven roubles a year; an officer around 300. Potemkin regularly received gifts of 100,000 roubles on his namedays, on holidays or to celebrate his particular help on a given project. He had a huge table allowance of 300 roubles a month. He lived and was served by the imperial servants in all the palaces for free. He was said to receive 12,000 roubles on the first of every month on his dressing table, but it is more likely that Catherine simply handed him thousands of roubles when she felt like it, as Vassilchikov had testified. Potemkin spent as easily as he received, finding it embarrassing on one hand, while, on the other, constantly demanding more. Yet he was still far from touching the ceiling of either his income or his extravagance. Soon there was to be no ceiling on either.[27]

Catherine made sure that Potemkin received as many Russian and foreign medals as possible – to increase his status was to consolidate hers. Monarchs liked to procure foreign medals for their favourites. The foreign monarchs resented handing them out – especially to the lovers of usurping regicides. But, unless there was a very good excuse, they usually gave in. The correspondence about these awards between monarchs and Russian ambassadors are most amusing studies in the tortuously polite, almost coded euphemism that was the language of courtly diplomacy.

'Good morning sweetheart,' Catherine greeted Potemkin playfully around this time, '... I got up and sent to the Vice-Chancellor asking for the ribbons; I wrote that they were for ... General Potemkin and I planned to put them on him after mass. Do you know him? He's handsome, he's as clever as he is handsome. And he loves me as much as he's handsome and clever and I love him too ...'.[28] That day, he got the Russian Order of St Alexander Nevsky and the Polish Order of the White Eagle, kindly sent by King Stanislas-Augustus. There was prestige in these orders, though the higher nobility regarded them as their due: one of Potemkin's more winning characteristics was his childish delight in medals. Soon he had collected Peter the Great's Order of St Andrew; Frederick the Great sent the Prussian Black Eagle; Denmark sent the White Elephant; Sweden the Holy Seraphim. But Louis XVI and Maria Theresa refused the Holy Ghost and the Golden Fleece respectively, claiming they were only for Catholics. In London, George III was shocked by his ambassador's attempt to procure Potemkin the Garter.[29]

'It seems the Empress is going to commit the reins of government to Potemkin,' Gunning told London. Indeed the unthinkable had happened: Potemkin was now Prince Orlov's superior. The foreign ambassadors could not swallow this. They had become so used to the Orlovs that they could not believe that they were not about to return to power at any minute. The Orlovs could not believe it either.

Prince Orlov stormed in to see Catherine on 2 June – an alarming sight, even for an Empress. 'They say', reported the well-informed Gunning, 'Orlov and Catherine had it out.'[30] Prince Orlov had always

been good-natured, but now he was permanently and dangerously irascible. His temper, once released, was fearsome. Indeed Catherine called
him a 'madcap' and was upset by whatever Orlov said to her. But she
was capable of dealing with him too: he agreed 'to travel abroad' again.
She did not care. She had Potemkin: 'Goodnight my friend. Send to tell
me tomorrow how you are. Bye – I'm very bored without you.'[31]

On 9 June, Rumiantsev took the offensive against the Turks, despat-
ching two corps across the Danube, which defeated their main army
near Kozludzhi. This cut the Grand Vizier off from the Danubian forts.
Russian cavalry galloped south past Shumla into today's Bulgaria.

Catherine and Potemkin were sorry to learn of the sudden death from
fever of Pugachev's vanquisher, Bibikov, but the Rebellion seemed over
and they appointed the mediocre Prince Fyodor Shcherbatov to succeed
him. Suddenly, in early July, Catherine learned that Pugachev, despite
his defeats, had resurfaced with another army. She sacked Shcherbatov
and appointed another, General Prince Peter Golitsyn: 'I'm sending you
my dear the letter that I've done to Prince Shcherbatov. Correct it
please and then I'll have it read to the Council.' The Empress wrote
optimistically to Potemkin, 'it'll hit the nail on the head'.[32]

On 20 June, the Turks sued for peace: usually this would have meant
a truce, a congress and the months of negotiating that had ruined the
last peace talks. This is where Potemkin's advice to 'empower' Rumiantsev bore fruit, because the Field-Marshal set up camp in the Bul-
garian village of Kuchuk-Kainardzhi and told the Turks that either they
signed peace or the two armies went back to war. The Ottomans began
to talk; news of a peace treaty was expected any day; Catherine's spirits
rose. Everything was going so well.

A new Pugachev crisis struck Catherine in mid-July. On the 11th, Pugachev appeared before the ancient and strategic city of Kazan with a
swelling army of 25,000. The supposedly defeated Pugachev was not
defeated at all, but he was being pursued by the true hero of the Rebellion,
the tirelessly competent Lieutenant-Colonel Ivan Mikhelson. Kazan was
a mere 93 miles from Nizhny Novgorod and that was just over a hundred
miles from Moscow itself. The old Tartar city, conquered by Ivan the
Terrible in 1556, had 11,000 inhabitants and mainly wooden buildings. It
happened that General Pavel Potemkin, the new appointee to run both
the Kazan and Orenburg Secret Commissions, had arrived in Kazan on 9
July, two days before Pugachev. The old Governor was ill. Pavel Potemkin
took over the command, but he possessed only 650 infantry and 200
unreliable Chuvash cavalry, so he barricaded his forces in the citadel. On

the 12th, Pugachev stormed Kazan, which was razed in an infernal orgy of violence that lasted from 6 a.m. to midnight. Anyone in 'German dress' or without a beard was killed; women in 'German dress' were delivered to the pretender's camp. The city was reduced to ashes before Pugachev's army escaped, leaving Pavel Potemkin to be rescued by Mikhelson.

The Volga region was now one teeming peasant rebellion. The Rebellion had taken an even nastier turn: it had started as a Cossack rising. Now it became a savage class war, a regular *jacquerie*, meaning a slaughter of landowners by peasants, named after the rebellion in northern France in 1358. The regime faced the prospect of the millions of serfs massacring their masters. This was a threat not just to Catherine but to the very foundations of the Empire. Factory serfs, peasants and 5,000 Bashkir horsemen now followed the flag of the pretender. Serfs rose in village after village. Gangs of runaway slaves roamed the countryside. Rebel Cossacks galloped through the villages urging the serfs to rise.* On 21 July, the news of the fall of Kazan reached Catherine in Petersburg. The authorities in the centre began to panic. Would Pugachev march on Moscow?[33]

The next day the Empress held an emergency Council meeting at Peterhof. She declared that she would travel directly to Moscow to rally the Empire. The Council heard this in smouldering silence. No one dared speak. The members of the Council were worried and uneasy. Catherine herself was rattled: Kazan made her seem suddenly vulnerable. Unusually for her, she showed it. Some of the magnates, especially Prince Orlov and the two Chernyshev brothers, bitterly resented Potemkin's rise and Panin's resurgence.

The Council was stunned by the Empress's wish to go to Moscow. Its defeated silence reflected the depth 'of the wordless depression'. Catherine turned to her senior minister, Nikita Panin, and asked his opinion of her idea. 'My answer', he wrote to his brother, General Peter Panin, 'was that it would not only be bad but disastrous,' because it smacked of fear at the top. Catherine passionately argued the benefits of her descent on Moscow. Potemkin backed her. The Moscow option may have been his idea because as the most old Russian among these cultured grandees, he instinctively saw Moscow as the Orthodox capital when the Motherland was in danger. Equally, he may simply have agreed with her because

---

* It was a mark of the anarchy engulfing the Volga region that yet another false Peter III, a fugitive serf, now managed to raise another rabble army and conquer Troitsk, south-east of Moscow, where he set up another grotesque Court.

he was too new there to risk independence of Catherine.

The reaction of most of the Council members was almost comical: Prince Orlov refused to give an opinion at all, claiming like a child that he felt off colour, had not slept well and did not have any ideas. Kirill Razumovsky and Field-Marshal Alexander Golitsyn, a pair of 'fools', could not summon up a word. Zakhar Chernyshev 'trembled between the favourites' – Orlov and Potemkin – and managed to emit 'half-words twice'. It was recognized that there was no one of any military weight on the Volga to co-ordinate Pugachev's defeat: 'a distinguished personage' was required. But who? Orlov presumably went off to get his beauty sleep while the downhearted Council resolved nothing, other than to wait for news of the Turkish peace treaty.[34]

Nikita Panin had an idea. After dinner, he took Potemkin aside and proposed that the 'distinguished personage' to save Russia was none other than his brother, General Peter Ivanovich Panin. There was something to be said for this: he was a victorious battle general with the aristocratic credentials necessary to soothe the fears of landowners. He was already in Moscow. But there was a problem with Peter Panin. He was a rude, arrogant and snobbish curmudgeon for whom the word 'martinet' might have been invented. Even for a Russian soldier in the eighteenth century, many of his loudly declared views were absurd: he was a pedant on the privileges of nobles and the minutiae of military etiquette and flaunted a stalwart belief that only men were qualified to be tsar. This harsh disciplinarian and spluttering tyrant was capable of appearing in the anteroom of his headquarters in a grey satin nightgown and a high French nightcap with pink ribbons.[35] Catherine loathed him, distrusted him politically and even had him under secret police surveillance.

So Nikita Panin, not daring to raise his brother aloud at the Council, cautiously approached Potemkin, who went straight to the Empress. She was probably furious at the very thought of it. Perhaps he persuaded her that they had little choice when they felt as if even her closest supporter were wavering. She agreed. When Nikita Panin spoke to her later, the Empress dissembled her real views and, ever the actress, graciously swore that she wanted Peter Panin to take supreme command of the Volga provinces and 'save Moscow and the internal parts of the Empire'. Nikita Panin immediately wrote to his brother.[36]

The Panins had pulled off what was almost a *coup d'état*, forcing Catherine to swallow the humiliation of the hated Peter Panin saving the Empire. They were now, in their way, as much of a threat to Catherine and Potemkin as Pugachev. Having gulped Panin's distasteful medicine, the lovers at once realized that they had to water it down. It was to get worse before it got better: the Panins demanded massive viceregal powers for the general over all towns, courts and Secret Commissions in the four huge provinces affected, and over all military forces (except Rumiantsev's First Army, the Second Army occupying the Crimea and the units in Poland), as well as power to issue death sentences. 'You see my friend,' Catherine told Potemkin, 'from the enclosed pieces, that Count Panin wants to make his brother the dictator of the best parts of the Empire.' She was determined not to raise this 'first-class liar . . . who has personally offended me, above all the mortals in the Empire'. Potemkin took over the negotiations with the Panins and the management of the Rebellion.[37]

Catherine and Potemkin did not know that, before Kazan had fallen, Rumiantsev had signed an extremely beneficial peace with the Turks – the Treaty of Kuchuk-Kainardzhi. On the evening of 23 July, two couriers, one of them Rumiantsev's son, galloped into Peterhof with the news. Catherine's mood changed from despair to gloating enthusiasm. 'I think today is the happiest day of my life,' she told the Governor of Moscow.[38] The Treaty gave Russia a toehold on the Black Sea, granting the fortresses of Azov, Kerch, Yenikale and Kinburn and the narrow strip of coastline between the Dnieper and Bug rivers. Russian merchant ships could pass through the Straits into the Mediterranean. She could build a Black Sea Fleet. The Khanate of the Crimea became independent of the Ottoman Sultan. This success was to make Potemkin's achievements possible. Catherine ordered extravagant festivities. The Court moved to Oranienbaum three days later to celebrate.

This strengthened Potemkin's position with Peter Panin, who waited excitedly in Moscow for confirmation of his dictatorial powers. The surviving drafts of these powers show that Catherine and Potemkin were equally excited about cutting the Panins down to size. They certainly did not hurry: Nikita Panin now realized that he might have overplayed his hand: 'I could see from the first day that this affair was considered . . . an extreme humiliation.' Potemkin was not overawed by the Panins: 'he doesn't listen to anything and doesn't want to listen but decides everything with his mind's impudence.'[39]

When Potemkin wrote to Peter Panin a few days later with the Empress's instructions, he spelt out, with all that 'impudence', that the appointment was completely thanks to his own efforts with the Empress: 'I'm absolutely sure that Your Excellency will treat my actions as a good turn to you.'[40] General Panin received his orders on 2 August – he was only to command forces already fighting Pugachev and enjoy authority over Kazan, Orenburg and Nizhny Novgorod. Potemkin still had his tough cousin Pavel Sergeievich in Kazan as a counterbalance to the overmighty Panin: authority was split between them. Panin's job was to destroy the Pugachev forces; Pavel Potemkin was to arrest, interrogate and punish. Not all the members of the Council quite understood that Peter Panin was not to be 'dictator': when Viazemsky suggested placing Pavel Potemkin's Secret Commission under Panin, he received a laconic rebuttal in the imperial hand: 'No, because it is under me.'[41]

The latest news from the Volga weakened the Panins yet further. It emerged that Mikhelson had beaten Pugachev several times right after the fall of Kazan, so that the news of its sacking was out of date by the time it rocked the Council in Petersburg. Far from marching on Moscow, Pugachev escaped southwards. Catherine's political crisis had passed. The celebrations for the victory over the Turks began at Oranienbaum on the 27th with parties for the diplomatic corps. But Catherine was still busy watching the strange disturbances on the Volga.

It was always hard to tell if Pugachev was fleeing or advancing. Even his flight resembled an invasion. Rabbles rallied to him, towns surrendered, manors burned, necks snapped, bells were rung. In the remote Lower Volga, the local towns kept falling, culminating on 6 August in the sack of Saratov, where renegade priests administered oaths of allegiance to Pugachev *and* his wife, which undermined his imposture even more. Twenty-four landowners and twenty-one officials were hanged. But Pugachev was doing what every cornered criminal does: heading home, to the Don.

The victors swiftly fell out among themselves: Peter Panin and Pavel Potemkin, both arrogant and aggressive, undermined each other wherever possible on behalf of their respective relations in Petersburg. This was precisely the reason Potemkin had divided their responsibilities.

Pugachev arrived in the land of the Don Cossacks before Tsaritsyn,* and learned the hard way that a pretender is never honoured in his own country. When he parleyed with Don Cossacks, they realized that 'Peter III' was the boy they remembered as Emelian Pugachev. They did not rally. Pugachev, still with 10,000 rebels, fled downriver and was then arrested by his own men. 'How dare you raise your hands against your emperor!', he cried. It was to no avail. The 'Amperator' had no clothes left. He was handed over to Russian forces in Yaiksk, where the Rebellion had started a year earlier. There was a glut of forceful and ambitious soldiers on the Lower Volga – Pavel Potemkin, Panin, Mikhelson and Alexander Suvorov – among whom there was an undignified scrummage

---

* Renamed Stalingrad in 1925. Since 1961, it has been called Volgagrad.

to claim credit for capturing the 'state villain' even though none of them had actually done so. Suvorov delivered Pugachev to Peter Panin, who refused to allow Pavel Potemkin to interrogate him.[42] Like children telling tales to their teachers, they spent August to December writing complaints to Petersburg. Often their contradictory letters arrived on the same day.[43] Now that the crisis was over and the lovers were in firm control, Catherine and Potemkin were half outraged, half amused by this squabbling. 'My love,' wrote Catherine some time in September, 'Pavel is right. Suvorov had no more part in this [capture of Pugachev] than Thomas [her dog].' Potemkin spoke for everyone when he wrote to Peter Panin: 'We are all filled with joy that the miscreant has come to an end.'[44]

Peter Panin had the bit between his teeth. He even killed some of the witnesses. When he got his hands on the pretender himself, who had served unnoticed under him at Bender in the war, he slapped him across the face and made him kneel. He brought him out and slapped him again for every curious visitor – except Pavel Potemkin, whose job it was to question him.[45] Catherine and Potemkin neatly cut this Gordian knot by dissolving the Kazan Commission to create the Special Commission of the Secret Department of the Senate in Moscow, which was to arrange Pugachev's trial. They appointed Pavel Potemkin to it[46] – but not Panin. Potemkin was obviously protecting his cousin's interests, and his own, for Catherine told him: 'I hope all Pavel's quarrels and dissatisfactions come to an end when he receives my orders to go to Moscow.' In the midst of the politics, she added: 'Sweetheart, I love you very much and wish that pill would cure you of all illness. But I ask you to abstain: eat just soup and tea without milk.'[47]

Peter Panin 'now decorated rural Russia with a forest of gallows', according to one modern historian.[48] 'The murderers [of officials]', declared Panin in a circular that was not approved by Catherine, 'and their accomplices shall be put to death first by cutting off their hands and feet and then their heads and placing the bodies on blocks beside thoroughfares ... those villages in which they were murdered or betrayed shall ... hand over the guilty by drawing lots, every third man to be hanged ... and if by this means they still do not give them up, then every 100th man by lot shall actually be hanged from the rib and all remaining adults to be flogged ...'.

Panin boasted to Catherine that he did not shrink from 'spilling of the damned blood of state miscreants'.[49] The hanging from the rib, which he specified, was performed on a forgotten delicacy – the *glagoly*, a special form of gallows in the shape of a small letter 'r' but with a longer arm, from which victims were hanged by the rib, held in place by a metal hook that was inserted behind their ribs and threaded through.[50] This macabre exhibition was the last thing Catherine wanted Europe to see, but Panin claimed that it was only to act as a deterrent. Rebels were trussed up on gallows on rafts and sent down the Volga, their corpses decaying on these amphibious gibbets. In fact, far fewer miscreants were executed that one might expect, though there must have been many cases of rough justice. Only 324, many of them renegade priests and nobles, were officially sentenced to death, which, considering the scale of the Rebellion, compares well to the English reprisals after the 1745 Battle of Culloden.[51]

The Yaik Cossack Host where the Rebellion had begun was abolished and renamed. In a foretaste of the Soviet fashion for renaming places after their leaders, Catherine ordered that Zimoveyskaya stanitsa,[52] Pugachev's home village on the far bank of the Don, should be renamed Potemkinskaya, erasing, in Pushkin's elegant words, 'the gloomy remembrance of the rebel with the glory of a new name that was becoming dear to her and the Motherland'.[53]

The 'state miscreant' was despatched to Moscow, staring like a wild animal out of a specially constructed iron cage. When he arrived at the beginning of November, the angry Muscovites were already relishing the prospect of a particularly sadistic execution. This began to worry Catherine, who knew that the Rebellion was already an embarrassing blight on her Enlightened reputation.

Catherine and Potemkin secretly resolved to reduce the cruelty of the execution – admirable at a time when judicial killing in England and France was still astonishingly vicious. Procurator-General Viazemsky was sent to Moscow, accompanied by the 'Senate secretary', Sheshkovsky, the feared knout-wielder who, Catherine chillingly informed Pavel Potemkin, 'has a special gift with common people'. However, Pugachev was not tortured.[54]

Catherine tried to oversee as much of the trial as she could. She sent Potemkin her Pugachev Manifesto to read – if he was not too ill. The hypochondriac did not reply, so the Empress, who obviously needed his approval, sent him another note: 'Please read it and tell us now what you make of it: is it good or bad?' Later that day or the next, the Empress became impatient – 'it's twelve o'clock but we haven't got the end of the Manifesto so it can't be written out in time and can't be sent to the Council ... If you like the drafts, we ask you to send them back ... If you don't like them, correct them.' Potemkin may really have been ill or perhaps he was working on the peace celebrations to be held in Moscow. 'My dear soul, you begin new enterprises every day.'[55]

The trial opened on 30 December in the Great Kremlin Hall. On 2 January 1775, Pugachev was sentenced to be quartered and beheaded. There was no 'drawing', or disembowelling while alive, in Russia: that was part of English civilization. However, the 'quartering' meant that all four limbs would be cut off while the victim was alive. Muscovites were enthusiastically anticipating this grisly spectacle. Catherine had other ideas. 'As regards executions,' she wrote to Viazemsky, 'there must be no painful ones.' On 21 December, she was at last able to tell Grimm that 'in a few days, the farce of the "Marquis de Pugachev" will be finished. When you receive this letter, you can count on it that you won't hear any more talk about that particular gentleman.'[56]

So the last setpiece scene of the 'farce of the Marquis de Pugachev' was prepared in the Bolotnaia Square below the Kremlin. On 10 January 1775, the crowds gathered, keen to witness the dismemberment of the living 'monster'. Pugachev, 'besmeared all over with black', was drawn in 'a kind of dung-cart', in which he was fastened to a stake. There were two priests with him and the executioner stood behind. Two gleaming axes lay on the block. 'Not a trace of fear' was discernible on his serene face 'in the hour approaching dissolution'. The 'monster' climbed up the ladder to the scaffold, undressed himself and stretched out, ready for the executioner to begin his carving.

Something 'strange and unexpected' happened. The executioner swung his axe and, contrary to the sentence, beheaded Pugachev without 'quartering'. This outraged both the judges and the crowd. Someone, possibly one of the sentencing judges, called out to the executioner and 'threatened him in severe terms'. Another official shouted, 'Ah, you son of a bitch – what have you done?' And then added: 'Well hurry up – hands and feet!' Witnesses said it was generally believed that the executioner 'will lose his tongue ... for his neglect'. The executioner paid no attention and dismembered the corpse, before moving on to cut off the tongues and clip the noses of the other miscreants who had avoided the death penalty. Pugachev's diverse quarters were exposed at the top of a pole in the middle of the scaffold. The head was stuck on an iron spike and displayed.[57] The Pugachevschina – the Time of Pugachev – was over.

Some time in the last stages of the crisis, Catherine wrote this letter to Potemkin: 'My dear soul, *cher Epoux*, darling husband, come and snuggle up, if you please. Your caress is sweet and lovely to me ... Beloved husband.'[58]

9

MARRIAGE: MADAME POTEMKIN

My marble beauty ... my beloved, better than any king ... no
man on earth can equal you ...
Catherine II to G. A. Potemkin

Catherine and Potemkin planned a secret rendezvous that must have
filled them with a sense of mounting anticipation, jubilation and anxiety.
On 4 June 1774, the Empress, still recovering in Tsarskoe Selo from her
blistering confrontation with Prince Orlov, wrote this cryptic note to
Potemkin, who was in the city: 'My dear, I'll come tomorrow and I'll
bring with me that which you wrote about. Order them to prepare Field-
Marshal Golitsyn's boat opposite the Sieverses' landing-stage, if it will
be possible to pull in to the shore not far from the palace ...'.[1] Alexander
Golitsyn, Potemkin's first commander in the war, was Governor-General
of the capital, so he had his own boat. Count Yakov Sievers had a landing
stage on the Fontanka, beside the Summer Palace.

On 5 June, as promised to Potemkin, the Empress returned to St
Petersburg. Next day, a Friday, she held a small dinner for her senior
courtiers in the little garden of the Summer Palace, perhaps to say
goodbye to Prince Orlov, about to 'travel abroad'. On Sunday, 8 June,
Catherine and Potemkin attended a dinner in honour of the Izmailovsky
Guards: the toasts were answered by salvoes of cannon; the meal on a
silver service from Paris was accompanied by Italian singers. Afterwards,
Catherine walked on the banks of the Fontanka beside Count Sievers's
house.[2]

At midnight on that summer's evening, the Empress set off on a
mysterious boating trip from the Summer Palace on the Fontanka. She
often visited her courtiers in their houses on the Neva or on the islands
that made up St Petersburg. But this was different. It was late for a
woman who liked to be in bed by 11 p.m. She left secretly, her face
probably hidden by a hooded cloak.[3] It is said that she was alone –
except for her loyal maid, Maria Savishna Perekushina. General-en-Chef
Potemkin, who had been with her all day, was absent. He had slipped
away at dusk to a boat waiting on the river, which had borne him into
the mist and then out of sight.

Catherine's boat struck out of the Fontanka, past the Summer Palace with its gardens, into the Great Neva river, heading for the unfashionable Viborg Side. The boat moored at the one of the little jetties on the Little Nevka. There the Empress climbed into an unmarked carriage, waiting with the curtains drawn. As soon as Empress and maid were inside, the postillions whipped the horses and the carriage headed briskly down the road. It stopped on the right outside the Church of St Sampsonovsky. There was no one around. The ladies disembarked and entered St Sampsonov. The church had been built by Peter the Great, unusually in the Ukrainian style, in wood (it was rebuilt in stone in 1781), to celebrate the saint's day of the Battle of Poltava. Its most striking feature was a high bell tower, painted in lilac blue, white and green.[4]

The Empress found Potemkin inside the church, illuminated by candles. 'The greatest nailbiter in the Empire' would have chewed his fingers to the quick. Since they had attended the Izmailovsky Guards dinner earlier, both would still be in their 'regimentals' – Potemkin in his uniform of a general-en-chef – green coat with red collar, braided with gold lace, red breeches, high boots, sword, hat with gold border and white feathers. We know from the Court Journal that Catherine was wearing her 'long Regimental Guards uniform' all day: it was 'trimmed in gold lace made in the form of a lady's riding habit'.[5] The Empress could now hand the hooded cloak to her maid, knowing that she looked most fetching in 'regimentals'. Perhaps her dress reminded them of the day they met.

There were just three other men in the church. A nameless priest and the two 'grooms'. Catherine's 'groom' was Chamberlain Evgraf Alexandrovich Chertkov; Potemkin's was his nephew, Alexander Nikolaievich Samoilov. It was the nephew who read the portion from the Gospel. When he reached the words 'wife be afraid of her husband', Samoilov hesitated and glanced at the Sovereign. Could an empress be afraid of her husband? Catherine nodded and he continued.[6] The priest then commenced the marriage ceremony. Samoilov and Chertkov stepped forward to hold the crowns over their heads as in a traditional Orthodox wedding. When the long ceremony was finished, the wedding certificates were signed and distributed among the witnesses. All were sworn to secrecy. Potemkin had become the secret consort of Catherine II.

This is the legend of Potemkin and Catherine's wedding. There is no conclusive proof that they married, but it is almost certain they did. However, secret marriages have always been the stuff of royal myth. In

Russia, Empress Elisabeth was said to have married Alexei Razumovsky. In England, the Prince of Wales was soon to marry Mrs Fitzherbert in a secret ceremony, the validity of which was much debated.

There are many versions of the marriage: some say they married in Moscow the next year or in Petersburg in 1784 or 1791.[7] The Moscow version takes place in the Church of the Ascension of our Lord near Nikitsky, with its distinctive round dome, painted yellow. This was close to the house of Potemkin's mother, where he lived in Moscow. The church was later embellished with Potemkin's money,[8] in his mother's memory. It is most famous now as the church where Alexander Pushkin married Natalia Goncharova on 18 February 1831 – one of many links between them.*

A secret marriage could well have taken place on many another day during their relationship and the details of it concealed in the routine account of their activities. However, this time and place are the most likely. The letter from Catherine mentioned a secret enterprise and the Sieverses' jetty. The Court Journal of 8 June showed her embarking and disembarking there. There is time in the early or late evening for the secret boat trip. All the oral legends, handed down by the wedding guests and their descendants and recorded by Professor Bartenev in the nineteenth century, mentioned the St Samsonov Church, mid- to late 1774, and the same four witnesses. But where are the certificates? Potemkin's was supposed inherited by his dearest niece, Alexandra Branicka. She told the secret to her son-in-law Prince Michael Vorontsov, and left the certificate to her daughter, Princess Lise. Count Orlov-Davydov remembered a visit to Count Samoilov, who showed him a jewelled buckle. 'This', he said, 'was presented to me by the Empress in memory of her marriage with my late uncle.' Samoilov's certificate was buried with him, according this his grandson Count A. A. Bobrinsky. Chertkov's copy passed into obscurity.

The disappearance of the evidence and the secrecy are not as dubious as they might seem, because no one would have dared expose this during the strict, militaristic reigns of Tsars Paul, Alexander I and Nicholas I – or afterwards. The 'Victorian' Romanovs were embarrassed by Catherine's love life, which, through the doubts about Paul's paternity, questioned their legitimacy. As late as the 1870s, Professor Bartenev had to ask

---

* There is another possible Moscow venue. During the nineteenth century, a Prince S. Golitsyn, a collector, used to invite visitors to his palace on Volkonsky Street, said to be one of the places where Catherine stayed in Moscow during 1775. He used to show them two icons supposedly given by Catherine to his chapel to celebrate her marriage there to Potemkin.

the Emperor's permission even to do the research and it could not be published until 1906: only in the interim between the 1905 and 1917 Revolutions, when the Autocracy was on its last legs, did Nicholas II permit its publication.[9]

The strongest evidence of their marriage lies in Catherine's letters; the way she treated Potemkin; how he behaved; and how their relationship was described by insiders. She signed her letters 'devoted wife' and called him her 'dear husband' in at least twenty-two letters, naming him her 'lord' or 'master' in hundreds of others.[10] 'I'll die if you'll change ... my dear friend, loving husband'[11] is an early mention of the word in their love letters. 'Father, *Ch[er] Ep[oux]* – [darling husband] – ... I've sent Kelhen to cure your chest, I love you very much, my beloved friend,' she wrote.[12] She called Potemkin's nephew – '*our* nephew'[13] (author's italics). Monarchs, more than normal mortals, have a very precise definition of who is or is not a member of their family. She was to treat some of his family as if they were her own until her death – so much so that there were rumours that his niece Branicka was her own child.[14] Her most revealing and specific letter on the subject probably dates from a year later, possibly in early 1776:

> My Lord and *Cher Epoux* ... Why do you prefer to believe your unhealthy imagination rather than the real facts, all of which confirm the words of *your wife*. *Was she not attached to you two years ago by holy ties?* I love you and *I am bound to you by all possible ties. Just compare, were my acts more meaningful two years ago than they are now?*[15] (author's italics)

The marriage, as both no doubt hoped, seemed to bring them even closer together. Probably Potemkin, in love with Catherine, tormented by jealousies and the fragility of his position, and ambitious to play an independent role, was soothed by it. He may have been as dissolute as he was pious, but he was a practising Orthodox believer, which may have helped persuade her. For her part, it might seem that marriage would be odd after a relationship of just a few months, but one should also quote that mother's saying – 'you just *know* when it is the right person'. Moreover Catherine had known Potemkin for twelve years and had loved him for some time: she knew him very well already. Their love was not only overwhelming but they were, as she put it, 'twin souls'. At last she had found an intellectual equal with whom she could share the burden of ruling and the warmth of family.

The best piece of evidence is that, whether or not one accepts there was a ceremony, Catherine treated Potemkin for the rest of their lives as if there had been. Whatever he did, he never fell from power; he was treated like a member of the imperial family and had absolute access to the Treasury as well as the ability to make independent decisions. He behaved with extraordinary confidence, indeed insouciance, and deliberately presented himself in the tsarist tradition.

The foreign ambassadors suspected something: one diplomat learned from a 'person of credit' that Potemkin's 'nieces were in possession of the certificate',[16] but such was the awe for monarchs in those days that they never mentioned 'marriage' specifically in writing, saving it up to tell their Courts directly. Thus the French Ambassador, Comte de Ségur, informed Versailles in December 1788 that Potemkin 'takes advantage of ... certain sacred and inviolable rights ... The singular basis of these rights is a great mystery which *is known to only four people* in Russia; a lucky chance enabled me to discover it and when I have thoroughly sounded it, I shall, on the first occasion ... inform the King'[17] (author's italics). The Most Christian King already knew: by October, Louis XVI was calling Catherine 'Madame Potemkin' to Comte de Vergennes, his Foreign Minister – though he meant it partly as a joke.[18]

The Holy Roman Emperor, Joseph II, soon found out too. He explained the riddle of Catherine and Potemkin, while strolling in the Viennese Augarten, to the British envoy Lord Keith like this: 'for a thousand reasons and as many connections of every sort, she could *not easily get rid of him, even if she harboured the wish of doing so.* One must have been in Russia to comprehend all the particulars of the Empress's situation'[19] (author's italics). This was presumably what was also meant by Charles Whitworth, the British Ambassador to Petersburg, when he reported in 1791 that Potemkin was unsackable and unaccountable.[20]

Potemkin hinted that he was almost royal. During the Second Russo-Turkish War, the Prince de Ligne suggested to Potemkin that he could become Prince of Moldavia and Wallachia. 'That's a joke to me,' replied Potemkin. 'I could be King of Poland, if I wanted; I refused to be Duke of Courland; *I am far more than all that*'[21] (author's italics). What could be 'far more than' being a king if not being the consort of the Empress of Russia?

Now the couple got back to work. After the wedding, they, as usual, revelled in the suspicions of others: did anyone notice how crazily in love they were? She wondered what 'our nephew' – possibly Samoilov – thought about their behaviour. 'I think our madness seemed very strange to him.'[22]

On another occasion, someone had guessed a great secret. 'What can we do darling? These things often happen,' Catherine mused. 'Peter the Great in cases like that used to send people out to the market to bring back information he alone thought was secret; sometimes, by combination, people just guess...'.[23]

On 16 January 1775, as soon as she knew Pugachev was dead, the Empress, accompanied by Potemkin, set out from Tsarskoe Selo for Moscow, where they were to hold celebrations for the victory over Turkey. Catherine had been planning to go to Moscow ever since the peace was signed but her dear 'Marquis de Pugachev' had delayed matters. Potemkin, according to Gunning, had encouraged her to visit the old capital, presumably to celebrate the opening of a window on to the Black Sea and to project the fact that government was in charge after Pugachev.

On the 25th, she staged a ceremonial entry with Grand Duke Paul. In case she forgot that she was now in the heartland of old Russia, Paul was warmly welcomed wherever he went while, according to Gunning, Catherine 'passed with scarcely any acclamations amongst the populace or their manifesting the least degree of satisfaction.'[24] But the Pugachev Rebellion had shown her that the interior needed some attention: she was to spend most of the year there. She stayed in the Golovin and suburban Kolomenskoe Palaces, where Potemkin was also given apartments designed by her, but she found them uncomfortable and unfriendly, a metaphor for all she disliked about Moscow.

Empresses do not honeymoon, but she and Potemkin obviously wanted to spend some private time together. In June she bought Prince Kantemir's estate, Black Earth, where she decided to built a new palace: she renamed it Tsaritsyno. Those who believe she married Potemkin, whether in Moscow or Petersburg, claim that this was where they had their version of a honeymoon. They wanted to live cosily, so they stayed there for months on end in a cottage with just six rooms, like a couple of bourgeois.[25]

Honeymoon or not, they were always planning, imagining, drafting: we can follow how hard they worked together in their letters. Catherine did not always agree with her pupil nor he with her. 'Don't be angry if you find that all my proposals are mad,' she told him while discussing the problem of licensing salt production and agreeing to his proposal that Pavel Potemkin and his brother Mikhail should investigate it. 'I couldn't invent anything better.' Potemkin was always off the mark with finance – whether his own or the state's. He was an entrepreneur, not a manager. When he proposed taking on the salt monopoly, she warned

him: 'Don't burden yourself with it because it will provoke hatred ...'.
He was hurt. She soothed him – but firmly: 'I don't want to make you
look like a fool or have the reputation of one ... You know very well you
wrote nonsense. I ask you to write a good law ... and you scold me.' If
he was lazy, for example in editing the Pugachev amnesty, she hectored
him: 'Monday to Friday is enough time to read it.'[26]

Catherine's solutions to the Pugachevschina were administrative and
involved the restructuring of local government and increasing the par-
ticipation of nobles, townspeople and state peasants in judiciary and
welfare. She boasted to Grimm of suffering from 'a new sickness called
legislomania'.[27] Potemkin corrected her drafts, as he did later with her
Police Code and her Charters to the Nobility and Towns: 'We ask you to
put + near the articles and it will mean you agree. If you put # near articles,
they are to be excluded ... write your changes clearly.' His changes impressed her: 'I see in them fervent zeal and your great intellect.'[28]

The couple now arranged a piratical game of international kidnapping.
In February 1775, the Empress commissioned Alexei Orlov-Chesmensky
to seduce a peculiar young woman in Leghorn, Italy, where Scarface
commanded the Russian Fleet, and bring her back to Russia.

She was twenty, slender, dark-haired, with an Italianate profile, an
alabaster complexion and grey eyes. She sang, painted and played the
harp. She affected the chastity of a vestal virgin while simultaneously
taking lovers like a courtesan. The girl used many names, but only one
mattered. She claimed to be 'Princess Elisabeth', the daughter of the
Empress Elisabeth and Alexei Razumovsky. She was the very quint-
essence of the eighteenth-century adventuress: every epoch is a balance
of opposites so that this golden age of aristocrats was also the ripest
season for impostors; the age of pedigree was also that of pretence. Now
that travel was easier while communications were still slow, Europe
was plagued, and embellished, by young men and women of dubious
ancestry taking advantage of the long distances to claim aristocracy or
royalty. Russia, as we have seen, had its own history of pretenderism and
the lady with whom Orlov-Chesmensky was now to rendezvous was one
of the most romantic of its impostors.

She first emerged using the name 'Ali Emena' – claiming to be the
daughter of a Persian satrap. On ligging jaunts from Persia to Germany,
she appeared and disappeared with a vanity case filled with Ruritanian
titles: Princess Vladimir, Sultana Selime, demoiselles Frank and Schell;
Countess Treymill in Venice; Countess Pinneberg in Pisa and then
Countess Silvisky. Later she was Princess of Azov, a Petrine name for

this was the port on the Sea of Azov conquered and lost by Peter the Great. As ever with hucksters who manage to convince many of their inherent truth, she was obviously charismatic and it helped that the 'Princess' possessed soulful delicacy. She was everything that a mysterious princess should be. On her travels, credulous older aristocrats fell under her spell, protected her, financed her . . .

Towards the end of the Russo-Turkish War, she headed for the land of disguise – Italy, the realm of Cagliostro and Casanova, where adventurers were as common as cardinals. No one ever discovered who she really was, but it was not long before every diplomat in Italy was investigating her origins: was she the daughter of a Czech coffee-house owner, a Polish innkeeper, a Nuremberg baker?

She hooked Prince Karol Radziwill, who was an anti-Russian Confederate Pole. Accompanied by an entourage of Polish nobles in their national costume, she became a political weapon against Russia. However, she made the mistake of writing to the British Ambassador to Naples. Aesthete and later cuckolded husband of Nelson's mistress Emma, Sir William Hamilton was particularly susceptible to lissom adventuresses and he gave her a passport, but he then wrote to Orlov-Chesmensky, who immediately informed Petersburg.[29]

The Catherine who replied was the ruthless usurper usually hidden from view. After Pugachev she was in no mood to take risks with pretenders, however feminine and young: the swaggering almost gangsterish tone of the letter gives us a glimpse of how she might have behaved behind closed doors with the Orlovs. If those Ragusans do not hand over the miscreant, 'one can toss a few bombs into the town', she told Orlov-Chesmensky when the woman visited Ragusa. But it would be much better to capture her 'without noise if possible'.[30]

Scarface devised a devious plan to play on this adventuress's delusions of grandeur and on her romantic dreams. He had two advisers as subtle as he was brutal: José Ribas, said to be a Spanish–Neapolitan cook's son, joined the Russian Fleet in Italy. This talented mountebank, who later became a successful Russian general and one of Potemkin's closest cronies, worked with a deft adjutant named Ivan Krestinek, who ingratiated himself into the ersatz Princess's suite and enticed her to meet Orlov-Chesmensky in Pisa.

Scarface courted her, wrote her love letters, let her use his carriage and took her to the theatre. None of the Russians was allowed to sit down in her presence, as if she really was a member of the imperial family. But he also claimed to be furious that Potemkin had replaced his brother Prince Orlov and offered to use his fleet to help her mount the throne in order to return his family to their rightful place beside a new empress. His deception may have been a most pleasurable game: it seems she did become his mistress and that the affair lasted eight days. Maybe the girl believed that he *was* in love with her and *she* was successfully gulling him. In such heartless matters of state, Scarface was a master. His marriage proposal baited the trap.

He invited her to inspect his fleet at Livorno. She accepted. The squadron was commanded by a plainspoken Scottish vice-admiral, Samuel Greig, one of the architects of Chesme. Greig agreed to welcome the Princess, two Polish noblemen, two valets and four servants, all Italians, aboard with imperial honours. There she found a priest awaiting them, surrounded by the crew in ceremonial uniforms. Imperial salvoes were fired; sailors hailed her, 'Long Live the Empress!' The priest chanted a blessing over 'Princess Elisabeth' and Orlov-Chesmensky. It is said she wept with joy as all her dreams came true.

When she looked around, the Count was no longer beside her. His myrmidons seized 'the villain', as Orlov-Chesmensky reported to his Empress in Moscow, and took her below. As the ship headed for Petersburg, we know that Potemkin was in correspondence with Orlov-Chesmensky – some of the letters have survived and they would certainly have discussed this affair. Catherine shared Scarface's letters with him. 'My honey, my sweetheart,' she wrote at the time of the kidnapping, 'send me the letter[s] from ... Co[unt] Al[exei] Gr[igorevich] Orlov.' In April, the couple discussed the reward due to Krestinek for his effective if distasteful work in reeling in the adventuress. Many felt that Greig's role in this dubious kidnapping on foreign soil was unbecoming in a British officer, but no evidence has reached us that the admiral, who was set on making a career in Russian service, had any compunction about kidnapping a young woman, especially as he was personally thanked in Moscow by Catherine herself.

The 'Princess' arrived in Petersburg on 12 May and was immediately delivered under cover of darkness to the Peter and Paul Fortress, though legend says she was kept for a while in one of Potemkin's suburban residences. Field-Marshal Golitsyn, Governor of Petersburg, interrogated her to learn who backed her and if she really believed her story. It seems that, like many of those who are able to convince followers of deceptions, she believed her own stories: Golitsyn reported to Catherine that 'the story of her life is filled with fantastic affairs and rather resembles fairy-tales'. Catherine and Potemkin would have followed this interrogation with interest. In the fevered imaginations of Russian peasants, crazier stories had created armies. But when the 'Princess' wrote to

Catherine asking for an interview, and signed herself 'Elisabeth', the Empress turned on her: 'Send someone to tell the notorious woman that if she wishes to lighten her petty fate, then she should cease playing comedy.'[31]

While Catherine and Potemkin celebrated victory in Moscow, 'Princess Elisabeth', who already suffered from tuberculosis, was kept in a damp cell where she dwelt in her castles in the air. She pathetically appealed for better conditions in her letters to Catherine. But she did not exist any more. No one heard her. Just as Catherine had turned a blind eye to Peter's murder and had arranged for Ivan's jailers to kill him if necessary, now the consumptive girl was abandoned. There were two floods in St Petersburg in June and July of that summer and a greater one in 1777, so the legend grew that the shivering beauty had been gradually drowned as the waters rose in her subterranean cell. This was the image recreated in Flavitsky's chilling portrait. It was also claimed that she died giving birth to Orlov-Chesmensky's child and that he was tormented with guilt – an unlikely sentiment in his case.

She is known to history by one of the few imaginable titles she had not used herself: 'Princess Tarakanova', literally 'of the cockroaches'. The name derived from her claims to be the child of Alexei Razumovsky, whose nephews were called Daraganov – which may have become 'Tarakanov'. But 'Princess of the Cockroaches' could also have come from the image of the insects who were the sole companions of her last days.[32] While the Empress was preparing to return to the capital, 'Princess Elisabeth' perished of consumption on 4 December 1775. She was twenty-three. Her body was hastily and secretly buried – another inconvenience snuffed out.[33]

When the Grand Duke Paul and the Court returned from the Kolomenskoe Palace outside town on 6 July 1775, even dour Moscow must have been incandescent with excitement, teeming with soldiers, princes, ambassadors, priests and ordinary folk, all ready for ten days of partying. The celebrations, the first political spectacular arranged by Potemkin, were designed to reflect Russia's victorious emergence from six years of war, pestilence and rebellion. Eighteenth-century festivities usually involved triumphal arches and fireworks. The arches, based on the Roman model, were sometimes made of stone but more usually of canvas, wood-bunting or papier-mâché. Notes flew between Empress and Potemkin over every detail: 'Have you received the people working on the *feu d'artifice* for the peace?', she asked him.[34]

The intricacy and scale of the arrangements put everyone on edge.

When Simon Vorontsov arrived with his troops, 'I presented to ...
Potemkin the state in which my regiment was and he gave me his word
he would not make us do exercises or public inspections for three months
... But ten days later, against his word, he sent me to say that the Empress
with all her Court would come to see the exercises ... I understand that
he wanted me to lose face in public ...'. The next day, they argued
violently.[35]

On 8 July, the hero of the war, Field-Marshal Rumiantsev, approached
the city. Potemkin sent a fond, respectful note to 'batushka' Rumiantsev
arranging to meet him at Chertanova, 'where the marquee [of the triumphal arch] is ready', signing off, 'Your most humble and faithful
servant, G. Potemkin.' Potemkin then rode out and brought the Field-
Marshal to Catherine's apartments.

On the 10th, the imperial entourage walked from the Prechinsky
Gate to the Kremlin. Potemkin had stage-managed a splendid show to
convince foreign observers of the ascendancy of this victorious Empress.
'Every street in the Kremlin was filled with soldiers ... a great dais ...
draped in red cloths, and all the walls of the cathedrals and other
buildings, were lined with rows of tiered seats to create a vast amphitheatre ... But nothing can compare with the magnificent sight which
greeted us with the procession of the Empress ...'. As the earth literally
shook with the 'sound and thunder' of ringing bells, the Empress,
wearing a small crown and purple cloak lined with ermine, progressed
back to the Cathedral with Rumiantsev on her left and Potemkin on her
right. Over her head, twelve generals bore a purple canopy. Her train
was carried by Chevaliers-Gardes, in red and gold uniforms with glittering silver helmets and ostrich plumes. Her entire Court followed 'in
gorgeous dress'. At the door of the Uspensky, the Empress was greeted
by her bishops. Solemn mass was performed, the 'Te Deum' sung. 'We
were entranced,' recalled a spectator.[36]

After the service, the Empress held a ceremony of decoration in the
Faceted Hall. Catherine surrounded by her four field-marshals, dis-
tributed the prizes of victory. She granted Rumiantsev the title suffix of
'Zadunaisky' – literally 'Beyond the Danube'. This dashing surname was
Potemkin's idea – Catherine asked him earlier: 'My friend, is it still
necessary to give the Marshal the title "Zadunaisky"?'[37] Once again,
Potemkin was supporting Rumiantsev, not trying to ruin him. Zadunaisky also received 5,000 souls, 100,000 roubles, a service of plate and
a hat with a wreath of precious stones worth 30,000 roubles. Prince
Vasily Dolgoruky received the title 'Krimsky' for taking the Crimea in
1771. But the most significant prizes went to Potemkin: the diploma of

his first title, count of the Russian Empire, along with a ceremonial sword. The Empress emphasized his political work, specifically citing his contribution to the Turkish treaty. As she told Grimm, 'Ah – what a good mind that man has! He's played more part than anyone in this peace.'[38] After one of their rows, she had promised, 'I'll give you the portrait on the day of the peace – adieu my jewel, my heart, dear husband.'[39] So now Potemkin received the Empress's miniature portrait, decorated with diamonds, to wear on his breast. Only Prince Orlov had had this privilege before, and Count Potemkin wore it in all his portraits and for the rest of his life – whenever, that is, he deigned to dress properly.

The festivities were to last two weeks: Potemkin had planned a rollicking and bucolic fairground on the Khodynskoe fields, where he had erected two pavilions to symbolize 'The Black Sea with all our conquests'. He created an imperial theme park with roads representing the Don and Dnieper, theatres and dining-rooms named after Black Sea ports, Turkish minarets, Gothic arches, Classical columns. Catherine enthusiastically praised Potemkin's first chance to display his unrivalled imagination as an impresario of political show business. Long lines of carriages were driven by coachmen 'dressed as Turks, Albanians, Serbs, Circassians, Hussars and "genuine Negro servants" in crimson turbans'. Catherine wheels exploded into light and as many as 60,000 people drank wines from fountains and feasted on roast oxen.[40]

On 12 July, the celebrations were delayed when Catherine fell ill. There is a legend that this was to disguise the birth of a child by Potemkin. She was a past mistress at concealing embarrassing pregnancies in the folds of clothes already designed for her plumpness. The cabinets of Europe were certainly gossiping that she was pregnant. 'Madame Potemkin is a good 45 years old – a fine age for having children,' Louis XVI had earlier joked to Vergennes.[41] The child was said to have been Elisaveta Grigorevna Temkina, who was brought up in the Samoilov household, so she had some connection to the family. Illegitimate children in Russia traditionally adopted their father's name without the first syllable; thus Ivan Betskoi was the bastard of Prince Ivan Trubetskoi, Rontsov the son of Roman Vorontsov.

However, this story is unlikely. Potemkin was very family-minded and made a fuss of all his relations, yet there is no record of him paying any attention to Temkina. Catherine also would have cherished her. But there was a separate ancient Temkin family that had nothing to do with the Potemkins. Furthermore, in that time, it was not regarded as reprehensible to have a 'fille naturelle' or 'pupille'. Bobrinsky, Catherine's son with Prince Orlov, was not hidden, and Betskoi enjoyed a successful public career. If she was Potemkin's daughter by a low-born mistress, there was even less reason to conceal her. Temkina remains an enigma – but not one necessarily connected to Catherine and Potemkin.[42] In Moscow, meanwhile, the Empress was confined to her apartments in the Prechistensky Palace for a week and then recovered. The festivities continued.

In Moscow, Count Potemkin was approached by the British with a strange request. In 1775, Britain's American colonies had rebelled against London. This was to distract the Western world from Russian affairs for eight years, a window of opportunity which Potemkin was to use well. France and its Bourbon ally, Spain, at once saw the possibility of avenging British victory in the Seven Years War twelve years earlier. London had turned down Panin's suggestion of an Anglo-Russian alliance because Britain refused to undertake the defence of Russia against the Ottoman Empire. But now George III and his Secretary of State for the North, the Earl of Suffolk, were suddenly faced with the American Revolution. Since Britain had the best fleet in the world but a negligible army, it traditionally hired mercenaries. In this case, it decided to procure Russian troops.

By 1 September 1775, Suffolk was complaining that 'the increasing frenzy of His Majesty's unhappy and deluded people on the other side of the Atlantic' meant that Russian assistance was needed immediately. Specifically, Britain wanted '20,000 disciplined infantry completely equipped and ready to embark as soon as the Baltic navigation opens in the spring'. When Panin showed no interest, Gunning approached Potemkin, who was intrigued. Ultimately Catherine refused, writing George III a polite letter and wishing him luck.[43]

Poor Gunning had to write home a few weeks later: 'I can scarcely entertain any hopes at present ... could not His Majesty make use of Hanoverians?'[44] Finally, the desperate British hired the army of that mercenary state of Hesse. The Americans with their united ideals and irregular tactics defeated the rigidly drilled, demoralized British, but one wonders if the hardy, brutal and homogeneous Russians, backed by Cossacks, could have beaten them. The tantalizing possibilities of this stretch out all the way to the Cold War and beyond.

Catherine and Potemkin's relationship was so all-consuming that it was beginning to burn them both. 'We would be happier', said Catherine, 'if we loved each other less.'[45] The sexual cauldron of the first eighteen months could not be sustained, but there was evidence too that the tensions of his role as official favourite were taking a toll on their affair. The teacher–pupil relationship that Catherine so enjoyed was becoming irksome if not intolerable to a man as masterful, confident and able as Potemkin. Even the marriage could not change the realities of court politics and his complete dependence on her whim. Yet she loved his wildness – the very thing that made him want to escape. Was he withdrawing from her or did he just need space to breathe?

She tried desperately to restore their happiness. 'It's time to live in harmony. Don't torment me,' she wrote. When he was outraged at his subordinate position, the Empress promised: 'I will never order you to do anything, you fool, because I don't deserve such coldness ... I swore to give only caress for caress. I want cuddles and loving cuddles, the best sort. Stupid coldness and stupid spleen will only produce anger and vexation in return. It's difficult for you to say "my dear" or "my honey". Is it possible that your heart is silent? My heart does not keep silent.'[46] Catherine was cut to the quick by his increasing harshness: was her consort falling out of love with her?

She did all she could to please him: during autumn 1775, when she was about to embark on a trip out of Moscow, reported Gunning, 'it had been forgotten that the succeeding Wednesday was Count Potemkin's nameday, the recollection of which determined her to postpone her intended excursion ... to admit of the Count's receiving the compliments of the nobility'. Gunning added that the Empress had also given him a present of 100,000 roubles – and appointed a Greek archbishop for Potemkin's southern provinces on his recommendation. This was Potemkin at his most demanding: typical of him to change an empress's timetable, receive a prince's ransom of a present – and not forget to achieve a political appointment.[47]

Sometimes, Catherine complained that he humiliated her in front of the Court: 'My dear Lord, Grigory Alexandrovich, I wish Your Excellency happiness. This evening, you had better lose at cards because you absolutely forgot me and left me alone as if I was a gatepost.' But Potemkin knew how to play her, replying with a line of Arabesque symbols – possibly a sexual code in their secret language, adding: 'That's the answer ...'.[48] But what was the answer? How could she keep her consort and yet make him happy?

The couple developed their own way of communicating their feelings – his obscure and passionate, hers understanding and accommodating – the epistolary duet:

Potemkin	*Catherine*
My precious soul	I know
You know that I am	
Absolutely yours	I know, I know
And I have only you	It is true.
I will remain faithful	
To you until death	I don't doubt you.
And I need your	
Support	I believe it.
For this reason, and	
Because of my wish,	
Serving you and applying	
My abilities is most	
Pleasant to me.	That was proved long
	Ago.
Doing some-	
Thing for me	With gladness, but
	What?
You'll never regret	
It and you'll see	
Only benefits.	My soul is glad but unclear.
	Tell me more clearly.[49]

Potemkin was somehow withdrawing from her. It is said that he claimed to be ill to avoid her embraces. As he became restless, Catherine tired of his endless tempers. The towering, eye-flashing rages that are so attractive at the beginning of a love affair became irksome exhibitionism in the middle of a marriage. Potemkin's behaviour was impossible, but Catherine was partly to blame. She was slow to understand the constant tension of Potemkin's political and social position which was to break so many of her later lovers. Catherine was just as emotionally greedy as he was. They were both human furnaces requiring an endless supply of fuel in the form of glory, extravagance and power on one hand, love, praise and attention on the other. It is these gargantuan appetites that made their relationship as painful as it was productive. Potemkin wanted to govern and build, but loving Catherine was a full-time job. It was a human impossibility for each of them to give each other enough of what they required. They were too similar to be together.

In May 1775, before the peace celebrations had started, Catherine did her Orthodox duty by leading a pilgrimage to the forbidding Troitsko-Sergeevna Monastery, an obligatory trip back into the Muscovite dark ages when women were kept in the seclusion of the *terem* and not on thrones. The visit brought out Potemkin's Slavic disgust for worldly success, his Orthodox yearnings and probably his discontent with his place. Succumbing to his coenobitic instincts and ignoring Catherine, he temporarily abandoned the Court and prayed in seclusion in a monk's cell.[50]

The rapidity of his mood changes must have been exhausting for both of them. Perhaps this was what she meant when she said that they loved each other too much to be happy: the relationship was so combustible that it was not settled enough to serve either of them well. They continued to love each other and work together throughout 1775, but the stress was rising. Catherine understood what was happening. She had found a partner in Potemkin – a rare diamond – but how was he to find a role? And how were they to satisfy their demanding natures and yet remain together? While they struggled, they looked around them.

The day before the peace celebrations, Count Potemkin received a sad note from his brother-in-law Vasily Engelhardt telling him of the death of his sister Elena Marfa. They had six daughters (the eldest was already married) and a son in the army. The five younger daughters were aged between twenty-one and eight. 'I ask you to take care of them and to take the place of Marfa Alexandrovna . . .', Engelhardt wrote to Potemkin on 5 July. 'By your order, I'll send them to your mother.' There was no reason why their father could not bring them up in Smolensk, but Engelhardt, a man of the world, realized his daughters would benefit from life at Court. Potemkin summoned them to Moscow.

The Empress, like any dutiful wife, was meeting the Potemkin family. When her formidable mother-in-law, Daria Potemkina, who still lived in Moscow,* was presented, Catherine was at her thoughtful and sensitive best: 'I noticed your mother was most elegant but that she has no watch. Here is one which I ask you to give her.'[51] When the nieces arrived, Catherine welcomed them warmly and told Potemkin, 'To make your mother happy you can nominate as many of your nieces as you want as Maids-of-Honour.'[52] On 10 July, the climax of the peace celebrations, the eldest of this brood, Alexandra Engelhardt, twenty-one, was appointed a *frele* or maid-of-honour to the Empress.[53] The second and most decorous, Varvara, was soon to join her. As soon as they arrived, the nieces were hailed as Russia's superlative beauties.

Meanwhile, Catherine was busy drafting her legislation, aided by two

---

* Catherine granted Daria a house on Prestichenka where she lived until her death.

young secretaries she had recently borrowed from Rumiantsev-Zadunaisky's staff: Peter Zavadovsky and Alexander Bezborodko. The latter, cleverest of the two, was so ugly and ungainly as to be somewhat fascinating. But Zavadovsky was methodical, cultured and good-looking. His pursed lips and humourless eyes suggested he was a sanctimonious plodder – the precise opposite of Potemkin, perhaps even antidote to him. During the many hours of drafting and during the tiresome journey back to St Petersburg, as they left grim Moscow at last, Catherine, Potemkin and Zavadovsky became an odd threesome.

We can imagine the scene in Catherine's apartments: Potemkin, stretched out on a divan in a flowing dressing gown, a bandana round his head, no wig and tousled hair everywhere, chewing radishes and imitating courtiers, bubbles with ideas, jokes and tantrums, while Zavadovsky perches stiffly and patiently in his wig and uniform, writing at his desk, his eyes fixed with labrador devotion on the Empress . . .

10

HEARTBREAK AND
UNDERSTANDING

My soul, I'm doing everything for you so at least encourage me
a little with affectionate and calm behaviour ... my little dear
lord, lovable husband.
Catherine II to Count Potemkin

But in such matters Russia's mighty Empress
Behaved no better than a common sempstress ...
Lord Byron, *Don Juan*, Canto IX: 77

'My husband just said to me "Where should I go, what should I do?" ',
Catherine wrote to Count Potemkin around this time. 'My darling and
well-loved husband, come to my place and you will be received with
open arms!"[1] On 2 January 1776, Catherine appointed Peter Zavadovsky
as adjutant-general. This *ménage-à-trois* puzzled the Court.

The diplomats realized that something was happening in the Empress's private life and presumed that Potemkin's career was over: 'The
Empress begins to see the liberties of her favourite [Potemkin] in a
different light ... It is already whispered that a person placed about her
by Mr Rumiantsev bids fair to gain her entire confidence.'[2] There were
rumours that Potemkin would lose the College of War, either to Alexei
Orlov-Chesmensky or to Panin's nephew Prince Repnin. But an English
diplomat, Richard Oakes, noticed that Potemkin was expanding his
interests, not reducing them, and 'seems to interest himself more in
foreign affairs than he at first affected to do.'[3] While the Anglo-Saxons
could not quite grasp what might be happening, the waspish French
envoy, Chevalier Marie Daniel Bourrée de Corberon, who kept an invaluable diary of his life at Court, suspected that it would take more than
Zavadovsky to destroy him. 'Better in face than Potemkin,' he observed.
'But his favour not yet decided.' Then in the sarcastic tone that diplomats
habitually adopted when discussing the imperial sex life: 'His talents
have been put to the test in Moscow. But Potemkin ... still has the air of
credit ... so Zavadovsky is probably only an amusement.'[4]

Between January and March 1776, the Empress avoided large gatherings as she struggled to work out her relationship with Count Potemkin.

That January, Prince Orlov reappeared after his travels and this muddied the waters even further because there were now three present or former favourites at Court. Grigory Orlov was back in his hearty old form, but he was no longer the man he had been: overweight and struck by attacks of 'palsy', he was in love with his cousin Ekaterina Zinovieva, aged fifteen, one of the Empress's maids-of-honour, whom some accounts claim he had raped. The ruthless competition at Court is reflected in the rumours that Potemkin was poisoning Orlov – something completely against his nature. Orlov's paralysis sounds like the later stages of syphilis, the sickly fruit of his well-known lack of discernment.

Catherine appeared only at small dinners. Peter Zavadovsky was frequently present; Potemkin was there less than before – but still too much for the former's liking. Zavadovsky must have felt inadequate between two of the most dynamic conversationalists of their time. Potemkin was still Catherine's lover, while the earnest Zavadovsky was increasingly in love with her. We do not know when (or if) she withdrew from Potemkin and took Zavadovsky as a lover – it was some time during that winter. Indeed, it was most likely that she never completely ceased to sleep with the man she called 'my husband'. Was she playing off one against the other, encouraging both? Naturally. Since by her own account she was one of those who could not contemplate a day without somebody to love her, it would have been only human for her to cast her eyes at her secretary when Potemkin was parading his lack of interest.

In some ways, their relationship is at its most moving in this tense six months because they still loved one another, regarding each other as husband and wife, drifting apart yet trying to find a way to stay together for ever. Count Potemkin sometimes wept in the arms of his Empress.

'Why do you want to cry?', she sweetly asked her 'Lord and Darling Husband' in the letter that reminded him of the 'sacred ties' of their marriage. 'How can I change my attitude towards you? Is it possible not to love you? Have confidence in my words ... I love you.'[5]

Potemkin had watched the closeness develop between Catherine and Zavadovsky and at least tolerated it. He continued to be as difficult as usual, but he clearly did not mean to kill Zavadovsky as he had once threatened to do to his successor. The letters reveal a crisis in their relationship and a certain amount of jealousy towards Zavadovsky, but Potemkin appears to be so dominant that the other man does not really threaten him. It seems most likely that Potemkin approved of the new relationship – up to a point. It was simply a question of finding it.

'Your life is precious to me and I don't want to remove you,'[6] the

Empress told him specifically. They liked to settle rows with their dia-
logue letters: the second that has survived reads like the climax of a
discussion, the calm reconciliation after a frantic storm of insecurities.
This is much more specific than the earlier epistolary duet. The Empress
is lovingly patient with her impossible eccentric, Potemkin is tender and
gentle with her – incongruous qualities in such a man:

Potemkin	*Catherine*
Let me my love say this which	I allow it
will, I hope, end our argument	The sooner the better
Don't be surprised if I am	
Disturbed by our love.	Don't be disturbed
Not only have you showered	
Me with good deeds,	So have you on me
You have placed me in your	You are there firmly and
heart. I want to be	strongly and will
There alone, and above everyone	
else,	Remain there
Because no one has ever loved	I see it and believe it
you so much; and	
As I have been made by your	In my heart, I shall be
hands, I want my peace	
To be the work of your hands,	Happy to do so
that you should be	
Happy in being good to me;	It will be my greatest pleasure
That you should find rest from	
the great	
Labours arising from your high	
station	
In thinking of my comfort.	Of course
Amen	Give rest to our
	Thoughts and let
	Our feelings act freely
	They are most tender and
	Will find the best way.
	End of quarrel.
	Amen.[7]

He was not always so kind. Potemkin, feeling vulnerable, lashed out
at her cruelly. 'I ask God to forgive you your vain despair and violence
but also your injustice to me,' she replied. 'I believe that you love me in

spite of the fact that often there is no trace of love in your words.' Both
suffered bitterly. 'I am not evil and not angry with you,' she tells him
after one of their discussions. 'It depends on your will, how you treat me.'
But she suggested that they could not sustain this tumultuous tension
indefinitely: 'I want to see you calm and be in the same state too.'[8]

The Court searched for signs of Potemkin's fall or Zavadovsky's rise,
while the couple debated what to do. Potemkin wanted to remain in
power, so he had to keep his apartments in the Winter Palace. When he
became upset, she told him what so many ordinary lovers have told their
agonized partners – 'it's not difficult to decide: stay with me'. Then she
typically added this reminder of their amorous–political partnership:
'All your political proposals are very reasonable.'[9] But Catherine finally
lost her cool too.

> The way you sometimes talk, one might say I am a monster which has
> all the faults and especially that of stupidity ... this mind knows no
> other way of loving than making happy whoever it loves and for this
> reason it finds it impossible to bear even a moment's breach with him
> whom it loves without – to its despair – being loved in return ... My
> mind is busy trying to find virtues, some merits, in the object of its
> love. I like to see in you all the marvels ...

After this expression of her hurt, as Potemkin fell out of love with her,
she defined the heart of their problem: 'The essence of our disagreement
is always the question of power and never that of love.'[10]

This has always been taken at face value, but it is a tidy feminine
rewriting of their history. Their love was as stormy as their political
collaboration. If power was the subject of their quarrels, then removing
the love but keeping the power would also perpetuate their rows. Perhaps
it was truer to say that the essence of their disagreement was the end
of the intensely physical phase of their relationship and Potemkin's
increasing maturity and need for freedom. Maybe Catherine could not
bring herself to admit that he no longer wanted her as a woman – but
they would always argue about power.

None of this satisfied him. Potemkin appears to have been in a permanent rage. 'You are angry,' she wrote in French. 'You keep away from
me, you say you are offended ... What satisfaction can you want more?
Even when the Church burns a heretic, it doesn't claim any more ...
You're destroying all my happiness for the time that is left to me. Peace,
my friend. I offer you my hand – will you take it, love?'[11]

*

On her return to Petersburg from Moscow, Catherine wrote to Prince Dmitri Golitsyn, her envoy in Vienna, that she wished to 'get His Majesty [Holy Roman Emperor Joseph II] to raise General Count Grigory Potemkin, who has served myself and the State so well, to the dignity of Prince of the Holy Roman Empire, for which I will be most indebted to him'. Joseph II reluctantly agreed on 16/27 February, despite the distaste of his prim mother, the Empress–Queen Maria Theresa. 'It's fairly droll', smirked Corberon, 'that the pious Empress–Queen recompenses the lovers of the non-believing sovereign of Russia.'

'Prince Grigory Alexandrovich!' Catherine acclaimed her Potemkin. 'We graciously permit you to accept the title of Prince of the Holy Roman Empire.'[12] Potemkin was henceforth known as 'Most Serene Highness', or in Russian, 'Svetleyshiy Kniaz'. There were many princes in Russia but from now Potemkin was '*The* Prince' – or just 'Serenissimus'. The diplomats presumed that this was Potemkin's golden adieu because Orlov had been granted use of his title only on his dismissal. Catherine also gave Potemkin 'a present of 16,000 peasants who can make annually five roubles a head', and then Denmark sent him the Order of the White Elephant. Was Potemkin being dismissed or confirmed in office? 'I dined at Count Potemkin's,' said Corberon on 24 March, 'It's said his credit falls, that Zavadovsky is still in intimate favour and that the Orlovs have a lot of credit to protect him.'[13]

Serenissimus desired to be a monarch as well as a prince: he already feared that Catherine would die and leave him at the mercy of the bitter Paul, from whom 'he can expect only Siberia.'[14] The solution was to establish himself independently, outside Russian borders. The Empress Anna had made her favourite, Ernst Biron, Duke of Courland, a Baltic principality, dominated by Russia but technically subject to Poland. The ruling Duke was now Biron's son Peter. Potemkin decided that he wanted Courland for himself.

On 2 May, Catherine informed her ambassador to Poland, Count Otto-Magnus Stackelberg, that 'wishing to thank Prince Potemkin for his services to the country, I intend to give him the Duchy of Courland' and then suggested how he should manoeuvre. Frederick the Great ordered his envoy in Petersburg to offer help to Potemkin in this project and, on 18/29 May, he wrote warmly to him from Potsdam. Yet Catherine never pulled out the stops: Potemkin had not yet proved himself a statesman and she had to tread carefully, in Courland as well as Russia. This quest for a safe throne abroad was a leitmotif of Potemkin's career. But Catherine always did her best to keep his mind on Russia – where she needed it.[15]

At the beginning of April 1776, Prince Henry of Prussia arrived to consolidate his brother Frederick's alliance with Russia. The Russo-Prussian relationship had lost its glow when Frederick had undermined Russian gains during the Russo-Turkish War. Frederick's younger brother was a secret homosexual, energetic general and clever diplomat who had helped to initiate the Partition of Poland in 1772. He was a caricature of Frederick, but fourteen years younger and bitterly jealous of him – the fate of younger brothers in the age of kings. Henry had been among the first to cultivate Potemkin. It was a mark of Potemkin's new and increasing interest in foreign affairs that he now arranged Henry's trip. 'My happiness', Prince Henry wrote to Potemkin, 'will be great if during my stay in St Petersburg, I get the chance to prove my esteem and friendship.' The moment he arrived on 9 April he demonstrated this wish by presenting Potemkin with the Black Eagle of Prussia to add to his growing collection of foreign orders: this gave Frederick II and Potemkin the excuse to exchange flattering letters. No doubt, Prince Henry also encouraged the Courland project.[16]

Just as the foreigners thought Potemkin had lost his credit, the unpredictable lovers seemed to be enjoying a little Indian summer. In perhaps the best and simplest declaration of love that anyone could give, she wrote: 'My dear Prince! God nominated you to be my friend before I was even born because he created you to be for me. Thank you for the present and for the hug ...'.[17] It sounds as though they were having a secret reunion – but the painful negotiations between them continued. Potemkin's eclipse and Zavadovsky's rise were widely expected. Neither Catherine nor Potemkin could take much more of this agonizing limbo. The morning after Prince Henry arrived, tragedy intervened.

At four o'clock in the morning on 10 April 1776, Grand Duchess Natalia Alexeevna, Paul's pregnant wife, went into labour. The Empress put on an apron and rushed to Natalia's apartments. She stayed with her and Paul until eight in the morning.[18]

The timing was inconvenient because Prince Henry had to be entertained. That night, the Empress and Prince Henry attended a violin concert by Lioli in 'the apartment of His Excellency Prince Grigory Alexandrovich Potemkin', recorded the Court Journal. Prince Henry and Potemkin discussed the alliance, as Catherine had suggested: on Frederick's instructions, Prince Henry made sure he got on well with the favourite.[19] That night, it looked as if the Grand Duchess was about to deliver an heir for the Empire.

Grand Duchess Natalia had already proved a disappointment to Cath-

Serenissimus Prince Grigory Potemkin in his prime when
he was already Catherine the Great's secret husband and
increasingly her partner in power. Catherine called him her
'marble beauty' and he was said to have the most beautiful
head of hair in Russia. Yet he was shy about his blind eye
and was always painted from this angle to hide it.

Catherine the Great, dressed in Guardsman's uniform, on 28th
June 1762 – the day she seized power from her husband,
Emperor Peter III. This was the occasion she met Potemkin for
the first time. As she reviewed her troops outside the Winter
Palace in St Petersburg, she noticed she was missing her
sword-knot. Young Potemkin galloped up and offered her
his own. She did not forget him.

Top: Countess Alexandra 'Sashenka' Branicka, clever, lithe and formidable, was Potemkin's niece, probably his mistress, but certainly his best friend after Catherine herself. He died in her arms.

Right: The Heir – Grand Duke (later Emperor) Paul, Catherine's unstable, embittered son who so hated Potemkin, he boasted he would toss him in jail.

Potemkin's palaces: his northern and southern houses.

Clockwise from left: the neo-Classical Taurida Palace in St Petersburg, the scene of the Prince's sumptuous ball in 1791; the Bablovo Palace in ruins near Tsarskoe Selo; his first palace, the Anichkov in Petersburg; the Ostrovki Castle. Both the Bablovo Palace and the Ostrovki Castle were inspired by Walpole's Gothic Strawberry Hill.

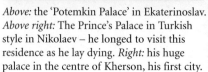

Above: the 'Potemkin Palace' in Ekaterinoslav. *Above right:* The Prince's Palace in Turkish style in Nikolaev – he longed to visit this residence as he lay dying. *Right:* his huge palace in the centre of Kherson, his first city.

The Empress aged 58 in her travelling costume during Potemkin's magnificent 1787 tour of the Crimea where she met Emperor Joseph II.

Field Marshal Potemkin during the Second Turkish War – the victor at his apogee. He wears Catherine's portrait set in diamonds – his proudest possession.

Below: his signature.

The ageing Empress during the 1790s: still majestic and dignified but growing fat and breathless. As she told Potemkin, she was so in love with her talentless young lover, Zubov, that she felt like a fat fly in summer. She yearned for his approval of her last favourite ...

This dashing, dynamic and triumphant warlord, late 1780s. The ebullient
Prince Potemkin sports the sumptuous (self-designed) white uniform of
the Grand Admiral of the Black Sea Fleet and his portrait of Catherine on
his chest while he points to Sebastopol and his new cities. Catherine said
his victories made him 'even more handsome'; his enemies admitted
'women crave the embraces of Prince Potemkin'.

Left: the monuments by the roadside (in Moldova) where Potemkin died on 5th October 1791.

Below: his coffin in the tomb beneath the Church. The Bolsheviks stole the icons ...

Left: this board announced Potemkin's death and listed all his titles during his lying-in-state in October 1791. The author found it in the Golia Monastery in Jassy (Romania) behind a piano.

Below: the trapdoor in St Catherine's in Kherson (Ukraine) leading to Potemkin's tomb.

The ruined church in Potemkin's home village of Chizhova, near Smolensk in Russia where he was christened, learned to read, and where his heart is probably buried.

erine. Though Paul appeared to love her, she was an intriguer who had not even bothered to learn Russian. Catherine and Potemkin suspected she had been having an affair with Andrei Razumovsky, Paul's closest friend and a suave womanizer. Nonetheless, on the 11th, Catherine donned her apron again and rushed to do her duty, spending six hours at the bedside, then dined in her apartments with her two Princes, Orlov and Potemkin. She spent all the next day with the Grand Duchess.

The foreign diplomats felt rather cheated that 'the accouchement' had suspended 'the fall of Potemkin', as Corberon put it. The Grand Duchess was crying out in agony. The Empress was worried. 'A meal was laid inside Her Majesty's apartments but she didn't want to eat,' records the Court Journal. 'Prince . . . Potemkin ate.' When he was hungry, there was not much that could put him off his food.

The doctors did what they could according to the science of solicitous butchery that then passed for medicine. Forceps were already in use in the mid-eighteenth century.* Caesareans, though desperately dangerous, had been successfully completed since Caesar's time: the mother virtually always perished of infection, shock and loss of blood, but the child could be saved. Now, nothing was tried and it was too late. The baby had perished and the foetus infected the mother. 'Things are very bad,' Catherine wrote, possibly the next day, in a letter marked 5 a.m., already thinking about how to cope with Paul afterwards. 'I think the mother will go the same way as the child. Keep silent about it . . .'. She ordered the commandant of Tsarskoe Selo to prepare Paul's apartments. 'When things are clear, I'll bring my son there.'[20] Gangrene set in. The stink was intolerable.

Prince Potemkin was playing cards while they awaited the inevitable denouement. 'I'm assured', said Corberon, 'that Potemkin lost . . . 3,000 roubles at whist when all the world were crying.' This was unfair. The Empress and her consort had much to arrange. Catherine compiled a list of her six candidates for Paul's new wife, which she sent to Potemkin. Princess Sophia Dorothea of Württemberg, whom she had always wanted Paul to marry, was first of the six.[21]

At 5 p.m. on 15 April, the Grand Duchess died. Paul was half mad with grief, ranting that the doctors had lied: she must be alive still, he wanted to be with her, he would not let her be buried – and all the other fantasies that people use to deny mortal reality. The doctors bled him. Twenty minutes later, Catherine accompanied her stricken son to Tsarskoe Selo.

---

* Until 1733, forceps had been the secret weapon, as it were, of a surgical dynasty, the Chamberlens. In that time, even the doctors were hereditary.

Potemkin travelled down with his old friend, Countess Bruce. 'Sic transit gloria mundi,' Catherine commented briskly to Grimm. She had not liked Natalia, but now diplomats criticized her for the conduct of the Grand Duchess's accouchement: had she allowed her daughter-in-law to perish? The post-mortem revealed that there was an abnormality which meant Natalia could never have given birth – thus she could not have been saved by the medicine of the day. But since this was Russia, where emperors died of 'piles', Corberon reported that no one believed the official story.*

'For two days, the Grand Duke has been in inexpressible distraction,' wrote Oakes, 'Prince Henry of Prussia has scarcely quitted him.' Prince Henry, Catherine and Potemkin united to promoted Paul's immediate remarriage to the Princess of Württemberg. 'The choice of a Princess will not be long delayed,' reported Oakes a few days later. Amid the mourning, Catherine, Potemkin and Prince Henry appreciated the harsh reality that the Empire needed an heir, so Paul urgently needed a wife.

Paul was understandably reluctant to marry again. Such personal scruples were removed when Catherine, so loving to her adopted families, so cruel to her own, showed him Natalia's letters to Andrei Razumovsky which were found among her effects. Catherine and Potemkin arranged to send Paul on a trip to Berlin to approve the bride. The Hohenzollern brothers were delighted to have the chance to influence the Russian Heir – Princess Sophia was their niece. Paul's placidity was probably aided by his Prussophilia and worship of Frederick the Great, like his father before him. The Court reverted to its favourite sport – plotting the fall of Potemkin.[22]

Grand Duchess Natalia and her still-born child lay in state at the Alexander Nevsky Monastery. She wore white satin. The foetus, which turned out in the autopsy to be perfectly formed, lay gruesomely at her feet in the open coffin.[23] Serenissimus remained at Tsarskoe Selo with Catherine, Prince Henry and Paul, who was grieving not only for his wife but also for the broken illusion of his marriage. Corberon could not comprehend how both Zavadovsky and Potemkin were with the Empress: 'the reign of the latter is at its end,' he crowed, 'his position as Minister of War

---

* Potemkin was said to have arranged this death and mysteriously visited the midwife. Medical murder is a recurring theme in Russian political paranoia – Stalin's Doctor's Plot of 1952/3 played on the spectre of 'murderers in white coats'. Prince Orlov, Grand Duchess Natalia, Catherine's lover Alexander Lanskoy and Potemkin himself were all rumoured to have been murdered by the doctors caring for them. Potemkin was said to have been involved in the first three deaths.

already given to Count Alexei Orlov,' but he worried that Potemkin seemed to be putting a very good face on matters.[24] Both Corberon and the British reckoned that Prince Henry was backing Potemkin against the Orlovs, contributing 'much to the retarding of the removal of Prince Potemkin whom the ribbon [the Black Eagle] has bound to his interests'.

Natalia's funeral was held on 26 April at the Nevsky Monastery. Potemkin, Zavadovsky and Prince Orlov escorted Catherine – but Paul was too distraught to attend. The diplomats scanned every mannerism of the leading players for political nuance, just as Kremlinologists would later dissect the etiquette and hierarchy at the funerals of Soviet General Secretaries. Then as now, Kremlinologists were frequently wrong. Here, Corberon noticed a telling sign of Potemkin's falling credit – Ivan Chernyshev, President of the Navy College, gave 'three big bows' to Prince Orlov but only 'a light one to Potemkin who bowed at him incessantly'.

Serenissimus could play the game with secret confidence. He was still in power on 14 June when Prince Henry of Prussia and Grand Duke Paul set off on their uxorious voyage to Berlin. The mission was successful. Paul returned with Sophia of Württemberg – soon, as Grand Duchess Maria Fyodorovna, to be his wife, and mother of two emperors.*

Meanwhile Prince Orlov and his brother, scenting blood, were said to be tormenting Potemkin with jokes about his imminent fall. Potemkin did not rise. He knew that, if things went according to plan, their jokes would soon not matter.[25] 'Rumours reach us from Moscow', Kirill Razumovsky wrote to one of Potemkin's secretaries, 'that your chief is beginning to ruin himself by drinking. I don't believe it and reject it because I think his spirit is stronger than that.'[26] Corberon reported Potemkin sinking into 'decadence'. It was true that Potemkin shamelessly pursued pleasure at times of personal strain – debauch was his way of letting off steam.[27] Catherine and Potemkin discussed the future in an exchange of insults and endearments. The doomsayers were right in that these were the days when the foundations of the rest of his career were laid.

'Even now,' the Empress assured him, 'Catherine is attached to you with her heart and soul.' A few days later: 'You cut me all yesterday without any reason ...'. Catherine challenged the truth of his feelings for her:

---

* Paul and Maria Fyodorovna were married in Petersburg on 26 September 1776. The two emperors were Alexander I and Nicholas I, who ruled until 1855. Their second son Constantine almost succeeded but his refusal of the throne sparked off the Decembrist Revolt in 1825.

'Which of us is really sincerely and eternally attached to the other; which of us is indulgent and which of us knows how to forget all offences, insults and oppressions?' Potemkin was happy one day and then exploded the next – out of jealousy, over-sensitivity or sheer bloody-mindedness. His jealousy, like everything else about him, was inconsistent but he was not the only one who experienced it. Catherine must have asked about another woman and Potemkin rubbed her nose in it. 'That hurt me,' she said. 'I didn't expect, and even now I don't know why, my curiosity is insulting to you.'[28]

She demanded his good behaviour in public: 'The opinion of the silly public depends on your attitude to this affair.' It is often claimed that Potemkin was now faking his jealousy in order to make his deal while protecting Catherine's pride as a woman. He suddenly demanded Zavadovsky's removal. 'You ask me to remove Zavadovsky,' she wrote. 'My glory suffers very much from this request ... Don't ask for injustices, close your ears to gossip, respect my words. Our peace will be restored.'[29] They were getting closer to an understanding, yet they must have decided to be apart like a couple who know they must not prolong the agony by constant proximity. Between 21 May and 3 June, Potemkin was not registered at Court.

On 20 May, Zavadovsky emerged as Catherine's official favourite, according to Oakes, and received a present of 3,000 souls. On the anniversary of the accession, he was promoted to major-general, receiving another 20,000 roubles and 1,000 souls. But now Potemkin did not mind. The storm was over: Potemkin was letting her settle down to her relationship with Zavadovsky because husband and wife had finally settled each other's fears and demands. 'Matushka,' he thanked her, 'this is the real fruit of your kind treatment of me during the last few days. I see your inclination to treat me well ...'.

However, an apologetic Potemkin could not keep away: he reappeared at Tsarskoe Selo on 3 June: 'I came here wanting to see you because I am bored without you. I saw my arrival embarrassed you ... Merciful Lady, I would go through fire for you ... If at last I'm determined to be banished from you, it would be better if it did not happen in public. I won't delay leaving even though it's like death to me.' Beneath this passionate declaration, Catherine replied, 'My friend, your imagination tricks you. I'm glad to see you and not embarrassed by you. But I was irritated by something else which I will tell you another time.'[30]

Serenissimus lingered at Court. Poor Zavadovsky, now in love with Catherine, and her official companion, disappeared from the Court Journal on the day Potemkin returned: had he fled before the ebullient giant? The diplomats did not notice: as far as they were concerned, it was only a matter of time before Potemkin resigned all his offices. Their expectations appeared to be confirmed when Catherine presented the Prince with a palace of his own: the 'Anichkov house', a massive, broken-down palace in St Petersburg that had belonged to Elisabeth's favourite Alexei Razumovsky. It stood (and still stands) on the Neva, beside the Anichkov Bridge. This suggested that Potemkin was about to vacate his rooms in the imperial places and go 'travelling' to the spas of Europe.

In an absolutist monarchy, proximity to the throne was imperative, the *sine qua non* of power. Potemkin was known to mutter that, if he lost his bed at the Palace, he would lose everything. Catherine constantly reassured her highly strung friend: 'Batinka, God is my witness, I am not going to drive you out of the Palace. Please live in it and be calm!'[31] He later moved out of the favourite's apartment but never left the Winter Palace and never lost his access to Catherine's boudoir.

They arranged a new residence that perfectly suited their situation. For the rest of his life, his real home was the so-called 'Shepilev house', a separate little building, formerly stables, facing on to Millionaya Street, which was linked to the Winter Palace by a gallery over the archway. The Empress and Prince could walk to each other's rooms along a covered passageway from beside the Palace's chapel, in privacy and, in Potemkin's case, without dressing.

Everything was settled. On 23 June, Potemkin set off on an inspection tour of Novgorod. A British diplomat noticed some furniture being removed from his apartments in the Winter Palace. He had fallen and was off to a monastery. But the shrewder courtiers, like Countess Rumiantseva, noticed that his journey was paid for, and serviced, by the Court. He was greeted everywhere with triumphal arches like a member of the imperial family, and that could only be the result of an imperial order.[32] They did not know that Catherine sent him a present for his departure, begged him to say goodbye and then wrote a series of affectionate notes to him: 'We grant you eternal and hereditary possession of the Anichkov house,' she told Potemkin, plus 100,000 roubles to decorate it. In his two years of favour, the financial figures are impossible to calculate because so often the Empress presented him with cash or presents that are unrecorded – or directly paid off his debts. But he now inhabited an unreal and opulent world in which the Croesian scale of riches was shared only by monarchs: he often received 100,000 roubles from Catherine when a colonel lived on 1,000 roubles a year. The Prince is estimated to have received as many as 37,000 souls, vast estates around Petersburg and Moscow and in Belorussia (the Krichev estate, for example, boasted 14,000 souls), diamonds, dinner services, silver plate and as much as nine million roubles. All this was never enough.[33]

The Prince returned a few weeks later. Catherine welcomed him with a warm note. He moved straight back into his Winter Palace apartments. This confounded his critics: Serenissimus 'arrived here on Saturday evening and appeared at Court the next day. His returning to the apartments he before occupied in the Palace made many apprehensive of the possibilities of his regaining the favour he had lost.'[34] They would have been even more surprised to learn that he was soon correcting Catherine's letters to Tsarevich Paul in Berlin.

There is little doubt that they were playing one of their prearranged games, like celebrities today who delight in tricking the press. Having started the year afraid of losing their love and friendship in a frenzy of jealousy and regret, they had now managed to arrange their unique marriage in their own manner. Each could find his own happiness while keeping the services – personal and political, affectionate and practical – of the other. This had not been easy. Affairs of the heart cannot be drilled like regiments, or negotiated like treaties – especially those of two such emotional people. Only trust, time, nature, trial and error, and intelligence had achieved it. Potemkin now made the difficult transformation from an influential lover to 'minister–favourite' who ruled with his Empress.[35] They had managed to gull everyone.

The day Serenissimus returned to Court, the couple knew they would be watched for any hint of his fall or recovery. So the Prince strolled into her apartments 'with the utmost composure' and found the Empress playing whist. He sat down right opposite her. She played him a card as if nothing had changed – and told him he always played luckily.[36]

Part Four

THE PASSIONATE PARTNERSHIP
1776–1777

11

HER FAVOURITES

And Catherine (we must say thus much for Catherine)
Though bold and bloody, was the kind of thing
Whose temporary passion was quite flattering
Because each lover looked a sort of king ...
Lord Byron, *Don Juan*, Canto IX: 70

An order from Her Majesty consigned
Our young Lieutenant to the genial care
Of those in office. All the world looked kind
(As it will look sometimes with the first stare,
Which youth would not act ill to keep in mind,)
As also did Miss Protassoff then there,
Named from her mystic office l'Eprouveuse,
A term inexplicable to the Muse.
Lord Byron, *Don Juan*, Canto IX: 84

The love affair of Prince Potemkin and Catherine II appeared to end there, but it never truly ceased. It simply became a marriage in which both fell in love and had sexual affairs with others, while the relationship with each other remained the most important thing in their lives. This unusual marital arrangement inspired the obscene mythology of the nymphomaniac Empress and Potemkin the imperial pimp. Perhaps the 'Romantic Movement', and the serial love marriages and divorces of our own time, have ruined our ability to understand their touching partnership.

Zavadovsky was the first official favourite to share the Empress's bed while Potemkin ruled her mind, continuing to serve as her consort, friend and minister. During her sixty-seven years, we know that Catherine had at least twelve lovers, hardly the army of which she stands accused. Even this is deceptive because, once she had found a partner with whom she was happy, she believed it would last for ever. She very rarely ended the relationships herself – Saltykov and Poniatowski had been removed from her; Orlov had been unfaithful and even Potemkin had somehow contrived to withdraw. Nonetheless, after Potemkin, her relationships with men much younger than her were obviously abnormal, but then so was her situation.

The reality was very different from the myth. She did make her lover into an official position, and Potemkin helped her. The triangular relationship between Catherine, Potemkin and her young lovers has been neglected by historians – yet this became the heart of her own 'family'.

Catherine's affair with Zavadovsky was the test case for the imperial *ménage-à-trois*. Potemkin's presence made life for the favourites more difficult and humiliating, because they could not avoid Catherine's intimacy with him. Their relationship with Serenissimus was almost as important as their love for the Empress. Even without Potemkin, this was a difficult role and Zavadovsky was soon deeply miserable.

Catherine's letters to Zavadovsky give us a wonderful glimpse into the suffocating world of the favourites. He lasted barely eighteen months in favour but his love for Catherine was genuine. Her letters to him reveal she loved him too. But there was less equality between them. Even though he was the same age as Potemkin, he was in awe of her and she treated him patronizingly, thanking him for his 'most affectionate little letter' as if he was clever to have known his alphabet. While Potemkin wanted time and space to himself, Zavadovsky longed to be with her every moment of the day, like a lapdog, so she had to write and explain that 'Time belongs, not to me, but to the Empire'. Yet they worked together – he still toiled in her secretariat all day before retiring with her at ten, after playing three rubbers of whist. It was a routine that was both tiresome and hard work.

The new favourite was also supposedly far less sexually experienced than the Prince, which is perhaps why he fell in love with her so absolutely. 'You are Vesuvius itself,' she wrote. His inexperience perhaps caused him to lose control, for she added: 'when you least expect it an eruption appears but no, never mind, I shall extinguish them with caresses. Petrusha dear!' She corresponded less formally with Zavadovsky than with Potemkin. While the former called her 'Katiusha' or 'Katia', the Prince had always used 'Matushka', 'Sovereign Lady'. The Empress's letters to Zavadovsky seem more sexually explicit: 'Petrushinka, I rejoice that you have been healed by my little pillows and if my caress facilitates your health then you will never be sick.' These 'pillows' may have meant her breasts – but she also embroidered herb-filled cushions, an example of the comical dangers of biographers making sexual interpretations of personal letters.[1]

Zavadovsky, who loved her so much, was often sick, more from nerves than anything else. He was not suited to being the subject of such intrigue and hatred. While she repeatedly declared her love for him in her letters, he could not relax in his position: his private life was 'under a micro-scope'.[2] She did not understand what he was up against and he did not have the strength that Potemkin employed to get what he wanted from everyone. Above all, he had to tolerate Potemkin's omnipresence. It was a threesome and, when Potemkin wanted attention, he presumably got it. When they had crises in their relationship, it was Potemkin who sorted them out: 'both of us need a restoration of spiritual peace!' wrote Catherine. 'I have been suffering on a par with you for three months, torturing myself ... I will talk to Prince Gri[gory] A[lexandrovich Potemkin].' This talk with Potemkin about Zavadovsky's private feelings could hardly have helped *his* spiritual peace. Afterwards, Zavadovsky claimed that he was quite unfazed by Potemkin's ever present flam-boyance, but the evidence suggests that he was intimidated and upset by him and hid when he was near by. 'I do not understand', the Empress wrote to Zavadovsky, 'why you cannot see me without tears in your eyes.' When Potemkin became a prince, Catherine invited, or rather ordered, Zavadovsky: 'If you went to congratulate the new Highness, His Highness will receive you affectionately. If you lock yourself up, neither I nor anybody else will be accustomed to see you.'[3]

There was a story, told years later, that Potemkin lost his temper with the Empress, told her to dismiss Zavadovsky, stormed through their apartments, almost attacked them and then tossed a candlestick at Cath-erine.[4] This sounds like one of Potemkin's tantrums, but we cannot know what provoked it. Potemkin may have decided that Zavadovsky was a bore; it may also have had something to do with his friendship with Potemkin's critics like Simon Vorontsov. Zavadovsky certainly had a mean-minded, parochial streak that was utterly alien to Serenissimus – and it may have irritated Catherine herself.

The diplomats noticed Zavadovsky's plight. Even in mid-1776, when he had only just been unveiled, as it were, Corberon was wondering 'the name of the new favourite ... because they say Zavadovsky is well on the decline'. The diplomatic business of analysing Catherine's favour-itism was always an inexact mixture of Kremlinology and 'tabloid-style' gossip – a question of reading bluffs and double-bluffs. As the French-man put it, 'they base his disgrace on his promotion'.

Within a year, though, an upset Catherine noticed his misery too. In May 1777, she wrote to Zavadovsky: 'Prince Or[lov] told me that you want to go. I agree to it ... After dinner ... I can meet with you.' They had a painful chat which Catherine, of course, reported in detail to Potemkin: 'I ... asked him, did he have something to say to me or not? He told me about it,' and she let him choose an intermediary, like a cross between a literary agent and a divorce lawyer, to negotiate his terms of dismissal. 'He chose Count Kirill Razumovsky ... through tears ... Bye, bye dear,' she added to Potemkin. 'Enjoy the books!' She had obviously sent him a present for his growing library. Once Razumovsky had negotiated Zavadovsky's retreat, Catherine gave him 'three or four thousand souls ... plus 50,000 roubles this year and 30,000 in future years with a silver service for sixteen...'.

This took an emotional toll on Catherine. 'I'm suffering in heart and soul,' she told Potemkin.[5] She was always generous to her lovers but, as we shall see, she gave far less to Zavadovsky than to anyone else except Vassilchikov. There was truth in the canard of Masson, the Swiss tutor: 'Catherine was indulgent in love but implacable in politics.'[6]

Zavadovsky was distraught. Catherine assumed the tone of a Norland nanny and told him to calm himself by translating Tacitus – a therapy unique to the age of neo-Classicism. Then, inevitably, she consoled the unhappy man by adding that, in order that Prince Potemkin 'be friendly with you as before, it is not difficult to make the effort ... your minds will share the same feeling about me and therefore become closer to one another'. There can be little doubt that the prospect of having to win over Potemkin can only have made Zavadovsky's wounds even more raw. He was heartbroken: 'Amid hope, amid passion full of feelings, my fortunate lot has been broken like the wind, like a dream which one cannot halt: [her] love for me has vanished.' On 8 June, Zavadovsky retreated bitterly to the Ukraine. 'Prince Potemkin', said the new British envoy, Sir James Harris, 'is now again at the highest pitch.'[7] It goes without saying that Catherine, who could not be 'without love for an hour',[8] had already found someone else.

On Saturday, 27 May 1777, the Empress arrived at Potemkin's new estate of Ozerki, outside Petersburg. When they sat down for dinner, there was a cannon salute to welcome her. Potemkin always entertained opulently. There were thirty-five guests, the top courtiers, the Prince's nieces Alexandra and Ekaterina Engelhardt, his cousins Pavel and Mikhail Potemkin – and, at the very bottom of the list, Major of the Hussars Semyon Gavrilovich Zorich, a swarthy, curly-haired and athletic Serb aged thirty-one. It was his first appearance at an official reception, yet it seems that Catherine had already met him. Zorich, a handsome daredevil already known as 'Adonis' by the ladies at Court and as a 'vrai sauvage' by everyone else, was something of a war hero. Potemkin remembered him from the army. Zorich had been captured by the Turks. Prisoners were often decapitated in the exuberance of the moment, but noblemen were preserved for ransom – so Zorich loudly proclaimed himself a count and survived.

On his return, this ambitious rogue wrote to Potemkin and was appointed to his entourage. Potemkin's aides-de-camp were obviously introduced to Court – and the Empress noticed him. Within a few days, Zorich was the new official favourite and his life changed instantly. He was the first of Catherine's succession of so-called favourites or *mignons* who took the role as an official appointment. While raving about Zorich's looks and calling him 'Sima' or 'Senyusha', Catherine was missing her Potemkin. 'Give Senyusha the attached letters,' she asked her consort. 'It's so dull without you.'[9] Just as modest Zavadovsky was an antidote to the ebullient Potemkin, so the excitable Serb was a relief after the moping Zavadovsky. The latter heard about the emergence of Zorich and rushed back to Petersburg, staying with his friends, the Vorontsovs.

Zavadovsky suffered like 'a stricken stag' – and the Court treated him like one. He was told to behave himself. The Empress 'respected' him but suggested that he restrain himself 'in order to extinguish the alarm.'[10] What alarm? The Empress's perhaps. But surely also the hypo-chondriacal, nailbiting Potemkin. In any case, Zavadovsky learned that, since he was not going to be reinstated, the courtiers no longer paid him much attention. He went back to his work. One warms to Zavadovsky for his diligent state service and his romantic pain, but he also spent the next twenty years moaning to his friends about Potemkin's omnipotence and extravagance. He remained devoted to Catherine and did not marry for another ten years. And when he built his palace at Ekaterinodar (Catherine's Gift) – with its 250 rooms, porcelain stones, malachite fireplaces, full library – its centrepiece was a lifesize statue of Catherine.[11] But he was not a typical favourite because, while the Empress never gave him independent political power as she did to Potemkin, he enjoyed a distinguished career under Catherine and afterwards.*

Catherine was in love with Zorich. Potemkin was happy with his former adjutant and gave him a plume of diamonds for his hat and a superb cane.[12] Catherine, who was to work so hard to make her favourites respect Potemkin, wrote: 'My dear Prince, I have received the plume, given it to Sima and Sima wears it, thanks to you.' Since the vain King Gustavus III of Sweden was on a visit, she laughingly compared the two dandies.[13] Zorich, who liked to strut around in the finest clothes, resembled nothing so much as a finely feathered fighting cock, but the *vrai sauvage* was soon out of his depth. He also suffered from the

* Alexander I appointed him Russia's first Minister of Education.

addiction of the age: gambling. Once Catherine had recovered from her early delight in his looks and vigour, she realized he was a liability. It was not the gambling that mattered – the Empress played daily and Potemkin all night – but his inability to understand his position vis-à-vis the Prince.[14]

Within a few months, everyone knew he would have to be dismissed and the diplomats were once again trying to guess the next lover. 'There is a Persian candidate in case of Monsieur de Zorich's resignation,' wrote Sir James Harris as early as 2 February 1778. But Zorich swaggered around, announcing in a loud voice that, if he was dismissed, he was 'resolved to call his successor to account' – in other words to challenge him to a duel. This muscular braggadocio would really bring Catherine's court into contempt. Far from delaying his fall, as he no doubt thought, this was precisely the sort of behaviour that made it inevitable. 'By God,' he threatened, 'I'll cut the ears of whoever takes my place.' Soon Harris thought he had spotted another candidate for favourite. Like all the diplomats, Sir James believed that it was 'probable that Potemkin will be commissioned to look out for a fresh minion and I have heard ... that he already has picked on one Acharov – a Lieutenant of Police in Moscow, middle-aged, well made, more of a Hercules than Apollo.'[15]

Three months later, with the Court at Tsarkoe Selo for the summer, Zorich remained in place. When the Empress attended the theatre, Harris claimed the Prince presented to her a 'tall hussar officer, one of his adjutants. She distinguished him a good deal.' The moment Catherine had gone, Zorich 'fell upon Potemkin in a very violent manner, made use of the strongest expressions of abuse and insisted on his fighting him'. Potemkin refused this insolent request with contempt. Zorich stormed into the imperial apartments and boasted what he had done. 'When Potemkin appeared he was ill-received and Zorich seemed in favour.'

Potemkin left Tsarskoe Selo and returned to town. But, as so often with Potemkin and Catherine, appearances were deceptive. The *sauvage* was ordered to gallop all the way to St Petersburg in the Prince's wake and humiliatingly invite him to supper to make friends. Serenissimus returned. The supper was held: 'they are apparently good friends'. Zorich had made the mistake of crossing Prince Potemkin, though that in itself was not decisive, since virtually all the favourites crossed him at one time or another. But Sir James had the measure of Potemkin: 'an artful man', who, 'in the end, will get the better of Zorich's bluntness'.[16]

Sure enough, just six days later, Harris reported Zorich's dismissal, 'conveyed to him very gently by the Empress herself'. Zorich exploded in bitter reproaches, probably about Potemkin. He had already been granted the exceedingly valuable estate of Shklov, with 7,000 souls and an 'immense sum of ready money'. He was last recorded at Court on 13 May.[17] A day later, Catherine met Serenissimus for dinner at the Kerekinsky Palace on the way home from Tsarkoe Selo: 'The child had gone and that's all,' she wrote after discussing Potemkin's military plans, 'as for the rest, we'll discuss it together . . .'. She was most likely referring to the object of her new-found happiness.

At the Kerekinsky, Prince Potemkin arrived with 'Major Ivan Nikolaevich Rimsky-Korsakov'. Naturally, by the time Catherine parted with Zorich, she was already infatuated with a new friend. Zorich was still making blustering threats when Rimsky-Korsakov was appointed Potemkin's adjutant on 8 May.[18] Far from being a heartless hedonist, Catherine always experienced emotional crises, if not complete collapse, during these changes. Zorich was still brooding in St Petersburg when, according to Harris, Catherine contemplated recalling 'the plain and quiet' Zavadovsky. Potemkin 'who has more cunning for effecting the purposes of the day than any man living, contrived to effect these good resolutions . . .'. He 'introduced' Korsakov 'at the critical moment'.

A couple of days later, the Empress, along with her Court and many of Potemkin's family, including two of his nieces, set off to stay at another of the Prince's estates 'to forget her cares . . . in the society of her new minion'. Potemkin's estate was Eschenbaum (Osinovaya Rocha) 'on the confines of Finland'. If one reads Catherine's letter to Grimm from Eschenbaum, in which she raved about the views of lakes and woods from her window while grumbling that her entourage had to squeeze into a mere ten bedrooms, one would have no idea that her new passion had already hit a snag. Two grand and libidinous middle-aged women were competing for the attentions of Potemkin's pretty adjutant.[19]

There were twenty guests out at Eschenbaum, including of course Potemkin's old friend Countess Bruce, supposedly the sampler of Catherine's lovers. Someone else – it must be Countess Bruce – was also attracted to the fine Korsakov. Catherine had noticed and hesitated before letting herself go. 'I'm afraid of burning my fingers and it's better not to lead into temptation . . .', she wrote to Potemkin in an enigmatic appeal in which she seemed to be asking him to get someone to keep her distance: 'I'm afraid that the last day dispelled the imaginary attraction which I hope is only one-sided and which can easily be stopped by your clever guidance.' She obviously wanted the 'child' herself, but 'I don't want, wanting and I want, without wishing . . . that's as clear as the day!'

Even in this oblique gibberish, it was clear she was falling in love – but wished the competition to be removed.

Potemkin's 'clever guidance' did the trick. Countess Bruce, if it was she, backed off and Catherine claimed her new *mignon*.[20] The house-party ended. Two days later, on 1 June, Korsakov was officially appointed adjutant-general to the Empress. In an age of neo-Classicism, Rimsky-Korsakov, aged twenty-four, immediately struck her with his Grecian 'ancient beauty', so that she soon nicknamed him 'Pyrrhus, King of Epirus'. In her letters to Grimm, she claimed he was so beautiful that he was 'the failure of painters, the despair of sculptors'.[21] Catherine seemed to choose alternate types because Korsakov was as elegant and artistic as Zorich has been muscular and macho: portraits show his exquisitely Classical features. He loved to sing, and Catherine told Prince Orlov that he had a voice 'like a nightingale'. Singing lessons were arranged. He was showered with gifts – 4,000 souls and presents worth half a million roubles. Arrogant, vain and not terribly clever, he was 'good-natured but silly'.[22]

Once again, Catherine was wildly happy with her new companion: '*Adieu mon bijou*,' she wrote to Potemkin in a summary of their special marriage. 'Thanks to you and the King of Epirus, I am as happy as a chaffinch and I want you to be just as happy.'[23] With the Empress happy, the Prince, increasingly busy running the army and governing the south, was so supreme that when Zavadovsky finally returned to Petersburg to find another favourite ensconced in his old apartment, he was shocked that Potemkin 'doesn't have any balance against him. In all the centuries', he grumbled to Rumiantsev-Zadunaisky, 'God has not created such a universal person as this. Prince P is everywhere and everything is him!'[24]

Catherine wrote passionately to her 'King of Epirus': 'my impatience to see the one who for me is the best of God's creatures is so great: I longed for him more than 24 hours and have gone to meet him.' Or as Harris put it drily: 'Korsakov enjoys all the affection and favour which attend novelty.' Korsakov was certainly enjoying his role, perhaps too much: Potemkin suggested that he should be made gentleman of the bedchamber, but Korsakov wanted to jump straight to chamberlain. When the *mignon* got his way, Catherine gave Pavel Potemkin the honour as well, to compensate Serenissimus. Soon Korsakov was a major-general; the King of Poland sent him the Golden Eagle, which he always wore. Catherine's hunger for Korsakov sings through the letters. She sounded pathetically grateful, writing: 'Thank you for loving me.'[25]

There were already ominous signs which the Empress alone could not, or would not, see. Even in her letters, Korsakov never seemed to be with her and she never seemed to know where he was. Here is a glimpse of her suffocating neediness and his avoidance of her companionship: 'I'm unable to forget you for a moment. When will I see you?' Soon she sounded almost feverish: 'If he doesn't come back soon, I'll run away from here and go looking for him in every place in town.' It was this emotional appetite that ruled Catherine and made her surprisingly vulnerable – the Achilles' heel of this otherwise indestructible political machine.[26]

It was not long before Catherine, hooked on the shallow youngster, was upset again. In early August 1778, just a few months after Korsakov's appointment, Harris reported to London that the new favourite was already in decline and that Potemkin, Grigory Orlov and Nikita Panin were each struggling to sponsor the replacement. Within a couple of weeks, he even knew 'the secret in Count Panin's office by name Strackhov ... first noticed at a ball at Peterhof on 28 June'. If the connection lasted, Harris told his Secretary of State for the North, the Earl of Suffolk, 'it must end in the fall of Potemkin'. By the end of the year, Harris decided that Korsakov was safe again but 'entirely subservient to the orders of Prince Potemkin and Countess Bruce'.

The mention of Countess Bruce was ominous. By the end of January, the candidates for favourite were multiplying: there was still Strackhov, whose 'friends were in great hope', but then there was also Levashev, a major in the Semenovsky Guards, who might have become favourite 'if a young man by name Svickhosky, patronised by Madame Bruce ... had not stabbed himself through disappointment. The wound is not mortal.' These rumours of Catherine's affairs were often based on a whisper of gossip which had little foundation, but the diplomatic scandal-mongering signified intense political struggles at Court, even if it was not necessarily what was happening in the imperial bedchamber. Nonetheless Harris was better informed than most because of his friendship with Potemkin. By this time, even a new diplomat in town like Harris knew that Countess Bruce had returned to her 'violent passion for Korsakov'.

The whole of Petersburg, except sadly the Empress herself, must have been aware that Countess Bruce had only restrained herself from Korsakov for a short time. Since both lived in the Palace only a few yards from the Empress's bedroom, they conducted their liaison right under Catherine's nose. Small wonder that the Empress was always looking for the favourite. Countess Bruce, the same age as Catherine and formerly a courtier of discretion and experience, must have lost her head to the beauties of the 'King of Epirus'.[27] Serenissimus and Countess Bruce fell out at this time, possibly over Korsakov. Potemkin, who would have known about the affair almost as soon as it started, wanted to remove Bruce. He must have tried to hint about it delicately to the Empress earlier in September. They rowed. The diplomats thought it was because he was jealous of Panin's candidate Strackhov.[28]

The Prince, who did not wish to hurt the Empress nor again lose credit for trying to help, decided to fix the matter. When the Empress was looking around the Palace for the elusive Korsakov, someone loyal to Potemkin would direct her towards a certain room. This person was probably Potemkin's favourite niece, Alexandra Engelhardt, who was a maid-of-honour. Harris would have heard this story from Alexandra herself since she was the secret recipient of English money.[29] Catherine surprised her lover and Countess Bruce in a compromising position, if not *in flagrante delicto*. There ended the short reign of 'silly' Korsakov.

The Empress was wounded and angry but never vindictive. As late as 10 October 1779, she still wrote kindly to Korsakov: 'I'm repeating my request to calm yourself and to encourage you. Last week, I demonstrated that I'm taking care of you ...'. Despite munificent presents, Korsakov lingered in Petersburg and even boasted of his sexual antics with the Empress in the salons in the most degrading way. Word of it must have reached the protective Potemkin, who loved Catherine too much not to do something about it. When she was discussing whether to reward her next favourite, Serenissimus suggested there should be limits to her generous treatment of Korsakov and the others. Once again, he hurt Catherine's pride. Her generosity was partly a shield to conceal the depth of her own emotional wounds – and partly an effort to compensate for her age and their youth. According to Corberon, the two argued but later made up.

Korsakov was not finished. He had the effrontery not just to cuckold the Empress but also to cuckold the cuckoldress, Countess Bruce, by beginning an adulterous affair with a Court beauty, Countess Ekaterina Stroganova, who left her husband and child for him. This was too much even for Catherine. The ingrate was despatched to Moscow. An era of Catherine's private life ended when Countess Bruce, now in disgrace, left the capital to pursue the 'King of Epirus' to Moscow. He no longer wanted her and she returned to her husband, Count Yakov Bruce.[30] The Court cheerfully plunged into the amorous guessing game that was just as popular as whist and faro.

The bruised Catherine enjoyed an unusual six months without being in love with anyone. It was at times of unhappiness like this, commented Harris, that Potemkin became even more powerful: did he return to Catherine's bed to comfort his friend?

It is most likely they temporarily resumed their old habits as they were to do throughout their lives: this is suggested in her letters to Potemkin, which joke about the delicious effects of the 'chemical medicines of Cagliostro'. The notorious charlatan, Count Cagliostro, rose to European fame in 1777 and became fashionable in Mittau, the Courland capital, before coming to Petersburg at precisely this time.* Catherine raved about 'Cagliostro's chemical medicine which is so soft, so agreeable, so handy that it embalms and gives elasticity to the mind and senses – enough, enough, *basta, basta, caro amico*, I mustn't bore you too much . . .'.[31] This tonic is either a jocular reference to some mystical balm sold by that necromancing snake-oil salesman – or one of Potemkin's sexual specialities. Since Catherine had little patience for Cagliostro's alchemy, Freemasonry and marketing of eternal life, but a proven tolerance for Potemkin's love-making, one can guess which it was.

Meanwhile the courtiers manoeuvred to find the Empress a new favourite. This time there were several candidates, including a certain Staniov, afterwards lost to history, then Roman Vorontsov's natural son, Ivan Rontsov, who, a year later, emerged in London as the rabble-rousing leader of a Cockney mob in the Gordon Riots. Finally, in the spring of 1780, she found the companion she deserved, a young man named Alexander Dmitrievich Lanskoy.

Aged only twenty to Catherine's fifty-one, this 'very handsome young man', according to an English visitor, was the gentlest, sweetest and least ambitious of Catherine's favourites. Sasha Lanskoy 'of course was not of good character', said the fast-rising Bezborodko, Catherine's secretary, but, compared to those who came later, 'he was a veritable angel'. Bezborodko, who saw everything in Catherine's office, had reason to know. Though Lanskoy did become embroiled in at least one intrigue against

* The letters mentioning Cagliostro are usually dated to 1774 by V.S. Lopatin and others because of their obvious sensual passion for Potemkin. But Count Cagliostro emerged in London only in 1776/7, so they could not have discussed him in 1774. Cagliostro travelled through Europe in 1778, finding fame in Mittau through the patronage of the ducal family and Courland aristocracy before coming to Petersburg, where he met Potemkin: their relations are discussed in the next chapter. If her wish that, instead of 'soupe à la glace' – Vassilchikov – they had begun their love 'a year and a half ago' is translated as 'a year and a half before', the letter could date from 1779/80, when their reunion would have reminded Catherine of that wasted year and a half.

Serenissimus, he was also the favourite who was happiest to join the broader Catherine–Potemkin family.[32]

Lanskoy, another Horse-Guardsmen, had been one of Potemkin's aides-de-camp for a few months, which is probably how Catherine noticed him. Yet, according to Harris, who was seeing Potemkin on a daily basis at this time, he was not his first choice. The Prince was persuaded to acquiesce only by imperial gifts of land and money on his birthday that Harris claims came to 900,000 roubles, a sum that beggars avarice. Whether Potemkin did have another candidate, he was eminently flexible in all matters of the boudoir: he supported Lanskoy.

Soon a lieutenant-general, he was Catherine's ideal pupil and companion. He was not highly educated but keen to learn. He liked painting and architecture. Unlike the others, he tried to avoid politics – though that was not completely possible – and he made an effort to stay friends with Potemkin, though that was not completely feasible either.[33] Despite his taste for splendour and his greedy family, Lanskoy was the best of the minions because he truly adored Catherine and she him. For the next four years, Catherine enjoyed a stable relationship with the calm and good-natured Lanskoy at her side.

In May 1781, there was a slight blip in Catherine's relationship with Lanskoy. Harris heard the usual rumours that Catherine was having an affair with a new favourite, Mordvinov, but that Potemkin helped to steer the Empress and Lanskoy through this rough patch in their relationship. If Catherine flirted with someone else, Lanskoy was 'neither jealous, inconstant, nor impertinent and laments the disgrace ... in so pathetic a manner' that Catherine's love for him revived and she could not bear to part with him.[34] They settled down happily into a relationship that she hoped would continue until she died.

Potemkin benefited enormously from Catherine's system of favouritism. When she was in a stable relationship, it gave him time to win his place in history. During her happy years with Lanskoy, Potemkin became a statesman – he changed the direction of Russian foreign policy, annexed the Crimea, founded towns, colonized deserts, built the Black Sea Fleet and reformed the Russian army. However, by the end of her life, Catherine's sexual career was already both a legend and a joke.

Inside Russia, the disapproval of Catherine's and Potemkin's moral conduct often coincided with political opposition to their rule among critics, like Simon Vorontsov and the entourage of the 'Young Court' of Grand Duke Paul, both excluded from power. The view of a traditional Orthodox aristocrat is expressed in Prince Mikhail Shcherbatov's *On the*

Corruption of Morals (published long after Catherine's death) which blamed virtually the entire morality of the eighteenth century on Catherine and Potemkin. Her critics charged that favouritism affected the whole atmosphere of the court: 'she has set other women the example of the possession of a long ... succession of lovers', grumbled Shcherbatov. As for the wicked puppetmaster, Potemkin radiated 'love of power, ostentation, pandering to all his desires, gluttony and hence luxury at table, flattery, avarice, rapaciousness'. In other words, the Prince was the source of 'all the vices known in the world with which he himself is full'.[35]

This titillating humbug reached its greatest extent during the later years of the Empress when no foreigner could discuss Russia without bringing the subject round to Catherine's sexuality. When the gossipy Oxford don John Parkinson visited Russia after Potemkin's death, he picked up and popularized any tidbit he could find and linked it all to Catherine's love life, even canal building: 'A party was considering which of the canals had cost the most money; when one of them observed there was not a doubt about the matter. Catherine's Canal (that is the name of the one of them) had unquestionably been the most expensive.' Even the distinguished ex-Ambassador Sir George Macartney, later celebrated for his pioneering mission to China, who had been recalled for siring a child with an imperial maid-of-honour, degraded himself by claiming that Catherine's taste for Russian men was due to the fact that 'Russian nurses it is said make a constant practice of pulling it when the child is young which has the great effect of lengthening the virile instrument'.[36] The diplomats sniggered in their despatches about 'functions' and 'duties' and coined puns that would shame a modern tabloid newspaper, but they were usually misinformed and historians have simply repeated the lies that seem to confirm every male fantasy about the sexual voracity of powerful women. There are few subjects in history that have been so wilfully misunderstood.

The nature of 'favouritism' derived from the Empress's peculiar position and her unique relationship with Potemkin. It was undeniably true that anyone becoming a favourite of Catherine's was entering a relationship in which there were three, not two, participants. Favouritism was necessary because Catherine lived in a man's world. She could not publicly marry again and, whether in law or spirit, she already had a husband in Potemkin. Their egos, talents and emotions were too equal and too similar for them to live together, but Catherine needed constant loving and companionship. She yearned to have an effective family around her and she had strong maternal instincts to teach and nurture.

These emotional longings were easily as strong as her famed sexual appetites. She was one of those who must have a companion, and often did not change partners without finding a new one first. Usually such habits are more based on insecurity than wantonness, but perhaps the two are linked. There was another reason why Catherine, as she got older, sought younger lovers, even at the cost of her dignity and reputation. She touched on it herself when she described the temptations of Elisabeth's Court. The Court was filled with handsome men; she was the Sovereign. Catherine did it because she could – like the proverbial child in the candyshop. Who would not?

The position of Catherine's favourite evolved into an unusual official appointment. 'Loving the Empress of Russia', explained the Prince de Ligne, the ultimate charmer of the Enlightenment who adored Potemkin and Catherine, 'is a function of the Court.'[37] Instead of having a disorderly court, Catherine appointed her lover publicly. She hoped her system of favouritism would pull the sting of sleaziness. In a sense, she was applying the tenets of the Enlightenment to her loins, for surely clarity and reason would prevent superstition in the form of innuendo and gossip.

Appearances had to be maintained but this was an age of sexual frankness. Even the Empress–Queen Maria Theresa, the ultimate Catholic moralist, who presided over a court of stifling rectitude, gave Marie-Antoinette astonishingly frank gynaecological advice on her marriage to Louis XVI. Catherine herself was prudish in public. She reprimanded the Comte de Ségur for making risqué jokes, though she could make the odd one herself. When she was inspecting a pottery, Corberon recounted that she made such a shocking joke that he recorded it in code in his original diary: it sounds as if she chuckled that one of the shapes resembled a vagina. Later, her secretary recorded her laughing at how, in mythology, women could blame their pregnancies on visits from gods. In a lifetime in the public gaze, a couple of dirty jokes is not much – though one cannot imagine Maria Theresa making any.

Behind the façade, Catherine enjoyed a discreet earthiness with her lovers. Her letters to Potemkin and Zavadovsky displayed her animal sensuality such as when she said her body had taken over from her mind and she had to restrain every hair. She obviously enjoyed sex, but, as far as we know, it was always sex while she believed herself to be in love. There is *no evidence* at all for her *ever* having sex with a man for its own sake without believing it to be the start of a long relationship. The diplomats bandied names around and said they performed certain 'functions', which has been believed ever since.

However, there must have been transitory relationships and 'one-night stands' in the quest for compatibility, but they would have been rare because they were difficult to arrange. In the Winter Palace for example, it would have been surprisingly complicated to let in – and let out – a lover, even if he was a Guardsman, without other Guards, maids, valets and courtiers knowing about it. For example, when Catherine went to see Potemkin in 1774, she could not go into his rooms because he was with adjutants, who would be shocked to see the Empress appearing in his apartment: she had to return secretly to her rooms even though he was her official favourite. Later, when one favourite spent the night in her boudoir, he came out in the morning and met her secretary, and *he* recorded it in his diary.

Catherine spent her whole life in public in a way that makes even our own age of paparazzi seem private. Inside her Palace, every move she made was watched and commented upon. It is likely there would be much more evidence if there were regiments of Guardsmen being smuggled in and out of her apartments. Only Potemkin himself could wander into her bedroom whenever he liked because he had a covered passageway that led directly from his rooms to hers, and everyone accepted he was unique.[38]

This is how the favourites rose to the imperial bedchamber and how they lived when they got there. Catherine's love affair became a Court institution on the day that it was announced in the Court Journal that the young man in question, usually a Guardsman of provincial gentry and therefore not a magnate's scion, had been appointed adjutant-general to the Empress. In several cases, as we have seen, the gentlemen were already aides-de-camp to Potemkin, an appointment that brought them into regular contact with Catherine.[39] So, whenever the diplomats wrote feverishly that Potemkin had presented an officer to Catherine, it could mean everything or nothing.* However, one senses Catherine preferred choosing her lovers from among Potemkin's staff, because they were somehow touched by a whiff of the Prince himself and they knew the form.

Before the appointment to adjutantcy, the young man would have

---

* Catherine's handful of adjutants included her favourite of the moment and also the sons of magnates and several of Potemkin's nephews. This was further complicated because in June 1776 Potemkin created the rank of aide-de-camp to the Empress whose duties (written out in his own hand and corrected by Catherine) were to aid the adjutants. The Prince of course had his own aides-de-camp, who often then joined Catherine's staff.

jumped through several hoops. The legend claims that Potemkin simply selected the boy out of a list of candidates. Then if Catherine liked him, the 'éprouveuse' or sampler – her lady-in-waiting, first Countess Bruce and later Anna Protasova – would try him out. Saint-Jean, a dubious memoirist who apparently worked in Potemkin's chancellery, claimed the Prince became a sort of sex therapist: a prospective favourite stayed with Potemkin for six weeks to be 'taught all he needed to know' as Catherine's lover.[40] He would then be checked by Dr Rogerson, Catherine's sociable Scottish doctor, and finally be sent to the Empress's room for the most important test of all. Almost all of this legend, particularly Potemkin's role, is false.

How were they selected? By chance, taste and artifice. Potemkin's pimping was widely believed: 'he now plays the same role that La Pompadour did at the end of her life with Louis XV', claimed Corberon. The truth was far more complicated because it involved the love, choice and emotions of an extremely dignified and shrewd woman. Neither Potemkin nor anyone else could actually 'supply' men to Catherine. Both of them were too proud to play the procuring game. He did not 'supply' Zavadovsky, who already worked with Catherine. As her consort and friend, he ultimately sanctioned it, though not before trying to get rid of the dull secretary. It was said that Zorich was 'appointed' by Potemkin. Earlier on the day of his dinner party at Ozerki just before Zorich became favourite, a written exchange between Catherine and the Prince holds a clue.

Potemkin wrote to his Empress humbly asking her to appoint Zorich as *his* aide-de-camp, 'granting him whatever rank Your Imperial Majesty thinks as necessary'. Potemkin was testing to see if Catherine approved Zorich or not. She simply wrote, 'Promote to Colonel.'[41] Potemkin wanted Catherine to be happy *and* to preserve his power. Perhaps this indirect route, not the smutty innuendo of the diplomats, was the subtle way that Potemkin tested the waters, asking if Catherine wanted this young man around Court or not, but without demeaning her dignity. Once she had found her favourite, she often looked to Potemkin for what she called his 'clever guidance'.[42] This was how these two highly sophisticated politicians and sensitive people communicated in such matters.

She made her own choices: when Lanskoy was chosen, he was one of Potemkin's aides-de-camp, but the Prince actually wanted someone else to be favourite. However it worked out, there was much competition, among Panins and Orlovs, to introduce potential favourites to Catherine since they were regarded as having much more influence than they probably did. Rumiantsev and Panin both hoped to benefit from Potemkin's rise: he was the downfall of both of them.

Were the favourites sampled by the 'éprouveuse'? There is no evidence at all of any 'trying out', but there is plenty of Catherine's jealous possessiveness of her favourites. This myth was based on Countess Bruce's possible earlier relationship with Potemkin, her mission to summon him to the Empress's favour from the Nevsky Monastery, and her affair with Korsakov well *after* Catherine's relationship with him had started. Did Korsakov, boasting after his dismissal, invent this arrangement, perhaps to excuse his own behaviour? As for the medical check, there is no proof of it, but it would seem sensible to have a rollicking Guardsman checked by Dr Rogerson for the pox before sleeping with the Empress.

After this, the lucky man would dine with the Empress, attend whatever receptions she was gracing and then adjourn to the Little Hermitage to play cards with her inner circle – Potemkin, Master of the Horse Lev Naryshkin, assorted Orlovs, if they were in favour, a handful of Potemkin's nieces and nephews, and the odd favoured foreigner. She sat for some rubbers of whist or faro or played rhyming games or charades. Everyone would be watching – though Potemkin would probably already know. At 11 p.m., Catherine rose and the young man accompanied her to her apartments. This would be the routine of their life virtually every day they were in Petersburg, unless there was a special holiday. Catherine was always grateful to Potemkin for his advice, kindness and generous lack of jealousy in such private matters – as she wrote to him after falling in love with Korsakov: 'He's an angel – big, big, big thanks!'[43]

The favourite derived massive benefits from his gilded position, but these were balanced by dire disadvantages. The advantages were enough land, serfs, jewels and cash to found an aristocratic dynasty. The disadvantages were, simply put, Catherine and Potemkin.

The first advantage – and the real mark of the position – was possession of the most potent piece of real estate in all the Russians. As in all property, location was paramount. Apartments in the Empress's wing of her palaces were as valuable as those at Versailles. The new favourite would take possession of the beautifully decorated, green-carpeted apartment linked to Catherine's by the notorious staircase. There, it was claimed, he would find a certain sum of money as a welcoming present – 100,000 roubles or 10,000 roubles every week. But there is no evidence for this golden hello, though we know from Vassilchikov's 'kept woman' complaint that she regularly gave generous cash presents on birthdays, and she certainly paid for their fine clothes and granted them a monthly table allowance. Legend claims that, in gratitude for their privileged position, the favourites would then pay Potemkin a bribe-payment of around 100,000 roubles as if they had bought a tax farm – or as if they were renting *his* place. Even the unreliable Saint-Jean does not believe this story, which is saying something as he believes virtually everything else.[44] Since the favourite would later receive untold riches, he might well thank the person who had sponsored his arrival in the highest circles, as anyone might thank a patron – but it is unlikely a penniless provincial would have 100,000 roubles to pay Potemkin even if the system existed. The only evidence of this payment was that, when they were appointed, one later favourite gave Potemkin a teapot, and another thanked his patron with a gold watch. Usually, Potemkin received nothing.

The favourite and his family would become rich. 'Believe me, my friend,' said Corberon, 'over here, this profession is a good one!'[45] Foreigners were dazzled by the costs of maintaining, and especially dismissing, the favourites. 'Not less than a million roubles yearly, exclusive of the enormous pensions of Prince Orlov and Prince Potemkin,' calculated Harris, who estimated that the Orlovs had received seventeen million roubles between 1762 and 1783.[46] The figures are impossible to verify, but Catherine was exceedingly generous even when she had been ill-treated, perhaps out of guilt or at least awareness that it was not an easy role. Maybe she hoped her magnanimity would demonstrate that she herself was not hurt. However, there was no shortage of ambitious young men eager for the position. Indeed, as the Empress was selecting a new lover, Potemkin's adjutant (and cousin of his nieces) Lev Engelhardt noticed that, 'during the church service for the court, lots of young men, who were even the slightest bit handsome, stood erect, hoping to regulate their destiny in such an easy way.'[47]

The arrangement may sound cold and cynical but the relationship of Catherine and favourite could not have been more indulgent, loving and cosy. Indeed, Catherine was passionately enamoured with each one and bathed them in loving and controlling attention, spent hours talking to them and reading with them. The beginning of each affair was an explosion of her maternal love, Germanic sentimentality and admiration for their beauty. She raved about them to anyone who would listen and, because she was Empress, everyone had to. Even though most of them were too spoiled and stupid to govern, she loved each one as if the relationship would last until the day she died. When her relationships fell apart, she became desperate and depressed, and often little business was achieved for weeks.

The imperial routine became excruciatingly boring after a while – endless dinners, games of whist, and sexual duties with a woman who, for all her charm and majesty, was increasingly stout, tormented by indigestion and in her early fifties by 1780. Once the excitement of luxury and the proximity to power had worn off, this could not have been easy for a young man in his early twenties. Catherine's affection sounds stifling, if not suffocating. If a favourite had the slightest ability and character, it must have been exceedingly difficult to accompany, day after day, an ageing empress who treated him like a cross between a pretty pupil and a 'kept woman'. One favourite called it a tedious 'prison'. The Court was malicious. Favourites felt as if they were living among a 'pack of wolves in a forest'. But it was also inhabited by the richest and most fashionable noble girls, while the favourites had to spend their nights with a stout old lady. Thus the temptations to cuckold the Empress must have been almost irresistible.[48]

Potemkin's role in Catherine's life made it worse. It must have been intolerable to learn that, not only were they expected to be the companion to a demanding older lady, but the real benefits of her love were bestowed on Potemkin, whom they were ordered to adore as much as she did. Most of the favourites – we have seen Vassilchikov's comments – had to admit that, while they were spoilt and kept, Potemkin was always Catherine's 'master', her husband. Catherine herself called him 'Papa' or 'My lord'. There was no room for another Potemkin in the government of Russia.

Even if the favourite was in love with the Empress, as Zavadovsky and Lanskoy were, there was no guarantee of privacy from Potemkin, whose rooms were linked to hers by the covered walkway. He was the one man in Russia who did not have to be announced to the Empress. By the late 1770s, he was often away, which must have been a relief, but when he was in Petersburg or Tsarskoe Selo, he was continually bursting in on the Empress like a dishevelled whirlwind in his fur-lined dressing gowns, pink shawls and red bandannas. This would naturally ruin the favourite's day – especially since he was unlikely to be able to equal the Prince's wit or charisma. No wonder Zavadovsky was reduced to tears and hiding.[49] Catherine made sure that the favourites paid court to Potemkin, with the humiliating implication that he was the real man in the household. Each of them wrote Potemkin complimentary letters and Catherine ended most of her letters to him by passing on the favourite's flattery and enclosing his little notes.

There is a strong sense that Catherine almost wanted the favourites to regard her *and Potemkin* as parents. Her own son Paul had been taken away from her and then become alienated from her, and she could not bring up Bobrinsky, so it was understandable that she treated the favourites, who were as young as her sons, as child substitutes. She claimed maternally that 'I'm benefiting the state by educating this young man',[50] as if she was a one-woman finishing-school for civil servants.

If she was mother, then her consort, Potemkin, was the father of this peculiar 'family'. She often called her favourites 'the child' and they respectfully called Potemkin, clearly on Catherine's urging, 'Uncle' or 'Papa'. When Potemkin was ill, Lanskoy had to write, 'This moment I have heard from Lady Mother that you, Father Prince Grigory Alexandrovich, are ill, which troubles us greatly. I wish you wholeheartedly to be better.' When he did not call him Father, Lanskoy wrote, 'Dear Uncle, thank you very much for the letter which I have received from you.' Then Lanskoy, just like Catherine, added: 'You can't imagine how dull it is without you, Father, come as soon as possible.' Later, when Potemkin was critically ill in the south, Lanskoy wrote to him that 'our incomparable Sovereign Mother . . . cries without interruption'. Lanskoy might have resented this but his affectionate nature made him take to what was effectively a makeshift family. As we will see in the next chapter, its strange symmetry was completed by the addition of Potemkin's nieces.

It was not one way. Serenissimus treated the favourites like his children too. When the prancing Zorich was dismissed, Potemkin generously wrote to King Stanislas-Augustus in Poland to make sure the fallen favourite received a decent welcome. The Prince explained to the King that this 'unhappy business' had made Zorich 'lose for a time in this country the advantages he deserved for his martial qualities, services and conduct beyond reproach'. The Polish King took care of Zorich during his travels. 'There is a pleasure in obliging you,' he told Potemkin. We know from Lanskoy's thank-you letters that the Prince sent him kind notes and oranges and supported the promotion of his family.[51]

The favourites suited Potemkin for the simplest of reasons: while they had to accompany Catherine through her dinners and make love to her at night, Potemkin had the power. It took years for courtiers and diplomats to realize that the favourites were *potentially* powerful but only if they could somehow remove Potemkin. The Empress's ladies-in-waiting, doctors and secretaries all had influence, but favourites had marginally more because she loved them. However these 'ephemeral subalterns' had no real power, even in her old age, *as long as Potemkin was alive*. They were, Count von der Goertz told Frederick II, 'chosen expressly to have neither talent nor the means to take ... direct influence.'[52]

To exercise power, a man requires the public prestige to make himself obeyed. The very openness of favouritism ensured that their public prestige was minimal. 'The definitive way in which she proclaimed their position ... was exactly what limited the amount of honour she bestowed upon them,' observed the Comte de Damas, who knew Catherine and Potemkin well. 'They overruled her daily in small matters but never took the lead in affairs of importance.'[53] Only Potemkin and, to a lesser extent, Orlov increased their prestige by being Catherine's lovers. Usually, the rise of a new favourite was 'an event of no importance to anybody but the parties concerned', Harris explained to his Secretary of State, Viscount Weymouth. 'They are ... creatures of Potemkin's choice and the alteration will only serve to increase his power and influence.'[54] So, if they survived, they were his men; if they were dismissed, he benefited from the crisis. That at least was the theory, but things were never so neat.

The legend says Potemkin could dismiss them when he wished. Provided Catherine was happy, Potemkin could get on and run his part of the Empire. He tried to have *every* favourite dismissed at one time or another. Yet Catherine only dismissed *one* favourite because Potemkin demanded it. Usually she was in love with them and rejected his grumbles. Serenissimus, who was neither rigid nor vindictive, would then happily coexist with them until another crisis blew up. He knew the sillier favourites thought they could overthrow him. This often ended in their departure.

The favourites usually accelerated their own fall, either through cuckolding the Empress like Korsakov, becoming deeply unhappy like Zavadovsky and Potemkin himself, or getting embroiled in clumsy intrigues against Potemkin, as Zorich did, which caused the Empress to tire of them. When Potemkin demanded their dismissal, which he did quite frequently, she probably told him to mind his own business and gave him another estate or admired the latest plans for his cities. At other times, she criticized him for *not* telling her when they were deceiving her, but he probably knew that she was so in love at the time, there was no point.

The Prince liked to boast that Catherine always needed him when things were not going well, politically or amorously. During crises of the boudoir, he was especially indispensable, as Harris reported to London during Catherine's hiccup with Lanskoy in May 1781: 'These revolutions are moments when the influence of my friend is without bounds and when nothing he asks, however extravagant, is refused.'[55] But it was undoubtedly more than that.

In times of crisis, such as her humiliation by Korsakov, he became her husband and lover again. 'When all other resources fail him to achieve what he wants,' the Austrian envoy, Count Louis Cobenzl, who was one of the few foreigners who really knew Catherine and Potemkin intimately, told his Emperor Joseph II, 'he retakes for a few days the function of favourite.'[56] The letters between Empress and Prince suggest that their relationship was so informal and intimate that neither would have thought twice about spending the night together at any time throughout their lives. Hence some writers call him 'favori-en-chef' and the others just 'sous-favoris'. No wonder the 'sous-favoris' failed to understand Potemkin's role and tried to intrigue against him.

Potemkin and Catherine had settled their personal dilemma in this formal system, which was supposed to preserve their friendship, keep imperial love out of politics and reserve political power for Potemkin. Even though there was a system which worked better than most marriages, it was still flawed. No one, not even those two deft manipulators, could really control favouritism, that sensitive and convenient fusion of love and sex, greed and ambition.

Nonetheless, it was their cure for jealousy. While Catherine was truly happy at last with Lanskoy in 1780, she was equally unjealous about Potemkin's scandalous antics. 'This step has increased Potemkin's power,' Harris told Weymouth, 'which nothing can destroy unless a report is true . . .'. The report? That Potemkin might 'marry his favourite niece'.[57]

12

HIS NIECES

There was a man, if that he was a man,
Not that his manhood could be called in question ...
Lord Byron, *Don Juan*, Canto VII: 36

When the five Engelhardt sisters arrived at Court in 1775, these mother-less, barely educated but beautiful provincial girls were instantly trans-formed by their uncle into sophisticates and treated as if they were members of the imperial family – 'almost as Grand Duchesses'.[1] When Potemkin ended his relationship with the Empress of Russia, he almost at once became very close to his striking teenage niece Varvara Engel-hardt. It was not long before Court gossip claimed that the degenerate Prince had seduced all five of these girls.

Now he was a semi-single man again, Potemkin immediately plunged into an imbroglio of secret affairs and public liaisons with adventuresses and aristocrats that were so intertwined that they fascinated his own times and are still difficult to unravel. 'Like Catherine, he was an Epi-curean,' wrote Count Alexander Ribeaupierre, son of one of Potemkin's adjutants, who married his great-niece. 'Sensual pleasures had an important part in his life – he loved women passionately and nothing could stand in the way of his passions.'[2] Now he could return to the way he preferred to live. Rising late, visiting Catherine through the covered passageway, he swung constantly between frenetic work and febrile hedonism, between bouts of political paperwork and strategic creativity, and then love affairs, theological debates, and nocturnal wassails, until dawn, at the green baize tables.

Nothing so shocked his contemporaries as the legend of the five nieces. All the diplomats wrote about it to their captivated monarchs with ill-concealed relish: 'You will get an idea of Russian morality', Corberon told Versailles under its prim new King Louis XVI, 'in the manner in which Prince Potemkin protects his nieces.' In order to underline the horror of this immoral destiny, he added with a shiver, 'There is one who is only twelve years old and who will no doubt suffer the same fate.' Simon Vorontsov was also disgusted: 'We saw Prince Potemkin make a harem of his own family in the imperial palace of which he occupied a part.' What 'scandalous impudence!' The scandal of the nieces was accepted by contemporaries as true – but did he really seduce all five, even the youngest?[3]

The 'almost-Grand-Duchesses' became the gilded graces of Catherine's Court, the richest heiresses in Russia and the matriarchs of many of the aristocratic dynasties of the Empire. None of them ever forgot who they were and who their uncle was: their lives were illuminated and mythologized by their semi-royal status and the prestige of Serenissimus.

Only five of the Engelhardt sisters mattered at Court because the eldest, Anna, left home and married Mikhail Zhukov before Potemkin's rise, though he looked after the couple and promoted the husband to govern Astrakhan. The next eldest, the formidable Alexandra Vasilievna, twenty-two in 1776, became Potemkin's favourite niece, his dearest friend apart from the Empress. She was already a woman when she arrived, so it was hardest for her to adapt to Court sophistication. But she was as haughty as Potemkin had been, and 'clever and strong-willed'. She used her 'kind of grandeur' to conceal 'her lack of education'.[4] She had a head for business and politics and a talent for friendship. Her portraits show a slim brunette, hair brushed back, with high cheekbones, bright intelligent blue eyes, a broad sensual mouth, small nose and alabaster skin, graced by a lithe body and the grandness of a woman who was an honorary member of the imperial family and the confidante of its greatest statesman.

The third sister was Varvara, twenty, who charmed her way through life. 'Plenira aux chevaux d'or' – 'the fascinatress with the golden hair' – was what the poet Derzhavin called her; she was celebrated for her radiant blondeness. Even in middle age, she kept her slender figure, and her features were described by the memoirist Wiegel as 'perfect ... with the freshness of a twenty-year-old girl'. No statesman like her sister Alexandra, she was excitable, flirtatious, capricious, hot-tempered and incessantly demanding. No one could criticize her ill-temper and bad manners when the Prince was alive, but on one occasion she pulled a friend by the hair; on another she whipped one of her estate managers. She was harsh to the pompous or corrupt but very kind to her servants[5] – though not necessarily to her serfs. Years later, force was required to suppress a peasant revolt on her estates.

Nadezhda, fifteen, contrived to be both ginger and swarthy and must have suffered from being the ugly duckling in a family of swans, but Potemkin made her a maid-of-honour like the others. She was headstrong and irritating: Nadezhda means 'hope' in Russian so Potemkin, who coined nicknames for everyone, cruelly called her 'bez-nadezhnaya' – or Hopeless. The fifth sister was the placid and passive Ekaterina, who was already the physical paragon of the family: her portrait by Vigée Lebrun, painted in 1790, shows her seraphic face surrounded by bright auburn-blonde curls, looking into a mirror. Ekaterina, wrote Ségur, the French envoy, might 'have served as a model for an artist to paint the head of Venus'. Lastly, Tatiana was the youngest – aged seven in 1776 – but she grew up as good-looking and intelligent as Alexandra. After Potemkin withdrew from Catherine's alcove, he fell in love with Varvara.[6]

'Little Mother, Varenka, my soul, my life,' wrote Potemkin to Varvara. 'You slept, little fool, and didn't remember anything. I, leaving you, kissed you and covered you with the quilt and with a gown and crossed you.' It is just possible to claim that this was the letter of an uncle who has simply kissed his niece good night and tucked her in, though it really reads as if he is leaving in the morning after spending the night with her.

'My angel, your caress is so pleasurable so lovable, count my love to you and you'll see you are my life, my joy, my angel; I'm kissing you innumerable times and I think about you even more . . .'. Even in the age of *sensibilité* and written by an emotional and uninhibited Prince, these sentiments were not those of a conventional uncle. Often he called her 'my honey' or 'my treasure', 'my soul, my tender lover', 'my sweetheart goddess' and 'lovable lips' and frequently signed off, 'I am kissing you from head to foot.' The letters are shamelessly sensual – and yet familial too: 'My honey, Varenka, my soul . . . Goodbye, sweet lips, come over to dinner. I have invited your sisters . . .'. In one letter, he told her: 'Tomorrow I'm going to the *banya*.' Recalling his rendezvous in the Winter Palace *banya* with Catherine, was he arranging to meet his niece there too?

The Prince was now thirty-seven, seventeen years older than Varvara, so, in age at least, there was nothing remarkable in their love affair. The sisters and their hulking brother, Vasily, were now at Court every day and in Potemkin's homes – the Shepilev house, the Anichkov – every evening. They attended his dinners and watched him playing cards with the Empress in her Little Hermitage. They were his most precious ornaments as well as his friends, family, entourage. As far as we know, he had no children: they were his heirs too. It was no coincidence that it was Varvara who became his mistress, for she was the family flirt, he the family hero.

The letters are clearly those of an older man and a younger woman;

for example, when Potemkin told her that the Empress had invited her to a dinner, he added, 'My dear, dress yourself very well and try to be kind and beautiful,' telling her to watch her 'ps and qs'. From outside town, possibly Tsarskoe Selo, he asked: 'I'm planning to come into town tomorrow ... Write to me where you plan to visit me – at the Anichkov or the Palace?' Varenka frequently saw the Empress and Serenissimus together. 'The Empress was bled today so there's no need to bother her,' he told her. 'I'm off to the Empress and then I'll come and see you.'

Varenka was in love with him too – she often called him 'my life' and worried, like all his women, about his illnesses while basking in his luxury: 'Father, my life, thank you so much for the present and the letter ... I'm kissing you a million times in my mind.' However, she began to suffer and make trouble. 'It's useless caressing me,' she said. 'Listen, I'm telling you seriously now ... if you loved me once, I ask you to forget me for ever, I've decided to leave you. I wish you to be loved by another ... though no one will love you as I've loved you ...'. Was this minx of the Engelhardt sisters jealous of another woman, for there were indeed others, or simply pretending to be?

'Varenka, you are a fool and an ungrateful rascal,' Potemkin wrote, perhaps at that moment. 'Can I say – Varenka feels bad and Grishenka feels nothing? When I come, I'll tear your ears off for it!' Was it when he arrived in a temper after this that she told him: 'Good my friend, then if it is me who has angered you, then go!' But then she said she had slept too much and perhaps that was why she was in a bad mood. So Varenka sulked and postured while Potemkin suffered the tortures of every older man who falls in love with a spoilt girl. The Empress, who invited Varvara to everything and knew of their relationship, did not mind when Potemkin was happy. Indeed she did everything she could to make sure that the niece was close to both of them. When one of the courtiers moved out of the palace, Potemkin asked the Empress to 'order Madame Maltiz [Mistress of the Empress's maids-of-honour] to give Princess Ekaterina's apartments to my Varvara Vasilievna'. Catherine replied: 'I'll order it ...'.[7]

News of the scandalous affair reached Daria Potemkina in Moscow. The Prince's appalled mother tried to stop it. A furious Serenissimus tossed her unread letters into the fireplace. Daria also wrote to Varvara to reprimand her. 'I've received grandmother's letters,' Varvara told Potemkin, 'which made me very angry. Was this the reason for you going?' Then the girl offered herself again: 'My darling little *méchant*, my angel, don't you want me, my adored treasure?'

When Potemkin started to spend more time in his southern provinces,

Varvara sulked at Court. Catherine decided to intervene. Harris got wind of this: 'Her Majesty reproached Prince XXX with the irregularity of his conduct with his niece and the dishonour it brought ...'. Harris was projecting English priggishness on to a relationship he did not understand. Catherine's indulgent teasing of Potemkin about his niece–mistress revealed their open relationship: 'Listen, my little Varenka is not well at all; it's your departure that is the cause. It's very wrong of you. It will kill her and I am getting very fond of her. They want to bleed her.'[8]

Was Varenka wasting away out of love for her uncle? Or was there another reason? The wily girl may have been playing a double game with the Prince. At the beginning, love pervaded her letters to him. Later, their tone changed. Potemkin was still in love with her – but he knew she would soon have to marry: 'Your victory over me is strong and eternal. If you love me, I'm happy, if you know how I love, you would never wish for anything else.' Now she was a woman, she did wish for more. She had already met Prince Sergei Fyodorovich Golitsyn, another of that populous and powerful family, and had fallen in love with him.

We do not know if Potemkin was heartbroken for long, but he had resolved that the girls should make magnificent marriages, settling fortunes on them to ease the way. The end of the affair was required by family duty. 'Now all is finished,' she wrote to him. 'I waited for it every moment for a month when I began to notice your changes towards me. What have I done now when I'm so unhappy? I'm returning all your letters to you.' So it was a two-way street. 'If I behaved badly,' she wrote, 'you have to remember who was the cause of it.'

Potemkin behaved generously. In September 1778, 'he prevailed on a Prince XXX to marry her'. Prince XXX – Sergei Golitsyn – agreed. 'They were betrothed with great pomp at the Palace the day before yesterday,' observed Harris. In January 1779 as with all the Engelhardt marriages, the Empress was present when Varvara married. Varvara and Potemkin remained close for the rest of his life, and she continued to write him affectionate, flirtatious letters: 'I'm kissing your hands and asking you to remember me, father. I don't know why but it seems to me that you forget me ...', and then, like everyone else who knew him, she wrote: 'Come, my friend, as soon as possible, it's so dull without you.' She still signed herself 'Grishenkin's pussycat'.[9]

Varvara and Sergei Golitsyn were happily married and had ten children. The Empress and Serenissimus stood as godparents to the eldest, named Grigory and born that year: contemporaries suggested he was Potemkin's son. This was certainly possible. Child and man, Grigory

Golitsyn bore an uncanny resemblance to his great-uncle – another mystery of consanguinity.

Following Varvara's marriage, Harris saw that 'Alexandra Engelhardt seems to have still greater power over' Potemkin. It seemed that the Prince had moved on to the niece with whom he had most in common. We do not have their love letters and no one knows what happens behind bedroom doors, but contemporaries were convinced they were lovers (though that does not mean they were). Alexandra, or 'Sashenka', 'is a young lady of a very pleasing person, of good parts and a very superior aptitude in conducting a Court intrigue', added Harris with admiration tinged with envy, for he was an avid if unsuccessful intriguer himself. He was sure Alexandra had nudged Catherine towards the room where she found Countess Bruce and Korsakov together.

Sashenka became inseparable from Empress and Serenissimus. 'If her uncle does not change his sentiments for her,' noted Harris, 'she is likely to become [Catherine's] female confidante.' So close did this relationship become that a silly legend was passed down and apparently believed among some Polish families that Alexandra was Catherine's daughter. Grand Duke Paul and Alexandra were born in 1754, so when, the story goes, Catherine gave birth to a girl instead of the expected male heir, she hid the child and replaced her with the son of a Kalmuk peasant-woman who grew up to be Emperor Paul I.[10] The simpler explanation is that she was Potemkin's niece and a fascinating woman in her own right. Sashenka's position as an unofficial member of the imperial family was still recognized forty years later.

Now she became Potemkin's hostess. A dinner given by her was a sign of his favour. Alexandra, Harris delicately told London, 'has a very notion of the value of presents'. She accepted gifts and money from the British envoy – and he recommended her to Alleyne Fitzherbert, his successor, as an intelligence source. She was an able businesswoman who made millions by selling grain and timber – yet she was celebrated for her generosity to her serfs.[11] In late 1779, Potemkin's intense relationship with Sashenka ended, but they remained the closest friends.

The Prince now embarked on a long relationship with the fifth sister – Ekaterina – though again there are no love letters to prove it. 'They even talk of the marriage between Potemkin and his little niece with whom he is more in love than ever.'[12] Ekaterina – 'Katinka', 'Katish' or the 'kitten', as the Empress and Potemkin called her – was the Venus in a family of them. 'Graced with her ravishing face,' wrote Vigée Lebrun, 'and her angelic softness, she had an invincible charm.' Potemkin called her his 'angel incarnate' – 'and never had anyone ever been more justly named', the Prince de Nassau-Siegen later told his wife.[13]

She was uneducated and incurious, but thoroughly seductive. Her temperament was like that of a blonde mulatto – eternal languor and nonchalant sexuality. 'Her happiness', recalled Vigée Lebrun, 'was to live stretched out on a *canapé*, enveloped in a big black fur without a corset.' When visitors asked why she never wore the 'enormous diamonds ... the most sumptuous you can imagine' which 'the famous Potemkin' gave her, she lazily replied: 'To what good, for whom, for what?' She was 'the kindest of the three' niece–mistresses and 'believed in Potemkin's love so as not to pain him'. She was too dreamy and passive for Potemkin, who only fell in love with passionate or shrewd women. So, while Potemkin loved her least of the three, she lasted the longest. Serenissimus declared that to be her lover was to taste the quintessential delights of the flesh, an ungallant compliment from an undoubted connoisseur.[14]

Late in 1780, the diplomats claimed that Potemkin's 'family harem' caused a 'diabolical row' at Court. The headstrong Varvara Golitsyna, defiantly respectable now that she was married, expressed her views on the Empress's life. This blundering tactlessness irritated Catherine. Varvara compounded her pigheaded folly by loudly proclaiming that one could hardly be knouted for telling the truth. Potemkin was furious too and sent her off to Golitsyn's estates. At this embarrassing moment, the 'angel-incarnate' Ekaterina allegedly became pregnant by her uncle. Dr Rogerson prescribed taking the waters at a spa. Serenissimus persuaded Varvara to take her sister. Corberon admired Potemkin's typical manipulation of what could have been a disaster by giving the impression that Varvara was just accompanying her sister on a medical mission instead of being exiled, and that Ekaterina was not being sent away to conceal her belly, merely going on a jaunt with the Golitsyns. By the time Ekaterina left, she was supposedly six months gone.

Catherine now made a suggestion that upset Potemkin and caused yet another row. When Ekaterina was appointed maid-of-honour in the summer of 1777, she immediately attracted the attention of Catherine and Prince Orlov's son, Bobrinsky, much to the amusement of the Empress, who joked about it in her letters to Potemkin.[15] Bobrinsky fell in love with the girl. The Empress, according to Corberon, had even promised that he could marry her. Bobrinsky was an insubstantial playboy who was a victim of the birth that made him everything yet nothing. Plenty of royal bastards found brilliant careers in those days – none greater than Louis XV's Marshal Maurice de Saxe, son of Augustus the Strong of Poland and Saxony – but Bobrinsky did not and was a notorious wastrel. Did he now refuse to marry a girl pregnant by her uncle? Or did Potemkin object because he considered Bobrinsky a fool – and, worse, an Orlov? This moral, sexual and familial maze presents a little kaleidoscope of Court morals.[16]

Alexei Orlov-Chesmensky, who had retired to Moscow and hated Potemkin, scented blood in the water and arrived in town in September 1778 hoping to overthrow the Prince. Serenissimus displayed the 'highest good humour and indifference' as the two giant opponents, Cyclops and Scarface, publicly served at the Empress's table. 'It is beyond the description of my pen', observed Harris, 'to describe . . . a scene, in which every passion that can affect the human mind, bore a part which, by all the actors, was concealed by the most masterly hypocrisy.' Orlov-Chesmensky was determined to make one last attempt to overthrow Serenissimus, whom, he told Catherine, had 'ruined your army': 'his only superior talent is cunning' and his only aim to 'invest himself with sovereign power'. Catherine was displeased by this but she tried to conciliate. 'Be friends with Potemkin,' she begged Orlov-Chesmensky. 'Prevail on that extraordinary man to be more circumspect in his conduct . . . [and] pay more attention to the duties of the great offices he fills . . .'.

'You know Madam,' Scarface said, 'I am your slave . . . if Potemkin disturbs your peace of mind, give me your orders. He shall disappear immediately . . .'. The offer to kill Potemkin may be merely diplomatic gossip, but everyone knew that Orlov-Chesmensky was quite capable of delivering. Catherine was unimpressed and this marked the last gasp of Orlov power.[17]

Despite the rows, Potemkin and the Empress were so involved at that time in recasting foreign policy that his political position was entirely stable. When the row got hottest, Potemkin simply absented himself in a diplomatic sulk until the Empress had calmed down. Ekaterina returned with no sign of a baby, so far as we know.

The youngest niece, Tatiana, was already 'full of spirit' when, aged twelve in 1781, she was appointed a maid-of-honour. When her uncle was in the south, she wrote him letters, in big girlish handwriting, which provide clues to the nature of Catherine and Potemkin's 'family'. She usually signed off as she did on 3 June 1785: 'I want your return with the most lively impatience.' Like everyone else, Tatiana was bored without Serenissimus: 'I don't know, my dear Uncle, when I will have the happiness to see you but those I ask tell me they know nothing and say you'll stay all winter. Ah! How long that time seems to me if it's true but I don't believe these clowns.' He gave her generous presents: 'My dear Uncle, a thousand, thousand and million thanks for your gracious present, I will never forget your kindness and beg you to continue for ever. I will do everything possible to deserve them.' She never became his mistress.[18]

The entire Potemkin clan was treated as a member of the extended Catherinian family that included Lanskoy, her lover. The Empress made a fuss not just of the Engelhardt sisters but also of Potemkin's other family – his cousin Pavel Potemkin, after serving against Pugachev, became viceroy of the Caucasus, and his brother Mikhail Chief Inspector of the College of War and one of Catherine's inner circle. The Prince's stalwart nephew Alexander Samoilov, son of his sister Maria, became secretary to the State Council and a general – 'brave but useless'. Other nephews, such as Vasily Engelhardt and Nikolai Vysotsky, son of his sister Pelageya, served as Catherine's aides-de-camp, being treated almost as family.

The Empress's favourite Sasha Lanskoy was very kind to Potemkin's nieces, as we know from Tatiana's letters, which have not been cited before this. 'Monsieur Lanskoy has had all sorts of attention,' she reported innocently. In one letter, Tatiana told her uncle how the Grand Duke and Duchess 'met me in the garden – they found me very grown up and spoke to me with a lot of kindness'.[19] When, a couple of years later, Ekaterina was married and pregnant, it was Lanskoy who sent Potemkin reports on the birth. 'Father,' he wrote, 'the Sovereign has kindly ordered a bow to you and to baptize the baby . . . here I'm sending a letter from Ekaterina Vasilievna . . .'. A few days later he told him that the Empress had a fever but the niece was feeling better each day.

There is a sense that, away from the harsh political struggles, the Empress, to some extent, succeeded in creating a patchwork family out of her – or, as she put it, 'our' – Potemkin 'relatives' and her beloved Lanskoy. She chose her family as others choose their friends. There was a symmetry between Catherine's favourites and Potemkin's nieces. When the politics allowed some serenity, she treated the nieces like daughters and he the favourites like sons. Together, they were almost the children of that unconventional, childless marriage.[20]

Potemkin's relationships with his nieces were irregular and idiosyncratic but not unusual for his time, and certainly Catherine did not seem shocked by them. She tells in her *Memoirs* how, during her own child-hood before leaving for Russia, she had flirted (and possibly more) with

THE PASSIONATE PARTNERSHIP

her uncle, Prince Georg-Ludwig of Holstein, who wanted to marry her.*
Such behaviour – and worse – was not uncommon among royal families.
The Habsburgs regularly married their nieces. Earlier in the century, the
Regent of France, Philippe, Duc d'Orléans, was supposed to have had
affairs with his daughter, the Duchesse de Berry.†

Augustus the Strong, the King of Poland, Elector of Saxony and duplicitous ally of Peter the Great, set an unbeatable incestuous precedent for
vigorous degeneracy that not even Potemkin could equal. Augustus,
an art-loving, impecunious and politically slippery *bon vivant* whom
Carlyle called that 'cheerful Man of Sin, gay eupeptic Son of Belial', had,
according to legend, not only fathered an heir and 354 bastards through
a legion of mistresses but also supposedly made his daughter Countess
Orczelska his mistress. To add insult to incest, the daughter–mistress in
turn was in love with Count Rudorfski, her half-brother, another of his
natural children. It was different for commoners, though in seventeenth-
century France Cardinal Mazarin had made his nieces – the Maza-
rinettes – into the richest heiresses in France and there were rumours
about his relationship with them. Meanwhile, Voltaire was having the
last affair of his long life with his promiscuous, greedy niece, Madame
Denis, but he kept it secret – only their correspondence revealed all. In
the generation after Potemkin, Lord Byron flaunted his affair with his
half-sister, and Prince Talleyrand set up house with his nephew's wife,
the Duchesse de Dino.

In Russia, uncle–niece incest was much more common. The Orthodox
Church turned a blind eye. Nikita Panin was rumoured to have had an
affair with his niece (by marriage) Princess Dashkova – though she
denied it. Kirill Razumovsky kept house at Baturin with the daughter of
his sister Anna, Countess S. Apraxina, with whom he lived as man and
wife. Yet the incestuous relationship of this prominent, much admired
magnate was barely mentioned because it was done quietly in the
country; no one 'frightened the horses'. Potemkin's sin was the openness
with which he loved them. This shocked contemporaries just as it was
Catherine's openness with her favourites that made her so notorious:
they were the parallel lines of the same arrangement. Serenissimus
regarded himself as semi-royal, so he would do what he wished and
everyone could see him enjoying it.[21]

* This Georg-Ludwig was also the uncle of her husband Peter III, who brought him to
Petersburg during his short reign. Ironically, his orderly was young Potemkin.
† On her death, Orléans' enemies sang: 'La pleures-tu comme mari / Comme ta fille
ou ta maîtresse?' – Do you weep for her as a husband, for your daughter or your
mistress?

Wicked uncle Potemkin has been crucified by historians for his behaviour, but his nieces themselves were willing partners – Varvara was in love with him – and adored him throughout their lives. Far from being abused and damaged, Alexandra and Varvara enjoyed unusually happy marriages, while continuing to be close to their uncle. Ekaterina, occasional mistress for the rest of his life, was said to have merely 'tolerated' his embraces but she was a sleepy girl who 'tolerated' her husband, diamonds and everything else: that was her nature. They would surely have worshipped the protector of the family. In their letters, they always wanted to see him. Like Catherine, they found life was dull without him. No abuse is required to explain this peccadillo: in that place and time, it must have seemed natural.

The nieces were not his only mistresses after his withdrawal from Catherine's boudoir: Potemkin's archives are heavy with literally hundreds of unsigned love letters from unknown women who were obviously wildly in love with the one-eyed giant. There are two sorts of womanizer – the mechanical fornicator who despises his conquests, and the genuine lover of women for whom seduction is a foundation for love and friendship. Potemkin was very much the latter – he adored the companionship of women. Later, his Court was so crowded with foreigners that it was impossible to miss the identity of his paramours. But in the 1770s all we have left are yearning letters in curling feminine hands asking: 'How have you spent the night, my darling: better than me. I haven't slept for a second.' They were never satisfied with the time he gave them. 'I am not happy with you,' this one wrote. 'You have such a distracted air. There must be something on your mind . . '. His mistresses had to wait in their husband's palaces, hearing from their friends and servants exactly what Potemkin was doing: 'I know you were at the Empress's in the evening and you fell ill. Tell me how you are, it worries me and I don't know your news. Adieu, my angel, I can't tell you more, everything prevents it . . '. It ends abruptly – the lady's husband had surely arrived, so she sent off the unfinished letter with her trusted maid.

These women fussed about his health, travelling, gambling, eating. His ability to attract such attention was perhaps the result of growing up surrounded by so many loving sisters: 'My dear Prince, can you make me this sacrifice and not give so much time to gaming? It can only destroy your health.' The mistresses ached to see him properly: 'Tomorrow there's a ball at the Grand Duke's: I hope to have the pleasure of seeing you there.' Around the same time, another woman was writing:

It's such a pity that I only saw you at a distance when I wanted so much to kiss you, my dear friend ... My God, it's a shame and I can't endure it! Tell me at least if you love me, my dear. It's the only thing that can reconcile me to myself ... I'd kiss you all the time but you'd get bored of me soon; I write to you before a mirror and it seems as if I'm chatting with you and I tell you everything that comes into my head ...

In the billets-doux of these unknown women sitting in front of mirrors and pots of rouge, rolls of silk, puffs of powder, with a quill in their hands 200 years ago, we see Potemkin alive and reflected: 'I kiss you a million times before you go ... You work too much ... I kiss you thirty million times and with a tenderness that grows all the time ... Kiss me in your thoughts. Adieu, my life.'[22]

Yet they masked a poignant dilemma in Potemkin's unique position. No one else could ever really possess him. His affairs with his nieces made sense because he could never marry and have a normal family life. If he was unable to have children, this made it doubly suitable. He loved many – but he was married to Empress and Empire.

13

DUCHESSES, DIPLOMATS
AND CHARLATANS

Or in a gilded carriage
By truly splendid tandem drawn
With hound, companion or a jester
Or some beauty – better yet –
Gavrili Derzhavin, 'Ode to Princess Felitsa'

Your Lordship can conceive no idea of the height to which
corruption is carried in this country.
Sir James Harris to Viscount Stormont, 13 December 1780

In the summer of 1777, the sumptuous yacht of Elisabeth, Duchess of Kingston, also Countess of Bristol, moored in St Petersburg. The Duchess was a raddled temptress, regarded in London as adulterous, bigamous and brazen. However, Petersburg was a long way away and the Russians were sometimes astonishingly slow at exposing mountebanks in their midst. Not many English duchesses visited Russia at a time when English fashions were sweeping Europe. So many English merchants purveyed their goods to the Russians that they inhabited the famous 'English line' in Petersburg. At the Russian Court, Potemkin was the leading Anglophile.

Already as cosmopolitan as a man could be who had only once left his country, Potemkin was preparing himself for statesmanship by carefully studying the language, customs and politics of Westerners and filling his own Court – the 'basse-cour' or 'farmyard' as Catherine dubbed it[1] – with the dubious foreigners Russia attracted. In the late 1770s, Russia became a fashionable extension to the Grand Tour undertaken by young British gentlemen, and Potemkin became one of its obligatory sights. The Duchess was its pioneer.

Kingston was greeted by the President of the Naval College, Ivan Chernyshev (brother of Zakhar Chernyshev, whom Kingston had charmed when he was Ambassador to London). He presented her to Catherine, the Grand Duke and, of course, the Prince. Even Catherine and Potemkin were slightly impressed by the fabulous wealth of this celebrated aristocrat aboard her floating pleasure dome, packed with England's finest antiques, mechanical contraptions and priceless treasures.

The Duchess of Kingston was one of those specimens of eighteenth-century femininity who managed to take advantage of the male-dominated aristocracy through a career of seduction, marriage, deception, exhibitionism and theft. Elisabeth Chudleigh was born a lady in 1720 and, at twenty-four, secretly married Augustus Hervey, who placed a bed-curtain ring instead of a diamond on her finger. Heir to the Earl of Bristol, he was the scion of a family as shrewd at amassing wealth as it was voracious in abusing pleasure. Chudleigh was one of the most pursued and promiscuous women of her time, becoming an early celebrity in the penny prints: she sought publicity and they followed her antics in over-excited detail. Her legitimate period reached a naked apogee when she appeared wild-haired in a see-through gauze dress at the Venetian Ambassador's Ball in 1749, dressed as Iphigenia the Sacrifice – 'so naked', commented Mary Wortley Montagu, daughter of the first Duke of Kingston, 'that the high priest might easily inspect the entrails of the victim'. It was a sight of such voluptuous daring that she appeared smirking in a generation of best-selling prints. So wanton was this vision that she supposedly even managed the impressive feat of seducing old George II.

After years as the mistress of the Duke of Kingston, an ageing Whig magnate, she married him bigamously. When he died, there was an unholy fight for his fortune. His Pierrepont family uncovered her marriage to Hervey and brought her to trial before the House of Lords, where she was found guilty before 5,000 spectators. She would have been branded – but Hervey inherited his earldom just in time to give her immunity. She lost the duchy but got the lucre – and continued to call herself Duchess anyway. She escaped to Calais, pursued by outraged Pierreponts, and the 'Ducal Countess', as Horace Walpole dubbed her, fitted out her new yacht with a dining-hall, drawing-room, kitchen, picture gallery and organ, stealing what she liked from the Kingston mansion, Thoresby Hall. Her crew indulged in every imaginable shenanigan, including two mutinies, which meant the English sailors had to be replaced. Finally she set sail with a colourful entourage including a French crew, an English chaplain-cum-hack (who seemed to be an unofficial correspondent of the newspapers) and a set of caddish ne'er-do-wells.

On arrival in Russia, this circus caused something more familiar in the British Home Counties than the palaces of St Petersburg – a war of the vicars. Kingston held 'a magnificent entertainment on board her yacht' which was loyally recounted to *Gentleman Magazine* by her obsequious chaplain. 'As soon as dinner was served a band of music composed of fifes, drums, clarinettes, and French horns played some English marches ... After dinner, there were some concertos on the organ which is placed in the antechamber.' The British community in Petersburg was scandalized by the impudence of this bigamous parvenu which, according to *their* chaplain William Took, excited 'universal contempt'. But her 'ostentatious displays' went down well in Petersburg.

The Duchess and her entourage were given a house on the Neva by the Empress and began to spend much time with Potemkin. They actually fitted rather well into his dissolute *ménage*. Indeed Potemkin flirted with the deaf, over-rouged, over-painted Duchess, who still dressed like a young girl, but he was more interested in her antiques. One of his officers, Colonel Mikhail Garnovsky, 'took care' of her. Garnovsky was what might be called a tradesman–soldier: he was Potemkin's spy, adviser and commercial agent and now added gigolo to his *curriculum vitae*. He became the lover of the Duchess, who had to spend 'five or six hours at her *toilette*' and was almost a definition of 'mutton dressed as lamb'. She gave Potemkin treasures and presented Ivan Chernyshev with a Raphael. She wanted to take Potemkin's niece Tatiana, aged eight, home with her to give her a Kingstonian education, a contradiction that Serenissimus would not even contemplate.

Kingston, who was nine years older than Catherine, had planned to dazzle Petersburg and leave fast to the sound of trumpets. But this plan went amiss when, to the secret delight of observers like Corberon, the tempest of September 1777 ran her yacht aground. Then her French crew mutinied too and absconded, leaving the Empress to find a new crew and have the yacht repaired. By the time she departed by land, the Duchess was calling Catherine her 'great friend', and was enamoured of Potemkin, whom she called a 'a great minister, full of *esprit* ... in a word all that can make an honest and gallant man'. He and Catherine politely invited her back, though they were tiring of her. Garnovsky accompanied her to the border.

She returned two years later – like every bad penny, she took up any invitation, no matter how lightly offered. She ordered Potemkin a richly bound book with his titles in silver and diamonds, but typically it did not arrive. She decorated a 'most splendid' Petersburg mansion with, according to her former gardener at Thoresby, now working for the Empress, 'crimsons damask hangings' and 'five Musical Lustres! Good organ, plate, paintings!' She bought estates in Livonia, including one from Potemkin for over £100,000 sterling, according to Samuel Bentham, a young Englishman, and grandly called her lands 'Chudleigh'.

By 1780, Catherine and Potemkin were bored of 'Kingstonsha' – that Kingston woman. Samuel Bentham spotted the bedraggled old slattern at the Razumovskys, sleeping through a concert: 'She served the company to laugh at.' However, she retained her modern expertise in what we now call public relations and leaked untrue tales of her imperial intimacy to the London newspapers. 'The Empress is polite in public,' Bentham noted, 'but she had no private conferences [with Catherine], which ... is what she herself put in the English Papers.' She kept open house 'but cannot prevail on any but Russian officers, who want a dinner, to come ...'. She made a failed attempt to marry one of the Radziwills, visited 'Chudleigh', then left for Calais. She made her last visit in 1784. When she left finally in 1785, time had caught up with her. After her death in Paris in 1788, Garnovsky, who was left 50,000 roubles in her will, managed to commandeer most of the contents of 'Chudleigh' and three of her properties, on which he based his own fortune.[2]

The Prince's aesthetic tastes were influenced by the Duchess – indeed he inherited her most valuable treasures.* Potemkin's Peacock Clock by James Cox, brought to Petersburg by her in 1788, was one of the most exquisite objects ever made: a gold lifesized peacock with resplendent tail fan standing on a gold tree with branches and leaves and an owl, in a gold cage twelve feet high with bells around it. The face of the clock was a mushroom with a dragonfly keeping the seconds. When the time struck the hour, this delightful contraption burst into surprising movement: the owl's head nodded and the peacock crowed, cocked its head regally and then opened its tail to its glorious full extent.† She also brought an organ-clock, another object of breathtaking beauty, probably the one that played on her yacht: on the outside, the broad face made it appear like a normal clock, but it opened to become an organ that played like a high-noted church instrument.‡ When the Duchess died, the Prince bought these *objets* and ordered his mechanics to assemble them in his Palace.[3]

*

* Potemkin showed off many of Kingston's treasures at his ball in 1791, described in Chapter 32. The Hermitage today, which holds much of the contents of Potemkin's collections, is spotted with the former belongings of the Duchess of Kingston. Garnovsky was to be cursed for his avarice, for the Emperor Paul threw him into a debtor's prison and he died poor in 1810.

† The Peacock Clock is one of the centrepieces of today's Hermitage Museum. It still performs every hour on the hour.

‡ This now stands in the Menshikov Palace, part of the Hermitage, and is played at midday on Sundays. In its music, we can hear the sounds of Potemkin's salon two centuries ago.

The Duchess also left a more tawdry reminder of herself around Potemkin's person. When she returned in 1779, still in favour, she brought a plausible young Englishman who claimed to be an army officer, expert in military and commercial affairs. 'Major' James George Semple had indeed served in the British army against the Americans and he certainly was a specialist in commerce, though not of the kind he suggested. (A portrait in the British Museum shows him sporting an insolent expression, high hat, ruffled white shirt and uniform – the paraphernalia of the mountebank.) When he arrived in Russia, Semple was already a celebrated rogue known as 'the Northern Impostor and the Prince of Swindlers'. Indeed a few years later, a book was published about him: *The Northern Hero – Surprising Adventures, Amorous Intrigues, Curious Devices, Unparalleled Hypocrisy, Remarkable Escapes, Infernal Frauds, Deep-Laid Projects and Villainous Exploits.* Semple was married to a cousin of Kingston's, but he was in the debtor's jail at Calais when she was arranging her second Russian jaunt. She bought him out of the jail and invited him to travel with her to Petersburg. The jailbird probably seduced the Ducal Countess.[4]

Potemkin was immediately charmed. The Prince always relished swashbuckling heroes and Semple, like all rascals, lived on his blarney. In his early days as a statesman, when he was getting to know Westerners for the first time, Potemkin was certainly careless about his foreign friends, but he always preferred amusing hucksters to boring aristocrats. The Northern Hero and Prince of Swindlers joined the entertaining Anglo-French riffraff in the *basse-cour*, including an Irish soldier of fortune named Newton, who was later guillotined in the Revolution; the Chevalier de Vivarais, a defrocked French priest who was accompanied by his mistress,[5] and a mysterious French adventurer called the Chevalier de la Teyssonière, who helped Corberon advance French interests.[6] It is a shame that the era's premier adventurer, the cultivated and witty Casanova, had arrived too early for Potemkin: they would have enjoyed each other.

The international circus of the *basse-cour* was a grotesque microcosm of the cosmopolitan world of diplomacy. Serenissimus, while working seriously on military and southern affairs, now began to take an interest in Nikita Panin's responsibility – foreign affairs. As Countess Rumiantseva had shrewdly observed to her husband after the end of Potemkin's affair with Catherine, 'The impulsiveness, which excited him once, is over. He leads an absolutely different life. Doesn't play cards in the evenings; working all the time ... You'll never recognize him ...'.[7]

The Prince was a diplomatic neophyte, but he was well qualified for the nature of international affairs at that time. The diplomatic world of the eighteenth century is often described as an elegant ballet in which every dancer knew their steps down to the minutest detail. But this was something of an illusion for, if the steps were familiar, the music, by late in the century, was no longer predictable. The 'Old System' had been overturned by the 'Diplomatic Revolution' of 1756. The guiding light of diplomacy was the ruthless self-interest of *raison d'état*. All depended on the power of the state, measured in population, territorial aggrand-izement and size of army. The 'balance of power', maintained by the ever present threat of force, was really an argument for the relentless expansion of the Great Powers at the cost of lesser ones: it often meant that, if one Power made gains, the others had to be compensated for them, as Poland discovered in 1772.

Ambassadors were usually cultivated aristocrats, who, depending on distance from their capitals, possessed independence to pursue royal policy in their own way, but the initiatives of the diplomats could be recklessly out of kilter with government policy: treaties were sometimes signed by diplomats who were then disowned by their own ministries. This meant that policy developments were slow and ponderous as cour-iers dashed back and forth along muddy, potholed roads, dodging foot-pads and staying at the cockroach-infested, rat-teeming taverns. Diplomats liked to give the impression of being aristocratic amateurs. It was quite common for example for the British and French ambassadors to Paris and London to swap houses and servants until their missions were over. The Foreign Offices of the eighteenth century were tiny: the British Foreign Office in the 1780s, for example, boasted a mere twenty employees.

Diplomacy was regarded as the prerogative of the king. Sometimes monarchs pursued clandestine policies that were completely contrary to those of their own ministers: in this way, Louis XV's blundering anti-Russian Polish policy, known as 'le Secret', managed to waste the last vestiges of French influence in Warsaw. Ambassadors and soldiers served kings, not countries. As Potemkin's *basse-cour* and military entourage were to demonstrate, this was an age of cosmopolitanism when for-eigners could find service in any court, especially in diplomacy and the army. Contemporaries would have regarded our view that a man can only serve the country in which he was born as silly and limiting.

'I like to be a foreigner everywhere,' the Prince de Ligne, international *grand seigneur*, told his French mistress, 'as long as I have you and own some property somewhere.' Ligne explained that 'one loses respect in a country if one spends too much time there'.[8] Embassies and armies were filled with various nationalities who excelled in those services: Livonian barons, Italian marcheses, German counts and, the most ubiquitous of all, Jacobite Scotsmen and Irishmen. Italians specialized in diplomacy, while the Scots and the Irish excelled at war.

After the Fifteen and the Forty-Five Rebellions, many Celtic families found themselves spread across different countries: they were known as the 'Flying Geese' and many came to service in Russia.* Three families of 'Flying Geese' – the Laceys, Brownes and Keiths† – seem to have dominated the armies of Europe. The Keith brothers – George, the exiled Earl Marshal of Scotland, and his brother James – became Frederick the Great's intimate friends after they had served Russia against the Turks. When General James Keith saluted an Ottoman envoy during those wars, he was amazed to hear a broad Scottish reply from beneath the turban of the Turk – a renegade Caledonian, from Kirkcaldy.[9] At a typical battle such as Zorndorf in the Seven Years War, the commanders of the Russians, Prussians and nearby Swedes were called Fermor, Keith and Hamilton.

Beneath the turgid etiquette, the competition between the ambassadors was an unscrupulous tournament to influence policy and gather information, starring adventurers of ersatz aristocracy, pickpocketing actresses, code-breakers, galloping couriers, letter-opening postmasters, maids, temptresses and noblewomen paid by foreign governments. Most despatches were intercepted by the Cabinet Noir, a secret government bureau that opened, copied and resealed letters, then broke their cyphers. The Russian Cabinet Noir was particularly effective.‡ Kings and diplomats took advantage of this system by not using code when they were writing something they wished a foreign government to know – this was called writing 'en clair'.[10]

Rival ambassadors employed an expensive network of spies, especially

---

* There was a special Scottish relationship with Russia. The Scots often became Russianized. Empress Elisabeth's Chancellor Bestuzhev was descended from a Scotsman named Best; Count Yakov Bruce was descended from Scots soldiers of fortune; Lermontov, the nineteenth-century poet, from a Learmond named 'Thomas the Rhymer'.
† One Browne cousin was a field-marshal in the Austrian army, while George Browne joined Russian service, was captured by the Turks, sold thrice in Istanbul and then became governor of Livonia for most of Catherine the Great's reign, dying in his nineties. Field-Marshal Count Lacey became Joseph II's most trusted military adviser and correspondent, while another, Count Francis Antony Lacey, was Spanish Ambassador to Petersburg and Captain-General of all Catalonia.
‡ The British Cabinet Noir was much feared because it was based in George III's Electorate of Hanover, a crossroads allowing it to intercept mail from all over Europe.

domestic servants, and they spent a fortune on paying 'pensions' to ministers and courtiers. Secret service funds were used either to secure information (hence English gifts to Alexandra Engelhardt) or to influence policy (Catherine herself received English loans during the 1750s). These latter payments often had no effect at all on policy and generally the scale of bribery was vastly exaggerated.[11] Russia was reputed to be especially venal but it was probably no more so than France or England. In Russia, the main bidders for influence were England, France, Prussia and Austria. All were now to use every weapon in their arsenal to court the favour of Potemkin.

Europe faced three sources of conflict in 1778. France, eager to avenge the Seven Years War, was about to support the American rebels and go to war against England. (The war started in June 1778 and Spain joined the French side the next year.) However, Russia was much more concerned with the other two flashpoints. The Ottoman Sultan had never been reconciled to the terms of the 1774 Treaty of Kuchuk-Kainardzhi, especially the independence of the Crimea and the opening of the Black and Mediterranean Seas to Russian merchant ships. In November 1776, Catherine and Potemkin had to send an army to the Crimea to impose a khan of their choice, Shagin Giray, in the face of disturbances inspired by Constantinople. Now the Khanate was rebelling against Russia's protégé, and the Ottoman and Russian Empires moved closer to war.

The third axis of conflict was the rivalry for the mastery of Germany between Prussia and Austria. Russia always had a choice between alliance with Austria or Prussia: each had its own advantages. Russia had been allied with Austria from 1726, and it was only thanks to Peter III that it had switched to the Prussian option in 1762. Austria had not forgiven Russia for this betrayal, so Catherine and Frederick were stuck with each other. Foreign Minister Nikita Panin had staked his career on maintaining this alliance, but the Northern System – his network of northern powers including Britain – had never materialized beyond its Prussian fulcrum. Furthermore, it had given Frederick an influence over Russian policy in Poland and the Ottoman Empire that almost amounted to a veto.

However, Potemkin always believed that Russia's interests – and his own – lay southwards, not northwards. He cared about the Austrian-Prussian and Anglo-French conflicts only in so far as they affected Russia's relations with the Ottoman Empire around the Black Sea. The victories in the Russo-Turkish War had exposed the irrelevance of the Prussian alliance along with Frederick's duplicity.

Serenissimus began to study diplomacy. 'How courteous he is with everyone. He pretends to be jolly and chatty but it's clear that he is only dissembling. Nothing he wants or asks for will be refused.' In 1773–4, Potemkin had paid court 'most assiduously' to Nikita Panin.[12] The Minister was a dyspeptic monument to the slowness and obstinacy of Russian bureaucracy – piggy-eyed, amused and shrewd, he squatted astride Russian foreign policy like a swollen, somnolent toad. The diplomats regarded Panin as 'a great glutton, a great gamester and a great sleeper', who once left a despatch, unopened, in his *robe de chambre* for four months. He 'passes his life with women and courtesans of the second order' with 'all the tastes and whims of an effeminate young man'. In reply to the Swedish Ambassador's brave attempt to discuss affairs of state during a meal, he delivered the *bon mot*: 'It is evident, my dear Baron, that you are not accustomed to affairs of state if you let them interfere with dinner.' There was not a little admiration in Harris's tone when he told his Court that 'you will not credit me if I tell you that out of 24 hours, Count Panin only gives half an hour to the discharge of his duties'.[13]

Initially, Potemkin 'thought only of establishing his favour well and did not occupy himself with foreign affairs in the direction of which Panin showed a predilection for the King of the Prussia', noted the Polish King Stanislas-Augustus. Now he began to flex his muscles. Early in his friendship with Catherine, it is likely that Potemkin persuaded her that Russia's interests were to maintain Peter the Great's conquests on the Baltic and keep control of Poland, but then use an Austrian alliance to make the Black Sea a Russian lake. Catherine had never liked Frederick the Great nor trusted Panin, but Potemkin was suggesting a reversal of Russian policy in turning to Austria. This had to be done slowly – but tensions with Panin began to grow. When the Council sat one day, Potemkin reported that there was news of disturbances in Persia and suggested there might be benefits for Russia. Panin, fixated on Russia's northern interests, attacked him bitterly, and an angry Potemkin broke up the meeting.[14] The rivalry between the two statesmen and their two policies became more obvious.

Panin was not going to give up without a fight, and Catherine had to move cautiously because Potemkin was as yet unproven on the international stage. Panin grew nervous as it became clear that Potemkin was there to stay. In June 1777, Corberon wrote that Panin had even said to a crony: 'Wait. Things can't stay like this for ever.' But nothing came of it as Potemkin consolidated his power. Catherine was deliberately pushing Potemkin forward on foreign policy: she had asked him to discuss affairs with the visiting Prince Henry of Prussia. When Gustavus III of Sweden, who had recently retaken absolute power in a coup, arrived on an incognito visit calling himself Count of Gothland, Potemkin met him and accompanied him during his stay. Potemkin's challenge was to destroy Panin's power, overturn the Northern System and arrange an alliance that would let him pursue his dreams in the south.

The two eastern conflicts of Europe escalated simultaneously at the beginning of 1778 – in ways that made the Prussian alliance still more obsolete and freed Potemkin's hand to begin building in the south. In both cases, Catherine and Potemkin co-ordinated diplomatic and military action.

The first was the so-called 'Potato War'. The Elector of Bavaria died in December 1777. Emperor Joseph II, whose influence was growing as his mother Maria Theresa aged, had long schemed to swap the Austrian Netherlands for Bavaria, which would increase his power in Germany and compensate for Austria's loss of Silesia to Prussia. In January 1778, Austria occupied most of Bavaria. This threatened Prussia's new Great Power status in the Holy Roman Empire, so Frederick, now aged sixty-five, rallied the German princes, threatened by Austrian aggrandizement, and in July invaded Habsburg Bohemia. Austria's ally France was busy fighting Britain and would not support Joseph. Catherine was cool about aiding her Prussian ally too. Joseph marched towards Frederick. Central Europe was at war again. But neither side dared risk a pitched battle. There was skirmishing. The men spent a cold winter digging up paltry Bohemian potatoes, the only things left to eat – hence the 'Potato War'.

Meanwhile in the Crimea, now 'independent' of Istanbul after Kuchuk-Kainardzhi, the pro-Russian Khan Shagin Giray was overthrown by his own subjects. Potemkin ordered his troops in the Crimea to restore Shagin Giray. The Turks, who had even sent an abortive expedition in August 1777 to overthrow the Khan, needed a Western ally to support them against Russia, but Austria and Prussia were busy harvesting Bohemian potatoes and France was about to join the Americans in their War of Independence.

Potemkin and Panin, secretly emerging as leaders of pro-Austrian and pro-Prussian factions, agreed with Catherine that Russia, though obliged by treaty to aid its ally Prussia, did not want a German war, which would weaken its position in the Crimea. France also did not wish these flashpoints to lead to war. Its sole aim was to prevent Britain finding a Continental ally. Thus, instead of encouraging war, France worked to reconcile the differences in both disputes. Russia offered to co-mediate with France between Prussia and Austria. In return for Catherine not helping Prussia, France agreed to mediate between Russia and the Turks.

The mediators compelled Austria to back down. Catherine and Potemkin worked together while bickering about their own relationship, her favourites and his nieces. 'Batinka,' she wrote to the Prince, 'I'll be glad to receive the plan of operations from your hands ... I'm angry with you, sir, why do you speak to me in parables?'[15] Potemkin ordered a corps under Prince Repnin to march west to help Prussia. Both sides were supposed to have offered Potemkin vast bribes. The Austrian Chancellor Kaunitz offered 'a considerable sum', Frederick the Duchy of Courland. 'Had I accepted the duchy of Courland it would not have been difficult for me to obtain the crown of Poland since the Empress might have induced the king to abdicate in my favour,' Potemkin supposedly claimed later.[16] In fact, there is no proof any money was offered or taken, especially since Frederick's meanness was legendary.*

Peace was settled at Teschen on 2/13 May 1779 with Russia as guarantor of the status quo in the Holy Roman Empire. Russia and Turkey had come to an agreement in March at the convention of Ainalikawak, which recognized the independence of the Crimea with Shagin Giray as khan. Both these successes raised Catherine's confidence and prestige in Europe.

Serenissimus welcomed Prince Henry of Prussia back to Petersburg in 1778 to shore up the tottering Prussian alliance. The Hohenzollern did his best to cultivate Potemkin, flattering him that he ranked in a triumvirate with the two senior imperial figures. Henry was touched 'by the marks of the Empress's goodwill, the Grand Duke's friendship and the attention of you, my Prince'.[17] Henry knew Potemkin well by then. But one wonders if he was amused when Potemkin unleashed his pet monkey during discussions with the Empress, who started playing with it. Catherine revelled in the Hohenzollern's astonishment. But whether Prince Henry realized it or not, these simian tricks were a sign that Potemkin was no longer interested in the Prussian alliance. Serenissimus sought any means to undermine Panin and advance his new strategy.

On 15 December 1777, Potemkin found his unwitting tool in this struggle. Sir James Harris arrived in Petersburg as the new minister

---

* Indeed, 'travailler pour le roi de Prusse' was a popular euphemism for 'working without salary'.

plenipotentiary and envoy extraordinary of the Court of St James's. Harris was a very different species of Anglo-Saxon from Potemkin's friends Semple and Kingston. He was a fine advertisement for the suave and cultured English gentleman. Now aged thirty-two, he had made his reputation in a most eighteenth-century manner while on his first posting to Madrid. When Spain and Britain almost went to war over some obscure islands called the Falklands, he should have returned home but instead he lingered twenty miles outside Madrid conducting a love affair. He was therefore uncannily well placed to react quickly and adeptly when the war did not occur. His career was made.[18]

Britain was fighting the Americans, backed by France, in their War of Independence, so Harris's instructions from the Secretary of State for the North, the Earl of Suffolk, were to negotiate an 'Offensive and Defensive Alliance' with Russia, which was to provide naval reinforcements. Harris first applied to Panin, who was not inclined to help. Learning of Potemkin's 'inveterate hatred for Monsieur de Panin',[19] he decided to cultivate Serenissimus.

On 28 June 1779, Sir James screwed up his courage and approached the Prince in the Empress's antechamber with the cheek and flattery most likely to win his attention. 'I told him the moment was now come when Russia must act the greatest part in Europe – and he alone was adequate to direct the conduct of it.' Harris had noticed Potemkin's rising interest in international relations and admired his 'very acute understanding and boundless ambition'. This was the beginning of a close friendship that confirmed Potemkin's Anglophilia[20] – but never his real commitment to an English alliance.

Sir James Harris (like his French counterparts) presumed throughout his Russian mission that Potemkin's and Catherine's prime interest was the Anglo-French struggle, not Russia's Turkish conflict. Potemkin took advantage of the deluded Anglocentricity of a Whig gentleman in the last days of Britain's first world empire. So these two scenes – the rivalry of Western diplomats and the secret dreams of Potemkin and Catherine – were played out simultaneously, side by side. The only things Potemkin really had in common with Harris were love of England and hostility towards Panin.

Serenissimus was delighted by Harris's feelers and liked the Englishman, for he impulsively invited him to dinner in his family circle at a nephew's country house. Initially, the Englishman denounced the depravity of Catherine and the 'dissipation' of Potemkin, but now he almost fell in love with the exuberance of the man he proudly called 'my friend'.[21] Harris begged Potemkin to send 'an armament', a naval expedition to help Britain, in return for some yet undecided benefit, to restore the balance of power and raise Russia's influence. The Prince seemed struck with this idea and said, 'Whom shall we trust to draw up this declaration and to whom for preparing the armament? Count Panin has neither the will nor the capacity ... he is a Prussian and nothing else; Count Chernyshev [Navy Minister] is a villain and would betray any orders given him ...'.[22]

Potemkin was also being wooed by Corberon and the new Prussian envoy, Goertz, both of whom described his extravagance, fun and whimsy. But the Prussian was particularly impressed by a man 'so superior by his genius ... that everyone collapses before him'. Harris won this contest: Serenissimus agreed to arrange a private audience with the Empress so that the Englishman could put his case directly.[23]

On 22 July 1779, Korsakov, the favourite of the day, approached Harris after Catherine had finished her card game at a masquerade and led him through the back way into the Empress's private dressing-room. Harris proposed his alliance to the Empress, who was friendly but vague. She saw that Harris's 'Armament' would embroil Russia in the Anglo-French war. Harris asked Catherine if she would give independence to America. 'I'd rather lose my head,' she replied vehemently. The next day, Harris delivered a memorandum, putting his case, to Potemkin.[24]

Potemkin's rivalry with Panin, seemed to work to Harris's advantage – yet it should have made him cautious. When the Council met to discuss the British proposals, Catherine through the Prince asked Harris to produce another memorandum. When they talked about Panin's conduct, Potemkin bamboozled the Englishman by claiming that 'he had been so little conversant in foreign affairs that a great deal of what I said was entirely new to him'. But there was no quicker student than Potemkin.

The Prince and Sir James spent their days and nights chatting, drinking, plotting and gambling. Potemkin may have been playing Harris like a game of poker, but he was also truly fond of him. One has the distinct sense that, while Harris was talking business, Potemkin was taking a course in English civilization. Couriers rushed between the two. Harris's published letters give his official account of the friendship, but his unpublished letters to Potemkin in the Russian archives show the extent of their familiarity: one is about a wardrobe that one of Harris's debtors gave him instead of the 1,500 guineas he was owed. 'You'd give me incontestable proof of your friendship', wrote the Envoy Extraordinary, 'if you could get the Empress to buy it ... Forgive me for talking to you so frankly ...'. It is not recorded if Potemkin arranged this, but he was a generous friend. In May 1780, Harris sent his father, a respected Classical scholar, a 'packet of Greek productions given to me for you by Prince Potemkin'. When Harris's father died, Potemkin was assiduous in his sympathy. In an undated note, the envoy thanked him: 'I'm not yet in a state to come round to your place my Prince but the part you've been kind enough to play in my sadness has softened it infinitely ... No one could love you, esteem you, respect you more than I.'[25]

When they met in the Winter Palace, Potemkin pulled Harris into the Empress's private apartments as if they were his own and the two chatted there all evening.[26] They obviously caroused together. 'I gave a *soupe dansant* about three weeks ago to Prince Potemkin and his set,' Harris told his sister Gertrude in 1780, at which they drank 'three bottles of the King of Poland's tokay and a dozen of claret and champagne'. Harris claimed he drank only water.

This Anglo-Russian friendship intensified the diplomatic intrigue in Petersburg as the other diplomats frantically watched, eavesdropped and bribed to discover what they were talking about. The surveillance and espionage was so obvious it must have been comical, and we can almost hear the rustle of curtains and the flicker of eyes at keyholes. The French were most alarmed. Corberon was reduced to spying constantly on Potemkin's various houses: he noted down that Harris had a tent in his garden 'seating ten' that he claimed was a gift from Potemkin. Catherine's doctor, Rogerson, was definitely 'Harris's spy'. Corberon even called on Potemkin to accuse him of enmity towards France. He then 'took from his pocket a paper from which he read a list of the several times' Harris had been seen socializing with Potemkin. The Prince abruptly ended this otiose conversation by saying he was busy. Harris probably heard about this encounter from his spy, the Prince's omnipresent niece–mistress, Alexandra. The Englishman became so close to her that Corberon accused him of courting. The Prussians were also watching. 'For a month, the table and house of the British Ambassador are filled with the relations and creatures of the favourite,' Goertz told Frederick on 21 September 1779.[27]

This elegant skulduggery reached a new low when Harris delivered his second memorandum to Potemkin, who was said to have languidly placed it in his dressing-gown pocket or 'under his pillow'. Somehow, it was removed and given to the French chargé, Corberon, and thence to Panin. The Chevalier de la Teyssonière, *basse-cour* hanger-on, played some part, but it was another Frenchwoman, a mistress of the Prince and a governess of his nieces, Mademoiselle Guibald, who actually stole the document. It was later claimed that Panin then added notes contradicting the British arguments and left it on Catherine's desk so that she would believe the notes were Potemkin's advice. This is obviously designed to give Potemkin's house a disorderly air, hence most historians have dismissed it, and Guibald, as legends. Catherine would certainly have known Potemkin's handwriting and views, making the notes an unlikely detail. But Teyssonière was certainly skulking around Potemkin's Court and Tatania Engelhardt's letters to her uncle reveal that Miss Guibald did exist. Besides, virtually every member of Potemkin's household would have been receiving bribes from somebody, which is probably why Guibald was not dismissed. She remained in Potemkin's household for years after. The story may have some truth after all.[28]

Serenissimus did not spend all his time with Harris. In the midst of this intrigue, a European phenomenon arrived in Petersburg. The *soi-disant* Count Alessandro di Cagliostro, accompanied by a pretty wife and posing as a Spanish colonel, set up shop as a healer, purveyor of the Egyptian Masonic rite, alchemist, magus and necromancer. The famous charlatan's real name was probably Giuseppe Balsamo of Sicily, but this squat, swarthy and balding Sicilian with black eyes and a throbbing forehead clearly possessed plenty of *chutzpah* and charisma.

The Age of Reason had undermined Religion, but there was a natural yearning for spirituality to fill the void. This was one reason for the fashion for Freemasonry, manifested in both rationalist and occult varieties. The latter spread rapidly in all its esoteric diversity – hypnotism, necromancy, alchemy, Kabbalism, preached in cults such as Martinism, Illuminism, Rosicrucianism and Swedenborgism. These ideas were propagated through Masonic lodges and by a remarkable series of healers and charlatans. Some like Swedenborg, Mesmer and Lavater were magi whose knowledge of human nature, if not healing powers, helped people in an era when doctors and scientists could explain little.[29] Many were just charlatans like the lover Casanova and the notorious George Psalmanazar, travelling Europe deceiving innocent noblemen with their tales of the Philosopher's Stone and the Fountain of Youth. They always presented themselves as exotically titled men of wealth, taste and mystery. Each offered an enticing mixture of common sense, practical medical advice, promises of eternal youth, guides to the after-life – and the ability to convert base metals, and even urine, into gold.

Their doyen, the so-called Comte de Saint-Germain, who claimed to be almost two thousand years old and to have witnessed the Crucifixion in his youth (his valet remembered it too), impressed Louis XV by creating, out of ether, a diamond worth 10,000 livres. A substantial chunk of Europe's aristocracy at this time was somehow involved in these cults of Freemasonry.

Cagliostro had dazzled Mittau, capital of Courland, but he then had to leave swiftly. Now he hoped to reproduce his success in Petersburg. As Catherine told Grimm, the hierophant 'came at a good moment for him when several Masonic lodges wanted to see spirits ...'. The 'master sorcerer' duly provided as many as required, along with all sorts of tricks involving disappearing money, sales of mysterious potions and 'chemical operations that don't work'. She especially laughed at his claim to be able to create gold out of urine and offer eternal life.

Nonetheless Cagliostro conducted healings and won a distinguished following for his Egyptian Masonic rite. Corberon and courtiers like Ivan Yelagin and Count Alexander Stroganov ardently subscribed to the necromancer's powers. Many Russian nobles joined Masonic lodges. Some gradually evolved into something like an anti-Catherinian opposition, which explained her deep suspicion of Freemasonry.

Potemkin attended some of Cagliostro's seances but never believed in them, remaining one of the few senior courtiers who did not become a Mason. He and Catherine thoroughly enjoyed joking about Cagliostro's tricks.[30] Potemkin's real interest was in Countess Cagliostro. Serenissimus is said to have enjoyed an affair with the hierophant's wife, born Lorenza, renamed Serafina and sometimes calling herself Princess di Santa Croce. This may have damaged Cagliostro more than he realized. Catherine teased Potemkin about the time he spent at their house: perhaps he should learn to keep Cagliostro's spirits in check ... Did she mean the ersatz Princess–Countess?[31]

So often did he call on Cagliostro's luxurious, indebted establishment that, according to legend, one of Potemkin's highborn Russian mistresses decided to bribe the adventuress to give him up. In one of those poignant, almost respectful meetings between noblewoman and courtesan, the former paid Serafina 30,000 roubles, quite a sum, to leave. Potemkin was flattered. He told Cagliostro's girl that she could stay, let her keep the money – and paid back the full amount to the noblewoman. Some silly legends[32] claim that the 'noblewoman' was the Empress herself.

Debts and truth had a way of catching up with such characters, even in that louche century. Soon afterwards, the Spanish Ambassador complained that Cagliostro was neither grandee of Spain nor colonel.

Catherine cheerfully told Grimm that the sorcerer and his 'Countess' had been thrown out of Russia.*

When Panin summoned Harris in early February 1780 to read him a rejection of the British proposals for an alliance, Sir James rushed over to Potemkin to learn the reasons. Potemkin clearly (for once) stated that Catherine's fear of 'embarking on a fresh war was stronger even than her thirst for glory'. Harris did not seem to hear. Potemkin explained that the new favourite, Lanskoy, was desperately ill, which had 'unhinged' the Empress. Sir James believed him when he claimed: 'My influence is temporarily suspended.' Harris criticized these 'timid resolutions', at which 'The Prince caught fire' and boasted that before he slept he 'would have a trial of skill whether there was in the empire any influence more powerful than his'. Harris was most encouraged, but typically Potemkin became ill and did not receive him again for weeks.

Serenissimus then confided in the credulous Englishman that the Empress was an over-cautious woman capable of feminine hysteria about her *mignons*. Potemkin himself alternated between expressions of political impotence and explosions of bombast. He attacked Panin, that 'indolent and torpid minister' – while himself lying in bed in the middle of the day. Harris was almost bewitched by Potemkin's friendship, flamboyance and apparent honesty.[33]

In February 1780, Serenissimus summoned Harris to announce, 'with an impetuous joy analogous to his character', the despatch of an armament of fifteen ships-of-the-line and five frigates 'to protect Russian trade'. But Potemkin must have known that this was a fatal blow to Harris's entire mission.[34] It was the sequel to Catherine's successful mediation in the War of the Bavarian Succession. Britain claimed the right to detain neutral ships and condemn their cargo, but had made the mistake of detaining Russian ships. This maritime highhandedness angered neutrals, including Russia. In March 1780, Catherine therefore declared the principles of neutral rights at sea in her so-called 'Armed Neutrality', designed to puncture British arrogance, increase the Russian

* After Petersburg, Cagliostro toured Europe, causing a sensation everywhere, more like a pop star than a magus, but in Paris he became involved, through his patron the Cardinal de Rohan, in the Diamond Necklace Affair, the sting which so damaged Marie-Antoinette. Napoleon named it as one of the causes of the French Revolution. Cagliostro was actually found innocent in the trial that Marie-Antoinette so foolishly demanded and Louis XVI so rashly allowed, but he was ruined. He died a prisoner in 1795 in the Italian Papal fortress of San Leone.

merchant navy and raise her prestige. Harris would have to offer more to get Russian attention.

Sir James wondered if Potemkin had been bribed by France or Prussia. At the same time, the French and Prussians suddenly thought Potemkin had been bribed by the English. This venal paranoia unleashed an orgy of bribery which must have seemed like manna from heaven to the greedy servants of Petersburg who were its main beneficiaries.

Harris was sure Corberon had bribed all the '*valets de chambre* and inferior agents in the Russian houses ... being chiefly French'. Versailles was indeed determined to keep Russia out of the war and it was willing to throw money around St Petersburg to fix it – the French even boasted they had enough to buy Potemkin.[35] 'I almost suspect my friend's fidelity has been shaken,' Harris confided to Viscount Stormont, Secretary of State for the North. Corberon was already telling Versailles that Harris disposed of a credit of £36,000 and had paid 100,000 roubles to Potemkin. Orlov-Chesmensky accused the Prince of receiving 150,000 British guineas. Harris thought France was paying £4,000/5,000 to Panin's family.

At the end of March 1780, Harris could contain himself no longer. If the French were bribing 'my friend', then Britain should outbid them with a 'similar bait'. The bribe market in St Petersburg now boomed like a bourse. Reminding Stormont that he was dealing with a 'person immensely wealthy', Harris suggested 'as much as Torcy proposed, but without success, to Marlborough'.[36] Even the paymaster of Europe must have gulped.* The Prussians and Austrians were also paying court to Potemkin. Harris observed the Prussian envoy in daily conferences with Potemkin and heard he was again offering Courland or 'to insure him in the case of the Empress's demise for his person, honours and property' – that is, in the event of Paul's succession. The Austrians on the other hand were rumoured to be offering him another principality.[37]

Was Potemkin being bribed or not? The elephantine sums of 100,000 roubles or 150,000 guineas were mentioned in late 1779, but research into 'the Secret Service Funds' shows that, by November, Harris had drawn only £1,450 and was later told off for spending £3,000. Even put together, this might have pleased Sashenka Engelhardt, but was not even table money for the Prince himself. Harris's doubts 'disappeared' – he

---

* Stormont would have known that this was the positively imperial sum of two million francs. Louis XIV's minister at the Hague offered the century's most famous bribe to Marlborough in May 1709.

realized that Potemkin's 'immense fortune places him above the reach of corruption'. Rich men can often be bribed with a little bit more, but Harris was probably right when he said that Potemkin could 'only be attained by strict attention to his humour and character'. This was emphasized when Catherine gave her friend £40,000 sterling, according to Harris, to thank him for his help on the Armed Neutrality. It was a huge sum, but 'so spoilt is this singular man that he scarcely considers it worth thanks'. The Prussian Goertz agreed that Potemkin was unbribable: 'riches can do nothing – his are immense'.

Panin put all these figures into context when he disdainfully asked, 'Do you really believe that £50,000 sterling is enough to buy Prince Potemkin?' When Potemkin heard the rumour that Harris had given him two million roubles, he despised the very idea. The Englishman was convinced of Potemkin's nobility. Serenissimus was too proud and too rich to be bribed.[38]

Potemkin's tactics were telling on Panin. Both believed the other was receiving bribes. This led to a tumultuous confrontation at the Council when Potemkin accused Panin of accepting French money or, as he put it, 'the portraits of Louis XVI' are excellent to 'bet at whist'. Panin exploded that if he needed them, guineas were easier to get. Presumably Panin believed Potemkin was getting more than that laughable £50,000. The Empress was called to restore the peace.[39]

Harris decided to find out if Serenissimus really supported an English alliance, so he bribed 'the favourite secretary of Prince Potemkin … also the secretary to the Empress'. This was probably Alexander Bezborodko, who was becoming Catherine's leading factotum in foreign affairs as Panin dwindled. Stormont agreed on the offer of £500, though he added that it was rather a lot. When it came to it, Harris was fleeced of nearer £3,000, though he did get closer to the reality of Potemkin's policy. Bezborodko revealed that the monarchs of Europe, from Frederick to Joseph, were bombarding Potemkin with offers of thrones and money. No offer swayed him. He was not really zealous in the English cause, except when roused by rivalry with Panin. The 'spy' added that Potemkin lived by the 'impulse of the moment' and was quite capable of 'adopting the political principles of every country' but was keenest at that moment on Austria. There, at last, was the truth.[40]

The diplomats had already heard Potemkin talking about real plans in the south. Even when discussing English fleets, Harris observed that Potemkin's 'mind is continually occupied with the idea of raising an Empire in the East' and it was he 'alone who heated and animated the Empress for this project'.[41] Catherine was indeed infected with

Potemkin's exciting visions. When she talked to Harris, she 'discoursed a long while ... on the ancient Greeks, of their alacrity and superiority ... and the same character being extant in the modern ones'.[42] Corberon, who had heard it too, did not exaggerate when he wrote that 'romantic ideas here are adopted with a fury'.[43] But the diplomats did not understand the significance of Potemkin's 'romantic ideas' – his 'Greek Project' – that so excited Catherine. Serenissimus' mind was not on London, Paris, Berlin or Philadelphia. It was on Tsargrad, the city of emperors – Constantinople. The dismemberment of the Ottoman Empire was to be the dominating theme of the rest of his life and the foundation of his greatness.

Part Five

❧

THE COLOSSUS
1777–1783

14

BYZANTIUM

I was asked to a fête which Prince Potemkin gave in his orangery
... Before the door was a little temple consecrated to
Friendship which contained a bust of the Empress ... Where
the Empress supped was furnished in Peking, beautifully
painted to resemble a tent ... it only held five or six ... Another
little room was furnished with a sofa for two, embroidered and
stuffed by the Empress herself.
Chevalier de Corberon, 20 March 1779

When the Ottoman Sultan, Mehmed II, took Constantinople in 1453, he rode through the streets directly to the Emperor Justinian's remarkable Church of Hagia Sophia. Before this massive tribute to Christianity, he sprinkled earth on his head to symbolize his humility before God and then entered. Inside, his sharp eyes spotted a Turkish soldier looting marble. The Sultan demanded an explanation. 'For the sake of the Faith,' replied the soldier. Mehmed slew him with his sword: 'For you the treasures and the prisoners are enough,' he decreed. 'The buildings of the city fall to me.' The Ottomans had not conquered Byzantium to lose the greatness of Constantine.

Mehmed was now able to add Kaiser-i-Rum – Caesar of Rome – to his titles of Turkish Khan, Arabic Sultan and Persian Padi-shah. To Westerners, he was not only the Grand Seigneur or the Great Turk – henceforth he was often called Emperor. From that day on, the Ottoman House embraced the prestige of Byzantium. 'No one doubts that you are the Emperor of the Romans,' George Trapezountios, the Cretan historian, told Mehmed the Conqueror in 1466. 'Whoever is legally master of the capital of the Empire is the Emperor and Constantinople is the capital of the Roman Empire ... And he who is and remains Emperor of the Romans is also Emperor of the whole earth.'[1] It was to this prize that Potemkin and Catherine now turned their attention.

The Ottoman Empire stretched from Baghdad to Belgrade and from the Crimea to Cairo and included much of south-eastern Europe – Bulgaria, Rumania, Albania, Greece, Yugoslavia. It boasted the cream of Islam's Holy Cities from Damascus and Jerusalem to the Holy Places themselves, Mecca and Medina. The Black Sea was for centuries its 'pure and immaculate virgin', the Sultan's private lake, while even the Mediterranean shores were still dominated by his ports, from Cyprus all the way to Algiers and Tunis. So it was indeed an international empire. But it was wrongly called a Turkish one. Usually the only Turkish leader in its carefully calibrated hierarchy was the Sultan himself. Ironically, the so-called Turkish Empire was a self-consciously multinational state that was built by the renegade Orthodox Slavs of the Balkans who filled the top echelons of Court, bureaucracy and the Janissaries, the Praetorian Guards of Istanbul.

There was little concept of class: while the Western knights were tying themselves in knots of noble genealogy, the Ottoman Empire was a meritocracy which was ruled in the Sultan's name by the sons of Albanian peasants. All that mattered was that everyone, even the grand viziers themselves, were slaves of the Sultan, who *was* the state. Until the mid-sixteenth century, the sultans were a talented succession of ruthless, energetic leaders. But they were to be victims of their own Greek Project, for gradually the dirty business of ruling was conducted by their chief minister, the grand vizier, while they were sanctified by the suffocatingly elaborate ritual of the Byzantine emperors. Indeed when the French soldier Baron de Tott witnessed the coronation of Mustafa III in 1755, he recalled how the Sultan, surrounded by Roman plumage and even *fasces*, was literally dwarfed by the magnificence of his own importance. Based on the tenth-century order of ceremonies compiled by Constantine Porphyrogenitus, the blessing and curse of the Byzantines was to turn the Ottoman sultans from dynamic conquerors astride steeds at the head of armies to limp-wristed fops astride odalisques at the head of phalanxes of eunuchs. This was not all the fault of the Greek tradition.

At first there was no law of succession, which often meant accessions were celebrated with royal massacres. The new emperor would cull his brothers – sometimes as many as nineteen of them – by strangulation with a bowstring, a polite despatch that shed no imperial blood. Finally a sense of royal ecology stopped this foolish waste. Instead Ottoman princes were kept, like luxurious prisoners in the Cage, half embalmed by pleasure, half educated by neglect, half dead from fear of the bowstring. When they emerged into the light, like bleary-eyed startled animals, new sultans were terrified, until reassured by the corpses of their predecessors.

The whole state became a rigidly stratified hierarchy with the grand vizier, often of Slavic origin, at the top, with a household of 2,000 and a guard of 500 Albanians. Each top official, each pasha (literally 'the Sultan's foot'), displayed his rank in terms of horses' tails, a relic of the House of Othman's nomadic origins. The grand vizier displayed five;

lesser pashas between one and three. Viziers wore green slippers and turbans, chamberlains red, mullahs blue. The heads and feet of the Ottomans marked their rank as clearly as pips on an epaulette. Officials wore green, palace courtiers red. All the nationalities of the Empire wore the correct slippers: Greeks in black, Armenians in violet, Jews in blue. As for hats, the powers of the Empire were celebrated atop heads in a fiesta of bonnets crested with furs and feathers.

The sultan dwelt in a palace built on the Seraglio Point, appropriately on the Byzantine Acropolis. In Turkish style, the palace was a progression of increasingly rarefied courtyards, leading into the imperial Seraglio through a series of gateways. These gates, where Turkic justice was traditionally dispensed, thus became the visible symbols of Ottoman government. That is why it was known in the West as the Sublime Porte.

The lusts of the emperors were encouraged in order to deliver a rich reservoir of male heirs. Thus if the sultans looked for quality, the logic of the Harem demanded quantity. Incidentally, the eunuchs who ran the Court were apparently capable of sexual congress, merely being bereft of the means to procreate – so that they too had the run of the Harem. Just as the Palace School, which trained imperial pages who rose to run the Empire, was filled with Albanians and Serbs, so the Harem, which produced imperial heirs to rule the Empire, was filled with blonde-haired and blue-eyed Slav girls from the slave-markets of the Crimea. Until the late seventeenth century, the lingua franca of the court was, bizarrely, Serbo-Croat.

The Ottoman Sultanate was dying by strangulation – not by bow-string, but by tradition. By Potemkin's era, the sultans were constricted not just by Byzantinism but by a religious fundamentalism imposed by the Islamic court, the *ulema*, and by political conservatism enforced by the vested interests of court and military.

The Empire was ruled by fear and force. The sultan still had power over life and death and he used it liberally. Instant death was part of the Court's exquisite etiquette. Many grand viziers are more famous for being killed than for ruling. They were beheaded at such a rate that, despite the riches the position brought, it is surprising there were so many candidates for the job. Sultan Selim killed seven in one reign so that 'Mayest thou be Selim's vizier' came to mean 'Strike you dead!' in the vernacular. Viziers always carried their wills with them if summoned by the sultan. During Potemkin's coming war against the Turks, 60 per cent of the viziers were executed.

The sultan's death sentences, signified by a slight stamp of the foot in the throne room or the opening of a particular latticed window, were usually executed by the dreaded mutes, who could despatch with string or axe. The display of heads was part of the ritual of Ottoman death. The heads of top officials were placed on white marble pillars in the palace. Important heads were stuffed with cotton; middling heads with straw. More minor heads were displayed in niches while heaps of human giblets, noses and tongues, beautified the palace locale. Female victims, sometimes the gorgeous losers of the Harem, were sewn into sacks and tossed into the Bosphorus.[2]

The most direct threat to a sultan was the Janissaries of his own army, and the mob. Constantinople's people had always been a rule unto themselves, even under Justinian. Now the riffraff of Istanbul, manipulated by the Janissaries or the *ulema*, increasingly decreed policy. Potemkin's agent Pisani reported throughout the 1780s how viziers and others 'animated the *canaille*' to 'intimidate their Sovereign' by 'committing all sorts of excess.'[3]

Command was abysmal, discipline laughable and corruption endemic. The failure of command began at the top: in 1774, Abdul-Hamid I had succeeded the abler Mustafa III after being immured for forty-three years in the Cage. This gentle and frightened man was not equipped to be warlord or reformer, though he did rise to the occasion by fathering twenty-two children before his death.* He tippled wine and liked to say that, if he became an infidel, he would embrace Roman Catholic communion because the best wines grew in their countries: whoever heard of a Protestant wine? This plodding wit did not improve the discipline of his forces.

When Tott was forming a corps of artillery, he demanded an honest man to manage its funds. 'An honest man,' replied the Vizier. 'Where shall we find him? As for me I know none.' The Vizier turned at length to his Foreign Minister: 'And you? Can you name us an honest man?' 'Less than anybody,' laughed the Reis Effendi. 'I'm only acquainted with rogues.'[4] The intellectual power of the Ottoman Government had also atrophied: the ignorance of Ottoman officials was a diplomatic joke. At the Congress of Sistova, one Turkish negotiator thought Spain was in Africa; the Reis Effendi, the Foreign Minister of an international empire, thought warships could not sail the Baltic; and all of them believed that Gibraltar was in England.[5]

The Empire could no longer depend on its military power. The Ottomans solved this problem by becoming a European power like any other.

* One, who later reigned as Mahmud II, was supposedly the son of that favourite odalisque, Aimée Dubucq de Rivery, cousin of the future Empress Josephine.

Indeed they turned Clausewitz's dictum on its head: while, for most powers, war was diplomacy by other means, diplomacy, for the Ottomans, was war by other means. The rise of Russia had changed Ottoman priorities. Russia's potential enemies – France, Prussia, Sweden and Poland – became the four potential allies of the Sublime Porte. The game was simple: each offered subsidies to the Porte to attack Russia. None of these powers would sit by while Russia consumed the Turks.

The Empire was, according to one of Potemkin's envoys, 'like an ageing beauty who could not realize her time was past'. But it still possessed vast military resources, in terms of men, and fanatical spirit, in its Islamic faith. Ruled by the bowstring, the green slipper and the *canaille* of Constantinople, the Empire in 1780 was more like a leprous giant whose Brobdingnagian limbs were still awesome even as they gradually fell off its colossal body.[6]

On 27 April 1779, Grand Duchess Maria Fyodorovna gave birth to a son, whom Catherine and Potemkin named Constantine and designated to become emperor of Constantinople after the destruction of the Sublime Porte. The Grand Duchess had already produced an heir to the Russian Empire two years earlier – Catherine's first grandson, Grand Duke Alexander. Now she produced the Heir to the Byzantine Empire of the Greeks.

Using Classical history, Eastern Orthodoxy and his own romantic imagination, Potemkin now created a cultural programme, a geopolitical system and a propaganda campaign all in one: the 'Greek Project' to conquer Constantinople and place Grand Duke Constantine on its throne. Catherine hired Constantine a Greek nurse named Helen and insisted that he should be taught Greek.[7] Potemkin personally contributed to the Greek education of the Grand Dukes right through the 1780s. 'I should like to remind you', he wrote to the Empress about changing Alexander and Constantine's lessons, 'that in learning languages, the Greek one should be most capital as it is the basis of the others ... Where you mentioned reading the Gospel in Latin, the Greek language would be more appropriate as it was the language of the original.' Catherine wrote at the bottom: 'Change according to this.'[8]

We do not know exactly when the partners began to discuss Classical greatness and Byzantine restoration, but it was obviously at the very beginning of their relationship (when Catherine teased him as her 'giaour' – the Turkish name for an infidel). Catherine must have been impressed with the Project's odd mixture of imagination, history and practicality. Serenissimus was made for his Greek Project just as it was made for him. He was knowledgeable about the history and theology of Byzantine Orthodoxy. Catherine and Potemkin, like most educated people of their time, were brought up on the Classics, from Tacitus to Plutarch – hence Potemkin's nickname Alcibiades – though he read Greek and she did not. He often had his readers recite the Classical historians, and his libraries contained most of them. The Classical enthusiasts of the eighteenth century did not just read about ancient times: they wished to emulate them. They built like the Greeks and the Romans.* Now Potemkin was also making himself an expert on the Ottoman Empire.

The idea itself was not new: Muscovite propaganda had promoted Russia as the 'Third Rome' ever since the Fall of Constantinople, which Russians still called Tsargrad, city of Caesars. In 1472, the Grand Duke of Muscovy, Ivan III, married the last Emperor's niece, Zoë Palaelogina. His Metropolitan hailed him as the 'new Emperor of the new Constantinople – Moscow' and he used the title Tsar (Caesar), which Ivan the Terrible adopted. In the next century, Filofey, a monk, pointed out that 'two Romes have fallen, but the third stands and there will be no fourth'.[9] But the neo-Classical splendour, the daring symmetry of religion, culture and politics, the practicality of the Austrian alliance, and the specific plan of a partition, belong to Potemkin. His talent was not merely the impulsive conception of ideas but also the patience and instinct to make them real: he had been following this Byzantine rainbow ever since coming to power and it had taken him six years to circumvent the pro-Russian Panin.

As early as 1775, when Catherine and Potemkin celebrated the Turkish peace in Moscow, the Prince had befriended the Greek monk Eugenios Voulgaris, who would supply the Orthodox theology for the Greek Project. On 9 September 1775, Catherine appointed Voulgaris, on Potemkin's suggestion, as the first archbishop of Kherson and Slaviansk. These cities did not yet exist. Kherson, named after the ancient Greek city of Khersonesos and the birthplace of Russian Orthodoxy, was merely a Greek name in the fevered imagination of Potemkin.

Catherine's decree appointing the Archbishop proclaimed the dubiously Greek origins of Russian Orthodoxy, a piece probably written by Potemkin. One of his first acts on becoming favourite was to found a Greek gymnasium. He now appointed Voulgaris to direct it. Potemkin tried to get his Greek Archbishop to be his 'Hesiod, Strabo Chrysostomos' and write a history of the region, 'dig up the hidden past . . .' and show the link between the Ancient Scythians and the Graeco-Slavs.

---

* Even Potemkin's valet, Zakhar Constantinov, was a Greek.

Voulgaris never wrote the history, but he did translate Virgil's *Georgics* and dedicated the work to Potemkin, 'most high and eminent phil-hellenic prince', along with an ode to his new Athens on the Dnieper that ended: 'Here once again is to be seen the former Greece; Thou, famous Prince, be indeed victorious.'[10] All this was just part of Potemkin's philhellenic programme to form a Greek civilization in a new Byzantine Empire around the Black Sea.

The genesis of the Greek Project is a window into the way the Empress and the Prince worked together. Catherine's rising secretary Alexander Bezborodko actually drafted the 'Note on Political Affairs' in 1780 that laid out the Project and it has been claimed that he conceived the idea. This is to misunderstand the relationship of the troika that henceforth made Russian foreign policy.

Potemkin conceived the Greek Project almost before Bezborodko arrived in Petersburg, as shown in his letters and conversation, his patronage of Voulgaris, the naming of Constantine and the foundation of Kherson in 1778. Bezborodko's 'Note' was a feasibility study of the idea, based on an explanation of Byzantine–Ottoman–Russian relations since the mid-tenth century, clearly commissioned by Catherine and Potemkin. Bezborodko's draft of the Austrian treaty of 1781 reveals how they worked: the secretary drafted on the right hand side of the page. Then Potemkin corrected it on the left in pencil, which he addressed to Catherine. From now on, Potemkin conceived the ideas and Bezborodko drafted them. Thus, on the Prince's death, Bezborodko was speaking the literal truth when he said that Potemkin was good at 'thinking up ideas when someone else had actually to do them'.[11]

Bezborodko was an 'awkward, clownish and negligent' Ukrainian hobbledehoy with thick lips and popping eyes who blundered about, his stockings about his heels, with the gait of an elephant. However, as Ségur realized, he 'concealed the most delicate mind in the most oafish envelope'. He was said to relish regular orgies in the Petersburg brothel district. Indeed he often disappeared for thirty-six hours at a time. Italian opera-singers imported young Italian girls for his seraglio; he paid a soprano, Davia, 8,000 roubles a month which she repaid by cuckolding him with anyone she could find. 'Though richly dressed, he always appeared as if he had pulled on his clothes at the end of an orgy,' which he probably had.

Once he arrived home drunk to find an urgent summons from the Empress. At the Palace, Catherine demanded a document she had been promised. The factotum took out a piece of paper and read out the exquisitely drafted *ukase*. Catherine thanked him and asked him for the manuscript. He handed her the blank piece of paper and fell to his knees. Bezborodko had forgotten to write it, but she forgave him for his improvisation. He was an independent and outstandingly precise and sensitive intelligence who began as Potemkin's protégé and became his political ally, even though he was friends with enemies like the Vorontsovs. The gratitude in his letters for Potemkin's patronage showed that the Prince was always by far the senior partner.[12] 'He keeps treating me very well,' he wrote to a friend, 'and . . . I deserve it because very often I spend as much time on his private affairs as I do on European ones.'[13]

Serenissimus worked with Catherine's ministers, such as Procurator-General Viazemsky and President of the College of Commerce Alexander Vorontsov (Simon's brother). Potemkin, famed for his subtle political intrigues, disdained conventional Court politics: he regarded the ministers, particularly Vorontsov, 'with the greatest contempt' and he told Harris that 'even if he could get rid of them, he did not see anybody better to put in their places'.[14] Bezborodko was the only one he seemed to respect. Potemkin proudly told Catherine that he never tried to build a party in Petersburg. He regarded himself as a royal consort, not a jobbing politician or a mere favourite. The only other member of *his* party was Catherine.

The first step towards the Greek Project was a *détente* with Austria. Both sides had been moving in this direction for some time and making encouraging diplomatic signals. The Holy Roman Emperor and co-ruler of the Habsburg Monarchy, Joseph II, never gave up on the Bavarian scheme that had led to the Potato War. He realized he needed Potemkin and Catherine to win Bavaria, which would make his Habsburg lands more compact and coherent. To this end, Joseph had to coax Russia away from Panin's cherished alliance with Prussia. If, in the process, he could increase his realm at the expense of the Ottoman Empire, so much the better. All roads led to Petersburg.

Joseph and his mother Maria Theresa had for years regarded Catherine as a nymphomaniacal regicide whom they called 'The Catherinized Princess of Zerbst'. Now Joseph weighed up a Russian alliance over his mother's opposition. His instincts were backed by his Chancellor, Prince Wenzel von Kaunitz-Rietberg, who had engineered the Diplomatic Revolution of 1756 to ally Austria with its old enemy France. Kaunitz was a vain, cold-hearted and libidinous neurotic who was so afraid of illness that he made Maria Theresa close her windows. His elaborate teeth-cleaning exercises at the end of each meal were the most disgusting feature of public life in Vienna. Kaunitz made sure that Austria's envoy in Petersburg, Cobenzl, took care 'to place relations with Monsieur de Potemkin on the footing of good friendship ... Tell me how you are getting on with him now.'[15]

On 22 January 1780, Joseph sent a message to Catherine, through her envoy in Vienna, Prince Dmitri Golitsyn, that he would like to meet her. The timing was ideal. She agreed on 4 February, informing only Potemkin, Bezborodko and a discontented Nikita Panin. It was set for 27 May in Mogilev in Belorussia.[16]

Empress and Prince keenly anticipated this meeting. Between February and April, they discussed it back and forth. The tension told on both of them. They calmed each other like a married couple and then exulted in their schemes like a pair of conspirators. Some time in April, Catherine's lover Lanskoy told her that the sensitive Potemkin's 'soul is full of anxieties'. Probably he was worrying about the array of intrigues against his southern plans, but she soothed him with her 'true friendship that you will always find in my heart ... and in the heart attached to mine, [that is, Lanskoy's], who loves and respects you as much as I do'. She ended tenderly: 'Our only sorrow concerns you, that you're anxious.' Potemkin snapped at poor little Lanskoy, who ran to Catherine. She was concerned that her favourite had irritated the Prince: 'Please let me know if Alexander Dmitrievich [Lanskoy] annoyed you somehow and if you are angry with him and why exactly.' There were even hints of the old days when they were lovers, though perhaps they were just discussing their plans: 'My dear friend, I've finished dinner and the door of the little staircase is open. If you want to talk to me, you may come.'

At the end of April, Serenissimus rode off to prepare the reception for the Tsarina and the Holy Roman Emperor – in Mogilev. It was his policy, and Catherine gave him the responsibility to set the scene. As soon as he departed, Catherine missed her consort. 'I'm without my friend, my Prince,' she wrote to him. Excited letters flew between them. On 9 May 1780, Catherine left Tsarskoe Selo with a suite that included the nieces Alexandra and Ekaterina Engelhardt, and Bezborodko. Nikita Panin was left behind. As the Emperor Joseph arrived in Mogilev to be greeted by Potemkin, Catherine was approaching on the road from Petersburg. She and her consort were still discussing the last-minute details of the meeting and missing each other. 'If you find a better way, please let me know,' she wrote about her schedule – then she signed off: 'Goodbye my friend, we are sick at heart without you. I'm dying to see you as soon as possible.'[17]

15

THE HOLY ROMAN EMPEROR

Is it not you who dared raise up
The power of Russia, Catherine's spirit
And with support of both desired
To carry thunder to those rapids
On which the ancient Rome did stand
And trembled all the universe?

Gavrili Derzhavin, *The Waterfall*

On 21 May 1780, Prince Potemkin welcomed Emperor Joseph II, travelling under the incognito of Comte de Falkenstein, to Russia. It is hard to imagine two more different and ill-suited men. The uptight, self-regarding Austrian martinet wished to discuss politics immediately, while the Prince insisted on taking him off to the Orthodox Church. 'Just up to now, commonplaces have been all the conversation with Potemkin and he hasn't uttered a word of politics,' the Emperor, thirty-nine, balding, oval-faced and quite handsome for a Habsburg, grumbled to his disapproving mother, the Empress–Queen Maria Theresa. Joseph's impatience did not matter because Catherine was only a day away. The Emperor continued to chomp at the bit – but Potemkin displayed only an enigmatic affability: this was a deliberate political manoeuvre to let Joseph come to him. No one knew what Potemkin and Catherine were planning, but Frederick the Great and the Ottoman Sultan observed the meeting with foreboding, since it was aimed primarily at them.

The Prince handed the Emperor a letter from Catherine which plainly revealed her hopes: 'I swear at this moment there is nothing more difficult than to hide my sentiments of joy. The very name Monsieur le Comte de Falkenstein inspires such confidence . . .' Potemkin recounted his impressions of Joseph to Catherine, and the partners impatiently discussed their meaning. The Prince passed on Joseph's extravagant compliments about the Empress. The spirit of their unique partnership is captured in Catherine's letter when she was just a day away: 'Tomorrow I hope to be with you, everyone is missing you . . . We'll try to figure out Falk[enstein] together.'[2]

This was easier said than done: the Emperor's awkward character baffled contemporaries – and historians. No one so represented the incongruities of the Enlightened despot: Joseph was an uncomfortable cross between an expansionist and militaristic autocrat and a *philosophe* who wished to liberate his people from the superstitions of the past. He thought he was a military genius and philosopher–king like his hero Frederick the Great (the enemy who had almost destroyed Joseph's own inheritance). Joseph's ideals were admirable, but he despised his fellow man, was tactless and lacked all conception that politics was the art of the possible. His over-strenuous doctrinaire reforms stemmed from an austere vanity that made him somewhat ridiculous: he believed that the state was his person.

Joseph's incognito was the symbol of his whole philosophy of monarchy. He was as pompous and self-righteous about his name as he was about his living arrangements and his reforms. 'You know that ... in all my travels I rigidly observe and jealously guard my rights and the advantages that the character of Comte de Falkenstein gives me,' Joseph instructed Cobenzl, 'so I will, as a result, be in uniform but without orders ... You will take care to arrange very small and ordinary quarters at Mogilev.'[3]

This self-declared 'first clerk of the state' wore a plain grey uniform, travelled with only one or two companions, wished to eat only simple inn food and liked to sleep on a military mattress in a roadside tavern rather than a palace. This was to create a challenge for the impresario of the visit, Potemkin, but he rose to it. Russia had few of the flea-bittern taverns the Emperor expected, so Potemkin dressed up manorhouses to look like inns.

The Emperor prided himself on perpetually inspecting everything from dawn till dusk. He never understood that inactivity can be masterful – hence the Prince de Ligne's comment that 'he governed too much and did not reign enough ...'. Ligne understood Joseph well – and adored him: 'As a man he has the greatest merit ... as a prince, he will have continual erections and never be satisfied. His reign will be a continual Priapism.' Since the death of his father in 1765, Joseph had reigned as Holy Roman Emperor or, as the Germans called it, Kaiser, but had to share power over the Habsburg Monarchy – which encompassed Austria, Hungary, Galicia, the Austrian Netherlands, Tuscany and parts of modern Yugoslavia – with his mother, the formidable, humane and astute Maria Theresa. For all her prudishness and rigid Catholic piety, she had laid the foundations for Joseph's reforms – but he imposed them so stringently that they first became a joke and then a disaster. He later took steps towards the emancipation of the serfs and the Jews, who no longer had to wear the Yellow Star of David, could worship freely, attend universities and engage in trade. He disdained his nobles; yet his reforms rained on his peoples like baton blows. He could not understand their obstinate ingratitude. When he banned coffins to save wood and time, he was baffled by the outrage that forced him to reverse his decision. 'God, he even wants to put their souls in uniform,' exclaimed Mirabeau. 'That's the summit of despotism.'

His emotional life was tragic: his talented first wife, Isabella of Parma, preferred her sister-in-law to her husband in what seemed to be a lesbian affair, but he loved her. When she died young after three years of marriage, Joseph, then twenty-two, was inconsolable. 'I have lost everything. My adored wife, the object of all my tenderness, my only friend is gone . . . I hardly know if I am still alive.' Seven years later, his only child, a cherished daughter, died of pleurisy: 'One thing that I ask you to let me have is her white dimity dressing gown, embroidered with flowers . . .'. Yet even these sad emotional outbursts were about himself rather than anyone else. He remarried a hideous Wittelsbach heiress, Josepha, to lay claim to her Bavaria, then treated her callously. 'Her figure is short, thickset and without a vestige of charm,' he wrote. 'Her face is covered in spots and pimples. Her teeth are horrible.'

His sex life afterwards alternated between princesses and prostitutes, and, if he thought he might fall in love with a woman, he drained himself of any desire by visiting a whore first. Ligne recalled that he had 'no idea of good cheer or amusements, neither did he read anything except official papers'. He regarded himself as a model of rational decency and all others with sarcastic disdain. As a man, he was a bloodless husk; as a ruler, 'the greatest enemy of this prince', wrote Catherine, 'was himself'. This was the Kaiser whom Potemkin needed to pull off the greatest achievements of his career.[4]

On 24 May 1780, the Empress of Russia entered Mogilev through the triumphal arch, escorted by squadrons of Cuirassiers – a sight that impressed even the sardonic Kaiser: 'It was beautiful – all the Polish nobility on horseback, hussars, cuirassiers, lots of generals . . . finally she herself in a carriage of two seats with Maid-of-Honour Miss Engelhardt . . .'. As cannons boomed and bells rang, the Empress, accompanied by Potemkin and Field-Marshal Rumiantsev-Zadunaisky, attended church and then drove to the Governor's residence. It was the beginning of four days of theatre, song and of course fireworks. No expense was spared to transform this drab provincial capital, gained from Poland only in 1772 and teeming with Poles and Jews, into a town fit for Caesars. The

Italian architect Brigonzi had built a special theatre where his compatriot Bonafina sang for the guests.

Joseph put on his uniform and 'Prince Potemkin took me to court.'[5] Serenissimus introduced the two Caesars, who liked each other at once, both dreaming no doubt of Hagia Sofia. They talked politics after dinner, alone except for Potemkin and his niece–mistress Alexandra Engelhardt. Catherine called Joseph 'very intelligent, he loves to talk and he talks very well'. Catherine talked too. She did not formally propose the Greek Project or partition of the Ottoman Empire, but both knew why they were there. She hinted at her Byzantine dreams, for Joseph told his mother that her 'project of establishing an empire in the east rolls around in her head and broods in her soul'. The next day, they got on so well at an *opéra comique* that Joseph had confided plans that 'I don't dare publish' – as Catherine boasted to Grimm. They meant to impress each other. They had to like each other. They made very sure they did.[6]

There was still opposition to this realignment, not just from Panin and the Prussophile Grand Duke Paul. Rumiantsev-Zadunaisky inquired if these festivities augured an Austrian alliance – a query that was the prerogative of a prickly war hero. The Empress replied, 'it would be advantageous in a Turkish war and Prince Potemkin advised it'. Rumiantsev-Zadunaisky sourly recommended taking her own counsel instead. 'One mind is good,' replied Catherine laconically, 'but two, better.'[7] That was the way they worked together.

Joseph, the obsessional inspector, rose early and inspected whatever he could find. Like many a talentless soldier – Peter III and Grand Duke Paul come to mind – he believed that enough inspections and parades would transform him into Frederick the Great. Potemkin politely escorted him to inspect the Russian army, but evidently found his strutting pace tiresome. When Joseph kept mentioning one of Potemkin's 'magnificent regiments', which he had not yet inspected, the Prince did not want to go because of 'bad weather that was expected at any moment'. Finally, Catherine told him like a nagging wife to take Joseph, whatever the weather.

A splendid tent was erected for the two monarchs to view the display of horsemanship while the other spectators, including the King of Poland's nephew Prince Stanislas Poniatowski, to whom we owe this story, watched on horseback. There was a distant roar as Prince Potemkin, at the head of several thousand horsemen, galloped into view. The Prince raised his sword to order the charge when suddenly the horse buckled under the weight of his bulk and collapsed, 'like a centaur on to its hindlegs'. However, he kept his seat during this embarrassing moment and gave his command. The regiment began its charge from a league away and, with the earth trembling, stopped right in front of the imperial tent, in perfect formation. 'I've never seen anything like this done before by a cavalry regiment,' said Joseph. His comments on Potemkin's mount were not recorded.[8]

On the 30th, Catherine and Joseph left Mogilev and headed in the same carriage to Smolensk, where they temporarily parted. Joseph, with only five attendants, headed off to see Moscow. Catherine was not far from Potemkin's birthplace, Chizhova. There is a legend that Potemkin invited Catherine to visit the village, where with his nephew, Vasily Engelhardt, one of her aides-de-camp and now owner of the village, he greeted her at the gates and showed her the wooden bathhouse where he was born. The well was henceforth named for Catherine. They then split up – the Prince joined Joseph on the road to Moscow, while the Empress returned to Petersburg. 'My good friend,' she wrote to Potemkin, 'it's empty without you.'[9]

Joseph could not understand Potemkin. 'Prince de Potemkin wants to go to Moscow to explain everything to me,' Joseph told his mother. 'His credit is at an all-time high. Her Majesty even named him at table as her true student ... He has not shown any particularly impressive views so far,' added Joseph, but 'I don't doubt he'll show himself on the journey.' But, once again, Joseph was confounded. While he ceaselessly gave pedantic perorations of his own views, in between brisk expeditions of inspection, Potemkin drifted away into silent reveries. The Prince wanted Joseph's alliance, but he was no sycophant and was not as impressed as he should have been to have the head of the House of Habsburg in his company. Once in Moscow, Joseph told 'very dear mother' that Potemkin 'explains to me the necessary' about some sights but 'to others I go alone'. It was entirely characteristic of Potemkin to doze in bed while the inspector–Emperor rose at dawn for more inspections. By the time they left, Joseph was indignant that Potemkin 'very much took his ease. I've only seen him three times in Moscow and he hasn't spoken to me about business at all.' This man, he concluded, is 'too indolent, too cool to put something into motion – and insouciant'.[10]

On 18 June Joseph and Potemkin arrived in Petersburg, where the two sides began to explore what sort of friendship they wanted. At Tsarskoe Selo, Potemkin arranged a treat for the Comte de Falkenstein. He recruited Catherine's English gardener from Hackney (originally from Hanover), the appropriately named Bush, to create a special tavern for the Emperor, who loved inns. When Baroness Dimsdale, the English wife of the doctor who inoculated the imperial family, visited a year later, the gardener proudly told her how he had a hung a sign outside the building on which he wrote 'The Count Falkenstein Arms'. He himself wore a placard reading 'Master of the Inn'. Joseph dined at the 'Falkenstein Arms' on boiled beef, soup, ham and the most 'agreeable yet common Russian dishes'. One wonders if the humourless pedant got the joke.[11]

Throughout the fun, the Russian ministers and the diplomats were on edge as they sensed vast yet so far invisible changes. When the party returned to Petersburg, Joseph encountered Nikita Panin. 'This man', noticed the Kaiser, 'has the air of fearing that one address oneself to his antagonist Prince Potemkin.' By early July, the Prince himself was working between Emperor, Empress and the Austrian envoy, Cobenzl, on the beginning of a more formal relationship 'to re-establish the old confidence and intimacy between the two courts'. Catherine could see the Emperor's Janus-like personality, but, in the semi-public arena of her letters to Grimm, she declared his mind 'the most solid, most profound and most intelligent' she knew. By the time he left, the sides were closer, but nothing was decided. Maria Theresa still reigned in Vienna.[12]

After Joseph's departure, in the midst of the bidding for Russian alliance from Austria, Prussia and Britain, Daria, Potemkin's estranged mother, died in Moscow. When the Empress heard, she was on her way to Tsarskoe Selo and the Prince was at his nearby summer residence, Ozerki. Catherine insisted on telling him herself, so she changed route and joined him. The loss of a distant parent is often more painful than that of a close one: Potemkin wept copiously because 'this prince', observed Corberon, 'combines the qualities and faults of *sensitivité*'.[13] There was an understatement.

Joseph's successful visit truly put the cat among the pigeons. The Prussian party, Panin and Grand Duke Paul, were in disarray. Frederick the Great decided to send a Prussian prince to Petersburg to counteract the Habsburg success. Well before the Mogilev meeting, his envoy Goertz had been discussing such a visit with Potemkin and Panin. Instead of Prince Henry, who now knew Potemkin well, Frederick sent his nephew and heir, Frederick William. This was not a good idea. Joseph, for all his pedantry, was an impressive companion, but Frederick William, who had special instructions from the King to flatter Potemkin, was an oafish and stout Prussian boor without any redeeming social qualities. Prince Henry dutifully wrote to Potemkin asking him to welcome the uncouth nephew – in the tone of a man who reluctantly sends a cheap present but apologizes in advance for its disappointing quality.*

Potemkin and Panin welcomed the Prince of Prussia together on 26 August. However, Potemkin pointedly decreed that Alexandra Engelhardt would 'not give him a supper',[14] and Catherine nicknamed the 'heavy, reserved and awkward' Prussian, 'Fat Gu'. The Hohenzollern was soon boring the entire capital except for the Grand Duke, who was so impressed with Frederick the Great and his military drill that any Prussian prince would do. Besides, Frederick's plan had already been undermined by the arrival of Joseph II's secret weapon – the Prince de Ligne.[15]

Corberon and Goertz convinced themselves, with wishful thinking, that nothing would come of Joseph's visit. However, the Frenchman then went to dinner with the Cobenzls 'and the new arrivals, the Prince de Ligne and his son'. Corberon dismissed this '*grand seigneur* of Flanders' as an 'amiable *roué*', but he was much more than that.

Charles-Joseph, Prince de Ligne, now fifty, was an eternally boyish, mischievous and effortlessly witty aristocrat of the Enlightenment. Heir to an imperial principality awarded in 1602, he was raised by a nurse who made him dance and sleep naked with her. He married a Liechtenstein heiress but found marriage 'absurd for several weeks and then indifferent'. After three weeks, he committed his first infidelity with a chambermaid. He led his Ligne regiment during the Seven Years War, distinguishing himself at the Battle of Kolin. 'I'd like to be a pretty girl until thirty, a general ... till sixty,' he told Frederick the Great after the war, 'and then a cardinal until eighty.' However, he was eaten by bitterness about one thing – he longed to be taken seriously as a general yet no one, from Joseph to Potemkin, would ever give him an independent military command. This rankled.[16]

Ligne's greatest talent was for friendship. The charmer of Europe treated every day as a comedy waiting to be turned into an epigram, every girl as an adventure waiting to be turned into a poem, and every monarch as a conquest waiting to be seduced by his jesting. His flattery could be positively emetic: 'What a low and brazen sycophant Ligne is!', wrote one who observed him in action. But it worked. Friends with both Joseph II and Frederick the Great, no mean feat in itself, as well as with Rousseau, Voltaire, Casanova and Queen Marie-Antoinette, he showed how small the *monde* was in those days. No one so personified the debauched cosmopolitanism of the late eighteenth century: 'I like to be a foreigner everywhere ... A Frenchman in Austria, an Austrian in France, both a Frenchman and an Austrian in Russia.'

---

* Even Frederick the Great called him 'a cloud of boredom and distaste.'

Ligne's letters were copied, his *bons mots* repeated, across the salons of Europe – as they were meant to be. He was a superb writer whose bitchy portraits of the great men of his time, especially Potemkin, who fascinated him, were never bettered. His *Mélanges* are, along with Casanova's *Histoire*, the best record of the era: Ligne was at the top and Casanova at the bottom of the same faro society. They met the same charlatans and dukes, prostitutes and countesses at balls and card tables, operas and bordellos, roadside taverns and royal courts, again and again, across Europe.

Ligne entranced Potemkin. Their friendship, bringing together two of the best conversationalists of the age, would wax and wane with the intensity of a love affair, chronicled in Ligne's many unpublished letters contained in Potemkin's archives, written in his tiny hand but dripping with wit and intelligence before sinking again into illegibility. This 'jockey diplomatique', as he called himself, was invited to all the Empress's private card games, carriage rides and dinners at Tsarskoe Selo. The bovine Prince of Prussia did not stand a chance against the man Catherine called 'the most pleasant and easy person to live with I've ever known, an original mind that thinks deeply and plays all sorts of tricks, like a child'.

Grand Duke Paul alone took trouble with Frederick William, which only served to alienate him from Catherine and Potemkin all the more. When the Empress gave a spectacle, ball and supper at the Hermitage Theatre in the Prince of Prussia's honour, the Grand Ducal couple accompanied the guest but Catherine sighed to Harris, 'I want you to defend me from boors,' and did not bother to attend the show. Diplomats wondered where the Empress had gone. It turned out she was playing billiards with Potemkin and Ligne.[17]

Empress and Serenissimus were relieved when Frederick William finally departed, having achieved nothing. He had noticed the cold shoulder: as king, he would take his revenge. But the Russians almost refused to let Ligne go. Ever the gentleman, the 'jockey diplomatique' stayed a little longer. Finally, in October, he insisted, so Potemkin went with him to show off one of his regiments and only let him leave with a deluge of presents – horses, serfs and a box encrusted with diamonds. Potemkin missed Ligne and kept asking Cobenzl when he was returning.

This was exactly what the Austrians wanted. They fired a barrage of compliments at Potemkin: in a little illustration of the lubricious nature of diplomatic flattery, Cobenzl asked his Emperor to mention Potemkin favourably in as many of his *en clair* despatches as possible. The Russian, he flattered Joseph in turn, rated a word from the Kaiser more highly than anything from the Kings of Prussia or Sweden. But the direct compliments of the Emperor should be saved for special occasions. And Joseph should also send regards to the Engelhardt nieces.[18]

On 17/28 November 1780, Joseph was liberated from the sensible restraints of Maria Theresa. Her death, after a reign of forty years, gave Joseph the chance almost to ruin the Habsburg legacy in a way that even Frederick of Prussia could not have imagined. In the lugubrious letters of sorrow that passed between Vienna and Petersburg, the grins were only just concealed behind the grief. 'The Emperor', Ligne joked to Potemkin on 25 November, only a week after her death, 'seemed to me so profoundly filled with friendship for you ... that I have had real pleasure to remonstrate with him on your account in all regards ... Have me told from time to time that you haven't forgotten me ...'.[19] There was no question of that.

When the Empress–Queen's body was laid in the Kaisergruft – imperial vault – of Vienna's Capucin Church, Joseph knew he could embark on his rapprochement with Russia. Potemkin declared both his 'keenness' and 'seriousness' to Cobenzl. Catherine made sure that all the details went directly to her and not to Panin, 'that old trickster', as she called him to Potemkin.[20] Catherine and Joseph turned their attention to the coming struggle against the Sultan.

Sir James Harris, who thought an Austrian alliance would help his own mission, still could not understand Russia's reluctance to ally with Britain, even after Potemkin's return from Mogilev. The Prince cheerfully blamed Catherine's refusal on a raft of flimsy excuses, including the 'imbecility of the tale-bearing favourite' Lanskoy, her weakness induced by her 'passions' and the 'adroit flattery' of the Habsburg Emperor, who made her think she was the 'greatest Princess in Europe'. This diatribe displayed Potemkin's genuine frustration with the effort of managing Catherine, but it also rings of Potemkinian mischief. This is a clear example of Potemkin 'playing' poor Harris, because the couple's secret letters prove they were both pinning their entire political system on an alliance with Austria.[21] Harris at last realized the mistake of backing Potemkin against Panin, because the former was now uninterested, if friendly, while the latter was openly hostile.

Harris requested recall in the face of Panin's hostility. But London was still pressing him to find a way to win the Russian alliance. So in nocturnal conversations with Potemkin the ever resourceful Harris conceived an ambitious scheme. Potemkin's imagination was the source of what became official British policy. Britain, suggested the Prince, should offer Russia 'some object worthy of her ambition' to join the war. In cypher, Harris explained to his Secretary of State, Viscount Stormont, in November 1780: 'Prince Potemkin, though he did not directly say so, yet clearly gave me to understand that *the only cession*, which would induce the Empress to become our Ally, was that of Minorca.' This was not as far-fetched as it might sound because, in 1780, Potemkin was building his Black Sea Fleet and promoting trade through the Straits and out to Mediterranean ports such as Marseilles. Port Mahon in Minorca might be a useful base for the fleet. Russia had occupied Greek islands during the last war – but not kept any at the peace; Potemkin regularly offered Crete to France and England in his Ottoman partition plans; and Emperor Paul later occupied Malta. Besides he was careful, as Harris emphasized, never to suggest it directly. This was one of those fantastical empire-building games that Potemkin loved to play – at no cost to himself.

Potemkin was excited about the idea of a Russian naval base on Minorca, especially since Britain would leave large stores of supplies, worth £2,000,000, which would be at Russia's or Potemkin's disposal. He met Harris daily to discuss it and arranged the envoy's second *tête-à-tête* with Catherine on 19 December 1780. Before Harris was summoned, the Prince went down to see the Empress for two hours, returning with a 'countenance full of satisfaction and joy'. This was the climax of Harris's friendship with Serenissimus. 'We were sitting alone together very late in the evening when he broke out of a sudden into all the advantages that would arise to Russia . . .'. We can hear Potemkin's child-like delight, chimerical dreams and febrile exhilaration, as he lazed on a divan in his rooms, strewn with bottles of Tokay and champagne, cards on green-baize tables: 'He then with the liveliness of his imagination ran on the idea of a Russian fleet stationed at Mahon, of peopling the island with Greeks, that such an acquisition would be a column of the Empress's glory in the middle of the sea.'[22]

The Empress saw the benefits of Minorca, but she told Potemkin, 'the bride is too beautiful, they are trying to trick me'. It seemed that she could not resist Potemkin's excitement when they were together but would often think better of it when he had gone. Russia, with an unbuilt fleet, could hold it only at Britain's pleasure. She turned down Minorca. She was right: it was too far away and Britain itself soon lost the island.

Potemkin grumbled that Catherine was 'suspicious, timid and narrowminded', but again this was half play acting. Harris still could not resist hoping that the Prince was committed to England: 'Dined on Wednesday at Tsarskoe Selo with Prince Potemkin . . . he talked upon the interests of our two Courts in such a friendly and judicious manner that I regret more than ever his frequent lapses into idleness and dissipation.' He still had not registered that Potemkin's strategic emphasis was not western at all but southerly. Nonetheless, as the Prince secretly negotiated with the Austrians, Sir James kept trying.

Joseph and Catherine had meanwhile agreed the terms of a defensive treaty, including the secret clause aimed at the Sublime Porte – but Potemkin's grand enterprise now hit a snag that was very much of its time. This was the so-called 'alternative', a diplomatic tradition by which monarchs signing a treaty put their name first on one copy and second on the other. The Holy Roman Emperor, as Europe's senior ruler, always signed first on both copies. Now Catherine refused to admit Russia was lower than Rome, while Joseph refused to lower the dignity of the Kaiser by signing second. So, amazingly, the realignment of the East ground to a halt over a matter of protocol.

This was one of those crises where the difference between Catherine and Potemkin was clearest, because, while the Empress was obstinate, the Prince begged her to be flexible and get the treaty signed. The bickering of the partners echoes through their letters and Cobenzl's despatches. Potemkin rushed back and forth between the two sides. Catherine at one point told him to inform Cobenzl 'to give up such nonsense which will imminently stop everything'. Everything did stop.

The tension was not helped by Potemkin's demands for favours for his nieces Alexandra and Ekaterina, both of whom were about to get married. Soon even Catherine's favourite Lanskoy was embroiled in the rows. But Catherine devised an inspired solution for Potemkin to suggest to Joseph: they would each exchange signed letters, setting out their obligation to each other, instead of a treaty.[23]

The highly strung Prince, faced with this crisis in the scheme of a lifetime, collapsed with 'bad digestion'. Catherine visited Potemkin's apartments to make up and spent the evening with him 'from eight till midnight'. Peace was restored.

Just as the crisis over the Austrian treaty reached its climax, on 10 May 1781, Potemkin ordered Count Mark Voinovich, a Dalmatian sailor, to mount a small invasion of Persia. He was pursuing a secret Persian policy while he was trying to smooth the obstacles from the path of his Greek Project.

This scheme had run parallel to the Austrian negotiations for a full year. Ten days before Joseph II had suggested the Mogilev meeting with

Catherine, on 11 January 1780, Serenissimus ordered General Alexander Suvorov, his ablest commander, to assemble an invasion force at Astrakhan. He ordered the ships he had been building at Kazan on the Volga since 1778 to move southwards. The alliance with Austria might take more years to accomplish. In the meantime, Russia would probe the Persian Empire instead of the Ottoman.

The Persian Empire in those days extended round the southern end of the Caspian to include Baku and Derbent, all of today's Azerbaijan, most of Armenia and half of Georgia. The Armenians and Georgians were Orthodox Christians. As with the Greeks, the Wallachians and the Moldavians, Potemkin longed to liberate his fellow Orthodox and bring them into the Russian Empire. At the same time, he was meeting Armenian representatives in Petersburg, discussing the liberation of the Christians of Armenia from the Persian yoke.

The Prince was one of the few Russian statesmen who understood commerce at that time: he knew that a trading post on the eastern Caspian was just 'thirty days' march from the Persian Gulf, just five weeks to get to India via Kandahar'. In other words, this was Potemkin's first and admittedly minor blow in what came to be called 'The Great Game'. We know that Potemkin was juggling his Greek Project with a Persian one because he talked about it with his British friends. The French and British watched Potemkin's secret Persian plans with interest. Indeed, six years later, the French Ambassador was still trying to discover its secrets.

In February 1780, Sasha Lanskoy had fallen ill and Potemkin delayed his final orders to Suvorov, who was left to kick his heels in drab provincial Astrakhan. Once the anti-Ottoman Greek Project, and Joseph's visit, was confirmed, it would have been foolish for Potemkin to spread his forces too thinly. So the plan was changed. Early in 1781, the Prince cancelled the invasion and instead persuaded Catherine to send a limited expedition, commanded by the thirty-year-old Voinovich, 'a dangerous pirate' from Dalmatia to some, a 'sort of Italian spy of the ministers of Vienna' to others, who had fought for Catherine in the First Russo-Turkish War and temporarily captured Beirut, now the capital of Lebanon.

On 29 June 1781, this tiny naval expedition of three frigates and several transports sailed across the Caspian to found a trading post in Persia and lay the foundations of Catherine's Empire in Central Asia. Persia was in disarray, but the Satrap of the Askabad province across the Caspian, Aga-Mohommed-Khan, was playing many sides against the centre. This chilling and formidable empire-builder, who had been castrated as a boy by his father's enemies, hoped to become shah himself. He welcomed the idea of a Russian trading post on the eastern shores, perhaps to fund his own armies with Russian help.

Voinovich's expedition was an Enlightened mixture of Potemkin's scientific longing for knowledge, mercantile enthusiasm and purely imperial aggrandizement. The meagre expedition boasted just fifty infantrymen, 600 men in all, and Potemkin's respected German-Jewish botanist Karl-Ludwig Hablitz, who probably wrote the unsigned account of the Prince's Persian expedition in the Quai d'Orsay archive. Voinovich was unsuited to such a sensitive role, but the expedition was in any case too small and was now left to its own devices. Probably this was the result of one of the many compromises between Catherine's caution and Potemkin's imagination. By the time the expedition set off, both Empress and Prince were firmly concentrating on Tsargrad and Vienna rather than Askabad and Kandahar.

Voinovich had been ordered to use 'only persuasion' by the Prince, but on arrival 'he did precisely the opposite'. When he arrived on the other side of the sea and found Aga-Mohommed camped with his army, Voinovich proved he was as 'bad a courtier as politician'. The Persian prince was still interested in a Russian trading post and even suggested that his nephew should lead a mission to Petersburg. Voinovich instead had the imprudence to establish a fort, with just twenty cannon, as if his 650 men could possibly defy a Persian army. While he gave fêtes for the Persians and ostentatiously fired his cannons, he only managed to alarm the already suspicious locals, who heard that Suvorov was marching through Daghestan with 60,000 men. This piece of disinformation was probably the first British intrigue in the 'Great Game' and it worked. Aga-Mohommed decided to rid himself of these inept and obnoxious Russians.

The village chief invited Voinovich and Hablitz to dinner. They had scarcely arrived before the house was surrounded by 600 Persian warriors. Voinovich and Hablitz were given a choice of losing their heads or evacuating the fort and sailing away without delay. They were right to choose the latter since Aga-Mohommed was capable of unbridled savagery: he later blinded the entire male population – 20,000 men – of a town that resisted him. He also managed the rare feat of being the only eunuch in history to found a dynasty: the Qajars, descended from his nephew, ruled Persia until early this century, when they were replaced by the Pahlavis. It took another century before Russia conquered Central Asia.[24]

The flotilla sailed miserably for home. Potemkin must take the blame for this quixotic expedition that could easily have ended in catastrophe, yet it was his Byzantine style to run an alternative policy just in case anything went wrong in Vienna.[25]

It did not. Joseph agreed to sign the secret defensive treaty with the exchange of letters. For six months, Europe believed that the negotiations had collapsed but, secretly on 18 May, Catherine signed her letter to 'My dear Brother' – and Joseph reciprocated. She agreed that Russia would aid Austria against Prussia; but, more relevantly, for Potemkin, Joseph promised to defend Russia if it was attacked by the Turks – 'I am obliged three months after ... to declare war ...'. Austria therefore underwrote Russia's peace treaties with Turkey.[26] This realignment of Russian policy was Potemkin's personal triumph.

Catherine and Potemkin enjoyed fooling the international community. French, Prussian and British envoys tossed bribes around to learn what was happening. Harris suspiciously noticed that 'my friend' was in 'high spirits' but 'avoided every political subject'. Cobenzl, who knew everything of course, enjoyed himself too. 'The whole affair', he told his Emperor, 'is continuing to be a mystery here for everyone except Prince Potemkin and Bezborodko.'[27] It was not long before Joseph realized that Catherine usually got what she wanted. In spite of the priority of the Greek Project, she did not allow the Armed Neutrality to drop and persuaded both Prussia and Austria to sign. 'What Woman wants, God gives, goes the proverb,' mused Joseph, 'and once in their hands, one always goes further than one wants.' Catherine and Potemkin were exultant: Catherine was so excited by one flattering letter from Joseph that she actually blushed.

The treaty remained secret. It was 25 June, a month later, before Harris first suspected that a treaty had been signed, thanks to a bribe of £1,600 to Bezborodko's secretary, but amazingly the secret was kept for almost two years. Only Catherine, Potemkin and Bezborodko knew everything; Grand Duke Paul was not told. Panin withdrew to his Smolensk estates.[28] The partners congratulated each other. Catherine saw herself and Potemkin as the mythical best friends of the Classical world – Pylades and Orestes. 'My old Pylades', she congratulated him, 'is a clever man.'

However, they now faced a challenge from Grand Duke Paul, who was profoundly sceptical about southern expansion and Austrian alliance. Aping his father, he remained a 'Prussian'. In July, when Catherine invited the British doctor Baron Dimsdale, with his wife, to inoculate the young Grand Dukes Alexander and Constantine against smallpox, Nikita Panin demanded the right to come back and supervise, a trick he had arranged with Paul. 'If he thinks ever to be reinstated in his post of First Minister,' Catherine snapped, 'he is greatly deceived. He'll never be anything in my Court other than a sick-nurse.'

Catherine and Potemkin must have discussed how to protect their policy from Paul and, if possible, convert him to the Austrian cause. Why not send him and his wife on a Grand Tour to Vienna and Paris, avoiding old Frederick the Great in Berlin? If Catherine suggested it, the nervous Paul would regard it as a trick by Potemkin to remove him. Serenissmus was arranging the creation of his own kingdom, founding his first cities on the Black Sea and planning his nieces' marriages. Paul could not be allowed to derail any of these schemes. Potemkin devised a solution.[29]

16

THREE MARRIAGES
AND A CROWN

Or midst a lovely little orchard
An arbour, where a fountain plays
A sweet-voiced harp within my hearing
My thoughts ensnares for divers pleasures,
First wearies and then awakens my blood;
Reclining on a velvet divan,
A maiden's tender feelings coddling
I fill her youthful heart with love.

Gavrili Derzhavin, 'Ode to Princess Felitsa'

Soon after the Austrian treaty was signed, Catherine put her consort's plan into practice. She persuaded Prince Repnin, Panin's nephew, to propose the Austrian trip to Paul, as if it came to from himself. Paul swallowed the bait and begged the Empress to let him go. After pretending to be reluctant, Catherine agreed – but she also worried about the inevitable blunders of her bitter, unstable son. 'I dare to implore the indulgence of Your Imperial Majesty', she asked Joseph, 'for the ... inexperience of youth.' Joseph sent the invitation. Paul and Maria Fyodorovna were excited. They were even polite to Potemkin, who in his turn praised the Heir to everyone.[1]

Panin had heard about this plan. 'The old trickster' no longer cared to conceal his sourness. He hurried back to Petersburg and stirred up Paul's fears that the journey was a plot. Such trips could be dangerous for Russian princes: no one could forget that Peter the Great's son Alexei was brought back from Vienna and tortured to death. All this was real to a tsarevich whose father had been murdered by his mother and who could trust few. Panin suggested that Berlin would be a better idea than Vienna – and then hinted that Paul would not only be excluded from the succession and possibly murdered but that his children would be taken from him. Paul became hysterical.

At Tsarskoe Selo next morning, Sunday, 13 September, the Grand Duke and Duchess, both in a state of panic, refused to travel. They partly blamed the need to remain with the children after their inoculation.

Catherine brought in Doctors Rogerson and Dimsdale to reassure them. The Court was in uproar for three days and the diplomats analysed how the Heir was undermining the Austrian rapprochement, defying the Empress and her Prince. Potemkin was so 'perplexed, irresolute and even despondent' that he even considered letting Paul visit the wily fox of Berlin. Harris, who was with him in his apartments that Friday and believed the Austrian alliance gave Britain renewed hope, warned him that such weakness could bring him down. Potemkin paced up and down the room, 'as in his manner', without saying anything, and then bounded off to see the Empress. Catherine was no Peter the Great, but the refusal of Paul to obey her orders would have caused a serious succession crisis. The partners resolved to force Paul to go. When Potemkin rejoined Harris an hour later, everything was settled.

The departure was a little tragedy of the life of royal families, played out in front of the Court, Paul's entourage, and scores of horses and serfs. On 19 September, the Heir, travelling incognito as Comte du Nord, and his wife kissed their children goodbye. The Grand Duchess fainted away and was actually carried unconscious to the carriage. The Grand Duke followed his wife with an expression of abject terror. The Empress and her big guns, Potemkin, Prince Orlov and the traitorous Count Panin, bid him goodbye. As he climbed grimly into the carriage, Paul whispered something to Panin, who did not answer.

The Heir pulled down the blinds and ordered the coachman to drive away fast. The next morning, Panin was dismissed.[2]

Serenissimus, savouring his political victory, was arranging the marriages of both of his single mistress–nieces, Sashenka and Katinka. On 10 November 1781, Katinka 'the Venus' – Ekaterina Engelhardt, with whom half the Court, including at various times both Catherine's sons, Paul and Bobrinsky, were in love – married the sickly but rich Count Pavel Martynovich Skavronsky, in the Palace Chapel. Descended from the Livonian brother of Peter the Great's wife, Catherine I, Skavronsky was a sublime eccentric. Brought up in Italy, which he regarded as home, he suited Potemkin because he was a tolerant buffoon obsessed with music – a melomaniac who composed and gave concerts though he had no talent for music whatsoever. His servants were forbidden to talk and could only communicate in recitative. He gave all his orders in music and his visitors made conversation in the form of vocal improvisations. His singing dinner parties, ornamented by the sleepy coquettish Katinka, must have been zany.[3] Catherine had misgivings about Skavronsky's ability to please a woman – 'he's a bit silly and clumsy', she thought, adding that she only cared because it was an issue that was 'close to us', meaning she regarded Potemkin's nieces as semi-family. The Prince disagreed – Skavronsky's weakness and wealth suited him.[4]

Two days later, Sashenka married her uncle's Polish ally, Grand Hetman (or Grand General) of the Polish Crown, Ksawery Branicki, aged forty-nine, a good-natured, self-made and ambitious ruffian who had made his career as King Stanislas-Augustus' hard man. He was what Casanova called a dim but swashbuckling 'Polish bravo'. Casanova duelled with Branicki in Warsaw for insulting his mistress, an Italian actress called La Binetti. Both were wounded – Branicki seriously – but became friends.[5] When Ségur passed through Warsaw, Branicki appeared in his room in traditional Polish costume – red boots, brown robe, fur hat and sabre – and said, 'Here are two companions for your journey,' giving him two bejewelled pistols.[6]

Branicki had fallen out with the King of Poland and, seeing his future as a Russian ally, found a kindred spirit in Serenissimus. They first met in Petersburg in 1775 and Branicki had been currying favour ever since, working for Potemkin in Poland. On 27 March that year, he wrote to tell 'my dear General' that 'Poland has chosen me' to deliver the news that Potemkin had received the certificate of *indigenat* or Polish noble status, the first step in his long game to become either duke of Courland or king of Poland, his escape route should Catherine die.[7] Branicki's marriage to his niece was obviously designed to be Potemkin's family bridgehead in Poland.[8]

The Empress supervised Alexandra's wedding to the 'Polish bravo'. The bride was taken to Catherine's rooms that morning and 'very richly dressed in some of the Empress's jewels, put on by her own hands'. We have a description of a similar wedding of one of the Empress's closest maids-of-honour, Lev Naryshkin's daughter: 'This lady's dress was an Italian night-gown of a white silver tissue with hanging sleeves . . . and a very large hoop.' The bride dined with the Empress. In church, the bride stood on 'a piece of brocaded sea-green silk'. The couple held candles as crowns were held over their heads according to Orthodox tradition. They exchanged rings and the priest took a 'piece of silk 2 or 3 yards long and tied their hands together'. Once the wedding was over there was a feast, after which the bride returned the Empress's jewels and received 5,000 roubles.[9]

At almost the same time, the fourth sister, 'hopeless' Nadezhda who had married Colonel P. A. Ismailov less splendidly in 1779, lost her husband and then married an ally of Potemkin's, Senator P. A. Shepilev. The last niece, Tatiana, married her distant cousin Lieutenant-General

Mikhail Sergeievich Potemkin, who was twenty-five years older than her, in 1785. Serenissimus nicknamed him 'Saint' for his good nature, and their marriage was happy until his early death.[10]

While Varvara and Alexandra ended their liaisons with Potemkin, Countess Ekaterina Skavronskaya, as we will now call her, seems to have remained his mistress. 'Things are on the same footing between her and her uncle as they were,' Cobenzl told Joseph II. 'The husband who is very jealous does not approve but does not have the courage to prevent it.' Even five years later, Skavronskaya was still 'more beautiful than ever and the favourite Sultana-in-chief of the uncle'.[11]

Potemkin had Skavronsky appointed ambassador to Naples in 1784, which delighted him because it let him inhabit the land of maestros. But Skavronskaya was not interested in Italian opera, and Potemkin, while he ran several other mistresses, enjoyed his placid niece and did not wish to part from her. Finally she did go, but did not stay long. The husband sent notes to Serenissimus that are masterpieces of pitiful sycophancy: 'I cannot succeed in expressing all the joy and gratitude with which I read what you have deigned to write to me and how much I have been moved to see that you deign to grant me your kindness and memory which I have consecrated my life to deserve and on which I dare suggest that no one in the world could place a higher value.' More than that, Skavronsky desperately wrote to beg Potemkin to help him avoid diplomatic *faux pas*. The Prince must have chuckled as he read these letters, though he liked the sculptures Skavronsky sent him from Italy.[12] Remarkably the Count fathered a family in between arias in Naples, including a daughter who was one day to be notorious in Europe.

Skavronsky always took care to tell the Prince that his wife longed to rejoin him in Russia, which was probably true, because the dreamy 'angel' missed her Motherland. While she was in Naples, she kept a 'woman slave' under her bed who helped her get to sleep by 'telling her the same story every night'. By day she was 'perpetually idle', her conversation was 'as vacuous as you could imagine', but she could not help but flirt.[13] She became Naples's leading coquette, high praise in a city that was soon to experience the wiles of Emma, Lady Hamilton. But when Potemkin's successes gave him the chance to woo Europe, Katinka hurried back to share his limelight.

Countess Alexandra Branicka remained not just Potemkin's confidante and his Polish agent of influence, but Catherine's closest friend. While her spendthrift husband did his best to lose their fortune, she increased it prodigiously, which led to arguments with her uncle – but they were always reconciled.[14] For the rest of her life she was often with Potemkin and the Empress – though she lived on her Polish and Belorussian estates. Her almost illegible letters to him are very affectionate: 'My father, my life, I feel so sad to be so faraway ... I ask you one mercy – don't forget me, love me for ever, nobody loves you like me. My God, I'll be happy when I've seen you.'[15] She was widely respected. Contemporaries emphasized her good morals, 'remaining a model of faithfulness all her life',[16] something remarkable in those days, especially when she was married to an older Lothario. They had a large family. Perhaps she fell in love with Branicki's endearing roughness.

This troika of marriages sparked rows with the Empress about the medals and money bestowed on his family – '600,000 roubles, money, the Order of St Catherine for the future Grande Genérale [Alexandra] and the portrait [of the Empress] for the Princess Golitsyn [Varvara]'. Potemkin expected his nieces to be endowed by the state – were they not Catherine's extended family? He got his way after weeks of rows. He certainly believed in caring for his own.

Paul left Tsarskoe Selo harbouring a visceral hatred for Serenissimus. Yet, like a monarch more than a minister, Potemkin tried to preserve a balance among the Court factions and foreign powers. In November, he talked to Harris about restoring Panin to a degree of power, presumably to balance him against the rising Bezborodko.[17] One of his best features – and one lacking in many politicians, even democratic ones – was the absence of vindictiveness. Perhaps he simply did not want to see Panin humiliated any more. In any case, Potemkin's triumph had broken Panin: he fell ill in October.

Similarly, by early 1782, the confused Cobenzl was telling Joseph that Potemkin was leaning back towards Prussia. Both Cobenzl and Harris concluded their reports by confessing that they were unable to fathom the motives for Potemkin's manoeuvres, but the Prince, while favouring Austria, continued to steer a middle passage between these two German monarchies for the rest of his life.[18]

In Vienna, Paul appalled his hosts, particularly after Joseph confided the secret of the Austrian alliance. The Habsburg saw that the 'feebleness and pusillanimity of the Grand Duke joined to falseness' were unlikely to make this angry snub-nosed paranoid into a successful autocrat. Paul spent six weeks in Austria, where he lectured Joseph about his loathing for Potemkin. When he arrived in the Habsburg lands in Italy, he ranted to Leopold, Grand Duke of Tuscany, Joseph's brother, about his mother's

Court and denounced the Greek Project and the Austrian alliance. Catherine's plans 'for aggrandizing herself at the expense of the Turks and refounding the empire of Constantinople' were 'useless'. Austria had obviously bribed that traitor Potemkin. When he came to the throne, Paul would arrest him and clap him in prison!¹⁹ The Habsburg brothers were surely relieved when the Comte du Nord departed for Paris.

The Prince could insure himself against Paul only by changing the succession or by establishing a base outside Russia. He therefore pursued a different plan to discredit Paul once and for all – and possibly later remove him from the succession, leaving the throne to his son Alexander. When Potemkin heard that Paul's suite included Prince Alexander Kurakin, another Prussophile enemy and Panin's nephew, he asked the Austrians, via Cobenzl, to let him see the Cabinet Noir intercepts of Paul's post. The Austrian secret services passed on to Potemkin what they gleaned from Paul's contacts with Panin. The Prince was sure that he would catch Kurakin spying for the Prussians and therefore taint Tsarevich Paul.²⁰

Nikita Panin, ill as he was, knew that Kurakin's post would be opened, so he arranged for Paul to keep in contact with his supporters at home via a third party, Pavel Bibikov, son of the general. The letter that was opened in early 1782 from Bibikov to Kurakin was a bombshell that, more than the Saldern Plot, ensured Paul's exclusion from power for the rest of Catherine's life. Bibikov described Catherine's rule as 'the horrible situation in the Motherland' and criticized Potemkin, 'Cyclops *par excellence*' and 'le borgne', for ruining the army. 'If he breaks his neck', everything would return to its 'natural order'.

Catherine was alarmed and angry. Bibikov was immediately arrested. Catherine personally wrote out the questions for his interrogation by Sheshkovsky. Bibikov's excuse was that he was just unhappy at his regiment being stationed in the south. Catherine sent the results to the Prince, while ordering Bibikov tried in the Senate's Secret Expedition. The trial *in camera* found him guilty of treason and, under military law, of defaming his commander, Potemkin, and sentenced him to death.

The Prince's decency came into play. Even though Paul's circle had actually discussed breaking his neck, Potemkin asked Catherine for mercy on 15 April 1782: 'Even if virtue produces jealousy, it's nothing still compared to all the good it grants to those who serve it ... You have probably pardoned him already ... He'll probably overcome his dissolute inclinations and become a worthy subject of Your Majesty and I will add this grace to your other favours to me.' Admitting he was terrified of

Potemkin's vengeance, Bibikov wept under interrogation. He offered to apologize publicly.

'He shouldn't be afraid of my vengeance,' Potemkin wrote to Catherine, 'in so far as, among the abilities granted to me by God, that inclination is missing. I don't even want the triumph of a public apology ... He'll never find any example of my vengeance, to anybody, in my entire life.'[21] This was true – but, more than that, it displayed the statesman's measured moderation: he never pushed things too far and therefore never provoked an unwanted reaction.

Bibikov and Kurakin, recalled from Paul's suite in Paris, were exiled to the south. When the Heir returned to Petersburg at the end of the journey, his influence was broken, his allies scattered. Even his mother disdained her tiresome, unbalanced son and his wife as 'Die schwere Bagage' – the heavy luggage.[22] 'Prince Potemkin is happier', Cobenzl told Joseph, 'than I've ever seen him.'[23]

The secret Austrian treaty was soon tested – in the Crimea, the key to the Black Sea, the last Tartar stronghold and the nub of Potemkin's policy of southern expansionism. In May, the Prince headed beyond to Moscow 'for a short trip', visiting some estates. While he was on the road, the Turks again backed a Crimean rebellion against Catherine's puppet Khan, Shagin Giray, who was driven out once more, along with the Russian resident. The Khanate dissolved into anarchy.

The Empress sent a courier after the Prince. 'My dear friend, come back as soon as possible,' she wrote on 3 June 1782, adding wearily that they would have to honour their promise to reinstate the Khan – even though it was the third time they had done so. She told Potemkin the news that the British Admiral Rodney had defeated Admiral Joseph de Grasse's French fleet at the Battle of the Saints in the Caribbean on 1/12 April, which slightly alleviated Britain's plight as America won its freedom. In the Crimea, she realized that her policy of propping up Shagin Giray was obsolete but the delicate question of what to do depended on the Powers of Europe – and Potemkin. 'We could decide it all in half an hour together,' she told her consort, 'but now I don't know where to find you. I ask you to hurry with your arrival because nothing scares me more than to miss something or be wrong.' Never was their partnership, and his equality, more clearly stated.[24]

The Prince saw the Crimean tumult as a historic opportunity, because Britain and France remained distracted by war. He galloped back and almost bounded into town. He immediately sent this playfully Puckish letter to Sir James Harris in French, scrawled in his scratchy hand: 'Vive la Grande Bretagne et Rodney; je viens d'arriver, mon cher Harris; devinez qui vous écrit and venez me voir tout de suite.'*

Harris rushed through Tsarskoe Selo at midnight to visit 'this extraordinary man who', he told the new Foreign Secretary, his close friend Charles James Fox, 'every day affords me new matter of amazement'. Sir James found Potemkin in a state of almost febrile ebullience. Serenissimus insisted on talking throughout the night, even though he had just finished 'a journey of 3000 versts, which he had performed in 16 days, during which period he had slept only three times and, besides visiting several estates and every church he came near, he had been exposed to all the delays and tedious ceremonies of the military and civil honours which the Empress had ordered should be bestowed on him ... yet he does not bear the smallest appearance of fatigue ... and on our separation, I was certainly the more exhausted of the two'.[25]

The reunited Prince and Empress resolved to reinstate Shagin Giray as Crimean khan but also to invoke the Austrian treaty in case it led to war with the Sublime Porte. Joseph replied so enthusiastically to 'my Empress, my friend, my ally, my heroine',[26] that, while Potemkin organized the Russian military response to the Crimean crisis, Catherine took the opportunity to turn their Greek Project from a chimera into a policy. On 10 September 1782, Catherine proposed the Project to Joseph, who was shocked by its impracticality yet impressed by its vision. First, Catherine wanted to re-establish 'the ancient Greek monarchy on the ruins ... of the barbarian government that rules there now' for 'the younger of my grandsons, Grand Duke Constantine'. Then she wanted to create the Kingdom of Dacia, the Roman province that covered today's Rumania, 'a state independent of the three monarchies ... under a Sovereign of Christian religion ... and a person of loyalty on which the two Imperial Courts can rely ...'. Cobenzl's letters make clear Dacia was specifically understood to be Potemkin's kingdom.

Joseph's reply was equally sweeping: he agreed to the Project in principle. In return he wanted the fortress of Khotin, part of Wallachia, and Belgrade. Venice would cede Istria and Dalmatia to him and get Morea, Cyprus and Crete in return. All this, he added, was impossible without French help – could France have Egypt? Only war and negotiation could decide the details – but he did not reject it.[27]

Did Potemkin really believe that there would be a reborn Byzantine Empire ruled by Constantine, with himself as king of Dacia? The idea

---

* 'Long live Great Britain and Rodney. I have just arrived, my dear Harris. Guess who is writing to you and come and see me immediately!'

thrilled him, but he was always the master of the possible. The Dacian idea was realized in the creation of Rumania in the mid-nineteenth century, and Potemkin certainly planned to make that real. But he did not lose his head about it.[28] During 1785 he discussed the Turks with the French Ambassador Ségur and claimed that he could take Istanbul, but insisted that the new Byzantium was just a 'chimera'. It was all 'nonsense', he said. 'It's nothing.' But then he mischievously suggested that three or four Powers could drive the Turks into Asia and deliver Egypt, the Archipelago, Greece, all Europe from the Ottoman yoke. Many years later Potemkin asked his reader, who was declaiming Plutarch, if he could go to Constantinople. The reader tactfully replied it was quite possible. 'That is enough,' exclaimed Potemkin, 'if anyone should tell me I could not go thither, I would shoot myself in the head.'[29] He was always flexible – it was he who suggested in September 1788 that Constantine could be made king of Sweden, a long way from Tsargrad.[30] So he wished it to serve its strategic purpose and to be as real as he could make it.

Catherine the Great herself settles any argument about Potemkin's contribution to the Austrian alliance and the Greek Project. 'The system with Vienna's court', she wrote later, 'is your achievement.'[31]

On 7 August 1782, the Empress and Serenissimus attended the unveiling of Falconet's mammoth statue of Peter the Great – the Bronze Horseman – that still stands in Senate Square in Petersburg. It was a statement in stone of their ambitions to emulate the achievements of Peter, who had succeeded so brilliantly in the Baltic but failed in the south.

The Prince ordered his nephew, Major-General Samoilov, to begin preparatory action to restore order in the Crimea, but he decided to go south himself and conduct the main part. This trip marks the end of the domestic era of Potemkin and Catherine's partnership and the beginning of his time of colossal achievement. From now on, Catherine understood that they were to be apart as much as they were together. This was his path to greatness and contentment, although, as she sweetly admitted to him while he was far away, 'My dear master, I dislike it so much when you are not here by my side.' On 1 September 1782, the Prince left St Petersburg to subdue the Crimea.[32]

17

POTEMKIN'S PARADISE: THE CRIMEA

I now steal captives from the Persians
Or at the Turks direct my arrows . . .
Gavrili Derzhavin, 'Ode to Princess Felitsa'

The Crimea was what Potemkin called 'the wart' on the end of Catherine's nose – but it was to become his own Russian 'paradise'. The peninsula itself was not only dazzlingly and lushly beautiful but it was also a cosmopolitan gem, an ancient entrepôt that controlled the Black Sea. The Ancient Greeks, Goths, Huns, Byzantines, Khazars, Karaim Jews, Georgians, Armenians, Genoese and Tartars, who came later, were all just visitors there, trading and dealing, in a peninsula that seemed to belong to no one race. For a Classicist like the Prince, there were the ruins of Khersoneses and the mythical temple of Iphigenia, the daughter of Agamemnon. But he was most interested in the Crimea's strategic importance and its history as the Mongol stronghold that had terrorized Russia for three centuries.

The Tartar Khanate of the Crimea, known in the West as Crim Tartary, was a state that seemed archaic even in 1782 – the last Mongol outpost. Crimea's Giray dynasty were the second family of the Ottoman Empire because they were descended from Genghis Khan himself, which was much more distinguished a descent than the House of Othman. If Rome and Byzantium represented two of the three international traditions of imperial legitimacy, the blood of Genghis Khan was the third. The family owned estates in Anatolia, where the Ottomans conveniently imprisoned restless potential successors in a sort of Giray Cage. If ever the Ottomans became extinct, it was understood that the Genghizid Girays would succeed them. They were always more allies than subjects.

The Khanate had been founded in 1441 when Haci Giray broke away from the Golden Horde and made himself khan of the Crimea and the shores of the Black Sea. His successor Mengli Giray acknowledged the ultimate suzerainty of the Ottoman Emperor, and from then on the two states existed in a tense, respectful alliance. The Tartars guarded the Black Sea, defended Turkey's northern borders and provided a stream of blonde Slavic slaves to sell to the fleshpots and rowing-galleys of Constantinople. Between 1601 and 1655, it has been estimated, they kidnapped over 150,000 slaves. Their armies of 50,000–100,000 horsemen had the run of the eastern steppes, raiding into Muscovy whenever they needed more slaves to fill their markets. They bore six-foot-long square-shaped bows, with arrows two feet long; muskets and round, bejewelled shields, with pistols studded with lapis and emerald. Until that century, the Genghizid khans received tribute from the tsars of Russia and kings of Poland. The Girays believed their grandeur was second to none. 'His imperial star rose above the glorious horizon,' one khan wrote in an inscription in the Bakhchisaray Palace, where the Khans resided in their Seraglio like miniature Great Turks, guarded by 2,100 Sekbans, Janissaries from Constantinople. 'His beautiful Crimean throne gave brilliant illumination to the whole world.'

For 300 years, Tartary had been one of the most important states of eastern Europe, its cavalry supposedly the best in Europe. It was far larger than just the Crimea: at its apogee in the sixteenth century, it had ruled from Transylvania and Poland to Astrakhan and Kazan, and halfway to Moscow. Even in Potemkin's day, the Khanate ruled from the Kuban steppes in the east to Bessarabia in the west, from the tip of the Crimea to the Zaporogian Sech – 'all that territory that separates the Russian Empire from the Black Sea'. Often allied with Lithuania against Muscovy, in the sixteenth century Tartar khans had even burned the suburbs of Moscow.[1] But their state was fatally flawed. The khans were not hereditary but elective. Beneath the Girays were the *murzas*, Tartar dynasties, also descended from the Mongols, who elected one Giray as khan and another, not necessarily his son, as his heir-apparent, the Kalgai khan. Furthermore many of the khan's subjects were unbiddable Nogai Tartar nomads. It was only in times of war that the khan could really command.[2]

Baron de Tott, French adviser to the Ottomans, was seconded to the Crimea, where he rode, hawked and went greyhound coursing with the Khan, who was always accompanied by 6,000 horsemen. When the Sublime Porte declared war on Russia in 1768, Khan Kirim Giray, accompanied by Tott, galloped out of the Crimea at the head of an army of 100,000 to attack the Russian army on the Bessarabian–Polish border, where young Potemkin served. When Kirim Giray died (possibly of poisoning), the Tartars halted in Bessarabia to install the new Khan Devlet Giray, and the Baron was one of the last to witness the primitive magnificence of this Genghizid monarchy: 'Dressed in a cap loaded with two aigrettes enriched with diamonds, his bow and quiver flung across his body, preceded by his guards and several led horses whose heads were ornamented with plumes of feathers, followed by the standard of the Prophet and accompanied by all his Court, he repaired to his Palace where in the hall of the Divan, seated on his throne, he received the homage of all the grandees.' This noble scene of nomadic warriorship was incongruously accompanied by 'a numerous orchestra and a troop of actors and buffoons'. When he set off to war, the Khan resided in a tent like his Mongol forefathers 'decorated on the inside with crimson'.[3]

The initial raids were impressive but the Russo-Turkish War was a disaster for Crim Tartary. Devlet Giray also perished in his crimson-lined tent and was replaced with a lesser man. Tott was recalled to Constantinople, but unfortunately the Tartar army remained on the Danube with the main Ottoman armies, so that it was not there in 1771 when Vasily Dolgoruky occupied the Crimea. As we saw, Pugachev and the diplomatic conjuncture prevented the Russians keeping all their conquests in 1774. But Catherine, shrewdly advised by Potemkin, insisted in the Treaty of Kuchuk-Kainardzhi that Tartary be made independent of the Sultan, who would still keep nominal religious control as caliph. This 'independence' brought further ruin.

Crimea's tragedy had a face and a name. Shagin Giray, the Kalgai Khan or, as Catherine put it, Tartar 'Dauphin', had led the Crimean delegation to St Petersburg in 1771. 'A sweet character,' she told Voltaire, 'he writes Arabic poems ... he's going to come to my circle on Sundays after dinner when he is allowed to enter to watch the girls dance ...'. Shagin was not only handsome but had been educated in Venice. Thus he became the Russian candidate for khan when the Crimeans agreed to their independence from Istanbul in the Treaty of Karasubazaar in November 1772. That year, Shagin left the capital with 20,000 roubles and a gold sword.[4] However, the Ottomans never accepted the independence of the Crimea, despite agreeing to it in both the Treaties of Kuchuk-Kainardzhi and Ainalikawak. They handed over Kinburn on the Dnieper and two of their forts on the Sea of Azov. But they kept the powerful fortress of Ochakov from which to threaten the Russians, who occupied the land between the Dnieper and the Bug.

In April 1777, Shagin Giray managed to get himself elected khan. He had been far too impressed with the Russian Court. His veneer of Western culture did not long conceal his political ineptitude, military incompetence and unrestrained sadism. Like an Islamic Joseph II but without his philanthropy, Shagin set about creating an enlightened des-potism, backed by a mercenary army led by a Polish nobleman. Meanwhile the Russians had settled 1,200 of their Greek allies from the war in their town of Yenikale on the Sea of Azov: these 'Albanians', as they were called, soon argued with the Tartars. When the Ottomans sent a fleet with another ex-khan on board to replace Shagin, the Tartars rebelled and Shagin fled again. In February 1778, Potemkin ordered yet another operation, while the Ottomans comically declared that they could prove Shagin was an infidel because he 'sleeps on a bed, sits on a chair and does not pray according to the correct manner'.[5] The restored Khan, so deluded about his political abilities that according to Potemkin he thought he was a Crimean Peter the Great, murdered his enemies so savagely that he appalled even the Russians. Catherine hoped the Khan had learned his lesson.

Potemkin however worked to pull the rug from under the Khanate. Its economy depended on Greek, Georgian and Armenian traders and fruit-growers – all Orthodox. The Tartars, whipped up by their mullahs, baited by the 'Albanians' and provoked by Shagin's Polish myrmidons, turned against these Christians. In 1779, Russia sponsored the exodus of the 31,098 Christians, under the control of General Alexander Suvorov. The Christians were presumably happy to leave a chaotic Moslem quagmire to find refuge in an Orthodox empire. They were promised economic privileges in Russia. But the exodus sounds like a death march. Their homes were not ready and many died on the road. Potemkin and Rumiantsev-Zadunaisky, the senior political and military officials, must share responsibility for their misery. But Potemkin did settle the majority in Taganrog and his new town of Mariupol. In imperialistic terms, it worked splendidly: without either trade or agriculture, Shagin found himself impoverished except for Russian generosity. Shagin's brothers rebelled in the summer of 1782. When he fled again, begging for Russian aid, one of them, Bahadir Giray, was elected khan. His reign was to be short.

It took Potemkin, who now assumed complete command of the southern theatre, just sixteen days to make it across Eurasia from the Baltic to the Black Sea. He travelled at the galloping pace usually reserved for couriers – but he made it his own. He grumbled to Catherine about 'displeasing companions, bad weather, poor roads and slow horses'.[6] The displeasing companion was probably Major Semple. Potemkin quizzed him on the armies of Western Europe, and the rascal claimed to have advised him on Russian military reforms, though Potemkin's ideas predated Semple's arrival and he executed them after his departure. The Prince was losing patience with the conman. Potemkin and Catherine exchanged warm letters all the way. She wanted to hear about the Crimea but gave him the latest news about Katinka Skavronskaya, who was ill. Lanskoy visited her and then reported to Catherine and Potemkin that she was getting better – this was how their peculiar family worked.[7]

On 16 September 1782, Serenissimus entered his new city of Kherson. On the 22nd, he met Shagin Giray at Petrovsk (now Berdyansk) to negotiate Russian intervention. He then ordered General de Balmain to invade the Crimea. The Russians routed the rebels, killing 400 'rather wantonly' before taking the capital Bakhchisaray. Shagin Giray, guarded by Russian soldiers, took possession of his capital again. On 30 September, Potemkin's nameday, which he usually celebrated with Catherine in his apartments, she sent him some wifely presents – a travelling tea-set and a dressing case: 'What a wild place you've gone to for your nameday, my friend.'[8]

A measure of tranquillity was restored by mid-October and Potemkin returned to his new town, Kherson. For the rest of his life, he spent much of his time in the south. Catherine missed him deeply but 'my master, I have to admit that your four-week stay in Kherson has been immensely useful'.[9] He worked hard to accelerate Kherson's constructions and shipbuilding, and inspected the building of the Kinburn fortress opposite Ochakov, the Ottoman stronghold. 'How can this small town raise its nose against the young Colossus of Kherson?', asked Catherine as the partners waited to see if the Sublime Porte would go to war against her. Luckily the united front of Austria and Russia proved sufficient to intimidate the Porte.[10] The Colossus rushed back to Petersburg to persuade Catherine to annex the Khanate.[11]

It was a different Prince who returned to Petersburg in late October. He had a mission – and everyone noticed 'the character and conduct of Prince Potemkin are so materially changed within these six months,' Harris reported to Lord Grantham, the new Foreign Secretary. 'He rises early, attends to business, is become not only visible but affable to everybody'.[12]

Serenissimus even dismissed his *basse-cour*. Major Semple tried to use Potemkin's protection to squeeze the merchants of Petersburg and extort money from the Duchess of Kingston. When he threatened to send Russian soldiers to her house to get the money, Potemkin exposed the 'Prince of Swindlers', who fled Russia, defrauding merchants all the way home. Little is known about Semple's subsequent adventures, but Ligne later wrote to Potemkin that he had entertained 'one of Your Highness's Englishmen, le Major Semple, who told me he accompanied you to the conquest of the Crimea'. He was convicted of fraud in England, transported in 1795, escaped, then died in prison in London in 1799.[13] Serenissimus enjoyed his menagerie of mountebanks, learning all he could from them and storing it in his prodigious memory. They used him. But Potemkin always got the better deal.

Now he started to sell his houses, horses, estates, jewels, amassed 'loads of ready money', and declared that he wished to retire to Italy. He told Harris he had lost his power and that he had offered Catherine his resignation but she had rejected it. Potemkin was forever threatening resignation – Catherine must have been used to it. Nonetheless, no one was quite sure what was afoot.[14] He even paid his debts.

It seemed as if God was paying Potemkin's debts too. Prince Orlov had gone mad after the death of his new young wife in June 1781 and wandered ranting, through the corridors of palaces. Nikita Panin had a stroke on 31 March 1783. When these two eclipsed suns, who loathed one another, yet grudgingly admired Potemkin, died within a few days, Catherine thought they would be 'astonished to meet again in the other world'.[15]

The Prince was organizing his affairs because he was preparing himself for his life's work in the south. He was in his creative prime when Catherine's 'dear master' got back to Petersburg – ideas whirled out of him as forcefully and picturesquely as sparks from a Catherine wheel. He immediately set to work on her to settle the Crimean problem once and for all. Was Catherine the tough, obstinate strategist and Potemkin the cautious tactician, as historians would claim later? In this case, Potemkin took the tougher line and got his way – but in different cases they took different lines: it is impossible to generalize. When faced with a problem or a risk, the pair argued, shouted, sulked, were reconciled, back and forth, until their joint policy emerged fully formed.

In late November, the Prince explained to Catherine, in a passionate *tour de force*, why the Crimea, which 'breaks our border', had to be taken because the Ottomans 'could reach our heart' through it. This had to be done *now* while there was still time, while the British were still at war with the French and Americans, while Austria was still enthusiastic, while Istanbul was still wracked with riots and plague. In a stream of imperialistic rhetoric and erudite history, he exclaimed:

Imagine the Crimea is Yours and the wart on your nose is no more! ... Gracious Lady ... You are obliged to raise Russian glory! See who has gained what: France took Corsica, the Austrians without a war took more in Moldavia than we did. There is no power in Europe that has not participated in the carving-up of Asia, Africa, America. Believe me, that doing this will win you immortal glory greater than any other Russian Sovereign ever. This glory will force its way to an even greater one: with the Crimea, dominance over the Black Sea will be achieved.

And he finished: 'Russia needs paradise.'[16]

Catherine hesitated: would it lead to war? Could not they just take the port of Akhtiar instead of the whole Khanate? Potemkin lamented Catherine's caution to Harris: 'Here we never look forward or backward and are governed solely by the impulse of the hour ... If I was sure of being applauded when I did good or blamed when I did wrong, I should know on what I was to depend ...'. Harris at last came in useful when Potemkin extracted his assurance that Britain would not prevent Russian expansion at the cost of the Porte.[17]

Then, just a few weeks after Potemkin's return, Catherine gave him the 'most secret' rescript to annex the Crimea – but only if Shagin Giray died or was overthrown or he refused to yield the port of Akhtiar or if the Ottomans attacked or ... There were so many conditions that both knew that he was really free to pull off his prize if he could get away with it. 'We hereby declare our will', the Empress wrote to the Prince on 14 December 1782, 'for the annexation of the Crimea and the joining of it to the Russian Empire with full faith in you and being absolutely sure that you will not lose convenient time and opportune ways to fulfil this.' There was still a risk that the Ottoman Empire would go to war or that the Great Powers would prevent it.[18]

No wonder Potemkin was working so hard. He had to prepare for war with the Sublime Porte while hoping to avoid it. Catherine kept Joseph closely informed by letter on the shrewd calculation that, if he had received no surprises, he was less likely to bridle. If they were quick and the operation bloodless, they could get the Crimea before the rest of Europe could react. The clock was ticking because France and Britain were just negotiating peace in the American War. They signed the preliminaries on 9/20 January in Paris. The peace was not yet ratified, so the Russians could count on another six months. The diplomats tried to guess how far the partners would go: 'The views of Prince Potemkin extend themselves every day and are of such a magnitude', reported Harris, 'as to exceed the ambition of the Empress herself.'[19] Sir James understated the case when he wrote that 'notwithstanding the pains he took to dissemble it', Serenissimus was 'very sorry to see our war drawing so near to its end ...'.[20]

*

These were Potemkin's last opportunities to enjoy the companionship of Sir James Harris. The Englishman felt he had played his last hand in Petersburg. When his friend Charles James Fox returned to the ministry as one-half of the Fox–North coalition, pursuing a pro-Russian policy, Harris demanded to be recalled while relations with Russia were friendly. Sir James and the Prince saw each other for the last time in the spring, when the latter was increasingly occupied with his southern prep-arations. Harris received his farewell audience from the Empress after Potemkin's departure on 20 August 1783 and then left for home.*

Harris had made the mistake of basing his hopes on a man who was happy to advocate an English alliance, but who was really pursuing an entirely different policy in the south. When the Austrian alliance became active, Harris's beguilement by Potemkin was exposed.

Sir James left Petersburg with high credit in London because his role as Potemkin's friend and tutor in English civilization had brought him closer to the top than any other ambassador was ever to get in Russia. But he must have had mixed feelings about Potemkin, who had so played him. 'Prince Potemkin is no longer our friend,' he sadly told Charles James Fox. Potemkin's archives show they kept in cheerful contact long afterwards. Harris often recommended travellers to the Prince: one was Archdeacon Coxe, the memoirist. 'I know I owe you excuses,' wrote Harris, '... but I know how you like men of letters ...'. Catherine came to regard Harris as a 'trouble-maker and intriguer'. Potemkin had 'crushes' on his friends and then moved on. He told a later ambassador that he had done much for Harris, who had 'ruined everything', and he growled at Bezborodko that Harris was 'insidious, lying and not very decent'. Their friendship was later destroyed by Britain's growing hos-tility to Russia – just one more sad example of the special graveyard reserved for diplomatic friendships.[21]

The Prince spent February and March 1783 preparing military plans to cover Sweden and Prussia, potential Ottoman allies against Russia, while fielding armies against the Turks and sending the Baltic fleet back to the Mediterranean. The object of any war had to be the Ottoman fortress of Ochakov that dominated the Liman (estuary) of the Dnieper and there-fore access to the Black Sea. Potemkin also turned his reforming eye to

* One token of Harris's favour with Catherine and Potemkin can still be seen in London in the form of a gorgeous bauble. When Harris left, she presented him with a chandelier created in Potemkin's glass factories. Harris's descendant, the 6th Earl of Malmesbury, recently gave this to the Skinner's Company of the City of London where it now hangs in the Outer Hall.

the dress and arms of the Russian soldier: in one of his barnstorming memoranda to Catherine, using his common sense and colourful colloquialisms, he proposed to reduce the burden of the common soldier by cutting out all the foppish Prussian paraphernalia. Unusually for a Russian general and an eighteenth-century commander, he actually wanted to improve the comfort of his cannon-fodder.

The Russian infantryman was expected to powder his hair and braid it, which could take twelve hours, and wear the most impractical clothes including tight high boots, stockings, expensive deerskin trousers and the pointed triangular stiff hat that did not protect against the elements. All this 'could not be better invented to depress the soldier', wrote Potemkin, who proposed: 'All foppery must be eliminated.' His denunciations of the Prussian martial hairstyle are classic Potemkin: 'About the hairdo. To curl up, to puff, to plait braids – is that soldiers' business? They have no valets. And what do they need curls for? Everyone must agree it's healthier to wash and comb the hair than to burden it with powder, fat, flour, hairpins, braids. The soldier's garb must be like this: up and ready.' Only months after becoming favourite, he also ordered officers to instruct soldiers without 'inhumane beatings' that made service disgusting and unbearable. Instead he recommended 'affectionate and patient interpretation'. Since 1774, he had been lightening and improving the Russian cavalry too, creating new Dragoon regiments and making the equipment and armour of the Cuirassiers easier to handle.

Years ahead of his time and unaffected by the brutish Prussomania of most Western (and Russian) generals, Potemkin borrowed from the light costumes of the Cossacks instead of the rigid uniforms of Prussian parade grounds to design the new uniform, which was to be named after him: warm comfortable hats that could cover the ears, short haircuts, puttees instead of stockings, loose boots, no ceremonial swords, just bayonets. Potemkin's new uniform set the standard for 'the beauty, simplicity and convenience of the garment, accommodated to the climate and spirit of the country'.[22]

It was time to leave. He knew that if the Crimean adventure succeeded, 'I shall soon be seen in another light and then if my conduct is not approved I will retire to the country and never again appear at Court.'[23] But the Prince was dissembling again: he was convinced he could do anything. He left the capital at the height of his favour. 'They consider his eye, the eye omniscient,' Zavadovsky bitterly told Rumiantsev-Zadunaisky. Yet Harris knew there was a risk: 'Prince Potemkin will go and take the command of the army, however hazardous such a step may be to the duration of his favour.'[24]

Finally, the Prince had a haircut, perhaps to present a more states-manlike look. 'The Grand Duchess', Mikhail Potemkin wrote to Ser-enissimus, 'said that, after you'd had your hair cut, your image has changed for the better.' It is reassuring to see that hairstyles had political significance even two centuries before television.[25] All scores settled, all ties cut – mortal, political, financial and hirsute – Potemkin headed south on 6 April 1783, accompanied by a suite including his youngest niece Tatiana Engelhardt, to conquer 'paradise'.

Before attending a war, the Prince was going to attend a christening. The uncle and the sparky little Tatiana arrived at the Belayatserkov estate of Sashenka Branicka for the christening of her newborn child. Bezborodko followed Potemkin's movements from St Petersburg: 'We received a message that Prince Potemkin had left Krichev on 27 April,' the minister told Simon Vorontsov, 'and having acted as godfather in Belayatserkov, he had departed the very next day ...'. Rarely has a christening been watched so carefully by the cabinets of Europe.

The Prince's progress was unusually leisurely. He was pursued by the Empress's increasingly anxious letters. Initially, the partners relished their diplomatic balancing act like a pair of highwaymen planning a hold-up. They suspected Emperor Joseph envied Russian gains from Turkey in 1774, so Catherine told Potemkin, 'I've made my mind up not to count on anybody but myself. When the cake is baked, everyone will want a slice.' As for Turkey's friend France, she was as unperturbed by 'French thunder, or should I say heat lightning' as she was unworried about Joseph's shakiness. 'Please don't leave me without information both on you and business.' Potemkin always knew the worth of the Austrian alliance but thoroughly enjoyed himself laughing at Joseph and his chancellor's vacillations: 'Kaunitz is acting like a snake or a toad,' he wrote to Catherine on 22 April, but he reassured her: 'Keep your reso-lution, matushka, against any approaches, especially internal or external enemies ... You shouldn't rely on the Emperor much but friendly treat-ment is necessary.'[26]

Potemkin's agents were preparing the Tartars in the Crimea and the Kuban while his troops got ready to fight the Ottomans. Balmain was fixing the easiest piece of the puzzle: on 19 April, he procured the abdication of Shagin Giray in Karasubazaar in the Crimea itself, in return for generous subsidies and possibly another throne. 'My dove, my Prince,' exulted Catherine when she heard this news.[27] When the Prince finally reached Kherson in early May, he found that, as ever, Russian bureaucracy was incapable of achieving much without his driving energy. 'Lady Matushka,' he reported to Catherine in early May, 'Having reached Kherson, I'm exhausted as a dog and unable to find any sense in the Admiralty. Everything is desolate and there's not a single proper report.' Like any country boy, his thoughts about the ministers of Europe were populated with dogs, wolves and toads.

The Prince now threw himself, in a whirl of activity and anxiety, into seizing the Crimea without outside interference. The archives show this multi-talented dynamo at work. Potemkin's rescripts to his generals – Balmain in the Crimea, Suvorov and Pavel Potemkin in the Kuban – took care of every detail: the Tartars were to be treated kindly; regiments were positioned; artillery was to be brought up in case he needed to besiege Ochakov; a spy was on his way ('arrest him and send him to me'). When a colonel was too deferential to the deposed Khan, he received a dose of Potemkinian sarcasm: 'Are you the Khan's butler or an officer?' And he specified every step of the swearing of the oath of allegiance.[28]

Meanwhile to the east of the Crimea and the Kuban, south of the Caucasus mountains, he conducted negotiations with two Georgian kings about a Russian protectorate and with a Persian satrap, along with Armenian rebels, about fostering an independent Armenian state. On top of all this, an epidemic of plague struck the Crimea, brought in from Constantinople, so quarantines had to be enforced. 'I order precautions against it – repeat the basics, inspire hygiene, visit the plague hospitals thus setting an example,' Potemkin wrote to Bezborodko. These were just some of the myriad projects Potemkin was conducting at this time. 'Only God knows how I've worn myself out.' As if this was not enough for one man, he monitored the Powers of Europe – and coped with Catherine.[29] He chided her: 'You've always shown me favour ... so do not decline the one I need most – take care of your health.'

Frederick the Great now attempted to ruin Catherine's plans by egging on the French to stop her. Potemkin dared the old Prussian 'huckster ... to send French troops here – we'd teach them a lesson in the Russian way'. King Gustavus of Sweden, who hoped to emulate his hero Alexander the Great, insisted on visiting Catherine, looking for chances to take advantage of Russian trouble with Turkey to reclaim Sweden's lost Baltic Empire. But his visit was delayed when his horse threw him at a military parade and he broke his arm. 'What a clumsy hero,' Catherine chuckled to Potemkin. Alexander the Great never made such a fool of himself. By the time Gustavus arrived for his visit, the Crimean cake was baked and eaten.

The Comte de Vergennes, the French Foreign Minister, sought out the Austrian envoy to Paris to co-ordinate a reaction to Russian plans. Joseph II, pushed to a decision by Catherine and afraid of missing out on Ottoman gains, suddenly rallied and informed the horrified Vergennes of the Russo-Austrian Treaty. Without support from its ally Austria, an exhausted France lacked the will to act. As for Britain, relieved to have escaped its American quicksand, Lord Grantham told Harris that if 'France means to be quiet about the Turks ... why should we meddle? No time to begin a fresh broil.'

Joseph's alliance proved decisive. 'Your prediction has come true, my cheerful clever friend,' the Empress told her consort. 'Appetite comes with eating.' So it looked as if the partners would get away with it.[30]

Potemkin was so embroiled in his many activities that he now ceased writing his usual letters to Catherine. She fretted and wrote repeatedly throughout May and June, snapping, 'While you complain there's no news from me, I thought it's me who had no news from you for a long time.' The two were getting irritated with each other, as they always did during political crises. She wanted to know if the Khan had left the Crimea so that the Tartars could take the oath of allegiance and she could publish her Manifesto on the annexation.

Potemkin, toiling in Kherson, was trying to manage the departure of Shagin, who was now delaying the enterprise despite his 200,000 rouble pension. The Tartars would not co-operate while the Khan was still there. Even though he sent his baggage to Petrovsk, the Khan's officers were discouraging the mullahs from trusting Russia. Pavel Potemkin and Suvorov at last reported from the distant Kuban that the Nogai nomads were ready to take the oath to Catherine. Everything had to be co-ordinated. The Prince was determined that the annexation should be bloodless and at least appear to be the will of the Crimean people. Finally at the end of May, Potemkin wrote that he was leaving Kherson for the Crimea: 'Goodbye Matushka, darling ... The Khan will be off in a trice.'

The Prince arrived in the Crimea and set up camp at Karasubazaar, ready to administer the oath on 28 June, Catherine's accession day. But it dragged on. While working frantically and exhausting himself, the Prince presented a picture of Oriental languor. 'I saw him in the Crimea,' wrote one of his officers, 'lying on a sofa surrounded by fruits and apparently oblivious of all care – yet amid all the unconcern Russia conquered the peninsula.'[31]

Catherine veered between longing for Potemkin and despairing of him. 'Neither I nor anyone knows where you are.' In early June, she missed him. 'I often deplore that you are there and not here because I feel helpless without you.' A month later, she was angry: 'You can imagine how anxious I must be having no news from you for more than five weeks ... I expected the occupation of the Crimea by mid-May at the latest and now it's mid-July and I know no more about it than the Pope of Rome.'[32] Then she began to worry that he was dying of the plague. Presumably Potemkin had decided to wait until he could lay the entire Crimea and Kuban at Catherine's feet.

Across the ancient Crimean Khanate, the murzas and mullahs gathered in their finest robes to take the oath on the Koran to an Orthodox empress over a thousand miles away. Potemkin administered the oath himself, first to the clergy, then to the rest. The most striking sight was in the Kuban far to the east. On the fixed day, 6,000 Tartar tents of the Nogai Horde were pitched out on the Eysk steppe. Thousands of tough little Mongol horses cantered around the encampments. Russian soldiers were casually vigilant. Shagin's abdication was read to the Nogai, who then took the oath to the Empress in front of Suvorov. They returned to their Hordes, who also recited the oath. Then the feasting began: 100 cattle, 800 rams were cooked and eaten. The Nogai drank vodka – because wine was banned by the Koran. After many toasts and shouts of hurrah, the Cossacks and Nogai competed in horse races. Then the Nogai, having lost their freedom 600 years after Genghis Khan despatched his Hordes westwards, wandered away.[33]

On 10 July, the Prince broke his silence to the Empress: 'In three days, I will congratulate you with the Crimea. All the notables have already sworn, now all the rest will follow.' On 20/31 July, Catherine received Potemkin's report that the Crimean Tartars and the two Nogai Hordes had taken the oath. She was so relieved and worn out by the anticipation that she replied coolly, but, as it sank in and she received Potemkin's explanation, she appreciated his achievement. 'What a lot of glorious deeds have been accomplished in a short time.' His letters were immediately filled with his ideas for towns, ports and ships, laced with Classical references to his new territories. His ebullience was always infectious. When he wrote that the cowardly rumours about the plague were spread by poltroons in 'Spa and Paris', Catherine laughed at last.[34]

A few days later, Serenissimus pulled another golden rabbit out of the hat: in the Caucasus, the Kingdom of Georgia accepted Russian protection. The Caucasus, the isthmus between the Black and Caspian Seas, was a mountaineous patchwork of kingdoms and principalities, dominated by the empires around them – Russia, Turkey and Persia. In the north-west, Potemkin had just annexed the Kuban, ruled by the Crimeans. In the foothills, Russian generals struggled to control the wild Moslem mountaineers in Chechnya and Daghestan. South of the mountains, the Persian and Turkish empires divided the region among themselves. There, the two Orthodox Georgian kingdoms, Kartli-Kacheti and Imeretia, were almost mythical or Biblical in their romantic ferocity, so it was entirely appropriate that their tsars were named respectively Hercules and Solomon.

Hercules (Heraclius, or Erakle in Georgian), a remarkable empire-builder, seemed to be the last of the medieval knights alive and well in the century of Voltaire. The name suited the man. Scion of the Bagratid dynasty that provided Georgian monarchs for almost a thousand years, he was a warrior–king who owed his throne to his fighting for the Shah of Persia in India and had managed to create a mini-empire in the backyards of Persia and Turkey. Already an old man, 'of middle size, with a long face, large eyes and small beard, he had spent his youth', a traveller remarked, 'at the Court of Nadir Shah where he contracted a fondness for Persian customs . . .'. Hercules was 'renowned for his courage and military skill. When on horseback he always has a pair of loaded pistols at his girdle and, if the enemy is near, a musket flying over a shoulder . . .'. The other Georgian Tsar, Solomon of Imeretia, was just as striking for, repeatedly overthrown and then restored, he had 'lived like a wild man for sixteen years in caverns and holes and frequently, by his personal courage, escaped assassination'. He too lived with a musket over his shoulder.[35]

When the Russians went to war in 1768, Catherine had helped Hercules and Solomon but abandoned them after 1774 to the vengeance of Shah and Sultan. Potemkin was emboldened by his Austrian alliance and decided to increase the pressure on the Ottomans by talking to the Georgians. He corresponded with Hercules, inquiring if he was now at peace with Solomon: he wanted both kingdoms for Russia.

On 31 December 1782, King Hercules told the 'Merciful and Serene Prince' that 'I am entrusting myself, my children and my Orthodox nation' to Russia. Serenissimus ordered his cousin, who commanded the Caucasus corps, to conduct negotiations. On 24 July 1783, Pavel Potemkin signed the Treaty of Georgievsk with Hercules on the Prince's behalf.[36]

Serenissimus, still encamped at Karasubazaar in the Crimea, was delighted. His Classical-cum-Orthodox exuberance at the news of another magnificent present to the Empress was irresistible:

Lady Matushka, my foster-mother, the Georgia business is also brought to an end. Has any other Sovereign so illuminated an epoch as you have? But it is not just brilliance. You have attached the territories, which Alexander and Pompey just glanced at, to the baton of Russia, and Kherson of Taurida [Crimea] – the source of our Christianity and thus of our humanity – is already in the hands of its daughter.* There's something mystic about it. You have destroyed the Tartar Horde – the tyrant of Russia in old times and its devastator in recent ones. Today's new border promises peace to Russia, jealousy to Europe and fear to the Ottoman Porte. So write down this annexation, unempurpled with blood, and order your historians to prepare much ink and much paper.[37]

Catherine was impressed. Thanking him for his achievements, she ratified the treaty, which confirmed Hercules' titles, borders and right to coin his own currency. In September Pavel Potemkin built a road out of a bridlepath and galloped in an eight-horse carriage over the Caucasus to Tiflis (now Tbilisi). In November, two Russian battalions entered the capital. The Prince began to supervise the building of forts on Russia's new border while two Georgian tsareviches, sons of Hercules, set off to live at the cosmopolitan Court of Potemkin.[38]

And there was more. The failure of Voinovich's Caspian adventure two years earlier had not discouraged Potemkin's plans for an anti-Ottoman alliance with Persia. Bezborodko, one of the few who understood Potemkin's geopolitical schemes, explained that the Prince planned not only this eastern version of the Austrian alliance. He had persuaded Catherine, in the Crimean rescript, to authorize him to push for the Caspian to create two other principalities: one Armenian (today's Armenia) and another on the Caspian seashores (today's Azerbaijan) that might be ruled by Shagin Giray, the deposed Crimean Khan.[39]

By early 1784, Potemkin was negotiating with the Persian Khan in Isfahan about whether he might also join the Empire, giving him a chance to found his Armenian kingdom. 'Armenia raises its hands to the sacred throne of Your Imperial Majesty asking for deliverance from the Aga's yoke,' declared Potemkin to the Empress.[40] Negotiations with Persian potentates, the Khans of Shusha and Goya, and the Armenians

---

* Potemkin the Orthodox revelled in possessing the very place, the ancient town of Khersoneses in the Crimea, where Vladimir, Grand Prince of Kiev, had been baptized in 988, the moment when Christianity reached the land of Rus.

of the Karabak, continued well into 1784.* Potemkin sent an envoy to Isfahan, but the Khan died and the envoy came home. Ultimately, the Persian–Armenian Project led to nothing. For now, his gains were substantial enough.

Catherine was delighted and praised him as an empress, lover and friend: 'For all the labours exerted by you and the boundless care of my affairs, I cannot sufficiently express my recognition to you; you yourself know how sensitive I am to merit and yours are outstanding, just as my friendship and love for you are. Let God give you health and ever greater powers of body and soul.'[41]

In late August 1783, the Prince collapsed with a dangerous fever. Exhausted by his massive projects, perpetual travel, proximity to plague and bad water, Potemkin lay close to death in a pretty Tartar cottage amid the verdant pastures of Karasubazaar.

Potemkin could not rest – but his health improved in mid-September. Europe still rumbled at Russia's achievement. As his fever ebbed and flared up again, he inspected Russian forces. In what became a pattern, even a tradition, Catherine, Bezborodko and the ambassadors followed every spasm back in Petersburg. When he moved to the regional capital of the south, Kremenchuk, away from plague-ridden Crimea and Kherson, Catherine, ever the concerned wife, wrote, 'You never take care of yourself while recovering. Just do me this favour, for once remember the importance of your health: the well-being of the Empire and my glory.' She knew that the conquest and development of the south depended on him: 'The most important enterprise in the world will turn into nothing without you. I praise your moving to Kremenchuk but this should not be done in the very depth of dangerous illness, I was horrified to hear you had covered 300 versts in such a state.'[42]

The two Russian imperialists savoured their success. Potemkin lost himself in romantic neo-Classical dreams, while Catherine reacted with crude, almost Stalinesque satisfaction: 'Upon the envy of Europe, I look quite calmly – let them jest while we do our business.' She reaffirmed his permanence: 'Know that I am committed to you for a century.'[43] To show it, she allotted 100,000 roubles to build him a new house that was to become the Taurida Palace.[44]

He could not stop working. He knew that the Nogai Hordes would

---

* The Armenians of Nagorno-Karabak were still fighting to escape the Moslem control of the Republic of Azerbaijan and join the Republic of Armenia during a vicious war in the early 1990s.

always create instability in the Kuban, so in a move that foreshadowed later stains on Russian history he drew up a plan to move the nomads and resettle them between the Volga and the Urals. The rumours reached the Nogai. Meanwhile that irritating Genghizid popinjay, Shagin Giray, lingered in the Taman and kept in contact with the Nogai Hordes. Perhaps encouraged by him, these had barely left Suvorov's barbecued banquet on the steppe than they massacred their pro-Russian murzas. The energetic Suvorov immediately pursued the rebels and slaughtered them on 1 October.[45]

The Russian Ambassador to the Porte was Potemkin's university friend Yakov Bulgakov, who now monitored the Ottoman reaction while negotiating a trade agreement. He reported that the Turks 'won't quarrel over the Crimea if no new circumstance comes from Europe'. The final Treaty of Versailles ended the War of American Independence on 23 August/ 3 September, but it was too late. Prussia and France tried to raise some resistance and, in late September, Catherine still expected an Ottoman declaration of war 'at any minute', but Joseph had held firm against Vergennes and Frederick.[46] The Kaiser even acclaimed 'the success of Prince de Potemkin' to the Empress: 'I know very well the value and difficulty in finding such good and loyal *serviteurs* like him and how rare it is in our profession to find someone who understands us.' On 28 December 1783, the Turks implicitly recognized the loss of the Crimea in the new convention of Ainalikawak, negotiated by Bulgakov.[47]

Letters and praise poured into Potemkin's Chancellery. It was true that he had now 'risen to the highest degree of power that Sovereigns accord to individuals', as his general Igelstrom wrote to him.[48] More than that, 'what the centuries had not completed, what Peter I had not managed', wrote the writer Glinka, 'this giant of his time was able to achieve'.[49] Catherine missed him most of all, writing her simplest confirmation of their partnership in early October: 'Let God make you better and return here. Honestly when I am without you, I often feel I am without hands.' The Prince replied that 'Thank God, I get better every hour ... and when I'm fully recovered, I'm coming to see my dear matushka.'[50]

Prince Potemkin returned to Petersburg in late November 1783 to find courtiers hostile to him in paroxyms of jealousy. His ally Bezborodko was beleaguered, so Potemkin defended him, only to find himself beset by enemies. 'The envy of many', observed Bezborodko, grateful for Potemkin's support, 'is clear.' This took the form of an intrigue to discredit Serenissimus.

The Empress had been told that the outbreaks of plague in the south were somehow due to Potemkin's negligence. She was sensitive on the subject, after Moscow's Plague-Riot of 1770. There were allegations that Italian settlers arriving to farm the southern steppes had died because there were no houses for them. Both the allegations were false – he had worked especially hard to limit the plague, and had succeeded. It must have been depressing to achieve so much and travel so far only to find he had to fight his corner on his return. The plot, according to Bezborodko, was hatched by the Navy Minister, Ivan Chernyshev, who had most reason to resent Serenissimus' success because Grand Admiral Potemkin was building his own Black Sea fleet outside the remit of the Navy College. Princess Dashkova, back from her travels, and even Lanskoy were somehow involved too. These accusations led to a row between the partners and a coldness descended over these two proud statesmen.[51]

Potemkin stopped calling on Catherine. Lev Engelhardt, another cousin from Smolensk who had just joined the Prince's staff as an adjutant, left a graphic account of this time. Usually the road, known as Millionaya (Millionaire's Row), in front of Potemkin's house adjoining the Winter Palace was so crowded with carriages and petitioners that it was impossible to pass. But now, at the height of his success, it was deserted. His enemies rejoiced.

On 2 February 1784, Serenissimus woke up late as usual. His valet had placed a little envelope with the imperial seal beside his bed. The Empress, who had been up since seven, had typically ordered that the Prince should not be woken. Potemkin read the letter and called for his secretary, Vasily Popov. 'Read!', he said. Popov ran into the anteroom, where adjutant Engelhardt was on duty: 'Go and congratulate the Prince. He's promoted to field-marshal.' Engelhardt went into the bedroom and congratulated his master. The Prince–Field-Marshal jumped out of bed, threw on a greatcoat, wrapped his pink silk scarf round his neck and went off to see the Empress. He was also raised to President of the College of War. Furthermore, on his recommendation, the Empress created the province of Tauris, the Classical name for the Crimea, and added it to Potemkin's vast viceroyalty of New Russia. Within two hours, his apartments were full. Millionaya was blocked by carriages again. The courtiers who had been coldest grovelled the lowest.[52] On 10 February, Catherine dined as Potemkin's guest in one of his nieces' houses.

The Prince impulsively decided he wanted to see Constantinople, so he asked Bulgakov: 'What if I come as a guest to you from the Crimea by ship? Seriously I want to know if it is possible.' Potemkin's request was not merely romantic impulse – though much of it was his desire to see the city of Caesars. He knew now what he wanted to do, how much he wanted to build in the south, and for that he needed time and peace. He surely wanted to go to Tsargrad to negotiate this peace with the Sultan himself. Ambassador Bulgakov must have dreaded the very prospect. On 15 March, he replied from Istanbul that it would be exceedingly complicated. 'They think', he explained, 'that you are our Grand Vizier.'[53] Potemkin never saw Constantinople – but his destiny was in the south. From now on, he planned 'to pass the first four or five months of each year in his provinces'.[54] In mid-March, the Prince left St Petersburg again. There were cities to build, fleets to float, kingdoms to found.

Part Six

~

THE CO-TSAR
1784–1786

18

EMPEROR OF THE SOUTH

Is it not you who put to flight
The mighty hordes of vulturous neighbours
And from vast empty regions made
Inhabitable towns and cornfields
And covered the Black Sea with ships
And shook the earth's core with your thunder?
Gavrili Derzhavin, *The Waterfall*

'Every hour I encountered some fresh, fantastic instance of Prince Potemkin's Asiatic peculiarities,' wrote the Comte de Damas, who observed the energetic and creative way the viceroy of the south worked in the late 1780s. 'He would move a *guberniya* [province], demolish a town with a view to building it somewhere else, form a new colony or a new industrial centre, and change the administration of a province, all in a spare half-hour before giving his whole attention to the arrangement of a ball or a fête . . .' This was how Westerners saw the Prince – a wizardly satrap ordering cities as he commissioned ball-dresses for his mistresses. They always presumed that 'barbaric' Russians could never really do anything properly, not like Germans or Frenchmen, so that Potemkin's work must surely be flawed. When it turned out that Potemkin did do things properly and that his achievements appeared almost miraculous in their imagination and execution, jealous Westerners and Russian enemies propagated the big lie of his sham 'Potemkin Villages'.

The reality of Potemkin's achievements in the south, in the fifteen years allotted to him, was remarkable. 'Attempts have been made to ridicule the first foundations of towns and colonies,' wrote one of his earliest biographers. 'Yet such establishments are not the less entitled to our admiration ... Time has justified our observations. Listen to the travellers who have seen Kherson and Odessa . . .' The so-called 'Potemkin Villages' are cities today with millions of inhabitants.

Russia underwent two massive leaps of expansion in the south: the reigns of Ivan the Terrible, who annexed the Khanates of Astrakhan and Kazan, and of Catherine the Great. Potemkin was, as Pushkin and others recognized, the mastermind and energy behind Catherine's successes in the south. Potemkin did not invent these policies: as the Russian historian Kliuchevsky put it, colonization is 'the basic fact of Russian history'. But Potemkin was unique in combining the creative ideas of an entrepreneur with the force of a soldier and the foresight of a statesman. He also brought the south to the north: while, under Panin, Russia pursued the Northern System, under Potemkin the south *was* Russia's foreign policy.

The Prince became the Governor-General (*namestvo*) of New Russia, Azov, Saratov, Astrakhan and the Caucasus soon after rising to favour, but in the late 1770s and certainly after the annexation of the Crimea, he became the effective co-ruler of the Russian Empire. Just as Diocletian saw that the Roman Empire was so vast that it required Emperors of the East and West, so Catherine let Potemkin run the south and control it absolutely. Potemkin had grown since 1774 – in stature as well as girth. He was made for the wide open steppes of the south and he could not be confined to Court. Petersburg was now too small for the both of them.

Potemkin's power was both vertical and horizontal, for he was in charge of the army at the College of War and commander-in-chief of all irregular forces, especially the Cossacks. When he began to build the Black Sea Fleet, it reported not to the Admiralty in Petersburg but to him as Grand Admiral. However, most of all, his power depended on his own personality, the prestige of his successes, such as the Crimea, and his ability to create ideas and force their execution – and no longer just on his closeness to Catherine.

Serenissimus deliberately ruled his Viceroyalty – the names and borders of the provinces changed but, essentially, they comprised all the new lands annexed between 1774 and 1783, from the River Bug in the west to the Caspian Sea in the east, from the mountains of the Caucasus, and the Volga across most of the Ukraine almost as far as Kiev – like an emperor. It was unique for a Russian tsar, such as Catherine, to delegate so much power to a consort – but the relationship between them was unparalleled.[3]

Serenissimus set up his own Court in the south that rivalled and complemented Catherine's in the north. Like a tsar, he cared for the poor folk, disdained the nobility, and granted ranks and estates in his lands. Potemkin travelled with a royal entourage; he was greeted at towns by all the nobles and townsfolk; his arrival was marked by the firing of cannons and the giving of balls. But it went further than just the trimmings of royalty. When he issued his orders, he did so in the name of the Empress, but he also listed his endless titles and medals as a king might. His commands too were absolute: whether it was a gardener or an engineer, his subordinates usually had a military rank and their orders were military in style. 'Equalling in his power the mightiest kings,' recalled Wiegel, 'I doubt even Napoleon was better obeyed.'[4]

The Prince liked to appear majestically languid – as he is remembered in so many memoirs – but this was something of a pose. He ruined his health with the mammoth quantity of work he conducted. Probably, he was more like a school swot who tries to appear to do no work while cramming all night. By the early 1780s, he governed through his own private Chancellery, which had at least fifty clerks in it, including specialists in French and Greek correspondence.[5] He even had his own effective prime minister – the indefatigable Vasily Stepanovich Popov, whom he, and later the Empress, trusted absolutely. Like Potemkin, Popov gambled all night, slept half the day, never took off his uniform and was always ready even in the middle of the night to respond to the Prince's famous call, usually from his bed, of '"Vasily Stepanovich!" All you heard was "Vasily Stepanovich!"'[6] If Popov was his chancellor, the equally tireless Mikhail Leontovich Faleev, a young merchant he met during the First Russo-Turkish War, became his quartermaster, contractor and collaborator in gargantuan works. His portrait shows the weary, shrewd blue eyes, slim, disciplined, tidy and handsome face of this most unusual Russian entrepreneur, wearing his blue coat and white ruffles. Potemkin had him ennobled and he amassed a great fortune but, unusually for merchant princes, Faleev was honoured and loved in the town he built with Serenissimus – Nikolaev. They were in constant correspondence.[7]

Potemkin was in perpetual motion, except when paralysed by bouts of depression and fever. However many cities he founded, wherever he was, whether alone in a *kibitka* sledge, with the Chancellery hundreds of versts behind, or in a palace, the capital of this southern empire was the creative yet flawed and tormented figure of Potemkin himself.

Potemkin's career began and ended with his love for the Cossacks. First he destroyed the Zaporogian Cossacks and then he recreated them by rebuilding their Host at the heart of the imperial army. On an island in the midst of the broad Dnieper river – hence their name 'za-porogi', 'beyond the rapids' – lived a unique republic of 20,000 martial men, who controlled a huge triangle of barren territory north of the Black Sea. The Zaporogians did not farm, because farming was done by slaves and these were freemen – the very word Cossack deriving from the old Turkic for freeman. But, like most Cossacks, their Sech was a brutal democracy which elected a hetman – or ataman – in wartime. They had their own laws: treason was punished by being sewn into a sack and tossed into the rapids. Murderers were buried alive in the cold embrace of the cadavers of their victims, to whom they were bound.

They were unusual for Cossacks in many ways. They were as happy on their sixty-foot, reed-lined and oar-propelled boats – the *chaiki* or 'seagulls' – as on horseback. They were said to be the inventors of the first submarine, using sand as ballast and a wooden pipe through which to breathe. The Zaporogian Cossacks did not live with women. No female was allowed inside their *sech* or 'clearing' to preserve the military discipline they held paramount: 'they were bachelors', Lev Engelhardt explained, 'like the Knights of Malta'.

These 'Boat Cossacks' sported handlebar moustaches, shaven heads with one long ponytail, Turkish pantaloons with gold thread, silken cummerbunds, satin kaftans, high fur hats and turbans often with ostrich feathers and jewelled insignia. Their true profession was war. When they did not fight for themselves, they fought for others, sometimes as mercenaries – in the mid-seventeenth century, some Zaporogians were lent by the King of Poland to fight Spain at Dunkirk, under the Prince de Condé, and twice that century their fleet of almost 100 *chaiki* had raided Constantinople itself.

The Cossacks had developed as freebooting guards of the Russian frontiers, but by 1774 their unruly independent Hosts were no longer needed to protect against the Turks – and the Sech stood in the way of Russia confronting the Tartars. The Ukrainian Cossacks under Mazeppa had abandoned Peter the Great and joined Charles XII of Sweden. Cossack raiders had started the Russo-Turkish War in 1768 and the Zaporogians had several times robbed Russian troops on the way to the front. Recently, the Yaik and Don Cossacks begat Pugachev. During the war, Potemkin had developed special links with the Sech – he was an honorary Zaporogian. Indeed, in May 1774, he wrote to his Cossack friends from Tsarskoe Selo, telling them of his rise to power and promising that 'I have told the Sovereign about everything.' Nonetheless, as soon as the Pugachev Rebellion was suppressed, he changed his tune, warned them to stop their plundering and recommended the liquidation of the Sech and the reorganization of all the Cossack Hosts. Indeed they were a proven liability to the Russian state – and to Potemkin's plans to colonize and cultivate new territories.

At dawn on 4 June 1775, Russian troops under Potemkin's orders approached the Sech, surrounded it and ordered it to surrender or face destruction. The Sech that he called 'the foolish rabble' surrendered without resistance. Potemkin wrote Catherine's Manifesto for her, which was published on 3 August 1775 – 'all their violence should be cited – the reasons why such a harmful society will be destroyed'.[8] The Zaporogians were not killed: only three leaders, including their wealthy Hetman Kalischevsky, were despatched to the Arctic monastery of Solovki on the White Sea. They were resettled as Astrakhan Cossacks, but many of them fled to fight for the Turks: Potemkin was to lure them back in the 1780s.[9] Nor was the Sech alone: the Yaik Host was moved and renamed; the Don Cossacks were reformed too and brought under Potemkin's direct control: he appointed their new hetman and the committee that would manage their civil affairs.[10] The overmighty Don Hetman, Efremov, was arrested, though Potemkin protected him and his family.[11]

Potemkin immediately suggested that the loyal Zaporogians be formed into special regiments. Catherine feared the Cossacks after Pugachev, so he bided his time, but he built a Cossack flotilla on the Caspian and Azov Seas.[12] He treated the Cossacks so kindly that noblemen grumbled that he was in love with them. He certainly surrounded himself with loyal Zaporogians. He also made sure that runaway serfs, found among these frontiersmen, should not be returned to their masters. It says much that Potemkin was loved by them in his lifetime: he earned the title 'Protector of the Cossacks'.[13]

Yet the destruction of the Zaporogians is always listed as one of Potemkin's crimes – especially in modern Ukraine, where the Sech is regarded as the forerunner of the Ukrainian state. But the Sech and other Hosts were doomed after Pugachev, their territory was unsettled, uncultivated and in the way of Russia's drive to the Black Sea. Their removal allowed the annexation of the Crimea. Serenissimus is criticized for removing treasures from Zaporogian churches and distributing the lands to his cronies – yet, since he was not there himself, he ordered General Tekeli to inventory all church plate and give it to the Church.[14] (Anyway, the majority of their jewels were themselves stolen.) The distribution and cultivation of land was the entire point of the annexation. He resettled these lands with Greeks who had fought for Orlov-Chesmensky and, later, state peasants from the Russian interior, and began building fortresses to protect them. Indeed, one modern historian argues that it was cultivation of these steppes that provided Russia with the resources and food supply to defeat Napoleon in 1812.[15]

On 31 May 1778, Catherine approved Potemkin's plan for a Black Sea port called Kherson, a sonorous name, ringing with his neo-Classical and Orthodox dreams of Khersoneses. This was the city made possible by the peace with Turkey and the liquidation of the Zaporogians.[16] Docks were ordered. Carpenters were demanded from all over the empire. On 25 July, the Prince chose one of the Admiralty's officers to be its first governor – Ivan Abramovich Hannibal. Probably, Potemkin was attracted to the exotic history of this man and his connection to Peter the Great.

He was the half-black eldest son of Peter the Great's famous blackamoor, Abraham Hannibal, an Abyssinian prince bought in Istanbul for the Tsar and adopted by him. Naming him for obvious reasons after Scipio's adversary, Peter educated his ward, promoted him and stood as godfather to his son Ivan. Pushkin, who wrote the (uncompleted) '*Blackamoor of Peter the Great*', was the great-nephew of Ivan Hannibal. Pushkin's grandfather Osip Hannibal was a poor father, so the poet's mother was actually brought up in the household of Potemkin's first governor of Kherson. Ivan Hannibal was as proud of his ancestry as Pushkin. When he died in 1801, the tombstone read: 'The sultriness of Africa bore him, the cold calmed his blood.' His portrait in the Kherson State Historical Museum shows the dark skin and fine Abyssinian features of his father and the straight hair and stockiness of his Russian mother. Now Catherine ordered Hannibal to proceed with this massive task.

Potemkin's first town was designed to be both the base for his new Black Sea Fleet, which so far existed only in a small way in the minor Russian ports of the Sea of Azov, and an entrepôt for Mediterranean trade. The placing of this port was a difficult decision because Russian's gains in 1774 had given it a narrow corridor to the Black Sea. Its access was via the mouth of the Dnieper river, one of the great waterways of Rus, which reached the Black Sea through a narrow, shallow estuary called the Liman. At the end of the Liman on the Kinburn spit, Potemkin had built a small fortress. But the Ottomans kept the powerful fortress–town of Ochakov on the other bank, which effectively controlled the delta. There was no ideal place that was both defensible and a natural harbour. The naval engineers favoured Glubokaya Pristan, a deep harbour, but it was indefensible, so Potemkin chose a site further up the Dnieper where a fortress named Alexandershanz already stood. There was an island in the river that protected the port and docks. The Dnieper rapids made it hard to reach without using 'camels', while a bar beneath the town obstructed access to the Sea. Worse than that, Kherson was on the edge of the baking-hot steppes and marshy waterways and thousands of versts from the nearest ship timber, let alone food supplies.

The obstacles were overwhelming, but Potemkin repeatedly overcame them to build his city. No one in Petersburg believed it would be completed. Not for nothing did Catherine write to him: 'Kherson will never be built without you.' Simultaneously, the jealousy that was to ruin Potemkin's reputation rose even before the first stone had been laid. 'The foundation of Kherson will become famous,' fumed Zavadovsky. 'Its creator loves his project and pushes it.'[17] He was right: Potemkin almost willed the town into existence and drove Hannibal relentlessly. By August, the Russo-Abyssinian had established twelve teams of workers and bought timber on the upper Dnieper in Russian Belorussia and Poland. Everything had to be floated down the river to Kherson.

Potemkin hired over 500 carpenters and thousands of workers, founded the shipyards and planned the town. The first keels of warships were laid down in May 1779. Two more were on the way by 1781. Serenissimus decided to employ the army, which started with its own wooden barracks, using mud wattle for the walls at first. Next he imported 1,000 criminals to work the quarries.[18] Then he gave the merchant Faleev his big chance, persuading him to dynamite the rocky Dnieper rapids in return for a slice of Kherson's future trade. Faleev, who invested in its success, undertook this major work. Potemkin supplied the gunpowder. By 1783, Faleev had succeeded to the extent that some barges could sail straight down to Kherson. The Prince rewarded him with the rank of major, raising him to nobility.[19]

Potemkin's critics claimed that little was built and nothing was done well – and history has believed them. Fortunately, the well-born Westerners who visited Petersburg on their Grand Tours met Potemkin, who always directed them to Kherson. One of the first of these was a young English engineer, Samuel Bentham, brother of the utilitarian philosopher Jeremy, who was to work with Potemkin for five years. In 1780, he saw Kherson already had 180 houses and had launched one sixty-four-gunned ship-of-the-line and five frigates, and marvelled: 'He chose the spot not above two . . . years ago when there was not even a hut here.' The timber, he noted, had to be floated down from a town in Poland that was later to become famous – Chernobyl.[20]

Another intrepid Englishman, and a friend of Samuel Bentham, was Reginald Pole Carew, an Oxford graduate and Cornish landowner in his late twenties, who witnessed the next stage. He was the sort of young man who would later play the Great Game. Potemkin adopted Pole Carew, showing him his estates and *fabriks* (factories) round Petersburg before he headed south. Pole Carew's notes, still unpublished, read as if he was either writing a book or engaged in amateur espionage. By the time he arrived, there were already 300 houses in Kherson. Apart from nine regiments of soldiers, 'up to now the town is mainly inhabited by Polish Jews and Greeks ... Soldiers, sailors, peasants are all being used ... in building,' but he noticed that the work on the fortifications was being done too fast 'for fear of disgusting higher powers'.[21] These were his real feelings, but he also tactfully told the Prince that 'what I see here surpasses imagination'.[22]

Potemkin was determined to attract trade to his Viceroyalty. In 1781, Pole Carew discussed a potential trading business with General Hannibal, and with Kherson's two tycoons – Potemkin's merchant Faleev and the Frenchman Antoine. Faleev had founded the Black Sea Company to trade with the Ottomans and soon launched his frigate, the *Borysthenes*. He also had the brandy farm for Potemkin's three *guberniya* and supplied the soldiers with meat: Pole Carew reckoned he already made 500,000 roubles a year. Pole Carew listed the goods that could be traded in Kherson – wax, flags, rope, timber,[23] and was tempted by the trading opportunities. 'It is a bourgeois of Kherson who writes to you,' he told the Prince.[24]

Antoine of Marseilles, later Baron de Saint-Joseph, was the town's shipping magnate. Setting off to Petersburg, he called on the Prince proposing the creation of a trading post and free port at Kherson. Potemkin was delighted,[25] and invited Catherine to 'abolish internal customs duties and to reconsider external ones'.[26] However keen he was on Britain, the Prince realized that France dominated Mediterranean trade from Marseilles and this was to have political consequences. By 1786, Antoine told Potemkin that, in the last year, eleven of his French ships had arrived from Marseilles.[27]

Nonetheless, Kherson was a struggle. Potemkin supervised every detail when he had time: on 3 August 1783, he wrote to his engineer Colonel Gaks in Kherson, 'I'm confirming for the second time that the building of the hospital must be finished ...'. On 14 October, 'I am surprised that in spite of being assured by you that the hospital is finished, it has not even been begun ...'. Then he added: 'It's strange to me that sometimes orders are cancelled when they have been confirmed by me.' In other words, if there was any deception in the building of Kherson, Potemkin was its victim, but he could not be everywhere at once. A week later, he was ordering Gaks to build two baths to fight the plague – 'one for the absolutely healthy and another for the weak ...' and 'Don't forget to build breweries.' But Hannibal and Gaks were simply not getting things accomplished. Potemkin was frustrated. The next February, Potemkin sacked Gaks and appointed Colonel Nikolai Korsakov, a talented engineer educated in Britain. Potemkin confirmed the annual budget of 233,740 roubles, but wanted everything finished 'in a short time' while insisting on both 'durability' and 'beauty inside'.[28] The Prince himself approved every plan, each building façade – from the school to the archbishop's house to his own residence – and it began to take shape.[29]

A painting of Kherson in its Museum shows its central square as Potemkin designed it: there is the beautiful church of St Catherine's. Later, in 1790, the Prince was still beautifying it. When his favourite architect Ivan Starov came to the south, Potemkin ordered him to 'remake the cupola in the cathedral in Kherson' exactly like the one in his St Petersburg Palace, 'and fix a place for the belfry'.[30] It was done. The dome and the bell-tower remain exactly as the Prince ordered. Potemkin's palace stood at right angles to it.

His memoranda to his officials completely destroy the image of Potemkin in most Western accounts.[31] These are the works of a man aware of the difficulties his officials faced. He was certainly authoritarian, concerned with the smallest details, but surprisingly flexible in giving second chances to overworked officials. Potemkin was aware as anyone that Kherson's position made it extremely vulnerable to disease. Reading between the lines, it must have been a ghastly posting. Pole Carew recorded that the shipwrights sent from Kronstadt and Petersburg had 'died off'. When ships from Istanbul and soldiers from across the Empire poured into the area as Potemkin organized the taking of the Crimea, the threat of an epidemic became serious. By 1786, the French merchant Antoine had lost his brothers and many employees. Kherson 'resembled a vast hospital: one only saw dead and dying'. The Prince tried to control local health and keep the fevers at bay.[32] He took special care with hospitals and breweries (to provide drinking water), even telling the inhabitants to eat greens,[33] and personally appointed the doctors[34] to his hospitals.*

Everything was driven by the manic enthusiasm of the man Catherine called the 'young Colossus of Kherson'.[35] His infectious energy was the only thing that could triumph over the sloth of the Russian bureaucrat: returning from his new town, he spoke to James Harris 'with raptures of the climate, soil, and situation of Kherson.'[36] But every visit revealed more mistakes by his subordinates. That was why he began to spend

---

* When this author visited Kherson, it was still infested with insects: the bed and ceiling in its main hotel so teemed with mosquitoes that the white of the sheets and the paint were literally blackened.

more and more time away and why Catherine admitted that the trips were worth it, however much she missed him.[37]

It is usually claimed that Potemkin concealed the mistakes in Kherson. On the contrary. He confided a catalogue of failures to Catherine. He dismissed Hannibal – apparently for building the fortifications poorly; he could not find any sense in the Admiralty; too much money had been spent; there was not enough wood; the timber they had was unsound. 'Oh Matushka, what a mess and what dishonesty is here in the Admiralty!' It was too hot. The buildings still stood in a wilderness. 'Nobody has even had the sense to plant trees. I've now ordered it.'[38] He demanded more experts: 'send the staff according the enclosed list. There aren't enough smiths here. I've sent to Tula for them.'

The town continued to grow. When Kirill Razumovsky visited in 1782, he was amazed by the stone buildings, fortress, battleships, 'spacious suburb', barracks and Greek merchant ships: 'Imagine all this and you will understand my bewilderment for not so long ago there was nothing here but a building where beehives are kept for the winter.'[39] Francisco de Miranda, the South American revolutionary, who was also temporarily adopted by Potemkin, had the chance to examine Kherson in December 1786. He claimed it had 40,000 inhabitants – 30,000 military and 10,000 civilians. There were 1,200 'very good houses built on stone'.[40] After Potemkin's death, the English traveller Maria Guthrie and the Russian writer Sumarokov praised the 'handsome town'[41] with St Catherine's, fourteen churches, synagogue, 22,000 Orthodox inhabitants and 2,500 Jews.[42]

Potemkin learned from his mistakes in Kherson. He boasted that his use of soldier-labour saved the state money, but he had a tsar's conception of budgets. Work had to be done fast, but, if it was not done correctly, like the fortress, he insisted on starting again: results were paramount, costs irrelevant to a semi-emperor who was allowed to treat the imperial Treasury as his own. However, the best rebuttal of Potemkin's critics is today's shipbuilding city.*

---

* The centre of the town is still mainly as Potemkin planned it. The fortress has been destroyed: only its two gate forts remain. The huge well, possibly the one Potemkin ordered Colonel Gaks to construct, remains covered by a grid. During the Second World War, Nazis threw executed Russians down it when they retreated. Potemkin's immense Palace survived until 1922. The curving arsenal, the mint, admiralty and above all St Catherine's Church remain. The church, with its sandy-coloured stone, its pillars and its noble Starov dome, was once used as a museum of atheism to display the decaying bodies of those buried in its graveyard, but is once again used as a church. Korsakov the

Potemkin aged around 35 at the height of his passionate love affair with Catherine, wearing the gold breastplates and uniform of the Captain of the elite Chevalier-Gardes, who stood watch over the Empress's own apartments.

Daria Potemkina, the Prince's mother who disapproved of his affairs with his nieces and told him so. He tossed her letters into the fire ...

The Empress Elisabeth: statuesque, blue-eyed, blonde, shrewd and ruthless, a true daughter of Peter the Great with a taste for men, dresses, transvestite balls, and Orthodox piety. After being presented to her, young Potemkin lost interest in his studies ...

The Grand Duchess Catherine with her gawky husband Peter and their son Paul. She loathed her husband – and Paul was probably her son by Serge Saltykov, her first lover.

Field-Marshal Peter Rumiantsev in command at the Battle of Kagul against the Turks in 1770. General Potemkin's heroic exploits in this campaign made him a war hero.

The Orlov brothers who helped Catherine seize power. Good-natured Grigory (on the left) was her lover for twelve years. Brutal, scarfaced Alexei (on the right) helped murder Peter III and won the naval battle of Chesme against the Turks. Potemkin broke their influence.

A fanciful print of Catherine and Potemkin playing cards in her boudoir. In fact, they played usually in the Little Hermitage where the Empress made special rules for him – 'Do not break or chew anything' – because he liked to wander in, chewing a radish and wearing nothing but a dressing-gown and a pink bandanna.

Alexander Lanskoy, Catherine's lover 1780–1784. He was gentle, affectionate and unambitious. She was happiest with him. When he died, Potemkin rushed to console her, and courtiers heard them howling together with grief.

Count Alexander Dmitriyev-Mamonov, Catherine's penultimate favourite and kinsman of Potemkin. She nicknamed him 'Redcoat'. He broke the Empress's heart by falling in love with a lady-in-waiting. 'Spit on him,' said Potemkin.

Potemkin's nieces were his family, friends and mistresses.

Left: Princess Varvara Golitsyna – he fell in love with his flirtatious, strong-willed niece after the end of his affair with Catherine.

Right: Countess Ekaterina Skavronskaya with her daughter, the future Princess Bagratian. Potemkin's languid and beautiful niece – mistress, known as his 'angel', was his 'sultana-in-chief' for many years ...

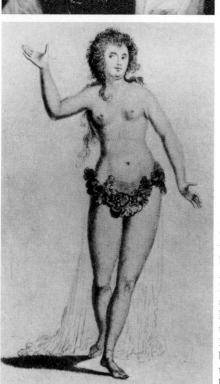

Left: The Duchess of Kingston (also Countess of Bristol) made her name when she was still Elisabeth Chudleigh by appearing naked at the Venetian Ambassador's Ball in London in 1749. By the time this ageing and slatternly self-publicist visited Petersburg in a luxurious yacht in the 1770s, she was the most scandalous woman in England, having been found guilty of bigamy. Potemkin, who fancied her art treasures, arranged for an adjutant to become her lover.

Above left: Princess Tatiana Yusupova, the youngest niece who adored her uncle and wrote that court was very dull without him. *Above right:* Countess Ekaterina Samoilova, the Prince's brazen but fascinating niece-by-marriage. She seduced the young Comte de Damas during the Siege of Ochakov in 1788 – and was said to be Potemkin's mistress soon afterwards.

Above: the Holy Roman Emperor Joseph II meets Catherine in a field near Kaidak during Potemkin's Crimean progress in 1787. That night, Joseph grumbled about Potemkin's cooking – yet he envied his vast achievements.

Left: Charles-Joseph, Prince de Ligne, socialite, Austrian soldier, renowned wit, 'jockey diplomatique', and the charmer of Europe, said that it took the materials for a hundred men to make one Potemkin.

Serenissimus commissioned two full-length icons for Kherson's fine neo-Classical church – one of St George, the other of St Catherine, he wielding a lance and wearing Roman military uniform, breastplate and red cloak, she in a golden dress and ermine-lined red cloak. His eyes are cast upward, she looks right at us. Then it strikes one: if St Catherine is a passable likeness of the Empress, St George[43] is unmistakably Potemkin.*

If the fall of the Zaporogians made Kherson possible, the end of the Crimean Khanate gave Potemkin his real chance to develop the south. It also made Kherson more of a commercial town and less necessary as a naval base because the Crimea was so well endowed with harbours. Kherson perched on the steppe, while the Crimea was the marketplace of the Black Sea, the hothouse and kitchen-garden of Constantinople.

Potemkin and his Empress longed to follow in Peter the Great's foot-steps. Peter had taken the Baltic from the Swedes, built a Russian fleet there and founded a city there. Now Potemkin had taken the Black Sea from the Tartars and Turks, built a Russian fleet and longed to found a Petersburg of his own. 'Petersburg established by the Baltic Sea is the Northern capital of Russia, Moscow the middle one and let Kherson of Akhtiar be the southern capital of my Sovereign,' he wrote to Catherine.[44] Kherson again! They loved the very word.

First, he attended to the creation of a port for his fleet. Akhtiar, Serenissimus told the Empress from the Crimea in June 1783, 'is the best harbour in the world'.[45] It was to be Russia's new naval base and Potemkin hurried to fortify it and build shipyards,[46] before he had even fully annexed the Khanate.[47] The Prince, of course, gave Akhtiar a Greek name: Sebastopol. He immediately founded a city in the 'natural amphi-theatre on the side of a hill'[48] and ordered his engineer Korsakov to build 'a strong fortification. The Admiralty must be conveniently located for unloading' and there must be a road through the peninsula 'as good as a Roman' one. 'I shall name it the Catherine Road.'[49] The engineer agreed with Potemkin's choice for the city: 'The most suitable place there is that which Your Highness has fixed . . .'.[50] Only four years later, when Potemkin visited the city with his friend Francisco de Miranda, the South American counted 'fourteen frigates, three ships-of-the-line of

engineer is buried in its churchyard. And the proudest boast of its priest and parishioners is that Potemkin its builder rests there beneath the church floor – see Epilogue.
* The author had heard the legend that the icons were by V. L. Borovikovsky and showed a saintly Potemkin and Catherine. The priest in the church had never heard it. It emerged that the icons from the church were stored in the Kherson Art Museum, where they are attributed to Mikhail Shibanov. Potemkin the dragon-slayer is instantly recognizable.

66 guns and a gunboat'. Miranda immediately grasped the value of Potemkin's new city: the harbour could hold a fleet of 'over 100 vessels'. If faced with disaster, a fleet could be repaired within a week.[51] Soon after Potemkin's death, Maria Guthrie[52] called it 'one of the finest ports in the world'. Sebastopol remains Russia's (and Ukraine's) greatest naval base.*

Serenissimus was ecstatic about his Crimea, touring the peninsula while ordering his favourite engineer Nikolai Korsakov to advise on fortifications, and his scientific experts such as the botanist Hablitz, who had endured the trauma of Potemkin's Persian expedition, to report on population and fauna.

'I don't describe the beauties of the Crimea because it would take too much time . . .', the Prince told his Empress in June 1783, as he annexed the peninsula and celebrated its charms, strategic potential and Classical history.[53] It is impossible not to share in Potemkin's feverish and exuberant fiesta of creation in that magical place with which he had fallen in love. Even today, it is easy to see why: as one passes through the Perekop Straits, past the salt lakes, which were the Khan's major source of income, the northern Crimea appears flat, arid, monotonous. But an hour to the south and it changes completely into a lush garden of Eden that most resembles the vineyards of southern Italy or Spain. Hills of greenery and vines rise to the battlements of medieval Genoese fortresses overlooking white cliffs and azure bays. Potemkin, who adored gardens, began to plant trees, celebrating the birth of the Grand Duke's children by laying out avenues of bay trees and olive groves. He imagined the Empress visiting his 'paradise'. The Romanovs in the next century and the twentieth-century Politburo apparatchiks were to make the Crimea their elite holiday resort, but Potemkin, to his credit, always wanted it to be far more than that.[54]

His first moves were to protect the Moslem Tartars from the brutish philistinism of his own soldiery: again and again, he ordered his generals to 'treat the inhabitants kindly and not to offend them. The chiefs of . . . regiments must set an example.'[55] He put special observers with regiments to keep an eye on their behaviour – or, as he put it, 'for the villages' protection' – and report to him 'all forbidden actions', and placed the

---

* Still a closed naval city, it is now shared by the Black Sea Fleets of Ukraine and Russia. None of Potemkin's original buildings survived the Anglo-French siege of the Crimean War and the Nazi siege of the Second World War. But there is a monument just above the port – crowded and grey with battleships – that reads: 'Here on 3 (14) June 1783 was founded the city of Sebastopol – the sea fortress of south Russia.'

Taurian region under Crimean murzas, especially the renegade Iakub Aga, who had become Yakov Izmailovich Rudzevich.[56] As he told Catherine, he gave money to maintain mosques and muftis. Indeed, when he travelled through the Crimea with Francisco de Miranda, he always met the local mufti and made a donation to his mosque.[57] Potemkin gave the Tartar murzas Russian nobility and the right to own land.[58] Typically, he formed a Tartar Crimean army, a little one for display.[59] It was traditional Russian imperialism to co-opt the Moslem hierarchies, but Potemkin's sensitive care for them is unusual in a Russian soldier of any epoch.

The Tartars were not farmers and never developed the land: 'This peninsula may become even better if we get rid of the Tartars by making them leave ... God knows, they are not worth this soil and the Kuban is a suitable place for them.' Potemkin shared the instincts of Russian imperialists to uproot people like chess pieces – but, he did not move them. In fact, he often favoured them and went to great lengths to make them stay. But thousands of the Tartars left anyway: their attitude was neatly put in the back-handed compliment of a Crimean mufti to Miranda: he remembered Potemkin taking the Crimea as 'a woman remembers the man who deflowers her'.[60]

Potemkin decided that the Crimean capital should be built on the Tartar town of Ak-mechet in the dry, flat middle of the peninsula: he called it Simferopol, still the capital today,[61] and still the same flat, carefully laid-out, dull city created by Potemkin.[62] The massive scale of Potemkin's plans extended from Kherson to Sebastopol, from Balaklava, Theodosia, Kerch, Yenikale and back to Kherson again. In all these places, new cities were founded or existing fortresses expanded into towns. But Colonel Korsakov was equal to all this. 'Matushka,' Potemkin raved to Catherine, 'we've never had an engineer like Korsakov before ... This man has to be looked after.'[63] Within five years, Sebastopol and its fleet were ready to be inspected by the two Caesars of the east.

In 1784, Potemkin decided to build a sumptuous capital for this southern Empire – a veritable new Athens – on the site of a small Zaporogian village called Palavitsa. He wished to call it 'Ekaterinoslav'. Incapable of doing anything by halves, he fell in love with the name because it meant 'Catherine's Glory' and he wanted to use it everywhere. (Indeed he also used it to rename his entire Viceroyalty.) 'Most Merciful Sovereign,' wrote the Prince, 'where, if not in the land devoted to your glory, should there be a city with magnificent buildings? That is why I undertook the development of projects that would suit the high name of this city.' Potemkin envisaged a neo-Classical metropolis: its law courts were to resemble 'ancient basilikas', its marketplace a huge semi-circle 'like the Propylaeum, or threshold of Athens'. The governor-general's house would be in 'Greek and Roman style'.[64]

Catherine, whose visions of Classicism and altruism were the same as his, approved his plans.[65] Serenissimus considered possible designs for over a year. Finally, in 1786, the French architect Claude Giroir produced his design for a central square and a grid of streets at right angles to the Dnieper, but Potemkin's architect Starov perfected the final plans. In January 1787, the Prince proudly displayed them to Francisco de Miranda, who was impressed with their 'Roman grandeur and architectural taste'. Potemkin wanted to employ 16,000 workmen for nine or ten years. Miranda wondered if it would ever be completed.[66]

Nothing in his career provoked such mockery as Ekaterinoslav. The building of a town here was necessary to develop the empty Zaporogian steppes, but the sin was its grandeur. Even the anti-Potemkin lies are interesting because of the light they shed on the extent to which Potemkin's enemies would go to blacken his name. Most histories claim Potemkin founded Ekaterinoslav in an unhealthy place and almost immediately had to move it, due to his own incompetence. It is true that in 1778, six years earlier, he had allowed a provincial governor to found a settlement for Armenians and Greeks, the Crimean refugees, on the River Kilchen, using the name 'Ekaterinoslav'. Now he simply took the name for his 'famous city', but he did not move the original one, which already had Greek, Armenian and Catholic quarters with three churches[67] and almost 3,000 inhabitants. He simply renamed it Novo-moskovsk.[68]

His enemies said the Prince planned to build a cathedral in the middle of this heretofore empty steppe larger than St Peter's in Rome, like the African dictator of a penniless state building the biggest cathedral in the world in the middle of the jungle. Ever since, historians, even Potemkin's only modern biographer George Soloveytchik, have repeated this embarrassing ambition as a sign of the Prince's overweening delusions of grandeur.[69] However, Potemkin may have mentioned St Peter's but he never actually proposed building it: in his letter to Catherine, he wrote, 'I imagine here an excellent cathedral, a kind of imitation of *St Paul's-outside-the-walls-of-Rome*, devoted to the Transfiguration of God, as a sign of the transformation of this land by your care, from a barren steppe to an ample garden, and from the wilderness of animals to a home, welcoming people from all lands.'[70] San Paolo-fuori-le-mura was admittedly an ambitious undertaking, but not quite as absurd as St Peter's. It is unlikely Catherine would ever have signed off on a copy of St Peter's nor assigned the huge tranches of two and three million roubles to the development of the south if Potemkin's ideas were so ludicrous. Somehow, St Peter's was substituted.

The only part of the city that existed from the beginning was the University of Ekaterinoslav, with its own musical *conservatoire*.[71] He immediately moved the Greek gymnasium, founded on his Ozerki estate as part of the Greek Project, to his New Athens, saying he had saved enough to rebuild the school there.[72] The *conservatoire* was closest to his lyrical heart. 'It's the first time', sneered Cobenzl to Joseph in November 1786, 'someone has decided to establish a *corps de musique* in a town before it's even been built.'[73] Potemkin hired Giuseppe Sarti, his personal composer–conductor, as the first head of the *conservatoire*. It was not just Sarti: the Prince really was hiring musical staff in Italy before a city was constructed. 'Enclosed, I have the honour of presenting you, Monseigneur, the bill of 2800 Roubles for the order of Your Highness,' wrote a certain Castelli from Milan on 21 March 1787, 'to Monsieur Joseph Canta who has passed them to the four Professors of Music … They plan to leave for Russia on the 26th …'.[74] The destiny of the four Milanese professors is unknown.

In 1786, he ordered local Governor Ivan Sinelnikov to enrol two painters, Neretin and Bukharov, as professors of art at the university, with salaries of 150 roubles. Even in the midst of the war in January 1791, he ordered Ekaterinoslav's Governor to employ a Frenchman named de Guienne as 'historian at the Academy' on a salary of 500 roubles. As Potemkin told Sinelnikov, the public schools had to be improved to provide the university with good students. Overall, 300,000 roubles was assigned to the educational establishments alone.[75] This was derided. Yet it is hard to fault Potemkin's priorities when he paid as much attention to teachers as to battleships.

All this was undoubtedly eccentric, but an ability to turn his ideas into reality was at the heart of Potemkin's genius. Much that seemed ridiculous after his death seemed possible during his life: the scale on which he created not just cities but the Black Sea Fleet sounded unlikely but he alone made it happen. So the university and city could have been built – but only in his lifetime. His vision was a noble one, far wider than just the *conservatoire*: it was to be an international Orthodox college where Potemkin believed 'young people' from Poland, Greece, Wallachia and Moldavia could study.[76] As ever with the Prince, his choice of students was closely connected to his aims for the Empire and for himself. He was always trying to train better sailors for his ships. In 1787, after Catherine's visit, he united all the naval academies in the region and

Petersburg and moved them to Ekaterinoslav. This was to be the academy of the Greek Project, the school for Potemkin's kingdoms.[77]

The work did not begin until mid-1787, then was delayed by the war so that little of it was built. But not as little as everyone thinks. In 1790, Starov arrived in the south, and laid new plans for the whole city, especially its cathedral and the Prince's Palace, all approved by Potemkin, on 15 February 1790. The professors' residences and the administrative buildings for the university were finished. By 1792, there were 546 state buildings and just 2,500 inhabitants.[78] Its Governor, Vasily Kahovsky, reported to the Empress after the Prince's death that the town was laid out and continuing. Without its master, would it continue?[79] By 1815, a travelling official reported that it was 'more like some Dutch colony than a provincial administrative centre'.[80] Yet something of his Athens remains.

Ekaterinoslav never became a southern Petersburg; its university was never the Oxford of the steppes. The gap between hope and reality made this Potemkin's biggest failure and it has been used to discredit much else that was done well. Yet none of the historians of the last two centuries had visited Ekaterinoslav, which, like Sebastopol, was a closed city in Soviet times. When one looks more closely at the city, now called Dniepropetrovsk, it becomes clear its position was admirably chosen on the high and green bank of a bend of the Dnieper, where the great river is almost a mile wide. Potemkin's main Catherine Street became the modern Karl Marx Prospekt, still called 'the longest, widest, most elegant avenue in all the Russias' by locals. (William Hastie, the Scottish architect, expanded on this grid in his 1816 city plan.)[81]

In the middle of the city stands an eighteenth-century church, now newly alive with Orthodox worshippers. Its name – Church of the Transformation – is the one Potemkin suggested in 1784. It is a grand and imposing edifice, completely in proportion to the size of its city. It has a high spire, Classical pillars and golden cupola, based on Starov's original plans. Begun in 1788 during the war, completed long after Potemkin's death, in 1837, there stands the Prince's noble cathedral in the midst of the city that was supposed never to have been built.[82] Not far from the church is a hideous yellow triumphal arch of Soviet design that leads to Potemkin Park, which still contains the massive Potemkin Palace.[83] It was to be another eighty years after Potemkin's death before musical *conservatoires* were opened in St Petersburg and

Moscow. But Ekaterinoslav was to flourish most under Soviet planning when it became a toiling industrial centre – as Potemkin had wanted.*

Potemkin's cities advanced as he gained territory. The last cities he sponsored were made possible by the conquests of the Second Turkish War – Nikolaev, by the fall of the fortress of Ochakov, and Odessa, by the push round the Black Sea.

On 27 August 1789, the Prince scrawled out the order to found Nikolaev, named after St Nikolai, the saint of seafarers on whose day Potemkin finally stormed Ochakov. Built on a high, cool and breezy spot where the Ingul river meets the Bug about twenty miles upriver from Kherson and fifty from the Black Sea, Nikolaev was the best planned and most successful of his cities (except Odessa).

It was built by Faleev on Potemkin's precise orders, sweeping in vision, precise in detail. In a twenty-one point memorandum, he ordered Faleev to build a monastery, move naval headquarters from Kherson to Nikolaev, construct a military school for 300, fund a church from the income of local taverns, recast the broken bell of the Mejigorsky Convent, adding copper to it, cultivate the land 'according to the English method as practised by three British-educated assistants of Professor Livanov', build hospitals and rest-homes for invalids, create a free port, cover all fountains with marble, build a Turkish bath and an admiralty – and then establish a town council and a police force.

Faleev amazingly was able to parry these thrusts of energy one by one. He answered Potemkin's specific orders, 'Your Highness ordered me to' and then reported that virtually all had been done – and more, from settling Old Believer priests to sowing kitchen gardens. Shipyards were built first. Peasants, soldiers and Turkish prisoners built the city: 2,500 were working there during 1789. Faleev evidently worked them too hard because Serenissimus ordered their protection and daily rations of hot wine. There is a contemporary print in the Nikolaev Museum showing the soldiers and Turkish prisoners-of-war working on foot, supervised by mounted Russian officers. Another shows oxen dragging logs to build the city.

* Dniepropetrovsk was noted in the Soviet era for providing the USSR with its clique of leaders in the 1970s. In 1938, a thirty-two-year-old Communist apparatchik named Leonid Brezhnev stepped over the corpses of his liquidated superiors in the midst of Stalin's Great Purge to become chief of propaganda in Dniepropetrovsk. There he gathered together the cronies who were to dominate the Soviet Union in 1964–80: the 'Dniepropetrovsk Mafia'. Locals today recall that Brezhnev especially enjoyed entertaining in the Potemkin Palace.

By October, Faleev could tell the Prince that the landing stage was finished and that the earthmoving by the conscripts and Turks would be finished within a month. There were already nine stone and five wooden barracks. In 1791, the main shipyards were moved from Kherson to Nikolaev.[84] Here we see how Potemkin worked. There is no trace of the layabout, nor of the clown who performed for Westerners, nor of the grandiose autocrat who paid no attention to detail. Potemkin pushed Faleev. 'Work quickly,' he wrote about one battleship he needed and 'Strain all your forces.' Next, he thanked him for the watermelons he had sent but added, 'You cannot imagine how my honour and the future of Nikolaev shipyard depends on this ship.'[85] The first frigate from his new city was launched before his death – and his own palace was almost complete.

Four years later, the visiting Maria Guthrie acclaimed its 10,000 inhabitants, 'remarkably long, broad, straight streets' and 'handsome public buildings'. The city's position even today is ideal: it is well laid out and planned, though few of Potemkin's buildings survive. Its shipyards still work where they were built by him 200 years ago.[86]

Odessa was conquered by Potemkin, who ordered a town and fortress to be built there – though it was neither named nor started until after his death. When the Prince took the Ottoman fort of Hadjibey in 1789, he recognized that it was an outstanding and strategic site, ordered the old castle to be blown up and personally chose the site of the port and settlement. Work was to start immediately.

This was being done when he died, but the town was formally founded three years later by his protégé José (Osip) de Ribas, the Spanish adventurer from Naples who had helped Orlov-Chesmensky kidnap 'Princess Tarakanova'. 'General (later Admiral) de Ribas was accomplished in mind, artifice and talent, but no saint,' according to Langeron. His portrait by Lampi shows his foxy, ruthless and subtle face. In 1776, he married the illegitimate daughter of Catherine's friend and artistic supremo Ivan Betskoi, who had had an affair with the Empress's mother. They became one of the most politically adept couples in Petersburg. Henceforth, wherever the Prince was, Ribas was never far away. Always vigorous and competent, whether building Potemkin's ships, commanding his fleets or procuring his mistresses, Ribas joined Popov and Faleev as Potemkin's three superlative men of action.*

Catherine named the port after Odessos – the Ancient Greek town

---

* Today Deribas is one of Odessa's most elegant boulevards.

that was believed to be nearby – but she feminized it to Odessa. It remains one of the jewels of Potemkin's legacy.[87]

'I report that the first ship to be launched will be called the *Glory of Catherine – Ekaterinoslav*,' wrote Potemkin over-enthusiastically to his Empress. 'Please allow me to give it this name.' The name 'Ekaterinoslav' had become an obsession. Cities, ships and regiments groaned under its grandeur. This concerned the prudent Empress: 'Please don't give too grandiose names to the ships, lest such loud names become a burden to them ... Do what you like with the names but free the reins because it's better to be than to seem.'[88] But Potemkin was not going to change *Catherine's Glory* even to protect the glory of Catherine at her own behest. So he ignored her request and, in September, proudly announced the launch from his Kherson shipyards of the sixty-six-gun ship-of-the-line named *Catherine's Glory*.[89] This is a most characteristic exchange.*

The Prince was right to be excited because ships-of-the-line, those hulking floating fortresses with their rows of over forty or fifty guns, the same as some entire armies, were the eighteenth century's most prestigious weapons – the equivalent of aircraft carriers. (Catherine granted Potemkin the initial 2.4 million roubles to finance this on 26 June 1786.) The construction of a whole fleet of them has been compared by a modern historian to the cost and effort of a space programme. However, Potemkin's critics claim that the ships were rotten, if they were built at all. This was nonsense. Pole Carew carefully examined the shipbuilding in progress. There were three ships-of-the-line of sixty-six guns in an 'advanced state' while frigates of thirty and forty guns had already been launched. Four more keels were laid. The state was not the only shipbuilder there – Faleev was building his merchantmen too. Down at Gluboka, thirty-five versts towards the sea, there were already seven more frigates of between twenty-four and thirty-two guns. When Miranda, who had no European prejudices and broad military experience, visited five years later, he reported that neither the timber nor the design of the ships could be bettered and considered the workmanship of a better standard than those of either Spanish or French vessels. They were built, he said, offering the highest praise one could give a ship in those days, 'in the English manner'.[90]

This showed that he knew what he was talking about, for the German,

---

* In Kherson today, on the site of the first docks stands a hideous concrete Soviet sculpture of a sailing ship. Its inscription of course does not mention Potemkin but it acclaims him nonetheless. 'Here in 1783', it reads, 'was launched the first 66-gun ship-of-the-line of the Black Sea Fleet – "Glory of Catherine".'

French and Russian critics of Potemkin's ships did not realize that his timber came from the same places as timber for English warships. Furthermore, they were built by sailors and engineers trained in England such as Potemkin's admiral Nikolai Mordvinov (who married an English girl) and the engineer Korsakov. Indeed, by 1786, Kherson had an English ambience. 'Mordvinov and Korsakov both are much more like Englishmen than any foreigners I ever met,' decided that ardent traveller Lady Craven.[91] Yet Kaiser Joseph, who was no expert on naval matters, claimed the ships were 'built of green timber, worm eaten'.[92]

By 1787, the Prince had created a formidable fleet that the British Ambassador put at twenty-seven battleships. If one counts ships-of-the-line as having over forty guns, he had twenty-four of them, built in nine years, starting at Kherson. Later Sebastopol's perfect harbour became the naval base of Potemkin's fleet and Nikolaev its main shipyard. This, together with the thirty-seven ships-of-the-line of the Baltic Fleet, instantly placed Russian seapower almost equal to Spain, just behind France – though far behind the 174 ships-of-the-line of Britain, the world's only naval superpower.

Potemkin is the father of the Black Sea Fleet, just as Peter the Great created the Baltic one. The Prince was proudest of his fleet. It was his special 'child' and he poses in Lampi's rare portrait in his white uniform as Grand Admiral of the Black Sea and Caspian Fleets with the Euxine (Black) Sea behind him. Catherine knew it was his creation. 'It might seem an exaggeration,' a British envoy recorded Serenissimus saying, at the end of his life, 'but he could, almost literally, say that every plank, used in building the fleet, was carried on his shoulders.'[93]

His other Herculean effort was to attract the ordinary folk to populate these vast empty territories. The settlement of colonists and ex-soldiers on the frontiers was an old Russian practice but Potemkin's campaign of recruitment, in which Catherine issued manifestos offering all manner of incentives to settlers – no taxes for ten years, free cattle or farming equipment, spirits or brewery franchises – was astonishing in its imagination, scale and success. Hundreds of thousands were moved, housed, and settled, and received welfare gifts of ploughs, money and oxen. Frederick the Great had set the standard of colonization during the *rétablissement* of his war-torn territories by tolerating all sects, so that, by the time of his death, 20 per cent of Prussians were immigrants. The Prince had a modern understanding of the power of public-relations. He advertised in foreign newspapers and created a network of recruiting agents across Europe. 'The foreign newspapers', he explained to Catherine, 'are full of praises for the new settlements set up in New Russia and Azov.' The public would read about the privileges granted to the Armenian and Greek settlers and 'realize their full value'. He also recommended the modern idea of using Russian embassies to help recruitment. Potemkin had been an enthusiastic colonist since coming to power. Even in the mid-1770s, he was recruiting immigrants for his new settlements on the Mozdok Line of the north Caucasus.[94] His ideal settlers would plant, plough, trade and manufacture in peacetime, and, when war came, ride out against the Turks.[95]

Potemkin's first settlers were the Albanians, from Orlov-Chesmensky's Mediterranean fleet of 1769, and the Crimean Christians. The former initially settled in Yenikale, the latter in their own towns like Mariupol. The Albanians were soldier–farmers. Potemkin founded schools and hospitals as well as towns for these immigrants. Once the Crimea was annexed, Potemkin formed the Albanians into regiments and settled them at Balaklava. The Prince specifically designated Mariupol for the Crimean Greeks. As with all his towns, he supervised its development, adding to it throughout his career. By 1781 the Azov Governor reported that much of it was built. There were four churches, the Greeks had their own court and it grew into a prosperous Greek trading town. Later Potemkin founded Nachkichevan, on the lower Don near Azov, and Gregoripol (named after himself, of course), on the Dniester, for the Armenians.[96]

Serenissimus racked his brains to find productive citizens inside the Empire, attracting noblemen and their serfs,[97] retired and wounded soldiers, Old Believers* or *raskolniki*,[98] Cossacks and, naturally, women to make homes for them. The girls were despatched southwards like the mail-order brides of Midwestern settlers in nineteenth-century America.[99] Typically, Potemkin also targeted impoverished village priests.[100] Outside the Empire, he offered amnesty to exiles, such as fugitive serfs,[101] *raskolniki*, and Cossacks who had fled to Poland or Turkey. Families, villages and whole towns of people moved, or returned, to settle in his provinces. It is estimated that, by 1782, he had doubled the population of New Russia and Azov.[102]

Potemkin's campaign intensified after the conquest of the Crimea – and, using a burgeoning network of middlemen, he extended it to the whole of Europe. The population of the Crimea had been halved

---

* These worshipped according to the old rites of Orthodoxy. They had been excluded from mainstream Russian life for a century, often living in remote Siberian settlements to worship freely. Fascinated by their faith, Potemkin protected and tolerated them.

throughout its troubles to about 50,000 males.[103] The Prince believed
that the territories boasted only 10 per cent of the populations they
should contain. 'I am using all my powers,' he told Catherine. 'From
diverse places, I have summoned colonists knowledgeable in all spheres
of the economy . . .'. He wielded his massive powers to decide who should
and should not be taxed and how much land settlers, whether noblemen
or foreigners, should receive. Immigrants were usually freed from taxes
for a year and a half, later raised to six years.[104]

The agents were paid five roubles per settler. 'I have found a man who
is charged to bring foreign colonists to the Crimea,' one of them wrote the
Prince. 'I've agreed with him to pay thirty roubles per family delivered in
those places.' Later he sent Potemkin another agent with whom 'I've
agreed 200 souls but he promises he can bring considerably more.'[105]

The peasants of southern Europe were particularly fertile ground. In
1782, sixty-one Corsican families arrived to be settled near Kherson.[106]
In early 1783, Potemkin was making arrangements to receive Corsicans
and Jews recruited by the Duc de Crillon. But the Prince decided, 'I do
not consider it necessary to increase the number of these inhabitants
except those already sent by Count Mocenigo' (who was the Russian
minister in Florence). In the Prince's archives, we can follow this strange
trade in honest farmers and opportunistic rascals. Some wrote directly
to the Prince's Chancellery. In a typical letter, potential Greek settlers,
named Panaio and Alexiano, asked to bring their family from 'the Archipelago' so that they 'can all come to make a colony bigger than that
made with the Corsicans.'[107] Some of the agents were the worst sort of
fairground hucksters: how many innocents did they gull? One suspects
that landowners saw this as a convenient way to rid their estates of
rogues. Potemkin did not mind. 'They will be transported to Kherson,'
he wrote, 'where everything is ready to receive them.'[108]

The Prince also managed to attract the most industrious, sober settlers
any empire-builder could wish for: the Mennonites of Danzig, who
asked for the right to have their own churches and no taxes for ten years.
Potemkin's agent George Trappe gave them their terms – they would
receive money for travel and houses when they arrived. The privileges
were granted. Potemkin's letter to his Scottish banker, Richard Sutherland, shows how the chief minister of the Empire personally arranged
the details of moving relatively small numbers of people across Europe:
'Monsieur, As Her Imperial Majesty has deigned to accord privileges
to the Mennonites who wish to come to settle in the Government of
Ekaterinoslav . . . be so good as to prepare the necessary sums, in Danzig,
Riga and Kherson, for their voyage and settlement . . . Following the

mercy that Her Imperial Majesty had deigned to grant to these good farmers, I trust there will be no obstacle in delivering the sums ... to prevent their settlement in Ekaterinoslav.'[109] There are many such unpublished letters in the archives. The 228 families, probably 2,000 people, set off on their long journey to found eight colonies in early 1790.[110]

At the same time, over in Kherson, he was ordering the incompetent Colonel Gaks to welcome a party of Swedes for the Swedish settlement, 'where they will find not only houses ... For foodstuffs, give five roubles to everyone.'[111] Another 880 Swedes were settled in the new city of Ekaterinoslav. Thousands of Moldavians and Wallachians, Orthodox Rumanians under Ottoman rule, also flocked across the borders. By 1782, some 23,000 had arrived. Many lived in Elisabethgrad, where they outnumbered Russians. 'A Greek of Bulgaria', reads a typical letter to Potemkin from one of his agents in 1785, 'has told me there are a number of Moldavians on the frontiers of Moldavia – it would be easy to persuade them all to come as immigrants.' No doubt they came.[112]

Almost uniquely among Russian soldiers and statesmen, Potemkin was more than just tolerant of Jews: he studied their culture, enjoyed the company of their rabbis, and became their champion. The Enlightenment had already changed attitudes to Jews. Empress Elisabeth had banned all these 'enemies of Christ' from the Empire in 1742. Maria Theresa hated Jews so much that, as late as 1777, when Potemkin was giving them privileges for settlement, she wrote: 'I know of no greater plague than this race.' She could not bear to set eyes on a Jew: she spoke to her banker Diego d'Aguilar from behind a screen. But her son Joseph II greatly improved their lot.[113] When Catherine usurped the throne, playing the Orthodox card, she was in no position to favour the Jews. Her October 1762 decree invited all settlers 'except Jews', but she secretly let them in by ordering Count Browne, her Irish Governor-General of Livonia, specifically *not* to ask the religion of potential settlers.[114]

The Partition of Poland in 1772 brought large numbers of Jews – about 45,000 – into Russia for the first time. Potemkin first encountered the many who lived on his Krichev estate in ex-Polish lands. When the Prince invited settlers to the south as early as 1775, he added the rare coda: 'even Jews'. On 30 September 1777, he set the policy: Jews were allowed to settle in his lands, sometimes in 'the empty smallholdings left by Zaporogian Cossacks', providing they brought five Polish settlers each and money to invest. Later he made this more appetizing: no taxes for seven years and the right to trade in wines and spirits; they would be protected from marauding soldiers; have their disputes adjudicated by rabbis; be permitted synagogues, graveyards and the right to import their wives from Jewish communities in Poland. These immigrants were useful: apart from commerce, brickmaking, which Potemkin needed for his new towns, was a Jewish trade. Soon Kherson and Ekaterinoslav, melting-pots of Cossacks, *raskolniki* and Greeks, were at least partly Jewish towns.[115]

Serenissimus became especially friendly with Joshua Zeitlin, a remarkable Jewish merchant, and Hebraic scholar, who travelled with the Prince, managed his estates, built towns, arranged financial deals for supplying his armies, and even ran the restored mint at Kaffa in the Crimea – he appears throughout the archives. Zeitlin 'walked with Potemkin like a brother and friend' – a relationship unique in Russian history because the Jew remained proudly unassimilated, steeped in rabbinical learning and piety, yet standing near the top of the Prince's entourage. Potemkin promoted him to the rank of 'Court advisor', thereby giving him noble status and allowing him to own serfs and estates. Russian Jews called Zeitlin, 'Ha-sar' – Lord. The Prince enjoyed Zeitlin's ability to do business as well as discuss Talmudic theology and they were often together. As the two inspected new roads and towns, Zeitlin 'would ride on a majestic horse alongside Potemkin.' While the Prince accepted petitions, the noble and plutocratic rabbi 'would accept halakhic queries from ... scholars. He would get down from his horse and compose halakhic responses in a kneeling position,' and then remount and ride on with Serenissimus. It is hard to overstate what an astonishing vision of tolerance this was, not merely for Russia, but for Europe.

Potemkin helped the Jews and repeatedly intervened to defend them. During Catherine's visit to the south in 1787, he even sponsored the delegation, led by Zeitlin, that petitioned her to stop Jews being called '*zhidy*' – 'Yids'. Catherine received them and decreed that henceforth they should be called '*evrei*' – 'Hebrews'. When Zeitlin clashed with the Prince's banker, Sutherland, Potemkin even backed his beloved Jews against his beloved British.[116] A variety of Jewish rabbis soon joined Zeitlin in Potemkin's bizarre court of mullahs and priests. It was this peculiar tolerance that led his anti-Semitic noble critics to sneer that the Prince favoured any foreigners with 'a big snout' – but Potemkin was never bound by the prejudices of others.[117]

No wonder the Prince became a Jewish hero. Wherever he went, particularly in Belorussia, crowds of excited Jews prepared such elaborate welcomes that they sometimes irritated him. They would offer him 'big trays of silver, bread, salt and lemons', which Miranda, who observed these rituals in Kherson, drily described as 'doubtless some kind of hospitality ceremony'.[118]

On Potemkin's death, Zeitlin retired to his sumptuous palace at Ustye in Belorussia, where this unusual financier patronized Jewish learning in his Hebraic library and synagogue, conducted scientific experiments in his laboratory, and held his own court, with the eccentricity and magnificence of a Jewish Potemkin. The position of Russian Jews again deteriorated. They were never again to have such an eminent protector.[119]

Next, the Prince had the idea of importing British convicts to settle the Crimea.

19

BRITISH BLACKAMOORS
AND CHECHEN WARRIORS

But I not rising until noontime
Drink coffee and enjoy a smoke;
I make vacations of my workdays
And spin my thoughts in chimeras ...
Gavrili Derzhavin, 'Ode to Princess Felitsa'

Serenissimus heard that the American War was preventing Britain from transporting its convicts to the Colonies and he saw an opportunity. His friend the Prince de Ligne was probably the source of this information, because Joseph II had considered settling them in Galicia and then decided against it. One day, Simon Vorontsov, now ambassador in London, was visited by an Irish adventurer named Dillon, who claimed that Ligne had assigned him to procure 'delinquents ... and black-amoors' to settle in the Crimea. Vorontsov, who disliked Potemkin, was appalled at the possible 'shame of Russia: all of Europe will get to know what kind of monsters were settled'. Their dissipation would make them ill and they would have to maintain themselves with their 'old pro-fession – robbery and swindles'.*

In October 1785, Vorontsov was amazed to receive an imperial order, via Bezborodko, to negotiate the sending of these British criminals to Riga for transport to the Crimea. The British Government was to pay for their journey. Vorontsov saw a chance to undermine Potemkin, so he wrote to the Empress warning of the effect on her European reputation. 'Despite the prodigious influence and power of Prince Potemkin', boasted Vorontsov, the Empress decided he was right – it might damage her image in Europe. 'It is true', trumpeted Vorontsov years later, 'that Prince Potemkin never forgave me.'[1]

This story was propagated by Vorontsov – and has been repeated ever since – to show Potemkin's clownish incompetence and lack of judgement. However, it was not a foolish or disgusting idea. Most of

* Who were these 'blackamoors'? Was Potemkin really trying to import black settlers – slaves from Africa? 'Blackamoor' surely meant 'street arabs' or urchins from London's streets, whom today we would call vagrants.

these 'delinquents' were not hardened criminals – this was a time when unfortunates were deported from England in chains on grisly prison-ships for stealing a handkerchief or poaching a rabbit. The ultimate penal colony, Australia, which was to become the destination of these very convicts, has flourished. The Empress, Ligne and Bezborodko, none of them fools, supported Potemkin's idea. Besides, it was a familiar concept because many Russian criminals were sent to Siberia as 'settlers'.

Some of the settlers were already semi-criminals anyway. In 1784, a shipload of what Samuel Bentham called 'ragamuffin Italians', mainly Corsicans, arrived from Leghorn. They had mutinied on the way, killing their captain, but were captured and brought to Kherson, where they were put to work building the town. Out of this débâcle comes a story that speaks for itself. There was an Englishman among these cut-throats – there is always an Englishman in Potemkin's schemes. Since he was said to be a coal-miner, he was ordered to search for coal. Bentham found him 'almost naked and living on five kopeks per day', so he mentioned his miserable compatriot to the Prince, who 'promised him a good salary, and when I said he was almost naked, he ordered me to give him 300 roubles to buy clothes. This, I think, proves no small degree of generosity – as well as a favourable disposition towards us English.'[2]

There is a revealing American postscript. In 1784, Americans loyal to the British Crown, who had to leave the United States, petitioned Pot-emkin to be welcomed as settlers. Potemkin worried that 'they may be the descendants of those people who migrated from England during the civil wars in the last century and who may be supposed to entertain opinions by no means compatible with the spirit of [Russia]'.[3] So British criminals were sought, respectable American loyalists rejected. But Pot-emkin, who regarded Cromwell, Danton and Pugachev as much the same, was being consistent: political rebellion was much more dangerous than mere crime.

Serenissimus specified to his governors precisely how these settlers were to be welcomed at the end of their long journeys. 'The new subjects who don't know our language or customs demand defence and pro-tection . . .', he told his Crimean Governor Kahovsky. The Prince certainly decided the settlers' destinies on a whim: 'I offered to settle them on the left bank of the Dnieper. But now I think it would be easier to move them into the empty Greek lands in Taurida itself where there are already buildings.'[4] He was constantly thinking of ways to improve their lot: 'Be so kind as to distribute bullocks, cows and horses, left behind by depart-ing Taurida Tartars, among the new settlers,' he ordered Kahovsky, 'trying, not merely to be equable, but to help the poor.'[5] To the Governor of Ekaterinoslav, Sinelnikov, he commanded each family to receive the same plus eight desyatins of land per head. 'A further 40 families are now coming down the Dnieper; do not fail to receive them yourself . . .'.[6] Again, this personal greeting by a busy governor sounds more like touchy-feely modern welfare than military settlement on Russian steppes.

Potemkin is often accused of abandoning these people to their fates. He could not see everything and his officials frequently lied to him. This was the reason he was perennially on the road – to ensure nothing was concealed from him. Nonetheless there must have been thousands of little miseries for some of these people. The departure of some of the settlers from the Crimea 'proves their unhappiness', Potemkin wrote to Kahovsky. 'Understand the reasons for it and carry out your duties with firmness, satisfying the offended.'[7] His military order to 'understand' demonstrates the contradiction of trying to foster psychological sensitivity by military command.

However, many others settled happily. The archives prove that, whenever Potemkin found a lapse, he reacted immediately, like the note to Kahovsky in which he suggested five ways to overcome the villagers' 'great privations' because the state had failed to provide enough cattle: 'Only three pairs of oxen, one plough and one cart have been given to four or even more families . . .'.[8] It is remarkable to find the co-ruler of an empire actually ordering his generals to correct such a mistake and give a certain number of oxen to a specific peasant family in one village. That is what happened again and again.

He did solve security problems by transporting peoples – some of the Nogai Hordes were resettled in the Urals, Taman and north Crimea, and then moved again. Their sin was being unreliable and too close to the turbulent Caucasus. These migrations must have been sad processions, for which Potemkin bears responsibility, just as contemporary British ministers, for example, bear the shame of the slave trade.

Overall, Potemkin cared enormously and did as much as an administrator in that century could do. Later, possibly during the building of his last city Nikolaev, there is a melancholic note to Faleev about the conditions of his ordinary people: 'You have to tell me the truth. I can't just know but you should be ashamed to conceal the truth from me. I employed people to work, promising them to pay them salaries; but it was turned into hard labour. Unluckily, my name is everywhere, so that they could begin to think I am a tyrant . . .'.[9]

*

The Prince planned to turn the Crimea and the south into the orchard of the Empire. 'This is an unbelievably good and fertile place,' he told Catherine. The Prince was evidently an early Green: at least, he instinctively understood what is now called ecology. To plant a tree to him was to help build the future of his lands, so he frequently ordered his men to 'plant paradise trees' or 'chestnuts'. On 5 August 1785, Potemkin printed an address to the nobles in the Crimea in which he autocratically required them to plant and create prosperity: 'I consider tillage the first source of riches.' It was a reliable business because the army always needed provisions and it was a service to the state. But if the land was not sown, 'it shames its owner and reproaches him with laziness'.[10]

He practised what he preached. 'Wishing to promote the settling of Perekop steppe and set an example', Potemkin himself took over forests and 6,000 desaytin 'for picking of canes'.[11] He continually ordered the directors of Crimean Agriculture, Professors Livanov and Prokopovich (who studied in England, along with students sent by Potemkin), and the botanist Hablitz, to travel the peninsula improving anything they could suggest. Apart from ordering Korsakov to build salt bridges to make the collection of salt more efficient, he sent engineers to seek bituminous coal along the Donetz and Lugansk rivers. The Taurida region even had a resident mining expert.[12]

The Prince was obsessed with using his estates and those he gave to others as trading posts between south and north. 'The boats that carry the supplies from the estates and factories of Prince Potemkin [from Belorussia] for the navy in Kherson are filled on their return with salt . . .', a French diplomat explained to Paris. With his acquisition of the empty steppes of the Crimean Khanate and the Zaporogian Sech, Potemkin intended to use grants of land to encourage trade and manufacturing, especially among foreigners like the Benthams. In this too he favoured Anglo-Saxons. 'The Russians are unfit for commerce,' Potemkin later told a British envoy, 'and he was always of the opinion that the foreign trade of the empire should be carried on entirely' by Englishmen.[13]

Potemkin ordered that no land should be given out without his command. There were many ways to settle these vast lands: first, he granted massive estates to magnates, officials (like his secretary Popov and his ally Bezborodko, who was delighted with his 'almost royal' estate), foreign friends (like the Prince de Ligne), Cossack cronies and renegade Tartars – and he gave himself 73,000 desaytins on the mainland, 13,000 on the peninsula.[14] If landowners did well, Serenissimus lifted taxes on them, as he did for three students of English agriculture 'for their great progresses'.[15] If they wasted their gift, Potemkin was tempted to take it away from them. Many foreigners, from Genoese noblemen to English peeresses, bombarded the Prince with schemes and demands for land – but they got them only if they had an entrepreneurial plan.

'I have, my Prince, a great desire to become a proprietor of some estates here,' the seductive and pushy Countess of Craven wrote to him from the Crimea. This daughter of the Earl of Berkeley, with her curly Medusan head of hair, was already a favourite beauty of the London scandal-sheets, not unlike the Duchesses of Kingston and Devonshire, but this talented and independent woman was also a courageous traveller and an early best-selling travel-writer. After an exceedingly short marriage with the peer whose name she shamelessly used, she had been caught *in flagrante* with a French duke, an envoy to London, but she was also notoriously 'democratic' in her tastes, supposedly even having working-class lovers. Then she went travelling with a young lover while writing colourful letters to her suitor, the Margrave of Anspach, brother-in-law of Frederick the Great. These were later published as her *Journey through the Crimea to Constantinople*. She ended her geographical, amorous and literary voyage in 1791 by marrying the Margrave, with whom Potemkin was also in correspondence, thereby joining the ranks of imperial petty-royalty.[16]

Elisabeth Craven met the Prince in Petersburg and travelled to the Crimea with his blessing. She saw the opportunities there. 'I would make a colony of honest and industrious people of my country,' she suggested. 'I'd be very happy to see my own land flower ... I tell you frankly, my Prince, I'd like to have two estates in different places of Taurida.' She appealed to his well-known romanticism, calling this her 'beautiful dream'. Her Ladyship suspiciously begged him 'not to share this with [Harris's successor as British envoy to Russia] Mr Fitzherbert nor my compatriots', presumably because she did not wish it to reach the London newspapers. In case Potemkin was not sufficiently tempted by her offer, Her Ladyship ensured that he knew exactly who she was, signing each letter, 'Elisabeth Craven, Peeress of England, *née* Lady Elisabeth Berkeley.' Potemkin's reply is unknown, but she never settled her family in the Crimea. Perhaps the Prince, who was no longer the neophyte charmed by Semple, thought this 'Peeress of England' protested too much.[17]

The Prince dreamed of filling his lands with prospering plantations and industrious factories: this time he wanted not soldiers but experts on agriculture. Catherine quoted Potemkin to her German friend Dr Zimmerman: 'In Taurida, the principal matter must ... be the cultivation of the land and nurture of silkworms and consequently mulberry plantations. Cloth could be made here ... cheese-making would also be very desirable ... gardens, above all botanical gardens ... we need sensible and knowledgeable people.'[18]

When the Spanish officer Antonio d'Estandas requested land to found china factories not far from Simferopol, the Prince at once ordered his governor to provide 'as much land as necessary' but 'with the obligation that the factory is established without delay'.[19] He stressed agriculture, orchards and flocks of sheep instead of herds of cattle,[20] believing the Crimea was ideal for wool and sheepbreeding. 'Making wool better with simple and correct methods,' he boasted to Catherine, 'we'll beat every country in Europe with our cloth. I ordered males from everywhere where they have the best sheep and I'm waiting for them next summer.'[21]

The Prince fostered various industries himself – particularly wine and silk. He behaved as a mixture of autocrat, banker, entrepreneur and customer. When he decided to manufacture silk, as he was already successfully doing in Astrakhan, he made an agreement with the Italian Count of Parma to produce it on a large estate. The Prince provided twenty families of peasants from his Russian estates, promising to add another twenty after five years, and lent the Count 4,000 roubles as seed money. To encourage the industry, he then bought all the silk produced locally at an inflated price.[22] As for Potemkin's success, Maria Guthrie found the 'zealous' Count still producing fine silk at the turn of the century.[23]

The Prince wanted to make Ekaterinoslav the marketing centre for the silk from his Crimean mulberry plantations. A silk-stockings factory was built at a cost of 340,000 roubles and he soon sent the Empress a pair of stockings so fine that they could be preserved in the shell of a nut. 'When, my Merciful Mother,' the Prince wrote, 'you visit the dominions over which I preside, you will see your path covered with silk.'[24]

As for wine, the Prince planted 30,000 vines of Tokay wine, imported from Hungary with Joseph's permission, in four places across the peninsula. He had been planting orchards and vineyards for years in Astrakhan, whence he brought his French viticulturist Joseph Banq to Soudak, the lush Crimean seaside village, beneath a ruined Genoese fortress, which became his wine centre. It is a tribute to Potemkin's activity that he had the gardener in place buying estates by September 1783, weeks after annexing the Khanate. Banq's sorry letters, scattered among the Potemkin archives, are bad-tempered, poorly written and often stained, as if he was writing them while watering his vines. They demonstrate the difficulties of putting Potemkin's schemes into reality. Poor Banq bitterly missed his wife – 'without my family, I cannot stay at Soudak if His Highness offered me all the world'. In any case, the work was impossible without twenty workers – not soldiers! But the workers were rude to Banq and he had to complain to the Prince again. When the vines flourished, he proudly sent Serenissimus 150 bottles of his red Soudak wine.[25]

Banq's job was to expand the vineyards, to plant fruit orchards and raisin plantations and, as a profitable sideline, to 'build a factory of vodka as in France'. His salary in this five-year mission was 2,000 roubles a year (much more than the average Russian officer's) plus an apartment, firewood, a pair of horses and forty litre barrels of wine.[26] On arrival, the Frenchman grumbled that the gardens bought for him were 'not worth anything ... it hasn't been cultivated for three years ... it's a waste of time to make wine this year'.[27] Finally Potemkin sacked the unfortunate, who may have been caught stealing, because he begged for forgiveness while feeling 'the most horrible despair'. His fate is unknown, but another Frenchman replaced him.[28] 'The wine of Soudak', declared the French envoy, Comte de Ségur, in a report to Versailles, 'is very agreeable' – Maria Guthrie concurred at the turn of the century.[29]

Even in the middle of the Second Russo-Turkish War in 1789, as he advanced into Ottoman territory, the Prince found time to order Faleev 'to plough the best fertile ground and prepare enough string beans for sowing next summer. I shall send you the seeds from Jassy. I am going to arrange a school of husbandry here ...'.[30] The planter and builder never rested and never ceased to enjoy creating.

Potemkin's empire within an empire was not confined to New Russia: he also ran the military frontiers of the Caucasus and the Kuban, which were almost permanently at war throughout the 1780s as the Chechens and other mountain peoples resisted the Russian advance. The Russian solution was to maintain a line of forts across the Caucasus, manned by military outposts of hardy Cossack settlers. As soon as he came to power in the 1770s, Potemkin reconsidered the defence plans for the Caucasus. He decided to advance the border defences from the old Tsaritsyn Line to the new Azov–Mozdok Line.

The Prince already thought beyond mere guns and towers. The Line, he wrote, 'gives the opportunity to set up vineyards, silk and cotton plantations, to increase stock-breeding, stud-farms, orchards and grain production, joins Azov with Astrakhan Province, and in time of war ... restrains their pressure on our lands'.[31] The new Line was started in the summer of 1777 with the construction of a series of forts at Ekaterinograd, Georgievsk and Stavropol. The Kabardian, Cherkess and Nogai tribesmen rebelled and were suppressed. In 1780, Potemkin moved the first civilian settlers, often state peasants from the interior, into the towns that were to grow into major provincial centres.* When the fortifications were nearly complete in late 1782, the Empress decreed that Potemkin should have 'sole supervision' of assignment of land there.[32] The Prince moved Cossacks up to the Line from their settlements on the Volga. When he created the fortress of Vladikafkaz in 1784, he gave it a name that threw down a gauntlet to the tribesmen of the hills: 'Master of the Caucasus'.

The Georgievsk Treaty of 1783 with King Hercules advanced the Russian borders, leap-frogging over the Caucasus to Tiflis. By this time, Potemkin's projects and territories were so vast that he recommended to the Empress that she form a separate viceroyalty for the Caucasus, containing the Caucasus, Astrakhan and Saratov provinces – under his ultimate control of course. The Prince's dynamic cousin Pavel Potemkin was appointed viceroy: after creating the Georgian Military Road over the mountains to Tiflis, he settled state and church peasants to people his new towns. In 1786 alone, 30,307 settlers were available from inside Russia for the Prince to assign to the Caucasus (and to Ekaterinoslav). Pavel Sergeievich was a true Potemkin: he raised Ekaterinograd to be his viceregal capital, holding court there in a splendid palace.[33]

Russian advances into the Caucasus provoked an Islamic rebellion among the Chechens, Avars and other tribes: in 1785, a mysterious leader in a green cloak using the name Sheikh Mansour – 'Victor' – emerged from the mountains, preaching the ideals of the Nazshbandi brotherhood of mystical Sufism and declaring a *Ghazavat* – holy war – against the Russians. No one will ever know who he really was: he was probably a Chechen shepherd named Ushurma, born around 1748, but some said he was an Italian notary's son from Monteferrat named Giovanni Battista Boetti, who ran away to become a Dominican missionary, converted to Islam, studied the Koran in the *medressah*s of Bokhara and ended as a Moslem warrior. Some Russians did not believe he existed at all: he was just a symbol wrapped in a green cloak.† He and his warriors, precursors

---

* Stavropol's most famous son is Mikhail Gorbachev. Though General Suvorov was responsible for building some of these forts in his Kuban Line and was given credit as their founder in various Soviet histories, it was Potemkin who ordered their construction.

† Sheikh Mansour and the nineteenth-century leader against the Russians, Imam Shamyl, an Avar, are the two great heroes of today's Chechen rebels. When the author was in Grozny before the Chechen War in 1994, portraits of Sheikh Mansour's finely

of the Murids, who, under Shamyl defied Russia in the nineteenth century, managed to eliminate one column of 600 Russian troops, but he was defeated more frequently than he was victorious. Nevertheless, he led his coalition of mountain tribesmen with a daring flair that made him a legend.

The war against Sheikh Mansour was directly run by Pavel Potemkin from Ekaterinograd. But Potemkin's archives show that the Prince ultimately oversaw this perennial war, which kept the Caucasus and Kuban corps in constant action. Before the Russo-Turkish War broke out again in 1787, a defeated Mansour fled to raise the Cherkess in Ottoman territory. When the war began, he was ready to fight again.[34] The Russians never permanently suppressed these guerrilla fighters, spending much of the next century fighting the so-called Murid Wars. At the time of writing, this war is still going on.

The Prince also built his own palaces across the south, fit for a viceroy if not a tsar. He had 'the large house' at Kremenchuk, visited by Lady Craven and Francisco de Miranda;[35] a vast palace at Kherson* with two wings, each with two storeys and a central portico of four storeys, which was the centrepiece of the new city. Then there was the glory of his 'Athens', the monumental Ekaterinoslav† Palace, designed by Ivan Starov with two wings that extended 120 metres from the portico with six columns reached by two stone staircases: Potemkin's gardener William Gould followed Starov with his hundreds of workers. In Ekaterinoslav, he built an English Garden and two hothouses around the Potemkin Palace to match all its 'practicality and loveliness', as the gardener told the Prince.[36]

Oddly, Potemkin did not build for himself on a particularly grand

featured and heavily bearded visage adorned the offices of the President and ministers. Grozny's airport was named after him during Chechnya's short independence in the 1990s.

* The Kherson State History Museum has prints that show it in its nineteenth-century glory. But it does not stand any more. Plundered for its firewood and hated for its grandeur, it was destroyed during the Civil War.

† 'Potemkin's Palace' still stands in the centre of Dniepropetrovsk. The local museum contains some of the gold-encrusted mirrors, possibly made in his own factories, with which Potemkin planned to decorate the palace. On Potemkin's death, only one storey was finished. The rest was built according to Starov's plans during the 1830s: it became the House of the Nobility. In 1917, it became the House of Rest for Working People. It remains the House of Students. Ruined in the war, it was rebuilt in 1951. The two hothouses of the Winter Garden in Ekaterinoslav crumbled in 1794. Today, Gould's garden, now a Park of Culture, is called 'Potemkin Park' and still has an English air.

scale in the Crimea, but Starov did build him a now vanished pink marble palace at Karasubazaar.[37] His last palace was in Nikolaev.* Built when Potemkin was almost becoming an Ottoman sultan, he ordered a Moldavian–Turkish style from local architects – a dome with four towers, like a mosque. Its high, sunny but cool and breezy position above the meeting of the two rivers was scenic. Since it was on the banks of the Ingul river, it had two storeys at the front rising to a third – but one at the back. In his last months, the Prince ordered Starov to add a *banya* and fountain 'like mine at Tsarskoe Selo'.[38] It was Starov's last work for his master.†

The Prince himself always believed that the south was his life's work. In his last days in Petersburg in June 1791, he subjected the British envoy William Fawkener, who never got a word in edgeways, to an exuberant soliloquy that showed he never lost his enthusiasm. Potemkin displayed all the excitement, energy, imagination and arrogance that made him a great imperial statesman. He had to head to the south to continue his great projects, he said, 'the success of all which depended solely on him ...'. There was the fleet he had built almost with his own hands, and 'the population of his Government has increased since his appointment from above 80,000 to above 400,000 fighting men and the whole might amount to nearly a million ...'.[39]

Before the lies had overpowered the truth, the French Ambassador, Ségur, who sent Versailles a report on Potemkin's gargantuan achievements, enthused that 'when he took possession of his immense viceroyalty, there were only 204,000 inhabitants and under his administration the population in merely three years had grown to 800,000. This growth is composed of Greek colonists, Germans, Poles, invalids, retired soldiers and sailors.'

Potemkin increased the estimated population of the Crimea from

---

* This survived long after his death. The author found the place where it had stood: today, locals swim and dive from its seafront. Two storeys of white stone steps that led to the house survive along with Starov's ornate white fountain, dated 1792. A basketball court stands on the palace's foundations. The house was the Ship-Owners Club during the nineteenth century, but it was destroyed in the Revolution: a photograph shows it being dismantled for firewood. Ironically, today Moldavian-style mansions of New Russian millionaires are springing up, like distortions of Potemkin's Palace, around the suburbs of Nikolaev.

† Potemkin's two creative planners, Starov and Gould, did well like everyone else who worked with him. He was evidently a very generous employer, as the fortunes of Faleev, Zeitlin, Shemiakin, Garnovsky and many others prove. Ivan Starov was a rich man, dying in 1808.

52,000 males in 1782 to 130,000 by 1795. In the rest of New Russia during the same period, the male population increased from 339,000 in the same period to 554,000, which meant that Potemkin almost managed to double the population of the Viceroyalty from 391,000 to 684,000 in just over a decade. Another reputable historian estimates that the male population rose from 724,678 in 1787 to 819,731 in 1793. Whatever the true figures, this was an awesome achievement. 'Until the invention of steamships and railroads in the nineteenth century opened up ... distant regions such as the American Middle West ... to commercial farming, this Russian expansion', writes a modern historian, 'remained unparalleled in scale, scope and rapidity.'[40]

He founded literally hundreds of settlements – 'one Frenchman', recorded Ségur, 'told me every year he found new villages established and flourishing in places that had formerly been deserts'[41] – and several big ones. Most still flourish today: Kherson, 355,000 inhabitants; Nikolaev, 1.2 million; Ekaterinoslav (now Dniepropetrovsk), 600,000; Sebastopol, 375,000; Simferopol, 358,000; Stravropol, 350,000; Vladikafkaz (capital of North Ossetia), 300,000; and Odessa, 1.1 million. Most still contain shipyards and naval bases.

The construction of Russia's Black Sea Fleet, as well as an oar-propelled flotilla, in less than ten years, was an equally astounding achievement that was to have far-reaching consequences down to the Crimean War and beyond. The effects of the Fleet and of harnessing the immense agricultural power of the steppes resounded and resounds into this century. Russia became a Near Eastern power for the first time. 'The truly enormous achievement', writes a modern historian, 'made Russia ... the arbiter of eastern Europe and allowed Russian might to outstrip Austrian and eclipse Ottoman power.'[42] But Potemkin's love of the south was never just about raw power: there was much romance in it. Sometimes he turned his hand to poetry. As he wrote for the Empress about the foundation of Ekaterinoslav:

> Scattered stones of ancient ruins
> Will answer your divine inspiration
> In pleasant, brilliant ways
> They'll create a New Athens.[43]

20

ANGLOMANIA: THE BENTHAMS
IN RUSSIA AND THE EMPEROR
OF GARDENS

*My love affair is at an end ... I must certainly quit Petersburg
... So it is lucky that an offer of Prince Potemkin offers me a
good opportunity ...*

Samuel Bentham to his brother, Jeremy Bentham

On 11 December 1783, Prince Potemkin summoned to his apartments in
Petersburg a young Englishman named Samuel Bentham, whose love
affair and now broken heart had been followed by all society like a
running soap opera, and offered him a glorious new career. This offer
led, not only to the most adventurous life in war and peace ever enjoyed
by an Englishman in Russia, but also to a farce in which an ill-sorted
company of Welsh and Geordie artisans were settled on a Belorussian
estate which they were to develop into Potemkin's own industrial empire.
The experiences of Samuel Bentham, soon to be joined on Potemkin's
estate by his philosopher brother Jeremy, reveal not just Serenissimus'
boundless dynamism but the way he used his own estates as the arsenal
and marketplace of the state, with no boundary between his own money
and that of the Empire.

Samuel Bentham was the youngest of seven children – Jeremy was the
eldest – and they were the only two who survived. Their father Jeremiah
was a well-connected lawyer whose patron was the future Whig Prime
Minister, the original but devious Earl of Shelburne, nicknamed the
'Jesuit of Berkeley Square' by his many enemies. They were a touchingly
close family, writing to each other constantly, worrying about Samuel's
escapades in Russia. The brothers shared a brilliant intelligence, a driving
energy and an outstanding inventiveness, but personally they were
opposites: Jeremy, now almost forty, was a shy, scholarly judicialist.
Samuel was loquacious, sociable, irritable and amorous. Trained as an
engineer but uninhibited by the profession, he was an inventive poly-
math and entrepreneur. In some ways he shared Potemkin's restless
ebullience – he was 'always running from a good scheme to a better ...
life passes away and nothing is completed'.[1]

In 1780, while Jeremy worked on his judicial reforms in London, Samuel, aged twenty-three, departed on a voyage that took him to the Black Sea coast (where he observed the burgeoning Kherson) and thence to St Petersburg, where he called on Potemkin. He hoped to make his fortune, while Jeremy wanted him to propose his legal ideas to the Empress.[2] Serenissimus monitored young Bentham's progress. The Englishman realized that the Prince was the man who could put his ideas into practice. Potemkin wanted his help with the Dnieper rapids and his estates and made a vague offer to him soon after meeting him.[3] But Samuel wanted to travel so, in 1781, the Prince despatched him on a trip to Siberia to analyse its industries, providing him with a couple of soldiers as guards. On his return, the Prince gave his papers on Mines, Fabricks and Salt-Works[4] to the Empress.

Potemkin was looking for talented engineers, shipbuilders, entrepreneurs and Englishmen: Samuel was all of these things. Writing to his brother Jeremy from Irkutsk in Siberia, Samuel boasted about his new contact – 'the man in power'.[5] It was obvious to the excited traveller that he and this anonymous potentate were made for each other:

> This man's business is to greater amount than any other's I have heard of in the Empire. His position at Court is also the best on which account, as well as that of his riches, Governors of course bow down to him. His chief affairs lie about the Black Sea. He there farms the duties on some articles, builds ships for the Crown, supplies the army and the Crown in general with all necessaries, has fabricks of various kinds and is clearing the waterfalls of the Dnieper at his own private expense. He was very anxious to have assistance in his undertakings before I left St Petersburg.[6]

However, on his return Bentham was distracted by something much more alluring.

The object of his affections was Countess Sophia Matushkina, pretty niece and ward of Field-Marshal Prince Alexander Golitsyn, the Governor of Petersburg whose failures of command during the Russo-Turkish War were now obscured by the prestige of age. Samuel and the Countess, roughly the same age, met in the Field-Marshal's salon, fell in love and managed to meet twice a week. Their passion was fanned by the operatic intrigues made necessary by the disapproval of old Golitsyn and the interest shown by the whole Court. The Field-Marshal was against any courtship, yet alone marriage, between his ward and this

English golddigger. The Empress, however, who combined mischief with a certain amorousness herself, let the Court know that she was thoroughly enjoying the scandal.

At this point, Samuel's ambitious imagination ran wild. 'If you have anything to say to me for or against a Matrimonial Connection,' he asked Jeremy, 'let me know.' He loved the girl – and her position, for he added disarmingly: 'She is heiress to two Rich People.' Samuel decided his love affair had caused such interest that it would help him get a job from the Empress, a novel sort of *curriculum vitae*, though one not unknown in Russia: 'I am fully disposed that a desire Her Majesty has to assist my Match goes a great way in disposing her in my favour . . . she fully believes it was my Love induced me to offer my Services.' He also wrote letters to Field-Marshal Golitsyn declaring, 'it's already more than five months since I loved your niece'. This can only have further incensed the Field-Marshal, who banned the couple from seeing each other.

The courtiers relished this forbidden romance as much as the Empress – and, even while annexing the Crimea, Potemkin was also kept informed. It was a wonderful moment to be an Englishman in Petersburg and Samuel lived a dizzy social existence, bathing in the attention of magnates and countesses. Petersburg was full of Englishmen – Sir James Harris, and his successor as British envoy Alleyne Fitzherbert, patronized him. His only enemy among them was the permanent Scotsman at court – Dr Rogerson, that accomplished gambler and usually fatal doctor. Perhaps suspecting Bentham's motives, Rogerson told Catherine that Samuel was not worth meeting because he had a speech defect.[7] This did not hold him back. Samuel's two best Russian friends were on Potemkin's staff, Princess Dashkova's son, Prince Pavel Mikhailovich Dashkov, and Colonel Korsakov, the engineer, both educated in Britain. The Russians took Bentham to the salons of all the magnates who kept open tables for foreigners. Here is a typical undated day in Samuel's social whirl: 'Breakfasted at Fitzherbert, dined by invitation at the Duchess of Kingston's [back on another visit], then to Prince Dashkov's, to Potemkin's but as he was not at home, went to Baroness Stroganov and from there to supper at Dashkov's.'[8]

Probably at Catherine's prompting, her favourite, Lanskoy, now intervened on Samuel's behalf, telling Sophia's aunt and mother that 'the Empress thought they did wrong to oppose the young Countess's inclinations . . . This only irritated the aunt more.' There were few cities in the world, even in Italy, as well arranged for intrigue as Petersburg, where the Court itself set the pace and where battalions of servants made the business of sending notes, eavesdropping and watching for secret signs at windows cheap and comprehensive. So, aided by his friends, Samuel and Sophia enjoyed *Romeo and Juliet* scenes on balconies in the dim gardens of palaces. Valets and coachmen bore secret letters that were pressed into manicured hands. Countess Sophia let down perfumed epistles to Sam from her windows.[9] Samuel, intoxicated by the grandeur of those involved in his affairs, suffered from the delusion common to many in love that they are the centre of the known world. He felt the very cabinets of Europe had forgotten wars and treaties, and were exclusively discussing his trysts.

Therefore when Potemkin returned triumphantly with the Crimea and Georgia at his feet, Samuel was convinced that Serenissimus' first question would be about his love. The Prince was much more interested in the Englishman's shipbuilding potential. But he knew from his court-iers that Bentham's affair was doomed. The Empress may have liked teasing the Golitsyns – but she was never going to support an Englishman against the scions of Gedimin of Lithuania. So Lanskoy, imperial inter-vention manifested in flesh, intervened again: the affair must end.

On 6 December, the crestfallen Samuel called on the Prince, who had Korsakov offer him a job at Kherson. Samuel resisted Potemkin's offer – still hoping Countess Sophia's love would lead to marriage. But it was all over. Petersburg was no longer such fun. Samuel resolved to leave 'out of delicacy' to the pining Countess, so he accepted the job. Potemkin appointed him lieutenant-colonel with a salary of 1,200 roubles a year and 'much more for table money'. The Prince had many plans for young Samuel – he was going to move his dockyards below the bar in the Dnieper and he wanted Samuel to erect his various mechanical inven-tions 'under his command'.

The fortunate Colonel was now almost in love with Potemkin, like so many Westerners before and after him. It is interesting how Bentham perceived the Prince's unique position: 'his immediate command is all the Southern part of the country and his indirect command is the whole Empire'. The melodramatic lover of the months before was now replaced by Potemkin's self-congratulatory protégé: 'While I enjoy the share of the Prince's good opinion and confidence which I flatter myself I possess at present, my situation cannot be disagreeable. Everything I propose to him, he accedes to.' When the Prince was interested in someone, he treated him with more respect than all the generals of the empires of Europe put together: now Samuel was that person. 'I go to him at all times. He speaks to me whenever I come into the room giving me the *bonjour* and makes me sit down when the stars and ribbons may come ten times without his asking them to sit down or even looking at them.'

Potemkin's idiosyncratic management style bemused Colonel Bentham: 'as to what employment I am to have at Kherson or elsewhere ...'. Serenissimus also mentioned 'an Estate on the Borders of Poland ... One day he talks of a new port and dockyard below the Bar, another he talks about my erecting windmills in the Crimea. A month hence I may have a regiment of Hussars and be sent against ... the Chinese and then command a ship of 100 guns.' He was to end up doing almost all of the above. He certainly could not complain that working for Potemkin was going to be boring. However, as to his immediate destiny, he could only inform his brother: 'I can tell you nothing.'

On 10 March 1784, the Prince abruptly departed from Petersburg for the south, leaving Bentham's arrangements to Colonel Popov, his head of Chancellery.[10] At midnight on Wednesday, 13 March, Bentham followed in a convoy of seven *kibitka*s. Samuel kept a diary of these days: he arrived in Moscow on Saturday to meet Potemkin. When he presented himself to the Prince on Sunday morning in his usual frockcoat, Serenissimus called in ever-ready Popov, told him to list the boy in the army, cavalry or infantry, whichever he liked – he chose the infantry – and put on his lieutenant-colonel's uniform.[11] Henceforth Bentham always wore his green coat with scarlet lapels, scarlet waistcoat with gold lace, and white breeches.[12]

A season of travelling with the Prince round his empire was a privilege accorded to very few foreigners – but Potemkin only tolerated those who were the best company. For six months, Samuel travelled round the Empire 'always in the same carriage' as Potemkin: 'The journey I have been making this spring with the Prince, to me who do not think much of fatigue, has been in every respect highly agreeable ... I had not for a long time spent my time so merrily.'[13] They headed south via Borodino, Viazma and Smolensk, passed through Potemkin's estates at Orsha on the upper Dnieper, noting that Potemkin's leather tannery already employed two tanners from Newcastle. They then headed off to Potemkin's southern headquarters, Kremenchuk. Bentham must have been with the Prince when he inaugurated his new Viceroyalty of Ekaterinoslav. They were in the Crimea by early June: they must have visited the new naval base at Sebastopol together. On the road, Lieutenant-Colonel Bentham experienced the way that Potemkin ran his empire from the back of a speeding sledge that travelled thousands of versts in a spray of ice.

Somewhere in this perambulating horse-powered seat of government, the Prince decided that Lieutenant-Colonel Bentham was not to stay in Kherson. In July, Bentham arrived at his new posting – Krichev. Potemkin's sprawling estate 'on the borders of Poland' was another world, all of its own.[14]

Bentham was appointed the sole master of an estate that was 'larger than any county of England' and indeed than many German principalities: Krichev itself was, according to Bentham, over 100 square miles, but it was right next to another Potemkin estate, Dubrovna, which was even larger. At Krichev, there were five townships and 145 hamlets – 14,000 male serfs. Together, the population of these two territories was 'upwards of 40,000 male vassals', as Samuel put it, which meant that the whole number of inhabitants must have been at least double that.[15]

The Krichev–Dubrovna estates were not only big but also strategically vital: when Russia annexed these Polish territories in the First Partition of 1772, Catherine gained control of the upper reaches of two of Europe's greatest trading rivers: the right (north) bank of the Dvina that led to Riga on the Baltic and the left or east bank of the Dnieper, on which Potemkin was to build so many of his cities. When Catherine granted lands to Potemkin in 1776, he may have requested estates that happened to have access to both rivers and therefore were potential trading stations with both the Baltic and the Black Sea: ideal for making small ships, Potemkin's lands flanked the north bank of the Dnieper for an awesome fifty miles.

Potemkin was already the master of an industrial empire, best known for its factories making Russia's most beautiful mirrors, a sign of the boom in demand for looking-glasses that literally reflected the eighteenth century's new self-awareness.* And then there was Krichev.[16] Bentham found a brandy distillery, factory, tannery, copperworks, textile mill with 172 looms making sailcloth, a rope walk with twenty wheels, supplying Kherson's shipyards, a complex of greenhouses, a pottery, a shipyard and yet another mirror-factory. Krichev was an extension of Kherson. 'The estate ... furnishes all the principal naval stores in the greatest abundance by a navigable river which ... renders the transport

---

* Potemkin took Reginald Pole Carew on a tour of his industrial holdings in 1781, including his glass and brick factories near Schlüsselburg, another glass factory near the Alexander Nevsky Monastery, and his iron foundry twenty miles outside Petersburg on his Eschenbaum estate, which was run by an Englishman, Mr Hill. Pole Carew also visited Krichev and Potemkin's other estates down the Dnieper, and suggested founding an English colony on a formerly Zaporogian island where Potemkin later settled immigrants.

easy to the Black Sea.'[17] The trade went in both directions: there was already a surplus of cordage and sailcloth that was traded on to Constantinople, while there was a booming import–export business to Riga. This was Potemkin's imperial arsenal, his manufacturing and trading headquarters, his inland shipyard and the chief supplier of his new cities and navy on the Black Sea.

Krichev was another world from the salons of Petersburg, yet alone the chambers of Lincoln's Inn, but it must have been even more of a shock to Bentham's recruits from England. Bentham moved into what was called 'Potemkin's house' but which was really just a 'tottering barn'.[18] The enthusiastic and arrogant Englishman had landed at one of Europe's crossroads: not only did the riverways converge there, but the place was a cultural cauldron too. 'The situation is picturesque and pleasant, the people ... quiet and patient to the last degree ... industrious or idle and drunken.' There were forty poverty-stricken Polish noblemen who worked on the estate 'almost as slaves'. It teemed with different races and languages.

This was all most confusing and alarming to a newly arrived artisan from Newcastle, who had never travelled before. 'The heterogeneous mixture of people here is surprising,' Beaty, a Geordie heckler, confessed. There were Russians, Germans, Don Cossacks, Polish Jews – and the English. At first 'I thought it a collection of the strangest sounds that ever invaded my English ears.' The Jews, from whom 'we had to buy all the necessities of life', spoke German or Yiddish.[19] Beaty could only muse that 'on a Market Day when I behold such an odd Medley of Faces and Dresses, I have more than once started and wondered what brought me amongst them'.[20]

Samuel's responsibilities over all these people were equally extensive: firstly he was now the 'Legislator, Judge, Jury and Sheriff' of the local serfs. Then, 'I have the direction and putting in order of all the Prince's fabriks here.' The factories were lamentable.[21] So Bentham offered to take them over. 'Extremely agreeable,' replied Potemkin from Tsarskoe Selo, professing himself 'charmed with your activity and the project of your obliging responsibility'.[22]

The Prince was always thinking of improving his cities and warships. Disproving his supposed allergy to detail or to seeing his projects through, he turned to the cordage factory: 'They tell me the cordage ... is scarcely fit for use.'[23] He begged Bentham to improve it and sent him an expert from Kronstadt. When Samuel's friends Korsakov and the sailor Mordvinov, both senior officers of Potemkin's, visited on the way to Kherson, Bentham reported to Serenissimus that he was supplying them with whatever they needed for their shipbuilding.[24] After almost two years, Samuel was doing so well with his mills that he suggested a deal to the Prince: he would actually take over the less successful factories for ten years while Potemkin kept the profitable ones. All the buildings and materials would be supplied along with 20,000 roubles (about £5,000) of capital, which he would gradually repay. In the deal signed in January 1786, Serenissimus asked for no income whatsoever during the ten years – he simply hoped to receive the factories back in a profitable state at the end. His real interest was not profit but imperial benefit.[25]

One of Bentham's suggestions was to import potatoes and plant them at Krichev: Potemkin approved. The first twelve acres were sown in 1787 and a 'much pleased' Prince kept growing them on his other estates afterwards. Some histories claim that Potemkin and Bentham brought potatoes to Russia. This is not true – Catherine arranged their import during the 1760s, but the Prince was the first to cultivate them and it was probably thanks to him that they became part of the staple Russian diet.[26]

Bentham's main task was to build ships for Potemkin – all sorts, any sort at all. 'I seem to be at liberty to build any kind of ship ... whether for War, Trade or Pleasure.' The Prince wanted gun frigates for the navy, a pleasure frigate for the Empress, barges for the Dnieper trade and ultimately luxury barges for the Empress's long-planned visit to the south. It was a tall if not towering order. There was a priceless moment of Potemkinish exasperation when Bentham tried to pin down the Prince about the ship design. Did Serenissimus want one mast, two masts, and how many guns? 'He told me by way of ending the dispute that there might be twenty masts and one Gun if I pleased. I am a little confused ...'[27] What inventor could want for a more indulgent, and maddening, master?

Soon Samuel realized he needed help. His ships required rowers, whether peasants or soldiers. This was no problem: the Prince delivered, as if by magic, a battalion of Musketeers. 'I give you the command,' wrote Serenissimus from Petersburg in September. Potemkin was always thinking about his beloved navy: 'My intention, sir, is that they shall be capable one day of serving at sea, therefore I exhort you ... to qualify them for it.'[28] Bentham naturally had no idea how to command soldiers or speak Russian, so when a major asked for orders on parade, Samuel replied: 'Same as yesterday.' How was this manoeuvre to be conducted? 'As usual,' ordered Bentham.[29] There were only 'two or three Sergeants' who could write, yet alone draw, plus the two leather-makers from

Newcastle at Orsha, a young mathematician from Strasbourg, a Danish brass-founder and a Scottish watchmaker.[30] Samuel bombarded the Prince with requests for artisans: 'I'm finding it very difficult to recruit people of talent,'[31] he complained in one unpublished letter. The Prince replied that he could hire workmen on whatever terms he liked.

The Prince's obsessional Anglomania now exploded into one of the most energetic recruitment campaigns ever designed to lure British experts to distant climes. Anglophilia ruled Europe.[32] In Paris, men sported 'Windsor collars' and plain frockcoats, ladies drank Scotch whisky, took tea while betting on jockeys at the races and playing whist.* Potemkin did not care about the details but he knew that he wanted only Englishmen, not only to drive the looms of Krichev but also to run his botanical gardens, dairies, windmills and shipyards from the Crimea to Krichev. The Benthams placed advertisements in English newspapers. These advertisements unconsciously catch the capricious demands of Potemkin. 'The Prince wants to introduce the use of beer,' announced one. Or he 'means to have an elegant dairy' with 'the best of butter and as many kinds of cheese as possible'. Soon the advertisements had expanded to anyone British: 'Any clever people capable of introducing improvements in the Prince's Government might meet with good encouragement,' read one Bentham advertisement in Britain. Finally Potemkin just declared to Samuel that he wished to create a 'whole colony of English' with their own church and privileges.[33] Potemkin's Anglophilia of course extended to his subordinates. Local landowners wanted their peasants trained with English smiths so Dashkov's serfs were sent over to learn English carpentry.[34] After Potemkin's future Admiral Mordvinov married Henrietta Cobley, Nikolai Korsakov confessed to Samuel that he too 'was exceedingly desirous of an English wife'.[35] Gardeners, sailors and artisans were not enough. The Russians wanted wives too.

Bentham's budget was limitless. When he bothered Serenissimus to fix some bounds on the credit, '"What is necessary" was the only answer I could get.' Sutherland, Potemkin's banker, simply arranged the credit in London.[36] Samuel Bentham immediately saw opportunities for him and his brother Jeremy to trade in goods between England and Russia and to be the middlemen of Potemkin's recruiting campaign. Within weeks of the first advertisements, Samuel was sending Jeremy shopping

---

* Card games followed political fashions. For example, the Comte de Ségur explains in his *Mémoires* how in Paris the faro of high aristocracy gave way to English whist, representing moderate liberty as explained by Montesquieu, but when the American War showed that Kings could be defied, 'boston' became the fashion.

lists by the dozen: one, for example, demanded a millwright, a windmill expert, a cloth-weaver, barge-or boat-builders, shoemakers, bricklayers, sailors, housekeepers, 'two under-maids, one to understand cheese-making, the other, spinning and knitting.'[37]

Father and brother, Jeremiah and Jeremy Bentham, enthusiastically scoured Britain. Old Jeremiah excelled himself – he called on Lord Howe at the Admiralty, then invited Under-Secretary of State Fraser and two recently returned Russian veterans, Sir James Harris and Reginald Pole Carew, to his house to discuss it. He even roped in the former Prime Minister Shelburne, now first Marquess of Lansdowne[38] – 'all to procure shipwrights to be sent to my son's assistance'. The Marquess thought Potemkin was interesting but untrustworthy and his compliments about the Bentham brothers were distinctly back-handed: 'Both your sons are too liberal in their temper to adopt a mercantile spirit and your Sam's mind will be more occupied with fresh inventions than with calculating compound interest which the dullest men in Russia can perhaps do as well . . .', wrote Lansdowne from Weymouth on 21 August 1786. 'He is spending his best years in a changeable country and relying on men of changeable tempers.'[39]

The whole frantic project now assumes some of the absurdity of an eighteenth-century situation comedy in which a mixed group of philosophers, sailors, phoneys, hussies and workmen are dropped without a word of any foreign language into a multilingual Belorussian village owned by an often invisible but impulsive Serenissimus. Each of these characters turns out to have a completely different agenda to the one assigned by the Benthams.

Jeremy became possessed by a sort of Catherinian graphomania and kept writing to Samuel with interminable superfluous details on a parade of candidates for posts varying from chief of botanical gardens to milk-maid: 'With the respect to the Botanist, I conceive there cannot be the least difficulty in finding a man of science' and then debated the costs of 'The Dairy Lady'. Finally, Jeremy recruited a Logan Henderson to run the said botanical garden. Naturally such an adventurous expedition attracted a motley crew: Henderson for example was a Scotsman who claimed to be an 'expert' on gardens, steam-engines, sugar-planting and phosphorous fireworks. He signed up, promising also to deliver his two nieces, the Miss Kirtlands, as dairymaids. Dr John Debraw, the ex-apothecary of Addenbrooke's Hospital, Cambridge, and revered author of that significant work, *Discoveries on the Sex of Bees* (just published to mixed reviews), signed up as Potemkin's experimental chemist along with gardeners, millwrights, hecklers, mostly from Newcastle or Scotland: the first tranche reached Riga in June 1785.

Jeremy Bentham longed to join Samuel in Belorussia: he saw not only mercantile opportunities but peace in which to work on his treatises, and statesmen like Potemkin who could put his utilitarian ideas into practice. (His utilitarian theory measured the success of rulers by their ability to provide the greatest happiness for the greatest number.) Potemkin's estates sounded like a philosopher's dream. Jeremy decided to bring out another group of his recruits. By the time he set off, Samuel was exasperated with his brother's ludicrous letters. Things really deteriorated when the philosopher began to write directly to the Prince himself suggesting quixotic ideas and telling him about gardeners and chemists: Potemkin's archives contain many of these unpublished works of Jeremy Bentham. They are priceless both as historic documents and as works of comic entertainment: the phrase 'mad professor' comes to mind.

Jeremy planned to buy a ship to bear the Prince's artisans, proposing to name it *The Prince Potemkin*. Then to business: 'Here, Monseigneur, is your Botanist. Here is your milkmaid. The milk is good in Cheshire, county of cheese ...'. Mademoiselle Kirtland, the milkmaid who was also an admirable chemist, stimulated this Benthamite exposition of feminism: 'Knowledgeable women so often lose the perfection of their own sex by acquiring those of ours ... That is scarcely true with Mademoiselle Kirtland.' The philosopher really wanted to sell Potemkin a 'machine de feu' or, even better, the latest steam-engine of Watts and Bolton, explaining that these were mechanisms 'which play by the force of water reduced to vapours in boiling. Of all the machines of modernity ... the easiest to construct is the *machine de feu*', but the hardest and costliest was the Watts and Bolton. If the Prince did not want the steam-engine, how about setting up a printing press in the Crimea with a Mr Titler? What would this printing press publish? Jeremy suggested *Project of the Body of the Laws* by one J. Bentham. Jeremy apologetically signed himself, 'Here for the fourth time, Your Eternal Correspondent'.[40]

Samuel panicked. Serenissimus hated long letters and wanted results. Colonel Bentham feared his career was being ruined by the 'Eternal Correspondent' so he told off his bungling brother. The Prince would have found the details 'troublesome' and 'expected to hear no more until the people made their appearance'. Samuel was anxious because Potemkin had not replied: 'I fear the worst ... I hope to lay the blame on your over-zeal.'[41] But the philosopher finally received a courteous letter from the Prince via the Russian Embassy in London. 'Sir,' the

Prince wrote to Jeremy, 'I have to thank you for the care you have given yourself in the execution of the Commissions ... on my account. The time did not permit me to come to a resolution sooner ... but now I have to beg you to engage Mr Henderson to accompany the Persons ...'. Indeed, Jeremy Bentham's long but brilliant letters were exactly the sort of fascinating distraction that the Prince relished: he sent word he enjoyed them immensely and was having them translated into Russian.[42]

Jeremy Bentham was most proud of recruiting a landscape gardener for Krichev named John Ayton, because, as he boasted to his father, 'our Gardener is Nephew to the King's Gardener at Kew'.[43] This was a time when there was an aristocracy of gardeners too. Yet Ayton did not become the Prince's star gardener. Potemkin's green-fingered factotum had already arrived in Russia in 1780, at about the same time as Samuel Bentham. His name was William Gould, a protégé of Lancelot 'Capability' Brown, the master of the English garden. During the 1770s, Catherine and Potemkin simultaneously became avid devotees of the English garden. In no other field was the Prince's Anglomania so marked as in his addiction to creating English gardens wherever he was.

The natural, picturesque (but intricately planned) chaos of the English garden, with its lakes, grottoes, landscaping and ruins, was now gradually vanquishing the formal precise French garden. The fortunes of the gardens followed those of the kingdoms: when Louis XIV dominated Europe, so did French gardens. As France declined and Britain conquered its empire, its gardens also triumphed. 'I adore English gardens,' Catherine told Voltaire, 'with their curved lines, *pente-douces*, ponds like lakes (archipelagoes on dry land); and I despise deeply straight lines and identical *allées* ... In a word, anglomania is more important to me than "plantomania".'[44]

The Empress approached her new gardening hobby with her usual levelheaded practicality, while Potemkin vaulted it with his typical obsessional singlemindedness. In 1779, the Empress had hired John Bush and his son Joseph to landscape her gardens at Tsarskoe Selo. On her other estates, she hired other green-fingered Englishmen with garden names – Sparrow and Hackett. It was a mark of his Anglomania that Potemkin clearly regarded an English gardener as the equal of a Russian aristocrat: such was his respect for these lords of the flowerbed that he dined at the Bushes' with two of his nieces, one of their husbands Count Skavronsky, and three ambassadors, a social puzzle that alarmed a supposedly more democratic English visitor, Baroness Dimsdale.[45] She observed that Potemkin relished Bush's 'excellent dinner in the English taste' and ate as much as he could. (Serenissimus so relished English cooking that, when his banker Sutherland gave him roast beef for dinner, he took the rest home with him.) Soon Potemkin's gardening requirements were so great that he recruited Ayton from England and borrowed Sparrow from Catherine.[46]

None of these became as famous as Potemkin's Gould, who is still celebrated in distant corners of Russia and Ukraine today: in 1998, this author heard his name in places as far apart as Petersburg and Dneipropetrovsk. Gould was lucky to be recruited by a man described by the *Encyclopaedia of Gardening* (1822) as 'one of the most extravagant encouragers of our art that modern times can boast'. But Potemkin was also fortunate to find his gardening *alter ego* – the capable and grandiose creator of massive English gardens across the Empire that defied distance and imagination.

Gould employed a staff of 'several hundred assistants' who travelled in Potemkin 's wake.[47] He planned and executed gardens in Astrakhan, Ekaterinoslav, Nikolaev and the Crimea, including on the estates on the lush Crimean coast at Artek, Massandra and the site of the Alupka Palace.* Local *cognoscenti* still breathe his name with reverence two centuries after he last hoed.[48] Potemkin discovered the ruins of one of Charles XII's castles, perhaps near Poltava. He not only had it repaired but had Gould surround it with yet more English gardens.

Gould's extraordinary speciality was building English gardens overnight, on the spot, wherever Potemkin stayed. The *Encyclopaedia of Gardening*, which gave one of Gould's junior gardeners, Call, as its source, claims that wherever Potemkin stopped he would set up a travelling palace and Gould would create an English garden, composed of 'shrubs and trees, divided by gravel walks and ornamented with seats and statues, all carried with his cavalcade'. Most historians have presumed that the stories of Potemkin's instant English gardens were simply legends – it was surely impossible that Gould travelled with a convoy of oak trees, rockeries and shrubberies. But here Legend and Reality merge: the State Archives in Petersburg, which contain Potemkin's accounts, show that Gould constantly travelled with Potemkin to places where we know from other sources that these gardens were indeed laid out in a matter of days. There was something of Haroun al-Rashid about

---

* Alupka is the remarkable Crimea palace built in a mixture of Scottish baronial, Arabesque and Gothic architecture by Prince Mikhail Vorontsov and his wife Lise, who was Potemkin's great-niece. It is now a museum. See Epilogue.

Potemkin. He was, as Elisabeth Vigée Lebrun put it, 'a sort of enchanter such as one reads about in the *Arabian Nights*.'*

Gould now rushed across Russia, working in tandem with the Prince. Gould became 'the [Capability] Brown of Russia' but, warned the *Encyclopaedia of Gardening*, 'a foreigner established as head gardener to an Emperor becomes a despot like his master'. One senses a gardener's jealousy of one of their kind raised to the level of a tsar of shrubberies, the Potemkin of gardens.[49]

Naturally, Potemkin pursued his Anglomania in painting too. He collected pictures and engravings and was said to own works of Titian, Van Dyck, Poussin, Raphael and da Vinci. The Prince used merchants and Russian ambassadors as his art dealers: 'I've not yet found the landscape painting you wanted, my Prince, but I hope to have it soon,'[50] wrote the Russian Ambassador in the Baroque capital of Saxony, Dresden.

Now Potemkin's English network led him to Sir Joshua Reynolds. When Harris returned to London in 1784, he gave John Joshua Proby, Lord Carysfort, a letter of introduction to Potemkin: 'the bearer of this letter is a man of birth – a peer of Ireland'.[51] Carysfort arrived in Petersburg and suggested to both the Empress and the Prince that their collections lacked English works: what about his friend Reynolds? Both agreed. The subjects were left to the artist – but Potemkin wanted something from history which suited Reynolds's taste. Four years later, after many delays, Catherine received one painting and Potemkin two. Carysfort and Reynolds wrote to the Prince in French as the paintings set off aboard the ship *Friendship*. Thanking him for his hospitality in Russia, Carysfort explained to Potemkin that Catherine's painting was 'a young Hercules who strangles the Serpent', adding, 'It would be superfluous to remark to Your Highness, who has so perfect a knowledge of Ancient Literature, the story that the Painting has taken from the Odes of Pindar.'† Reynolds himself told Potemkin that he was going to do him the same painting, then decided on something else. This turned out to be the *The Continence of Scipio*. Carysfort also sent him Reynolds's

* We can follow some of Gould's adventures in the archives: in 1785, he is paid 1,453 roubles for a tool needed in the Crimea; the next year, 500 roubles for gardeners coming from England to join the team. In 1786/7, Gould headed from Petersburg to the Crimea with 200 roubles for the journey and 225 for his carriage. Then he joined the Prince in Moldavia during the war, travelling with him to Dubossary in 1789 (800 roubles) and the next year to Jassy (650 roubles).

† The bitchy Horace Walpole laughed at the appropriateness of the subject since two tsars had been killed, at least one strangled, to secure Catherine's crown.

The Nymph whose Belt is Untied by a Cupidon. 'Connoisseurs', wrote Carysfort, 'who have seen it have found it a great beauty'.[52]

It was indeed a 'great beauty'. Both paintings seem appropriate for Potemkin. *The Nymph*, or *Cupid Untying the Zone of Venus* as it now called, depicts the lively little Cupid undoing the belt of a glowing, bare-breasted Venus. In the other painting, *Scipio*, Potemkin's ideal Classical hero – who defeated the Carthaginians as he was defeating the Turks – fights off the temptations of women and money, two things Potemkin could never resist.[53] Neither Catherine nor Potemkin was in any hurry to pay: Reynolds charged Carysfort £105 for the *Nymph*. Catherine paid Reynolds's executors.* Later, Potemkin added a Kneller and a Thomas Jones to his English collection.

Serenissimus also patronized the best English artist in Petersburg, Richard Brompton, a Bohemian 'harum-scarum ingenious sort of paint-er', according to Jeremy Bentham, whom Catherine rescued from debt-or's prison. Potemkin almost became Brompton's agent, even advising him what to charge. He commissioned him to paint Branicka: the splen-did full-length canvas, now in the Alupka Palace in the Crimea, catches Sashenka's pert prettiness, her clever haughtiness. Brompton also painted the Empress but, Potemkin personally ordered changes to her hair. Joseph II bought the painting, only to complain that this 'daubing' was 'so horribly painted that I wanted to send it back'.[54] Brompton often appealed to Potemkin in scrawled unpublished letters that fret about money and imperial patronage.[55] When he died leaving 5,000 roubles' debts, Potemkin gave his widow 1,000 roubles.[56]

The enthusiasm with which Potemkin and Catherine shared their artistic tastes is another charming aspect of their relationship. When the two of them retired alone for two hours in 1785, the diplomats thought a war had started, until they learned that the couple were happily perusing some Levantine drawings brought by Sir Richard Worsley, an English traveller. Given their shared enjoyment, it was fitting that, after the Prince's demise, his collection joined Catherine's in the Hermitage.[57]

Meanwhile, on 28 July 1785, Jeremy Bentham set out from Brighton, bearing Shelburne's wordly advice: 'get into no intrigues to serve either England or Russia, not even with a handsome lady'.[58] He met up with Logan Henderson and the two lissom Miss Kirtlands at Paris and

---

* Potemkin's paintings were admired in the Hermitage by Parkinson in 1792. None of the three Reynoldses is now on display in the Hermitage, but they are exhibited abroad. When the author searched for them in 1998, they were in a dusty corridor used as a storeroom, leaning forlornly against the wall.

travelled on via Nice and Florence (where he spotted a 'poor old gentleman' at the opera – the Young Pretender). The group sailed from
Leghorn to Constantinople. Thence Jeremy sent Henderson and the two
Miss Kirtlands by sea to the Crimea. He made his own way overland:
after a dramatic journey with the sister of the Hospodar of Moldavia
and twenty horsemen, he reached Krichev in February 1786.[59] It was a
joyous reunion: the Bentham brothers had not seen each other for five
and a half years.

Once the party was complete, the Belorussian village seemed to turn
into a Tower of Babel of quarrelling, drinking and wife-swapping. The
recruits were as ragged a crew as could be expected, and few were
quite what they claimed: Samuel tried to control this 'Newcastle mob –
hirelings from that rabble town'.[60]

Jeremy confessed to Samuel that Henderson's milkmaid 'nieces', who
had so impressed him with their femininity and knowledge, were neither
cheesemakers nor any relation to the gardener: they were apparently
troilists. Henderson did not turn out successfully. Potemkin settled the
gardener and the two milking 'nieces' in the Tartar house near Karasubazaar. The sentimental Prince remembered his recovery from fever
there in August 1783 and bought it. However, he soon learned that
Henderson was a 'shameless impostor' who had not even 'planted a
single blade of grass and Mamzel [one of the girls] has not made a single
cheese'.[61]

Roebuck, another recruit, travelled with his 'soi-disant wife', who
turned out to be a thorough slattern. She offered 'her services to either
of the Newcastle men', wishing to be rid of her ruffian husband.[62] Samuel
managed to pass her on to Prince Dashkov: these Russian Anglophiles
were grateful for a gardener's wench – if she came from the land of
Shakespeare. Samuel suspected 'the very quarrelsome' Roebuck of stealing diamonds at Riga – he was 'not the most honest'. When Potemkin
summoned Samuel, Jeremy was left in charge, which led to more bad
behaviour. Dr Debraw, the bee sexologist, proved an utter nuisance. He
stalked into Jeremy's study 'with a countenance of a man out of Bedlam'
and demanded a pass to leave. This stew of crooks even stole Samuel's
money to pay off their debts.[63] There were rebellions against the
Benthams led by Benson the general factotum, who again 'like a man let
loose from Bedlam' abused Jeremy, who had never seen him before in his
life.[64] Then 'the termagant cook–housekeeper' joined 'the male seducers'
by luring 'old Benson' to her bed.[65] The word 'Bedlam' appeared with
ominous and appropriate frequency in the Benthams' letters.

Despite the capers of these expatriates, the Benthams achieved an immense amount, both literary and mercantile: 'The day has an abundance more hours in it at Krichev or rather at our cottage three miles off where I now live,' wrote Jeremy. 'I rise a little before the sun, get breakfast done in less than an hour and do not eat again until eight . . . at night.' He was working on his *Code* of civil law, a French version of the *Rationale of Reward* and the *Defence of Usury*. But he had also 'been obliged to go a begging to my brother and borrow an idea . . .'. This was the *Panopticon* – Samuel's solution to supervising this rabble of Russians, Jews and Geordies: a factory constructed so that the manager could see all his workers from one central observation point. Jeremy the legal reformer could immediately see its use in prisons. He worked from dawn till dusk on the *Panopticon*.[66]

Both Jeremy and Samuel were also pursuing another great ambition that was close to Potemkin's heart: to become landowners in the Crimea. 'We are going to be great farmers,' announced Jeremy. 'I dare say he would give us a good portion of land to both of us if we wish it . . .'.[67] But despite Potemkin's cruelly teasing Samuel – 'you have only to say of which kind'[68] – the Benthams never became Crimean magnates – though they did get a share in one of Korsakov's estates.

Samuel meanwhile was running the factories, trading with Riga and Kherson in foreign exchange (changing Potemkin's 20,000 roubles for ducats) and English cloth, and building *baidak*s (riverboats) for the Dnieper. Despite the 'Bedlamite' behaviour of his recruits, he often praised other workers who helped him to achieve so much. In the first two years he had already built two big vessels and eight *baidak*s; in 1786, he produced an impressive twenty *baidak*s.[69] It was all so dramatic and exciting that old Jeremiah Bentham decided he might to come out too. But two Benthams were enough.

In 1786, Potemkin's orders changed. Since 1783, Catherine and Potemkin had been debating when the Empress should inspect her new domains in the south. The trip had always been delayed but now it looked as if it would actually happen. Samuel was already an expert at building barges and *baidak*s for the Dnieper. Now Potemkin ordered him to produce thirteen yachts and twelve luxury barges in which the Empress could cruise down the Dnieper to Kherson. Samuel had been experimenting with a new invention which he called 'the vermicular', which is best described as 'an oar-propelled articulated floating train, a series of floating boxes cunningly linked together'.[70] Samuel set to work and managed to fulfil Potemkin's massive order, to which he added an imperial vermicular – a six-section barge, 252 feet long, driven by 120 oars.

*

Jeremy Bentham, who wanted to meet the famous Potemkin, was waiting for Serenissimus to visit the estate while Samuel was away, testing his ships. Since it seems that most of Russia spent much of this period feverishly anticipating the arrival of the 'Prince of Princes', this was not surprising. Meanwhile, that incongruous British community, the rebellious Belorussian Bedlam, behaved worse than ever now that they were being nervously managed by the philosopher of utlitarianism on a part-time basis.

Potemkin had not paid them yet. Dr Debraw, gardener Roebuck and butler–factotum Benson were now in open rebellion. Many of the British clearly enjoyed a traditional expatriate life of abandoned debauchery. Soon they began to perish prolifically, a misfortune that Samuel said had more to do with their intemperate lifestyle than with the unwholesome climate. Debraw had just been made physician-general to the army when he died, possibly a mercy for the Russian soldiers. The rest either expired or were dispersed.[71]

'We have been in hourly expectation of the Prince on his way to his Governments for a considerable time . . .', wrote Jeremy Bentham, but, as so often, the Prince was always delayed.[72] A few days later, Potemkin's niece–mistress Countess Skavronskaya stopped at Krichev on her way to Petersburg from Naples and told them that 'the Prince of Princes had given up his intentions of coming'.[73] Some biographers have claimed that Potemkin and Jeremy Bentham had long philosophical discussions,[74] but there is no account of such a meeting. If they had met, it is hard to believe that Jeremy would not have written about it.*

Finally, after more than a year in Potemkin's world, Jeremy Bentham departed through Poland, staying in lots of 'Jew inns'. Dirty houses and filthy animals had their consolations: gorgeous Jewesses. Here's a typical entry: 'Pretty Jewess, hogs in the stable . . . fowls free in the house.'[75] The philosopher even managed a singular compliment for a travelling Englishman of his century: one household of Jewesses were so magnificent that 'the whole family, fine flesh and blood, [were] *not inferior to English*' (author's italics).

The estate flourished: in Krichev, Potemkin had taken advice from his Swiss medical adviser Dr Behr on reducing mortality, possibly by inoculation. The male serf population had risen from 14,000 to 21,000 in just

---

* Potemkin may never have got the chance to encounter Jeremy Bentham. But we can: he rests, stuffed, pale and desiccated but clearly recognizable, his 'auto-icon', in the corridors of University College, London.

a few years.[76] Its estate and financial accounts show its importance to the Kherson fleet, while Bentham's unpublished letters in Potemkin's archives reveal how the Black Sea cities used Krichev as their supply yard. In the two years and eight months up to August 1785, Bentham's enterprise sent Kherson rigging, sailcloth and riverboats worth 120,000 roubles and cable and canvas worth 90,000 roubles. In 1786, Bentham delivered 11,000 roubles's worth of *baidaks*. When Samuel had moved on, its canvas production trebled, its ships' tackle doubled. Many of the factories were highly profitable by 1786: the brandy distillery made 25,000 roubles per annum; the 172 looms made another 25,000 roubles; and the ropewalk produced 1,000 poods or sixteen tons a week, creating maybe 12,000 roubles.[77] However, profit and loss accounts meant little to Potemkin: his sole criterion was what brought glory and power to the Empire – which meant his army, navy and cities. By this criterion, this imperial arsenal and factory was an outstanding success.

Suddenly, in 1787, the Prince sold the entire complex, for 900,000 roubles, in order to purchase even bigger estates in Poland. He had received the estate for nothing and, though he had invested a lot, it is unlikely that hiring English artisans cost anything close to that. As always with the Machiavellian Prince, there were grand political reasons for the sudden sale of what he had built up so carefully. He moved some of the factories to his estates in Kremenchuk, leaving others to continue under new management. When the estate was sold, Krichev's Jews tried to raise a purse to buy the estate themselves 'to enable Sam[uel Bentham] to buy up this town'. But nothing came of it.

This was the end of the Krichev adventure for Jeremy Bentham and his British recruits. But it was far from the end for Potemkin's two favourite Englishmen – Samuel Bentham and William Gould. Both were to play large roles in his future. The Prince had so far used Sam Bentham as a Siberian mining consultant, factory-manager, shipbuilder, colonel of Musketeers, agronomist and inventor. Now he was to bring his barges up the river on a special mission and then become a quartermaster, artillery expert, fighting naval officer, Siberian instructor and Chinese–Alaskan trader, in that order.

Gould, his team constantly increasing with more experts from England, became an indispensable part of the Prince's entourage – the harbinger of Potemkin himself, arriving with tools, workmen and trees, a few weeks before the great man himself. In the coming war, none of Potemkin's peripatetic headquarters was complete without a Gould garden. But his masterpiece was to be the Winter Garden at the Taurida Palace.

Serenissimus occasionally neglected his British guests because of the necessity of his juggling Petersburg politics with southern enterprise. At the very beginning of Samuel Bentham's adventure, when he was travelling with Potemkin on the way back from the Crimea, Potemkin promised to accompany him to Krichev to decide what to do there. They stopped in Kremenchuk, where news reached Potemkin from Petersburg that changed everything.

Without a word of goodbye, the Prince left Kremenchuk with the 'utmost expedition', taking just one servant with him.[78] Only one person in the world could make Potemkin drop everything like that.

21

THE WHITE NEGRO

Besides the Empress sometimes liked a boy
And had just buried the fair faced Lanskoi . . .
Lord Byron, *Don Juan*, Canto IX: 47

On 25 June 1784, Lieutenant-General Alexander Lanskoy, Catherine's twenty-six-year-old favourite, died at Tsarskoe Selo with the Empress beside him. His illness was sudden: he had come down with a sore throat less than a week earlier. Lanskoy seemed to know he was going to die – though Catherine tried to dissuade him – and he did so with the quiet dignity he had brought to his awkward position.[1] Yet the most malicious rumours were soon abroad about his demise: he had died 'in place' with Catherine, he had ruined his fragile health by taking dangerous aphrodisiacs to satisfy his nymphomaniacal old mistress. As he died, it was claimed he 'quite literally burst – his belly burst'. Soon after death, 'his legs dropped off. The stench was also insufferable. Those who gave him his coffin . . . died.' These were rumours of poisoning: had Potemkin, already blamed for bringing on Prince Orlov's madness by slow poison, killed another rival? Judging by Catherine's tragic account to Grimm and other witnesses, Lanskoy probably died of diphtheria. Thanks to the baking summer and the delay before Catherine could bear to bury him, the stench is only too believable. The innards of unburied corpses do tend to swell in the heat.[2]

The Empress collapsed in a paroxysm of overpowering grief. Her courtiers had never seen her in such a state. The imperial body-physician Rogerson and minister Bezborodko, gambling and drinking partners, consulted, no doubt in the quick whispers that must have been the background music of Court crises. Rogerson let loose his often fatal laxatives and bleeding, but both men sensed an emotional prescription would heal her better.* The Empress naturally thought of her 'husband', her 'dearest friend'. In her desperate unhappiness, she kept asking

---

* Dr Rogerson had just claimed another victim. Soon after seeing off Samuel Bentham's love for his niece, Field-Marshal Prince Alexander Golitsyn died in Rogerson's care, probably bled and purged to death. 'I'm afraid', Catherine half joked to Potemkin, 'that anybody who gets into Rogerson's hands is already dead.'

touchingly if Potemkin had been told. Rogerson informed Bezborodko that it was 'most necessary' to try to calm the Empress's sorrow and anxiety: 'And we know there is just one way to achieve this – the soonest arrival of His Highness.' As soon as Lanskoy was dead, Bezborodko despatched the Court's fastest courier southwards. Catherine inquired like a child if the Prince could be expected soon. Yes, they surely replied, the Prince is on his way.[3]

The courier found Serenissimus, accompanied by Samuel Bentham, at Kremenchuk in the midst of arranging the foundation of Sebastopol and the management of Krichev. The Prince left immediately. Two indivisible sentiments, as always, dominated his actions: his beloved friend needed him and his power depended on it. Potemkin prided himself on being the swiftest traveller across Russia. If the couriers usually took ten days, Potemkin made it back in seven. On 10 July, he arrived at Tsarskoe Selo.

As Potemkin galloped across the steppes, Catherine had to face the tragic loss of the favourite who had made her happiest. 'Cheerful, honest and gentle' Lanskoy was her beloved pupil, with whom she let her maternal, pedagogic instincts run free, and he had truly become part of the Catherine–Potemkin family. He was strikingly handsome – his portraits show his refined, gamin features. Catherine thought she had found her Holy Grail – a companion for the rest of her life. 'I hope,' she told Grimm just ten days before Lanskoy's sore throat, 'that he'll become the support of my old age.'[4]

Potemkin found the Court paralysed by the prone Empress, haunted by the unburied and decomposing Lanskoy, and infected by a plague of vicious, sniggering lies. Catherine herself was inconsolable. 'I have been plunged into the most acute sorrow and my happiness is no more,' she told Grimm. Lanskoy 'shared my pains and rejoiced in my joys'.[5] The nobles in both St Petersburg and Tsarskoe Selo became worried by Catherine's emotional collapse. Weeks after the death, courtiers reported that 'the Empress is as afflicted as the first day of M. Lanskoy's death'. Catherine was almost mad with grief, continually asking about her lover's body, perhaps hoping his death would prove a lie. She did not leave her bed for three weeks. When she finally got up, she did not go out. No one saw her for months. There was no entertainment, Court was 'extremely sad'. Catherine became ill. Dr Rogerson bled her and prescribed his usual panaceas, which no doubt explained her wind and weakness. At first, only Potemkin and Bezborodko saw her at all. Later Fyodor Orlov, gentlest of the brothers, called in the evenings. The Prince comforted Catherine by sharing her mourning: it was said the courtiers heard Potemkin and Catherine 'howling' together for the dead favourite.

Catherine felt no one could imagine her suffering. Initially, even Potemkin's sympathy hurt her, but finally his care managed to guide her through the misery and 'thus he awakened us from the sleep of the dead'.[6] He was there with her, every morning and every night: he must have almost lived with her for those weeks.[7] Probably this was one of those crises, as Count Cobenzl told Joseph II, when Potemkin returned to his old role as husband and lover.[8] Their relationship defies the form of modern customs but was closest to the Gallic *amitié amoureuse*. This was not necessarily a time for love-making, but very much for loving. These were the moments when Potemkin achieved 'unbounded power', as he once told Harris:[9] 'When things go smoothly, my influence is small but when she meets with rubs, she always wants me and then my influence becomes as great as ever.'[10]

Gradually Catherine improved: Lanskoy was buried near Tsarskoe Selo in her absence more than a month after his death. Catherine left her summer residence on 5 September, saying she could never return. When she reached the capital, she could not bear to stay in her own apartments, with all their memories of Lanskoy, so she moved into her Hermitage. For almost a year after Lanskoy's death, there was no favourite. Catherine was mourning. Potemkin was with her: in a sense, they were reunited for a while. There was relief when the Empress finally emerged in public: she went to church three days later. This was the first time the Court had seen her for two and a half months.

Potemkin had to return to the south to finish his projects there: he left in January 1785. Even at such a distance, he acted as her comfort. Some of their letters, which probably date from these months, approach the chivalry and playfulness, but not the frantic passion and guffawing laughter, of their affair ten years earlier. There was an autumnal tone to this resurgence of romance as if both felt older. First he sent her a snuff-box and she thanked him for the beautiful thing 'with my whole heart'. Then he sent her a dress made with silk from his southern factories and romantically invited her down the road, 'bespread with silk', to the south.[11]

Serenissimus returned at the beginning of the summer of 1785, when Catherine was on form again. The two old lovers played their familiar games. 'I'm now on my way to confession. Forgive me, Lady Matushka, for all my sins – either deliberate or unconscious,' wrote Potemkin in old Southern Slavonic script. The Prince had done something mischievous. Catherine replied: 'I equally ask you to forgive me and God bless you. The rest of the aforementioned, I can figure it out all right but I understand nothing or very little. I laughed a lot when I read it.'[12] That was Potemkin: often incomprehensible but always stimulating. Laughter was very much part of her therapy. But she missed his company during his six months in the south.

Catherine's habit of making the favourite into a semi-official position meant that the Court was now so used to it that the courtiers expected the place to be filled. This may have put a strange pressure on her to find someone. A year after Lanskoy's death, Potemkin understood that she, who could not be 'without love for a single hour', needed more permanent love than he could give. If Potemkin was to achieve glory in the Empire, he needed someone to take care of Catherine. When Catherine went to church at this time, young men preened and stood erect in their best uniforms, hoping to be noticed as she passed.[13] Catherine always found it hard to concentrate in church – as Casanova spotted. This was a distasteful but understandable scene. The men's posing makes clear that candidates for favourite were not fixed by Potemkin, as malicious gossip claimed – they were simply noticed around Court, though a clever patron would place them in the Empress's path.[14] Nonetheless the hunt was on. The disappearance of Lanskoy marked the beginning of the apogee of Catherine's splendour but also of her slide towards indignity. Her loves were never so equal again.

Once Serenissimus was back in the capital, the Empress did notice some of the Guards officers on duty. There was Prince Pavel Dashkov, Bentham's Edinburgh-educated friend and son of Princess Dashkova, and two Guardsmen – Alexander Petrovich Yermolov, and Alexander Matveevich Dmitriyev-Mamonov, who was Potemkin's distant cousin. All three served on the Prince's staff. This now became something like an imperial beauty contest, in which the prize would be announced at a masquerade ball.

Catherine had had a soft spot for Dashkov for some time. She regularly inquired about his 'excellent heart'.[15] Five years earlier, Prince Orlov had bumped into Princess Dashkova travelling with her son in Brussels – two semi-exiled Russian magnates. Orlov had teased the self-regarding Princess by suggesting to the boy that he could become favourite. As soon as her son was out of the room, Dashkova subjected Orlov to a prudish tongue-lashing: how dare he speak to a seventeen-year-old boy of such disgusting matters? 'As for favourites,' she concluded, 'I bade him recollect that I neither knew nor acknowledged such persons . . .'. Orlov's obscene reply to this grandiosity was 'unworthy of repetition' – but much deserved.[16] Now Orlov was dead, Princess Dashkova had returned from years of travelling and Dashkov was twenty-three.

It is hard to avoid the impression that Princess Dashkova, while regarding favouritism with ill-concealed disdain, could not overcome her ambition for her son to fill that position. Potemkin still made the Empress laugh with his mimicry of top courtiers – but his impersonation of Dashkova's pomposity was his star turn and Catherine often requested it specially. So Serenissimus must have particularly relished hoisting this humbug by her own extremely grand petard.[17]

Princess Dashkova called on Potemkin and was most charming. Potemkin evidently encouraged the Princess in her ambitions and mischievously gave her reasons to hope that the Dashkov family was about to be honoured. Between such discussions, Potemkin probably bounded along to Catherine's apartments to give wicked impersonations of the Princess, to gales of imperial laughter. Unbeknown to Dashkova, Catherine was flirting with Yermolov and Mamonov, who were also handsome – but lacked the grisly mother. All had high hopes that their candidate would be chosen, though Potemkin apparently had no preference.

Princess Dashkova, revelling in her resurgent favour, claimed in her *Memoirs* that Potemkin sent round his nephew Samoilov at the 'lover's hour' after dinner, 'to inquire whether Prince Dashkov was at home'. He was not. So Samoilov left a message that Potemkin wished to see him at his house as soon as possible. The Princess, writing years later, claimed that Potemkin was offering her son the disgusting post of favourite, which she denounced to Samoilov thus: 'While I love the Empress and dare not oppose her will, I have too much self-respect ... to take part in any affair of such a nature.' If her son did become favourite, she added, the only use she would make of her influence would be to ask for a passport to go abroad.

This dubious anecdote has spawned the myth that Potemkin sent youths over to Catherine at the 'lover's hour'. Since Dashkov was Potemkin's adjutant, there was nothing sordid in such a summons. It is far more likely that Potemkin was teasing the Princess. No doubt her answer was immediately repeated in his 'Dashkova-voice' to Catherine.[18]

Serenissimus held a masquerade at his Anichkov Palace – he never lived in this colossal residence,* on the corner of Nevsky Prospect and

---

* On his death, the Palace passed to the Romanovs: it was the Petersburg residence of Alexander I's adored sister Catherine until her death in 1818. Then it belonged to Nicholas I until his accession and was then used to hold the Empress's dances: Pushkin and his wife often danced there. Later, it belonged to Tsar Nicholas II's mother, the Empress Maria Fyodorovna, until 1917. In February 1914, Prince Felix Yusopov, the future killer of Rasputin, married Grand Duchess Irina there.

the Fontanka, but he kept his library there and used it for entertaining. He ordered his architect Starov to construct a third floor and alter the façade to add more of his beloved Doric columns. When Potemkin was low on funds, he repaid his debts to his merchant friend Nikita Shemiakin with the Anichkov. But Catherine repurchased it for him. This trading of palaces for debts happened periodically and the Empress always obliged.[19]

Two thousand people arrived all evening in costumes and dominoes. He arranged the orchestra, in the Anichkov's huge oval gallery, around a richly decorated pyramid. Over 100 musicians, conducted by Rosetti, played horns and accompanied a choir. The star of the orchestra was a 'silk-clad blackamoor playing a kettle drum' atop the pyramid. A curtain divided the room. Couples danced the quadrille: the courtiers watched Prince Dashkov partner a teenage girl named Princess Ekaterina Bariatinskaya, an outstanding beauty, who was coming out for the first time. She was to be one of Potemkin's last mistresses.

When the Empress arrived with Grand Duke Paul, everyone watched to see if any of the three young men would be favoured. Lev Engelhardt, who kept a graphic account of the evening, noticed Yermolov. Potemkin had ordered his staff to wear light cavalry uniforms, but Yermolov was dressed as a Dragoon, flouting the Prince's command. Engelhardt rushed to warn him to go home and change. 'Don't worry,' replied Yermolov confidently. 'But thanks all the same.' This daring arrogance puzzled Engelhardt.

Princess Dashkova buttonholed Potemkin: together they admired the athletic figure of her son, but then she pushed her luck either by presuming her son had been selected or by asking the Prince to propose another of her family. Potemkin turned to her sarcastically in front of everybody. There is no vacancy, he said. The post has just been filled by Lieutenant Yermolov. *Who*, stammered the humiliated Princess, *who?*

Potemkin abandoned her, took Yermolov by the hand and walked off into the crowd with him 'as if he was some high nobleman'. The Prince led Yermolov up to the table where the Empress was playing whist and deposited him, as it were, just four steps behind her chair, ahead of the senior courtiers. At that moment, everyone, even Dashkova, realized the Empress had taken a new favourite. The curtain was drawn to reveal the resplendently set table. Empress, Grand Duke and the courtiers sat at a special round table while forty others were laid out for the rest. The ball went on until three.[20]

The next morning, eleven months after the death of the much mourned Lanskoy, Yermolov moved into his old apartment in the Winter

Palace and was nominated adjutant-general to the Empress. He was thirty-one years old, tall, blond, with almond-shaped eyes and a flat nose – Potemkin nicknamed him the 'white negro'. He was neither as decent nor as pretty as Lanskoy, nor as clever as Zavadovsky: 'he's a good boy', noted Cobenzl, 'but quite limited'. Soon promoted to major-general and decorated with the Order of the White Eagle, Yermolov was the nephew of one of Potemkin's friends, Levashov, but equally friendly with Bezborodko. Probably Potemkin was relieved that Catherine had found someone acceptable after that mournful year. Though the simpler historians have repeated Potemkin's jealousy of each favourite, shrewder observers like Cobenzl understood that he was pleased that Yermolov would prevent the Empress 'from falling into melancholy' and would stimulate her 'natural gaiety'.[21]

The ascension of Yermolov placed Potemkin at the height of his power. When the Prince was ill a few days later. Catherine 'went to see him, forced him to take medicine and took infinite care of his health'.[22] But at last Potemkin's position was unchallenged. Court was harmonious. The Prince could return to running his provinces and armies because Catherine the woman was happily settled.

Catherine's Court had reached a height of extravagance and splendour in the mid-1780s: 'a great display of magnificence and state with the great taste and charm of the Court of France', wrote Comte de Damas. 'The splendour of the ceremonial was enhanced by Asiatic luxury.'[23] Catherine and Potemkin both enjoyed holding masquerades, fêtes and balls at vast expense: the Empress herself had a taste for transvestite balls. 'I've just had a pleasant idea,' she wrote, earlier in her reign, 'we must hold a ball in the Hermitage ... we must tell the ladies to come less dressed and without *paniers* and *grande parure* on their heads ... French comedians will make market stalls and they will sell on credit women's clothes to men and men's clothes to women ...'.[24] This was perhaps because the plump Empress knew that she cut a fine figure in male attire.

If one was to meet the Empress of all the Russians at the Court ball during the 1780s, one might find her 'dressed in a purple tissue petticoat and long white tissue sleeves down the wrist and the body open ... of a very elegant dress', sitting 'in a large elbow chair covered with crimson velvet and richly ornamented', surrounded by standing courtiers. The sleeves, skirt and body of the dress were often of different colours. Catherine now always wore these long old Russian gowns with long sleeves. They concealed her corpulence, but they were also much more comfortable than corsets and *paniers*. Princess Dashkova and Countess

Branicka copied her in this dress, but Baroness Dimsdale noted that the other ladies 'wore [it] very much in the French fashion' – though 'French gauzes and flowers were never', decreed Lady Craven, 'intended for Russian beauties'. There were card tables all round; everyone played whist while the Empress toured the room, graciously insisting that no one should stand – which of course they did.[25]

The Court moved between the Winter and Summer Palaces in St Petersburg during the winter. It followed the same weekly programme – the big gatherings in the Hermitage on Sundays with all the diplomats; Mondays, the ball at the Grand Duke's and so on. When Potemkin was in the capital, he usually spent his Thursday evenings wandering in and out of the Empress's Little Hermitage, where she continued to relax with her lover Yermolov and close friends like Naryshkin and Branicka. Conversation there was private. No servants eavesdropped. At dinner, the guests ordered their food by writing on little slates with a pencil, placing them in the midst of the special mechanical table and sending them down on a dumb waiter, whence came their meals a little later.[26]

During the summer months, the entire Court travelled the twenty or so miles out to the imperial resorts near by. Catherine loved Peterhof on the Gulf of Finland, but the Court's main home at that time of year was Tsarskoe Selo, where Catherine usually stayed in Elisabeth's Baroque wedding cake, the Catherine Palace, named after the Empress Elisabeth's mother, Peter the Great's peasant-born Empress.

'The place is a magnificent building,' wrote Baroness Dimsdale, 'the brick edifice stuccoed while ... outside pillars all gilded.' Inside, some rooms were simply 'superb'; one in Chinese taste struck her, but she would 'never forget' the little suite 'like an enchanted palace' with 'its sides inlaid with foil red and green so it dazzles one's eyes'. The tapestries in the Lyons room were supposed to have cost 201,250 roubles. Catherine had had the whole place redesigned by her Scottish architect Charles Cameron, and the gardens were of course English, laid out by Mr Bush, with lawns, gravel walks, follies and woods – and a very large lake in the middle. Cameron's Gallery was like an ancient temple, hanging in the light on top of its pillars, giving an impression of lightness and space. Inside was Catherine's gallery of busts including Demosthenes and Plato. The park was filled with monuments and follies to Russia's victories, so that this magical vista was not unlike an imperial version of a Disney theme park, the theme in this case being the aggrandizement of Empress and Empire. There was the Chesme Column, designed by Antonio Rinaldi, rising with impressive dignity out of an island amid the Great

Pond, and the Rumiantsev Column dedicated to the Battle of Kagul. There were Siberian, Turkish and Chinese Bridges, a Chinese village, a Ruined Tower, a pyramid and a mausoleum to three of her English greyhounds, engraved: 'Here lies Zemira and the mourning graces ought to throw flowers on her grave. Like Tom, her forefather, and Lady, her mother, she was constant in her loyalties and had only one failing, she was a little short-tempered . . .'. Not far away was the mausoleum of Lanskoy. There were even fairground games like the Flying Mountain – a sort of big dipper.[27]

The Empress rose early there and walked with her greyhounds in her long coat, leather shoes and bonnet, as shown in Borovikovsky's painting and described in Pushkin's novella, *The Captain's Daughter.* Later in the day, there might be military parades. While Baroness Dimsdale was there, Catherine stood on the balcony to review Potemkin leading her Guards.

The Prince had his own houses around Tsarskoe Selo, and the Empress often stayed in them too. Sometimes they built their palaces next door to each other – for example, she constructed Pella next to his Ostrovky so they could easily visit one another. As he based himself in his apartments within the imperial palaces, his many residences were mere caravanserai for this itinerant sultan – but he was constantly acquiring more, building and rebuilding them on a whim or to follow English fashions. The first was the little palace at Eschenbaum on the Finnish coast, 'given to my Prince Potemkin' in 1777, where Catherine stayed when she began her affair with Korsakov. 'What a view from each window,' she exclaimed to Grimm. 'I can see two lakes from mine, three manticules, a field and a wood.'[28] This was probably where Harris stayed with Potemkin's family. He had another residence on the Peterhof road,* which he bought in 1779: Starov knocked down a Baroque palace there and rebuilt it in neo-Classical style.

However, in the 1780s, Potemkin fell in love with the neo-Gothic style typified in Britain by Walpole's Strawberry Hill. So Starov rebuilt two of his palaces as neo-Gothic castles, Ozerki and Ostrovky.† Ostrovky had towers and spires, arches and battlements. Only one of the Prince's Gothic castles survives: he owned a large estate in Bablovsky woods adjoining Tsarskoe Selo. In 1782–5, he commissioned Ilya Neyelov (just

---

* A hideous Soviet cinema stands there today.
† There was a sinister tradition that 'Princess Tarakanova' was kept here for a while, with the child supposedly fathered by Alexei Orlov-Chesmensky, but there is no evidence for this stay or the child. Ostrovky survived until the Nazis destroyed it, but luckily it was photographed during the 1930s.

back from viewing the stately homes of England) to create his own Strawberry Hill. Bablovo* was a picturesque, asymmetrical palace with Gothic turrets, towers, arches and arched windows: its two wings extend out from a central circular medieval tower. Through the woods, it looks today like a cross between a ruined church and a magical castle.[29]

When it was time for the Court to return to Petersburg, a flunky in a scarlet-trimmed uniform with gold fringe placed a little stool of crimson velvet for the Empress to step into a coach pulled by ten horses. Fifteen coaches followed in its wake. For every one of these journeys, the cavalcade included more than 800 horses. A hundred cannons were fired, trumpets played and crowds cheered. There were palaces on the road to Petersburg where the Empress could rest on the way.[30]

It was more than ten years since Potemkin and Catherine had fallen in love: Catherine was fifty-seven years old. Everyone in her presence, wrote Damas, was struck by 'the dignity and stateliness of her bearing and the kindness and gentleness of her expression'.[31] Bentham thought 'her eyes the finest imaginable and her person altogether comely'.[32] Her blue eyes and formidably mannish forehead were as striking as ever, but she was small, increasingly fat and constantly tormented by indigestion.[33]

Her attitude to power remained the same mixture of ruthless aggrandizement and *raison d'état* combined with a shrewd and utterly disingenuous modesty. When Ligne and Grimm started spreading the name 'Catherine the Great' round the salons, she affected her customary humility: 'Please don't call me the sobriquet Catherine the Great because (i) I don't like any nickname (ii) my name is Catherine II and I don't want people to say of me like Louis XV that they thought me wrongly named ...'[34] (Louis was not very *Bien-Aimé* by his death.) Her sole weakness remained her eternal and endearing quest for love. 'It would be better if she had only these loves for the physicality,' wrote a French diplomat, 'but it's rare thing among older people and when their imagination is not dead, they make a hundred times more a fool of themselves than a young man.' From now on, she began to make a fool of herself, as much as an Autocratrix could.

Potemkin knew exactly how to handle her, and she him. By the mid-1780s their relationship depended as much on being apart as being together. The Prince knew 'that it was never in the Empress's vicinity that his power was greatest since then he had to share it with her',

---

* The author found its ruins in the Bablovsky Park. There is a surprise inside the tower: a circular red granite bowl with a diameter of about ten feet. This was the early version of a swimming pool built by Alexander I, where he used to swim privately during hot Tsarskoe Selo summers.

explained Damas. 'This was why he latterly preferred to be away from her. When he was at a distance, all details of administration and military affairs were in his hands.'[35] Potemkin respected her 'excessive penetration' and ability to spot any inconsistencies in arguments, but he also followed the Disraelian dictum about handling royalty with trowels of flattery. 'Flatter as much as you can,' he advised Harris, 'you cannot have too much unction but flatter her for what she *ought* to be not for *what she is.*' He also disloyally criticised her timidity and femininity: 'talk to her passions, to her feelings ... she asks for nothing but praise and compliment, give her that and she will give you the whole force of her Empire'.[36] But this was Potemkin playing a role with Harris, perhaps prearranged with Catherine. If flattery had been the key, Harris would have been more successful, and Potemkin less so, because the Prince and the Empress were constantly arguing among themselves.

When he wrote to her, he revealingly called her his 'kormilitsa', his nurse or foster-mother; she still called him 'gosudar' – 'lord' – or used a nickname, but she saw the two of them as Pylades and Orestes, the David and Jonathan of mythology. She behaved as both empress and wife to Potemkin: when he was away she darned his elbows on his jackets like a *Hausfrau*, sent him endless coats and told him to take his medicines like a child.[37] Politically, she regarded him as the essential man of business of her government, her friend – the consort. She constantly told him that 'without you I feel as if I'm without hands', or just begged him to come back to Petersburg to see her. Often she wished he was with her, not in the south, so that they could settle complex matters in 'half an hour'. Her admiration for his inventiveness, intelligence and energy are plain in their letters, and she frequently worries she will do something wrong without him: 'I find myself at a loss as I never am myself when I am with you. I keep fearing I've missed something.'[38] Their 'two minds' were ever 'better than one'. She thought he was 'cleverer than I am, everything he's done has been carefully thought out'.[39] He could not force her to do things she did not wish to, but they had their own way of coaxing and arguing through problems until they found a solution. Personally, 'he is the only man that the Empress stands in awe of, and she both likes, and fears him.'[40]

She was tolerant of his debauched lifestyle, indulgent of his idiosyncrasies and knew well that he was almost an emperor. 'Prince Potemkin has retired to his place at eleven in the evening under the pretext of going to bed,' she told Grimm on 30 June 1785 from Peterhof, where she stayed with her new lover Yermolov, 'though one knew perfectly well that he is putting together a party of the night' to look at maps and decide state business. 'One's even heard him named more than a king.'[41] She was under no illusions about his unpopularity among some high nobility – but she seemed secretly pleased when her valet told her he was hated by everyone except her.[42] His disdain for popularity attracted her and his ultimate dependence on her soothed her fear of his power. Indeed she liked to say, 'Even if the whole of Russia rose against the Prince, I'd be with him.'[43]

When he returned to Petersburg from his trips, he often facilitated her business: Catherine decided that she wished to appoint her tedious co-conspirator, Princess Dashkova, director of the Academy of Sciences. The Princess wrote a letter refusing the job, which she felt was beyond her, and went off to Potemkin's house to explain her refusal, but Potemkin interrupted, 'I have already it from Her Majesty.' Serenissimus read Dashkova's letter and then 'tore it to pieces' in front of her. 'In utter astonishment and rage', Dashkova demanded to know how he dared tear up a letter addressed to the Empress.

'Be composed, Princess,' said he, 'and hearken to me. You are sincerely attached to Her Majesty ... why then will you distress her on a subject that, for these last two days, has occupied her thoughts exclusively and on which she has fixed her heart? If you are inexorable, here is pen, ink, and write your letter anew. But I'm only acting the part of a man devoted to your interests.' Then he added this piece of Potemkinish stroking: the Empress had one other reason for wanting Dashkova in Petersburg. She wanted to be able to talk to her more because, 'to tell the truth, she is worn out with the society of those fools who eternally surround her'. This did the trick. 'My anger', wrote Dashkova, '... subsided.' Serenissimus could be irresistible when he wanted. Naturally, she accepted the post.[44]

As soon as Yermolov had settled into his new quarters, the Empress, accompanied by the Court, the new favourite, Serenissimus and the ambassadors of Britain, France and Austria, set off on a cruise from Lake Ladoga to the upper Volga. Catherine and Potemkin liked to see things for themselves – as the Empress put it, 'the eye of the master fattens the horse'. This trip neatly shows how the Court entertained themselves – and how Potemkin made policy. The main challenge of Court life was fighting boredom.

The three envoys were paragons of Enlightened wit. The Austrian Ambassador remained the hideous, charming womanizer Louis Cobenzl, who, despite being middle-aged, dreamed of the stage and took singing lessons. When imperial couriers arrived from Vienna, they were never surprised to find the Ambassador before his mirror, singing, disguised in full drag as the Countess d'Escarbagnas.[45] Alleyne Fitzherbert's 'caractère vraiment britannique' meant that he was 'nonplussed by the Prince's habits',[46] but Potemkin found a new friend in the French envoy, who was different from his mediocre predecessors. Round-faced, with his eyebrows always raised, and a permanently amused expression like a smiling marmoset, Louis-Philippe, Comte de Ségur, aged thirty-two, was an ornament to the epoch which he recorded so elegantly in his *Mémoires*. Son of a French marshal and war minister, friends with Marie-Antoinette, Diderot and D'Alembert, and a veteran of the American War, he became an intimate member of Catherine and Potemkin's circle.

On the cruise, the courtiers amused themselves with card games, concerts and especially word games. They sound contrived today, but the ambassadors could change their king's relations with Russia by being good at them: for example, Fitzherbert was given the task of creating a poem with lines ending with the words *amour, frotte, tambour* and *garde-note*. His reply, combining flattery, French and all four words, was regarded as so brilliant that Catherine repeated it to Grimm:

> D'un peuple très nombreux Catherine est l'amour
> Malheur à l'enemi qui contre elle se frotte;
> La renomme usa pour elle – son tambour
> L'histoire avec plaisir sera – son garde-note.

Some of these ponderous *bons mots* were invented on the spot, but more usually, like supposedly live comic television shows today, they were laboriously invented offstage and then delivered in public as if pulled effortlessly out of the air. But Fitzherbert was not the master of these poetic drolleries: he was out-drolled by the 'amiable and witty' Ségur, whom Catherine acclaimed as the genius of the genre: 'He makes us poems and songs . . . Prince Potemkin has been dying of laughter during the whole trip.'[47]

As the barges sailed down the Volga, Ségur witnessed how Potemkin's excitable whims seemed to make instant policy. Joseph II had helped Potemkin annex the Crimea, so Catherine was obliged to back him in his recurring project to exchange the Austrian Netherlands for Bavaria. He had tried it before in 1778, but it had ended in the Potato War with Prussia. Now, once again, Frederick the Great, in his last bow on the stage he had dominated for almost half a century, foiled Joseph's plan to annex Bavaria, by negotiating a League of German Princes to prevent it. It happened that the Anglo-Russian Trade Treaty was up for renewal, but Catherine was now demanding better terms. However, Hanover, of which George III was elector, joined Frederick in his anti-Austrian league. This was no less than a kick in the teeth to Catherine – and even more so to the Anglophile Potemkin.

When this news reached the imperial barge, it sent the couple into a sulk. After dinner, Ségur followed Potemkin on to his galley, where Serenissimus exploded, denouncing British egotism for this 'perfidious trick'. 'I've told the Empress long ago but she did not want to believe me.' The new twenty-six-year-old British Prime Minister, William Pitt, 'who doesn't like her personally', was sure to put obstacles in the way of Russian policies in Germany, Poland and Turkey. This analysis of Pitt's eastern approach was accurate. The Prince declared he would give anything to avenge himself on 'perfidious Albion'. What about a Franco-Russian trade treaty, suggested Ségur? Potemkin burst out laughing: 'The moment is favourable. Seize it!' Foreigners liked to present the Prince as a capricious child, but actually he was already encouraging Kherson's trade with France, certain Marseilles, not London, was the key to Russia's Black Sea commerce. He immediately recommended that Ségur write out a secret draft of a treaty: 'Don't even sign it. You risk nothing ... The other ministers won't know ... Get quickly to work!' Ironically, Ségur had to borrow Fitzherbert's writing-desk with which to draft this anti-British ambush.

The next day, Potemkin bounded into Ségur's cabin to inform him that, the moment they returned to Petersburg, the Empress would order the treaty signed. Sure enough, when they arrived back on 28 June, Ségur was attending a Court masquerade when Bezborodko waddled over and whispered in his ear that he had received the orders to negotiate the treaty at once. It took time but was signed in January 1787.

'The credit of Yermolov seemed to rise fast,' noticed Ségur on his return to Petersburg. 'The court, astonished at such a change, turned towards the rising sun.' By the spring of 1786, just under a year into Yermolov's tenure, the young favourite had begun to play a dangerous game: he had decided to unseat Potemkin. 'The Prince's friends and relations were in consternation.'[48] Yermolov remained Potemkin's creature until the Prince caught the favourite's uncle Levashov cheating at cards. Potemkin threw him out and the uncle grumbled to the bumptious Yermolov. It was claimed he refused to forward Serenissimus' requests for favours. But Potemkin could do that perfectly well himself. It is more likely the unintelligent Yermolov was reluctant to be a junior member of the Catherine–Potemkin family, was jealous of the Prince's power – and was manipulated by his rivals.[49]

The invisible hands behind Yermolov's intrigue were probably Alexander Vorontsov, President of the Commerce College and brother of Ambassador to London Simon, and the ex-favourite Zavadovsky, both of whom worked with Potemkin but loathed him. They used Potemkin's distrait finances to suggest that he was embezzling Treasury funds – specifically three million roubles for southern development – but their evidence was a letter from the deposed Crimean Khan, Shagin Giray, who claimed that the Prince was stealing his pension.[50] This was no evidence, as they well knew, because all Treasury payments, even those to Potemkin, and indeed Shagin Giray, were often years late. This was one reason why it was meaningless to analyse Potemkin's finances, since he used private money for state purposes and then repaid himself when the state funds arrived. Besides, he did not need to embezzle – Catherine granted anything he required. However, the plotters persuaded Yermolov to lay Shagin Giray's letter before the Empress. While the Court was at Tsarskoe Selo, he did so and managed to sow some doubt in her mind. The die was cast.[51]

Catherine became cool to Potemkin. The Prince, having done so much to build up the south, was proudly aloof. They barely spoke and he rarely called on her, though his decline was exaggerated. Even in late May, the nadir of this crisis, Catherine said to her new secretary, Alexander Khrapovitsky, 'Prince Potemkin looks like a wolf and is not liked much for that but he has a kind heart . . . he would also be the first to ask mercy for his enemy.'[52] Nonetheless, the courtiers smelled blood. His anterooms emptied. 'Everyone distanced themselves,' recalled Ségur. 'As for me, I redoubled my assiduity to the Prince. I saw him every day.' This was not merely friendship on Ségur's part, for he had divined that the relationship between Prince and Empress was based on a secret and invisible tie. Nonetheless, the noose appeared to be tightening. Ségur begged him to be careful. 'What – you too!' replied Potemkin. 'You wish me to beg shamefully after such great services rendered under the whim of an offensive injustice? I know they say I'm lost but they're wrong. Let me reassure you – a mere child won't overthrow me!'

'Be careful!', warned Ségur again.

'Your friendship touches me,' said the Prince. 'But I disdain my enemies too much to fear them.'[53]

On 17 June, the Empress, Grand Duke, Potemkin, Yermolov and Ségur left Tsarskoe Selo for Pella. The next day, she visited Potemkin's neighbouring palace at Ostrovky, more evidence that Potemkin's true position was not nearly as disastrous as gossip suggested. On their return to Tsarskoe Selo, Potemkin attended all Catherine's dinners for the next three days. Presumably, the conspirators were now pushing Catherine to act on their evidence. Even in the sunny Catherine Palace, Potemkin was being cold-shouldered.

The next day, he simply left Court without a word and travelled towards Narva on the Baltic. He established himself back in the capital at the palace of the Master of Horse, Naryshkin, occupying himself with 'parties, pleasure and love'. Potemkin's 'enemies sang victory'. Catherine presumably was used to his sulks and did nothing. But when he did not appear on 28 June – Catherine's Accession Day – she surely realized that the masterful politician was calling her bluff.

'I am very anxious if you are well?', Catherine wrote secretly to Potemkin, answering his challenge. 'I haven't heard a word from you for so many days.'[54] The letter was warm. It was one of those signs that he understood perfectly. Potemkin waited a few days.

Then he suddenly appeared at Court – a Banquo's ghost who turned out not to be a ghost at all. The Prince supposedly stormed directly into the Empress's boudoir in 'a fury'[55] and shouted something like this: 'I come, Madame, to declare to Your Majesty that Your Majesty must this instant choose between Yermolov and me – one of us must this very day quit your Court. As long as you keep that White Negro, I will not set my foot within the Palace.'[56] Then he stormed out again and left Tsarskoe Selo.

On 15 July, the Empress dismissed Yermolov through one of his puppet-masters, Zavadovsky. The White Negro departed the next day, burdened with 4,000 peasants, 130,000 roubles and an order to travel.* That very evening, the other young officer with whom Catherine had flirted with a year earlier, Alexander Dmitriyev-Mamonov, arrived with Potemkin. Mamonov was his adjutant (and distant kinsman). Potemkin is said to have sent Mamonov to Catherine bearing a watercolour, with the saucy question, what did she think of the picture? She viewed his looks and replied: 'The contours are fine but the choice of colours less fortunate.' This is a legend, but it does sound like one of the games that Potemkin alone could play with the Empress. The next day, the Empress wrote to Mamonov...

That night, Mamonov passed his friend Khrapovitsky, the Empress's

* Yermolov's demand for an audience with George III when he visited London caused some awkwardness a year later. He later settled in Vienna.

secretary, as he was escorted into Catherine's bedchamber – either an awkward or a triumphant moment to meet a close friend. It was indeed a very small world which the diarist Khrapovitsky recorded in fascinating detail. Next morning, the punctilious secretary noted archly: 'They s[lep]t until nine o'clock' – in other words, the Empress spent an extra three hours in bed. Next day, 'they closed the door. M–v was there at dinner and according to custom – [she was] powdered', according to Khrapovitsky, whose eyes almost never leave the imperial keyhole.[57]

The handover to Mamonov was so seamless that it is quite possible that Potemkin's 'fury' had been much earlier and that the crisis was never about embezzlement at all but about Yermolov himself. It is likely that Catherine was romancing Mamonov while Yermolov and his plotters were singing with victory. This explains Potemkin's unusual absence of nerves about the conspiracy – another example of his play-acting. Potemkin threatened, at one time or another, to have every one of the favourites dismissed, from Zavadovsky onwards. Usually Catherine reassured him that his power was secure – so he should mind his own business. She forced the favourites to flatter him, while he was flexible enough to befriend them and work with them. He succeeded in deposing Yermolov probably because that minion refused to live within Potemkin's system – and because Catherine did not really love him. However arranged, it was a political victory.

'Matushka having walked around Petersburg, Peterhof, Oranienbaum, I've returned and I kiss your feet. I've brought Paracletes safe, healthy, merry and lovable.' Paracletes – matushka's little helper, Mamonov – was already with the Empress, who replied, 'It's a great joy, batinka: how are you feeling without any sleep, my lord? How glad I am you've arrived!'[58]

'Prince Grigory Alexandrovich has returned,' wrote Khrapovitsky on 20 July. Mamonov gratefully presented the Prince with a golden teapot engraved 'More united by heart than by blood', because they were such distant relations.[59] Mamonov, aged twenty-six, was an educated Francophile from the middling gentry, with an exquisite rosebud mouth and tidy little nose. He was much more cultured and intelligent than Yermolov and widely liked for his charm, looks and courtesy. Catherine showered him with honours: the Adjutant-General was made a count of the Holy Roman Empire and he soon owned 27,000 serfs while receiving 180,000 roubles a year with a table budget of 36,000 roubles. Did she feel she had to compensate her lovers more for her own ageing? Catherine fell in love with him and was soon raving about him. She nicknamed him 'Mister Redcoat', because he liked to wear one that went well with his black eyes. 'The red coat', she exulted to Grimm on 17 December, 'covers a man with an excellent heart ... the wit of four people ... an inexhaustible well of merriment.' Mamonov made Catherine happy and Potemkin secure. He became a member of their unusual family, like Lanskoy, helping the nieces Branicka and Skavronskaya,[60] and writing warm letters to the Prince, which Catherine enclosed with her own. Sometimes she added postscripts to Mamonov's letters, which he usually signed 'with absolute devotion'.[61]

Soon after the fall of the White Negro and the installation of Mister Redcoat, Potemkin invited Ségur for dinner. 'Well Monsieur Diplomat,' the Prince greeted him, 'at least in this case ... my predictions are better than yours!' Then, embracing his friend warmly, Potemkin boomed: 'Was I mistaken in anything, batushka? Did the child overthrow me? Did my bravery sink me?'[62]

His bravery had indeed paid off handsomely. Serenissimus could return to the south. He was away so much that Colonel Mikhail Garnovsky, his *homme d'affaires* in Petersburg who made a fortune out of the Duchess of Kingston, sent him secret reports on the politics of the Court. Garnovsky particularly monitored the behaviour of the favourite and noticed that, when toasts were drunk, he carefully drank only to the Prince. Catherine showed state papers to Mamonov, but he was no statesman. Potemkin's enemies Alexander Vorontsov and Zavadovsky courted him, hoping he would do a Yermolov. He remained loyal but he suffered. He was jealous if Catherine paid attention to anyone else, but found Court life lonely and cruel: he was right when he said the courtiers were like 'wolves in a forest'.[63]

Catherine and Potemkin decided the time had come for her to inspect his achievements in the south and demonstrate Russia's undying commitment to controlling the Black Sea. The date kept changing, but finally they agreed that she would visit Kherson and Crimea in the summer of 1787. On the eve of Catherine's departure on this remarkable and glorious expedition, Serenissimus was now at the height of his power, exercising, 'in Russia, a power greater than ... Wolsey, Olivares and Richelieu',[64] wrote one foreigner. For years, diplomats described him as 'Grand Vizier',[65] others called him 'Prime Minister',[66] but none of these quite caught his unique position. Saint-Jean was closest to the reality: 'People realized they could not overthrow Potemkin ... He was tsar in all but name.'[67] But was he happy? How did he live? Who was Potemkin the man?

22

A DAY IN THE LIFE OF
GRIGORY ALEXANDROVICH

Tis you, the bravest of all mortals!
Mind fertile with a host of schemes!
You did not tread the usual paths
But did extend them – and the roar
You left behind to your descendants.
Tis you, Potemkin, wondrous leader!

Gavrili Derzhavin, *The Waterfall*

MORNING

The Prince woke late when he resided at the 'Shepilev house', linked by its covered passageway to the Empress's apartments in the Winter Palace. The anterooms were already crowded with dignitaries. He received favoured ones lying in bed in his dressing gown. When he arose, he liked to have a cool bath followed by a short morning prayer. His breakfast was usually hot chocolate and a glass of liqueur.

If he decided to hold a large audience, he reclined in his reception room, studiously ignoring the keenest sycophants. But they were in trouble if they ignored him. One young secretary, educated at both Cambridge and Oxford, was waiting to see the Prince with a briefcase of papers among all the generals and ambassadors. They sat in sepulchral silence because everyone knew the Prince was still asleep. 'Suddenly the door of the bedroom ... was loudly opened and the huge Potemkin appeared on his own in a dressing gown, calling for his valet. Before he even had time to call, in a sudden moment, everyone in the hall – generals and noblemen – competing in their speed, rushed headlong out of the room to find the Prince's valet ...'. Since everyone else had scampered off, the secretary remained frozen there in Potemkin's presence, 'not even daring to blink'.

Serenissimus gave him a menacing glance and strode off. When he reappeared in full uniform. Potemkin called him over: 'Tell me, Alekseev, do you know how many nut-trees there are in my Taurida Palace garden?' Alekseev did not know. 'Go to my garden, count them and report to me,' ordered the Prince. By nightfall, the youngster returned and gave the Prince the number. 'Good. You fulfilled my order quickly and well. Do you know why you were given such an order? To teach you to be more prompt because I noted this morning, when I cried for my valet and generals and noblemen rushed to find him, you didn't move, you greenhorn ... Come tomorrow with your papers because today I am not disposed to examine them. Goodbye!'[1]

The petitioners were puzzled by the looks and character of this Prince – he was unpredictable, fascinating, alarming. He exuded both menace and welcome: he could be 'frightening',[2] crushingly arrogant, wittily mischievous, warm and kind, manic and morose. When Alexander Ribeaupierre was eight, he was taken to see Potemkin and never forgot his animalistic power and affectionate gentleness: 'I was terrified when he lifted me up in his mighty hands. He was immensely tall. I can see him now in my mind's eye wearing his loose dressing gown with his hairy chest naked.'[3] Ligne said he was 'tall, erect, proud, handsome, noble, majestic or fascinating', while others described him as a hideous Cyclops. Yet Catherine constantly talked of his handsomeness and he was amply endowed with 'sex appeal', to judge by the female letters that fill his archive.[4] He was undeniably vain about his fame, but shy about his appearance, particularly his one eye. When someone sent him a courier with one eye, Serenissimus immediately suspected that they were trying to make fun of him and was deeply hurt by this 'ill-judged wit' – this when he was the most powerful man east of Vienna.[5] That is the reason there are so few portraits of him.

'Prince Potemkin has never consented to be painted,' Catherine explained to Grimm, 'and if there exists any portrait or silhouette of him, it is against his wish.'[6] She persuaded him around 1784 and again in 1791 to sit for Giambattista Lampi, the only artist he trusted.[7] But Serenissimus, ever shy of his eye, would only sit three-quarter face – even though his useless, half-closed eye was not particularly repulsive.* Foreigners thought his eyes represented Russia, 'the one open and the other closed, [which] reminded us of the Euxine [Black Sea] always open and the Northern Ocean so long shut up with ice'. Lampi's portrait of him as Grand Admiral, bestriding the Black Sea, is the dynamic Potemkin that history has ignored. Lampi's later paintings show the fuller, older face.[8] But the best is the unfinished portrait of the Prince in his mid-forties –

---

* Giambattista Lampi, 1751–1830, was one of the most fashionable portrait painters in Vienna – Joseph II and Kaunitz sat for him. Potemkin seemed to have shared him with the Austrians, sometimes asking Kaunitz to send him over. The paintings done in 1791 before he died were copied by painters like Roslin and sold in prints.

the long, artistic face, full lips, dimpled chin, thick auburn hair. By the late 1780s, his immense girth matched his giant stature.

The Prince dominated every scene he graced. 'Potemkin created, destroyed or confused, yet animated, everything,' wrote Masson. 'The nobles who detested him seemed at his glance to sink into nothing.'[9] Virtually everyone who ever met him used the words 'extraordinary', 'astonishing', 'colossus', 'original' and 'genius' – but even those who knew him well found it hard to describe him. There was and is no way to categorize Potemkin except as one of history's most exhilarating originals. That was, after all, how Catherine saw him. Yet the best observers are agreed only that he was 'remarkable' – simply a phenomenon of nature. 'One of the most extraordinary men, as difficult to define as rare to encounter,' thought the Duc de Richelieu. He remains, as Lewis Littlepage of Virginia wrote, 'that indescribable man'.[10]

Everything about the Prince was a study of the wildest contrasts: he was a living *chiaroscuro* – 'an inconceivable mixture of grandeur and pettiness, laziness and activity, bravery and timidity, ambition and insouciance', wrote Ségur. Sometimes he showed the 'genius of an eagle', sometimes 'the fickleness of a child'. He was 'colossal like Russia'. In his mind, 'there were cultivated districts and deserts, the roughness of the eleventh century and the corruption of the eighteenth, the glitter of the arts and the ignorance of the cloisters'.[11] On the one hand he was 'bored with what he possessed', on the other, he was 'envious of what he could not obtain'. Potemkin 'wanted everything but was disgusted by everything.' His lust for power, wanton extravagance and towering arrogance were always made bearable by his exuberant brilliance, Puckish humour, caressing kindness, generous humanity and absence of malice. Richelieu saw that 'his nature always carried him more towards Good than Bad'.[12] The fame of the Empire was increased by his conquests – but he knew, as Ségur predicted, that 'the admiration they excited' was for Catherine and 'the hatred they raised' was for him.[13]

Everything had to be complicated with Potemkin.[14] His eccentricities may have irritated the Empress, but overall, Ségur noticed, they made him far more interesting to her. Richelieu thought him a man of 'superiority' but 'an astonishing confection of absurdity and genius'.[15] 'At times,' observed Littlepage, 'he appeared worthy of ruling the Empire of Russia, at times scarcely worthy of being an office clerk in the Empire of Lilliput.'[16] But the most striking feature of all his eccentricities – and the one we must never forget – is that he somehow found the time and energy to conduct colossal amounts of work and almost achieve the impossible.

*

The petitioners waiting his attention were accustomed to hearing the Prince's orchestra. He liked to begin the day with music, so he would order his ever present musicians and one of his collection of choirs to perform for him. They also played during dinner at 1 p.m. and had to be ready at 6 p.m. to play wherever the Prince appeared – and they travelled with him whether he was in the Crimea or at war. Music was intensely important to him – he wrote it himself and it soothed him. Potemkin had to have music wherever he went and he often sang to himself.

He managed the musical entertainment at Court because the Empress happily admitted to being tone-deaf. 'Sarti, Marchese the singer and Madame Todi were the delight not of the Empress whose ear was insensible to harmony,' Ségur remembered of one concert, 'but of Prince Potemkin and a few enlightened music lovers …'.[17] He paid 40,000 roubles for the Razumovskys' orchestra. But his musical passion really took off when he hired the celebrated Italian composer–conductor Giuseppe Sarti in 1784. The orchestra itself, between sixty and a hundred musicians, played 'that extraordinary music', recalled Lady Craven, 'performed by men and boys, each blowing a straight horn, adapted to his size. 65 of these musicians produce a very harmonious melody, something like an immense organ.'[18] Potemkin made Sarti his first director of music at the unbuilt Ekaterinoslav University. His expenses show him importing horns and paying for carriages to take 'Italian musicians Conti and Dophin' to the south. There Potemkin gave Sarti and three of his musicians 15,000 desyatins of land: 'I grant the village … for the four musicians … Be happy and tranquil in our country.' Thus Potemkin settled what was surely history's first musical colony.[19]

Potemkin and his circle were continually sending each other opera scores, as music lovers today give each other new CDs. Catherine enjoyed Potemkin sending music to her friend Grimm, who called him 'my benefactor in music'.[20] Music was a way to curry favour. Prince Lubomirski, a Polish magnate whose estates provided Potemkin's timber, frequently sent him horn music: 'If this genre of music is to the taste of Your Highness, I will take the liberty of following it with another.'[21] The Austrians used music as a diplomatic weapon. When Cobenzl, himself an opera fanatic, was at home in Vienna, he reported to Potemkin: 'We've heard the details of the charming show' of Sarti and Marchesini in Petersburg. The opera in Vienna could not equal it, the envoy claimed tactfully. Later, when the war began, Kaiser Joseph thought it worth while to send Cobenzl 'two choral pieces for Prince Potemkin's orchestra'.[22] Just as Russian ambassadors found his art deals and did his shopping, so they also were always looking for new musicians for him.[23]

Serenissimus took a personal pride in Sarti's work, especially since he wrote parts of it himself. He had always written love songs, like the one to Catherine, and religious music, like the 'Cannon to Our Saviour', published by his own printing press. It is hard to judge the quality of Potemkin's composition but, since his critics did not mock his music, he was probably talented, as Frederick the Great was with his flute. Indeed, Miranda, Potemkin's cynical travelling guest and a just witness, was impressed by his musical talents. He met Sarti in the south and watched Potemkin 'writing scores here and there, then gave them back to Sarti indicating the tone, rhythm and melody of the two points composition written on the spur of the moment, which gives some idea of his fecundity and great skill'. Sarti presumably then took Potemkin's ideas and arranged them for the orchestra.[24]

Certainly Catherine was proud of his musical abilities. 'I can send you the tune of Sarti,' she wrote to Grimm, 'composed on the notes put together haphazardly by Prince Potemkin.' The Prince, who always wanted an immediate reaction, 'is very impatient to know if all the music has been delivered to you'.[25] Sarti and his itinerant hornblowers were with Potemkin to the end, but later he was also offered the greatest musical genius of his time – Mozart.

At about 11 a.m., the ritual moment arrived that defined Potemkin's mysterious power. The Prince was 'receiving all the great nobles at his *lever*, wearing their decorations', recalled the Comte de Damas, 'while he sat in the middle of the circle with his hair unbound and a great dressing gown around him with no britches underneath.' In the midst of this Asiatic scene, the Empress's *valet de chambre* appeared and whispered in the Prince's ear: 'he quickly wrapped his dressing gown more closely round him, dismissed everyone with a bow of farewell, and, disappearing through the door that led to the privy apartments, presented himself to the Empress'.[26] She had already been awake for about five hours.

He might then decide to get dressed – or not. Potemkin adored shocking everyone, thought Ligne, so he affected 'the most attractive or the most repulsive manners'. He enjoyed dressing up and down. On formal occasions, no one was more richly clothed than Potemkin, who adopted 'the style and manners of a *grand seigneur* at Louis XIV's court'. When he died, the clothes in his palace were listed: there were epaulettes set with rubies worth 40,000 roubles and diamond buttons worth 62,000 roubles, and he always wore his diamond-set portrait of the Empress worth 31,000 roubles. He had a hat so heavy with jewels that only an adjutant could bear it, worth 40,000 roubles. Even the garters for his stockings were worth 5,000 roubles. His full-dress wardrobe was worth 276,000–283,000 roubles. Yet he was often seen 'hair loose, in dressing gown and pantaloons, lying on a sofa'. He also favoured furs – the Prince was 'unable to exist without furs; always without drawers in his shirt – or in rich regimentals embroidered on all the seams'.[27] Foreigners implied that a man in a dressing gown was obviously not working, but this was not so: wearing wraps or regimentals, Potemkin usually worked extremely hard.

When Ségur arrived in Petersburg, Serenissimus appalled the French Ambassador by receiving him in his fur wrap. So Ségur invited Potemkin to dinner and Ségur greeted him in the same garb, which the Prince enjoyed immensely – though only a friend of Marie-Antoinette could have got away with it. There was political method in this sartorial madness: at a time when the ritual of Catherine's Court was getting richer, more stratified, the courtiers competed to follow etiquette while dressing as ostentatiously as possible. Catherine's favourites were always keenest to display their prosperity and power in lace, feathers and diamonds. Favourites used dress to symbolize their affluence and influence.[28] Potemkin's shaggy furs announced that he was no mere favourite. It emphasized his superiority: he was above the Court. He was the imperial consort.

The Prince had now been up for a few hours, reviewing papers with Popov, receiving petitioners and meeting the Empress. But there were days when he was too depressed to get out of bed at all. Once he summoned Ségur to his bedroom, explaining that 'depression had prevented him from getting up or dressing ...'. Harris believed that his illnesses arose solely from 'his singular manner of living'.[29] Serenissimus certainly lived on his nerves. The life of a favourite, let alone a secret consort, was extremely stressful, for he was the man to destroy and he had to defend himself against all comers.* The work of a chief minister, in an era when states were expanding so fast, but the bureaucracies had not caught up, was debilitating – no wonder leaders like Pitt and Potemkin died at the ages of forty-six and fifty-two.[30]

Potemkin had to be doing something with his hands and mouth, so he was either 'gnawing his nails or apples and turnips'. He even bit his

* The great favourites of earlier epochs, such as the Count-Duke of Olivares and Cardinal Richelieu, both suffered recurring nervous collapses.

nails in the company of monarchs, a winning trait.[31] But he overdid it and often suffered from infected hangnail. Catherine saw it as just another part of his unique charm.[32] When Grand Duke Alexander was born, the Empress joked that 'he chewed his nails just like Prince Potemkin'.[33]

His moods were ever changing – from 'distrust, to confidence, to jealousy or to gratitude, to ill-humour or pleasantness', recalled Ligne. Crises or bursts of work were usually followed by bouts of illness, which afflicted other politicians such as Sir Robert Walpole, whose feverish attacks always struck after anxiety was eased by success. These were partly the result of the malarial fevers he contracted in 1772 and 1783. The exhaustion of travelling vast distances at high speed, along with tireless inspections, political tension, heat and cold, and bad water, was enough to make anyone ill: indeed the other most widely and swiftly travelled Russian leader, Peter the Great, whom Potemkin in some ways resembled, was constantly ill with fevers on his journeys. The Prince's need to bestride Russia made his life much harder because he almost literally had to be in two places at once.

His temperament was abnormally turbulent, swinging from wild exuberance to the depths of depression in moments. 'On some occasions, he was insouciant to the point of immobility and on others capable of putting forth incredible exertions.' When he was depressed, he brooded silently and often felt desperate, even frantic. Twenty adjutants were summoned, then he would not speak to them. Sometimes he did not speak for hours. 'I sat next to Prince Potemkin at dinner,' wrote Lady Craven, 'but except for asking me to eat and drink, I cannot say I heard the sound of his voice.'[34]

He may have been cyclothymic, even manic-depressive, swerving between lows of depression, inactivity and despair on one hand, and hypomania, a whirl of energy, elation and activity, on the other. He was frequently described as manic, and his euphoria, intense loquacity, insomnia, wild spending of money and hypersexuality were all characteristics of cyclothymic behaviour. But so was 'the intense creativity' that enabled him to do several things at once and, during his periods of activity, to do much more than a normal person could. His excessive optimism was often self-fulfilling. It also contributed to the aura of seductiveness and sexual enjoyment that made him so attractive. Such characters are difficult to live with – but are often talented.* They

---

* Oliver Cromwell, the Duke of Marlborough and Clive of India are among the many gifted leaders who are said to have displayed cyclothymic traits.

sometimes possess outstanding powers of leadership, precisely because they suffer from this manic condition.[35]

People who knew Potemkin admired his 'agile imagination' but attacked his fickleness. 'Nobody thought out a plan more swiftly, carried it out more slowly and abandoned it more easily,'[36] said Ségur, an attitude that is disproved by the scale of his actual achievements. But that was certainly the impression Potemkin gave. Ligne was nearer than truth when he said Serenissimus 'looks idle and is always busy'.

He was quite capable of doing many things at once: when Ségur visited him to help the French merchant Antoine in Kherson, he told the diplomat to read his memorandum aloud. But Ségur was 'greatly surprised to see the Prince beckon into the room one after another, and give orders to a priest, an embroiderer, a secretary and a milliner'. The Frenchman was annoyed. Potemkin 'smiled and said he had heard everything quite well'. Ségur was not convinced, until three weeks later Antoine wrote from Kherson to say that every request had been fulfilled by the Prince. Ségur went round to Potemkin's to apologize: 'As soon as he caught sight of me he flung his arms open and came towards me saying, "Well batushka did I not listen to you? ... Do you still think I can't do several things simultaneously and are you still going to be put out with me?"'[37] But he worked when he wanted and if he wanted.

If he was in a state of depressive collapse or just relaxing, no papers were signed and part of Russian government came to a halt. The secretaries in his Chancellery were frustrated, so one bright spark, who was nicknamed 'the Hen', probably for his busy-body bustle, boasted he could get them signed. Finding the Prince, the Hen explained how necessary it was to sign the papers. 'Ah! You've come to the point. I have free time' – and Potemkin tenderly took the boy to his study and signed everything. The secretary boasted of his achievement back in the Chancellery. But when the office began to process the papers, the unfortunate official discovered that Potemkin had signed every one, 'Cock, Cockerel, Hen.'[38] He could be shamelessly childish.

Every day, he studiously ignored and disdained the many of the princes, generals and ambassadors who crowded his anterooms to win his favour. Lying half naked and fur-wrapped on his divan, he might summon one of them with his finger.[39] Diplomats so feared being made to look silly that they hid in their carriages outside the Palace and sent in their underlings to wait until Potemkin deigned to receive them.[40]

Serenissimus would not tolerate sycophancy and devised appropriate punishments to tease those who practised it, but he respected and rewarded courage. 'I'm bored with these nasty people,' he grumbled one day. The witty but sycophantic writer Denis von Vizin saw his opportunity: 'Why do you let such scoundrels in? You should order them barred.'

'Really?' said the Prince. 'I'll do it tomorrow.' The next day, von Vizin arrived at the Palace, satisfied at having expelled his rivals from the Prince's circle. The Guards would not admit him.

'There must be some mistake,' said von Vizin.

'No,' replied the doorman. 'I know you, and His Highness ordered me not to admit you, thanks to your own advice yesterday.'[41]

A general, kept waiting for hours in the antechamber, shouted that he would not be treated 'like a corporal' and demanded to be received, whatever the Prince was doing. Potemkin had him shown into his office. When the general came in, the Prince got up, an unheard-of honour. 'Your Highness, please!', said the general.

'I'm on my way to the lavatory,' laughed the Prince.*

When an impoverished old colonel burst into his office to ask for a pension, Potemkin snapped, 'Get him out of here.' An adjutant approached the Colonel, who punched him and went on hitting him even on the floor. Potemkin ran over, pulled them apart and led the veteran into his apartments. The Colonel received a new job, travel expenses and a bonus.[42]

Serenissimus feared no one and felt that, like a tsar, he was on a different level from the aristocracy: indeed, he identified much more with the Russian peasant or the European cosmopolitan than the Russian nobleman. At Mogilev, when he caught a provincial governor cheating at faro, he grabbed him by the collar and cuffed him. He once struck a *grand seigneur*, a Volkonsky, because he clapped at one of Potemkin's jokes. 'What, you applaud me as if I was a jester.' Slap! 'There ... that's the way to treat this sort of scoundrel.' The chastized nobleman kept away from the Prince's table for a week but was soon back.[43]

MIDDAY

Once the audiences were over, Popov reappeared with piles of papers to sign. Potemkin shared with Kaunitz the distinction of being Europe's most flamboyant hypochondriac: he always saw his doctors while going over state papers. 'A torrent of correspondence fell on Prince Potemkin and I don't know how he could be so patient with all the idiots who

---

* In our times, this resembles President L.B. Johnson humiliating his cabinet from his lavatory seat.

attack him everywhere,' observed Miranda.[44] These varied from German princes and Russian widows to Greek pirates and Italian cardinals. All used the word 'importune' in their requests, which were often requesting lands in the south or the opportunity to serve in the army. One has the impression that Potemkin was in correspondence with virtually every prince in the Holy Roman Empire, which he called 'the archipelago of princes'. Even kings apologized if their letters were too long. 'I know by experience', wrote King Stanislas-Augustus of Poland, 'how one doesn't like long letters when one is busy . . .'.

He received many ludicrous letters of over-the-top flattery such as the Samgrass-like Professor Bataille who sent an ode to Catherine adding: 'Could I, Monseigneur, write without a mention of Your Highness? Deign you, Monseigneur, to cast a glance on my work.'[45] Potemkin's fifty-strong perambulant Chancellery answered many of these, but he was also notorious for forgetting to reply to eminent people like the King of Sweden: Field-Marshal Loudon, an Austrianized Scotsman, complained to Joseph II that 'Prince Potemkin had had the politeness not to reply to two letters he had sent him.'

There were also tragic requests for help from unfortunates of all ranks which give a glimpse of life in that time: a male protégé of Potemkin's thanked him for his help in marrying one of the Naryshkin girls, who suddenly revealed that she had 20,000 roubles of debts, obviously from playing cards, probably faro, the heroin addiction of its day. Some were from aristocrats in trouble like the Princess Bariatinskaya, who wrote from Turin, 'I struggle against the horrors of misery,' but 'you alone my Prince can make a woman happy who has been unhappy all her life'. Another German count, dismissed by the Empress, wrote, 'I can no longer have the means to sustain a wife always ill, a girl of 14, sons . . .'. An ordinary man wrote: 'I beg you to have pity on us . . .'.[46] But, being Potemkin, there was always some exotica: one mysterious correspondent was Elias Abaise, *soi-disant* Prince of Palestina, who confessed, 'I am forced by misery lacking so greatly money, credit and all the basic necessities, to implore the high protection and benevolence of Your Highness . . . and to aid my departure . . . winter is coming.' It was signed in Arabic. Was this a Wandering Jew or Arab from the Ottoman province of Palestine? If so, what was he doing in St Petersburg in August 1780? And would Potemkin help him? 'Your Highness', reads the next letter, 'has had the favour to give me gracious help.'[47]

The Prince wrote many replies himself, in his scratchy, slanted hand, in Russian or French, but Popov was so trusted that the Prince told him his wishes and the secretary sent them out in his own name. Potemkin was extremely tolerant towards his subordinates[48] – even when they were making a mess of things. First he gave them their orders again. If tolerance did not work, he tried biting, if droll, sarcasm. When Admiral Voinovich made excuses after a ship ran aground, the Prince replied: 'I am very pleased to learn the ship *Alexander* is wedged off a sandbar but it would've been better not to have run into it ... I like your view that this accident will make officers more diligent but I wish and demand diligence without accidents ... And if Captain Baronov is such an experienced seaman I would be more convinced ... if he ran Turkish ships on to sandbars and not his own.'[49]

Before dinner, the Prince liked to be alone for an hour. It was then that he came up with the richness of political ideas that distinguished him from Catherine's other advisers. Popov and his secretaries seldom interrupted him. This was a golden rule: one secretary who did not get the message was actually sacked for speaking. Potemkin would call for his jewels.

Jewels calmed the Prince as much as music. He sat there with a little saw, some silver and a box of diamonds.[50] Sometimes visitors noticed him sitting alone like a giant child, playing with them, pouring them from hand to hand, making them into patterns and drawings until he had worked out the problem.[51]

He showered his nieces with diamonds. Vigée Lebrun said that Skavronskaya's jewellery box in Naples was the richest she had ever seen. Ligne marvelled that he had a 100,000 rouble fleece of diamonds in his collection.[52] Jewels were another good way to win favour. 'I send you a little red ruby and bigger blue ruby,'[53] wrote Sashenka's husband, Branicki, in one of his shockingly obsequious letters. Potemkin's correspondence with his jewellers showed his impatient enthusiasm. 'I'm sending Your Highness the ruby of St Catherine,' wrote Alexis Deuza, probably a Greek craftsman working in Potemkin's stone-cutting *fabrick* at Ozerki, 'It's not as fine as I'd like, to perfect this sort of work, one needs a cylinder and the one Your Highness ordered won't be ready for ten ... days and I did not think I should wait. It seems Your Highness wants it urgently.'[54] His spending reveals his passionate pursuit of brilliants: he owed a procession of merchants money for 'diamonds, gems, amethyst, topaz and aquamarine, pearls'.[55] Everything had to be exquisite and beautiful. Here is a typical bill from Duval, a French jeweller, in February 1784:

A big sapphire of 18.3/4 carats – 1500 Roubles
Two diamonds of 5.3/8 carats – 600 R

10 diamonds of 20 carats – 2200 R
15 diamonds of 14.5 carats – 912 R
78 diamonds of 14.5 carats – 725 R ...[56]

It was not just jewels: a bill from his bankers Tepper in Warsaw lists two gold snuff-boxes engraved with diamonds, a gold watch, a golden repeater clock engraved with diamonds, a 'souvenir-à-brilliants', some music, eighteen pens, customs for paintings imported from Vienna, payments to a Polish agent of influence, 15,000 roubles payed to 'the Jew Hosias' for unnamed work, all totalling almost 30,000 roubles.[57]

Potemkin's payment for all this was so hit-and-miss that it too has gone into legend. There were virtually always unpaid jewellers and crafts-men among the petitioners crowding his apartments. It was said that when a creditor arrived Potemkin used to signal to Popov: if the sign was an open hand, the merchant was paid. If it was a closed fist, he was sent away. None of them dared confront him directly at Court. But the Swiss court jeweller Fasi was said to have slipped his bill under Potemkin's plate at the Empress's table. Serenissimus thought it was a billet-doux and was furious when he read it. Catherine laughed and Potemkin always admired courage so he paid the bill. But, to teach the jeweller for his insolence, he delivered it in copper coins, enough to fill two rooms.[58]

DINNER

At about 1 p.m., the jewels were put away and the Prince's guests arrived for dinner, the main meal in the eighteenth century, at a table set for eighteen, usually officers, visitors and his best friends of the moment, from Ségur or Ligne to Lady Craven or Samuel Bentham. Potemkin's friendships, as we saw with Harris, were as intense as love affairs – and tended to end in disillusionment. 'The true secret of winning his friendship', said Ségur, 'was not fearing him.' When he arrived in Peters-burg and called on Potemkin, Ségur was kept waiting so long that he stormed out. Next day, the Prince sent him an apology, invited him back and greeted him a gorgeous suit in which every seam was embroidered with diamonds. When Potemkin was lying in bed, depressed, he said to Ségur: 'My dear Comte, let us lay aside all ceremony ... and live like two friends.' Once he had befriended someone, he favoured his companion above all the highest imperial grandees, as Sam Bentham discovered.[59] Potemkin was a loyal friend: in private, he was caressing and warm but in public he seemed 'haughty and arrogant'. This was probably due to that surprising shyness.[60] Miranda actually saw him blush bashfully at the obsequious attention he received.[61]

The Prince was a master of conversation in an era when wit was especially prized. 'Sometimes serious, sometime hilarious,' recalled Ségur, 'always keen to discuss some ecclesiastical question, always switching from gravity to laughter, wearing his knowledge lightly.' Ligne said that if he wanted to charm someone, he possessed 'the art of conquering every heart'. He was an immensely rewarding, enjoyable and impossible companion, 'scolding or laughing, mimicking or swearing, engaged in wantonness or prayers, singing or meditating'. He could be 'uncommonly affable or extremely savage'. But, when 'savage', his harshness often concealed 'the greatest benevolence of heart'. Bentham had never known such 'merriment' as he did travelling in Potemkin's carriage. The poet Derzhavin remembered Potemkin for 'his kind heart and great generosity'.[62] He was also deeply kind: 'The more I see of his Character,' Sam Bentham told Pole Carew, 'the more reason I have to esteem and admire it.'[63]

His geniality was combined with a heartfelt humanity and care for ordinary people, especially soldiers, that was rare in the age of cannon-fodder. Ligne noticed he was 'never vengeful, asking pardon for a pain he has inflicted, quickly repairing an injustice'. When Potemkin bought Prince Lubomirski's estates in Poland, he ordered that 'all the gallows ... must be destroyed as soon as possible without trace', wishing that the peasants obey him 'through respect for their duty and not from fear of punishment'.[64] His military reforms were designed to give more comfort to his troops, quite a new notion in that century, though he was also increasing their effectiveness. But his constant orders to be more lenient in punishments were unique in the Russian army: again and again, he ordered that beatings should be reduced. 'All compulsion ... must be eradicated,' he wrote in one order. 'Lazy ones can be forced by the stick but not more than six lashes. Every kind of compulsion ... has to be eradicated.'[65] His repeated orders to feed the troops with warm nourishing food, regarded by Russian generals as mollycoddling, sound absolutely modern.[66]

'He was neither vindictive nor rancorous yet everybody was afraid of him,'[67] recalled the memoirist Wiegel, who believed that this explained the ambiguous attitude to Potemkin. His very tolerance and good nature confused the Russians. 'The way he looked at people, his movements, it seemed, said to all those around him "You're not worth my anger." His lack of severity and indulgence clearly originated from his unlimited disdain.'[68]

Dinner was served at about 1.30 p.m. and even if there were only a total of sixteen guests, as when Lady Craven attended such an event at the

Taurida, the sixty-strong horn orchestra played during the meal.[69] The Prince was a notorious Epicurean and trencherman – Shcherbatov called him 'the omnipotent glutton'.[70] As political tensions rose, he must have eaten for comfort or as a locomotive consumes coal. He never lost his taste for simple peasant food, yet he also served caviar from the Caspian, smoked goose from Hamburg, cucumbers from Nizhny Novgorod, pastries from Kaluga, oysters from the Baltic, melons and oranges from Astrakhan and China, figs from Provence. He loved *pain doux de Savoie*[71] for dessert and expected to eat his favourite dish, sterlet soup from the Caspian, made with the young sturgeon fish, wherever he was. Soon after his arrival in St Petersburg in 1780, Reginald Pole Carew attended 'an ordinary' dinner at Potemkin's and listed the 'exquisite and rare dishes': 'remarkable, fine white veal from Archangel, a joint of delicious mutton from Little Bokhara, a suckling pig from Poland, conserves from Persia, caviar from the Caspian'.[72] All was cooked by Ballez,* his French *chef de cuisine*.[73]

Serenissimus also appreciated wine, not just his own from Soudak in the Crimea, but, as Carew Pole recorded,[74] from all the 'Ports of Europe and the Grecian isles, the Cape and the borders of the Don'. No toast was complete without champagne.[75] If a Russian ambassador in southern Europe, like Skavronsky in Naples, wanted to win favour, he sent a Classical column – and some barrels of wine.[76]

One day, at the height of his fortunes, Serenissimus sat down to dinner. He was very cheerful, playing the fool until towards the end of the meal when he became quiet. He started biting his nails. Guests and servants waited to see what he would say. Finally, he asked:

> Can any man be more happy than I am? Everything I have ever wanted, I have; all my whims have been fulfilled as if by magic. I wanted high rank, I have it; I wanted medals, I have them; I loved gambling, I have lost vast sums; I liked giving parties, I've given magnificent ones; I enjoy building houses, I've raised palaces; I liked buying estates, I have many; I adore diamonds and beautiful things – no individual in Europe owns rarer or more exquisite stones. In a word, all my passions have been sated. I am entirely happy!

* The Prince loved his food and when Monsieur Ballez's much anticipated arrival from France was delayed by his being stranded at Elsinor in Denmark, Potemkin mobilized the Russian Ambassador and various special envoys to get him quickly overland to Petersburg.

At this, the Prince swept the priceless china plates on to the floor, smashed them all, stormed off to his bedroom and locked himself inside.

Potemkin suffered from his own surfeit of everything: he regarded himself as 'fortune's child'; indeed he often used the phrase. But sometimes the scale of his success seemed to disgust him. Perhaps this was deeply Russian: he was ashamed of his vast power and proud of his turbulent soul, repulsed by the cold machinery of state, proud of his boundless capacity for suffering and self-abasement in which the greatness of the Russian character resides. His appetites for fame, fortune and pleasure were insatiable – yet they did not make him happy. Only massive accomplishment, whether in statesmanship or battle, aesthetic beauty, in music or art, or the serenity of religious mysticism, seemed to excuse the obscenity of mere power.[77]

Once he called for his adjutant and ordered coffee. Someone rushed out to get it. Then he asked again. Another courier was despatched. Finally he ordered it again and again, almost in a frenzy. But when it arrived he said, 'It's unnecessary. I only wanted to wait for something but now I've been deprived even of that pleasure.'[78]

AFTERNOON: THE LOVER'S HOUR

The afternoon was traditionally the 'lovers' hour' in Russia, like the Gallic *cinq-à-sept* or the Spanish *siesta*. There must have been much coming and going of closed carriages and ladies' maids bringing billets-doux to Potemkin's house. Still more married women were now sending him love letters, begging to see him. One of them always hailed him: 'Hello, my unique friend!' These unpublished notes, handwritten in an argot of French and Russian but always unsigned and undated, fill an entire section of the archive. 'I have not been able to give you pleasure because I've had no time, you left so quickly,' wrote another in a big girlish hand. This was repeated in all the love letters. When the same woman wrote again, she declared, 'I wait with the most tender impatience the moment when I can come to kiss you. While waiting, I do it in my imagination and with equal tenderness.'

Serenissimus' whims and moods tormented his mistresses. 'You're rendering me mad with love,' wrote one. His restlessness and long departures to the south made him unobtainably attractive: 'I'm so angry at being prevented from [having] the pleasure of embracing you,' wrote one girl. 'Don't forget that I beg you to be persuaded that I am involved only with you!' But it seemed that Potemkin had soon forgotten that. 'Don't forget me,' she beseeched him later. 'You *have* forgotten.' Yet another declared melodramatically that 'if I didn't live in the hope of being loved by you, I would give myself to Death'. Finally, driven to the edge by Potemkin's impossible lack of commitment, the girls had to retreat and become friends again: 'I don't want to recall the past and I forget all except that I loved you and that suffices to wish sincerely for your happiness ... Adieu, mon Prince.'[79]

He was accustomed to languish on his divan surrounded by women like a sultan, though he called his harem 'the hen-run'. He always enjoyed the company of women and saw no need to restrain his 'Epicurean appetites'.[80] Diplomats always called his maîtresse en titre 'sultana-in-chief'. But he behaved 'nobly' to his mistresses, according to Samoilov, who had reason to know since his wife was probably one of them: his affairs were always questions of passion, not merely vanity, 'as they are for many famous people'.[81] His subordinates knew they had to keep their wives at a distance if they wanted to preserve their virtue. Potemkin's 'wandering and capricious glance sometimes stopped, or better to say, slid, upon my mother's good-looking face', recalled Wiegel. One day, a 'fool' in his entourage told him that Wiegel's mother had the most exquisite feet. 'Indeed,' said Potemkin, 'I hadn't noticed. Some time I'll call her over and ask her to show me them without stockings.' Wiegel's father quickly despatched her to their estates.[82]

If Potemkin was bored, he often went over to the palace of Catherine's buffoonish friend, the Master of Horse, Lev Naryshkin, where eating, drinking and dancing went on all day and night. Potemkin treated it like his private club – he usually sat in his own special alcove – as it was the ideal place to meet high-born married mistresses. 'It was the foyer of all pleasure,' wrote Ségur, 'the rendezvous of all the lovers because, in the midst of so many happy people, secret trysts were 100 times easier than at balls or salons where etiquette reigned.' The Prince relaxed there, sometimes in silence, sometimes 'very cheerful, chatting to women, he who never talked to anyone'. Potemkin, whom 'one hardly saw anywhere else', was drawn by the Naryshkin daughters, with whom he was 'always' in 'tête-à-tête'. He seemed to work his way through the Naryshkin girls: 'he consoles himself for the absence of his niece with Madame de Solugub, daughter of Madame Naryshkina', reported Cobenzl to his Emperor. Ivan Solugub was one of his generals. All his officers had to endure his conquests both on the battlefield and in their own households.[83]

The Prince still dominated the lives of all his nieces and insisted on running their households whenever possible. His 'angel of fleshly delights', Katinka Skavronskaya, was inconveniently visiting her operatic husband in Naples, but we can follow her movements across Europe by Potemkin's instructions to his bankers to pay for her expenses. When she passed through Vienna, even Emperor Joseph had to entertain[84] 'your kitten', as Catherine tolerantly called her.[85] By 1786, Katinka was 'more beautiful than ever', according to that connoisseur Cobenzl, and always 'favourite sultana-in-chief' of her uncle's harem.[86]

The spirited Sashenka Branicka was as imperious as her uncle: they were always arguing, even though they were closest of all. In 1788, Serenissimus tried to remove Mademoiselle Guibald from one of the Engelhardt households. Guibald was the Frenchwoman in Potemkin's entourage who had supposedly stolen Harris's letter and became a companion for the nieces and a seraglio-manageress for the Prince. Branicka refused to dismiss her, so he wrote to insist because Guibald 'wants my niece to remain a child for ever'. We do not know which niece was being discussed, but all were married by then. Branicka evidently reassured the French lady, which made Potemkin furious: 'I'm master of my house and I want what I wish. I don't understand how Countess Branicka dared to calm her against my will ...'. The Prince believed that 'my exalted station confers benefits on my relatives; they owe me everything and they'd be in a paltry state without me ...'. He stated simply: 'There are a lot of reasons but the main one is that I wish it to be so.'[87]

EVENING

At about 10.30 p.m., when the Empress retired with her favourite, Potemkin, who usually spent the early evening in attendance, whether at the Little Hermitage or at a ball, received his 'pink ticket'. His real day, as it were, was just beginning. He woke up at night, his most creative hours. One could define absolutism as the power to overrule even the laws of time. Potemkin paid no attention to the clock and his subordinates had to do the same: he was an insomniac, said Ligne, 'constantly lying down, but never sleeping whether day or night'.[88]

NIGHT

Sir James Harris experienced the Prince's nocturnal habits: 'His hours for eating and sleeping are uncertain and we were frequently airing in the rain in an open carriage at midnight.'[89] There is no more Potemkinish scene than that.

Potemkin was relentlessly curious and was always asking questions, teasing and provoking his companions, discussing religion, politics, art and sex – 'the biggest questioner in the world'. His questions reminded Richelieu of 'a bee, which with the help of the flowers, whose pollen it sucks, creates an exquisite substance'. In this case the 'honey' was Potemkin's racy and pungent conversation, aided by a flawless memory and a whimsical imagination.[90]

Everyone who met Potemkin and even those who loathed him had to admit that he was gifted with admirable mental equipment: 'Potemkin joined the gift of prodigious memory with that of natural, lively, quick mind . . .'.[91] Ligne thought he had 'natural abilities, an excellent memory, much elevation of soul; malice without the design of injuring, artifice without craft, a happy mixture of caprices', concluding that he had 'the talent of guessing what he is ignorant of and a consummate knowledge of mankind'. Not every Westerner liked Potemkin: Sir John Sinclair called him 'a worthless and dangerous character', but even he thought Potemkin had 'great abilities'.[92] His more intelligent Russian opponents agreed: Simon Vorontsov believed the Prince had 'lots of intelligence, intrigue and credit' but lacked 'knowledge, application and virtue'.[93]

Ségur was often astonished by Potemkin's knowledge 'not only of politics but travellers, *savants*, writers, artists and even artisans'. All those who knew him acclaimed his 'vast erudition on antiquities'. His travelling companion in the south, Miranda, was amazed by his knowledge of architecture, art and music. 'It seems this man of so much intelligence and prodigious memory also wanted to study sciences and arts in depth and that he has achieved this to some extent,' wrote the Venezuelan after they had discussed the music of Haydn and Boccherini, the paintings of Murillo and the writings of Chappe d'Auteroche – he turned out to be profoundly knowledgeable on all of them.[94] It was no wonder that Damas owed 'the most instructive and agreeable moments of my life' to the 'strange' Prince.[95]

His knowledge of Russian history was equally impressive. 'Thanks for your chronology, it's the best part in my Russian history,' wrote Catherine about her *Notes on Russian History*, with which he helped her. The partners loved history. 'I've spent years researching this subject,' Catherine told Seinac de Meilhan, the French official and writer. 'I've always loved to read things no one else reads. I've only found one man who has the same taste – that's Marshal Prince Potemkin.'[96] Here was another pleasure they shared. When the translator of the *History of Armenia*, one of Potemkin's pet subjects, was hanged by the Turks, 'Prince Potemkin', joked Catherine to Grimm, 'was very angry about it.'[97]

He always wanted to set up his own printing press, and Jeremy Bentham tried to help him find one.[98] Just before the war started, Potemkin at last acquired his press, which was to follow him around throughout the war, printing political journals and classics in Russian, French, Latin and Greek, as well as his own compositions.[99]

Ségur and his friend Ligne claimed that Potemkin 'had less acquired his knowledge from books than from men'. This was clearly untrue. The Prince was widely read. Pole Carew, who spent so much time with him at the start of the decade, stated his culture came from 'copious reading in his earlier years' – hence his 'knowledge and taste for the Greek language'.[100] Potemkin's advice to Catherine on a Greek education for the little Grand Dukes shows his artistic ear for the Greek language: 'It's hard to imagine how much knowledge and delicate taste one can get from learning it. The language has the loveliest harmony and much play of thought.'[101]

His library, which he gradually expanded by buying collections from scholars and friends like Archbishop Voulgaris, reveals his broad interests: there were all the classics from Seneca, Horace and Plutarch to *Les Amours de Sappho*, published in Paris in 1724; many works of theology, war, agriculture and economics including *Coutumes monastiques*, manuals of artillery, *Uniformes Militaires* and *La Richesse des Nations de Schmitt* (Adam Smith); many works on Peter the Great, but also the masterpieces of the *philosophes* from Voltaire and Diderot to Gibbon's *Decline and Fall of the Roman Empire*. His Anglophilia and his obsession with English gardens were covered in histories of England, the works of Locke and Newton, the *Caricatures de Hoguard* (Hogarth) and of course *Britannia Illustré ou deux livres des vues des principales maisons et jardins ... de la Grande Bretagne.* By the time he died his huge collection contained 1,065 foreign works and 106 in Russian: it filled eighteen carriages.[102]

His political ideas were quintessentially Russian, despite imbibing the tolerance of the *philosophes* and the utilitarianism of Bentham. He believed that absolutism was the best system for an empire the size of Russia. The ruler was a woman and a state and he served both. The three revolutions – the American, French and Polish – appalled and fascinated him. He cross-examined Ségur about the Americans, for whom the Frenchman had fought, but 'did not believe that republican institutions could have a long life in a land so vast. His mind, so accustomed to absolute despotism, could not admit the possibility of a union of order and liberty.'[103] As for the French Revolution, Potemkin simply told the Comte de Langeron: 'Colonel, your countrymen are a pack of madmen.'[104] The Prince believed that politics was the art of infinite flexibility and philosophical patience in order to attain a fixed objective. 'You must have patience,' he lectured Harris, 'depend on it. The chapter

of accidents will serve you better than all your rhetoric.' Potemkin's
political motto was 'Improve events as they arise.'[105]*

The Prince liked to talk 'divinity to his generals and tactics to his
bishops', said Ligne, and Lev Engelhardt observed him 'playing off' his
'erudite rabbis, Old Believers and different scholars against each other'.[106]
His 'favourite topic' was the 'separation of the Greek and Latin Churches',
the only sure way to win his attention was talk about 'the Councils of
Nicaea, Chalcedon and Florence'. Sometimes he wanted to found a
religious order, sometimes wander Russia as a monk. This was why
Frederick the Great had ordered his ambassador in the 1770s to study
Orthodoxy, the best way to befriend the Prince.

He joked about religion – teasing Suvorov for observance of fasts –
'You wish to enter paradise astride a sturgeon' – but essentially he was a
serious 'son of the Church', never joining the Masonic lodges.[107] He
may have swung between being a coenobite and a sybarite, but he was
certainly a believer, who could tell Catherine during the coming war,
'Christ will help, He'll put an end to our adversity. Look through your
life and you can see what a lot of unexpected benefits came to you
from Him in misfortune . . . It was a mere chance that your coronation
coincided with the feast of the Apostles' – and who could then quote the
appropriate chapter 16 verse 1 from the Epistle of Paul to the Romans.[108]
He often dreamed of retiring to the Church. 'Be a good mother,' he asked
Catherine, 'prepare a good bishop's mitre and a quiet tenure.'[109] Potemkin
never let religion ruin his pleasures – Ségur 'saw him spend a morning
examining models of hats for dragoons, bonnets and dresses for his
nieces, and mitres and habits for priests'. He staggered from church to
orgy and back, 'waving with one hand to the women that please him
and with the other making the sign of the Cross', observed Ligne, 'embracing the feet of a statue of the Virgin or the alabaster neck of his mistress'.[110] A religious man and a great sinner, he was the 'epitome of the
Russian's staggering ability to live upright within while enveloped in
unceasing sin'.[111]

The Prince also passed much of the night at the green baize tables. If
French was the language that united Europe, faro was the game: a squire
from Leicestershire, a mountebank from Venice, a planter from Virginia
and an officer from Sebastopol played the same game that required no
language. A night of faro at Potemkin's Palace in the mid-1780s was

---

* This was an earlier, more proactive version of British Prime Minister Harold Mac-
millan's description of politics as 'Events, dear boy, events.'

probably very much like a game at Chatsworth with Georgiana, Duchess of Devonshire, who was also a compulsive gamester. The players would sit at an oval table covered in green baize with a wooden rim across it to separate the cards. A *tailleur* (banker) sat opposite the *croup* and the players bet on the cards turned up on either side of the rim. The players could double stakes all the way up to a *soixante et le va* – sixty times the stake, all of which was wordlessly announced by complicated mutilations, or bending, of the cards. Thus faro peculiarly suited Potemkin: the taking of vast risks without the need to speak a word.

He used gambling in a very Potemkinish manner. One occasion was recounted later by Pushkin. A young man, named 'Sh.', was about to be ruined by the debts owed to 'Prince B.', who was going to complain to the Empress. The young man's family begged Potemkin to intercede. He sent a message to 'Sh.' to visit him during the card game the next day and insisted, 'Tell him to be bolder with me.' When 'Sh.' arrived, Potemkin was already playing. When 'Prince B.' arrived, he was poorly received, so he sat and watched the game. Suddenly Potemkin called 'Sh.' over and, showing him his cards, asked, 'Tell me, brother, how would you play this hand?' Young 'Sh.', remembering his instructions, replied rudely, 'What affair is it of mine? Play the best you can!' Everyone watched Potemkin to see how he would react to this insolence. 'Dear me,' said Serenissimus, 'one can't say a word to you, batinka. You fly straight off the handle!' When 'Prince B.' saw this, he realized that 'Sh.' must be in the highest favour with Potemkin and Catherine. He never called in the debt.[112] Gamblers played for *rouleaux* of banknotes, but the Prince had long since forgotten the value of money. So he insisted that they play for gemstones, which sat beside him on the green baize in a glistening pile.[113] Debts were settled among adventurers by duels – but not by a man of Potemkin's stature. Nonetheless, his fellow gamblers risked cheating because, while Potemkin was playing for fun backed by Catherine's bottomless purse, they were placing their entire family fortunes at the mercy of the dice. When one player (possibly Levashov, Yermolov's uncle) paid his winnings with rhinestones, Potemkin said nothing but arranged his vengeance with the coachman. That afternoon during a storm, the Prince went riding alongside the cheat's carriage. When the carriage was in the midst of a flooded field, Potemkin yelled, 'Off you go,' to the coachman, who galloped off with the horses, leaving the victim behind. When he finally walked home, hours later, his silk clothes soaked, the bedraggled cheat was greeted with gales of laughter from the Prince at the window. But nothing more was ever said about his cheating.[114]

Potemkin's games could not be interrupted. When summoned to the Council, he simply refused to go. When the messenger humbly asked the reason, Potemkin snapped, 'In the 1st Psalm and 1st verse.' When the Council looked it up, this read: 'Beatus vir qui non abiit in consilio impiorum,'* thereby simultaneously displaying his wit, memory, arrogance, theological knowledge and gambling mania.[115]

Somehow, between sunset and sunrise, the Prince also sliced through swathes of papers – it was probably when he did the greatest part of his work. His secretaries were on duty and Popov, in between gambling bouts, often stood behind his chair with pen and pad, awaiting his orders, recording his ideas.

DAWN

When this insomniac finally went to sleep, the carriage of one of his mistresses sometimes stood on Millionaya Street outside the Winter Palace. Inside it, the lady longingly and lovingly watched the candles still burning, just before dawn. 'I passed your house and I saw all the lights on. No doubt you were playing cards. My dear Prince … give me this pleasure, do something for me and don't stay up as you do until four or five in the morning … my darling Prince.'[116]

Since the Prince could not live without his English gardens, the travels of his gardener William Gould were a weathervane of Potemkin's intentions. In late 1786, the English 'Emperor of Gardens' set off for the south in style with his 'general staff' of gardeners and workmen. The *cognoscenti* knew this meant that something important was afoot.[117] The Empress was about to depart on her grandiose journey to the Crimea to meet the Holy Roman Emperor under the gaze of Europe. In November 1786, Serenissimus, the impresario of this imperial progress, departed to make the last checks on the route. On this trip, he excelled himself in his flamboyant choice of carriage companions: a Venezuelan liberator and mountebank who kept a diary of his Ukrainian whorings, and an aspiring king of Ouidah and freebooter, who had been seduced by the Queen of Tahiti.

---

* 'Blessed is he who does not go to the council of the ungodly.'

Part Seven

THE APOGEE
1787–1790

23

THE MAGICAL THEATRE

Louis XIV would have been jealous of his sister Catherine II,
or he would have married her ... The Empress received me ...
She recalled to my mind a thousand things that monarchs alone
can remember for their memory is always excellent.
Prince de Ligne

On 7 December 1786, Francisco de Miranda, aged thirty-seven, a cultured, cynical and rakish revolutionary of dubious Creole nobility, who
had been cashiered from the Spanish army and was travelling from
Constantinople to raise support for a free Venezuela, awaited Potemkin
in Kherson. The whole town was preparing for the arrival of the Prince,
who was on his final tour of inspection before the visit of Catherine II
and the Holy Roman Emperor to his territories. Everyone was waiting.
The cannons were primed, the troops were drilled. There were rumours
that he was on his way, but still the 'mysterious godhead', as Miranda
called him, did not come. 'No one knew where he would be going next.'
Waiting for Serenissimus was one of the hallmarks of Potemkin's power.
Nothing could be done without him. The more powerful he became,
the more everything stopped in anticipation of his arrival. Potemkin
had to be welcomed like a tsar or at least a member of the imperial
family – on Catherine's orders. His whims were unpredictable, his travelling so swift that he could descend on a town without warning – hence
everything had to be kept in a state of the highest readiness. 'You don't
ride,' Catherine teased him. 'You fly.'[1]

Twenty days later, on 28 December, Miranda was still waiting. Then
at sundown 'the much desired Prince Potemkin' arrived to the boom of
cannons. Soldiers and officials went to pay their respects to the 'favourite
idol'.[2] Miranda was taken by his friends to the Prince's exotic Court,
inhabited by all the 'cretins and respectable people' Kherson could hold.
'My goodness, what a bunch of sycophants and crooked rascals,' wrote
Miranda, 'but anyway what most amused me was the variety of costumes
that could be seen there – Cossacks, Greeks, Jews' – and Caucasian
ambassadors in uniforms *à la Prusse*. Suddenly a giant emerged, bowing
here and there, not speaking to anyone. The Venezuelan was introduced

to the Prince as a Spanish count (which he was not). Potemkin said little – but his curiosity was aroused.

On 31 December, Potemkin's aide summoned Miranda, only for the Venezuelan to find Potemkin taking tea with Prince Charles de Nassau-Siegen.[3] 'Give me strength!', thought Miranda at the sight of Nassau, whom he knew from Spain and Constantinople, and regarded with the disdain that only one adventurer can feel for another. They had both led tumultuous lives. Miranda had fought for the Spanish as far as afield as Algiers and Jamaica, and knew Washington and Jefferson from his years in America. Nassau-Siegen, aged forty-two, impoverished heir to a tiny principality, become a soldier of fortune at fifteen, joined Bougainville's expedition of global circumnavigation during which he killed a tiger, tried to make himself king of Ouidah in west Africa,[4] and made love to the Queen of Tahiti. On his return, he commanded the unfortunate Franco-Spanish assault on Gibraltar in 1782 and launched a raid on Jersey. Ruthless and reckless in war and intrigue, Nassau moved east. He wooed Princess Sangushko, a Polish widow. Each thought the other was rich. Once they were married, both discovered the other was not as advertised. But it turned out to be a happy marriage of strong characters and they impressed the salons of Warsaw by keeping fifty bears on their Podolian estate to repel Cossacks. Nassau-Siegen had recently become Potemkin's travelling companion when King Stanislas-Augustus sent him to ask the Prince to bring his Polish clientele to order. But Nassau also hoped to inveigle himself into Potemkin's favour to win trading rights in Kherson.[5]

The Prince was interrogating Miranda about South America when Ribas, his Neapolitan courtier, rushed in and announced that his mistress had arrived. She called herself 'Countess' Sevres, but 'whatever her origins', wrote Miranda, 'she is a whore.' That did not matter: everyone rushed to court her. Her companion was Mademoiselle Guibald, the governess of Potemkin's nieces and now the itinerant manageress of his southern seraglio. Potemkin kissed his mistress and sat her on his right – 'he sleeps with her without the slightest ceremony', noted Miranda. A quintet began playing Boccherini. Over the next few days, the exuberant Potemkin, holding court at 'Countess' Sevres's apartments in his Palace, could not be without the company of his two new friends, Miranda and Nassau-Siegen. Both, in their different ways, were remarkable – Nassau-Siegen was known as the 'paladin' of the age and Miranda was the father of South American liberation, so we are lucky that the latter recorded his experiences in his sceptical and unprejudiced diaries. Potemkin even prepared them a fricassee with his own hands while discussing Algerian pirates and Polish aspirations. Miranda was pleased that the courtiers were 'exploding' with jealousy at this new friendship.[6]

The Prince invited Nassau and Miranda to accompany him on his lightning inspection of the imperial route. Potemkin knew that the success or failure of Catherine's journey would either make him unassailable – or ruin him. The cabinets of Europe were watching. England, Prussia and the Sublime Porte stirred uneasily as Potemkin created new cities and fleets to threaten Constantinople. The Empress's Crimean trip had been delayed because of plague, but there was always a suspicion that it could not take place because nothing in the south had been done – 'there are people who supposed', Cobenzl told Joseph, 'that all necessary to make the tour cannot be ready'.[7]

At 10 p.m. on 5 January 1787, Potemkin, Miranda and Nassau set off, crossing frozen rivers at high speed – three of the most extraordinary men of their epoch in one carriage. They galloped all night, thrice changing horses, stopping at a house of Potemkin's on the way, to reach Perekop, the gateway to the Crimea, at 8 a.m., having covered 160 miles in twenty hours.[8] They crossed short distances in a roomy travelling coach, but since it was now midwinter they often used *kibitka*s (light carriages) mounted on sleighs – their wheels were removed – to glide swiftly over the snowy steppes, almost alone. Travelling in a *kibitka* was like lying in a space capsule: 'they are exactly like cradles, the head having windows to the front', Lady Craven recalled. 'I can sit, or lie, at length, and feel in one like an overgrown baby, comfortably defended from the cold by pillows and blankets.' The rough terrain and high speed made it even more risky. Passengers were subjected to continuous 'shaking and violent thumps ... the hardest head might be broken. I was overturned twice.' But the Russian postillions thought nothing of it: they just got silently off their horses, set the carriage up again and 'never ask if the carriage is hurt'.[9] They would then hurtle away again.

The Prince inspected the Crimea, where Miranda saw the new fleet, troops, cities and plantations. He admired the palaces prepared for the Empress at Simferopol, Bakhchisaray, Sebastopol and Karasubazaar, and the English gardens that William Gould was laying out around them. When they arrived at Sebastopol, the officers insisted on giving a ball for the Prince, who blushed when a toast was given in his honour. Miranda laughed at some of the officers, who 'jumped and hopped about' like 'Parisian *petit maîtres*'. They then inspected Inkerman before galloping back to Simferopol, where the travellers went hunting for two days as Potemkin worked.[10]

Potemkin was accompanied everywhere by Tartar horsemen in regular cavalry squadrons: 'fifty escorted the carriage at every moment', Nassau-Siegen told his wife, 'and the Tartars of every locality where we passed arrived from every direction so the countryside was covered in men who, running, from every direction, gave it an air of war.' The 'paladin' thought it was all 'superb'.[11] Miranda also noticed how Potemkin carefully cultivated all the local Islamic muftis in each town. Serenissimus was accompanied by his court artist, Ivanov, who painted as they travelled, and music – ranging from string quartets to Ukrainian choirs – played wherever they stopped. One day Miranda found Potemkin admiring 'a very famous pearl necklace embellished with diamonds'.[12] The Venezuelan had never seen a 'more noble or beautiful adornment in my life'. It was indeed so valuable that when it was bought from Mack, the Viennese Court jewellers, the identity of the buyer was kept secret. Even Joseph II wanted to know who had bought it. Finally Cobenzl revealed the secret to his Emperor: Potemkin was planning to present it to the Empress on her tour.[13]

The three travellers took tea at the English dairy run for Potemkin by Mr Henderson and his two dubious 'nieces', recruited by the Benthams, then headed for the vineyards of Soudak. He presented a vineyard to Nassau, who at once ordered vines from Constantinople. The soldiers they inspected impressed Miranda – the Kiev and Taurida Regiments 'could not have been better'. Then the party visited Potemkin's mint at the old slave-market at Kaffa, run by his Jewish merchant Zeitlin, and his new town of Theodosia.

Serenissimus occupied every night and every carriage-ride with political and artistic discussions with his companions, ranging from the virtues of Murillo to the sins of the Inquisition. The three companions in the Potemkin carriage got on well, perhaps too well, so the Prince entertained himself by provoking a row between Nassau and Miranda. Potemkin baited the Franco-German Nassau by attacking the French for their ingratitude to Russia. The Venezuelan joined in. Nassau was enraged and told Miranda that Spanish women were all prostitutes and most were infected with venereal diseases. Indeed when he met the notorious Duchess of Alba, a Spaniard immediately warned him that she was 'infested'. This incensed Miranda, and the two argued over whose nation was more poxed. No doubt Potemkin enjoyed all this hugely and the journey passed all the more quickly.[14]

On the 20th, Potemkin's party set off across the steppes back to Kherson: as usual they travelled all night through the isthmus and rested for breakfast at Perekop, where Miranda admired one of Potemkin's new breed of lambs. It was so cold, the travellers' faces were frozen. 'They rubbed snow and fat on them which is the treatment used here.' Bauer, Potemkin's adjutant, awaited them. He had made it from Tsarskoe Selo in seven and a half days to announce that the Empress was on her way to rendezvous with Potemkin at Kiev.[15]

At 11 o'clock on the freezing morning of 7 January, fourteen carriages, 124 sledges (and forty reserves) set off from Tsarskoe Selo to the sound of cannon salutes. Five hundred and sixty horses awaited them at each post. Catherine's entourage of twenty-two consisted of her senior court-iers and Ségur, Cobenzl and Fitzherbert, the ambassadors of France, Austria and England. All were wrapped in bearskins and sable bonnets. They were accompanied by hundreds of servants, including twenty footmen, thirty washerwomen, silver polishers, apothecaries, doctors and blackamoors.

The Empress's carriage, drawn by ten horses and lined with cushioned benches and carpets, was so cavernous that a man could stand up in it. It was a six-seater. Every seat mattered.* On that first day, it bore the Empress herself, 'Redcoat' Mamonov, Lady-in-Waiting Protosova, Master of the Horse Naryshkin, Chief Chamberlain Shuvalov and Cobenzl. The key to the bone-jolting royal travel of those days was to fight boredom without offending diplomacy. So, every other day, Shuvalov and Naryshkin swapped places with Ségur and Fitzherbert,[16] whom Catherine called her 'Pocket Ministers'.[17] Each knew that they were about to witness the spectacle of a lifetime.

When it got dark at 3 p.m., the carriages and sledges rushed along icy lanes through the cold winter nights illuminated by bonfires of cypresses, birch and fir, on both sides of the road, to form 'avenues of fire brighter than daylight'. Potemkin had ordered them to be stoked night and day. The Empress tried to follow the same routine as she did in Petersburg, rising at 6 a.m., then working. She breakfasted with her 'Pocket Min-isters' before resuming the journey at 9 a.m., halting at 2 p.m. for dinner, then travelling until 7 p.m. Everywhere there were palaces prepared for her: their stoves were so piping-hot that Ségur was 'more alarmed at the heat ... than the cold outside'. There were cards and conversation until

* The Empress's trip was the cause of another row with her Heir: she wanted to take the little princes, Alexander and Constantine, with her. Grand Duke Paul bitterly objected: he wished to come on the trip as well, but Catherine was not going to allow 'Die schwere Bagage' to spoil her glory. Paul even appealed desperately to Potemkin to stop the children going, a humiliating recognition of his power. Potemkin probably helped the children stay with the parents, a sign of kindness overcoming expediency; but Alexander fell ill, which actually solved the problem.

9 p.m., when the Empress withdrew to work until bedtime. Ségur enjoyed the experience, though none of his risqué jokes were tolerated; the melancholy Fitzherbert, feeling liverish and leaving a Russian mistress behind, was bored. He complained to Jeremy Bentham about 'the same furniture, same victuals': it was 'only St Petersburg carried up and down the empire'.[18] While she settled down with 'Redcoat' in her palace, the ambassadors were as likely to find themselves in a fetid peasant cottage as in a manorhouse.[19]

Heading south-west towards Kiev, the foreigners observed traditional Russia: 'a quarter of an hour before Her Majesty comes up to them', the peasants 'lay themselves flat on the ground and rise again a quarter of an hour after we have passed'.[20] Crowds gathered to welcome the Empress but, like Frederick the Great, she disdained their admiration: 'They'd come out in crowds to watch a bear too.'[21] The Empress passed through Potemkin's estate, Krichev, and Jeremy Bentham saw her progress down the main street, 'edged with branches of firs and other evergreens, and illuminated with tar barrels'.[22] There were balls every day, everywhere: 'that's how we travel', she boasted to Grimm.[23]

On 29 January, she arrived at Kiev, where the Court was to reside for three months until the ice on the Dnieper melted. A 'multitude of travellers from all parts of Europe' awaited her – including Ligne.[24] The roads to Kiev were jammed with grandees. 'I have never in my life met with so much gaiety, so much charm and wit,' wrote a Polish noblewoman on her way to court Catherine and Potemkin.* 'Our little dinners in these squalid Jewish inns are quite exquisite ... If one closes one's eyes, one imagines oneself in Paris.'[25]

Catherine received this letter from Potemkin in the Crimea: 'Here the greenery in the meadows is starting to break through. I think the flowers are coming soon ... I pray to God that this land will be lucky enough to please you, my foster-mother. That is the source of all my happiness. Goodbye, my dear Matushka.'[26]

Accompanied by music and the bickering of his companions about national venereal customs, Potemkin travelled day and night, 'at the speed of the devil' according to Nassau, to reach Kremenchuk.[27] Regard-

---

* This was Countess Mniszech, née Urszula Zamoyska, the King of Poland's niece. Stanislas-Augustus claimed that Potemkin had proposed marriage to her back in 1775. For obvious reasons, this was unlikely. Now Potemkin, who evidently bore no ill feelings, had her decorated by Catherine, along with Alexandra Branicka.

less of the vast responsibilities on his shoulders, with emperors, kings and half the courtiers in Europe converging to view his works, the Prince appeared to spend his days listening to concerts. 'We had music and more music,' marvelled Miranda – hornplayers one day, a Sarti oratorio the next, a Ukrainian choir, then more Boccherini quartets. But beneath the nonchalance Potemkin must have been working and biting his nails like never before. Not everything was perfect: two days after Catherine arrived in Kiev, he inspected ten squadrons of Dragoons. 'It was horrible,' noted Miranda. 'PP was not very happy.' Another squadron of Cuirassiers near Poltava was too much of a mess to be inspected at all.

As the Empress waited in Kiev, the Prince's arrangements accelerated with the unpredictability that was his only rhythm. He ordered Nassau and Miranda to meet the Empress with him. On 4 February, after inspecting troops and attending parties, Potemkin met the exiled Moldavian Hospodar, Alexander Mavrocordato, who had just been deposed by the Turks contrary to the spirit of Kuchuk-Kainardzhi – a reminder of the rising tension between Russia and the Sublime Porte.

Miranda rushed to get courtier's suits made. When he got home, he found his servant had procured him a Russian girl 'who owes nothing in bed to the most lascivious Andalusian'. Next morning, an adjutant announced that Potemkin had left in a *kibitka* at 5 a.m. 'without saying anything to anybody'. At 3 p.m., Nassau and Miranda set off in pursuit, each in their own *kibitka* capsule. They never caught up of course, because no one had reduced the hours of eighteenth-century travel to such a fine art as Potemkin. The snow was soft. The sledges got stuck or overturned. New horses were ordered. There were delays of hours. When Miranda arrived at the Kiev customs two days later, he found that Nassau had commandeered Potemkin's messages – typical of that unscrupulous intriguer. 'What a mess,' wrote Miranda.[28]

Kiev, on the right bank of the Dnieper, was a 'Graeco-Scythian' vision of 'ruins, convents, churches, unfinished palaces', an ancient Russian city fallen on hard times.[29] When everyone had arrived, there were three luxurious *tableaux*: first, 'the eye was astonished to see, all at one time, a sumptuous court, a conquering Empress, a rich and quarrelsome nobility, proud and luxurious princes and grandees' and all the peoples of the Empire: Don Cossacks, Georgian princes, Kirghiz chieftains and 'savage Kalmyks, true image of the Huns'. Ségur called it a 'magical theatre that seemed to confuse and mix antiquity with modern times, civilization and barbarism'.[30]

Cobenzl's house was like a gentleman's club for the foreigners, though the other two 'Pocket Ministers' each had a little mansion of his own. There were French, Germans, lots of Poles and some Americans, including the diminutive and aptly named Lewis Littlepage, recently appointed chamberlain to Stanislas-Augustus, King of Poland. Aged twenty-five, this Virginian gentleman and friend of George Washington had fought the British at Gibraltar and Minorca, and was an enthusiastic amateur actor–producer, who staged the Polish première of the *Barber of Seville* at Nassau's house. Now he became Stanislas-Augustus' eyes at the Court of Potemkin.[31] The doyen of these foreigners was the Prince de Ligne – 'affectionate with his equals, popular with his inferiors, familiar with princes and even sovereigns, he put everyone at their ease'. Not everyone was so charmed by charm itself: Miranda found him a nauseating flatterer.[32]

Then there was the Court of Potemkin. That coenobite moved directly into the massive monastery of the Caves, half-church, half-fortress, a sepulchral medieval labyrinth of subterranean halls, churches with twenty-one domes, and troglodyte cells, many of them cut into the caves beneath the city. Seventy-five saints lay undecayed in silk, cool in their catacombs. When Potemkin received his courtiers there, it seemed 'one entered an audience with the vizier of Constantinople, Baghdad or Cairo. Silence and a sort of fear ruled there.' The Prince appeared at Court in his marshal's uniform, clanking with medals and diamonds, laced, powdered and buckled; but at his monastery he stretched out on a divan in his favourite *pelisse*, thick hair uncombed, pretending to be 'too busy playing chess to notice' his Court of Polish princelings and Georgian tsareviches. Ségur worried he would be mocked for exposing the dignity of the King of France to such hauteur, 'so this was the way I played it . . .'. When Potemkin did not even raise his eyes from the chessboard, Ségur approached him, took his leonine head in his hands, embraced him and sat down casually beside him on the sofa. In private, Serenissimus dropped his haughtiness and was his old cheerful self,[33] surrounded by nieces Branicka and Skavronskaya, Nassau, Miranda and his composer Sarti, 'dressed as a ridiculous macaroni'. He cherished his dear friend Ségur 'like a child'.*

---

* Once in this intimate circle, Ségur noticed that Potemkin kept slipping away to a back room. When he tried to follow, the nieces detained him with 'charming cajolery'. Finally he escaped to discover the Oriental scene of a room filled with jewels and forbidden merchandise, surrounded by merchants and onlookers. At the centre of it was his own valet Evrard, who had been caught red-handed smuggling and whose goods were thus being sold off, with Potemkin doubtless getting the best of the gems. The highly embarrassed Ségur sacked his valet on the spot, but the nieces, who were evidently

Kiev became the Russian capital. Even Ligne was amazed at the sights: 'Good Heavens! What a retinue! What noise! What a quantity of diamonds, gold stars and orders! How many chains, ribbons, turbans and red caps brimmed with furs or sharp-pointed!'[34] Potemkin took his guests, Miranda and Nassau, on a roving debauch of card games, dinners and dances. The nieces were more than ever treated like grand duchesses: at Branicka's house, where ambassadors and Russian ministers gathered, Miranda could barely believed the 'wealth and magnificence' of the Polish 'kinglets' like Potocki and Sapieha.[35]

On 14 February, Potemkin had Miranda presented to the Empress. She was taken with his machismo, questioning him about the Inquisition, of which he claimed to be a victim. From then on, Miranda was included in Catherine's intimate circle as well as Potemkin's. Soon he was rather blasé. 'Whist with the usual people,' he wrote. Nassau complained to his wife that the stakes were a 'bit expensive – 200 roubles'. What did he expect if he played with the Empress and Serenissimus? Most evenings ended in relaxed decadence at Lev Naryshkin's – just like in Petersburg.[36]

There was the usual fascination with Catherine's and Potemkin's sex lives. The ambassadors scribbled reports back to their Courts and all the travellers recorded anything they could glean. Catherine was always accompanied by Mamonov, who 'owes his fortune to Prince Potemkin and knows it', according to Nassau, but this did not prevent false rumours about Miranda. 'Nothing escaped his penetration, not even the Empress of all the Russias,' claimed a young, envious American diplomat, Stephen Sayre, 'a mortifying declaration for me to make who was 21 months in her capital without ever making myself acquainted with the internal parts of her extensive and well known dominions.'[37]

The *soi-disant* 'Countess' Sevres, escorted by Mademoiselle Guibald, began the Kiev sojourn in possession of Potemkin's 'momentary adoration'. Then there were his two nieces, but Sevres was soon replaced as 'favourite sultana' by a Naryshkina,[38] who was admired by Miranda at one of Naryshkin's fêtes. The Empress dined there. 'There were games and music with dancing.' Catherine played whist with Potemkin, Ségur and Mamonov and then summoned Miranda to discuss the architecture of Granada. When she left as usual at 10 p.m., the real fun began. Naryshkina danced a Cossack jig then a Russian one, 'which was more lascivious', thought Miranda, 'than our fandango . . . what a good dancer

delighted with the latest fashions from Paris, dissuaded him. 'You had better be nice to him,' said Potemkin, 'since by a strange chance, you find yourself to be his . . . accomplice.' His valet may have been caught with contraband, but the Ambassador of the Most Christian Majesty had clearly been set up for one of Potemkin's jokes.

... what a soft movement of the shoulders and back! She could raise the dead!'

Serenissimus evidently shared Miranda's admiration for her res- urrectory talents for he spent 'an hour *tête-à-tête* with Mademoiselle M. Nari ... to persuade her of some political affair'. Miranda could hear her 'giving sighs' and exclaiming '*if that was true!*' to Potemkin's stories.[39] A dubious source also claimed that Potemkin pounced on Zakhar Cher- nyshev's daughter right outside Catherine's rooms.* The girl screamed, waking up Catherine. This is unlikely since he was hardly short of female company.[40]

The Prince's entourage, including Miranda and Nassau, lodged with him at the Monastery – but none behaved like monks. Kiev buzzed with merriment – a bonanza for the whores of the Ukraine. Miranda and Kiselev, one of Potemkin's adjutants, 'went to the house of a Jewish woman of Polish descent who had very good girls and offered the best tonight', but when they returned after the afternoon at Field-Marshal Rumiantsev-Zadunaisky's, 'I only found a very average Polish woman.' Miranda was surprised that even the girls in Ukrainian provinces wore French fashions: 'God damn it! How far has hellish Gallic frivolity contaminated the human race?' There was such competition for Kiev's overworked *horizontales* between different courtiers that, just as Miranda and Potemkin's adjutant turned up, Catherine's young cham- berlains arrived in force and hogged all the girls. Miranda was furious: he took his pleasures seriously. Finally he found his Polish-Jewish procuress, but, when he tried to explain to the pander what services Kiselev desired, the Russian officer too became angry. 'Oh, how difficult it is for men to act liberally in matters of love and sexual preference!', grumbled Miranda. The two Lotharios had better luck a few days later at a house with an eighteen-year-old courtesan and her maid. Kiselev tackled the maid. Miranda 'tried to conquer the mistress who in the end agreed on three ducats (she wanted ten)'. He stayed happily 'with my nymph in bed ... she was very good and I enjoyed it', but perhaps not as much as he wished: 'she did not let me put it in'. Early next morning: 'Holy Thursday. We attended a solemn mass in the Church of Pechersky with the Empress present ...'. Such, from Polish-Jewish trolls to solemn imperial mass, was life in Kiev.[41]

There was seething intrigue behind the pleasure-seeking. The ambas-

* This resembles Lord Palmerston's attempt to ravish one of Queen Victoria's ladies- in-waiting at Windsor – except that Catherine was probably as amused as the Queen was not.

sadors tried to learn what was really happening, but 'political secrets remained concealed between Catherine, Prince Potemkin and Count Bezborodko'. When Ségur announced that in faraway Paris Louis XVI had called the fatal Assembly of Notables, the first step towards the French Revolution, the Empress congratulated him. 'Everybody's mind was secretly stirred up by liberal sentiments, the desire for reform.' Catherine and Potemkin talked reform but understood the ominous signs in Paris. 'We're not impressed,' Catherine told Grimm, promising that Potemkin would send him some 'Dervish music'.[42]

Icy realities were manifested in the presence there of the richest and most restless of Poland's overmighty 'kinglets'. 'Half Poland is here,' Catherine told Grimm. The Empress was in the process of arranging to meet her ex-lover from the 1750s, King Stanislas-Augustus of Poland. Potemkin decided to see him first in order to discuss the agenda for the summit with Catherine. Serenissimus was continuing to cultivate Poland as a personal insurance policy as well as increasingly conducting Russian policy there. He had that special Smolensk *szlachta* sympathy for Poland from his childhood, but his two immediate aims were to build up a personal position as a Polish magnate and to win Polish support for the coming war against the Turks.

Polish affairs were so complex and unstable that Potemkin remained uncommitted to any one policy, preferring to move in mysterious and flexible ways. He conducted at least three policies simultaneously. He continued to run the pro-Russian Polish party, which was hostile to King Stanislas-Augustus, around his nephew Branicki and a camarilla of magnates.[43]

In late 1786, he began to pursue a second policy – the purchase of huge estates in Poland itself, made possible by his *indigenat* of 1775. (He had sold some Russian estates in 1783 and was about to sell the Krichev complex.) Now he told Miranda that he had just bought Polish estates that extended over 300,000 acres and cost two million roubles.[44] The rumour went round Kiev that these estates contained 300 villages and 60,000 souls.[45] In late 1786, the Prince made a complicated deal with Prince Ksawery Lubomirski to buy the massive Smila and Meschiricz estates on the right bank of the Dnieper in the triangle of the Polish Palatinate of Kiev that jutted into Russian territory. Smila alone was so extensive that, at his death, it contained 112,000 male souls, giving it a total population the size of a small eighteenth-century city. It had its own baronial Court, its own judicial system and even a private army.[46]

He bought the estates with his own money, but it all derived from the

Treasury in one way or another and he regarded this purchase as an imperial, as well as a private, enterprise. Lubomirski was already one of the main contractors of timber for Potemkin's Black Sea Fleet, so he was buying his own suppliers to create a semi-private, semi-imperial conglomerate.[47] But there was more to it than that: the deal made Potemkin a Polish magnate in his own right – the foundations of his own private principality outside Russia. It was also a form of privatized annexation of Polish territory – and a Trojan Horse that would give him the right to penetrate Polish institutions. Catherine had tried to give Potemkin the Duchy of Courland and the new Kingdom of Dacia, if not the crown of Poland itself. 'From his newly bought lands in Poland,' she commented in Kiev to her secretary, 'Potemkin will perhaps make a *tertium quid* independent of both Russia and Poland.' She understood the danger of Paul's accession to her dear consort – but it also made her uneasy. Later that year, he explained to her that he had bought these lands 'to become a landowner and to gain the right to enter both their affairs and their military command'.[48] Like everything connected with Poland, the Smila purchase proved to be a quagmire, igniting a series of court cases and family arguments among the Lubomirskis that embroiled Potemkin in four years of negotiations and litigation.[49]

King Stanislas-Augustus represented the third strand of Potemkin's Polish policy. While undermining him with Branicki and his land purchases, Potemkin had always had a soft spot for Stanislas-Augustus, that powerless aesthete and overly sincere patron of the Enlightenment: their correspondence was warmer than just diplomatic courtesy, at least on Potemkin's side. The Prince believed that a treaty with Stanislas-Augustus would buy Polish support against the Turks and keep Poland in the Russian sphere of influence and out of the greedy paws of Prussia. Personally, Potemkin could then command Polish troops as a magnate. All this could be most easily achieved through King Stanislas-Augustus.

The Poles themselves were in Kiev to undermine their own king before the meeting with Catherine, and win Serenissimus' favour.[50] 'These first-rank Polish are humble and sycophantic before Prince Potemkin,' observed Miranda at a dinner at the Branickis'. Politics and adultery were the undercurrents, as all the Poles 'tricked themselves, and were tricked, or tricked others, all very amiable, less so it is true than their wives ...'. Indeed their entire display was to raise their prestige in the eyes of Potemkin, 'but his glance is hard to catch', joked Ligne, 'since he has only one eye and is short-sighted'.[51]

Potemkin demonstrated his power by favouring one Pole and humiliating another. Everyone was jealous of Potemkin's attention. Ligne,

Nassau and Lewis Littlepage intrigued with the Poles on behalf of their masters. Branicki envied Nassau, because the latter was staying with Potemkin – and therefore was 'master of the field of battle.'[52] Branicki and Felix Potocki tried to persuade Potemkin that Stanislas-Augustus opposed his land acquisitions, which had understandably caused some unease in Warsaw.[53] Alexandra Branicka was already so close to the Empress that Polish gossip claimed she was her natural daughter.[54] The Prince was irritated by Branicki's bungling intrigues, so there was a 'terrible scene', which made Alexandra ill.[55] Yet he had Branicki and Felix Potocki received warmly by the Empress, while she 'did not even cast a glance' at his critics, Ignacy Potocki and Prince Sapieha.[56]

Even Miranda managed to become caught up in this Polish game. He greeted the Prince in front of some Polish magnates without standing up. Miranda should have known that royalty, of whom Potemkin was by now almost one, are touchy about etiquette. Strangers could never take Potemkin's favour for granted. Rumours that Miranda was neither a Spanish count nor a colonel may have also played some part in this cooling. Potemkin gave him the icy treatment.[57]

In early March, the Prince, accompanied by Nassau, Branicki and Stackelberg, the Russian Ambassador to Warsaw, travelled the twenty-eight miles to Chwastow to meet the King of Poland, who nervously awaited his rendezvous with Catherine after so many years.[58] Potemkin wore the uniform of a Polish *szlachta* of the Palatinate of Bratslav and his Polish orders. He treated the King, accompanied by Littlepage, like his own monarch. The two men agreed on Potemkin's suggestion of a Russo-Polish treaty against the Ottomans. Serenissimus let Stackelberg sound out Stanislas-Augustus on his plans to set himself up in a feudal principality at Smila. The King responded that he wanted Russian agreement on reforming the Polish constitution. Potemkin denounced Ignacy Potocki as 'a *scelerat*' – a fossil, Felix Potocki was 'a fool', but Branicki was really not a bad fellow.[59] Potemkin was 'enchanted' by the King[60] – 'for at least a moment'.[61] The coming meeting with Catherine was confirmed.

Back in Kiev two days later, Miranda awaited Potemkin's return nervously. But the Prince, whose sulks never lasted long, greeted him like a long-lost friend: 'it seems a century since we last saw each other', he boomed.[62] As Catherine's departure got closer, it was time to leave Miranda behind. The Empress, via Mamonov, offered him Russian service, but he revealed his hopes for a Venezuelan revolt against Spain. Catherine and Potemkin were sympathetic to this anti-Bourbon project.

'If the Inquisition is so necessary, then they should appoint Miranda as Inquisitor,' joked Potemkin. Catherine offered him the use of all Russian missions abroad and he cheekily requested 10,000 roubles of credit. Mamonov told Miranda that Serenissimus would have to approve, more evidence of Catherine's and Potemkin's near equality. Potemkin agreed. On 22 April, the future (if short-lived) dictator of Venezuela took his leave of Empress and Prince. The Spanish caught up with Francisco de Miranda in the end. Later that year in Petersburg, the two Bourbon ambassadors threatened to withdraw unless the fake Count–Colonel was expelled. In the end, he never got the full 10,000 roubles – but he did keep in contact with Potemkin: the archives reveal that he sent him a telescope from London as a present.[63]

Just as everyone was getting exceptionally tired of Kiev, which Catherine called 'abominable',[64] artillery salvoes announced that the ice had melted and the show could begin. At midday on 22 April 1787, the Empress embarked on her galley in the most luxurious fleet ever seen on a great river.

24

CLEOPATRA

The barge she sat in, like a burnish'd throne,
Burn'd on the water, the poop was beaten gold,
Purple the sails, and so perfumed, that
The winds were lovesick with them, the oars were silver
Which to the tune of flutes kept stroke, and made
The water which they beat to follow faster,
As amorous of their strokes. For her own person,
It beggar'd all description . . .
William Shakespeare, *Antony and Cleopatra*

At midday on 22 April 1787, Catherine, Potemkin and their entourage boarded the dining barge, where a feast for fifty was laid out. At 3 p.m., the fleet moved off. The seven imperial galleys of the Prince's sublime fleet were elegant, comfortable and majestic, painted in gold and scarlet on the outside, decorated in gold and silk inside, propelled and served by 3,000 oarsmen, crew and guards, and attended by over eighty other boats.[1] Each had its own orchestra, always on deck, which played as the guests embarked or disembarked. On Catherine's barge, the *Dnieper*, the orchestra was conducted by Potemkin's maestro, Sarti. Her boudoir had twin beds for her and Mamonov. Each barge had a communal drawing room, library, music-room and canopy on deck. The sumptuous bedroom suites were hung with Chinese silk, with beds in taffeta; the studies had mahogany writing-tables, a comfortable chintz-covered divan and even lavatories with their own water-supply, a novelty on land let alone on the Dnieper. The floating dining-hall could seat seventy.

The dazzling, almost mythical, memory of this cruise remained with all its guests for the rest of their lives. 'A multitude of sloops and boats hovered unceasingly at the head and sides of the fleet which looked like something out of a fairy-tale,' remembered Ségur. Onlookers gave 'thundering acclamations as they saw the sailors of her majestic squadron rhythmically dip their painted oars into the waters of the Dnieper to the roar of the guns'. It was like 'Cleopatra's fleet . . . never was there a more brilliant and agreeable voyage', thought Ligne. 'It's true', Nassau told his wife, 'that our gathering on this galley is one of the most unique things ever seen.'

The Prince presented a perpetual spectacle along the riverside: as they set off to cannon salvoes and symphonies, small squadrons of Cossacks manoeuvred over the plains. 'Towns, villages, country houses and some-times rustic huts were so wonderfully adorned and disguised with gar-lands of flowers and splendid architectural decorations that they seemed to be transformed before our eyes into superb cities, palaces suddenly sprang up and magically created gardens.'

Potemkin's barge, the *Bug*, housed himself, his nieces, their husbands and Nassau-Siegen. The tedium of Kiev was left behind, but the malice and mischief cruised down the Dnieper with them. 'I love being with the Prince, who really likes me,' Nassau told his wife, 'despite my companions who loathe me.' Later he made friends with Branicki. The ex-lover of the Queen of Tahiti and almost-King of Ouidah drew a picture for his wife of their living quarters on the 'big and ornate' barge: Potemkin occupied the largest suite and no one could reach their rooms without passing through his salon. Catherine's first rendezvous was with the King of Poland five days downriver, and Potemkin's barge was a floating confederation of Polish intrigues. Nassau, still on his mission for Stanislas-Augustus against Branicki and trying to make his fortune, always awoke early and roused Potemkin to get him on his own.

The mornings were free. At midday, the Empress's galley fired a cannon to announce dinner, sometimes for only ten guests, who were rowed over. Afterwards, Nassau was conveyed to the barge of Ligne and Ségur, where the former would read out his diaries. At 6 p.m., it was back to the Empress's boat for supper. She always retired at 9 p.m. and 'everyone goes to Prince Potemkin's'. But, despite this unprecedented pomp, the tour was intimate. One night, Mamonov, bored with his early imperial lights-out, asked Nassau and some others to stay for a game of whist. Scarcely had they begun to play in Catherine's salon than she entered with her hair down, holding her bed bonnet and wearing an apricot-coloured taffeta dressing gown with blue ribbons. This was a unique glimpse of how the older Catherine looked to her young lovers behind bedroom doors. 'Having her hair uncovered makes her look younger,' remarked Nassau. She hoped she was not disturbing them, sat down, excused her 'déshabillé' and was 'very cheerful'. She retired at 10 p.m. The whist ended at 1.30 a.m.

'The journey is truly a continual party and absolutely superb,' Nassau reported. 'A charming society because Ligne and Ségur make it great.' The pair, who shared the *Sejm*, were to become the naughty schoolboys of the tour, always up to horseplay. Every morning, Ligne knocked on the thin partition separating their bedrooms to recite impromptu poems to Ségur and then sent over his page with letters of 'wisdom, folly, politics, pretty speeches, military anecdotes and philosophical epigrams'. Nothing could have been stranger than this sunrise correspondence 'between an Austrian general and a French ambassador lying side by side on the same barge, not far from the empress of the North, sailing down the Dnieper, through Cossack country, to visit the Tartars'. Ségur thought the visions of the cruise almost poetical: 'The beautiful wealth, the magnificence of our fleet, the majesty of the river, the movement, the joy of countless spectators along the riverside, the military and Asiatic mixture of costumes of thirty different nations, finally the certainty of seeing new things each day, stirred and sharpened our imagination.' The sheer success of these spectacles reflected on the magnificent showman: 'The elements, seasons, nature and art all seemed to conspire to assure the triumph of this powerful favourite.'[2]

After three days of Cleopatran cruising, the King of Poland, Stanislas-Augustus, touched with romantic memories and political panaceas, waited at Kaniev on the Polish bank to meet the Empress. There was pathos in this meeting: when they had last met, he was a young Polish dreamer and she the oppressed wife of an imbecilic bully. Now he was a king and she an empress. He had not seen the woman he never really stopped loving for twenty-eight years and had probably indulged himself with fantasies of a reunion. 'You can easily imagine', the King confessed to Potemkin in an unpublished note back in February, 'with what excitement I await the moment which should give me this joy.' It was the sort of doomed sentimentality that would have struck a cord in Potemkin.[3]

Stanislas-Augustus remained handsome, sensitive, cultured, but above all he wanted to do the best that he could for Poland. Potemkin and Stanislas-Augustus shared interests in opera, architecture and literature, yet the latter could not afford to trust the former. The King's lot was nothing but frustration and humiliation. Politically, he had been dealt the weakest imaginable hand. Personally he was no match for politicians like Potemkin. Catherine found the King's political dilemmas irritating and inept – and his personal sincerity almost unbearable. Perhaps, having once loved him so much in the prison of her miserable marriage, the very thought of her impotent naivety in those times embarrassed her.[4]

The real purpose of the meeting was not amorous nostalgia but the survival of Poland. The sprawling chaos, feeble grandeur, stubborn liberty and labyrinthine subtleties of the Commonwealth made it the only political issue that confounded Catherine's orderly mind. Yet these were the very conditions in which the serpentine Potemkin flourished. The plan of the King and Prince, sealed at Chwastow, to form an anti-Turkish alliance and reform the Polish constitution, might have prevented the tragedy of Poland's destruction. But this was an occasion where personal awkwardness undermined political understanding.

The flotilla dropped anchor off Kaniev. At 11 a.m. on 25 April, Bezborodko and Prince Bariatinsky, Marshal of the Court, collected the King in a launch. 'Gentlemen, the King of Poland has asked me to commend Count Poniatowski to your care,' he said, assuming his original name, since kings of Poland could not leave Polish soil. When the King met the Empress, Ségur and the others formed a circle around them to witness their first words 'in circumstances so different from those in which they first met, united by love, separated by jealousy and pursued by hatred'. But their expectations were immediately crushed. There was no spark now. The monarchs walked stiffly on deck. Probably his surging nostalgia could not resist some painful allusions to the past for, when they returned, she was strained and embarrassed, and there was a 'certain trace of sadness' in his eyes. Some said that she used his blandishments to make Mamonov jealous. 'It was thirty years since I'd seen him,' Catherine wrote afterwards, 'and you can imagine that we found each other changed.'[5]

There was one touching moment, after Stanislas-Augustus awkwardly awarded Potemkin's nephew, Engelhardt, the White Eagle. It was time for dinner. The King looked for his hat. Catherine handed it to him. 'To cover my head twice,' he quipped – the first being his crown. 'Ah, madame, that is too much bounty and goodness.' Stanislas-Augustus rested on another barge, then was rowed to Potemkin's floating residence. Serenissimus tried to reconcile the King with Branicki, but the latter behaved so insolently that Stanislas-Augustus left the room. Potemkin rushed after him, apologizing. The Empress and the Prince sharply reprimanded Branicki – but he was family: their Polish creature remained in their entourage.

At 6 p.m., the King returned to Catherine's barge for the political negotiations. He proposed the Russo-Polish alliance, strolling on deck. She promised an answer. The Prince himself nonchalantly played cards near by. Catherine was furious that he did not come to her assistance. 'Why did Prince Potemkin and you have to leave us all the time like that?', she berated Ligne. Stanislas-Augustus begged Catherine to come for supper in Kaniev, where he had almost bankrupted his meagre resources by laying on two days of dinners and fireworks, but Catherine snubbed him. She told Potemkin she did not care to do things in a rush as they did in Poland; 'you yourself know any change of my intentions is unpleasant for me'. Potemkin, whether out of respect for Stanislas-Augustus or out of anger with Catherine for ruining his Polish strategy, kept playing cards and saying nothing. Catherine became angrier and quieter. The King got glummer. The courtiers fidgeted and eavesdropped. 'Prince Potemkin didn't say a word,' Catherine muttered to her secretary the next day. 'I had to talk all the time; my tongue dried up; they almost made me angry by asking me to stay.' Catherine finally deigned to watch Poland's costly fireworks from her barge.

The broken-hearted and humiliated King took his leave. 'Don't look so distressed,' Ligne whispered to him bitchily. 'You're only giving pleasure to a Court which ... detests you.' Catherine remained furious with Potemkin. He sulked on the *Bug*. She sent him a series of notes: 'I'm angry with you, you're horribly maladroit today.' The flotilla waited to watch the fireworks culminating in a simulated eruption of Vesuvius. Thus the King had, in Ligne's inimitable description, 'been here for three months and spent three million to see the Empress for three hours'. Stanislas-Augustus sent this pathetic note in a semi-legible scrawl to Potemkin a few days later: 'I was pleased when I saw the Empress. I don't know her any more, but although one is sad, I count on having Prince Potemkin as a friend.'[6]

Kaiser Joseph II and Tsarina Catherine II, the Caesars of the East, were getting closer. On 30 April, the flotilla rowed late into Kremenchuk, delayed by a high wind. Joseph, again in incognito as Comte de Falkenstein, waited downriver at Kaidak, bristling with military impatience.

Joseph's despotic but rational reforms had already driven several of his provinces into rebellion. He had not wanted to come to Russia at all, but his presence was the most important for the Russians since the Austrian alliance was their main weapon against the Ottomans. 'Perhaps one can find time', Joseph suggested to Chancellor Kaunitz, 'to find an excuse.' The pompous Habsburg thought Catherine's invitation 'most cavalier' so he told Kaunitz his answer would be 'honest, short but will not refrain from letting this Catherinized Princess of Zerbst know she should put a little more consideration ... in disposing of me'. He then accepted enthusiastically. He was keen to inspect Russian military forces but, in his heart, was determined to find they could not do anything properly, unlike his Austrians. He wrote ironically to Potemkin that he looked forward to seeing his 'interesting arrangements and surprising creations'. Now the inspector-maniac consoled himself for the wait by inspecting Kherson on his own.[7]

Catherine fretted – where was Joseph? Cobenzl sent his emperor reassuring letters. Potemkin seemed to live only for the moment – though there were rumours that he was short of horses for the rest of the journey. The Empress landed at Kremenchuk and inspected an elegant palace surrounded, of course, by an 'enchanted English garden' of shady foliage, running water and pear trees. Potemkin had had huge oak trees, 'as broad as himself' joked Ligne, transported from afar and assembled into a wood. William Gould had been there. 'Everything is in flower,' the Empress told Grimm. Catherine then inspected 15,000 troops, including seven regiments of Potemkin's new light cavalry, which Cobenzl acclaimed for its men and horses. After giving a ball for 800 that night, Catherine headed downriver for her imperial reunion.[8]

Just as the boats disappeared down the river, Samuel Bentham, leaving brother Jeremy to manage Krichev, sailed into view with his proudest creation: the six-link state vermicular for Catherine.* Among so many wonderful sights, the young Englishman, high on a platform, barking orders through a trumpet, must have provided another. Potemkin ordered him to moor near his barge. Next morning, he inspected it and 'was pleased, as can be', according to Samuel. When the flotilla set off again, Bentham went too. He claimed the Empress noticed his vessels and admired them – but Potemkin was possibly consoling him for missing his moment.

Twenty five miles short of Kaidak, where they were to meet the Emperor, some of the barges ran aground. The flotilla anchored. Potemkin realized they could not go all the way by river. There was a danger that the spectacular would descend into embarrassing chaos: one Empress was grounded; one Emperor was lost; there was a shortage of horses; and the barges containing the food provisions and kitchen grounded on sandbanks. Bentham's 'floating worm' saved the day.

Leaving the Empress behind, Potemkin changed boats and, to Bentham's delight, pushed ahead in the vermicular to find the Emperor. When he got nearer Kaidak, very close to the Sech of the vanquished Zaporogians, he elected to stay on board rather than in one of his local palaces. Next morning, he went off and found Joseph II. That evening, the Emperor returned the compliment on Bentham's vermicular. Bentham was puffed up by the praise of two Caesars and one Prince – but they were much more interested in meeting each other than in viewing ingenious English barges.†

---

* The whole floating worm was 252 feet long and almost 17 feet wide, propelled by 120 rowers.

† 'There is no doubt', Samuel told Jeremy Bentham, deluding himself winningly, 'that the Emperor as well as everybody else praised the invention.'

Potemkin and Joseph decided that the Emperor would 'surprise' the Empress. Monarchs do not appreciate surprises, so Serenissimus sent a courier hotfoot to warn Catherine, and Cobenzl sent a courier back to warn Joseph that Potemkin had warned her: such are the absurdities of serving kings. On 7 May, Catherine abandoned the barges and proceeded by carriage towards this achingly unspontaneous 'surprise'.[9]

Catherine, accompanied by Ligne, Mamonov and Alexandra Branicka, crossed a field and came 'nose to nose' (in her words) with Joseph, who was with Cobenzl. The two Majesties, reunited in one carriage, then headed the thirty versts to Kaidak. There Joseph was appalled to discover that the kitchens and cooks were far behind on the grounded barges. Potemkin galloped off to make arrangements and forgot to eat. Now the Tsarina and Kaiser were without any hope of food. 'There was no one', Joseph noted, 'to cook or serve.' So much for the Emperor who liked to travel without ceremony. The imperial tour threatened to subside into farce.[10]

Potemkin was the master of improvisation just as necessity is the father of invention. 'Prince Potemkin himself became the *chef de cuisine*,' Catherine laughingly told Grimm, 'Prince de Nassau, the kitchen-boy, and Grand General Branicki, the pastry-maker.' The imbroglio in the kitchen, created by a one-eyed Russian giant, an international lion-slaying paladin and a bewhiskered 'Polish bravo', must have been an alarming but comical glimpse of culinary Hades. Potemkin did manage to present a *girandole*, a revolving firework spinning round Catherine's initial, surmounted by 4,000 rockets, and yet another exploding volcanic hill. For eighteenth-century royalty, fireworks and ersatz volcanoes must have been as boring as visits to youth centres and factories today. One wonders if it took their mind off Potemkin's cooking: the three mad cooks had indeed spoiled the broth. Catherine thought 'the two Majesties had never been so grandly and *badly* served' but it was such fun that it was 'as good a dinner as it was bad'. One person – the most important – did not agree.

'The dinner was constructed of uneatable dishes,' the unamused Emperor told Field-Marshal Lacey, but at least 'the company is quite good'. But the Emperor of *Schadenfreude* was secretly delighted – 'the confusion that reigns on this voyage is unbelievable'. He noticed there were 'more things and people on the boats than the carriages could contain and there aren't horses to carry them'. Joseph, twisted with German superiority over the blundering Russians, was 'curious how it will all succeed in the end', but, he ended with a martyred sigh, 'This will truly be a time of penitence.'[11]

Joseph drew Ligne aside when he got the opportunity: 'It seems to me these people want war. Are they ready? I don't believe so; in any case, I'm not.' He had already seen Kherson's ships and forts. The Russians were involved in an arms race, but he believed the whole show was 'to throw dust in our eyes. Nothing is solid and all is done in a hurry in the most expensive way.' Joseph could not quite bring himself to admit that he was impressed. He was right if he thought the magnificence of the tour and Potemkin's achievements were moving Catherine towards war. 'We can start it ourselves,' she told her secretary.

Potemkin wanted to discuss the possibility of war with Joseph himself, so one morning he went to see the Emperor and explained Russian grievances and territorial demands against the Ottomans. Potemkin's shyness prevented him saying all he wanted, so he asked Ligne to do it for him. 'I didn't know he wanted so much,' muttered Joseph. 'I thought taking the Crimea would suffice. But what will they do for me if I have war with Prussia one day? We'll see . . .'[12]

Two days later, the two Caesars arrived, in a grand black carriage with Catherine's crest on the doors, a leather ceiling and red velvet seats, at the desolate foundations of Potemkin's grandiose Ekaterinoslav.* When the two Majesties laid the foundation stones for the cathedral, Joseph whispered to Ségur, 'The Empress has laid the first stone, and I the last.' (He was wrong.) The next day they headed across the steppes, stocked with 'immense herds of sheep, huge numbers of horses',[13] towards Kherson.

On the 12th, they entered Potemkin's first city in a ceremonial procession through an arch emblazoned with an unmistakable challenge to the Sublime Porte: 'This is the road to Byzantium.'[14] Joseph, who had already inspected the town, now had a chance to inspect Catherine's entourage. 'Prince Potemkin alone, mad for music, has 120 musicians with him,' observed the Kaiser, yet 'it took an officer whose hands were horribly burned with gunpowder four days to get help'. As for the Empress's favourite, Joseph thought Mamonov was 'barely intelligent . . . a mere child'. He liked Ségur, thought Fitzherbert was 'clever' though clearly bored, and praised the 'jockey diplomatique', who possessed of all the wit and *joie de vivre* the Emperor lacked: 'Ligne is marvellous here and counts well for my interests.' But Joseph's peripatetic inspections and secret jealousy were not lost on the Russians. Catherine rolled her eyes at her secretary: 'I see and hear everything but I don't run around like the Emperor does.' It was no wonder, she thought, he had driven the burghers of Brabant and Flanders to rebel.[15]

---

* The carriage is in the Dniepropetrovsk State Historical Museum.

Ségur and Ligne were dazzled by Potemkin's achievements there: 'we could not have prevented our plain astonishment', wrote Ségur, 'to see such great new imposing creations'. The fortress was almost finished; there were houses for 24,000; 'several churches of noble architecture'; there were 600 cannons in the Arsenal; 200 merchant ships in the port and two ships-of-the-line and a frigate, ready to launch. The surprise in Catherine's entourage was due to the probably almost universal presumption in Petersburg that Potemkin's achievements were fraudulent. Now Ségur said they all recognized the 'talent and activity of Prince Potemkin'. Catherine herself, who had evidently been told by Potemkin's enemies that it was all lies, told Grimm, 'They can say all they like in St Petersburg – the attentions of Prince Potemkin have transformed this land which, at the peace [1774] was not more than a hut, into a flourishing town.' The foreigners realized the port's limitations – 'they've built a lot at Kherson in the short time since its foundation', wrote Joseph, ' – and it shows.'

On the 15th, Catherine and Joseph launched the three warships from three seaside canopies decorated with 'gauze, laces, furbelows, garlands, pearls and flowers', which Ligne thought looked as if 'they had just come from the milliners' shops in the rue St Honoré'. One of the ships-of-the-line with eighty guns was named *St Joseph* in the Kaiser's honour, but he thought the 'wood is so green ... the masts so bad' that they would soon fall to pieces. They did not.[16]

Before they departed, there was an ominous moment when Catherine decided she wanted to visit her strategic fortress of Kinburn at the mouth of the Dnieper. But an Ottoman squadron cruised the Liman, so the Empress could not go. The Russians were more aware of Turkish eyes watching them than they let on to foreigners. The Russian Ambassador to the Sublime Porte, Yakov Bulgakov, sailed from Constantinople to discuss Turkish policy. Potemkin teased Ségur about the French encouraging the Turks, who had 'good reason to worry'.[17]

After Kherson, the two Caesars headed across the bare steppe towards the Crimea. When Ségur rashly joked about the deserts, Catherine snapped: 'Why put yourself out Monsieur le Comte. If you fear the boredom of deserts, what prevents you leaving for Paris?"[18]

Suddenly the imperial carriage was surrounded by 3,000 Don Cossacks in full regalia, led by their Ataman, in a single row, ready to charge. Among them, there was a squadron of another of Potemkin's favourite steppe horsemen: the ferocious Kalmyks, 'resembling Chinese' thought Nassau. The Cossacks charged and charged again, giving warlike whoops that thrilled Potemkin's guests. Then they split into two halves and

fought a battle. Even Joseph was impressed with their force and endurance: they could do sixty versts a day. 'There's no other cavalry in Europe',
said Nassau, 'who can do it.'

At Kizikerman,* seventy-five versts north-east of Kherson, they came
upon a small stone house and an encampment of tents braided with
silver, the carpets sprinkled with precious gems. When the Cossack
officers were presented to the Empress next morning by Alexandra
Branicka, the diplomats were excited by the Ataman's women: his wife
wore a long dress like a priest's habit, made of 'a brocade of gold and
money'. She wore a sable hat with its base covered in pearls. But Nassau
was most taken with the 'four fingers of pearls' that dangled erotically
over her cheeks, all the way down to her mouth.[19]

At dusk, Joseph and Ségur walked out into the flat, apparently endless
wasteland, nothing but grass all the way to the horizon. 'What a peculiar
land,' said the Holy Roman Emperor. 'And who could have expected to
see me with Catherine the Second and the French and English Ambassadors wandering through a Tartar desert? What a page of history!'

'It's more like a page from the *Arabian Nights*,' replied Ségur.

Then Joseph stopped and rubbed his eyes: 'I don't know if I'm awake
or whether your remark about the Arabian Nights has made me dream.
Look over there!'

A tall tent appeared to be moving towards them, gliding all on its own
over the grass. Kaiser and Count peered at this magical sight: it was an
encampment of Kalmyks who moved their tents without dismantling
them. Thirty Kalmyks came out and surrounded the two men, with no
idea that one of them was an emperor. Ségur went inside. Joseph preferred to wait outside. When Ségur finally emerged, Joseph joked that he
was relieved the Frenchman had been released from his 'imprisonment'.[20]

The Caesars had no sooner passed the Perekop Lines into the Crimea
than there was a roar of hooves and a cloud of dust through which
galloped 1,200 Tartar cavalry. Potemkin's 'Tartar ambuscade' surrounded
the imperial conveyance completely, armed with jewel-encrusted pistols,
engraved curved daggers, lances and bows and arrows, as if the travellers
had suddenly passed backwards into Europe's dark past.

'Wouldn't it cause uproar in Europe, my dear Ségur,' said Ligne, 'if the
1200 Tartars surrounding us decided to gallop us to a small port near by
and there embark the noble Catherine and the great Roman Emperor
and take them to Constantinople for the amusement and satisfaction of

* Potemkin preferred its Greek name, Olviopol.

Abdul-Hamid?' Luckily Catherine did not overhear Ligne's musings. A guard of Tartar *murza*s, sporting green uniforms richly braided with golden stripes, now formed Catherine's personal escort. Twelve Tartar boys served as her pages.[21]

The carriages and Tartar horsemen seemed to be going faster and faster. They had turned down the steep hill that led to the ancient capital of the Giray Khans: Bakhchisaray. The horses on Catherine and Joseph's eight-seater carriage bolted down the hill. It careered off the road, veering dangerously between rocks. The Tartars galloping alongside tried to get control of it. Catherine showed no fear. The Tartars somehow managed to calm the horses, for they stopped, as suddenly as they had bolted, in the Crimean capital.[22]

The Khan's Palace was an eclectic compound of palace, harem and mosque, built by Ukrainian slaves, to the plans of Persian and Italian architects, in Moorish, Arabian, Chinese and Turkish styles, with peculiar Western touches like Gothic chimneys. Its layout was based on the Ottoman palaces of Constantinople, with their gates and courtyards leading inwards into the Khan's residence and his harem. Its courtyards were silent and serene. Towering walls surrounded secret gardens, soothed by the trickle of elaborate fountains. The hints of Western influence and the thickness of the walls reminded Joseph of a closed Carmelite convent. Beside the khans' mosque, with its high minarets, stood the haunting, noble graveyard of the Giray dynasty: two octagonal rotundas were built around the mausoleums of khans in a field of intricately carved gravestones. Sweet scents rose from burning candles beneath the windows. Around the Palace stood a Tartar town with its baths and minarets, in a valley wedged between two sheer cliffs of rock.* Potemkin had covered these with burning lanterns so that the travellers really felt they resided in a mythical Arabian palace in the middle of an illuminated amphitheatre.[23]

Catherine was staying in the Khan's own apartments, which included the Girays' 'magnificent and eccentric audience chamber' – big and richly ornamented with the defiant Giray declaration that threw down the gauntlet of supremacy to all the dynasties of the East: 'The jealous and envious will have to admit that neither at Ishfan nor Damascus nor Istanbul will they find its equal.' The Habsburg lived in the rooms of a khan's brother. Potemkin, appropriately, lived in the Harem with Ligne,

* Potemkin had Catherine's Crimean progress marked by milestones, engraved in Russian and Turkish and placed every ten kilometres. Only three survive: one stands today outside the Khan's Palace in Bakhchisaray. The Giray graveyard also remains intact, if somewhat overgrown.

who was captivated by the magic of the place. So was Catherine. The delicious sweet scents of the gardens – orange trees, roses, jasmine, pomegranates – pervaded every apartment, each of which had a divan round its walls and a fountain in the middle. At Catherine's dinners, she received the local muftis, whom she treated respectfully. She was inspired by the imams calling the faithful to prayer five times a day outside her window to write a bad, if rhyming, poem to Potemkin: 'Isn't this a place for paradise? My praise to you, my friend.'

After dinner, Joseph rode off to inspect the nearby Chufut Kale, home of the eighth-century Karaite Jewish sect that rejected the Talmud, believed only in the original Torah and lived in joyous isolation in abandoned castles on Crimean mountaintops. Back in Bakhchisaray, Nassau, Ségur and Ligne explored the town, like schoolboys on an exeat. Ligne, despite being twenty years older than Ségur, was the most mischievous, hoping to spot a Tartar girl without her face covered. But that alluring prospect would have to wait. Back in the Harem, Potemkin reclined to watch 'Arab dancers', who, according to Nassau-Siegen, 'did disgusting dances'.[24] After just two nights in Bakhchisaray, the Caesars set off at 9 a.m. on 22 May, surrounded by pages, Tartars and Don Cossacks, to view Potemkin's greatest show of all.

Tsarina and Kaiser were dining splendidly in a pretty palace built on the Heights of Inkerman on a spit of land that jutted out over the sea. Potemkin's orchestra played. The hillsides swarmed with jousting and charging Tartar cavalry. Serenissimus gave a sign. The curtains were drawn back, the doors thrown open on to a balcony. As the monarchs peered out, a squadron of Tartar cavalry in mid-skirmish cantered aside to reveal 'the magnificent sight' that took their breath away.

The amphitheatre of mountains formed a deep and glittering bay. In the midst of it, a numerous and formidable fleet – at least twenty ships-of-the-line and frigates, thought Joseph – stood at anchor, in battle order, facing the very place where the monarchs dined. At another hidden signal from the Prince, the fleet saluted in unison with all its guns: the very sound, remembered Ségur, seemed to announce that the Russian Empire had arrived in the south and that Catherine's 'armies could within 30 hours . . . plant her flags on the walls of Constantinople'. Nassau said the moment was 'almost magical'. This was the naval base of Sebastopol founded three years before. Potemkin had built this entire fleet in just two.

As soon as the guns were silent, Catherine was stimulated by this vision of raw Russian power to rise and offer an emotional toast to her 'best friend', looking at Joseph without naming him.* One can imagine Joseph cringing at her passion, sneering jealously at the Russian success, itching to inspect it himself. Fitzherbert remained utterly phlegmatic.[25] All eyes turned to Potemkin: it was his achievement, a remarkable feat given the sloth of Russian officialdom, the breadth of his responsibilities, the lack of Russian naval expertise, and the distance from the nearest timber in faraway Poland. The Russians present must have thought of Peter the Great's conquest of the Baltic and the foundation of the Russian fleet there. Which courtier would say it first? 'Madam,' said Ségur, 'by creating Sebastopol, you have finished in the south what Peter the Great began in the north.' Nassau embraced Potemkin and then asked to kiss the Empress's hand. She refused. 'It's Prince Potemkin to whom I owe everything,' she said again and again. 'So you must embrace him.' Then she turned laughingly to her dear consort. 'I hope no one is going to say that he's lazy any more,' she said, warning against any hint that his achievements were not real. Potemkin kissed her hands and was so moved that his eyes filled with tears.[26]

Serenissimus led the Tsarina and Emperor down to a landing-stage and on to a rowing-boat, which set off towards Sebastopol and the new fleet. The rest followed in a second sloop. They passed right under the bows of three sixty-six-gun ships-of-the-line, three frigates of fifty guns and ten of forty guns, which saluted the Empress in three more salvoes; sailors cheered her. They disembarked at a stone staircase that led straight up to the Admiralty, where she was staying. Around them was the new city of Sebastopol, 'the most beautiful port I have seen', Joseph wrote. At last, he was full of admiration: '150 ships were there ... ready for all events of the sea.' The port was defended by three batteries. There were houses, shops, two hospitals, and barracks. Cobenzl estimated there would soon be twelve ships-of-the-line. Even Joseph admitted they were 'very well built'. It seemed impossible to Ségur that Potemkin had done this in such a short time. Everything was well done where only three years earlier there had been nothing. 'One must do justice to Prince Potemkin,' Catherine wrote that day to Grimm in Paris. 'The Empress', noted Joseph, 'is totally ecstatic ... Prince Potemkin is at the moment all-powerful and fêted beyond imagination.'

The Caesars and the Prince thought of war. Catherine and Potemkin felt that they could beat the Turks on the spot. The Empress asked Nassau

---

* The Prince de Ligne saw a universal rule about women here: 'The flattery made her drunk ... the inconvenience of women on thrones.'

if he thought her ships were equal to the Ottoman ones at Ochakov. Nassau replied that the Russian vessels could put the Turkish fleet in their pocket if they liked. 'Do you think I dare?', she smiled at Ligne with chilling flirtatiousness. Russia was ready for war, Potemkin 'ceaselessly' told Ligne. If it was not for France, 'we'd begin immediately'.

'But your cannons and munitions are so new,' said Ligne, restraining him on behalf of his Kaiser.

'Everything is there,' replied Serenissimus. 'All I have to do is say to 100,000 men – March!'

Catherine kept her head enough to order Bulgakov to send the Sultan a reassuring note. Neither she nor Potemkin were as warlike as they appeared. Nonetheless, the 'Pocket Ministers', the Sublime Porte and the chancelleries of Europe could have been forgiven for believing that Russia was chomping at the bit.[27]

Catherine retired to talk alone with the overawed Emperor about the timing of war. Potemkin joined them, emphasizing his semi-royal status. Joseph urged caution, citing France and Prussia. Frederick William of Prussia (Frederick the Great had died in 1786) was 'too mediocre' to stop them, claimed Catherine. France will make 'a lot of noise', agreed Potemkin, but 'end up taking part of the cake'. He suggested that France swallow Egypt and Candia (Crete) in the coming carve-up. Besides, added the Empress threateningly, 'I'm strong enough, it suffices that you won't prevent it.' Joseph, terrified of being left out, assured them Russia could count on Austria.[28] Little did any of them realize that the same debate – war or peace – was simultaneously raging, beside the same sea, one day's sailing away, in the Divan of the Sublime Porte. The *canaille* of Constantinople were rioting for war, as thousands of soldiers marched through the streets on their way to the fortresses of the Black Sea and the Balkans.

Joseph invited the diplomats to trot around Sebastopol to discuss the enigma of Potemkin in private. The ability of this exotic eccentric to achieve so much confounded the Emperor. Potemkin was all the more 'extraordinary for his genius for activity', he told Nassau. 'In spite of his bizarreness', Joseph declared to Ségur, 'that unique man' was not only 'useful but necessary' to control a barbaric people like the Russians. Joseph yearned to find some fault, so he suggested to Nassau, who had commanded at sea, that the ships were surely not ready to sail. 'They are ready and entirely armed,' replied the paladin. Joseph for once had to admit defeat: 'The truth is that it is necessary to be here to believe what I see.'[29]

Nassau and Ligne rode off, escorted by Cossacks and Tartars, to inspect

Partheniza and Massandra, the estates given to them by the Prince. Partheniza, Ligne's property, was supposedly the site of the Temple of Diana, where Iphigenia was sacrificed. Ligne was so moved that he wrote a poem to Potemkin. The guests visited the ruins of the ancient city of Khersoneses. Serenissimus headed for the hills for a day, taking Nassau up to relax at an estate so fine he called it 'Tempted'.[30]

25

THE AMAZONS

Assemblage étonnant des dons de la nature
Qui joignez la génie à l'âme le plus pure
Délicat et sensible à la voix de l'honneur
Tendre, compatissant, et rempli de candeur
Aimable, gai, distrait, pensif et penseur sombre
De ton charmant, ce dernier trait est l'ombre
Apprends-moi par quel art, tout se trouve en ta tête?
The Prince de Ligne's poem to Prince Potemkin, written on the
Crimean journey

A regiment of Amazons rode out to meet the Kaiser when he pushed ahead
to inspect Balaclava. Joseph was astonished by this trick of Potemkinian
showmanship. The Prince's Greek, or 'Albanian', military colony there
already sported a neo-Classical costume – breastplates and cloaks, along
with modern pistols. These Amazons were 200 female 'Albanese', all
'pretty women', according to Ligne, wearing skirts of crimson velvet, bordered with gold lace and fringe, green velvet jackets, also bordered with
gold, white gauze turbans, spangles and white ostrich feathers. They were
armed to the teeth 'with muskets, bayonets and lances, Amazonian breastplates and long hair gracefully platted'. This caprice originated in a discussion between Catherine and Potemkin, in Petersburg before the trip,
about the similarities between modern and Classical Greeks. He praised
the courage of his Greeks and their wives. Catherine, no feminist, doubted
the wives were much use. The Prince resolved to prove her wrong.*

The awkward Kaiser so admired this vision that he rewarded the
beautiful nineteen-year-old Amazon commander, Elena Sardanova, wife
of a captain, with a most unimperial kiss on the lips. Then he galloped
back to meet the Empress. She encountered Potemkin's Amazons on her

* Herodotus writes that the Amazons, led by their queen Penthesilea, crossed the Black
Sea, fought the Scythians and then settled with them not far from the Sea of Azov. So
Potemkin would have known that the Crimea was, as it were, the natural habitat of
Amazons. When Potemkin took Miranda to the Crimea, they met a German colonel,
Schutz, whose wife had 'followed him in campaign dressed as a man and been injured
twice – she has a bit of a manly look'. Did Frau Schutz advise on Potemkin's Amazon
Regiment? It seems a coincidence that there should be two households of Amazons in
one small peninsula.

next stop at the Greek village of Kadykovka as she processed down an avenue of laurels, oranges and lemons. Potemkin told her that the Amazons would like to demonstrate their shooting prowess. Catherine, probably secretly bored with military demonstrations, refused. Instead, she embraced Sardanova, gave her a diamond ring worth 1,800 roubles, and 10,000 roubles for her troop.[1]

The Amazons joined Catherine's escort of Tartars, Cossacks and Albanians for the rest of the trip. As the imperial procession trundled along the fecund, mountainous south-eastern shore of the Crimea, its most paradaisical countryside, where they passed Potemkin's vineyards, it must have been quite a sight. The aura of success about the 'Road to Byzantium' allowed the two Caesars to relax. Joseph even admitted that Potemkin kept him waiting in his anteroom like an ordinary courtier but said he could not help but forgive that extraordinary man – quite a departure for a petulant Habsburg.[2]

Bouncing along in their carriage, Catherine and Joseph discussed the sort of things that heads of state have in common. Ligne sat in a royal sandwich between them, drifting off to sleep, only to wake up hearing one say, 'I have thirty million subjects, only counting the male population,' while the other admitted to only twenty million. One asked the other: 'Has anyone ever tried to assassinate you?' They discussed their alliance. 'What the deuce shall we do with Constantinople?', Joseph asked Catherine.[3]

At Kaffa, the old slave port refounded by Potemkin as Theodosia, Serenissimus played one of his tricks on Ségur. As the party climbed into the carriages that morning, Ségur bumped into an exquisite young girl in Circassian dress. The colour drained from his face: she was the precise image of his wife. 'I thought for a moment Madame de Ségur had come from France to meet me. Imagination moves fast in the land of marvels.' The girl disappeared. A beaming Potemkin took her place. 'Isn't the resemblance perfect then?', he asked Ségur, adding that he had seen the wife's portrait in his tent.

'Complete and unbelievable,' replied the stunned husband.

'Well, batushka,' said Potemkin, 'this young Circassian girl belongs to a man who will let me dispose of her and, as soon as you reach St Petersburg, I will give her to you.'

Ségur tried to refuse because his wife might not appreciate this expression of affection. Potemkin was hurt and accused Ségur of false delicacy. So Ségur promised to accept another present,* whatever it might be.[4]

---

* It turned out to be a Kalmyk boy called Nagu, later captured at the storming of Ochakov, to whom Ségur taught French and then managed to unload on a delighted Countess Cobenzl, back in the north.

The party climbed into the rolling, green hills of the interior to view Potemkin's gardens, dairies, flocks of sheep and goats, and his pink 'Tartar' Palace at Karasubazaar.* This, according to an Englishwoman visiting a decade later, was 'one of those fairy palaces' that arose 'as if by magic by the secret arrangement of Potemkin, to surprise and charm'.[5]

They found an English island here. Capability Brown would have recognized the English gardens – 'clumps of majestic trees, a most extensive lawn', leading to 'woods which make a delightful pleasure ground laid out by our countryman Gould', and there was Henderson's English dairy. Potemkin's idyll was incomplete without a full English tea too. Henderson's 'nieces', who had travelled out with Jeremy Bentham, caught Ligne's experienced eye: 'Two heavenly creatures dressed in white' came out, sat the travellers down at a table covered in flowers 'on which they placed butter and cream. It reminded me of breakfast in English novels.' There were barracks and soldiers to inspect for Joseph, but he was completely uncharmed. 'We had to go through mountain roads,' he grumbled to Field-Marshal Lacey, 'just to make us see a billy-goat, an Angora sheep and a sort of English garden.'[6]

Potemkin laid on a *feu d'artifice* that impressed even these firework-weary dignitaries. In the midst of a banquet, 20,000 big rockets exploded and 55,000 burning pots crowned the mountains twice with the initials of the Empress, while the English gardens were illuminated as if it was daylight. Joseph said he had never seen anything more awesome and could only marvel at the power of Potemkin, and therefore the Russian state, to do exactly what he wished, regardless of cost: 'We in Germany or France would never have dared undertake what is being done here ... Here human life and effort count for nothing ... The master orders, the slave obeys.'[7]

When they were back again in Bakhchisaray, Tartar women again occupied the minds of the worldly courtiers. Ligne, younger at fifty than when he was thirty, could no longer restrain his curiosity. 'What's the use of going through an immense garden when one is forbidden to examine the flowers? Before I leave the Crimea, I must at least see a Tartar woman without her veil.' So he asked Ségur: 'Will you accompany me?' Ligne and Ségur set off into the woods. They came upon three

---

* The exact position of this 'fairy abode' – built on the site of the Tartar hut where Potemkin almost died in late 1783 – is now unknown. But when the author visited Beligorsk, Karasubazaar's present name, he found a verdant spot near a river and orchard that fitted the description of the English visitor Maria Guthrie. The Tartars, deported by Stalin, have returned to the village.

damsels washing, with their veils on the ground beside them. 'But alas,' recalled Ségur, none was pretty. Quite the contrary. 'Mon Dieu!', exclaimed Ligne. 'Mahomet was quite right to order them to cover their faces.' The women ran away screaming. The peepers were pursued by Tartars shrieking curses and throwing stones.

Next day at dinner, Catherine was silent, Potemkin sulky – both probably exhausted. Ligne thought he would cheer them up with his naughty escapade. It displeased the Tsarina: 'Gentlemen, this joke was in poor taste.' She had conquered this land and commanded that Islam should be respected. The Tartars were now her subjects under imperial protection. If some of her pages had behaved so childishly, she would have punished them.[8]

Even the Kaiser was affected by the voluptuous atmosphere. Catherine let Joseph, Ligne and Ségur (perhaps as a consolation after their reprimand) watch her audience with a Giray princess. But they were disappointed with this descendant of Genghis: 'her painted eyebrows and shining cosmetics made her look like a piece of china in spite of her lovely eyes', thought Ségur. 'I would have preferred one of her servants,' Joseph told Lacey. The Kaiser was so taken with the beauty of Circassian women that this supposed pillar of the Enlightenment decided to buy one:* he gave one Lieutenant Tsiruli money to set off into the Kuban and purchase a 'pretty Circassian woman'. Potemkin approved it. That mission's outcome is unknown. However, Joseph did return to Vienna with what sounds like a different Circassian girl, aged six, whom he bought from a slave-trader.[9] She was baptized as Elisabeth Gulesy, was educated at Court, and was left a pension in his will of 1,000 Gulden a year, not bad since Mozart's pension, granted in 1787, was only 800. Later she married a nobleman's majordomo and is lost to history.

On 2 June, Their Imperial Majesties finally parted on the steppes at Kizikerman. Joseph headed west towards Vienna, Catherine north towards Moscow. On 8 June, the Empress reached Poltava, the site of Peter the Great's victory over Charles XII of Sweden. Potemkin re-enacted the battle in what Ségur called a huge 'animated tableau, living

---

* Western monarchs often procured Eastern slave girls, despite their disgust for Oriental slavery. There must have been quite a traffic in these girls, who were either captured in war or bought by ambassadors to the Sublime Porte. Hence Potemkin's offer of a girl to Ségur. Frederick the Great's Scottish Jacobite friend Earl Marshal Keith travelled with a Turkish slave girl picked up in the Russo-Turkish Wars, and, as we will see, one of the most cultivated men of the era, King Stanislas-Augustus of Poland, was sent a regular supply.

and moving, almost a reality' with 50,000 troops playing Russians and Swedes. Catherine's eyes shone with Petrine pride. Then Serenissimus presented her with the pearl necklace that he had shown Miranda. In return, Catherine issued a charter acclaiming Potemkin's achievements in the south, granted him 100,000 roubles and the new surname title of 'Tavrichevsky' – he was henceforth known as Kniaz Potemkin-Tavrichesky, Prince Potemkin of Taurida.*

'Papa,' she wrote on 9 June, 'I hope that you let me leave tomorrow without big ceremonies.' Next day, on the approaches to Kharkov, the weary pair parted. Catherine, accompanied by Branicka and 'your kitten' Skavronskaya, as well as the 'Pocket Ministers', met her grandsons, Alexander and Constantine, in Moscow. When she reached Tsarskoe Selo on 22 July, all the travellers on this magical voyage 'had to return to dry political calculations'.[10]

The driest of these calculations was the persistent allegation that Potemkin had deceived Catherine: the calumny of the 'Potemkin Village'. As soon as they arrived back, the 'Pocket Ministers' were interrogated by Potemkin's enemies to learn if Kherson, Sebastopol, the flocks and fleets, were real. But the 'Potemkin Village' was invented by a man who had never visited the south, let alone seen Potemkin's achievements for himself.

Even in the 1770s, malicious rumours had alleged that Potemkin had done nothing in the south. That was manifestly untrue, so now his foes, and those of Russia, whispered that the whole show was a stupendous fraud. The embittered Saxon envoy Georg von Helbig, who was not on the journey, now coined his phrase 'Potemkinsche Dörfer', a concept so suited to political fraud, especially in Russia, that it entered the language to mean 'a sham, a façade, an unreal achievement'. Helbig did not stop at using his clever phrase in his diplomatic despatches but also published a biography, *Potemkin der Taurier*, in the magazine *Minerva* of Hamburg, during the 1790s, which was taken up by the enemies of Russia. Later a full version was published in German in 1809, which was expanded and published in French and English in the nineteenth century. It thus laid the foundation of a historical version of Potemkin that was as fabricated and unjust as it claimed his villages to be. It did not fit Serenissimus – but the mud stuck.[11]

* This translates awkwardly into English but sounds better in German – 'Potemkin der Taurier' – and in French 'le Taurien', the Taurian. Catherine and Grimm discussed how to translate it and the *philosophe* suggested it should be 'Tauricus' or 'le Taurien'.

The cruise along the Dnieper provided the basis of the 'Potemkin Villages': Helbig claimed the settlements there were composed of façades – painted screens on pasteboards – that were moved along the river and seen by the Empress five or six times. Helbig wrote that thousands of peasants had been torn from their homes inside Russia and driven along the riverbank at night with their flocks to be ready for the arrival of the Empress next morning – 1,000 villages had been depopulated and many died of hunger during the resulting famine. The foreigners simply saw the same peasants every day.

The accusation of 'Potemkin Villages' had already been alleged *years before* the trip ever happened. When Kirill Razumovsky visited Kherson in 1782, the very existence of the town was a 'pleasant surprise', evidently because he had been told the project was just a mirage.[12] All foreign visitors to the south were warned in Petersburg that it was a big lie: Lady Craven reported, *a year before* Catherine set off, that 'those at Petersburg who were jealous of Potemkin's merit' told her there was no water in the Crimea – 'his having the Government of Taurida, and commanding the troops in it, may have caused the invention of 1000 ill-natured lies about this new country ... to lessen the share of praise, that is his due'.[13] The Empress had been told for years – whether by the Heir's circle or by envious courtiers – that Potemkin was inventing his achievements. Garnovsky reported to the Prince, *before* Catherine departed, that she was being told that she would see only *painted screens, not real buildings*. In Kiev, the stories became more insistent. One of the reasons Catherine was so keen on the trip was surely to check on things for herself: when Potemkin tried to delay her departure from Kiev because arrangements were not complete, she told her secretary Khrapovitsky that she wanted to see for herself 'in spite of its non-readiness'.[14]

There is absolutely no evidence in Potemkin's own orders or in the accounts of eye-witnesses for the 'Potemkin Villages'. He certainly began his preparations for Catherine's visit as early as 1784, so it is not necessary for us to believe that the whole show was created overnight: that year, General Kahovsky reported that palaces had been built or old houses redecorated for her imminent visit. Potemkin used travelling palaces – but most of Catherine's palaces were permanent: the ones at Kherson survived for more than a century afterwards. In Bakhchisaray, the Khan's Palace was to be 'repaired' and 'repainted'. The next year, in a list of improvements across the Crimea from building new salt stores in Perekop to Gould's chestnut-tree 'paradise' in Kaffa, Potemkin was ordering that, in Bakhchisaray, Kahovsky was to build up 'the large street where the Empress will pass' with 'good houses and shops'.[15] This order to improve some existing buildings is the nearest the thousands of documents in Potemkin's archives yield as evidence of cosmetic presentation. Miranda is a key, unprejudiced witness because he accompanied Potemkin on his pre-trip inspection, but saw nothing being falsified. On the contrary, this witness testifies to the massive reality of Potemkin's work.

What about the dancing peasants and their herds on the riverbanks? It was simply impossible to move such numbers around in those days, especially at night. Cattle and sheep perish if so driven. Potemkin's inability to conceal the fiasco of the lost kitchen of Kaidak, where he himself had to cook dinner for the two monarchs, is more evidence that he was unlikely to have been able to move thousands of men and animals across vast distances to deceive his guests.[16] Nor were these flocks completely new: the nomads there had always kept cattle and sheep. Potemkin added to them and improved their quality: Miranda saw the flocks of sheep on the steppe,[17] while, a year earlier, Lady Craven proves that Potemkin did not need to use magic on the riverbanks and steppes: she watched huge, grazing herds of 'horses, cows and sheep approaching, making at once a simple and majestic landscape full of peace and plenty'.[18] The flocks were there already. They were real.

The crowds did not need to be forced to see the Empress. No tsar had visited the south since Peter the Great sixty years earlier, so who would not hurry to gawp at not one, but *two* Caesars? Even in Smolensk, crowds turned out to see the Empress from twenty leagues away.[19] Besides, the local peasants surely wished to sell produce to the imperial kitchens. When Lady Craven visited Bakhchisaray a year earlier, a solitary, unknown foreigner, the streets were lined by curious and enthusiastic Tartars and soldiers, so their reaction to the arrival of two monarchs was only slightly greater.[20] This is not to say there was no element of show on the banks of the Dnieper: on the contrary, Potemkin beautified and ornamented everything that he could. He was a political impresario who understood the power of presentation and enjoyed the aspect of 'play' in politics, which was entirely self-conscious and deliberate.[21]

Today, a visit by a head of state is routinely prepared and minutely choreographed in detail, houses repainted, streets cleaned, tramps and whores arrested, banners festooned across streets. Brass-bands play, indigenous schoolchildren dance, and the stops at well-stocked shops are prearranged.[22] In many ways, this was the first such visit. Everyone knew that the Amazons, Cossacks and instant English gardens were shows, just as Queen Elizabeth II knows that the Zulu *impis* with *assegai* and shields who perform on her trips are not typical inhabitants of

Johannesburg.* This was what Ségur meant when he said that Potemkin had 'an amazing knack of overcoming all obstacles, conquering Nature ... cheating the eye of the dreary uniformity of the long stretches of sandy plain'.[23]

It is certainly true that, wherever the Empress went, the local officials tidied up the streets, added a lick of paint to buildings and concealed ugliness. In two towns, Kharkov and Tula, not part of Potemkin's show-route, the governors did conceal things from her and may have built false houses.† Thus it is ironic that the sole accounts of 'Potemkin villages' suggest they were not perpetrated by Potemkin at all.[24] One could argue that Potemkin was the inventor of modern political spec-tacle – but not that he was a fairground huckster.

Serenissimus did not *need* to falsify towns and fleets, as the foreigners, from Miranda to Joseph, testify.[25] The Empress could not visit every site and even Potemkin was deceived by his officials, but Kaiser Joseph made a point of inspecting everything and admitted that all was real – though he revealingly added that, if he had not seen things with his own eyes, he would not have believed it.[26] Ligne also went out on his own and discovered 'superb establishments in their infancy, growing manu-factures, villages with regular streets surrounded with trees and irrigated ...'.

Catherine, among other allegations, had been specifically told that Potemkin had ruined the army by reforming the cavalry. When she saw his magnificent light cavalry at Kremenchuk, she felt anger at those who had lied to her, exclaiming to Ligne, 'Wicked people – how they deceived me!'[27] This was the reason for Catherine's double joy at finding that the rumours were lies and her keenness to tell her grandsons and officials like Count Bruce what she had seen: 'It is nice to see these places with my own eyes. They warned me against the Crimea, scaring me and

---

* But not even this was all show: when Lady Craven visited the Albanians in April 1786, they already wore a 'kind of Roman warrior's dress' and had 'Oriental and Italian poniards' while the Cossacks performed for her just for the fun of it.

† There was indeed a famine in certain areas, notably around Moscow, not in Potemkin's richer southern provinces, after a bad harvest in 1786, which was why Catherine hurried back to the capital. When she arrived in Tula, far from Potemkin's Viceroyalty, the local governor concealed local poverty with false façades but also did not inform her of the rising food prices. When Lev Naryshkin told her the bread prices, she, to her credit, cancelled the ball given for her that night. Both Catherine and Potemkin felt the suffering of ordinary people, when they heard about it, but neither would let a minor famine interfere with the glorious aggrandizement of the Empire nor with the magnificence of their lifestyles. But this was a characteristic of all eighteenth-century governments, however enlightened.

dissuading me from seeing it for myself. Having arrived here, I wonder the reason for such rash prejudice.' She even admitted 'her great surprise' that Kherson was so developed. But her assertions did not stop the calumnies against Potemkin.[28]

'Already the ridiculous story has been circulated that pasteboard villages were painted on our roads ... that the ships and guns were painted, the cavalry horseless,' Ligne wrote to Paris. He touched at once on the reasons for it: 'Even those among the Russians, ... vexed at not being with us, will pretend we have been deceived.' Ligne knew 'very well what legerdemain tricks are', but the achievements were real.[29] Potemkin was well aware of the lies spread about him by his enemies. 'And the main thing', he wrote to Catherine afterwards, 'is that malice and jealousy could never harm me in your eyes.' The Empress said he was right: 'You've smacked your enemies' fingers.'[30]

Their fingers might have been smarting, but that did not stop them for long. Back in Petersburg, Potemkin's enemies were determined to discredit him, despite all the evidence. Overexcited courtiers like Evgraf Chertkov (the witness at Potemkin's wedding to Catherine) did not help by telling everyone, 'I saw miracles, which appeared there only God knows how ... It was like a dream ... Only he [Potemkin] is able to do such things.'[31] This was exactly what enemies like Grand Duke Paul wanted to hear.

The Tsarevich summoned Ligne and Ségur to question Potemkin's achievements. He was not going to let the truth interfere with his prejudices. 'In spite of all these two travellers have been able to tell him, he *does not wish* to be persuaded that things are in as good a state as one tells him.'[32] When Ligne conceded that Catherine could not see everything, Paul exploded: 'Oh! I know it very well. It's why this bitch of a nation does not want to be governed only by women!'[33] This determination, even at Court, explains the persistence of the lies even when eye-witnesses disproved them. The lies were amplified by critics of Russian expansion. It is easy to imagine how, once Potemkin and Catherine were dead, this calculated disinformation became transformed into the gospel of history. Even the 1813 English adaptation of Helbig's work concluded that the 'envy which fastens itself upon great men has magnified what was but show, and diminished what was real'.[34] Potemkin was a victim of his own overwhelming triumph. The 'Potemkin Village' is itself one of history's biggest shams.

The new Prince of Taurida sank into one of his bouts of depressed exhaustion, a symptom of the anti-climax after such manic overwork and dazzling success. He remained a few days in Kremenchuk and, in mid-July, set up Court at Kherson, where he fell ill, languishing on his divan, brooding and playing with diamonds. This was not an ideal time for the Prince to be depressed. Since October 1786, he had been in charge of all Ottoman policy and 'arbiter of peace and war'. Now the Ottoman Empire was moving towards war. Ever since the loss of the Crimea and Georgia, and the admission of Russian influence in the Danubian Principalities, the Ottomans had sought the chance to claw back these shameful concessions.[35]

There was tumult in Istanbul as early as March and into May. 'Here, the public talk only of war,' reported Potemkin's best agent, N. Pisani, a scion of one of Istanbul's professional diplomatic families who interpreted and spied for everyone. Sultan Abdul-Hamid, pressured by his pro-war Grand Vizier, Yusuf-Pasha, and the muftis, was deliberately testing Russian resolve: in 1786, the Hospodar of Moldavia Mavrocordato was driven out; Russia gave him refuge. The Georgian Tsar Hercules was being attacked by the local Pasha. The Turks backed Sheikh Mansour and his Chechens, so Potemkin strengthened his Mozdok Line. The Porte refortified its bases from the Kuban to the Danube, from Anapa and Batumi to Bender and Ismail, and rebuilt its fleets, hence the show of strength off Ochakov on Catherine's visit. 'The warriors', added Pisani, 'become daily more insolent and commit all sorts of excesses.'[36]

Potemkin, feeling strong with his new fleet and Catherine's imminent visit, had certainly played a part in this escalating brinkmanship. In December 1786, he had ordered Bulgakov, envoy to the Porte, to demand that these pinpricks in the Danubian Principalities and the Caucasus cease forthwith.[37] He offered either war or the guarantee of Russian Black Sea possessions in return for security for the Ottoman Empire. At that moment, the Sublime Porte leaned towards security. His language was strong, but not excessively provocative. If it had been so, the Ottomans would have attacked during Catherine's visit. Cobenzl thought Potemkin's demands 'very minor'.[38] In March, Potemkin ordered Bulgakov: 'We do everything to avoid war but it will certainly follow if they ignore our requests ... Try to explain to the Sultan how minor and just they are.'[39] When Bulgakov consulted with Potemkin at Kherson that June, the aim was to avoid war, not cause it. In August, Potemkin specifically told Bulgakov to 'win another two years'.[40] Delay was necessary, preparations unfinished.[41]

Serenissimus' martial boasting may have looked like a longing for war, but he had gained the Sech, Crimea and Georgia with the *threat* of war, without losing the bones of a single Ekaterinoslav Grenadier. He knew that ultimately he would have to fight the Turks because their resentment increased with each Russian success. But it is clear that he talked war in order not to have to fight it. However, Potemkin has been blamed for causing the war through his blunderingly aggressive diplomacy. This view is partly based on the hindsight that Russia was bullying the weak Turks, while in fact the Porte was raising armies and fleets that were much improved since their dismal performance in the First Turkish War. It is also based on ignorance of the war fever in Istanbul and the Ottoman policy of provoking Russia in the Caucasus and on the Danube. If the Prince is guilty of anything, it was creating the Black Sea Fleet and arranging the imperial visit to the Crimea: these declared that the Russian presence on the Black Sea was permanent, but also suggested that this was the Porte's last chance to dislodge it. So the arms race and provocations were mutual and simultaneous. The war was caused by a mutual tightening of the screw so that ultimately it came before either side was fully ready for it.

The Russian envoy returned to find Constantinople infected with war fever. Grand Vizier Yusuf-Pasha, supported by the Janissaries and the imams, was deliberately, according to Pisani on 1 June 1787, 'animating the *canaille* ... to intimidate their Sovereign to make him believe the people want war and that otherwise they will rebel against him'. The mob was rioting. Recruits from Asia poured through the city on their way to Ismail, the main fortress of Moldavia. Ottoman armies numbered 300,000. Only the peaceful resolve of the Sultan and his prestigious Capitan-Pasha (Grand Admiral) Hassan-Pasha restrained them.[42] Prussia, Sweden, Britain and France encouraged the Turks – indeed Pisani reported, 'I have in my hands the notebook of the plan' by French officers to retake the Crimea. Finally, the Sultan buckled. The Porte made impossible demands to Bulgakov, such as the return of Georgia and the acceptance of Turkish consuls in Russian cities. Bulgakov rejected them, was arrested on 5 August and thrown into the Seven Towers. On the 20th, Ottoman ships attacked two Russian frigates off Ochakov. After a six-hour battle, the Russians escaped. It was war.[43]

'I am afraid you have no more nails on your fingers,' Catherine declared to Potemkin on 24 August, writing to discuss their strategy, and membership of her Council. 'You've chewed them all off.'[44] How well she knew him. The relationship between Catherine and Potemkin entered a new phase that month: their letters became much longer as the theatre of operations and diplomacy broadened. More than ever, they became

Right: Potemkin's 'Matushka' and 'foster-nurse'. Catherine in the 1780s as she could be seen around the park at Tsarskoe Selo, in a bonnet and walking shoes with her beloved English greyhounds.

Below: Potemkin, in the helmet in the centre, leads the storming of the powerful Turkish fortress of Ochakov in 1788. The Turkish dead were so numerous, they were piled into pyramids on the ice where they froze solid.

Left: Count Alexander Suvorov, Russia's most brilliant general. Tough, cultured and wildly eccentric, he used to perform naked somersaults in front of his army every morning. 'You can't over-Suvorov Suvorov,' said Potemkin.

Below: The invitation to Potemkin's famous ball in the Taurida Palace on 28th April 1791. Catherine and Potemkin wept as he knelt at her feet to say goodbye.

Генералъ Фелдмаршалъ Князь Потемкинъ
Шаврическій проситъ здѣлать ему честь пожаловать
въ понедѣльникъ 28го дня сего Апрѣля въ шесть часовъ по по=
=лудни въ домъ его что въ Конной гвардіи въ маскерадъ,
который удостоенъ будетъ Высочайшаго присутствія

ЕЯ ИМПЕРАТОРСКАГО ВЕЛИЧЕСТВА и
ИХЪ ИМПЕРАТОРСКИХЪ ВЫСОЧЕСТВЪ

Princess Ekaterina Dolgorukaya, Potemkin's mistress near the end of his life. She was a paragon of aristocratic beauty with whom the Prince fell passionately in love, shocking observers by stroking her in public, building her an underground palace, ordering artillery salvoes to mark their caresses, and serving diamonds instead of pudding at her birthday ball.

Countess Sophia Potocka, the 'Beautiful Greek' and outstanding adventuress of the age, said to be the 'prettiest girl in Europe'. She was a spy and courtesan notorious for her 'beauty, vice and crimes' who was sold at the age of 14 by her mother, a fruit-seller in Constantinople, and became one of Potemkin's last mistresses before marrying the fabulously wealthy Polish Count Felix Potocki, seducing her stepson and building a huge fortune.

Prince Platon Zubov, Catherine the Great's last favourite who was vain, silly and politically inept. She nicknamed him 'Blackie'. Potemkin failed to remove him but, as Zubov admitted, Serenissimus remained Catherine's 'exacting husband'.

'Potemkin's death was as extraordinary as his life.' On 5th October 1791 Potemkin, weeping for the Empress, died on the Bessarabian steppes beside the road, in the arms of his favourite niece, Countess Branicka. Branicka fell into a faint. A Cossack commented, 'Lived on gold; died on grass.'

Potemkin's funeral in Jassy was magnificent – but the destiny of his body
was as restless as his life.

partners in both glory and anguish, public and private. They corresponded like an old couple who happen to rule an empire, loving yet often irritated, exchanging political ideas and gossip, giving each other confidence, praise, new clothes and sick remedies. But the Prince, sitting in Kremenchuk, shivered from spasms of fever, and sank deeper in dysphoric darkness. Contrary to the usual histories, he did not neglect his duties but became exhausted because he had concentrated so much power in his own hands. This worried Catherine: 'You do everything yourself so you have no rest.'[45]

Apart from Peter the Great himself, Potemkin was Russia's first commander-in-chief of both military and naval forces across several different theatres of war. As war minister, he was responsible for all fronts, from the Swedish and Chinese borders to those of Poland and Persia. There were two main armies facing the Turks. The Prince commanded the main Ekaterinoslav Army in the centre while Field-Marshal Rumiantsev-Zadunaisky commanded the smaller Ukraine Army that covered him in the west on the Moldavian border. In addition, Potemkin was his own grand admiral of the Black Sea Fleet. In the Caucasus and the Kuban, he commanded the corps fighting both the Ottomans and the Chechen and Circassian tribes led by Sheikh Mansour. None of these forces were complete or fully prepared – though fortunately this was equally true of the Turks. Potemkin amassed his forces and waited for the two out of every 500 levy from the interior to raise 60,000 new recruits. Furthermore he was in charge of co-ordinating operations with his Austrian allies and increasingly, of Russian policy in Poland. It was a gigantic command that required, not only the ability to supply these forces and co-ordinate land and sea operations, but also sweeping strategic vision.

The prime Ottoman aim was to recover the Crimea, using the powerful fortress of Ochakov as their base. They first had to take Potemkin's city of Kherson. The key to Kherson was Kinburn, the small Russian fortress on the end of a spit at the mouth of the Liman, the long estuary of the Dnieper river. Potemkin energetically ordered defensive measures. Forces were sent to Kinburn under Potemkin's best general, Alexander Suvorov. On 14 September, the Turks tried to land at Kinburn but were repelled. The Prince ordered the Black Sea Fleet to put to sea from Sebastopol to hunt the Ottoman fleet, said to be at Varna.[46] Yet Potemkin's fever and depression undermined his strength. 'The illness makes me weaker every day,' he confided in Catherine. If he did not recover, let her give the command to Rumiantsev.[47]

'God forbid to hear you are so sick and weak as to pass the

command to Rumiantsev,' Catherine replied on 6 September. 'You're on my mind day and night ... It's God I ask and pray to save you alive and unharmed – how necessary you are both for me and the Empire, you know that.' She agreed that they had to act defensively until the spring, but they worried whether the Turks would attack before the Russian forces were ready and whether Joseph would honour his side of their treaty.[48]

Her words encouraged him. 'You write to me like a real mother,' he replied and gave her a strategic overview in his usual colourful turn of phrase: Suvorov in Kinburn was 'a man who serves with his sweat and blood' while Kahovsky in the Crimea would 'climb astride a cannon with the same sang-froid with which he would lie on a sofa'. He advised Catherine to appease Britain and Prussia, already foreseeing their policies. Then he suggested that Russia should send its Baltic Fleet to the Mediterranean as it had during the last war. But, even as he wrote, he seemed to collapse again: he could neither sleep nor eat and was 'very weak, millions of troubles, hypochondria too strong. Not even a minute's rest, I'm not even sure I can stand it long.'[49] His letters ceased.

Then suddenly Potemkin's world collapsed. He learned that the Black Sea Fleet, his beloved creation and the very arsenal of Russian power, had been destroyed in a storm on 9 September. He became almost mad. 'I'm exhausted, Matushka,' he wrote on the 19th. 'I'm good for nothing ... God forbid, if any losses happen, if I haven't died of sorrow, I'll throw my merits at your feet and hide in obscurity ... let me rest, a little. Really I can't stand any more ...'. Yet he was also clear-minded and efficient – the armies were forming, manoeuvring and provisioning – and Kinburn was ready: he had done all he could but that did not help his physical and mental state.[50]

'Lady Matushka, I've become unlucky,' Potemkin, who so believed in Providence, wrote to his empress on 24 September. 'Despite all the measures I'm taking, everything's gone topsy-turvy. The Sebastopol Fleet has been crushed ... God defeats me, not the Turks.' His sensitive emotions dived towards the very bottom of his cyclothymic nature at the critical moment for which his entire career had been a preparation. He fell into deep despair, though historically his collapse puts him in good company: Peter the Great suffered almost suicidal emotional crises after Narva in 1700, so did Frederick the Great at both Mollwitz in 1740, whence he fled, and Hochkirch in 1758. In our century,[51] the best examples of such temporary breakdowns at similarly vital moments were those suffered by Joseph Stalin, faced with the German invasion on

22 June 1941, and Yitzhak Rabin, Israeli Chief of Staff, in May 1967, planning the pre-emptive strike of the Six Day War.*

The Prince was in such a manic state that he confided in Rumiantsev-Zadunaisky, his old teacher, 'My career is finished. I've almost gone mad.' He scrawled a second note to Catherine that day, suggesting that Russia abandon the Crimea, his prize, his own title – since, without a fleet in Sebastopol, what was the point of keeping so many troops cooped up there? 'Assign the command to someone else . . .', he beseeched her. On God's word he had always been devoted to her. But now: 'Really I'm almost dead . . .'.[52]

---

* When Hitler invaded Russia on 22 June 1941, Stalin almost disappeared, saw nobody and seemed overwhelmed by the scale of responsibility and a temporary loss of nerve. He was apparently suffering some sort of depression. In May 1967, Rabin was 'stammering, nervous, incoherent'. His biographer quotes an eye-witness as observing 'it was almost as if he had lost his nerve, was out of control'.

26

JEWISH COSSACKS AND AMERICAN ADMIRALS: POTEMKIN'S WAR

> Prince Potemkin formed the singular project of raising a
> regiment of Jews ... he intends to make Cossacks of them.
> Nothing amused me more.
> The Prince de Ligne

> You would be charmed with the Prince Potemkin than whom
> no one could be more noble-minded.
> John Paul Jones to the Marquis de Lafayette

Catherine rallied the Prince of Taurida. 'In these moments, my dear friend, you are not just a private person who lives, and does what he likes,' she told him on the very day he wrote so desperately. 'You belong to the state, you belong to me.' Nonetheless she sent Potemkin an order, authorizing him to transfer command to Rumiantsev-Zadunaisky if he wished.

When she received his most frantic letters, she displayed her cool good sense. 'Nothing is lost,' she said, like a strict but indulgent German schoolmistress. 'The storm that was so harmful for us was equally harmful for the enemy.' As for withdrawal from the Crimea, there seemed 'no need to rush to start the war by evacuating a province which is not in danger'.* She ascribed his depression to what she called the 'excessive sensibility and ardent assiduity' of 'my best friend, foster-child and pupil, who is sometimes even more sane than myself. But this time, I am more vigorous than you because you're ill and I'm well.'¹ This was the essence of their partnership: whoever was up would look after whoever was down. War had given the partners more worry but also more to share.

---

* Withdrawal of the 26 battalions of infantry, 22 squadrons of cavalry and 5 Cossack regiments, all cooped up in the Crimea, was not the cowardice of a hysteric, but sound military sense. Potemkin planned to let the Turks land on the peninsula before destroying them in a land battle. (This was precisely what Suvorov did on a smaller scale at Kinburn). Once the danger of a landing was over, they could have been moved, but Catherine rejects the idea for political reasons.

Their military discussion often alternated with the warmest declarations of love and friendship.

A week later, Potemkin emerged from his depression, partly thanks to Catherine's letters, but even more because it turned out the fleet was damaged but not ruined: only one ship had been lost. 'The destruction of the Sebastopol Fleet was such a blow I don't even know how I survived it,' he confessed to his empress. He was relieved he could hand over to Rumiantsev if it became too much. They agreed that she should despatch Prince Nikolai Repnin, a talented general and Panin's nephew, to command the army under him. Serenissimus apologized for giving her such a shock: 'It's not my fault I am so sensitive.'[2] She sympathized. In a very eighteenth-century diagnosis, Catherine blamed much of it on his bowels: his spasms 'are nothing but wind', she decreed. 'Order them to give you something to get rid of the wind ... I know how painful they are for people as sensitive and impatient as us.'[3]

Potemkin had just recovered when the war began in earnest. On the night of 1 October, after a bombardment and several false starts, the Turks landed 5,000 crack Janissaries on Kinburn's thin spit and tried to storm the fortress. The Turks constructed entrenchments. The Russians, under the brilliant Suvorov, charged thrice and finally managed to slaughter virtually the entire Ottoman force, but at a high cost. Suvorov himself was wounded twice. But the victory at Kinburn meant that Kherson and the Crimea were safe until the spring.

'I can't find words to express how I appreciate and respect your important service, Alexander Vasilievich,'[4] Potemkin wrote to Suvorov, who was nine years older. The two great eccentrics and outstanding talents of their time had known each other since the First Turkish War. Their tense relationship fizzed with mutual admiration and irritation. Suvorov was a wiry little general with a cadaverous comedian's face, brutal, intelligent eyes and repertoire of zany antics. 'Hero, buffoon, half-demon and half-dirt,' wrote Byron, 'Harlequin in uniform.'[5] He rolled naked on the grass every morning, doing somersaults in front of his army, jumped on tables, sang in the midst of high society, mourned a decapitated turkey by trying to return its head to its neck, lived in a straw hut on the beach, stood on one leg at parade and set his armies marching by crowing thrice like a cockerel. He asked his men mad questions such as 'How many fish are there in the Danube?' The correct answer was a firm one. 'God save us from the "Don't knows",' he used to exclaim.[6]

Soon after Kinburn, a young French volunteer was writing a letter when his tent was unceremoniously opened and a scarecrow entered, wearing just a shirt. This 'fantastical apparition' asked to whom he was writing. To his sister in Paris, he replied. 'But I want to write a letter too,' said Suvorov, grabbing a pen and writing her a complete letter. When the sister received it, she said it was mostly unreadable – and the rest utterly crazy. The Frenchman decided 'I had to deal with a lunatic.' Legend has it that Suvorov once heard Catherine saying, *vis-à-vis* Potemkin, that all great men were eccentrics. Suvorov immediately began daily affecting a new singularity which in the end became second nature. Yet he spoke six foreign languages and was a connoisseur of ancient history and literature.[7]

Suvorov, who like Potemkin advocated informal, easy clothes and simple tactics of attack, was unlike the Prince in his ruthless, very Russian lack of concern for the lives of his men. The bayonet was his favourite weapon: 'Cold steel – bayonets and sabres! Push the enemy over, hammer them down, don't lose a moment.' Never trust the musket, 'that crazy bitch'. He always wanted to storm and charge regardless of losses: speed and impact were everything. His greatest battles, Ismail and Praga, were bloodbaths.[8] Every commander-in-chief needs a Suvorov. Potemkin was lucky to have him but he used him skilfully.*

Serenissimus now hailed Suvorov as 'my dear friend' and sent him endless presents from a greatcoat to a hamper of 'pâté de Périgord' – *foie gras*.[9] He urged Catherine to promote Suvorov above his seniority: 'Who Matushka could have such leonine courage?' He should be given Russia's highest order, the St Andrew. 'Who has deserved the distinction more than him? ... I begin with myself – give him mine!'[10] Potemkin's alleged jealousy of his subordinate became part of the Suvorov legend, but there is no trace of it in any of Potemkin's letters and it would have seemed absurd during their lifetimes: Potemkin was supreme and Suvorov was just one of his generals. Suvorov was so moved by Potemkin's affectionate letters that he wrote back, 'I am a commoner! How can it be I was not flattered by Your Highness's favour! The key to the secrets of my soul lie in your hands for ever.'[11] Suvorov was Potemkin's match in eccentricity and talent: contrary to the mythology of their hatred, they admired each other. Indeed their passionate, half-mad letters almost read like a love affair. 'You can't oversuvorov Suvorov,' joked Serenissimus.

---

* Later, Suvorov became more than famous: he became Prince of Italy, a European star fighting the Revolutionary French in Italy and Switzerland. By 1799, he was *the* peerless Russian idol and remained so until 1917. Then in 1941, Stalin restored him to the status of national hero and instituted the Order of Suvorov. Soviet historians reinvented him as a people's hero. The result of this cult is that even today Suvorov is given credit for much actually done by Potemkin.

Potemkin inspected Kherson, Kinburn and the fleets on one of his flying tours and then established his headquarters at Elisabethgrad, where he held his winter Court and planned the coming campaign. But he kept up his inspections: after a thousand versts on the road in icy weather, he complained to Catherine of piles and headaches. But he was achieving miracles in terms of repairing the old fleet and building a new flotilla to fight on the Liman.

Grand Duke Paul declared he wished to fight the Turks and bring his wife to the front. Paul's companionship was a dire prospect for Serenissimus, with the risk that the Heir might try to undermine his command. Nonetheless he agreed in principle. Catherine loathed her son now, comparing him to 'mustard after dinner'. Despite two requests, she managed to put him off, using anything – from crop failure to the Grand Duchess's latest pregnancy – to spare Serenissimus this tedious and dangerous fate. Paul spent the rest of the war drilling his troops at Gatchina 'like a Prussian major, exaggerating the importance of every trivial and minute detail', while tormenting himself with his father's murder and threatening everyone with 'hardness and vengeance' on his accession. He had to bite his lip and congratulate Serenissimus on his victories, but his wife was grateful for Potemkin's kindness to her brothers, who served in his army. As Catherine grew older, Potemkin flattered Paul, who remained sour as ever – 'Heaven and Earth were guilty in his eyes.' He took every opportunity to denounce his mother's partner to anyone who would listen.[12]

Joseph had not yet accepted the *casus foederis* of the treaty, but still complained that Potemkin and Rumiantsev were doing nothing. The Russians and the Austrians were watching each other closely: each wanted the other to bear the brunt of the war without losing out on the rewards. Both sides sent spies to watch each other.[13]

Joseph's spy was the Prince de Ligne, who was ordered to use his friendship with Potemkin to get the Russians to do as much of the fighting as possible. 'You will report to me on a separate piece of paper in French,' Joseph secretly instructed Ligne, 'which will be concealed and placed in an ordinary packet with the envelope addressed carefully: For His Majesty Alone.'[14] The 'jockey diplomatique'[15] did not know that this fell into the hands of the Russian Cabinet Noir – it remains in Potemkin's archives – but he did notice Serenissimus' reserve when he turned up in Elisabethgrad. 'The Prince de Ligne, whom I love, is now a burden,' Potemkin told Catherine.[16] War was the ruin of their friendship.

Elisabethgrad was a godforsaken little garrison-town, forty-seven miles from the Ottoman frontier. 'What weather, what roads, what winter, what Headquarters I found in Elisabeth,' wrote Ligne, who embraced Potemkin and asked, 'When to Ochakov?' This was a ludicrous question given that it was mid-winter and the Austrians, who were as surprised and unprepared as the Russians, had so far not even declared war. 'My God,' replied the still-depressed Potemkin. 'There are 18,000 men in the garrison. I don't even have as many in my army. I lack everything. I'm the unluckiest man if God doesn't help me.' Potemkin listed the Turkish garrisons in the nearby Ottoman fortresses, Akkerman, Bender and Khotin. 'Not a word of truth in all of that,'[17] Ligne commented. He was wrong.[18] Pisani's reports from Istanbul testified that the fortress had been freshly manned and refortified.* Potemkin had no intention of wasting Russian lives to save Austrian reputations: one has the distinct impression that some of his depression was diplomatic madness to distract the Austrians.

Potemkin lived splendidly in the misery of Elisabethgrad in a wooden palace beside the old fortress. Foreign volunteers – Spaniards, Piedmontese, Portuguese and especially French aristocrats – poured into the frozen town along with a 'vile troop of subaltern adventurers'. On 12 January 1788, Roger, Comte de Damas, having run away from France to find *gloire*, arrived to offer his services. Aged just twenty-three, with a shock of black curls, graceful and fearless, Talleyrand's cousin was the lover of the Marquise de Coigny, a sometime mistress of Ligne whom Marie-Antoinette called 'queen of Paris'. On arrival, he asked for his mistress's friend Ligne. Up in the castle, he was told. Thence he was directed to Potemkin's palace. He passed two guards and entered an immense hall, full of orderlies. This led to a long suite that was as brightly lit as a 'fête in some capital city'.

The first room he saw was full of adjutants awaiting Potemkin; in the second, Sarti conducted his orchestra of horns; in the third, thirty to forty generals surrounded a huge billiard table.[19] On the left, Serenissimus gambled with a niece and a general. This Court was 'not inferior to a lot of Sovereigns of Europe'. Russian generals were so servile that, if Potemkin dropped something, twenty of them scrummaged to pick it up.[20] The Prince rose to meet Damas, sat him at his side and invited him to dinner

---

* This was just the first of the many occasions when Ligne's criticisms, widely propagated and accepted by history as truth, were factually wrong and based on his Austrian partisanship. His rightly famous accounts of Potemkin at war, which he repeated in his fine letters to Joseph, Ségur and the Marquise de Coigny and thus to the whole of Europe, never deliberately lied but they have to be read in the context of his job, which was to spy on his friend, and persuade him to take the heat off his own Emperor. He was also bitterly disappointed not to be given his own command.

with Ligne and his niece at a small table, while the generals ate at a bigger one. From then on, Damas dined with Potemkin every day for three months of luxury and impatience.[21] Ligne was the consolation of the foreigners – 'a child in society, Lovelace with the women'. There was no shortage.

Potemkin could never bear war without women. He was soon joined for the winter by a coterie of goddesses, all in their late teens or early twenties, who came to meet their husbands in the army. There was the Russian Aphrodite – Princess Ekaterina Dolgorukaya, wife of an officer and daughter of Prince Fyodor Bariatinsky, one of Catherine's senior courtiers. She was acclaimed for her 'beauty, grace, fine tastes, delicate tact, humour and talent'. Then there was the lissom and wanton Ekaterina Samoilova, wife of Potemkin's nephew and daughter of Prince Sergei Trubetskoi. She was the 'most adorable woman', with whom Ligne was soon in love and writing poems that catch the grimness of life there: 'Dromedaries, horses; Zaporogians, sheep; They're all we meet here.'[22] The third of this graceful troika was Pavel Potemkin's wife, Praskovia.[23] Ségur teased Potemkin from Petersburg on his affair with a girl with 'beautiful black eyes with whom it is claimed you try the Twelve Labours of Hercules'.[24] Damas said Potemkin 'subordinated the art of war, the science of politics and the government of the kingdom to his particular passions'.[25] This galaxy of Venuses revolved around Potemkin: who was to be the next sultana-in-chief?

Potemkin and Ligne tormented each other: Potemkin was pressuring the Austrians to enter the war 'against our common enemy'.[26] Ligne waved one of Joseph's letters, which contained a war plan, and demanded Potemkin's strategy. Potemkin delayed, and after two weeks Ligne claimed he was fobbed off with the statement: 'With the help of God I'll attack everything that is between the Bug and the Dniester.' This was another Ligne lie. In an unpublished letter, Potemkin had quite clearly laid out the Russian plan: 'We'll undertake the siege of Ochakov, while the army of the Ukraine covers Bender', and the Caucasus and Kuban corps would fight the mountain tribes and Ottomans to the east.[27]

Ligne however did not exaggerate Serenissimus' impossible moodiness towards him: they were 'sometimes fine, sometimes bad, arguing at daggers drawn or uncontested favourite, sometimes gambling with him, talking or not talking, staying up until six in the morning'. Ligne said he was the nurse for a 'spoilt child' and a malicious one at that. But Potemkin was equally fed up with Ligne's 'villainous ingratitude', because his Cabinet Noir had opened all Ligne's lying letters to his friends. Serenissimus grumbled to Catherine that the 'jockey diplomatique' could not make up his mind: 'in his eyes, I am sometimes Thersites and sometimes Achilles', the louche Thersites of *Troilus and Cressida* or the heroic Achilles of the *Iliad*. It was a love–hate relationship.[28]

Between conducting adulteries, laughing at dromedaries and playing billiards, Potemkin was achieving a miracle ready for the next year. First he was awaiting his reserves and his levy of recruits, so that gradually an army of about 40,000–50,000 assembled in Elisabethgrad. Across the Mediterranean, Potemkin's officers tried to recruit more men, particularly from Greece and Italy: for example, on the island of Corsica it is said that a young man offered himself for service to a Russian recruiter, General I.A. Zaborovsky. The Corsican demanded Russian rank equivalent to his position in the Garde Nationale Corse. He even wrote to his General Tamara about it.* But his request was refused and he remained in France. The name of this abortive recruit to Potemkin's army was Napoleon Bonaparte.[29]

Serenissimus was creating the Cossack Host he had been planning ever since destroying the Zaporogian Sech. An honorary Zaporogian himself, Potemkin had a 'passion for the Cossacks'. His entourage was filled with them, often old friends from the First Turkish War like Sidor Bely, Chepega and Golavaty. Potemkin believed that the old Cuirassier heavy cavalry was outdated and inconvenient in southern wars. The Cossacks had copied the horsemanship of the Tartars and now Potemkin had his light cavalry emulate the Cossacks. But he also decided to reharness the Zaporogian Cossacks, tempting back their brethren who had defected to the Turks. 'Try to enlist the Cossacks,' he ordered Bely. 'I'll check them all myself.' He also filled up their ranks by recruiting new Cossacks from among Poles, Old Believers and even coachmen and *petit bourgeois*. Overcoming Catherine's caution, he founded the new 'Black Sea and Ekaterinoslav Host' under Bely and his Cossack protégés. They were later renamed the Kuban Cossacks, Russia's second largest Host (the Don remained bigger) until the Revolution. It was Potemkin who made the Cossacks the pillars of the Tsarist regime.[30]

Potemkin decided to arm the Jews against the Turks. This 'singular project', probably his Jewish friend Zeitlin's idea, spawned in some rabbinical debate with the Prince, started as a cavalry squadron raised among the Jews of his Krichev estate. In December, he created a Jewish

---

* History hangs on such petty questions of rank. Count Fyodor Rostopchin, later the Governor of Moscow who burned the city in 1812, claimed in his *La Verité sur l'Incendie de Moscow* to have seen it: 'I've held this letter in my hands several times.' He regretted that Bonaparte did not join the Russian army.

regiment called the Israelovsky, a word reminiscent of the Izmailovsky Guards. But that was where the similarities ended. Commanded by Prince Ferdinand of Brunswick, their ultimate aim was to liberate Jerusalem for the Jews, just as Potemkin was to conquer Constantinople for the Orthodox. This sign of Potemkin's unique philo-semitism and of Zeitlin's influence was an awkward idea given Russian and especially Cossack anti-semitism, but it was surely the first attempt by a foreign power to arm the Jews since Titus destroyed the Temple.

The Prince wanted his Israelovsky to be half-infantry, half-cavalry, the latter to be Jewish Cossacks with Zaporogian lances: 'we already have one squadron', observed Ligne to Joseph II. 'Thanks to the shortness of their stirrups, their beards come down to their knees and their fear on horseback makes them like monkeys.' Joseph, who had loosened the restrictions of his own Jews, was probably amused.

By March 1788, thirty-five of these bearded Jewish Cossacks were being trained. Soon there were two squadrons, and Ligne told Potemkin there were plenty more in Poland. Ligne was sceptical, but he admitted he had seen excellent Jewish postmasters and even postillions. The Israelovsky evidently went out on patrol with the cavalry because Ligne wrote that they were as terrified of their own horses as those of the enemy. But five months later Potemkin cancelled the Israelovsky. Ligne joked that he did not dare continue them for fear of 'getting mixed up with the Bible'. So ended this rare experiment that says a great deal about Potemkin's originality and imagination.* Ligne thought the Jewish Cossacks were 'too ridiculous'. Instead, Potemkin concentrated on a 'great number of Zaporogians and other Cossack volunteers' pouring in to form the new Black Sea Host.[31]

The 'Prince–Marshal', as the foreigners called him, was now repairing the damaged fleet while preparing a huge new flotilla to fight in the Liman beneath Ochakov. The Russians were exposed in the Liman. The nature of this shallow estuary meant that Potemkin would have to fight a different sort of war with a different sort of fleet. Potemkin and his admiral Mordvinov turned to the most ingenious shipbuilder they knew:

* One wonders what happened to these Jewish Cossacks. Six years later, in 1794, Polish Jews raised a force of 500 light cavalry to fight the Russians. Their colonel Berek (Berko) Joselewicz joined Napoleon's Polish Legion in 1807. Berek won the Légion d'Honneur, but died fighting the Austrians in 1809. Did any of Potemkin's Jewish Cossacks fight for Napoleon? Later in the mid-nineteenth century, the great Polish poet Adam Mickiewicz formed another Jewish cavalry regiment called the Hussars of Israel among Polish exiles in Istanbul. A Lieutenant Michal Horenstein even designed an elegant grey uniform. During the Crimean War, the Jewish horsemen fought with the remaining Ottoman Cossacks against the Russians outside Sebastopol.

Samuel Bentham's vermicular barges had been left behind and forgotten when the Empress's tour headed for Kherson, leaving him to tag along behind.* Now he was needed again, but Serenissimus had forgotten to pay him. He was swiftly paid, but Potemkin was so embarrassed about the debts that he hardly spoke to Bentham. 'By order of His Highness', Sam was enrolled into the navy[32] – though 'I had rather continue on *terra firma*.'[33] Potemkin ordered him to create a light flotilla that could fight the Turkish fleet in the Liman.[34] While Potemkin appeared to be lazing around at Elisabethgrad having tantrums with Ligne, the archives show that he was driving the creation of this fleet with all his force. 'Fit them up completely as quickly as possible with rigging and all their armaments,' he ordered Mordvinov. 'Don't lose any time over it.'[35]

Joseph now accepted the *casus foederis* and launched a bungled pre-emptive strike against the Ottoman fortress of Belgrade in today's Serbia. The operation collapsed farcically when Austrian commandos, disguised in special uniforms, got lost in the fog. Potemkin was 'furious'[36] with Ligne about this military buffoonery, but it let the Russians off the hook. 'It's not very good for them,' Catherine told Potemkin, 'but it is good for us.' Joseph fielded his 245,000 men but went on the defensive across central Europe, which at least restrained the Turks, giving Potemkin time to fight the Battle of the Liman.[37]

This strategy drove the Austrians to despair. Potemkin was adamant to Catherine that 'nobody can encourage me to undertake something when there's no profit in it and nobody can discourage me when there's a useful opportunity'.[38] Ligne tried to persuade him, but Potemkin laughed maliciously: 'Do you think you can come here and lead me by the nose?'[39] The Austrian general Prince Frederick Joseph de Saxe-Coburg-Saalfeld failed to take Khotin too. A second lunge for Belgrade never even got started. The Austrian war was not going well.[40]

So Potemkin treated Ligne to two unpublished strategic memoranda that the 'jockey diplomatique' does not mention in his famous letters because they firmly restore the balance of Austro-Russian achievements: 'It seems to me that on several occasions one has not been on guard enough,' and Serenissimus proceeded to explain how the Turks fought: 'They like to envelope their enemy on all sides ...'. Potemkin's advice was to concentrate forces, not spread them out in thin cordons, as Joseph was doing. Whether Joseph ever saw these documents, he did exactly

---

* Samuel was so depressed that he wrote a letter to Prime Minister Pitt the Younger which offered to exchange his 'battalion of 900 Russians' in order to supervise a Panopticon 'of British malefactors'.

what Potemkin warned him against, with disastrous results.[41]

Ligne could do nothing but accuse the Prince of the vainglorious pursuit of medals and lying about his victories. When a courier arrived with news of a victory in the Caucasus, Potemkin beamed: 'See if I do nothing! I've just killed 10,000 Circassians, Abyssinians, Imeretians and Georgians and I've already killed 5,000 Turks at Kinburn.' Ligne said this was a lie, but the Prince's generals Tekeli and Pavel Potemkin had won a series of victories across the Kuban in September and November against the Ottoman ally, Sheikh Mansour.[42] Ligne simply had no conception of the breadth of Potemkin's command.*

It was now Catherine's turn to lose her confidence for a moment and Potemkin's to encourage her in his belief that the two of them were specially blessed. Christ would help her – as He had always done before. 'There were times', he reassured her, 'when all the escape-routes seem to be blocked. And then all of a sudden, chance intervened. Do rely on Him.' He thanked her for the fur coat she had sent. She missed him – especially in a crisis: 'without you, I feel as though I'm missing a hand and I get into trouble which I'd never get into with you. I keep fearing something is being missed.'[43] Later in the spring, she wrote a *postscriptum* to a short note, thanking him for his reassurances. 'I thought it would be nice to tell you that I love you, my friend, very much and without ceremony.' They were still so close that they usually thought the same way, and even suffered from the same ailments.[44]

A Polish delegation now arrived in Elisabethgrad: Potemkin kept them waiting for days and then shocked them by receiving them in a dressing gown without breeches. Nonetheless, Potemkin paid serious attention to the problem of Poland. The sprawling Commonwealth was moving towards the so-called 'Four Year Sejm', the long parliament that presided over the Polish Revolution and overthrew the Russian protectorate. This was what Potemkin and King Stanislas-Augustus' proposed alliance might have avoided. 'Make Poland join us in the war,' the Prince urged

---

* Ligne's letters give only half the story; Potemkin's archives hold the other half. Ligne's claims that Potemkin was lying about his victories on other fronts were accepted by historians but are actually themselves false. Potemkin's espionage network, revealed by his archives, kept him informed of events across his huge theatre of operations: he received regular reports from the Governor of the Polish fortress Kamenets-Podolsky, General de Witte, who explained how he had managed to get spies into Turkish Khotin in a consignment of butter – though the fact that the sister of Witte's Greek wife was married to the Pasha of Khotin might also have helped.

Catherine.[45] He offered the Poles 50,000 rifles to equip Polish forces, which would include 12,000 Polish cavalry to fight the Turks. Potemkin wanted to command some of the Poles himself – 'at least a single brigade. I am as much of a Pole as they are,' he protested, referring to his Smolensk origins and *indigenat* as a Polish nobleman.

This offer to command Polish troops was not a casual one. He was still developing his flexible plans for dealing with Poland and his own future under Paul, partly based on his new Podolian estates.[46] In any case, Catherine distrusted the plan, perhaps nervous about his vast Polish lands and schemes. She would only propose a treaty that specifically preserved the weak, chaotic Polish Constitution that served Russian ends. It was never signed.

There was always comedy with Serenissimus, even in war. When his Cossacks captured four Tartars, the prisoners expected to be killed. But Potemkin cheerfully had them thrown into a barrel of water and then announced they had been baptized. When a half-senile Frenchman arrived, purporting to be a siege expert, the Prince questioned him, only to learn that the sage had forgotten most of his knowledge. 'I should like to peep . . . and study the works that I have forgotten again,' said the old man. Potemkin, 'always kind and amiable' to characters, laughed and told him to relax: 'Don't kill yourself with all that reading . . .'.[47]

Samuel Bentham, working under Admiral Mordvinov and General Suvorov at Kherson, threw himself into creating a rowing flotilla, using all his ingenuity.* He adapted Catherine's 'cursed' imperial barges into gunboats, but his real work was to renovate a graveyard of old cannon and fit them on to any light boats that he could either convert or construct. 'I flatter myself I am the principal agent, filling out the Galleys and smaller vessels,' he wrote.[48]

Bentham's masterpiece was to arm his ships with far heavier cannon than usual on most gunboats.[49] 'The employment of great guns of 36 or even 48 pounds on such small vessels as ships' long boats', Bentham boasted justifiably to his brother, 'was entirely my idea.'[50] It was to Potemkin's credit that, when he came to inspect in October, he immediately understood the significance of Bentham's idea and adopted it in the construction of all the frigates and gunboats, including twenty-five Zaporogian *chaiki*[51] being built separately by his factotum Faleev. 'They respect the calibre of guns in the fleet, not the quantity,'[52] Potemkin

---

* In the process, he invented an amphibious cart, perhaps the first amphibious landing craft; a floating timebomb; an early torpedo; and bottlebombs filled with inflammable liquid that had to be lit and then thrown – 160 years before Molotov cocktails. Perhaps they should be called 'Bentham' or 'Potemkin cocktails'.

explained to Catherine. He managed to overcome his awkwardness and thank Bentham publicly for all he had done.[53] Bentham was delighted.

By the spring, Potemkin had created a heavy-armed light flotilla of about a hundred boats out of almost nothing.[54] Even Ligne had to agree that 'it needed a great merit of the Prince to have imagined, created and equipped' the fleet so fast.[55] The birth of the Liman fleet – another 'beloved child' – was perhaps the 'most essential service Potemkin rendered to Russia'.[56] Who was to command it? Nassau-Siegen arrived at Elisabethgrad in the New Year eager to serve. Potemkin enjoyed Nassau's pedigree – from the bed of the Queen of Tahiti to the raid on Jersey during the American War – but he knew his limitations. 'Almost a sailor',[57] he called Nassau – which made him perfect for his almost-fleet in the Liman. On 26 March, he placed Nassau, whose 'bravery' was 'renowned', in command of the rowing flotilla.[58]

Potemkin inspected and reinspected maniacally: 'The extent of his authority, the fear he inspired and the prompt execution of his wishes made his visits of inspections seldom necessary.'[59] By late March, everything was almost ready. 'Then we can begin the dance,' declared Nassau.[60] But, just as everything seemed arranged with the command, an American admiral appeared on the Liman.

'Paul Jones has arrived,' Catherine told Grimm on 25 April 1788. 'I saw him today. I think he'll do marvellous things for us.'[61] Catherine fantasized that Jones would slice straight through to Constantinople. John Paul Jones, born the son of a gardener on a Scottish island, was the most celebrated naval commander of his day. He is still regarded as one of the founders of the US Navy. His tiny squadron of ships had terrorized the British coast during the War of American Independence: his wildest exploit was to raid the Scottish coast, taking hostage the inhabitants of a country house. This earned him the enviable reputation in America as a hero of liberty, in France as a dashing heart-throb and in England as a despicable pirate. Prints were sold of him; English nannies scared their children with tales of this bloodsoaked ogre. When the War of Independence ended in 1783, Jones, living in Paris, found himself at a loose end. Grimm, Thomas Jefferson and the King of Poland's Virginian, Lewis Littlepage, had all helped direct him to Catherine, who knew that Russia needed sailors – and who could never resist a Western celebrity. Catherine is usually credited with hiring Jones without consulting Potemkin. But the archives show that Potemkin was simultaneously negotiating with him. 'In case this officer is now in France,' he told Simolin, the Russian envoy in Paris on 5 March, 'I ask Your Excellency to get him to come as early as possible so that we can use his talents in the opening of the campaign.'[62]

Jones duly arrived at Tsarskoe Selo, but Admiral Samuel Greig and the British officers of the Baltic fleet refused to serve with the infamous corsair, so Catherine sent Jones straight down to Elisabethgrad. On 19 May 1788, Potemkin gave Rear-Admiral Pavel Ivanovich Dzones the command of his eleven battleships, while Nassau kept the rowing flotilla.[63] Jones was not the only American fighting for Potemkin: Lewis Littlepage, whom the Prince knew from Kiev, arrived as the King of Poland's spy at Russian HQ. At the Battle of the Liman, he commanded a division of gunboats. The Prince appointed Damas, Bentham and another English volunteer, Henry Fanshawe (Potemkin called him 'Fensch'), a gentleman from Lancashire, to command squadrons under Nassau. 'Lieutenant-Colonels Fensch and Bentham finally agreed to serve on board the ships,' Potemkin informed Mordvinov.

Nassau and the other three proved inspired choices for the flotilla,[64] the two Americans less so. Jones generated resentment and excitement: Fanshawe and Bentham were not impressed with the 'celebrated, or rather notorious', Jones and the former declared that 'nothing but the presence of the enemy could induce us to serve *with* him and no consideration whatever could bring us to *serve under* him'.[65] In Petersburg, Ségur wrote a very modern if flattering letter about Fame to Potemkin: 'I did not expect having made war in America with Brave Paul Jones to meet him here so far from home but Celebrity Attracts Celebrity and I can't be surprised to see all those who love glory ... coming to associate their laurels with yours.' But Ségur presciently begged Potemkin to be fair to Jones and never 'condemn him without having heard him'.[66]

On 20 May 1788, Nassau saw the forest of masts of the Ottoman fleet in the Liman off Ochakov. 'We have to make a dance with the Capitan-Pasha,' Nassau boasted to his wife.[67] He swore to Damas that, in two months, he would either be dead or wearing the cross of St George.[68]

Ghazi Hassan-Pasha, the Capitan-Pasha, commanded eighteen ships-of-the-line, forty frigates and scores of rowing galleys that brought his flotilla to over 109 ships, considerably more than the Russians in numbers and tonnage.[69] The Capitan-Pasha himself, renegade son of a Georgian Orthodox servant on the Barbary Coast, was the outstanding Ottoman warrior of the later eighteenth century, the latest in the tradition of the Algerian pirates who had come to the Sultan's rescue. The 'Algerine renegado', instantly recognizable by his 'fine white beard', had seen the inferno of Chesme and rushed back to protect Istanbul; defeated the

Egyptian rebellions against the Sultan; and won the nickname 'the Crocodile of Sea Battles'.[70] He was the darling of the Istanbul mob. When Lady Craven visited his house in 1786, she recounted the magnificence of his lifestyle and bounty of diamonds in his wife's turban.[71] He was always accompanied by a pet lion that lay down at his command.

Potemkin, again suffering an attack of nerves, wondered if he should evacuate the Crimea. 'When you are sitting on a horse,' Catherine replied, 'there is no point in getting off it and holding on by the tail.' Potemkin sought reassurance from his Empress rather than actual evacuation – and that was what she gave him.[72]

The Liman or estuary of the Dnieper was a long, narrow and treacherous bay that stretched thirty miles towards the west before it opened into the Black Sea. It was only eight miles wide, but its mouth was just two miles across. The south shore was Russian, ending in Kinburn's narrow spit, but its mouth was dominated by the massive fortifications of the Ottoman fortress of Ochakov. It was of great strategic importance because Ochakov was the principal Russian war aim of the first campaign. But it could not be taken if the Ottomans controlled the Liman. Furthermore, the loss of the battle would leave the Turks free to attack Kinburn again, advance fifteen miles upstream to Kherson and possibly take the Crimea. Potemkin's strategy was to win naval control of the Liman and then besiege mighty Ochakov, which would open communications between Kherson and Sebastopol, protect the Crimea and win a new expanse of coastline. So all depended on the Prince de Nassau-Siegen, Rear-Admiral John Paul Jones and the Crocodile of Sea Battles.

On 27 May, Potemkin marched out of Elisabethgrad with his army as the Capitan-Pasha gathered his fleet. On the morning of 7 June, the Capitan-Pasha advanced along the Liman with his rowing flotilla backed by his warships. It was a gorgeous and impressive sight – 'better than a ball at Warsaw', thought Nassau, 'and I'm persuaded we'll have as much fun as Prince Sapieha dancing "l'Allemande" '. Nassau and Damas showed each other portraits of their women back home. The Turks opened fire. While Jones's squadron was held back by a contrary wind, Nassau used the light Zaporogian *chaiki* on his left to attack them all along the line. The Turks withdrew in chaos. The Capitan-Pasha fired on his own retreating forces. He was, after all, the man who had solved the problem of lazy firefighting in Istanbul by tossing four firemen into a blaze *pour encourager les autres*.

Nassau and Jones ordered their respective fleets to give chase. Bentham, who was commanding a division of seven galleys and two gunboats, saw his heavy artillery win the day but got his eyebrows singed when one of his cannons exploded.[73] The First Battle of the Liman was more of a stalemate than a rout – but it was encouraging.

'It comes from God!', exclaimed Serenissimus, whose army was camped at Novy Grigory, where he had consecrated a church to his patron St George. He embraced Ligne.[74] Surprisingly in a man notorious for his indolence, Potemkin's concept of command was all-embracing and was combined with a mastery of detail. He supervised the flotilla's manoeuvring, its formations and the signalling codes between ships and Kinburn. He thought first about the ordinary men: he ordered Nassau to let each man have a portion of *eau de vie* (spirits) daily and he specified that meals were to be served on time, always hot, and had to include vegetable soup and meat on holy days. When summer came, the men were to wash daily. But most remarkable were his views on discipline. 'I am entirely persuaded', he wrote, that 'sentiments of humanity' contributed to the health of the troops and their service. 'To succeed in this, I recommend you to forbid the beating of people. The best remedy is to explain exactly and clearly what you have done.' Contemporaries saw Potemkin's humanity and generosity to his men as mad, indulgent and dangerous. This would have been regarded as mollycoddling in the Royal Navy half a century later.[75]

Nassau and Jones became rabid enemies: the reckless paladin was not impressed with Jones's sensible preservation of his ships, while Jones thought Nassau hated him because he had 'extracted him out of his foul-up and peril'.[76] Both complained to the Prince, who tried to keep the peace while secretly backing Nassau. 'It is to you alone', he wrote two days later, 'I attribute this victory.'[77] But he also ordered him to get on with Jones: 'Moderate a little your fine ardour.'[78]

On 16 June, the Crocodile decided to overcome the stalemate by bringing his entire fleet, including battleships, into the Liman. 'Nothing could present a more formidable front that this line extending from shore to shore,' wrote Fanshawe, so densely packed that he could see no interval between their sails. The attack was imminent. That night, after the arrival of another twenty-two Russian gunboats, Nassau called a council of war. Jones declared, 'I see in your eyes the souls of heroes,' but advised caution. Nassau lost his temper, telling the American he could stay behind with his ships if he liked, and ordered a dawn pre-emptive strike. The two admirals were now fighting their own private war.

Damas led the assault on the right with his galleys, gun-batteries and bomb-ketches, while Bentham and Fanshawe backed by Jones's battleships, *Vladimir* and *Alexander*, attacked the hulking Turkish ships-of-the-line. The Turks advanced towards them blowing trumpets, clashing cymbals and shouting to Allah but, rattled by the Russian pre-emptive strike, they soon tried to retreat. The flagships of their Vice-Admiral and then Ghazi Hassan himself became stuck on shoals. Damas' gunboats pounced on them, but Turkish fire managed to sink a smaller Russian boat. When Jones noticed the shoals, he stopped the pursuit with his ships-of-the-line. Prudence won him no friends. Bentham, Fanshawe and the rest pursued in their lighter gunboats. But the *pièce de résistance* came in the afternoon when Damas succeeded in destroying the Crocodile's flagship. Its explosion was 'a magnificent spectacle', recalled Fanshawe.[79] The 'Algerine renegado' continued to command from the nearby spit. As night fell, the young Englishmen stepped up their chase. The Turks withdrew beneath the guns of Ochakov, leaving behind two destroyed ships-of-the-line and six gunboats.

Overnight, the old Crocodile withdrew the battleships that had lost him the battle, but as they passed the Kinburn spit Suvorov opened up with a battery, positioned for just such an opportunity. The two battleships and five frigates tried to avoid the bombardment but instead ran aground. They were clearly visible in the moonlight. During this lull, Jones made a secret reconnaissance and wrote in chalk on one warship's stern: 'To be Burned. Paul Jones 17/28 June'. Jones, Bentham and Damas rowed over to Nassau's flagship. There was another row between the admirals. 'I know how to capture ships as well as you!', shouted Nassau. 'I have proved my ability to capture ships that are not Turkish,' replied Jones pointedly. It was comments like this that made him enemies who would stop at nothing to destroy him.[80]

Nassau and the young bloods decided to attack. Off they went helter-skelter in their boats to bombard these beached whales. 'We had about as much discipline', wrote Bentham, 'as the London mob.' Samuel fired so many shells that he could not even see his targets for the smoke. He captured one ship-of-the-line, but the 'London mob' was so keen for blood that they blew up the other Turkish ships with 3,000 of their rowing slaves still chained on board. Their screams must have been appalling. 'Dead bodies were floating around for a fortnight afterwards,' Samuel told his father.[81] The rest of the fleet took refuge beneath the walls of Ochakov. The Capitan-Pasha executed a selection of his officers.[82]

'Our victory is complete – my flotilla did it!', declared Nassau, *soi-disant* 'Master of the Liman'. In two days of the Second Battle of the Liman, the Turks had lost ten warships and five galleys with 1,673 prisoners and over 3,000 dead, while the Russians had lost just one frigate,

eighteen dead and sixty-seven wounded. Damas was given the honour
of taking the news to the Prince, waiting at Novy Grigory to cross the
Bug.[83] This time Potemkin was beside himself. He kissed Ligne all over
again: 'What did I tell you of Novy Grigory? Here again! Isn't it amazing?
I'm the spoilt child of God.' Ligne coolly commented that this was 'the
most extraordinary man there ever was'.[84] The Prince of Taurida exulted,
'The boats beat the ships. I've gone mad with joy!'[85]

   That night, the jubilant Potemkin arrived from the shore to dine with
Nassau and Lewis Littlepage on Jones's flagship, the *Vladimir*. Potemkin's
flag as grand admiral of the Black Sea and Caspian Fleets was piped up.
Nassau and Jones were still at daggers drawn. 'So brilliant in the second
rank,' Nassau commented of Jones, 'eclipsed in the first.'[86] The Prince–
Marshal persuaded Nassau to apologize to the touchy American, but he
was sure that the victories belonged to Nassau. 'It was all his work,' he
reported to Catherine. As for the 'pirate' Jones, he was not 'a comrade-
in-arms'.[87] The victory truly owed more to Bentham's artillery than to
Nassau's 'mob'. Naturally Samuel thought so, and he was promoted to
colonel,* and awarded the St George with a gold-hilted sword.[88] Catherine sent Potemkin a golden sword 'garnished with three big diamonds,
the most beautiful thing possible', and a golden plate engraved 'To Field-
Marshal Prince Potemkin of Taurida, commander of the land army and
sea army victorious on the Liman and creator of the fleet'.[89] The prickly
Jones got less than the brazen Nassau: the snub was clear. The chastened
Crocodile of Sea Battles put to sea with the remains of his fleet.

   Just when things were going so well, dangerous news arrived from
Catherine: Gustavus III of Sweden had attacked Russia on 21 June,
providing his own pretext by staging an attack against his own frontier,
using Swedish troops in Russian uniforms.[90] Before leaving Stockholm
to lead his troops in Finland, Gustavus boasted he would soon be taking
'luncheon in St Petersburg'. The capital was exposed, for the crack
Russian forces were in the south, though Potemkin had left an observation corps guarding the border, and sent Kalmyks and Bashkirs, with
their spears and bows and arrows, to scare the Swedes. (They scared the
Russians just as much.) Fortunately, the Baltic Fleet, under Greig, had
not left to fight the Turks in the Mediterranean. Potemkin appointed
Count Musin-Pushkin to command the Finnish front against Gustavus.
Soon afterwards, Alexei Orlov-Chesmensky arrived in Petersburg to

---

* Potemkin wrote to him: 'Sir, Her Imperial Majesty distinguishing the bravery shown
by you against the Turks on the Liman of Ochakov ... has graciously been pleased to
present you with a sword inscribed to commemorate your valour ...'.

exploit the Prince's supposed negligence – an experience Catherine compared to having a 'load of snow'[91] landing on her head. Petersburg soon felt as if it was a fortified town, she reported. The first sea battle on 6 July at Gothland was a victory for Russia, 'so my friend', she told her consort, 'I've also smelt powder'.[92] But Gustavus was still advancing on land. In one of those moments when Potemkin envisaged ruthless evacuations of people, he half jokingly suggested depopulating Finland, dispersing its people and making it into a wasteland.[93]

Unfortunately, Sweden was just the tip of the iceberg. England, Holland and Prussia were about to sign a Triple Alliance that would turn out to be strongly anti-Russian. France was paralysed by imminent revolution. But Catherine found herself astride the two faultlines of Europe – Russia versus Turkey and Austria versus Prussia. The jealous Prussia, under its new king Frederick William, was determined to squeeze advantage out of Russo-Austrian prizes against the Turks and keen to feast again on the juicy cake of Poland – a menu of desires that the Prussian Chancellor Count von Hertzberg would bring together in his eponymous Plan. Austria felt exposed to Prussian attack in its rear, but Russia assured Joseph this would not be allowed to happen. The pressure increased on Potemkin again; Russia was back in crisis.[94]

On 1 July, Potemkin led his army across the Bug to invest Ochakov, while Nassau launched a raid on the ships left under its walls: after another battle, the Turks abandoned the ships and scampered back into the fortress. Two hours later, Fanshawe heard Potemkin attack the town.[95] Serenissimus mounted his horse and advanced on Ochakov at the head of 13,000 Cossacks and 4,000 Hussars. The garrison welcomed them with a barrage followed by the sortie of 600 Spahis and 300 infantry. The Prince immediately placed twenty cannon on the plain beneath the fortress and stood personally directing the fire, 'where all the immense diamonds of the beautiful portrait of the Empress that is always in his buttonhole, attracted fire'. Two horses and a cart driver were killed beside him.

Ligne acclaimed Potemkin's 'beautiful valour', but Catherine was unimpressed. 'If you kill yourself,' she wrote, 'you kill me too. Show me the mercy of forbearing from such fun in the future.'[96] So began the siege of Ochakov.

CRY HAVOC: THE STORMING
OF OCHAKOV

It began in the morning
At the rise of a red sun
When Potemkin speaks...
Our bravest leader
Only wave your hand and Ochakov is taken
Say the word and Istanbul will fall
We'll march with you through fire and rain...
Soldiers' marching song, 'The Fall of Ochakov'

The forbidding fortress of Ochakov was Russia's most pressing prize in 1788 because it controlled the mouths of the Dnieper and the Bug. This was the key to Kherson, hence to the Crimea itself. The Turks had therefore reinforced its network of defences, advised by 'a French engineer of note', Lafite. 'The town', observed Fanshawe, 'formed a long parallelogram from the crest of a hill down to the waterside, fortified with a wall of considerable thickness running round it, a double ditch ... flanked by six bastions, a spit of sand running out from the west flank into the Liman which flanks the sea wall and terminates in a covered battery.'[1] It was a considerable town of mosques, palaces, gardens and barracks with a garrison of between 8,000 and 12,000 Spahis and Janissaries, dressed in their green jackets and tunics over pantaloons with turbans, shields, curved daggers, axes and spears.* Even Joseph II, who inspected Ochakov on his visit, appreciated that it was not susceptible to a *coup de main*.[2]

As soon as he began to invest the fortress Serenissimus insisted on setting off with Ligne, Nassau and his entourage in a rowing boat to reconnoitre and test some mortars. Ochakov saluted the Prince with a bombardment and sent out a squadron of Turks in little boats. Potemkin haughtily ignored them. 'One could see nothing more noble and cheer-

---

* Today, though the fortifications are gone, one can stand on the ramparts where the walls stood and look down on the length of the Liman and the encampments of the Russian besiegers. Far to the left is the mouth of the Bug. Opposite on its own narrow spit stands the Russian fortress of Kinburn. Near by to the right, at the end of the Ochakov spit, the Hassan-Pasha Redoubt still has an awesome power. The cobbles of the streets are almost all that remain. The modern town of Ochakov is behind.

fully courageous than the Prince,' said Ligne. 'I loved him to madness that day.'[3] Potemkin's demonstrations of valour impressed everyone – especially a few weeks later when Sinelnikov, Governor of Ekaterinoslav, was hit in the groin by a cannonball while standing between an imperturbable Potemkin and an excited Ligne. Serenissimus ordered the reduction of a Turkish stronghold in the Pasha's gardens. This ignited a skirmish which Potemkin and 200 courtiers observed from amid the barrage. 'I've not seen a man', said Nassau, 'who was better under fire than he.'[4] Potemkin rushed to help Sinelnikov, who, ever the courtier, even in agony, asked him 'not to expose himself to such danger because there's only one Potemkin in Russia'. The pain was so excruciating, he begged Potemkin to shoot him.[5] Sinelnikov died two days later.[6]

The Prince extended both wings of his forces in an arc around the town and ordered a bombardment by his artillery. Everyone waited for the storming to begin – especially Suvorov, who was always longing to unleash the bloody bayonet, if not the 'crazy bitch' of the musket.

Next day, on 27 July, the Turks made a sortie with fifty Spahis. Suvorov, 'drunk after dinner', attacked them, throwing more and more men into a fierce fray, without orders from Potemkin. The Turks fled but returned with superior forces to pursue Suvorov and his Russians back to their lines, killing many of his best men, who were then beheaded. When Potemkin sent a note to inquire what was happening, Suvorov is supposed to have sent back this rhyming couplet:

> I am sitting on a rock
> And at Ochakov I look.[7]

Three thousand Turks fell on the fleeing Russians. Damas called it 'useless butchery'.[8] Suvorov was wounded and the rest of his division was saved only by Prince Repnin making a diversion. The heads of the Russians were displayed on stakes around Ochakov.

Serenissimus wept at the waste of 200 soldiers, 'due to the humanity and compassion of his heart', according to his secretary Tsebrikov. 'Oh my god!', cried Potemkin. 'You're happy to let those barbarians tear everybody to pieces.' He angrily reprimanded Suvorov, saying 'soldiers are not so cheap that one can sacrifice them . . .'.[9] Suvorov sulked and recuperated in Kinburn.*

---

* Since it became a rule of Russian history that Suvorov was a genius, it followed that he was simply trying to begin the storming of Ochakov out of frustration at Potemkin's inept hesitancy. This is possible but unlikely, since Suvorov had no artillery behind him. It was a bungled operation by a tipsy and fallible general who was capable of costly mistakes as well as brilliant victories.

Potemkin did not storm Ochakov. The pressure on him increased all the time: on 18 August, the Turks made another sortie. General Mikhail Golenishev-Kutuzov, later the legendary hero of 1812 and vanquisher of Napoleon, was wounded in the head for the second time – like Potemkin, he was blinded in one eye.* Nassau repulsed the Turks by firing on their flanks from his flotilla in the Estuary. As winter descended on Ochakov, the foreigners – such as Ligne and Nassau – grumbled bitterly about Potemkin's slow incompetence. Nassau considered Potemkin the 'most unmilitary man in the world and too proud to consult anybody'.† Ligne said he was wasting 'time and people' and wrote to Cobenzl in code, undermining Potemkin – though he did not dare sneak to Catherine.[10] 'It is impossible', wrote Damas, who thought the batteries badly laid out around the town, 'that so many blunders should have been made unless Prince Potemkin had personal reasons ... to delay matters.' But these foreigners were prejudiced against Russia. Potemkin's reasons were political and military.[11] Serenissimus was happy to let the Austrians absorb the first Ottoman attacks, especially since Joseph had failed in virtually all his plans except the meagre prize of Sabatsch and had himself gone on to the defensive. Catherine heartily agreed: 'Better be slower but healthy than quick but dangerous.'[12] Given the Swedish war, the increasingly hostile Anglo-Prussian alliance and the surprisingly strong performance of the Ottoman armies against Austria, Potemkin knew Ochakov would not end the war: there was every reason to husband resources until the end of the year.

Serenissimus was not a genius of movement, more a Fabius Cunctator, a patient delayer and waiter on events. This was an age in which officers like Ligne and Suvorov believed warfare was a glorious game of charges and assaults, regardless of the cost in men. Potemkin threw away the book of conventional Western warfare and fought in a way that suited the nature of his enemies – and himself. He much preferred to win battles without fighting them, as in 1783 in the Crimea. In the case of sieges, he preferred to bribe, negotiate and starve a fortress into submission. His attitude was not swashbuckling, but modern generals would recognize his humanity and prudence.[13] Potemkin specifically decided that he would not storm Ochakov until it was absolutely necessary, in order to save the blood of his men. 'I'll do my best', he told

---

* Most of the heroes of 1812 fought under Potemkin – the future Field-Marshal and Prince Mikhail Barclay de Tolly, Minister of War and Commander of the First Army under Kutuzov at Borodino, also served at Ochakov.

† Yet even Ligne had to admit to Joseph II that the camp was tidy, the soldiers well paid and the light cavalry in excellent state, even if they did no manoeuvres or practice.

Suvorov, 'to get it cheap.'[14] Potemkin's emissaries rode back and forth negotiating with the Turks. Serenissimus 'was convinced the Turks wish to surrender'.[15] Storming was his last resort.* The foreigners also had little concept of his vast responsibilities, commanding and provisioning armies and navies from the Caucasus to the Gulf of Finland, from managing Polish policy to driving Faleev to create another rowing flotilla, already looking ahead to the next year's fight up the Danube.[16]

'I won't be the dupe of the Russians who want to leave me alone to bear the entire burden,'[17] Joseph bitterly complained to Ligne. Joseph's desperation to share the burden was the reason for Ligne's frantic and venomous attempts to force Potemkin either to storm Ochakov or to bear the blame for Joseph's failures. In September, the ablest Ottoman commander, Grand Vizier Yusuf-Pasha, surprised Joseph in his camp and the Kaiser barely escaped with his life, fleeing back to Vienna. Joseph learned the hard way that he was not Frederick the Great. 'As for our ally,' Potemkin joked, 'whenever he's around, everything goes wrong.'† The Turks had certainly improved their military skills since the last war – 'the Turks are different', Potemkin told Catherine, 'and the devil has taught them'. The Austrians could not understand why Catherine did not order Potemkin to storm, but 'she negotiates with him for everything'. Half the time, he did not even reply to her letters. 'He has decided to do what he wants.'[18]

The Prince often played billiards with Ligne until 6 a.m. or just stayed up to chat. One night, Ligne gave him a dinner for fifty generals and all his exotic friends.[19] Potemkin was often depressed and then he would 'put his handkerchief dipped in lavender water around his forehead, sign of his hypochondria'. During the heat, he served icecreams and sorbets. At night, Ligne and the rest of them listened to his 'numerous and unique orchestra conducted by the famous and admirable Sarti'. There is a story that during one of these recitals, as the horns were piping, Potemkin in his dressing gown asked a German artillery officer: 'What do you think of Ochakov?' 'You think the walls of Ochakov are like those of Jericho that fell to the sound of trumpets?', replied the officer.[20]

There were consolations of the feminine kind when they were rejoined

---

* There were sound military reasons for not storming until the fleet had control over the Liman and until artillery had arrived, which did not happen until August.

† Potemkin was not alone in delaying: when Ligne rode off to join Rumiantsev-Zadunaisky, he found him just as inactive, while Count Nikolai Saltykov ostentatiously delayed his attack on Khotin. It was Russian policy as well as Russian habit – as Kutuzov was to demonstrate to such effect in 1812.

by the three graces, whom Ligne called 'the most beautiful girls in the Empire'.[21] The Prince was falling in love with Pavel Potemkin's wife. Praskovia Andreevna, *née* Zakrevskaya, had a bad figure but a 'superb face, skin of dazzling whiteness and beautiful eyes, little intelligence but very self-sufficient'. Her arch notes to Potemkin survive in the archives: 'You mock me, my dear cousin, in telling me as an excuse that you await my orders to come to see me ... I am always charmed.'[22] Damas was equally charmed by Potemkin's libidinous niece-by-marriage, the twenty-five-year-old Ekaterina Samoilova. Her portrait by Lampi shows a bold, full-lipped sexuality with jewels in her hair and a turban tottering on the back of her head. When she later had children, the wags joked that her husband, Samoilov, never saw her – but she still provided ample 'proof of her fecundity'.[23] After a freezing day in the trenches, Damas, who dashingly sported French and Russian uniform on alternate days, visited the ladies' tent: 'I hoped that a more energetic siege would make them surrender more quickly than the town.' He soon succeeded with Samoilova, but was then wounded again. Potemkin consoled his protégé by bringing Skavronskaya, another newly arrived sultana, to his sickbed.[24] The Prince did not want to deprive Damas of 'seeing one of the prettiest women in Europe'.*

The Capitan-Pasha met the Sebastopol Fleet off Fidonise, near the Danube delta, on 3 July and Potemkin's baby passed its first test – just. Ghazi Hassan withdrew and now returned to save Ochakov. The Crocodile delivered supplies and another 1,500 Janissaries for the garrison. Twice the supplies got through – much to the admirals' shame and Potemkin's fury. But the entire Turkish fleet was again cooped up under the walls of Ochakov and therefore neutralized: as ever, there was some method in Potemkin's madness.

On 5 September, the Prince, Nassau, Damas and Ligne sailed into the Liman to examine the Hassan-Pasha Redoubt and discuss Nassau's plan to land 2,000 men under the wall of the lower battery. The Turks opened up with grapeshot and shell. Potemkin sat alone in the stern, with his medals glittering on his chest and an expression of 'cold dignity that was deliberately assumed and truly admirable'.[25]

Potemkin's entourage, particularly his strange band of neophyte admirals and foreign spies, began to disband with mutual dis-

---

* Back at Gatchina, Grand Duke Paul's microcosm of Prussian paradomania, the Tsarevich was disgusted by this harem at war and sneeringly demanded where in Vauban's siege instructions did it say that nieces were necessary to take cities. This was rich since Paul himself had asked to take his wife to the war with him in 1787.

illusionment. Life at Ochakov became harder. 'We have no water,' wrote Ligne, 'we eat flies and we're a 100 leagues from a market. We only drink wine . . . we sleep four hours after dinner.' Bitter winter came early. Ligne burned his carriage for firewood. The camp became 'snow and shit'. Even the Liman was green from the burned bodies of Turks.[26]

Samuel Bentham, appalled by the stench of decay and dysentery, called war 'an abominable trade'. Potemkin indulgently sent him to the Far East* on the sort of mission that appealed to both of them.[27] The King of Poland's eyes, Littlepage, stormed off when Potemkin suspected him of trying to undermine Nassau. The little American protested he had never been 'a troublemaker'. Serenissimus soothed him and he went back to Stanislas-Augustus.[28] The real victim of this parting of the ways was America's famous sailor John Paul Jones, whose obscure origins meant he was always under pressure to prove himself. His thin-skinned, pedantic behaviour did not endear him to Serenissimus. When Nassau was promoted rear-admiral, Jones got into a ludicrous row about his own precedence and salutes – his account gave six reasons why he need not salute Nassau!

Soon anything that went wrong at sea was blamed on poor Jones. Potemkin ordered the American to destroy ships, moored off Ochakov, or at least spike their cannons. Jones tried twice but for some reason did not succeed. Potemkin cancelled the order and assigned it to Anton Golavaty and his beloved Zaporogian Cossacks, who accomplished it. Jones complained rudely to the Prince who replied: 'I assure you Mr Rear-Admiral that in command, I never enter into individual considerations, I give justice when I should render it . . . As for my orders, I am not obliged to give account of them and I changed these same orders according to circumstance . . . I've commanded a long time and I know very well its rules.'[29] Serenissimus decided Jones was 'unable to command' and had him recalled by Catherine.[30] 'I'll eternally regret having had the misfortune to losing your good graces,' Jones told Potemkin on 20 October. 'I dare say it's difficult but very possible to find sea officers of my skill . . . but you'll never find a man with a heart as susceptible to loyalty with more zeal . . .'.[31] At a last interview, Jones bitterly blamed

* Colonel Bentham was to command two battalions on the Chinese–Mongolian border, create a regimental school, discover new lands, form alliances with Mongols, Kalmyks and Kirghiz and open trading with Japan and Alaska. He also devised a Potemkinian plan to defeat China with 100,000 men. In 1790 he headed back via Petersburg to Potemkin's headquarters in Bender to report to the Prince and get permission to return to England, which he finally did. There ended a unique adventure in Anglo-Russian relations.

Potemkin for dividing the command in the first place. 'Agreed,' snapped the Prince–Marshal, 'but it's too late now.'[32] On 29 October, Jones departed for Petersburg,[33] where he soon learned the danger of making powerful enemies.

After another attempt to bombard the town into submission by land and sea, Nassau, irritated by the delay and out of favour as Potemkin discovered his devious manipulations of truth, stormed off to Warsaw. 'His luck didn't hold,' Potemkin told Catherine.[34]

Joseph's spy Ligne left too. Potemkin wrote him the 'sweetest, tenderest, most naive' goodbye. Ligne apologized for hurting his friend in an unpublished semi-legible note to the Prince – 'Pardon, 1000 Pardons, my Prince' – that has the air of a rejected lover on the eve of parting.[35] Potemkin, 'sometimes the best of men', seemed to awaken out of a dream to say goodbye to Ligne: 'he took me in his arms for a long time, repeatedly ran after me, started again and finally let me go with pain'. But when he reached Vienna Ligne told everyone that Ochakov would never be taken and set about ruining Potemkin's reputation.[36] So young Roger de Damas lost his two patrons. The Prince offered himself to replace them as 'friend and protector'. Thus Potemkin, who went from 'most perfect graciousness' to 'the most morose rudeness' in seconds, inspired 'gratitude, devotion and hatred at the same moment'.[37]

Catherine worried about her Prince's glory and consort's comfort: she sent him the commemorative dish and sword for the former, and a jewel and a fur coat for the latter. Potemkin was delighted: 'Thank you, Lady Matushka ...'. The jewels showed 'royal generosity' and the fur displayed 'maternal caring. And this', he added with feeling, 'is more dear to me than beads and gold.'[38]

The weather at Ochakov and the politics in Europe deteriorated together at the end of the October. The cold was now severe. When Potemkin inspected the trenches, he told the soldiers they did not need to rise at his approach: 'Only try not to lie down before the Turkish cannons.' Soon the sufferings of the army were 'inconceivable' in the snow and ice with temperatures of minus 15 degrees Centigrade. The men rolled up their tents and lived in burrows in the ground that shocked Damas, though actually these *zemlianka*s were the traditional Russian way for the troops to camp in the cold. There was hardly any food, meat or brandy. Potemkin and Damas received the latest news from France. 'Do you think that when your King has assembled the States-General ... he will dine at the hour that pleases him?' Potemkin asked him. 'Hell, he will only eat when they are kind enough to permit it!'

Soon it was so bad that even Samoilova had to go and camp with her husband, who commanded the left wing. This caused her lover Damas considerable inconvenience: 'I was forced to take my chance of being frozen in the snow in order to pay her the attentions she deigned to accept.'[39]

The misery of the army was the 'absolute fault of Prince Potemkin', Cobenzl told Joseph. 'It's he who lost a whole year before unhappy Ochakov where the army has suffered more by illness and lack of substance than it would have lost in two battles.'[40] Potemkin's critics, especially the Austrians, claimed his delay caused the death of 20,000 men and 2,000 horses, according to the prejudiced Frenchman, the Comte de Langeron, who was not even there.[41] Forty to fifty men were said to be dying daily in the hospital.[42] 'Scarcely any man recovers from dysentery.'[43] It is hard to discover how many really died, but Potemkin certainly lost fewer men than earlier generals like Münnich and Rumiantsev-Zadunaisky, both of whose armies were so decimated they could scarcely campaign. The Austrians, who damned him over Ochakov, were in no position to criticize: at exactly the same time, 172,000 of their soldiers were sick; and 33,000 died, more than Potemkin's entire army.[44]

Yet the foreigners mocked Potemkin's generosity and care of his troops while complaining simultaneously about his brutal indifference. Samoilov, who lived with his forces, admitted there was an 'extraordinary freeze but our troops did not suffer' because Potemkin ensured that they had trench fur-coats, hats and *kengi* – fur or felt galoshes pulled over their boots – in addition to special tents. They were supplied with meat and vodka and 'hot punch of Riga balsam'.[45]

Serenissimus distributed a great deal of money among the troops in the field, 'which made them spoilt ... without relieving their wants', claimed Damas, with breathtaking aristocratic prejudice and disdain for the ordinary soldiers.[46] Russians understood him better. Potemkin was, wrote his secretary, 'naturally disposed to love humanity'. As for the care of the dying, Tsebrikov saw forty hospital tents that were placed beside Potemkin's tent at his express order so they would be better treated: the Prince visited them to check, the sort of care and concern rarely shown by British generals sixty years later during the Crimean War. Yet Tsebrikov also met a convoy of carts returning from the army, each carrying the bodies of three or four men.[47] The army did suffer, many died, but Potemkin's medical care, money, food, clothes and humanitarianism, unparalleled in Russia, may explain the army's survival.

Finally a deserter informed Serenissimus that the Turkish Seraskier (commander) would never surrender and had executed the officers with whom he had been negotiating.[48] The Prince still waited.

The Empress herself was becoming impatient. Russia was still at war on two fronts, but the Swedish front had been improved by Greig's defeat of the Swedish navy at Gothland and by the intervention of Denmark, which attacked Sweden's rear. In August, England, Prussia and Holland concluded their Triple Alliance. In Poland, the pent-up resentment of Russian domination exploded in a celebration of liberty. 'A great hatred has risen against us in Poland,' Catherine told Potemkin on 27 November.[49] She tried to negotiate the treaty with Poland along the traditional lines, but Prussia outbid her by proposing a treaty that offered the Poles the hope of a stronger constitution and freedom from Russia. Catherine was losing Poland, but Potemkin could free her hands by making a quick peace with the Turks.

'Do please write to me about this quickly and in detail,' the Empress told the Prince, 'so I won't miss anything important and, after the capture of Ochakov, endeavour most of all to start peace negotiations.'[50] The ever adaptable Potemkin had already warned Catherine to realign herself closer to Prussia and proposed his Polish alliance: his suggestions had been ignored and his warnings had turned out to be right. He wanted to resign again.[51] The Poles, backed now by Prussia, demanded the withdrawal of all Russian troops from their Commonwealth, even though the Russian army in the south depended on Poland for its winter quarters and most of its supplies. It was a further blow. 'If you retire . . .', Catherine told him, 'I'll take it as a deathblow.' She begged him to capture Ochakov and place the army in winter quarters. 'There is nothing in the world I want more than your coming here . . .', partly to see him after such a long time and partly 'to discuss a lot with you tête-à-tête'.[52]

The Prince could not resist saying 'I told you so' to Catherine: 'It's bad in Poland which it wouldn't have been of course with my project but that's how it is.' He proposed pulling the teeth of the Triple Alliance by putting out feelers to Prussia and England and making peace with Sweden. His letter reads like an order to an empress: 'You'll work out later how to get revenge.'[53] The secret reports of his *homme d'affaires*, Garnovsky, from Petersburg suggested that the discontent about Potemkin's handling of Ochakov had now spread to Catherine. The Court had been displeased with the delay as early as August. Alexander Vorontsov and Zavadovsky undermined Potemkin's position and resisted his desire for rapprochement with England and Prussia. Catherine was 'dissatisfied'.[54] Only the arrival of Serenissimus himself would alleviate her state of confusion and vacillation.[55]

When the remains of the Turkish fleet retired to port for the winter on 4 November, leaving the garrison alone, Potemkin made his plans.[56] In late November, the entire cavalry was dismissed to go into winter quarters, a miserable and often fatal march through the snowy wilderness.[57] Back at the siege, the Turks made a sortie on 11 November against one of the Potemkin's batteries and killed General S.P. Maximovich, whose head then lolled forlornly on the battlements.[58] Lavish snowfalls delayed the denouement.*

On 27 November Catherine begged him: 'Take Ochakov and make peace with the Turks.'[59] On 1 December, Potemkin signed his plan to storm the fortress with six columns of roughly 5,000 men each, which would give 30,000, but Fanshawe claimed only 14,500 were left.[60] Samoilov, who led one of the columns, says the Prince had waited deliberately until the Liman itself was frozen, so that Ochakov could also be attacked from the sea.[61] On the 5th, the order of battle was set during a war council. Damas was assigned to spearhead the column storming the Stamboul Gate. He prepared to die by writing an adieu to his sister, returning the love letters of his Parisian mistress, the Marquise de Coigny – and then spending the evening with his Russian one, Samoilova, until 2 a.m., when he crept back to his tent.

Potemkin himself passed the most important night of his life so far in a dug-out in the forward trenches. The Prince's stubborn valet actually refused to admit Repnin, who had arrived to inform him that the assault was about to start, because he did not dare awaken his master: 'an example of passive obedience unimaginable in any country but Russia'. The Prince of Taurida prayed as the men advanced.[62]

At 4 a.m. on 6 December, three shells gave the signal. With shouts of hurrah, the columns charged forward towards the entrenchments. The Turks resisted wildly. The Russians gave them no quarter. Damas stormed the Stamboul Gate with his Grenadiers. The moment they were inside, 'the most horrible and unparalleled massacre began forthwith', earning Frederick the Great's nickname for them – 'les oursomanes', half-bear, half-psychopath.[63]

* But first, on 7 November, Potemkin ordered his Zaporogians to take the island of Berezan, which offered Ochakov a last potential source of support and provisions: the Cossacks rowed there in their 'seagulls' and took the island, making their distinctive menacing cries. They captured twenty-seven cannons and two months of provisions for Ochakov – showing it was a sound decision.

The Russian soldiers went almost mad with 'fury': even when the garrison surrendered, they ran through the streets killing every man, woman and child they could find – between 8,000 and 11,000 Turks in all – 'like a strong whirlwind', Potemkin told Catherine, 'that in a moment tossed people on to their hearses'.[64] This was literally havoc, justified by the Russians as holy war against the infidel. The Turks were killed in such numbers and in such density that they fell in piles, over which Damas and his men trampled, their legs sinking into bleeding bodies. 'We found ourselves covered in gore and shattered brains' – but inside the town. The bodies were so closely packed that Damas had to advance by stepping from body to body until his left foot slipped into a heap of gore, three or four corpses deep, and straight into the mouth of a wounded Turk underneath. The jaws clamped so hard on his heel that they tore away a piece of his boot.[65]

There was so much plunder that soldiers captured handfuls of diamonds, pearls and gold that could be bought round the camp the next day for almost nothing. No one even bothered to steal silver. Potemkin saved an emerald the size of an egg for his Empress.[66] 'Turkish blood flowed like rivers,' Russian soldiers sang as they marched into the next century. 'And the Pasha fell to his knees before Potemkin.'[67]

The Seraskier of Ochakov, a tough old pasha, was brought bare-headed before Serenissimus, who veered between grief and exultation. 'We owe this bloodshed to your obstinacy,' said the Prince. If Ochakov had surrendered, they could have avoided all this. The Seraskier seemed surprised to find a commander so moved by the loss of life. 'I've done my duty,' shrugged Seraskier Hussein-Pasha, 'and you yours. Fate turned against us.' He had only persisted, he added with Oriental flattery, in order to render His Highness's victory all the more brilliant. Potemkin ordered that the Seraskier's lost turban be found in the ruins.

By 7 a.m., after four hours of savage fighting, Ochakov was Russian.* Potemkin ordered a stop to the slaughter, which was instantly obeyed. Special measures were taken to protect the clothes and jewels of women and to look after the wounded. All witnesses, even the foreigners, agreed that Potemkin's assault was 'excellent' and shrewdly planned in relation to the fortifications.[68]

---

* The town no longer exists except for one building, a former mosque that has been converted into a museum. It is a typical mark of the blind Soviet prejudice against Potemkin that the museum is dedicated to Suvorov. In fact, Suvorov was not only *not* in command at the storming of Ochakov, he was *not even present* there. Yet the museum hails him as its victor and genius and barely mentions Potemkin. Such are the absurdities of the central state planning of truth.

The Prince entered Ochakov with his entourage and seraglio – 'handsome Amazons who delighted', according to the Grand Dukes' mathematics tutor Charles Masson, 'in visiting fields of battle and admiring the fine corpses of Turks as they lay on their backs, scimitars in hand'.[69] Stories already abounded, even before detailed reports had reached Petersburg, of Potemkin's luxurious negligence towards the wounded. 'As they rarely report the truth about me,' Potemkin corrected the gossip to Catherine, 'they lie here too.' Serenissimus turned his palatial tent into a hospital, moving to live in a small dug-out.[70]

Damas ran up to join Potemkin and his 'nieces' – especially Ekaterina Samoilova, who evidently gave him a delicious prize. 'This particular form of happiness ... has never before rewarded any man so promptly for a morning of such cruel joy. Most men have to wait until they return to their capital,' including Samoilova's long-suffering husband, no doubt.[71]

Lieutenant-Colonel Bauer, the fastest world traveller in Russia, galloped off to inform the Empress. When he arrived, Catherine was asleep, ill and tense. Mamonov awoke her. 'I was poorly,' said the Empress, 'but you have cured me.' Potemkin wrote to her the next day – 'I congratulate you with the fortress,' 310 cannons and 180 banners; 9,500 Turks were killed and 2,500 Russians. 'Oh, how sorry I am for them,' wrote the Prince.[72]

Massacres are easy to make and hard to clear up. There were so many Turkish bodies that they could not all be buried, even if the ground had been soft enough to do so. The cadavers were piled in carts and taken out to the Liman where they were dumped on the ice. Still moist with gore, they froze there into macabre blood-blackened pyramids. The Russian ladies took their sledges out on to the ice to admire them.[73]

Catherine was triumphant: 'I take you by the ears with both my hands and kiss you, my dear friend ... You've shut everybody's mouths and this successful event gives you the chance to show generosity to those who criticize you blindly and stupidly.'[74] No longer able to hide their incompetence behind Potemkin, the Austrians were almost disappointed. 'Taking Ochakov is very advantageous to continue the war,' Joseph told Kaunitz in Vienna. 'But not to make peace.'[75] Courtiers now laughed at Ligne, who had been 'singing at the top of his voice' that Ochakov would not be taken that year.[76] Potemkin's critics rushed to write sycophantic letters.[77] 'There's a man who never goes by the ordinary road,' said Littlepage, 'but still arrives at his goal.'[78]

'Te Deums' were sung on 16 December to the boom of 101 cannons. 'Public joy was great.' Bauer, promoted to colonel and presented with a gold snuff-box with diamonds, was sent back bearing a diamond-set star of St George and a diamond-encrusted sword, worth 60,000 roubles, for the Prince of Taurida.[79] Potemkin was exhausted but did not rest on his laurels. There was much to do before he could return to Petersburg. In one of his bursts of euphoric energy, he inspected the new naval yards at Vitovka, decided to found a new town called Nikolaev, then toured Kherson to review the fleet. But his most important job was to garrison Ochakov, send the fleet back to Sebastopol, convert the Turkish prizes into sixty-two-gun ships-of-the-line, and settle the army in winter quarters. This was no easy task, since Poland was increasingly hostile, emboldened by the Anglo-Prussian alliance.

The Prince called again for *détente* with Prussia. Catherine disagreed and suggested western European affairs were *her* department. 'My lady, I am not a cosmopolitan,' replied Potemkin. 'I don't give a jot about Europe but, when it intervenes in affairs entrusted to me, there's no way I can be indifferent.' This is clear evidence of the partners' division of responsibilities and Potemkin's refusal to be bound by even that. As for the Prussians, 'I'm not in love with the Prussian King' nor afraid of his troops. He just thought 'they should be disdained less than the rest'.[80]

At last, Serenissimus headed towards Petersburg. 'I shall take you there myself,' he told Damas. 'We mustn't be separated. I myself will undertake the arrangements.'[81] The sledges were ready. The Prince and Damas climbed into those cockpits like baby's cradles and wrapped themselves in furs and leather. 'Are you ready?', Potemkin's muffled voice called to Damas. 'I've ordered that you are to stay close to me.' A lackey jumped on to the seats on the back of the sledges and whipped the horses, which sped into the night, escorted on all sides by Cossacks holding burning torches. Damas was left behind, only catching up at Mogilev. He just wanted to sleep; but, wherever the Prince arrived, the local governors and nobility had the garrison on parade and a fête awaiting him. Damas was led straight out of his sledge and into a 'magnificent ball', where 'the whole town were assembled'. The Prince waved aside Damas' worries about either his clothes or his fatigue, summoned all the girls and 'without further ado, he brought me a partner, whereupon ... I danced until six in the morning'. By noon, they were on the road again.[82]

Petersburg awaited the Prince's return with the dread and excitement of the Second Coming. 'All the town is worried by waiting for His Highness,' reported Garnovsky. 'There is no other conversation except this.' The diplomats watched the road – especially the Prussians and the English. A British diplomat got drunk at Naryshkin's and shouted a toast to

Potemkin. One disappointed but ever hopeful American corsair, John Paul Jones, also eagerly anticipated the Prince, who would decide his destiny. 'The Prince has not yet arrived,' Zavadovsky complained to Field-Marshal Rumiantsev-Zadunaisky. 'Without him – nothing.'[83]

Catherine followed his swift journey, which reminded of her of a bird's migration, 'and you wonder why you get tired. If you arrive here ill, I'll pull your ears at our first encounter – however glad I am to see you.'[84] But Catherine remained edgy, besieged on all sides by wars, coalitions and Court intrigues. Mamonov was a comfort but little help in affairs of state: besides he was now always ill. Catherine fretted about her consort's welcome – especially when she realized that she had raised triumphal arches to Prince Orlov and Rumiantsev-Zadunaisky yet forgotten Serenissimus. 'But Your Majesty knows him so well that she does not need to keep accounts,' replied her secretary, Khrapovitsky. 'True,' she said, 'but he's human too and maybe he'd like it.' So she ordered the marble gate at Tsarskoe Selo illuminated and decorated with an appropriately ambiguous ode by her Court poet, Petrov: 'You'll enter Sophia Cathedral with clapping.' This referred to Istanbul's Agia Sophia again. Catherine mused that Potemkin might 'be in Constantinople this year but don't tell me about it all of a sudden'.[85] The road was lit up for six miles, day and night. The guns of the fortress were to be fired – the prerogative of the Sovereign. 'Is the Prince loved in the town?', she asked her valet, Zakhar Zotov. 'Only by God and You,' he bravely replied. Catherine did not mind. She said she was too ill to let him go to the south again. 'My God,' she murmured, 'I need the Prince now.'[86]

At 6 p.m. on Sunday, 4 February 1789, Serenissimus arrived in Petersburg in the midst of a ball for the birthday of Grand Duke Paul's daughter. Potemkin went straight to his apartments in the house adjoining the Winter Palace. The Empress left the festivities and surprised the Prince as he was changing. She stayed with him a long time.[87]

28

MY SUCCESSES ARE YOURS

We shall glorify Potemkin
We shall plait him a bouquet in our hearts.
Russian soldiers' marching song, 'The Moldavian Campaign of 1790'

The favour of the Empress was agreeable;
And though the duty waxed a little hard,
Young people at his time of life should be able
To come off handsomely in that regard.
Lord Byron, *Don Juan*, Canto X: 22

On 11 February 1789, two hundred Ottoman banners from Ochakov were marched past the Winter Palace by a squadron of Life-Guards accompanied by four blaring trumpeters. The parade was followed by a splendid dinner in Potemkin's honour.[1] 'The Prince we see is extremely affable and gracious to everyone – we celebrate his arrival every day,' Zavadovsky sourly told Rumiantsev-Zadunaisky. 'All faith is in *one person*.'[2] Potemkin received another 100,000 roubles for the Taurida Palace, a diamond-studded baton and, most importantly of all, the retirement of Rumiantsev-Zadunaisky, commander of the Ukraine Army. The Prince was appointed commander of both armies.

Potemkin liberally distributed honours to his men: he insisted Suvorov, whom he brought to Petersburg with him, should receive a plume of diamonds for his hat with a 'K' for Kinburn.[3] He ordered his favoured general straight down to Rumiantsev's old command, where the Turks were already launching raids.* The Prince promised Suvorov his own separate corps.[4]

The festivities could dispel neither the tension of Russia's international position nor Catherine's private anguish. After the dinner that night, Catherine quarrelled with her favourite, Mamonov. 'Tears,' noted Khrapovitsky, 'the evening was spent in bed.' Mamonov was behaving ominously: he was often ill, unfriendly or just absent. When Catherine asked

---

* Suvorov, according to the histories, was supposed to have complained to Catherine that jealous Potemkin was excluding him from senior commands. The truth was the opposite.

the Prince about it, he replied, 'Haven't you been jealous of Princess Shcherbatova,' (a maid-of-honour) adding, 'Isn't there an *affaire d'amour*?' He then repeated 'a hundred times': 'Oh Matushka, spit on him.'[5] Potemkin could hardly have warned her more clearly about her lover. But Catherine, tired and almost sixty, did not listen.

She was so used to hearing what she wanted and so accustomed to her routine with Mamonov that she did not rise to Potemkin's warnings. Besides, Serenissimus turned against every favourite at one time or another. So the trouble with Mamonov continued – 'more tears' recorded Khrapovitsky the next day. Catherine spent all day in bed and her consort came to the rescue. 'After dinner, Prince G.A. Potemkin of Taurida acted as peacemaker' between the Empress and Mamonov.[6] But he only papered over the cracks in the relationship. Nor could the Prince solve all of Russia's problems.

The leadership was divided over Russia's worsening position. While it held its own on two fronts against the Turks and Swedes, Russia's power was haemorrhaging in Poland. The Polish 'Four Year Sejm', now encouraged by Berlin, was enthusiastically, if naively, dismantling the Russian protectorate and throwing itself into the arms of Prussia. 'Great hatred'[7] of Russia was driving Poland towards reform of its constitution and war with Catherine. Prussia cynically backed the idealism of the Polish 'Patriots' – even though Frederick William's true interest was the partition, not the reform, of Poland.

That was not all: Prussia and England were also working hard to keep Sweden and the Turks in the war. Pitt now hoped to recruit Poland to join a 'federative system' against the two imperial powers. This alarmed Vienna, where Joseph's health was failing – he was 'vomiting blood'. The Austrians fretted that Potemkin had become pro-Prussian. All Joseph could suggest to his Ambassador was to flatter the vanity of the 'all-powerful being'.[8]

So should Russia risk war with Prussia or come to an agreement with it, which meant making peace with the Turks, betraying the shaky Austrians and probably partitioning Poland, which would be compensated with Ottoman territory? This was the Gordian knot that Potemkin's long-awaited arrival was meant to cut.

Potemkin had for some time been advising Catherine to soften her obstinate contempt towards Frederick William. The Council expected him to try to persuade her to cut a deal because he knew that Russia could not fight Prussia and Poland as well as Turkey and Sweden. Since it was not yet time to make peace with the Sultan, Potemkin had to avoid war elsewhere. Serenissimus did not want a return to Panin's Prussian system, so he advised Catherine: 'Provoke the Prussian king to take whatever from Poland.'[9] If he lulled the Prussian King into revealing the real greed of his Polish masquerade, the Poles would lose their love for Prussia.[10] 'Sincerity', he told his ally Bezborodko,[11] 'is unnecessary in politics.'[12]

This visit also saw the end of his friendship with the French envoy, Ségur, who had supported the criticisms of Ligne and Cobenzl during Ochakov. Ségur was hurt: 'Your friendship for me has cooled a bit, mine won't ever imitate it. I'm devoted to you for life.'[13] They had been discussing a Quadruple Alliance with the Bourbons and Habsburgs,[14] but Britain was ever stronger, France ever weaker. 'I would have advised my Sovereign to ally with Louis the Fat, Louis the Young, Saint Louis, clever Louis XI, wise Louis XII, Louis the Great, even with Louis le Bien-Aimé,' Serenissimus teased Ségur, 'but not with Louis the Democrat.'[15]

Poor Ségur, playing chess with the Prince, had to endure an entire evening of anti-French comic sketches from his Court 'fool' – Russian nobles still had clowns in their households. But he got his own back by bribing the fool to tease Potemkin about Russian military blunders. The Prince overturned the table and threw the chess pieces at the fleeing buffoon, but he saw Ségur's joke and the evening ended 'most gaily'.[16]

Ségur was about to turn detective, trawling the brothels and taverns of Petersburg on behalf of Potemkin's American 'pirate', Jones. In April, just as Potemkin was about to make Jones 'the happiest man alive' with a new job, the American was arrested and accused of paedophile rape. The story has the seedy gleam of a modern sex scandal. Jones appealed to Serenissimus: 'A bad woman has accused me of violating her daughter!' Worse, the daughter was said to be nine years old. He beseeched Potemkin: 'Shall it be said that, in Russia, a wretched woman, who eloped from her husband and family, stole away her daughter, lives here in a house of ill repute and leads a debauched and adulterous life, has found credit enough, on a simple complaint, unsupported by any proof, to affect the honour of a general officer of reputation, who has merited and received the decorations of America, France and this empire?' Jones, once a Parisian Lothario, admitted to Potemkin, 'I love women' and 'the pleasures that one only obtains from that sex, but to get such things by force, is horrible to me'.[17]

Potemkin, deluged with responsibilities and already disliking Jones, did not reply. The capital became a desert to Jones. Detective Ségur was the only friend who supported his old American comrade and resolved to investigate who had framed him. He discovered that Jones had told

Potemkin the truth – the accusing mother was a procuress who traded 'a vile traffic in young girls'. The girl, Katerina Goltzwart, was not nine but twelve, if not fourteen. She sold butter to guests at Jones's hotel, the London Tavern. In his statement to the chief of police three days after the incident, Jones admitted that the 'depraved girl' came several times to his room. He always gave her money. He claimed that he had not taken her virginity but 'each time she came *chez moi*, she lent herself with the best grace to all a man could want of her'.

Ségur asked Potemkin to reinstate Jones and not charge him. The latter was possible but not the former. 'Thanks for what you tried to do for Paul Jones, even though you did not achieve what I wanted,' Ségur wrote to the Prince. 'Paul Jones is no more guilty than I, and a man of his rank has never suffered such humiliation, through the accusation of a woman, whose husband certifies she is a pimp and whose daughter solicits the inns.'[18] Thanks to Ségur's investigations and Potemkin's tepid help, Jones was not prosecuted and was received by Catherine one last time on 26 June 1789. Who framed Jones? Potemkin was above such vendettas. The English officers hated the American corsair enough to frame him, but Ségur the detective concluded that Prince de Nassau-Siegen was the culprit.

Once back in Paris, Jones wrote a vainglorious account of the Liman and bombarded Potemkin with complaints about the medals he was owed. 'Time will teach you, my lord,' he wrote to Serenissimus on 13 July 1790, 'that I am neither a mountebank nor a swindler but a man loyal and true.'[19]

On 27 March, the pacific, wine-quaffing Sultan Abdul-Hamid I died. This made things worse, not better, for Russia because Selim III, his eighteen-year-old successor, was an aggressive, intelligent reformer whose determination to fight was buttressed by Moslem fanatics and the ambassadors of Prussia, England and Sweden. Austria and Russia wished to discuss peace with Selim in order to ward off a possible Prussian intervention in the Turkish War – but the augurs were not encouraging. The Austrian Chancellor, Kaunitz, wrote to Potemkin about Selim's ferocity, alleging that when he had once spotted a Polish Jew on the streets of Istanbul wearing the (wrong) yellow shoes, he had had him beheaded before the unfortunate had a chance to explain that he was a foreigner.[20] Peace could be won only on the battlefields in Potemkin's next campaign: no wonder Catherine was so anxious.

Potemkin and Catherine still flirted with one another. After her birthday reception at Paul's palace on 12 April, he sweetly boosted her flagging morale by complimenting the 'mother of her subjects, especially to me' and the 'angelic virtues' of the 'first-born eagle nestling', her grandson Alexander.[21] Before he left he gave her an exquisite present, 'a so-called bagetelle,' she wrote to him, 'which is of rare beauty and, more to the point, as inimitable as you yourself. I marvel at both – it and you. You really are the personification of wit.'[22]

On 6 May 1789, having laid plans with Catherine for every eventuality, including wars against Prussia and Poland, the Prince of Taurida left Tsarskoe Selo for the south. The old partners were not to meet again for almost two years.[23]

Serenissimus raced to the front, where he divided the combined Ukraine and Ekaterinoslav armies – about 60,000 men – into his own main army and four corps. The strategy was to fight round the Black Sea in a south-westerly direction through the Principalities of Moldavia and Wallachia (today's Moldova and Rumania), taking the fortresses on each river: Dniester, Pruth, then Danube. Potemkin's army was to cover the Dniester until the Turks were diminished enough to begin fighting up the Danube into modern Bulgaria – to the walls of Constantinople.[24]

The main Austrian army, under one of their many Scottish officers, Field-Marshal Loudon, was to attack Belgrade (in today's Serbia), while Prince Frederick Joseph of Saxe-Coburg-Saarlfeld co-operated with the Russians in Wallachia and Moldavia. The most important force, except Potemkin's own, was Suvorov's 'flying corps', the Third, which was to protect the 'hinge' with the Austrians on the Russian extreme left. Suvorov balanced himself across three parallel rivers – the Sereth, Berlad and Pruth – and waited.

The new Grand Vizier Hassan-Pasha Genase commanded an Ottoman army of 100,000: his strategy was to smash the Austrians where the link between the allies was weakest around the rivers Pruth and Sereth, close to Suvorov's 'hinge', while a new armada landed on the Crimea. Ex-Capitan-Pasha Ghazi Hassan, the white-bearded Crocodile of Sea Battles, took to the land in command of a 30,000-strong corps that was to distract Potemkin's main army while the Vizier broke through. The Turkish manoeuvres were unusually adept. The Russians were vigilant. On 11 May, Potemkin crossed the Bug, massed his forces at Olviopol and then advanced towards the powerful Ottoman fortress of Bender on the Dniester.

In the West, the world was changing. Potemkin was settling into his new headquarters at Olviopol when the Parisian mob stormed the Bastille on 3/14 July. The National Assembly passed the Declaration of the

Rights of Man on 15/26 August.[25] The Polish Patriots, who were opposed to Russia, were encouraged by the French Revolution – Warsaw enjoyed a febrile fiesta of freedom and hope. Poland demanded that Russia withdraw its troops and magazines. Potemkin carefully monitored Poland, yet he had no choice but to comply.[26] He continued to pursue his own Polish policies, vigorously expanding his Black Sea Cossacks to act as an Orthodox spearhead which would raise the pro-Russian eastern area of the Commonwealth when the time came.[27]

Potemkin 'flew' between his headquarters at Olviopol, where Russia, Poland and Turkey met, and Kherson, Ochakov and Elisabethgrad, checking and inspecting his vast front until he had exhausted himself with 'haemorrhoids and fever', as he told Catherine, 'but nothing can stop me except death'.[28] She encouraged him by sending one of his rewards for Ochakov, the diamond-studded field-marshal's baton.

The Grand Vizier stealthily pushed forward, with a corps of 30,000, to strike at Coburg's Austrians before they could join up with the Russians. At this vital moment, a long and anguished secret letter arrived from a frantic empress. Just as the Turks probed the weakest point of Potemkin's front, Catherine's relationship with Mamonov disintegrated in the most humiliating way.

Catherine finally understood that Mamonov was not happy: it is hard to blame him. The favourite always complained that life at Court was like surviving in the jungle.[29] His role as a companion to an older woman bored him, now that he was accustomed to luxury. Potemkin blocked any political role for him – on his last visit, the Prince had vetoed Mamonov's request to be a Court vice-chancellor. His sexual duties may have become tedious, even distasteful.

Catherine was turning sixty. She remained publicly majestic, privately simple and playful. 'I saw her once or twice a week for ten years,' wrote Masson, 'every time with renewed admiration.' Her modesty with her staff was admirable: Countess Golovina recalled how she and her fellow maids-of-honour were happily eating dinner when they noted that the 'beautiful' hand of the servant who handed them their plates wore a 'superb solitaire ring'. They looked up to find it was the Empress herself. She took care with her appearance, keeping her good skin and fine hands. Her now white hair was carefully dressed – but she was exceedingly fat; her legs were often so swollen that they 'lost their shape'. Her architects, including Cameron at Tsarskoe Selo, and nobles whose houses she visited, gradually installed *pentes douces* to make it easier for her to enter buildings. Her voice was hoarse, her nose may have become more 'utterly

Greek' or aquiline, she was cursed with wind and indigestion, and she had probably lost some of her teeth. She was older,* and time exaggerated both her affectionate nature and her emotional neediness.[30]

The Empress wrote Mamonov a letter generously offering to release him and arrange his happiness by marrying him to one of the richest heiresses in Russia. His reply devastated her. He confessed he had been in love with Princess Daria Shcherbatova, a maid-of-honour, for a 'year and a half' and asked to marry her. Catherine gasped and then collapsed at this shameless betrayal of her trust and feelings. Mamonov rushed after her, threw himself at her feet and revealed everything. Catherine's friend Anna Naryshkina shouted at the favourite. Deeply wounded but always decent to her lovers, Catherine agreed that he could marry Shcherbatova.

At first, she concealed this crisis from Potemkin, probably out of embarrassment and to see if a relationship developed with a new young person close to her. But on 29 June she told her staff she was going to write to Potemkin at Olviopol. By the time it reached him, she had supervised Mamonov's marriage on 1 July: the groom received 2,250 peasants and 100,000 roubles. Catherine wept at the wedding. 'I've never been a tyrant to anybody,' she told Potemkin sadly, 'and I hate compulsion – is it possible you didn't know me to such an extent, and that the generosity of my character disappeared from your mind, and you considered me a wretched egotist? You would have healed me by telling me the truth.' She remembered Potemkin's warnings – 'Matushka, spit on him' – which she had ignored. 'But if you knew about his love, why didn't you tell me about it frankly?'[31]

Serenissimus replied: 'When I heard last year he was sending her fruits from the table, I understood it at once but I had no exact evidence to cite in front of you, Matushka. However, I hinted. I felt sorry for you, my foster-mother, and his rudeness and feigned illnesses were even more intolerable.' Potemkin despised Mamonov's 'blend of indifference and egotism ... Narcissus to an extreme degree', advising her to make the ingrate envoy to Switzerland.[32] Instead Count and Countess Mamonov were sent to Moscow to stew in their own juices.

'A sacred place', Zavadovsky rightly said, 'is never empty for long.'[33] Catherine had already found Mamonov's replacement but she wanted to settle herself before telling Potemkin. Even in her first letter, Pot-

---

* Her courtiers were old too: Ivan Chernyshev left such a disgusting stench in the Empress's apartments that the floor had to be doused in lavender water every time he left.

emkin's eye must have been drawn to the reference to a young man she nicknamed 'le Noiraud' – 'Blackie' – with whom Catherine was getting acquainted. As early as three days after Mamonov's declaration, Catherine started to see more of Blackie: her valet and secretary both suspected an affair was developing.[34] He was a protégé of Anna Naryshkina and Count Nikolai Saltykov, head of the Grand Duke Paul's household and a critic of Potemkin. As the entire court knew that Mamonov was in love with Shcherbatova, they lost no time in pushing Blackie towards the Empress, because they knew that Potemkin would intervene if they waited. The Prince could not choose Catherine's lovers but he liked to ensure they were not hostile. There is no doubt that Blackie's backers intended to undermine Potemkin, knowing that war prevented him from returning as he had after Lanskoy's death. In June 1789, this ailing Empress, tormented with war and dyspepsia, was far more likely to take what she was offered than at any other time in her life. Perhaps her happiness became more important than her dignity.

Blackie was Platon Alexandrovich Zubov, Catherine's last favourite. He was probably the handsomest of all. Aged twenty-two, Zubov was muscular yet frail, pretty and dark – hence Catherine's nickname for him – but his expression was brittle, vain, cold. His frequent illnesses suited Catherine's maternal instincts. He had been at Court since the age of eleven – Catherine had paid for him to study abroad. This popinjay was clever in a shallow and silly way, but he was neither imaginative nor curious, nor able, merely greedy and ambitious. None of this mattered in a favourite. Potemkin helped her run the Empire and fight the war. Zubov was her companion and pupil in her work for the Empire. 'I'm doing quite well by the state,' she said disingenuously, 'by educating young men.'[35]

Zubov's ascension to greatness followed a familiar rhythm: the Court noticed the youngster offer his arm to Catherine in the evening. He wore a new uniform with a large feather in the hat. After her card game, he was summoned to accompany Catherine to her apartments and took possession of the favourite's rooms, where he possibly found a cash present. The day after that, the antechamber of the 'new idol' was filled with petitioners.[36] On 3 July, Zubov was promoted to colonel in the Horse-Guards and adjutant-general, and significantly he gave a 2,000 rouble watch to his sponsor Naryshkina. Zubov's patrons already feared Potemkin's reaction and warned him to show respect to 'His Highness'.[37]

Catherine fell in love.[38] She was almost swelling with admiration for Blackie. 'We love this child who is really very interesting,' she declared, protesting too much. Her joy had the mawkishness of an old woman in the throes of a sexual infatuation with a youth almost forty years younger, as she told Potemkin: 'I am fat and merry, come back to life like a fly in summer.'[39] Ordering some French books for Zubov, she even made a ponderous but unusually risqué joke to her secretary. One of the books was called *Lucine without commerce – a letter in which it is demonstrated that a woman can give birth without commerce with a man.* Catherine laughed: 'That's a revelation, and in ancient times, Mars, Jupiter and the other gods provided the excuse.'[40] But she nervously waited for the Prince of Taurida's reaction.

'Your peace of mind is most necessary,' he wrote cautiously, 'and for me it's dearer than anything,' but he did not expect any political harm since 'your mercy is with me.'[41] But Potemkin did not pass judgement on her choice of Zubov. Catherine could not quite bring herself to mention the youngster by name to Potemkin, but she could not resist raving about his prettiness: 'Blackie has very beautiful eyes.' She restated their secret partnership: 'You are right when you write that you have my mercy and there are no circumstances to harm you ... Your villains will have no success with me.' In return, she begged for Potemkin's approval of her new love: 'Comfort me, caress us.'[42]

Soon she was making Zubov write flattering letters to her consort, to recreate their 'family': 'Here I enclose for you an admiring letter from the most innocent soul ... who has a good heart and a sweet way of thinking.' She added hopefully: 'Think what a fatal situation it would be for my health without this man. *Adieu mon ami*, be nice to us.'[43] When he was 'nice', the Empress actually thanked him for his approval: 'It is a great satisfaction for me, my friend, that you are pleased with me and little Blackie ... I hope he doesn't become spoilt.'[44] That was too much to hope. Zubov spent hours in front of the mirror having his hair curled. He arrogantly let his pet monkey pull the wigs off venerable petitioners. 'Potemkin was indebted to his elevation almost solely to himself,' recalled Masson, who knew both men. 'Zubov owed his to the infirmities of Catherine.'[45]

Zubov's rise is always described as a political disaster for Potemkin, but its significance has been exaggerated by hindsight. The Prince's first interest was for Catherine to find a favourite to leave him to run the Empire and to make her happy. He was not sorry to see the end of Mamonov, originally his choice, because he had become disrespectful to Catherine. When he was in Petersburg in February, it was rumoured he was pushing his own candidate[46] – and one source suggests it was Zubov's younger brother Valerian, which would mean that, whoever their friends were, the Zubovs were not regarded as inherently hostile. Indeed Potemkin liked the brave and able Valerian and promoted him wherever possible.[47] Damas, who was with Potemkin, did not notice any particular antipathy towards the Zubovs.[48] Potemkin and Zubov now began the usual correspondence – young favourite paying court to older consort. Every favourite dreamed of supplanting the Prince. The danger was now greater because of Catherine's age. But Potemkin's prestige and power increased throughout the war. So Zubov was politically inconvenient – but no more than a pinprick.

Serenissimus granted his approval slowly: 'My dear Matushka, how can I not sincerely love the man who makes you happy? You may be sure I will have a frank friendship with him because of his attachment to you.' But he had more exciting news: victory.[49]

The Ottoman corps of 30,000 suddenly jabbed towards Fokshany in Moldavia, where 12,000 Austrians guarded Potemkin's right flank. Coburg, the stodgy Austrian commander, was in no doubt of his own limitations and called for Russian help. Potemkin had specifically ordered Suvorov to prevent any concentration of the Turks or attempt to divide the allied forces. As soon as Suvorov received Coburg's message, he informed Potemkin and force-marched his 5,000 Russians to intervene so aggressively that the Turkish commander presumed they must be the vanguard of an army. On 20/21 July 1789 at the Battle of Fokshany, Suvorov's tiny but disciplined corps, assisted by the Austrians, routed the Turks, killing over 1,500 while losing only a few hundred men. The Turks fled towards Bucharest.[50]

The Grand Vizier's huge army was on the move again. Suvorov hurried back to his post. Potemkin crossed the Dniester on 12 August and turned southwards to set up his headquarters at Dubossary. All eyes were on the Grand Vizier: Potemkin kept his army between Dubossary and Kishnev, and rushed over to Ochakov and Kherson to prepare them for the planned Turkish attack from the sea.

At his Headquarters at Dubossary, Serenissimus lived sumptuously in a residence 'as splendid as the Vizier's'. William Gould, the emperor of landscapers, created an instant English garden on the spot.[51] Sarti's orchestra played all day. Many generals have travelled with mistresses and servants, but only Potemkin went to war with an army of gardeners and violinists. It seemed as if he planned to spend the rest of his life there.[52]

The Vizier correctly identified the 'hinge' between the allied armies as Potemkin's weakest point, so he launched two thrusts. The old Crocodile,

Ghazi Hassan, sortied out of Ismail with a corps of 30,000, and lunged across the Pruth to draw Potemkin's main army. But Potemkin kept his army in place and despatched Repnin to parry the thrust and if possible take mighty Ismail: he pursued the now land-lubbing Algerian sailor and his corps all the way back to the fortress. Once there, Repnin wasted time and did nothing.

On 1 September, Potemkin gave specific orders to Suvorov about the Vizier's army. 'If the enemy appears anywhere in your direction, attack him, having asked for God's mercy, and don't let him concentrate.'[53] Just after getting Potemkin's orders on 4 September, Suvorov received a second call for help from Coburg. The Grand Vizier was approaching Fokshany, bearing down on Coburg's 18,000 with an army of 90,000. Suvorov replied to Coburg: 'Coming. Suvorov'.[54] He just had time to send off a courier to the Prince before he embarked his 7,000 men on a Spartan forced-march of 100 versts, across flooded rivers, which he covered in two and a half days.

Potemkin fretted that he would not make it in time.[55] On the same day that he ordered Suvorov to be ready, he devised a complex amphibious operation to attack a vital Ottoman fortified port called Hadjibey, the future Odessa. The land forces advanced from Ochakov supported by a flotilla made up of Zaporogian *chaiki* and other oar-propelled gunboats, commanded by that talented Neapolitan adventurer José de Ribas, whose rear was covered by the ships-of-the-line of the Black Sea Fleet. Potemkin himself led his army forward towards Kaushany in case Repnin or Suvorov required his assistance. These sophisticated manoeuvres belie Potemkin's unjust reputation as a military incompetent.[56]

Suvorov found Coburg cowed before the Grand Vizier's encampment on the River Rymnik. The Turks outnumbered the allies four to one. On 8 September, Potemkin ordered Suvorov to 'assist Prince Coburg in attacking the enemy but not in defence'. On 11 September, the allies attacked. The Turks fought with their old fanaticism, throwing wave after wave of Janissaries and Spahis against Suvorov's squares. They just held for two hours. Then the allied troops advanced, shouting 'Catherine' and 'Joseph'. Potemkin's new light forces – his Jaegers, mobile sharpshooters, and cavalry, Carabiniers and Cossacks – proved themselves as adept and swift as Ottoman forces. The Turks were annihilated, 15,000 died on the 'cruel battlefield'.[57] The Grand Vizier, as Potemkin boasted to his erstwhile friend Ligne, 'fled like a boy'.[58]

The elated Serenissimus lavished praise on Suvorov: 'I embrace and kiss you sincerely, my dear friend, your indefatigable zeal makes me wish I could have you everywhere!' Suvorov embraced him back: 'I'm kissing your precious letter and remain in deepest respect, Serenissimus, Merciful Lord!' Their exultation was based on mutual respect: the strategy was Potemkin's; the tactics belonged to Suvorov's genius. Potemkin followed up Suvorov's triumph on land and sea. He took Kaushany on 13 September. Next day, Ribas captured Hadjibey. The Prince ordered the Sebastopol fleet out to sea to attack the Ottomans.

He then advanced on the two most potent Ottoman fortresses on the Dniester. Wielding the memory of the bloodbath of Ochakov as his weapon, Potemkin hoped to get them 'cheap'. First there were the towering ramparts of Akkerman (Belgrade-on-Dniester) that commanded the mouth of the river. When the Turkish fleet headed back to Istanbul, Potemkin ordered the taking of Akkerman. It surrendered on 30 September. The Prince rushed down to inspect it and returned through Kishnev, struggling to arrange the provisioning of the armies as Poland closed its doors.*

Serenissimus turned to the greatest prize on the Dniester: the famous fortress of Bender, built high on an escarpment above the river in a modern fortified square with four formidable towers and a 20,000-strong garrison, a small army.[59] Potemkin moved to besiege the fortress, but he also opened negotiations. On 4 November, he got his wish. He later enjoyed telling Catherine the 'Miraculous Case' of Bender's eight generals, who dreamed that they had either to surrender or perish. They went to the Pasha and told him the story. The dreaming Turks were obviously looking for a somnolent excuse to avoid a Russian assault, but this life-saving parable amused Potemkin.[60] Bender surrendered; Potemkin took 300 cannons – in return for letting the garrison march out. The surrender document, now in Potemkin's papers,[61] catches the elaborate formality of the stultified Ottoman bureaucracy, but it also referred to the Prince in terms not given to the Grand Vizier but only to the Sultan himself.†

Bender was Potemkin's ideal conquest, not costing Russia a single man. Success was infectious: Joseph congratulated Potemkin, but in an unpublished letter to Ligne he grasped Potemkin's true achievement:

---

* Akkerman's massive fortress still stands.

† 'To his Highness Monseigneur Prince Potemkin: Representation of Ahmet Pasha Huhafiz of Bender. In rendering with deep respect the honours due to Your Highness, very generous, very firm, very gracious, ornamented of an elevated genius to devise and execute very great enterprises, whose authority is accompanied by the most dazzling dignity, Principal Minister, acclaimed with the very highest precedence and first representative of Her Imperial Highness, the Padishah of Russia, we represent ... the pity for children and women brings us to accept ... the proposition.'

'It's an art to besiege forts and take them by force ... but to make yourself master in this way is the greatest art of all.' It would be Potemkin's 'most beautiful glory'.[62]

The Grand Vizier would not have agreed: after Rymnik, the Sultan had him killed in Shumla, while the Seraskier of Bender was beheaded in Istanbul: four months later, the British Ambassador noticed his head still rotting outside the Seraglio.[63]

'Well Matushka, did it come off according to my plan?',[64] the euphoric Potemkin asked Catherine. Triumph made him playful, so he wrote her this ditty:

> Nous avons pris neuf lançons
> Sans perdre un garçon
> Et Bender avec trois Pashas
> Sans perdre un chat.[65]*

Serenissimus' reaction to Suvorov's victory at Rymnik could not have been more generous: 'Really Matushka, he deserves your favour and the fighting was vital, I am thinking what to give him ... Peter the Great granted Counts for nothing. How about giving him [a title] with the surname of "Rymniksky"?'[66] Potemkin was proud that Russians had rescued Austrians, who had been on the verge of running away. He asked her to 'show grace to Suvorov' and 'shame the sponger-generals who aren't worth their salaries'.[67]

Catherine got the message. She gave Suvorov the title and a diamond-studded sword engraved 'Conqueror of the Grand Vizier'. Potemkin thanked her for Suvorov's reward (Joseph made him an imperial count too) and gave every soldier a rouble.[68] When he sent all Suvorov's rewards – a 'whole wagon'[69] of diamonds and the Cross of St George 1st degree – he told the new Count, 'You would of course obtain equal glory and victories at any time; but not every chief would inform you about the rewards with pleasure as great as mine.' Once again, these two brilliant and overly emotional eccentrics outdid each other. 'I can hardly see the daylight for tears of joy!', declared Suvorov-Rymniksky. 'Long live Prince Grigory Alexandrovich ... He is an honest man, a kind man, a great man!'[70]

Potemkin was the hero of the hour, going from 'conquest to conquest', as Catherine told Ligne: he had now taken the entire Dniester and Bug

---

* 'We've taken nine launches, Without losing a boy, And Bender with three Pashas, Without losing a cat.'

and the land between them.[71] 'Te Deums' were sung in Petersburg; 101 cannons were fired. If power is an aphrodisiac, victory is love itself: Catherine wrote to him as if they were almost lovers again. 'Your present campaign is brilliant! I love you very, very much.'[72] But they were still discussing how to react to Prussian pressure to undermine Russian gains against the Turks. She told him she was taking his advice about the Prussians: 'We are caressing the Prussians,' though it was not easy to tolerate their 'abuse'. She told him that Zubov had wanted to see Potemkin's art collection and apartments in the house on Millionaya, so Catherine took him on a tour and noticed that the décor was a bit shabby for a conquering hero. She had it redecorated, lavishing white damask on the bedroom and hanging his collection for him. She signed off: 'I love you with all my heart.'[73]

Meanwhile the Austrians, now in the sure hands of Loudon, had taken the Balkan Belgrade on 19 September, while Bucharest fell to Coburg. The 'Te Deums' for the two Belgrades (the other was Akkerman – Belgrade-on-Dniester) were sung in Petersburg simultaneously.

Victory accelerated a cult of the Prince as Mars. Catherine had cast a medallion of his profile to commemorate Ochakov. The sculptor, Shubin, was carving a bust.[74] So she lectured Potemkin on stardom like the sensible mother of a famous son. 'Don't be too bumptious,' she wrote, 'but show the world the greatness of your soul.'[75] Potemkin understood that 'everything good is given to me by God', but he was a little hurt. He threatened to retire to a bishopric.[76] Catherine replied: 'A monastery will never be the home of a man whose name is trumpeted across Asia and Europe – it's too small for him.'[77]

In Vienna, where even Joseph was now popular, the Prince's name was cheered in the theatres and the women wore belts and rings emblazoned 'Potemkin'. He could not resist telling Catherine all about it and sent her Princess Esterhazy's 'Potemkin' ring. After her lecture, he was careful not to boast too much to the Empress, who was so like him in her love of glory: 'Since I am yours, then my successes too belong directly to you.'[78]

The ailing Kaiser urged Potemkin to make a peace rendered more desirable by 'the bad intentions of our joint enemies' – the Prussians.[79] Surely now the Turks would be ready. Potemkin set up Court in Jassy, the Moldavian capital, to winter like a sultan, revel in his mistresses, build his towns, create his regiments – and negotiate peace with the Sublime Porte. Now he was emperor of all he surveyed. He lived in Turkish palaces; his Court was ever more exotic – Kabardian princes and Persian ambassadors; his girls, whether Russian or not, behaved like odalisques. The heat, the distances, the years away from Petersburg, changed the man. His enemies began to compare him to the semi-mythical seventh-century BC Assyrian tyrant, famed for his capricious extravagance, voluptuous decadence and martial victories – Sardanapalus.

29

THE DELICIOUS AND THE
CRUEL: SARDANAPALUS

Now dreaming I a Sultan am
I terrify the world by glances ...
Gavrila Derzhavin, 'Ode to Princess Felitsa'

The despotism of vice
The weakness and the wickedness of luxury
The negligence – the apathy – the evils
Of sensual sloth produce ten thousand tyrants.
Lord Byron, *Sardanapalus*

'Be very careful with the Prince,' whispered Princess Ekaterina Dolgorukaya to her friend Countess Varvara Golovina when she arrived at
the court of Serenissimus in Jassy, the capital of Moldavia. 'He is like a
Sovereign here.'[1] Potemkin's chosen capital, Jassy (now Iaşi in Rumania),
could have been made for him. It was surrounded by three empires –
Ottoman, Russian and Habsburg – prayed in three religions – Moslem,
Orthodox and Jewish – and spoke three languages – Greek, Turkish and
French. Its marketplaces, dominated by Jews, Greeks and Italians, offered
'all the merchandise of the Orient in abundance'.[2] Its sophistication,
which consoled Ligne in 1788 for the miseries of Ochakov, had 'enough
of the oriental to have the *piquant* of Asia and enough civilization to add
to it some European graces'.[3]

The rulers, the Hospodars or Princes, of Wallachia and Moldavia, the
two Danubian Principalities, were Greeks from the Phanar District of
Constantinople and some of them were descended from Byzantine
emperors. These wealthy Phanariots bought their temporary thrones
from the Ottoman Sultan. Their Orthodox–Islamic, Byzantine–Ottoman
coronations in Istanbul were perhaps the only example of rulers crowned
in a country which they did not rule.[4] Once in Jassy or Bucharest, the
hydrid Greek-Turkish Hospodars taxed their temporary realms to fill
their coffers to cover the exorbitant price they had paid the Sultan for their
thrones: 'a prince leaves Constantinople with three million piastres of
debt and after four years ... returns with six million'.[5] They lived like
magnificent parodies of Ottoman–Byzantine emperors, surrounded by

Phanariot courtiers – their prime minister was called the Grand Postelnik, their police chief the Grand Spatar and their chief justice the Grand Hetman. Often they might rule in both places, or the same one, several times.

The aristocracy, the boyars, were Rumanians but were overlaid with rich Phanariot dynasties, some of whom were now based in Jassy, where they built their fine neo-Classical palaces. These Greek boyars, who looked like 'monkeys on a horse covered in rubies', lived in Turkish robes and pantaloons, grew their beards, shaved their heads and sported bonnets encircled with fur and rings of pearls. They waved flywhisks, nibbled sherbet and read Voltaire. Their women languished on divans, wearing diamond-infested turbans and short transparent petticoats, their necks and arms covered in gauze with pearls and coins sewn into them. They dangled fan-like chaplets made of diamonds, pearls, coral, lapis lazuli and rare wood. Connoisseurs of femininity like Ligne were fascinated by these 'pretty, tender – and apathetic' princesses whose only flaw was the protuberant belly regarded as a sign of beauty. Ligne claimed that their morals made the Paris of *Les Liaisons Dangereuses* appear monastic and that the Hospodar let his friends 'visit' the women in his wife's household – but only after a medical check. 'People took each other and left each other, there was neither jealousy nor bad temper.'[6]

It was not merely the cosmopolitanism and luxury that suited Potemkin, but also the politics. The throne of Moldavia was highly lucrative but extremely dangerous: heads were lost as quickly as fortunes were gained. Ligne overheard the ladies at court sighing, 'here my father was massacred by order of the Porte and here my sister by order of the Hospodar'. This was the battleground of both the Russo-Turkish wars, which placed the Hospodars in an impossible position. They trod a political tightrope between Orthodox God and Moslem Sultan. They had to play a complicated double game. The First Russo-Turkish War had won Russia rights to appoint consuls in these Principalities. One of the major causes of the outbreak of war in 1787 was the Ottoman overthrow of the Moldavian Hospodar, Alexander Mavrocordato, who was given sanctuary in Russia and sent Potemkin books and requests for money, while writing that 'philosophy alone sustains me'. The impermanence of these Hospodars, their Greek race and the Orthodoxy of the people attracted Potemkin.[7]

Serenissimus now ruled from Jassy as if he had, at last, found his kingdom. Dacia had been destined for him since the Greek Project of

1782. The rumours of Potemkin's potential crowns became ever more colourful – a Livonian duchy, a Greek kingdom of Morea and even a most Potemkinian project to buy two Italian islands, Lampedusa and Linosa, from the Kingdom of Naples and found an order of knighthood – but a variation on Dacia was much more likely.[8] Potemkin 'regarded Moldavia as a domain which belonged to him'.[9]

While the Hospodars of Moldavia and Wallachia corresponded with Potemkin from the Turkish camp, begging for peace,[10] the Prince himself adopted their resplendence, while ruling through a Divan of boyars, under his dynamic Georgian negotiator[11] Sergei Lazhkarev.* The Turks and Westerners knew that Potemkin wanted Moldavia; he coaxed and charmed the boyars, who[12] themselves were almost offering him the throne.[13] Their letters at this time thanked him for delivering them 'from the tyranny of the Turks. We beg Your Highness not to lose from your vigilant vision the little interests of our country which will always have Your Highness as Liberator.' Prince Cantacuzino, scion of Byzantine emperors, heralded this 'epoch of felicity – we dare to run to the wise lights of Your Highness, hero of the century'.[14]

Serenissimus now took the modern step of becoming a press baron. He created, edited and published his own newspaper called *Le Courrier de Moldavie*. Printed by his own movable printing press, *Le Courrier* was a tabloid emblazoned with the Moldavian crest that reported international and local news. The articles were moderately liberal, rabidly against the French Revolution and gently supportive of an independent Rumanian realm under Potemkin.[15] Some believed he even planned to create a Moldavian army by detaching crack Russian regiments.[16] His nephew General Samoilov, who was often with him at this time, states that he would only ever make peace if Moldavia – Dacia† – was granted independence.[17]

The Prince was never one to allow war, winter or the small matter of a new kingdom to interfere with his pleasures. 'Mister monk, no

---

* Lazhkarev, whom Westerners compared to a gypsy clown, once repelled an Islamic mob in Negroponte by leaping off a balcony with a basin of water, threatening them with the horror of instant baptism. Later, in Alexander I's entourage at Tilsit in 1807, it was he who met Napoleon and negotiated Russia's annexation of Bessarabia, ceded by the Porte in the 1808 treaty, in return for French domination of Europe.

† While Potemkin later came to represent hated Russian imperialism to the Rumanians, a French visitor, forty years on, found that the Jassy boyars still regarded him as an early father of Rumanian nationalism. This made sense since Dacia roughly forms Rumania. However, the sole legacy of the name was President Ceaucescu's decision to name the national make of car the 'Dacia'.

monkhood,' Catherine teased him in an imperial understatement.[18] He
resided in the palaces of either Princes Cantacuzino or Ghika and spent
hot days in Czerdak in the countryside nearby.* He was joined by
ten mechanics from Tula, twelve carriages of books, twenty jewellers,
twenty-three female carpet-makers, 100 embroiderers,[19] a mime troupe,
his 200 hornplayers (to play Sarti's 'Te Deum' to Ochakov, accompanied
by the firing of cannons, an idea borrowed by Tchaikovsky for his *1812
Overture*), a 300-voice choir, a *corps de ballet*,[20] gardener Gould, architect
Starov,[21] nephews, nieces and his chancellor Popov.

Only his English cooks refused to go,[22] so he had to make do with
English gardens and French meals – probably a much better idea anyway.
But he did receive hampers[23] of English delicacies as a consolation. One
such consignment – the bill is in his archives – contained smoked salmon,
dried salmon, marinated salmon, Dutch herrings, Livonian anchovies,
smoked souls, lampreys, eels, two barrels of apples, two bottles of
mussels, two bottles of tinto, two bottles of Lacrima Christi, two bottles
of champagne and six of Hermiatate, three bottles of red burgundy,
three of white burgundy, three bottles of Jamaican rum – and more.

'Parties, balls, theatres, ballets were organized ceaselessly.' When the
Prince heard that an officer 700 versts away played the violin well, he
sent a courier for the fiddler; when he arrived, he listened with pleasure,
gave him a gift and sent him straight back again.[24] This reflected Potemkin's pre-Napoleonic view that an army marches on its merriment,
not its stomach. 'A sad army can never undertake the toughest assign-
ments,' he wrote, 'and it's more likely to suffer illness.'[25]

The belles of Petersburg trooped down to entertain him and deceive
their husbands. Praskovia Potemkina of the flawless skin and perfect
face was now firmly esconced as 'favourite sultana',[26] and supplicants
waited in her antechambers to ask for favours.[27] Praskovia and the Prince
enjoyed a deep love affair in Jassy. 'You are my pleasure and my priceless
treasure, you are God's gift to me,' he wrote, adding that his love expressed itself to her, not in mad passion or drunkenness, but in 'never
ending tenderness'. Without her, 'I'm only half of myself . . . you are the
soul of my soul, my Parashinka.' He always enjoyed choosing dresses for
his nieces and designing habits for monks, and Praskovia must have
looked fetching in uniforms because he wrote to her: 'Do you know,
beautiful sweetheart, you are a Cuirassier in my regiment. The helmet
suits you perfectly, everything fits you. Today I shall put a bishop's hat

---

* The Ghika Palace still stands: it is now the Medical Faculty of Iași University. It has
been expanded, but it still has its original Classical portico.

on you ... Do me a favour, my unrivalled beauty, make up a dress of calico and purple satin ...'. He told her which jewels to wear – which to string, which to mount in a diadem. He even designed their imaginary house of love, which reveals the touching originality of this strange, sensitive man: 'I drew you patterns, I brought you diamonds, now I am drawing you a small house and garden in the oriental taste with all the magical luxuries ...'. There would be a big hall, the sound of a fountain. Upstairs, there would be a lighted gallery with 'pictures of Hero and Leander, Apollo and Daphne ... the most ardent poems of Sappho' and an erotic painting of Praskovia herself 'in a white short dress, girded by a delicate lilac belt, open at the breast, hair loose and unpowdered, the chemise held by a ruby ...'. The bed would be surrounded by 'curtains as thin as smoke' in a room with aquamarine glass. 'But the place where luxury will exhaust itself is the bath', which would be surrounded by mirrors and filled with water, scented with rose, lilac, jasmine, and orange'. Serenissimus was 'cheerful when you're cheerful, I'm full up when you're full up'.[28]

When the Prince was in love, he would do anything for his mistress. In March and April 1790, he even ordered Faleev to rename two of his ships after Praskovia.[29] 'The jewels, diamonds and all the treasures of the four parts of the world were used to decorate her charms.' When she wanted jewels, Colonel Bauer galloped off to Paris; when she talked about perfumes, Major Lamsdorf headed for Florence and returned with two fragrant carriages of it.[30]

Here is his Parisian shopping-list for one of those legendary missions, probably for Praskovia and other 'sultanas', in July 1790, second year of the French Revolution. The courier was Lamsdorf. When he arrived in Paris, the Russian envoy Baron Simolin was expected to drop everything. 'I have not ceased to occupy myself with him in the execution of the commissions Your Highness has wished to be discharged in Paris and to assist him with my advice and that of a lady of my acquaintance.' It sounds as if Simolin recruited his mistress to make sure he was buying the right stockings. Indeed, 'we have taken care to execute all things in the latest fashion'. Without the lady and Lamsdorf, Simolin admitted he could not have bought the following:

– fashion pieces [ballgowns] made by Mademoiselles Gosfit, Madame de
    Modes 14,333 livres
– fashion pieces [ballgowns] made by Henry Desreyeux 9,488 livres

- a piece of muslin from the Indies, embroidery from India in silk and
    silver (Henry Desreyeux) 2400 livres
- [fashion from] Madame Plumesfeur 724 lives
- seller of Rubies 1224 livres
- madame the florist 826 livres
- couturier for 4 corsets 255 livres
- shoemakers for 72 pairs of shoes [ball slippers] 446 livres
- embroiderer for 12 pairs of shoes [ball slippers] 288 livres
- a pair of ear muffs 132 livres
- the stocking maker for 6 dozen pairs 648 livres
- rubies 248 livres
- madame the gauze seller 858 livres
- the wrapping-up man Bocqueux 1200 livres.[31]

One suspects that not all of these were for the Prince himself. As soon
as all the craftsmen and seamstresses had finished their work, Lamsdorf
galloped them back to Jassy. These frivolous missions were also useful:
the couriers who brought delicacies and ballgowns from Paris bore
Potemkin's vast correspondence – twenty to thirty letters a day – and
collected intelligence and replies; for example, Stackelberg in Warsaw
reported that Potemkin's fastest courier had delivered an urgent despatch
on his way to the West.[32] This was a diplomatic, espionage, ballgown and
catering service, all in one.

Serenissimus was certainly extravagant. That trip cost 44,000 livres
for fourteen items, approximately £2,000, at a time when an English
gentleman could live comfortably on £300 a year. It was more than
the annual salary of a Russian field-marshal (7,000 roubles).[33] These
missions were quite frequent. Potemkin even sent Grimm regular shop-
ping-lists of female clothing, maps or musical instruments which Catherine's *philosophe* dutifully provided.[34] However, Potemkin's notorious
inefficiency in paying debts drove Simolin to distraction. On 25 December 1788, he was even forced to appeal to Bezborodko for help in getting
the Prince to pay for an earlier expedition that had cost another 32,000
livres.[35]

Potemkin's lifestyle had been royal if not imperial since 1774, and he
possessed 'a fortune greater than certain kings'.[36] It is impossible to work
out the exact sums: even on his death, his estate was unquantifiable. The
Prince was 'prodigiously rich and not worth a farthing', wrote Ligne,
'preferring prodigality and giving, to regularity in paying'.[37] This was
almost literally true, because he was essentially a member of the imperial
household – so that, the Treasury was his private bank. 'It is true Pot-

emkin had immediate access to the State Treasury,' claimed Masson, 'but he also spent a great deal for the State and showed himself as much a Grand Prince of Russia as a favourite of Catherine.'[38] Pushkin later recorded the story that, when a Treasury clerk queried Potemkin's latest request for money, he sent back a note that read: 'Pay up or fuck off!' It was said that Catherine ordered the Treasury to regard his requests like her own, but this was not quite so.[39]

There is no record of Catherine ever turning down any of Potemkin's requests for money, but he still had to apply for the money, even though he knew it would be granted. During the building of his towns and fleets and during the war, massive amounts of money poured through his hands, but the image of his wanton waste of public funds is not borne out by the archives, which show how the money was assigned by Catherine, via Procurator-General Viazemsky, and then distributed by Potemkin, via his offices and officials like Faleev, Zeitlin or Popov, down to the actual regiments and fleets. Much of it never actually reached the Prince himself – though he was too grand to concern himself with smaller sums and Viazemsky complained to the Empress that he had neglected to account for all of it. This touches on the question of his financial probity. In his case, it was a meaningless concept: Serenissimus used his own money for the state and the Treasury for his personal uses and saw little difference between the two.[40]

The Prince was hungry for money and he loved spending it – but it did not interest him for its own sake. He had to spend a fortune to maintain himself in the style of imperial consort when even senior courtiers strained themselves to keep up appearances. Furthermore, the delays in payments by the Treasury meant that, in order to push through his projects and raise his armies, he had to spend his own money. His avidity for riches was part of his insurance policy against the accession of Paul, one reason he invested in Polish land.

Once he was showing some officers round one of his palaces when they came upon a gold bath. The officers raved about it so much that Potemkin shouted: 'If you can shit enough to fill it up, you can keep it.' When a flatterer marvelled at the resplendence of some ball he gave, the Prince snapped: 'What, sir, do you presume to know the depth of my purse?' Potemkin himself never had any idea of its depth. He just knew there was almost no bottom: his fortune was variously estimated at nine, sixteen, forty and fifty million roubles. But given that during war and peace the whole military and southern development budgets of the Empire passed through his Chancellery, these figures are irrelevant and his debts enormous.[41]

Potemkin borrowed prodigiously and he tormented his Scottish banker, Richard Sutherland, who became rich on Potemkin's business and eventually rose to be Catherine's Court banker and a baron.* Bankers and merchants circled Potemkin like vultures, competing to offer goods and loans.[42] Sutherland worked hardest, and suffered most, to win Potemkin's business. On 13 September 1783, he begged Potemkin 'humbly to condescend to give orders to make payment to me of the rising claims which I have the honour to send him coming to 167,029 roubles and sixty kopecks', mostly spent on state business, settling immigrants. The anguished banker tried to explain, 'again I take the liberty of representing to Your Highness that my credit depends, and depends a lot, on the return of this money'.[43] Sutherland was evidently desperate, because he owed other bankers in Warsaw and beyond, and it often seems as if Potemkin was about to set off a chain-reaction banking crash across Europe – but it is worth noting that most of this money was not spent on baubles. Sutherland was the means by which Potemkin financed the settlement of immigrants, the procurement of timber and the building of his towns, the best example of how his personal and imperial spending were entangled.

By 1788, the Prince owed Sutherland 500,000 roubles. Three weeks later, Sutherland swore that things had reached such a 'critical and worrying point' as to force him to 'come importuning to my first benefactor ... to obtain ... the sum without which I would not know how to honour my affairs'. It was Potemkin himself who scrawled in French on the letter: 'Tell him he'll receive 200,000 roubles.'

Serenissimus was far from miserly – on the contrary, he was wildly generous. Saving was foreign to his nature. Only his death gave a snapshot of his fortune and even then it hardly enlightens us. Like the Empress herself, he was part of the state, and the Empire was his fortune.[44]

A country's enemies multiply in proportion to its successes. Russia's enemies, aroused by Potemkin's dangerous victories, did all they could to encourage the Ottomans to keep fighting. Meanwhile Russia's military activity became paralysed by the prospect of war against Prussia, Poland and England as well as Turkey and Sweden. So Potemkin spent the winter of 1789 and much of the following year trying to negotiate with the Sublime Porte. Initially, the Turks seemed sincere in their wish to make

* It was Sutherland's English roast beef which Potemkin so enjoyed, when he came for dinner, that he had it wrapped up and took it home with him.

peace. Sultan Selim freed the Russian Ambassador from the Seven Towers and appointed 'the famous Algerian knight',[45] ex-Capitan-Pasha Ghazi Hassan-Pasha, as grand vizier, to talk peace.

However, Prussian diplomacy aimed to undermine Russia and fulfil the so-called Hertzberg Plan, named after the Prussian Chancellor, which was designed to secure the Polish towns of Thorn and Danzig for Prussia in return for Austria ceding Galicia to Poland and Russia returning the Danubian Principalities to Turkey. This required a coalition against Russia, so the Sultan was offered an alliance to secure the return of the Crimea. Sweden was offered Livonia with Riga. Russia's ally Austria was threatened with Prussian invasion. Russia itself was forced to withdraw from Poland, leaving the field to Prussia, which found itself in the ironic situation of having the greatest influence in a country it wanted to carve up. It was only now, when Poland was offered constitutional reform and an alliance in return for the cession of Thorn and Danzig, that the Poles realized that they had been deceived: Prussia was not just as carnivorous as Russia but more so. Yet they were forced to accept the Prussian advances and turned on the Russians. England backed Prussia in demanding that Russia and Austria make peace with the Porte on the basis of the *status quo ante bellum*. There was no question of any Russian military operations: Potemkin had to move a corps to cover a possible attack by Poland and Prussia. By 24 December 1789, Catherine was telling her secretary: 'Now we are in a crisis: either peace or a triple war with Prussia.'[46]

Potemkin's agent for the peace negotiations was a truly Levantine operator and diplomatic entrepreneur named Ivan Stepanovich Barozzi, a Greek quadruple agent for Russia, Turkey, Austria and Prussia simultaneously. After meanderingly mysterious Potemkinian conversations in Jassy, where he was shocked by the Prince's lecherous behaviour, Barozzi headed for the Vizier's headquarters, Shumla, with Potemkin's terms.[47] The Dniester would be the new border. Akkerman and Bender would be razed. The Principalities would be 'independent'.*

Barozzi reached Shumla on 26 December 1789. The Prince's accounts show the way such discussions were lubricated with a shower of *baksheesh*. At least sixteen rings, gold clocks, chains, snuff-boxes, were

---

* Potemkin also suggested that, if the Turks would back a Russian nominee for King of Poland, Russia would consider keeping the Bug as the border. In other words, Russia would use Ottoman help to retake Poland and, in either case, Potemkin had the potential to secure a crown for himself – Poland or Dacia. Nonetheless, even for Poland, it is hard to believe Potemkin would have accepted the Bug border, which would have meant surrendering Ochakov.

designated for different Turkish officials, specified as 'Ring with blue ruby and diamond for first secretary of Turkish ambassador Ovni Esfiru', while Barozzi himself got a 'ring with a big emerald' either to present or to wear for his discussions with the Vizier.[48] Potemkin even offered to build a mosque in Moscow. However charming the brilliants, Potemkin's terms did not please the 'Algerine renegado'. Serenissimus, unimpressed with the counter-proposals, gave his new terms on 27 February 1790. 'My propositions are short,' he said, 'there is no need for a great deal of talk.' There would be no armistice – 'more the wish to gain time than make peace – from what I know of Turkish artifice'. Then came a Potemkinian phrase: 'The Turks like to take a chariot to chase a hare.' The Prince preferred to be defeated rather than tricked.[49]

Potemkin was right not to commit himself completely to the Barozzi talks. The Prince knew from the Austrians and his Istanbul spies that Sultan Selim regarded the Grand Vizier's peace talks as a secondary, parallel policy to his negotiations with the Prussian envoy, Dietz, in Constantinople. If the Turks could get help from Prussia and Poland, they could go on fighting. By the time Potemkin replied, the Sultan had already signed an aggressive alliance with Prussia on 20 January 1790 which committed Frederick William to help reconquer the Crimea and go to war against Catherine.

As this noose tightened around Russia, 'the health of the Emperor is the severest of all the storms which menace the political sky', Potemkin told Kaunitz that January. Joseph II was stricken, physically with tuberculosis, and politically with revolts across his Empire from Hungary to the Netherlands. He seemed to be recovering when he had to undergo an agonizing operation on an anal abcess that sapped his strength. The death scene was tragic. 'Has anyone wept over me?', he asked. He was told that Ligne was in tears. 'I did not think I was deserving of such affection,' replied the Emperor. He suggested his own epitaph: 'Here lies a prince whose intentions were pure but who had the misfortune to see all his plans collapse.' Catherine was 'sorry for my ally', who was 'dying, hated by everybody.'[50] When Joseph died on 9/20 February 1790, Kaunitz supposedly muttered: 'That was very good of him.'[51]

It may have been good for the Habsburg Monarchy but it was another blow to Russia. On 18/29 March, Prussia tightened its ring once again and signed a military alliance with Poland. Frederick William moved 40,000 men towards Livonia in the north and another 40,000 in Silesia, mustering a 100,000-man reserve. The new Habsburg monarch, Leopold, King of Hungary (until he was elected emperor), was alarmed and immediately wrote to Potemkin: 'You have lost a friend in my

brother His Majesty the Emperor, you have found another in me who
honours more than anyone your genius and nobility.' Serenissimus and
Leopold co-ordinated their defence of Galicia against the Poles – but the
King of Hungary's true concern was to prevent the Prussian invasion 'in
concert with Poland' and save the Habsburg Monarchy. He begged
Potemkin to make a peace that had already slipped away.[52]

In the midst of these upheavals, the Prince learned that an admirable
Englishman was dying of a fever near Kherson. John Howard was a
selfless prison-reformer, who had dared to expose the misery of jails
and hospitals on his travels across the world, not least in Potemkin's
Viceroyalty. Serenissimus sent his doctor to tend him, but Howard died.
The Duke of Leeds, the British Foreign Secretary, wrote to say that
'the British nation will never forget' such *sensibilité* and Potemkin
replied, 'Mr Howard had every right to my attentions. He was the famous
friend of Humanity and a British citizen and these, Monsieur le Duc,
are claims enough to acquire my esteem.' Howard became a Russian,
and Soviet, hero.[53]

The Prince of Taurida now turned his guns and imagination on to Russia's
once and future enemy, Poland. The so-called 'Patriots', elated at the prospect of gaining a strong constitution, expelling the Russians and receiving Galicia from Austria, controlled Warsaw. The strain of losing Poland
took its toll on Catherine and Potemkin – he suffered hangnail and
rheumatism. Catherine sweetly sent him a 'whole pharmacy of medicines'
and 'a fox fur coat with a sable hat'.[54] If it came to war against Prussia and
Poland, 'I will take command in person,' Potemkin told Leopold.[55] While
the Austrians panicked and asked for Russian assistance, military operations against the Turks were suspended.

Catherine regarded Poland as an enemy to be dealt with when she
had the chance, but Potemkin's protean imagination had for some time
been evolving a plan to insert a Trojan Horse into the Commonwealth.
The Trojan Horse was himself, backed by his Orthodox co-religionists
in eastern Poland and by his new Cossack Host. He would raise Orthodox
Poland in the Palatinates of Bratslav, Kiev and Podolia (where his huge
estates lay) against the Catholic centre, on behalf of Russia, in the Cossack
tradition of Hetman Bogdan Khmelnitsky. So, after taking Bender, he
asked Catherine to grant him a new title with special historic resonance:
grand hetman.[56]

'Your plan is very good,' replied the Empress, though she wondered
if the Hetmanate would provoke more hatred in the Polish Sejm.[57]
Nonetheless in January, she appointed him 'Grand Hetman of the Black

Sea and Ekaterinoslav Cossack Hosts'. Potemkin was delighted with his Hetmanate and designed a resplendent new uniform in which he posed round Jassy.[58] His own extravagance grated on his sometimes coenobitic nature: he had the sensitivity to notice that his poorer officers could not keep up, so he ordered everyone, including himself, to wear plain cloth tunics – much more Spartan, he told Catherine.[59] He had become careful to share his glory with the Empress. When she hailed him as 'my Hetman', he replied: 'Of course I'm yours! I can boast that I owe nothing to anyone except you.'[60]

Potemkin, who already effectively controlled Russian foreign policy towards Austria and Turkey, was taking over Polish policy too. He demanded the sacking of the Russian Ambassador in Warsaw, Stackelberg, whom he called a scared 'rabbit',[61] so Catherine appointed Potemkin's ally Bulgakov.[62] She knew that Potemkin had his own interests in Poland and remained sensitive to the possibility of his forming an independent duchy out of his lands. He reassured her that 'there's nothing I wish for myself here' and, as for the hetman title, 'if your welfare did not demand it', he did not need a 'phantom that was more comic than distinguished'. Meanwhile he spent the spring building up his own Cossack Host – even persuading some of his Zaporogian bachelors to marry.[63]

Potemkin's Hetmanate did outrage the Patriots in Warsaw. Rumours of his plans to become king of Poland reached a new intensity. The Prince indignantly denied this ambition to Bezborodko: 'It's forgivable for the King [of Poland] to think I want his place. For me, let the devil be there. What a sin it is to think that I may have other interests than those of the state.'[64] Potemkin was probably telling the truth: the crown of Poland was a fool's cap. A Ukrainian or Moldavian duchy loosely attached to Poland was more feasible. Besides, he had long since convinced himself of that statesman's vanity – that what was good for Potemkin was good for Russia.

The French and Polish Revolutions changed the atmosphere at Catherine's Court as well as her foreign policy. She was alarmed by the spread of French ideas – or 'poison' as she called them – and was determined to suppress them in Russia. In May 1790, when Russia was losing its Austrian ally, the Swedish War was critical, and the Prusso-Polish alliance threatened to open a new front, a young nobleman named Alexander Radishchev published an anonymous book, *A Journey from St Petersburg to Moscow*, which was veiled attack on Catherine, serfdom and Potemkin, whom he implied was an Oriental tyrant. However, it was the application of French Revolutionary principles to Russia, not merely the insults about Potemkin, that outraged her. Radishchev was arrested, tried for sedition and *lèse-majesté* – and sentenced to death.

The Prince intervened on the author's behalf, even though the Revolutions had made this a dangerous time to undermine the regime, even though he was personally attacked, and despite the pressure on him. 'I've read the book sent to me. I am not angry ... It seems, Matushka, he's been slandering you too. And you also won't be angry. Your deeds are your shield.' Potemkin's generous response and sense of proportion calmed Catherine. She commuted the sentence and Radishchev was exiled to Siberia. 'The monarch's mercy', wrote the writer's grateful brother on 17 May 1791, 'was obtained by Prince Grigory Alexandrovich.'[65]

The Prince was still negotiating with the Grand Vizier. Catherine decided that the demand for an independent Moldavia with its own prince (Potemkin) was excessive, given the Porte's new treaty with Prussia. The ever flexible Prince seamlessly switched policies and proposed instead that Moldavia be given to Poland as a morsel to tempt the Commonwealth back to the Russian fold. He lost nothing because it could still become his private Polish duchy.[66] Serenissimus was suffering. 'Anxiety of such uncertainty weakens me: deprived of sleep and food,' he told her, 'I'm worse than a baby in arms.' He did not forget Zubov either: Potemkin loved Catherine's young lover 'more and more, for he pleases you'.[67]

Once Sultan Selim was committed to fight on, backed by Prussia, the Grand Vizier's peace policy became obsolete. The ex-Capitan-Pasha was too prestigious to kill openly, so the Crocodile of Sea Battles perished mysteriously on 18 March 1790, probably of the Sultan's poison. This alarmed Catherine. 'For God's sake,' she warned Potemkin. 'Be on guard against the Turk ... He may poison you. They use such tricks ... and it's possible the Prussians will give them the opportunity' to exterminate the man 'whom they fear most'.[68] Meanwhile, the Turks in Moldavia took the opportunity to defeat Coburg's Austrian army, which provoked a Potemkinian outburst to Catherine that the Austrian Field-Marshal had 'gone like a fool and been thrashed like a whore'. But the inconsistent King of Prussia was shocked when he learned that his new treaty with the Porte committed him to fight Russia and disowned the alliance, recalling his envoy Dietz in disgrace. Frederick William was more interested in fighting the Austrians. In May, he assumed personal command of his army.[69]

The Habsburgs succumbed to the Prussian threat. Leopold abandoned Joseph's hopes of winning Turkish territory in order to restore order to his own provinces and negotiated a rapprochement with Prussia, therefore withdrawing from the Turkish War. On 16/27 July at Reichenbach, Leopold agreed to the Anglo-Prussian demands of instant armistice on the basis of the *status quo ante bellum*. Prussia celebrated this victory by raising the stakes: Frederick William ratified Dietz's Prusso-Turkish treaty after all. Russia stood alone in the cold war against Prussia, England and Poland, and in the hot one against Turkey and Sweden.

On 28 June, the Swedes for the first time defeated the Russian Baltic Fleet, now commanded by Nassau, whose recklessness caught up with him at Svensksund.[70] But Catherine, who hated admitting bad news, delayed telling Potemkin for three weeks.[71] However, this cloud had a silver lining – the Swedish victory saved Gustavus' reputation, therefore allowing him to seek an honourable peace, signed on 3/14 August at Verela, based on the *status quo ante bellum*. 'We've pulled one paw out of the mud,' exulted Catherine to Potemkin. 'When we pull the other one out, then we'll sing Hallelujah!'[72]

The withdrawal of Austria from the war had temporarily alleviated the threat from Prussia too. Potemkin and Catherine realized that, while Prussia and England cooked up their next move, there was a chance to break the Turks, who had strengthened their forces on the Danube and in the Caucasus. The Prince was as 'tired as a dog', travelling back and forth the 1,000 versts between Kherson, Ochakov and his new naval base, Nikolaev, to inspect his ships. Nonetheless, he created an amphibious strategy to reduce the Turkish fortresses on the Danube which would open the road to Constantinople.[73] The fleet was to patrol the Black Sea. The army was to take the Danubian fortresses. The flotilla – a most Potemkinian improvisation of converted imperial barges, Benthamite gunboats, Zaporogian *chaiki* and a Marseilles merchantman disguised as a warship, commanded by Ribas and his motley crew of 'Greek brigands, Corfiote renegades and Italian Counts'[74] – was to fight its way up the Danube to rendezvous with the army beneath the most formidable Turkish fortress in Europe: Ismail.

Potemkin personally devised the training for the amphibious troops on Ribas's flotilla over the summer: his instructions, which show that the Prince's ideas predated Suvorov's much more famous *Art of Victory*, reveal his modernity, imagination and military skill. 'Find out who's most fit for precise shooting, who's good at running and who is skilled in swimming,' he demanded in an order that shows he envisaged what we would call marine assault commandos, lightly armed and highly skilled. Simultaneously, in the Caucasus, he also ordered his Kuban and Caucasus generals to destroy the 40,000-strong army of Batal-Pasha before moving on the great Ottoman fortress of Anapa.[75]

In August, the Prince of Taurida established new headquarters in the captured fortress of Bender on the Dniester, a convenient place to supervise his armies and navies on all fronts while keeping in contact with Warsaw, Vienna and Petersburg. Here, in this half-destroyed Tartar town, surrounded by steppes, he indulged himself in a Sardanapalian effulgence that beggared even his Jassy Court.

New campaign, new mistress: his relationship with Praskovia Potemkin, whom he had loved for two years, ended in Jassy and she was sent to join her complaisant husband in the field. As armies marched, barges rowed and fleets sailed, Potemkin may have enjoyed a short affair with Ekaterina Samoilova, the lascivious niece-by-marriage who had loved Damas at Ochakov. Ligne wrote to say he 'tenderly loved' Potemkin and was jealous that he was missing 'the beautiful eyes, beautiful smile and noble indifference of Madame Samoilova'.

However, she did not last long because Praskovia's place as 'favourite sultana' was then taken by Princess Ekaterina Dolgorukaya, just twenty-one years old and said to be the prettiest girl in Russia. 'Her beauty struck me,' wrote the painter Vigée Lebrun. 'Her features had something Greek mixed with something Jewish about them, above all in profile.' Her long dark hair, let down carelessly, fell on her shoulders. She had full lips, light blue-grey eyes, ivory skin and splendid figure.[76] Potemkin's Court was also enlivened by the arrival of exiles from the French Revolution who had volunteered to fight for Russia.

One of them was Alexandre, Comte de Langeron, a veteran of the American War, who was precisely the sort of Gallo-centric aristocrat who sneered at primitive Russians – and was so outraged by Potemkin's sybaritic splendour that his account regurgitates every malicious lie he heard. Langeron's (and Ligne's) bitter memoirs of Potemkin have dominated his historical image in the West ever since. Yet Langeron ended a disappointed man, unjustly cashiered by Alexander I after the Battle of Austerlitz, then forgiven, and later appointed governor-general of the south, in which job he lasted a year. 'Incapable of commanding a corps,' wrote Wiegel, 'he got command of a country.' Only after these failures was he big enough to recognize Potemkin's greatness and pen a passionate tribute.

Langeron was joined by his more gifted compatriot, the twenty-four-year-old Armand du Plessis, Duc de Richelieu, who left us a less prejudiced account of life with Serenissimus. This admirable aristocrat, with fine, serious features, curly locks and sardonic eyes, was a great-nephew of Louis XIII's Cardinal and a grandson of Louis XV's swash-buckling Field-Marshal. He inherited the cool shrewdness of the former and the cosmopolitan tolerance of the latter.[77]

Ten days and nights on the road staying at dimly lit inns had not prepared Richelieu for the spectacle that struck his eyes on entering the Prince's salon in the Pasha's Palace in Bender: 'a divan stuffed with gold under a superb baldaquin; five charming women with all the taste and careless elegance possible, and the sixth dressed with all the magnificence of Greek costume, lay on sofas in the Oriental manner'. Even the carpet was interwoven with gold. Flowers, gold and rubies were strewn around. Filigree scent-boxes wafted exquisite Arabian perfumes – 'Asiatic magic'. Potemkin himself, wearing a voluminous sable-edged coat with the diamond stars of the Orders of St Andrew and St George, and little else, sat among them – but closest to Princess Dolgorukaya, who was daringly wearing Turkic costume like an odalisque (except the pantaloons). She never left his side.

Supper was served in a hall by tall Cuirassiers with silver belts and breastplates, red capes and high fur hats surmounted by a tuft of feathers. They walked 'two by two in pairs ... like the Guards in tragedy plays', while the orchestra performed. Richelieu was introduced to Potemkin, who greeted him shyly. He was then relieved to lose himself in the crowd and find his friends Damas and Langeron.[78] The Prince, wrote Richelieu, surpassed 'all that the imagination can define as the most absolute. Nothing is impossible to his power – he commands today from Mount Caucasus to the Danube and he also shares with the Empress the rest of the Government of the Empire.'[79]

Fifty officers were gathered at the end of the brightly illuminated salon keeping their distance and waiting on the Prince. 'Here one saw a dethroned Sultan, established for three years in the Prince's ante-chamber, then another Sovereign who became a Cossack Colonel, there one saw an apostate Pasha, here a Macedonian and then further along Persian ambassadors'[80] – and amid this bazaar sat Samuel Bentham, waiting for his papers to go home. Potemkin felt this Court lacked a painter, specifically the only artist ever allowed to paint him properly – Lampi. So he wrote to Kaunitz in Vienna, asking him to despatch the artist to Bender: 'It relaxes my mind to have good painters around me who work under my gaze.'[81]

'All that can serve the pleasure of a capital city', noted Richelieu, 'accompanies Prince Potemkin in the midst of camps and the tumult of armies.'[82] The surreal daily life there resembled Petersburg with its little suppers, musical recitals, gambling, love affairs, jealousies, 'all that beauty inspires with the delicious, cruel, and perfidious'.[83] The Prince existed in a bizarre world so rarefied that 'the word "impossible" had to be deleted from the grammar'. It was said that the magnificence with which he celebrated his love for Dolgorukaya 'surpassed all that we read in *1001 Nights*'.[84] Whatever she wanted from the four corners of the world, she got. There were no longer any limits. The Princess said she liked dancers. When Potemkin heard of two captains who were the best gypsy dancers in Russia, he sent for them by courier – even though they were in the Caucasus. When they finally arrived, they danced daily, after dinner – one dressed as a girl, the other as a peasant. 'I've never seen a better dance in all my life,' recalled Potemkin's adjutant, Engelhardt.[85]

The Prince decided to build a subterranean palace for the Princess: he was bored with moving between his palace and the residences of his sultanas, so two regiments of Grenadiers worked for two weeks to build this trogledytic residence. When it was finished, Potemkin decorated its interior with Greek columns, velvet sofas and 'every imaginable luxury'.[86] Even Russians were awestruck by such extravagance, but the entire Russian army spent the winter in their *zemliankas* and the officers' dugouts were 'as comfortable as houses' with thatched roofs and chimneys.[87] Potemkin of course went considerably further: there was a gallery for the orchestra but the sound was slightly 'dulled', which produced an even finer resonance. The inner sanctum of this underground pleasure dome was, like the seraglio, a series of more and more secret rooms: outside there were the generals. Then the apartment itself was divided into two: in the first men gambled day and night, but the second contained a divan where the Prince lay, surrounded by his harem, but always closer and closer to Princess Dolgorukaya.

Ignoring the rules of civilized adultery, 'alive with passion and reassured by his excess of despotism', Potemkin sometimes forgot that the others were even there and caressed the Princess with 'excessive familiarity' as if she was just a low-born courtesan, instead of one of Russia's grandest noblewomen. The Princess would then laughingly repulse him.[88] When her friend Countess Golovina arrived, she was repelled by this tainted passion 'based on vanity'. Virtuous Golovina initially believed Dolgorukaya's insistence that there was no sexual relationship with Serenissimus, who was thirty years older. But then Dolgorukaya could not restrain herself any longer and suddenly 'gave way to a coquetry so shocking' that all was revealed.[89] Her husband Vasily Dolgorukay interrupted Potemkin's fun whenever possible. Langeron says Serenissimus seized him by the collar and shouted: 'You miserable man, it's me who gave you all those medals, none of which you deserved! You are nothing but mud and I'll make of you what I wish!' The Frenchman commented, 'this scene would have caused some astonishment in Paris, London or Vienna'.[90]

On one occasion, maybe during Sarti's Ochakov cannonade, the Prince arranged his Ekaterinoslav Grenadiers with their hundred cannons and forty blank cartridges for each soldier in a square around the subterranean palace. The drummers drummed. He cavorted inside the underground palace with the Princess and, at a supreme moment, gave the sign to fire. When her husband heard of this orgasmic salvo, he commented with a shrug, 'What a lot of noise about nothing.'[91]

Potemkin excelled himself at Princess Dolgorukaya's birthday-dinner. Dessert was served. The guests were amazed to find their crystal goblets filled with diamonds instead of *bonbons*, which were served to them piled on long spoons. Even the spoilt Princess, sitting beside Potemkin, was impressed. 'It's all for your sake,' he whispered. 'When it's you I fête, what astonishes you?'[92]

Potemkin's indolence was always more apparent than real, but it served to confirm every foreign prejudice about Russian barbarism. Yet at the very moment when Langeron claimed he spent his time canoodling with Dolgorukaya, the archives attest that he had never worked so hard, or on such a colossal canvas. He was overseeing the building of his towns in such detail that he was specifying the shape of Nikolaev's churchbells, the position of its fountains and the angle of the batteries around its Admiralty; supervising Faleev's building of more gunboats and ships-of-the-line at the Ingul shipyards; reorganizing the war in the Caucasus and Kuban (sacking his commander there, Bibikov, for bungling the march on Anapa through 'incompetence and negligence', and appointing his successors), discussing the strategy of his flotilla with Ribas while ordering him to investigate financial abuse by officers. He also devised a new signalling system for the fleet and training for its gunners.

On Polish matters, he finally agreed with Princess Lubomirska to grant her his Dubrovna estate as part of the payment for Smila.* He was instructing the Russian ambassadors to Warsaw, Stackelberg, then Bulgakov, on Russian policy, and receiving secret reports from Baron

---

* Potemkin's Dubrovna appears in the history of Napoleon. The Emperor was to stay in Princess Lubomirska's manorhouse in November 1812 during the Retreat from Moscow.

d'Asch in Warsaw about the Polish Revolution, dealing with King Stanislas-Augustus' complaints about his Cossacks stealing Polish horses, and discussing his Hetmanate and secret Polish plans with pro-Russian magnates. Serenissimus was constantly reforming and improving the army, adding more light cavalry and ever more Cossacks, but he was also intent on deliberately watering down the aristocratic content of the elite Guards Regiments, promoting foreigners, Cossacks and Old Believers, much to the disgust of the higher nobility. He told Catherine that the officers of the Preobrazhensky had been 'weakened by luxury'. He was therefore involved in a little more than just the seduction of Dolgorukaya. 'My occupations are innumerable,' he told Princess Lubormirska in a slight exaggeration. 'They do not leave me a moment to think about myself.'[93]

Then there was the international situation. The Poles were arming themselves: if they backed Prussia too closely, 'it will be time to proceed to your plan', Catherine told Grand Hetman Potemkin.[94] Worst of all, the British and Prussians were now cooking up a war to stop the Russians. Catherine and Potemkin watched the storm clouds cautiously, though both had cheered up since the Swedish peace. Catherine confided that she was so 'merry' that her dresses were getting tight and needed to be let out. Nevertheless, she missed her consort: 'I often feel, my friend, that on many occasions, I would like to talk to you for a quarter of an hour.'[95] When the Prussian minister fainted and hit his head on the throne at Catherine's Swedish peace celebrations, they saw it as a good omen. But the 'extremely tired' Catherine, so like Potemkin, always became ill once the tension broke. Now she almost collapsed. She confided she had a 'strong bout of diarrhoea' and 'colic wind'.[96]

The Prince was now the bogeyman of Prussians and Polish Patriots, who were assailing his regal ambitions; and, since 1789, there had been moves afoot in the Sejm to annul his *indigenat* and confiscate his Polish estates, involving him in yet more complex negotiations.[97] Perhaps dreaming of retirement and security, he asked Catherine to grant him some southern land he had noticed: 'I've got enough but there is no place I could lay my head pleasantly.' She granted it and sent him a gold coffee set and a diamond ring.[98]

There was one more burst of negotiating before Potemkin realized that only war would force the Turks to the table while Prussia and England were encouraging them. 'I'm bored by Turkish fairy-tales,' Potemkin told his negotiator, Lazhkarev. 'Explain to them that if they want peace, do it more quickly – or I'll defeat them.'[99] It was to be war.

*

In March, he had assumed personal command of the Black Sea Fleet and appointed Rear-Admiral Fyodor Ushakov as his deputy – another of his outstanding choices. On 24 June, he ordered him to sea to 'confront the enemy'. After inspecting the fleet himself, he sent him out again on 3 July: 'Pray to God He will help us. Put all hopes in Him, cheer up the crews and inspire them for battle . . .'.[100] Ushakov twice defeated the Turks, on 8 July, and 28/29 August off Tendra, blowing up their flagship. It was only seven years since Serenissimus had founded the fleet. 'In the north you've multiplied the Fleet,' Potemkin told Catherine, 'but here you've created it out of nothing.'[101] She agreed that it was their baby – 'an enterprise of our own, hence close to our hearts'.[102] Potemkin now ordered his flotilla to fight its way into the Danube. 'I've ordered the Sebastopol Fleet to sea,' he told Ribas, 'and to make itself visible to you. You and your flotilla should be ready to join them at the mouth of the Danube . . . Inform me of everything.'[103] In September, Potemkin rushed down to Nikolaev and the Crimea to inspect the fleets and then ordered the army to advance south towards the Danube.

On another coast of the Black Sea, there was more good news: on 30 September, General Herman eliminated a 25,000-strong Turkish army and captured Batal-Pasha. 'We hardly lost 40 men!', Potemkin told Bezborodko.[104] Nearer home, he ordered the taking of Kilia on the Danube, which failed bloodily on the first attempt because Ribas had not yet managed to destroy the Turkish Danube flotilla. Potemkin attempted a second storming and Kilia fell on 18 October 1790.[105] Ribas broke into the Danube two days later and took Tulcha and Isackcha, as he worked his way up towards mighty Ismail. The Prince trusted and admired Ribas. 'Having you there,' he wrote, 'I leave it under your command.'[106] By the end of November, the entire lower Danube as far as Galatz was his – except for Ismail. Potemkin decided to take the fortress. 'I will make an attempt on Ismail,' he said, 'but I don't want to lose ten men.'[107]

Far to the west, Richelieu, Langeron and the Prince de Ligne's son Charles were dining in Vienna, where they had gone to grumble about Potemkin's inactivity, when they heard of Batal-Pasha's defeat and the investment of Ismail. They left immediately and galloped to re-enlist with Potemkin at Bender. 'I beg Your Highness to let me rejoin the army before Ismail,' Langeron wrote to him.[108] No young sabre wanted to miss the assault – the climax of Potemkin's military career and one of the bloodiest days of the century.

30

SEA OF SLAUGHTER: ISMAIL

All that the devil would do if run stark mad,
All that defies the worst which pen expresses,
All which by hell is peopled, or as sad
As hell, mere mortals who their power abuse
Was here (as heretofore and since) let loose.

Lord Byron, the storming of Ismail, *Don Juan*, Canto VIII: 123

On 23 November 1790, some 31,000 Russian troops, under Lieutenant-Generals Ivan Gudovich, Pavel Potemkin and Alexander Samoilov, and the flotilla, commanded by Major-General de Ribas, invested indomitable Ismail. The season was late; sickness decimated the hungry army. Only the tough and talented Ribas had the stomach for an assault. The other three generals argued among themselves. None had the prestige on his own to force through the storming of an almost impregnable fortress.[1] Ismail was built into a natural amphitheatre which was defended by 265 cannons and a garrison of 35,000 men, the strength of a medium-sized army. It was a semi-circle of formidable walls, deep ditches, interlocking towers, perpendicular palisades and redoubts, with the River Danube as the flat diameter. French and German engineers had recently reinforced its 'brilliantly constructed' battlements.[2]

Potemkin watched from Bender because, if Ismail did not fall, he did not wish the prestige of the entire army to be affected.[3] The Prince saw no need to live more austerely at this crucial moment. On the contrary, he continued to suffer from a surfeit of choice on the feminine front. His ardour for Princess Dolgorukaya was cooling. The rising 'sultana', Madame de Witte, remained at his side. Countess Branicka was said to be on her way, and 'Madame L.' – the wife of General Lvov – 'is coming and bringing a young girl of fifteen or sixteen, beautiful as Cupid', a courtesan and the 'Prince's latest victim', reported a well-informed if hostile witness.[4] He appeared as sybaritic as ever. He was 'enchanted' when Richelieu, Langeron and young Ligne arrived in Bender, but he did not mention whether he was going to storm Ismail or not. Langeron asked, but 'no one opened their mouths'. The three joined the army at Ismail.[5]

Unbeknown to the generals in Ismail and most historians of the siege, the Prince had already decided that the commanders on the scene were not capable of taking the city. He had therefore summoned the one man he knew could take it, Suvorov. 'With God's help, capture the town,' Potemkin wrote to him on 25 November, adding, 'there are a lot of generals there of equal rank and so it's turned into a sort of indecisive parliament'. The Prince advised Suvorov that Ismail's walls on the river side were the weakest and he recommended only two soldiers on the spot: 'Ribas will help you ... and you'll be pleased with Kutuzov.' On both counts, posterity would agree with Potemkin's judgement. 'Make the arrangements and, with a prayer to God, do it.'[6] Suvorov set off immediately for Ismail.

The camp there was a picture of Russian administrative chaos and poor leadership. The Prince had ordered the artillery forward and demanded the capture of the city 'at any cost'.[7] On 25 November (the same day Potemkin had summoned Suvorov), Gudovich chaired a faltering war council at which Ribas demanded a full assault and the others vacillated. Ribas appealed to the Prince, who secretly wrote back, on 28 November, that Suvorov was on his way and so 'all difficulties will be swept away'. On 2 December, Gudovich held another council and ordered a retreat. Ribas was furious. 'The comedy is over,'[8] wrote a disgusted officer to a friend. They repacked the artillery; the troops began to march away. Ribas appealed to the Prince while his flotilla rowed back to Galatz.[9]

At Bender, Potemkin maintained his insouciant and debauched façade, never letting on that Suvorov was on his way to take command. He was said to be playing cards with his harem when Madame de Witte, pretending to tell his fortune, foretold he would take Ismail within three weeks. Potemkin laughed that he had a more infallible way than fortune-telling – Suvorov – as if he had just had the idea over cards. Serenissimus enjoyed playing such games with his gullible courtiers – but his obscurity was deliberate. Indeed he boasted to Catherine that he had kept his true intentions from the enemy and his own staff. 'The slaughterer must never show his knife,' he once wrote. 'Secrecy is the soul of war.'[10]

When news of Gudovich's withdrawal reached the disdainful Prince, he treated the general to a dose of his sarcasm and appointed him to command the Caucasus and Kuban corps: 'I can see you had a huge discussion about actions against Ismail but I don't find anything harmful to the enemy ... As you have not seen the Turks at close quarters except after they've been captured, I'm sending you General Suvorov who will show you how ...'.[11] Potemkin knew it was impossible to 'oversuvorov Suvorov.'

Count Suvorov-Rimniksky approached Ismail, turned back the retreating troops and recalled Ribas's flotilla. Suvorov entered the camp on 2 December, looking more 'like a Tartar than the general of a European army', a little scarecrow riding all alone except for one Cossack orderly.[12] Despite (or perhaps because of) his peculiarities, spending nights singing, eating on the floor at odd times and rolling naked on the ground, Suvorov inspired confidence. He reorganized the artillery batteries, oversaw the making of ladders and fascines to fill the ditches, and trained the troops on mock-ups of the walls. Serenissimus waited tensely in Bender – but he deliberately gave Suvorov a narrow escape-route if he really judged Ismail impregnable. This was not uncertainty, simply a sensible reminder to Suvorov not to risk Russian men and prestige if the assault was impossible. After all, the Turks were convinced Ismail really was impregnable.[13]

On 7 December, a trumpeter was sent up to the fortress with letters from Potemkin and Suvorov demanding that Ismail surrender to avoid what the Prince called shedding the 'harmless blood of women and children'.[14] Suvorov was more direct: if Ismail resisted, 'nobody will be spared'.[15] The Turks responded defiantly by parading round the ramparts, already decorated by many banners – presenting, thought Richelieu, 'a most picturesque vision of this multitude of magnificently dressed men'.[16] When the Seraskier asked for a ten-day truce, Suvorov rejected this delaying tactic. Ribas planned the assault. After a war council on 9 December, Suvorov ordered the storming of Ismail from all sides – six columns on the land side and four across the Danube. 'Tomorrow,' Suvorov told the army, 'either the Turks or the Russians will be buried at Ismail.'[17] The Seraskier, like a voice already beyond the grave, declared: 'The Danube will stop its course, the heavens will fall to earth before Ismail surrenders.'[18]

At 3 a.m. on 11 December, the heavens did fall to earth. A sustained artillery barrage pounded the fortress before a rocket zigzagged across the sky to give the order to advance. The Turkish artillery took a murderous toll on the attackers. Ismail was, recalled Langeron, a 'spectacle of horror and beauty' as the ramparts were crowned with flames.[19] Damas, who commanded a column attacking across the Danube, was one of the first atop the walls: as Potemkin had seen, the river side was weakest. On the land side, the first two columns had broken into the town, but Kutuzov's spearhead was beaten back twice with terrible losses. Suvorov was supposed to have sent him a note congratulating him on taking Ismail and appointing him its governor. This encouraged him to throw himself at the walls a third and successful time. A priest brandishing a crucifix, with bullets ricocheting off it, brought up the reserve. By the time the sun rose, all the columns were on the ramparts, but several had not yet descended into the streets. Then the Russians poured into Ismail like a 'torrent that floods the countryside'. The hand-to-hand fighting between 60,000 armed soldiers now reached its bloodiest: even as late as midday, the battle was not decided.[20]

Ismail assumed the incarnadine horror of a Dantean hell. As the 'ursomaniacs' screamed 'Hurrah' and 'Catherine II', and the Turks fell back, they were overtaken again by the lust for havoc, a fever of blood madness to kill everything they could find. 'The most horrible carnage followed,' remembered Damas, 'the most unequalled butchery. It is no exaggeration to say that the gutters of the town were dyed with blood. Even women and children fell victims to the rage.' The screams of children did not stop the Russians. A Turk ran out of a building and pointed his gun at Damas, but it did not fire and the 'poor wretch' was killed instantly by his men.

Four thousand Tartar horses escaped from the underground stables to stampede over the dead and dying, their frantic hooves pulping the human flesh and shattering the skulls of the dying, until they themselves were butchered. The Seraskier and 4,000 men were still defending the bastion on which his green tent was pitched. When they were about to surrender, an English sailor in Russian service tried to capture the Turkish general and shot him down but was himself pierced with fifteen bayonets. At this the Russians sank into a grim orgy of death, methodically working their way through the entire 4,000 men, of whom not one survived.

The Turks awaited their death with a resignation that Richelieu had never seen. 'I won't try to paint the horror which froze all my senses.' But he managed to save the life of a ten-year-old girl whom he found soaked in blood and surrounded by four women with their throats cut. Two Cossacks were about to kill her when he took her hand and 'I had the pleasure to see that my little prisoner had no other harm than a light scratch on her face probably from the same sword that had killed her mother.' A Tartar prince, Kaplan Giray, and his five sons, proud descendants of Genghis Khan, made a last stand in the bastion: the father fell last surrounded by the wreath formed by the bodies of his brave sons.

The massacre resembled a macabre pantomime as the resistance ebbed. The blood-crazed Russians draped themselves in every piece of clothing they could find – masculine or feminine. They stripped their victims before killing them to preserve their clothes. They pillaged the

Turkish shops, so the delicious smell of spices pervaded the air torn by the cries of the dying. Unrecognizable Cossacks, more terrifying than ever in wigs and dresses, marauded through the fragrant spicy streets, knee deep in a marsh of mud-congealed cadavers, reeking of blood, wielding dripping swords and pursuing naked unfortunates as horses whinnied and galloped, dogs barked and children screamed.

> The heat
> Of carnage, like Nile's sun-sodden slime,
> Engendered monstrous shapes of every crime.

The bodies themselves were piled so high that Langeron found it impossible not to walk on them. Richelieu, still holding the hand of his child, met Damas, and the two had to clear bodies to let the little girl walk along. The massacre continued until four in the afternoon, when the Turks finally surrendered.

> The glow
> Of burning streets, like moonlight on the water,
> Was imaged back in blood, the sea of slaughter.

Ismail's surviving senior Pasha laid out some carpets on the ground in the middle of the ruined fortress, surrounded by the bodies of his massacred compatriots, and smoked a pipe as tranquilly as if he was still sitting in his seraglio. Thus was conquered 'one of the keys of the Ottoman Empire'.[21] Almost 40,000 died[22] in one of the greatest military massacres of the century.

On a scrap of paper, now yellowed and almost smelling of gunpowder, Suvorov told Potemkin: 'Nations and walls fell before the throne of Her Imperial Majesty. The assault was murderous and long. Ismail is taken on which I congratulate Your Highness.'[23]

The Prince was 'as happy, as affectionate as a Sultan'.[24] He ordered the guns to be fired to celebrate and at once wrote to Catherine, sending the new favourite's brother, Valerian Zubov, whom he liked, with the news – which he recounted with all due credit to Suvorov. 'I congratulate you with my whole heart,'[25] Catherine replied. The hostile Langeron claimed that the man who had not wanted to lose ten men a month earlier now boasted, 'What are 10,000–12,000 men to the cost of such a conquest?' Potemkin may have played the bloodthirsty conqueror, but it is more revealing that he never visited Ismail, despite planning to do so daily: he fell ill, as he often did after the suspense was over, but he also had no wish to parade through the 'hideous spectacle'.[26] He finally sent Popov instead. He was certainly delighted with his victory, but he was also profoundly upset about Russian casualties – he lost his great-nephew Colonel Alexander Raevsky, one of two brothers who were 'dearest of all his nephews'.* His attitude was more likely to have been that it was a dirty job well done. He was relieved it had fallen because he and Catherine hoped this would jolt the Turks into a generous peace. Potemkin was also delighted to hear that, when the news reached Vienna, the Prince de Ligne had had to eat his weasel words about his generalship.[27]

It is said that, when Suvorov arrived in Jassy right after the battle, Potemkin received him splendidly and asked, 'How I can reward you for your services?' Suvorov snapped, 'No, Your Highness, I'm not a merchant ... No one can reward me but God and the Empress!' This is fiction that has become history.† The two originals did not meet until February, and their notes to each other were jubilant. When both arrived almost simultaneously in Petersburg, Potemkin continued to praise and promote his favourite commander.[28]

Serenissimus moved the army into winter quarters and travelled over to his 'capital', Jassy. As the entourage approached, Richelieu noticed the light rising from the town, illuminated by torches of a fête in Potemkin's honour. However, the Prince was reluctant to linger in Jassy.[29]

Potemkin wanted to return to Petersburg with the prestige of a supreme commander who had won victories in a theatre of war 'making almost a quarter of the globe, everywhere with success'. He may not have had the bloodcurdling, bayoneting dash of Suvorov but, as a strategist and overall military and naval commander, he had not lost a single battle. In a letter to Catherine, he could not resist comparing his victories to those of Prince Eugene of Savoy and Frederick the Great, yet he claimed he was avoiding the sin of pride, after her 'maternal advice in the last

* The surviving brother, Nikolai Raevsky, was the heroic general of 1812 who held the Raevsky Redoubt at the Battle of Borodino. Much later, he befriended Pushkin, who travelled with him, enjoying his stories of Potemkin and 1812. The Raevskys were the sons of Samoilov's sister.

† Virtually every history, Russian or English, contains this piece of Suvorov legend. This was supposedly the end of their relationship, in which the jealous Potemkin got his comeuppance from the genius Suvorov. In fact, this encounter probably never happened. No witness in Jassy, such as Langeron, mentions it. Potemkin was in Bender not Jassy after Ismail. Recent research by V. S. Lopatin, who has completely disproved most of the accepted pillars of the Potemkin–Suvorov relationship, shows that the two could not have met for two months – that is, not until the first week in February.

campaign'. He looked back at his life and thanked Catherine for her favour, 'which you showed to me from my first youth'. He concluded: 'Since I belong to you, all my wonderful successes belong to you too.'

Catherine and Potemkin were not old, but they were no longer young. They lived on their nerves and the years of power had made them more imperious and more sensitive. Yet they still cared for one another, gently and lovingly. The siege of Ismail had taken a toll on both of them. The partners exchanged news of their illnesses. 'My health is improving,' Catherine wrote, 'I think it's gout which has reached my stomach and bowels but I cure it with pepper and a glass of malaga wine which I drink daily.' He was ill in Jassy but, when he heard about her illness, he agreed with her malaga wine and pepper, but added that she must 'always keep your stomach warm. I kiss your hands, foster-mother.'[30] He had been away from Petersburg for almost two years and asked Catherine if he could come home. 'It's extremely necessary for me to be with you for a short time,' he wrote from Jassy on 11 January 1791. Poland was probably the main subject he wanted to discuss with her in person. 'Let me have a look at you.'[31]

She wanted to see him – 'talking's better than writing', she agreed – but she asked him to wait a little. This has been interpreted as the beginning of his fall from grace and her apprehension that he would return to Petersburg to try to remove Zubov. But her letters do not read like that, though there were certainly tensions between them. He was frustrated at her rigidity towards appeasing Prussia. He also knew that, in the capital, the Prussians, the Poles and their friends, the Grand Duke Paul and various Masonic Lodges, were trying to undermine him, claiming he wanted to be king of Poland. He suspected Zubov too was plotting against him. But he remained confident of his eternal 'sacred' ties with the Empress: 'I don't doubt your permanent favour.'[32]

Catherine certainly did not act as if she was losing the fondness of a lifetime. On the contrary, she showered him with gifts and even bought the Taurida Palace again – for 460,000 roubles – to pay his debts. But an amused Potemkin noticed that the diamonds on the Order of St Andrew, sent by the Empress, were fakes, made of crystal – surely a symbol of an increasingly sclerotic Court.[33] She simply asked him to wait a few weeks in the south so as not to miss the chance of making peace with the Turks after the triumph of Ismail. Its fall had indeed shattered Istanbul.[34]

If a peace could be negotiated with the Porte, Russia could afford to turn to the problem of Poland: its Four-Year Sejm was drafting a constitution that it hoped would make it a strong and viable kingdom and therefore a threat to Russia. Potemkin, who dominated Russia's policies towards both Poland and the Porte, proposed to Catherine that they force the Turks to cede Moldavia to Poland and thus turn the Poles against the Prussians.[35] But it all depended on the Turks. Now Britain and Prussia threw them a lifeline – the 'Ochakov Crisis'.

Even before the fall of Ismail, the Triple Alliance had been planning to foil Russian aggrandizement. Until now, Prussia had driven the coalition against Russia and it was mainly due to Frederick William's inept, inconsistent diplomacy that more damage had not been done. Now Britain, freed from the Nootka Sound Crisis with Spain, took the lead against Russia for both commercial and political reasons. The worsening of relations between Britain and Russia had begun with Catherine's Armed Neutrality, and the ending of the Anglo-Russian commercial treaty in 1786, followed by the signing of a Franco-Russian one the next year. This led to a feeling that Britain was too dependent on Russian naval supplies and should instead trade more with Poland. Britain was alarmed by Russia's ascendancy over eastern Europe, especially after the fall of Ismail promised a victorious peace with the Turks. William Pitt, the Prime Minister, therefore aimed to create 'a federative system' of alliances with Poland and Prussia, among others, to force Russia to accept a peace based on the *status quo ante bellum*. If Russia did not agree to give up Ochakov and other gains, it would be attacked by the Royal Navy at sea and Prussia on land. It certainly looked as if Britain was going to war merely to 'pluck a feather from the cap of the Empress'.[36]

Selim III was unlikely to make peace with Russia when Britain was arming a fleet to bombard Petersburg. The Sultan executed his latest Grand Vizier, reappointed the hawkish Yusuf-Pasha and gathered another army. Pitt and the Prussians prepared their ultimatum, their armies and their warships. The Prince was needed in Petersburg: now he could go home.

On 10 February 1791, he set out from Jassy. It was said that he joked that he was going to Petersburg to remove Zubov and 'extract the tooth' – *zub* meaning tooth – though, in the midst of the Ochakov Crisis, he had more important matters to discuss. Petersburg waited his arrival with greater apprehension than ever. 'All the ministers are seized with panic,' fearing the Prince, wrote the Swedish envoy Count Curt Stedingk to King Gustavus III on 8 February.[37] 'Everyone is in agitation' at the prospect of the 'apparition of this phenomenon'. Government stopped: 'No one dares, and no one can, decide anything before the arrival.'[38]

'Madame,' Stedingk asked the Empress at Court, 'should one believe the gossip that Prince Potemkin will bring peace?'

'I know nothing of it but it's possible,' replied Catherine, adding that

Serenissimus was original and very clever and he would do everything he could and that she let him. Then she mused revealingly: 'He loves to prepare me surprises.'

The Court carriages were sent to await his arrival, the roads illuminated with torches nightly for a week. Count Bruce led the welcoming delegation, waiting in a hut by the roadside from Moscow, not even daring to undress. Bezborodko rode out to prearrange tactics with Potemkin.[39] Frederick William gathered 88,000 men in East Prussia, Lord Hood amassed an 'armament' of thirty-six ships-of-the-line and twenty-nine smaller vessels at Spithead – and the Prince of Taurida, trailing a dazzling new mistress, prepared for war and for the most extravagant ball in the history of Russia.[40]

Part Eight

THE LAST DANCE
1791

31

THE BEAUTIFUL GREEK

First, test yourself to see if you are a coward; if you aren't, fortify
your innate bravery by spending much time with your enemies.
Prince Potemkin's advice to his great-nephew N. N. Raevsky, the future
hero of 1812 and friend of A. S. Pushkin

When Potemkin swept into Petersburg on 28 February 1791 – his way
emblazoned with hundreds of torches[1] – the Empress hurried to meet
him. She presented him with the Taurida Palace once again – she had
only just bought it from him. The Anglo-Prussian coalition's threat of
war was Russia's gravest crisis since the days of Pugachev and the two
old partners met anxiously every day, while the nobility and diplomats
outdid each other to celebrate Serenissimus' return.

'In spite of the great expectation I had had of this event, and all I had
heard of the importance and power of this man, the train, the fracas,
the excitement, that accompanied him, amazed me, and I still have its
effects before my eyes,' wrote Jean-Jacob Jennings, a Swedish diplomat.
'Since this Prince arrived, there is no other subject of conversation in all
society, in all high houses or lower, than of him – what he does or will
do, whether he dines or will dine or has dined. The interest ... of the
public is on him alone – all the tributes, respects, offerings of all classes
of citizens – lords, artisans, merchants, writers – all sit at his door and
fill his anterooms.'[2]

The Prince of Taurida appeared all-conquering: 'His credit and
authority have never been greater,' noticed the Swedish envoy Stedingk.
'All that shone before his arrival is eclipsed and all Russia is at his feet.'[3]
There was an outpouring of admiration – and envy from some of the
magnates.[4] The Russian 'public', so far as it existed, meaning the lower
nobility and the merchants, hero-worshipped him. Ladies wore his
picture on medallions – 'Her pearl-like bosom heaving sighs,' wrote
Derzhavin, 'A hero's image animates.'[5] The specially written 'Ode to
Potemkin' was recited at receptions.[6] Every grandee had to give a ball in
what was called 'The Carnival of Prince Potemkin'.[7]

Catherine herself seemed relieved and delighted to see Serenissimus
after so long. 'Victory has embellished him,' she told Grimm. Potemkin
was now 'handsome as the day, gay as a lark, brilliant as a star, more

spiritual than ever, no longer biting his nails, giving parties every day. Everyone is enchanted, despite the envious.'[8] The Prince had never been more charming. Even Augustyn Deboli, the hostile envoy of Revolutionary Poland, reported that Potemkin was so polite that he mischievously asked everyone if they noticed how his behaviour was altered.[9]

This is how Potemkin appeared at his apogee in March 1791. 'I saw for the first time this extraordinary man last Sunday in the circle of the Grand Duke,' gushed Jennings. 'He had been described as very ugly. I did not find him so. On the contrary, he has an imposing presence and that eye defect does not influence his face as badly as you would expect.' Potemkin wore the white uniform of the Grand Admiral of the Black Sea Fleet, covered in diamonds and medals. As soon as this Grand Admiral appeared, the 'circle around the Grand Duke disappeared and it formed around Prince Potemkin exactly as if we saw in him the person of our Master'. Even princes of Württemberg stood upright and immobile 'like statues, eyes fixed on the great man, waiting for him to deign to gratify them with a look'.[10]

'The Potemkin Carnival' meant a fête every night. The courtiers – Nikolai Saltykov, Zavadovsky, Ivan Chernyshev, Bezborodko, Osterman, Stroganov and Bruce – competed to hold the most extravagant ball. Some almost ruined themselves, trying to keep up with the Stroganovs. But they were confused about the identity of the Prince's latest mistress. The courtiers prepared to give balls in honour of his 'sultana', Princess Dolgorukaya, until they noticed that he never visited her. She claimed to be ill – yet he still did not visit, not even once, at which point the cowardly courtiers cancelled their balls and the crestfallen Princess had to retire to Moscow.[11] On 18 March, the Prince de Nassau-Siegen gave one of the most expensive parties, with plates piled with sturgeon and sterlet, Potemkin's favourite delicacy. There, Serenissimus, wearing his superb jewel-encrusted grand hetman's uniform that Deboli claimed cost 900,000 roubles,[12] unveiled his other favourite dish: Madame de Witte, the most intriguing adventuress of all.

The appearance at Nassau's ball of 'this beauty of renown' was 'the greatest sensation', according to a goggle-eyed Jennings. When Potemkin had finished his card game, he rushed over to her and talked only to her, while everyone else stared: 'all the women were agitated, men too – the former with despair, irritation and a lot of curiosity, the latter with desire and expectation'.[13]

Sophie de Witte, now twenty-five years old, with blonde curls, a noble Grecian face and violet eyes, was 'the prettiest woman in Europe in that era'. She rose from teenage courtesan in Constantinople to one of the richest countesses of Poland: for forty years, she astonished and scandalized Europe with her 'beauty, vice and crimes'. Born in a Greek village on the outskirts of 'the city of the world's desire', she was nicknamed the 'Beautiful Greek' or 'La Belle Phanariote' after the Greek Phanar district. Her mother, who traded vegetables, sold her at twelve to the Polish Ambassador, who procured girls for King Stanislas-Augustus, while her equally fine sister was sold to a senior Ottoman pasha. From then on, every time she was bought, another man fell in love with her and outbid the first. So, on her way with the ambassadorial baggage, Sophie de Tchelitche, as she then called herself, was spotted by Major de Witte, son of the Governor of the Polish fortress of Kamenets-Podolsk, who bought her for 1,000 ducats and married her in 1779 aged fourteen. Witte sent her off to Paris with Princess Nassau-Siegen to learn manners – and French.

La Belle Phanariote bewitched Paris. Langeron saw her there and praised 'the tenderest and most beautiful eyes that nature had ever formed', but he was under no illusion about her cunning manipulations and the 'coldness of her heart'.[14] Some of her fascination was 'a sort of originality proceeding from either feigned naivety or ignorance'. In Paris, everyone praised her 'beaux yeux'. When someone asked about her health, she replied, 'My *beaux yeux* are sore,' which amused everyone enormously.[15] Back in Poland, when Potemkin's War began, her husband, now himself governor of Kamenets, was the linchpin of the Prince's espionage network in southern Poland: it was he who smuggled spies into Khotin hidden with the butter. But it was probably his wife who provided the information: her sister was married to the Pasha of Khotin, while Sophie herself became the mistress of the besieging general, Nikolai Saltykov.[16] But the sharp-eyed Ribas spotted her and introduced her to Potemkin at Ochakov. Visitors to Jassy and Bender noticed her Greek costume and how she posed melodramatically and 'flung herself around', to impress Serenissimus. She became the confidante of his affair with Dolgorukaya, whom she then supplanted.[17] Potemkin appointed the complaisant husband to be governor of Kherson.[18] It is likely he used her as a secret agent among the Poles and Turks.[19]

The Empress, used to her consort's latest paramours, gave the 'Beautiful Greek' a pair of diamond earrings.[20] This made Sophie's husband so proud that he boasted she would be remembered in history as the friend of royalty, adding: 'The Prince is not the lover of my wife but just a friend because, if he was her lover, I would break any connection with him.' This simple-minded wishful thinking must have provoked some sniggers. The courtesan–spy clearly fascinated Potemkin – she was an Oriental, an intriguer, a Venus and a Greek, any of which would have attracted him. 'You're the only woman', Potemkin told her, 'who surprises me', to which the minx replied, 'I know. If I'd been your mistress, you'd already have forgotten me. I am only your friend and always will be.' (Ladies are always bound to say this in public: no one close to them believed her.)[21] Perhaps she broke her own rule, because two weeks later diplomats noticed Potemkin suddenly began to lose interest: had she succumbed against her better judgement?[22]

Serenissimus decided to hold a ball to defy the Anglo-Prussian coalition and celebrate Ismail. He was supposed to be negotiating the subsidy that Russia would pay Gustavus III for a Russo-Swedish alliance. It was in Potemkin's interest to play this out because Britain was also offering Sweden a subsidy for the use of its ports in a war against Russia. The threat was serious enough for Potemkin to send Suvorov on 25 April to command the corps facing Sweden as a living warning to Gustavus. The Swedish King was trying to auction his services and Britain offered £200,000, but, once the Ochakov Crisis was over, the price would drop. So Potemkin deliberately delayed negotiations by forcing the Swedish envoy, Stedingk, to sit through the rehearsals for his ball at the Taurida Palace.

Thus Stedingk received a theatrical education – but no diplomatic satisfaction at all.[23] Serenissimus, covered in diamonds, seemed pre-occupied by diamonds – he looked at diamonds, admired the huge diamonds on his miniature portrait of Catherine, played with diamonds until the stones alone became the subject of conversation.[24] Potemkin made Stedingk 'walk through fifty apartments, see and admire everything [then] got me into his carriage, talking only of himself, the Crimea & the Black Sea Fleet.' Next, there were more rehearsals.[25] When the Prince got bored with his own spectaculars, his face revealed 'disgust boredom lassitude ... that came from having all desires satisfied, when one is blasé about everything and there is nothing left to want'.[26]

Then he gave an order: '200 musicians, placed in the gallery of the great hall, play ... with the two of us as their only audience. The Prince is in Seventh Heaven. 100 people arrive, they dance, they do another quadrille.' The rehearsals started at 3 p.m. and ended at 9 p.m. 'without one moment to fix the attention of the Prince on Sweden. Such Sire', Stedingk sorrowfully told his King, 'is the man who governs the Empire.'[27] Potemkin told everyone who would listen that he was not involved in foreign affairs but thought only about his entertainment.[28]

*

The real business was conducted in Catherine's apartments, where the partners struggled to counter an imminent Anglo-Prussian war. After two years apart, they were adapting their relationship to his overbearing dominance and her weary obstinacy. On 16/27 March, Pitt sent off his ultimatum to Petersburg, via Berlin. It was a rash act for the usually cautious British Prime Minister, but thirty-nine ships-of-the-line and 88,000 Prussians were no idle threat. The Empress was determined that there would be no concessions to the Prussians and the English.

In their struggle to find a way out of the trap, Potemkin and Catherine even turned to the leading statesman of the hated French Revolution, Honoré Gabriel Riqueti, Comte de Mirabeau. Potemkin thought 'France has gone mad,' and Catherine believed Mirabeau should be hanged, not from just one gallows, but many – *and then* 'broken on the wheel'. But it was fitting that Potemkin should be in secret contact with Mirabeau, who was his only European equal in terms of eccentric brilliance, physical scale and extravagant debauchery. (Ironically Mirabeau's father once muttered about his son: 'I know of nobody but the Empress of Russia for whom this man would make a suitable match.') The Prince paid fat bribes to 'Mirabobtcha', as he nicknamed him, in an attempt to persuade France to join Russia against Britain (while in fact Mirabeau advocated *entente* with London). Mirabeau, already bribed generously by the beleaguered Louis XVI, simply 'consumed' Potemkin's money to pay for his magnificent lifestyle and then fell ill. He died in Paris on 19 March/ 2 April 1791 – the day after Nassau's ball for Potemkin.[29]

Serenissimus knew that Russia simply could not fight the Triple Alliance and Poland as well as the Turks. So while he prepared the army for a broader war, placing corps on the Dvina and Kiev ready to advance across Poland into Prussia, he was prepared to buy off Frederick William to give Russia a free hand with the Turks and Poles. Catherine did not want to surrender to the coalition. This strained their friendship. Stedingk believed that 'even Her Majesty the Empress' was 'secretly jealous' of Serenissimus. Perhaps that was why Catherine said Potemkin did 'everything she *let him do*'. Stedingk reported that 'the Empress is no longer what she was ... Age and infirmities have rendered her less capable.' It was now easier to trick her, appeal to her vanity and mislead her. To paraphrase Lord Acton, absolute power coarsens, and both of them had become coarser – the destiny of statesmen who never leave government. Yet Potemkin proudly still treated her as a woman. 'What do you want?', he told the Swede. 'She is a woman – one's got to manage her. One can't rush anything.'[30]

Actually, it was less personal than that. She was anxious because there

516   THE LAST DANCE
```

was a real divergence in their views, something that had never happened before. She probably worried that he might win, and undermine her authority. Potemkin was irritated that her pride and obstinacy were threatening all their achievements. Would she surrender to Potemkin's superior knowledge of the military situation?[31]

The Prince also wanted to remove the Empress's companion, Platon Zubov, who was increasingly involved in intrigues against him. This must have added to the tension. A politician is never so exposed as when he appears invincible, for it unites his enemies, and Potemkin was beset by attempts to undermine him. Deboli recorded that Zubov, Saltykov and Nassau-Siegen were already intriguing against him, even though 'so many attempts against . . . Potemkin failed like this one'.[32] Yet Zubov was backed by his patron Nikolai Saltykov, Governor of the little Grand Dukes, and therefore connected to Paul, his pro-Prussian circle based at the Gatchina estate, and the Masonic Lodges, particularly the Rosicrucians, linked to Berlin.* Some of these Lodges[33] became rallying-points for criticism of the Catherine–Potemkin regime, especially since so many magnates were Masons – and the Prince was not.[34] Paul himself, who so hated Potemkin, was in treasonable correspondence with Berlin.[35]

Catherine and Potemkin now had little time for nostalgic endearments: they locked horns in bouts of argument and reconciliation as they had done since they fell in love seventeen years earlier. Catherine's belief all those years ago that their arguments were 'always about power, not love' was true enough now. When persuasion failed, Potemkin tried to bully her into changing her policy. Catherine resisted tearfully, though her tears were always as manipulative as his tantrums. Her refusal to make friendly noises towards a power that was about to invade an exhausted Russia was surely foolish. Potemkin, who knew the situation on the ground, was not suggesting surrender, merely sensible lulling of Frederick William until they had made peace with the Turks.

Potemkin told Catherine's valet, Zakhar Zotov, that there would have to be a row because of the Empress's postponing of the decision. She would not even correspond with Frederick William. Then Serenissimus muttered angrily about Zubov – why did Mamonov leave his place in

---

* It was no coincidence that the first and most vicious anti-Potemkin biography, written even before Helbig, *Panslavin Fürst der Finsternis (Panslavin Prince of Darkness)* was by a Freemason, J. F. E. Albrecht, probably a Rosicrucian. Mystical Freemasonry was surprisingly fashionable among the parodomaniacs of Prussia: the fat, dull and dim Frederick William of Prussia supposedly spent evenings communicating with the spirits of Marcus Aurelius, Leibniz and the Great Elector, from whom he hoped to learn greatness. If so, the lessons failed.
```

such a silly way and not wait for Potemkin for arrange things? If the war became absolutely imminent, Potemkin would protect his Turkish gains and satisfy Prussia with a Polish partition. But partition, which would ruin his subtler plans for Poland, was a last resort.[36]

Catherine and Potemkin argued for days on end. Catherine wept. Potemkin raged. He bit his nails while the tumult hit Catherine in the bowels. By 22 March, Catherine was ill in bed with 'spasms and strong colic'. Even when they rowed, they still behaved like an old husband and wife: Potemkin suggested she take medicine for her bowels but she insisted on relying 'on nature'. The Prince kept up the pressure.[37]

A little boy, the ten-year-old son of Potemkin's valet, witnessed a row and reconciliation that sound like any couple: the Prince banged the table and left the room slamming the door so hard that the glasses jumped. Catherine burst into tears. Then she noticed the alarmed child, who was no doubt wishing he was elsewhere. She smiled through her tears and gesturing at the absent Potemkin told the boy, 'Go and see how he is.' So the child obediently ran along to Serenissimus' apartments and found him sitting at his desk in the study.

'So it's she who sent you?', asked the Prince.

Yes, replied the child, with the open-hearted courage of the innocent; maybe Serenissimus should go and comfort Her Imperial Majesty because she was crying and apologizing.

'Let her blub!', said Potemkin callously – but he was too soft-hearted to leave her for long. A few minutes later, he calmed down and went to make friends again.[38] Such was their personal and political relationship towards the end of their lives.

'Obstinacy', recorded Catherine's secretary on 7 April, 'leads to new war.' But now the prospect of a war on several fronts – since there was every likelihood that Poland and Sweden would join England, Prussia and Turkey – made Catherine blink. She told her staff that there would no more 'beer and porter' – English products – but on 9 April Potemkin and Bezborodko drafted a memorandum to appease Frederick William enough to distract him from the war. 'How can our recruits fight Englishmen?', Potemkin had grumbled. 'Hasn't Swedish cannon-fire tired [anyone] here?' Catherine was indeed tired of shooting: she buckled and agreed secretly to renew the old Prussian treaty, encourage Poland to agree to the cession of Thorn and Danzig to Prussia, and make peace with the Porte, gaining Ochakov and its hinterland.[39] But they prepared for war. 'You'll have news of me if they attack on land or sea,' Catherine wrote to a friend in Berlin, deliberately *en clair*, and offering no concessions.[40]

The partners did not know that the coalition was collapsing. Before Catherine's proposal reached Berlin, the British faltered. Pitt's Government technically won the three Parliamentary debates on the Ochakov Crisis – but lost the argument. On 18/29 March, Charles James Fox scuppered the weak arguments for the naval expedition against Russia with a rousing speech, asking what British interests were at stake in Ochakov, while Edmund Burke attacked Pitt for protecting the Turks – 'a horde of barbaric Asiatics'. Catherine's envoy, Simon Vorontsov, rallied the Russian 'lobby' of merchants, from Leeds to London, and primed his own armament of hacks. Ink and paper proved mightier than Prussian steel and British gunpowder. Even the navy was against it: Horatio Nelson could not see 'how we are to get at her fleet. Narrow seas and no friendly ports are bad things.' Within days, 'no war with Russia!' was daubed on walls all over the Kingdom. Cabinet support waned. On 5/16 April, Pitt withdrew his ultimatum and despatched a secret emissary, William Fawkener, to Petersburg to find a way out of the débâcle that almost cost him his place.[41]

The Prince and Empress were jubilant. Catherine celebrated by placing Fox's statue in her Cameron Galley between Demosthenes and Cicero. Potemkin celebrated by happily boasting to the humiliated British envoy, Charles Whitworth, that he and Catherine were 'the spoilt children of Providence'. The Ochakov Crisis posed the Eastern Question to the British for the first time, but they were not yet interested in the survival of 'the sick man of Europe'. Jingo would have to wait. Potemkin had been wrong to force Catherine to negotiate – but only with hindsight. His advice had been sensible. They had just been fortunate. The Prince believed that he and the Empress shared a lucky star: 'in order to be successful', he told the Englishman, 'they only have to desire it'.[42]

His masquerade ball, which he had been rehearsing day and night since his return, was to mark Russian triumph over Turks, Prussians and Britons – Catherine and Potemkin's defiant celebration of Providence. His servants galloped around St Petersburg delivering this invitation:*

> The General–Field-Marshal Prince Potemkin of Taurida
> invites you to render him the honour of coming
> on Monday, 28th April at six o'clock
> to his palace on Horse-Guards
> to the masquerade which will be favoured by the presence of
> Her Imperial Majesty and Their Imperial Highnesses.[43]

* The author found what is probably the sole surviving copy of this card, addressed to Countess Osterman, in the archives of the Odessa State Local History Museum.

32

CARNIVAL AND CRISIS

That Marshal Prince Potemkin gave us a superb party yesterday
at which I stayed from seven in the evening until two in the
morning when I went home … Now I am writing to you to
improve my headache.

Catherine II to Baron Grimm

At 7 p.m. on 28 April 1791, the imperial coach arrived before the Classical
colonnade of the Prince's palace on Horse-Guards, which was illuminated with hundreds of torches. The Empress, wearing a full-length
long-sleeved Russian dress with a rich diadem, dismounted slowly in
the rain. Potemkin stepped forward to greet her. He wore a scarlet
tailcoat and, tossed over his shoulders, a gold and black lace cloak,
ornamented with diamonds. He was covered with 'as many diamonds
as a man could possibly wear'.[1] Behind him, an adjutant held a pillow
that bore his hat, which was so weighed down with diamonds that it
could barely be worn. Potemkin moved towards her through two lines
of footmen, wearing their master's livery of pale-yellow with blue and
silver. Each bore a candelabrum. Bathed in this imperial effulgence,
Potemkin knelt on one knee before Catherine. She brought him to his
feet. He took her hand.

There was a dull roar as 5,000 members of the public, more interested
in eating than in observing history, rushed forward to feast on tables of
free food and drink. There were swings, roundabouts and even shops
where people were given costumes, but now they wanted the food. The
Prince had ordered that it should be laid out after the Empress had
entered. But a steward mistook a courtier's carriage and started the feast
too early. There was almost a riot. For a second, Catherine, nervous of
the people as the French Revolution dismantled the Bourbon monarchy,
thought 'the honourable public' were stampeding. She was relieved to
see they were simply filling their pockets with food to take home.[2]

The Prince led his Empress towards the door of the Palace, later
named the Taurida, which set a new standard for Classical simplicity
and grandeur. 'All was gigantic.' That was its clear message: the façade
was plain and colossal, designed by the architect Ivan Starov to symbolize
Potemkin's power and splendour. Two long wings led out from a domed

portico supported by six Doric columns. Inside, the couple entered an anteroom and walked along a receiving line that led into the Cupola or Colonnade Hall, where the Grand Duke Paul and his wife along with 3,000 guests awaited Catherine in their costumes.

'Imagine it if you can!', Catherine dared Grimm. The Hall was the biggest in Europe – 21 metres high, its oval shape was 74.5 metres long and 14.9 metres wide, supported by two rows of thirty-six Ionic columns – the 'poetry of columns' that dwarfed the thousands of guests. (It could easily hold 5,000 people.) The floors were inlaid with precious woods and decorated with 'astonishingly huge' white marble vases, the ceilings hung with multi-tiered chandeliers of black crystal – treasures bought from the Duchess of Kingston. At each end was a double row of French windows.[3] The entire Hall was so bright it almost appeared to be on fire, illuminated by the massive chandeliers and fifty-six smaller ones each with sixteen candles. Five thousand torches burned. The wind orchestra of 300 musicians and an organ, accompanied by choirs – all hidden in the two galleries – burst into a concert of specially written choral pieces.

Straight ahead of her, the Empress could not miss the famous Winter Garden. This too was the biggest in Europe, for it was the same size again as the rest of a palace that covered 650,700 square feet. The huge glass hall was supported by columns in the form of palm-trees which contained warm water pipes. This was William Gould's *chef d'oeuvre* – an organized jungle of exotic plants, 'flowers, hyacinths and narcissuses, myrtles, orange trees in plenty' – where the walls were all mirrors that concealed more immense stoves.* Lamps and diamonds were hidden in mock bunches of grapes, clusters of pears and pineapples so that everything seemed alight. Silver and scarlet fishes swam in glass globes. The cupola was painted like the sky. Paths and little hillocks crisscrossed this arbour, leading to statues of goddesses. Its most striking effect was its 'infinite perspective', for Catherine could see straight through the brightness of the Colonnade Hall into the tropical lightness of the Winter Garden and, further, through its glass walls into the English Garden outside, where its 'sanded paths wind, hills rise up, valleys fall away, cuttings open groves, ponds sparkle',[4] its follies and hills, still snow-covered, rolling all the way down to the Neva. The tropical forest and the snowy hills – which was real?

---

* Potemkin's tsar of gardeners, William Gould, 'lived in splendour' in the Palladian villa Catherine had built for him in the grounds of the Taurida (still called the 'gardener's house') and 'gave entertainment to the nobility'. He died in luxurious retirement at Ormskirk in Lancashire in 1812.

In the midst of the Winter Garden stood a temple to the Empress on a diamond-studded pyramid. At the feet of Shubin's statue of Catherine the Legislatrix, a placard from Potemkin read: 'To the Mother of the Motherland and my benefactress'.[5] The Prince escorted Catherine to the left of the Colonnade Hall on to a raised dais, covered in Persian carpets, facing the garden. Out of the tropical gardens came two quadrilles, each of twenty-four children, 'the most beautiful in St Petersburg' according to Catherine, dressed in costumes of sky blue and pink, and covered from head to foot in 'all the jewels of the town and suburbs' – the boys in Spanish garb, the girls in Greek. Grand Duke Alexander, the future Emperor and vanquisher of Napoleon, danced a complicated ballet in the first quadrille, choreographed by Le Picq, the celebrated dancemaster. Grand Duke Constantine danced in the second. 'It's impossible', wrote Catherine afterwards, 'to see anything more gorgeous, more varied or more brilliant'. Then Le Picq himself danced a solo.

As darkness fell, Potemkin conducted the imperial family, followed by the entire party, into the Gobelins Room, where the tapestries told the story of Esther. In the midst of sofas and chairs stood a Potemkinian wonder: a life-sized gold elephant, covered in emeralds and rubies, with a clock concealed in its base, ridden by a blackamoor mahout in Persian silks who gave a signal at which curtains were raised to reveal a stage and amphitheatre with boxes. Two French comedies and a ballet were followed by a procession of all the peoples of the Empire, including captured Ottoman pashas from Ismail, in the Asiatic splendour of their national dress. While guests watched the show, servants in the other halls were lighting a further 140,000 lamps and 20,000 wax candles. When the Empress returned, the Colonnade Hall was bathed in a blaze of light.

The Prince took Catherine by the hand to the Winter Garden. When they stood before the statue in the temple, he again fell to his knees and thanked the Empress. She raised him to his feet and kissed him tenderly on the forehead: she thanked him for his deeds and devotion. Derzhavin's 'Ode' to Potemkin's victories was recited: 'Thunder of victory, ring! Brave Rus, rejoice!'[6]

Potemkin signalled the orchestra. The ball began at last. Catherine played cards with her daughter-in-law in the Gobelins Room, then went to rest. Just as *he* had apartments in *her* palaces, so Catherine had a bedroom in *his*. Their rooms here showed their cosy intimacy together. Both loved monumental palaces and tiny bedrooms: her bedroom was in Potemkin's wing and its ceiling was decorated with Classical symbols of voluptuousness, goats and shepherds. There was a secret door, concealed behind a rug hung on the wall, into Potemkin's anteroom, bedroom and study, so that they could enter each other's rooms. His bedroom was simple, snug and light, with walls of plain silk.* (Sometimes, when he was in residence, she is said to have stayed; she certainly held dinners there.)[7]

At midnight, Catherine returned for the supper in such high spirits that the forty-eight children returned to dance their quadrilles all over again. The Empress's table, placed where the orchestra in the amphitheatre had played, was covered in gold. Forty-eight magnates sat down around her. Fourteen tables surrounded hers. There were other tables and buffets in different halls. Each was illuminated by a ball of white and blue glass. On one table, a huge silver goblet stood between two more of the Duchess of Kingston's gargantuan vases. While waiters in Potemkin's livery served, the Prince stood behind the Empress's chair, looming over her like a diamond-glinting Cyclops, and served her himself until she insisted he sit down and join her. After dinner, there were more concerts and the ball began again. At 2 a.m., four hours after she usually left balls, the Empress rose to leave. The Prince of Taurida led her out as he had led her in.

In the vestibule, Serenissimus fell to his knees – the ritual submission of this scarlet-coated giant before his empress, in front of the great of the Empire and the cabinets of Europe. He had had her bedroom prepared if she wished to stay. It was unlikely, but he wanted to be able to offer it. She was too tired to stay any longer. The orchestra was primed with two different airs – one if the Empress stayed, and one if she left. If she was leaving, Potemkin had arranged to put his hand on his heart, and, when he did, the orchestra burst into the melancholic bars of a lover's lament, written, long before, by the Prince himself. 'The only thing that matters in the world', went the cantata, 'is you.' The magnificence of the ball, the sadness of the song and the sight of this unwieldy one-eyed giant on his knees touched Catherine. The partners felt old and had loved each other for a very long time. Both of them burst into tears. He kissed her hand again and again, and they sobbed together before she climbed into her carriage and drove away.[8]

This looked like a parting. It is often interpreted as a premonition of Potemkin's death. So much of this last stay in St Petersburg is distorted by hindsight.† But it was a most emotional night, the climax of their

---

* When the Emperor Paul set out to deface the building after his mother's death, these little rooms so disgusted him that he did not ruin them. He simply sealed them and they alone remain today.
† Indeed some histories claim that this was the last time they met. In fact, Potemkin remained in Petersburg for three more eventful months.

adventure together. Potemkin lingered among the debris of the party, touched by melancholy and nostalgia, almost in a trance.

When he came to say goodbye to one lady who knew him well – Countess Natalia Zakrevskaya – she noticed his air of sadness. Her heart went out to him. She knew him well enough to say: 'I don't know what will become of you. You are younger than the Sovereign. You'll outlive her: what will become of you then? You would never agree to be the second man.' Potemkin contemplated this dreamily: 'Don't worry. I'll die before the Sovereign. I'll die soon.' She never saw him again.[9]

'That fête was magnificent,' wrote Stedingk, who was there, 'and no other man could have given it.'[10] But it had been irresponsibly extravagant – Potemkin supposedly spent between 150,000 and 500,000 roubles during those three months. Everyone knew that the Treasury was paying for the ball as it paid all his bills, but it was soon widely believed that, as Stedingk reported, 'this prodigality displeases the Empress'.

Catherine was so overexcited when she got home that night that she could not sleep. She got over her 'little headache' by writing to Grimm to rave about the 'fête superbe' with the enthusiasm of a young girl the morning after her début. She even drew a map to show Grimm where she sat and told him how late she stayed: so much for her disapproval! Then she 'spun' Grimm the political purpose of what was clearly a joint Catherine–Potemkin production: 'There you are, Monsieur, that is how, in the midst of trouble and war and the menaces of dictators [she meant Frederick William of Prussia], we conduct ourselves in Petersburg.' There is no evidence that she grumbled about Potemkin's expenditure, colossal and excessive though it was, but she probably did. Like all of us, she may well have got a shock when she received the bill.

Just as she was writing to Grimm, a letter arrived bringing dramatic Polish news that meant that Potemkin would have to stay in Petersburg much longer.

On 22 April/3 May 1791, the Commonwealth of Poland and Lithuania had adopted a new constitution amid tumultuous scenes in the Sejm: one deputy even drew his sword in mid-debate and threatened to kill his son like Abraham and Isaac. Poland's 'May the Third' Revolution created a hereditary monarchy, in which the succession was to be offered to the Elector of Saxony or his daughter, with a strong executive, almost combining the powers of the English Crown and American presidency, and an army. Warsaw celebrated with the slogan 'The King with the Nation'. Those who had thought Poland was beyond help were impressed. 'Happy people,' wrote Burke, 'happy prince.'

The timing was useful for the Russians but unfortunate for the Poles, because the Anglo-Prussian coalition was about to free Russia's hands to deal with their awkward and recalcitrant satellite. Catherine shared Potemkin's disgust for the French Revolution: Republicanism was 'a sickness of the mind' she declared, and she was already cracking down on radical ideas in Russia itself. The Polish Revolution was actually politically conservative, strengthening, not weakening, the monarchy, decreasing, not increasing, the franchise. But Catherine chose to regard it as a Jacobin extension of the French Revolution into her sphere of influence: 'We're perfectly prepared,' Catherine signed off ominously to Grimm, 'and unfortunately, we don't yield to the very devil himself!'[11]

Potemkin, who was receiving almost daily reports from Bulgakov, Branicki and spies in Warsaw, was watching Poland closely too. He did not like what he saw[12] and resolved to take supreme control of Polish policy and put his secret plans into action. He had not yet succeeded in budging Zubov but he probably felt that an Ottoman peace and a Polish success would overpower his critics. So he stayed much longer than he had agreed with Catherine, to discuss Poland, which severely strained their partnership. But, before they could turn on Poland, they had to fight the Turks to a settlement and negotiate their way out of the Ochakov Crisis with Pitt's emissary, Fawkener, who was about to arrive.

'If you want to take the stone from my heart, if you want to calm the spasms,' Catherine told Potemkin in early May, 'then send couriers to the armies quickly and let land and sea forces start operations . . .' – otherwise they would never get the peace both wanted.[13] The Prince, in one of his moods of euphoric creativity, fired off orders to his forces while founding new settlements across the south. On 11 May, he ordered Admiral Ushakov to put to sea and pursue the enemy; Repnin, commanding the main army in his absence, to strike decisively across the Danube to destroy any concentration of Turkish forces; and Gudovich, commanding the Kuban corps, to take the strongest Ottoman fortress in those parts – Anapa.[14] Meanwhile the partners worked out their Polish plans.

On 16 May, when the Anglo-Prussian crisis was still unsettled. Catherine signed her first rescript to Potemkin on Poland. The Prince could intervene only if the Prussians moved into Poland, in which case Potemkin could offer the Poles the Ottoman principality of Moldavia in return for reversing their Revolution. If they did not take this bait, Potemkin could resort to 'extreme measures' in the traditional way, by arranging a confederation under his Polish allies, Branicki and Potocki. Catherine specifically added that among the 'extreme measures' she approved 'your secret plan' of raising the Orthodox in Kiev, Podolia and

Bratslav, under the banner of the 'Grand Hetman' of the Cossacks.[15] It is usually claimed that Potemkin did not receive the powers he wanted.[16] On the contrary, his powers were potentially vast, though conditional on the real if diminishing likelihood of Prussia and England attacking Russia. (Negotiations with Fawkener had not yet started.)* Besides, Potemkin did not 'receive' the rescripts like a schoolboy from a head-mistress: the couple worked on them together, correcting one another's drafts, as they always had. The rescripts and correspondence show that Catherine agreed with Potemkin's Cossack and Moldavian schemes, and had done so for more than two years.

Potemkin's Polish schemes are the mystery of his last year: he was weaving a tapestry of overlapping threads that no one has ever managed to untwine. His plans appear protean, shifting and exotic, but the Prince never saw the need to decide on a plan until the last moment. Meanwhile, he would run all of them simultaneously. He had been contemplating the Polish question since he came to power and his Polish policies existed on many different levels, but it is impossible to divorce them from his need for a principality outside Russian borders. All these plans contain slots for Potemkin's own realm. He had convinced himself that his 'independent' Polish duchy, built around his Smila estates, would be a camouflaged means for Russia to win swathes of central Europe without having to repay the other powers with a second partition of Poland.

There were four Potemkinian projects. There was annexation of Mol-davia by Poland. This duchy would have fitted well into the Poland envisaged by his ally, Felix Potocki, in a letter to Potemkin that May: a federal republic of semi-independent hetmanates. Simultaneously, there was the plan for a confederation, led by Branicki and Potocki, that would overthrow the new Constitution and replace it with the old version or a new federal one with Moldavia as a bribe. Even as early as February, Potemkin had been flattering Potocki, inviting him to a meeting 'on the veritable well-being of our common country'.[17]

Then there was Potemkin's idea of invading Poland as grand hetman of the Black Sea Cossacks to liberate the Orthodox of eastern Poland. This combined his Polish ancestry, his regal ambitions, his enjoyment

---

* Some Polish historians regard this condition as a sham to delude Potemkin, because Catherine already knew there would be no war with Prussia. This is clearly not so. England had blinked but not surrendered. The conditions placed on Potemkin's action were entirely reasonable. The accompanying documents discussing the creation of Polish forces to back up a Confederation show how they worked together just before his Taurida ball: he drafted a proposal that required recruitment of Polish forces, to which she added her thoughts in the margin.

of drama, his Russian instinct to break the Polish Revolution – and his 'passion for Cossacks'.[18] Even before procuring the Hetmanate, Potemkin had envisaged a special Polish role for Black Sea Cossacks, recruiting them in Poland.[19] On 6 July 1787, for example, Catherine let him establish four such squadrons from his own Polish villages,[20] where he already had his own forces: Smila's mounted and infantry militia.[21] Later, Alexandra Branicka explained that he 'wanted to unite the Cossacks with the Polish army and declare himself king of Poland'.[22]

This now seems the most unlikely of his plans but actually it was feasible. The Orthodox provinces of Podolia and eastern Poland, led by magnates like Felix Potocki and his old-fashioned vision of Polish freedom, were a long way from the sophisticated, Catholic Patriots who dominated the Four-Year Sejm in Warsaw with their new-fangled French concept of liberty (and who hated Potemkin). The mistake is to see this Cossack eruption in isolation: both Catherine and Potemkin clearly saw it as a way to mobilize the Orthodox population to break the power of the Revolution in Warsaw while possibly getting Serenissimus his own realm within a federated Poland, dominated by Russia.

The fourth possibility was the second partition of Poland: Potemkin was never shy about discussing a new partition and often dangled it in front of Prussian envoys; despite the views of nationalistic Polish historians, however, it was his last option. He might have made Poland cede Thorn and Danzig in April to avoid war on two more fronts in April, but that moment had passed. This proudly reborn scion of the *szlachta* understood that partition destroyed his ancient homeland – '*our* country' – and it also scuppered his personal base outside Russia. Strategically, it benefited Prussia more than any other state, bringing the Hohenzollerns nearer to Russia. He favoured the Petrine policy of keeping an independent Poland as a crippled and eccentric buffer-zone. Far from wanting partition, most of Potemkin's plans, such as the Moldavian option, involved enlarging Poland, not diminishing her. If he had lived longer, he might have succeeded and helped prevent partition. If Catherine had predeceased him, it is likely he would have moved to become a Polish magnate.

Potemkin stayed in Petersburg to hammer out a Polish policy, while the stories of his sinister plans circulated in febrile revolutionary Warsaw. The Polish envoy Deboli stepped up the tension by sending Stanislas-Augustus every rumour of Potemkin's royal ambitions. As his enemies united at Court to depose him at last, the scene was set for the bitterest crisis of his long friendship with Catherine.

*

'We were running things all right without you, weren't we?', Catherine replied to Potemkin, according to the hostile Deboli. The words ring true, though the tone is that of a wife wryly scolding her husband, not divorcing him.[23] William Fawkener, Pitt's special envoy, had arrived on 14 May, but the protracted negotiations to settle the Ochakov Crisis only really started in early June, when Catherine and Potemkin held long conversations with him. In his unpublished despatches, Fawkener observed their different styles but united message: during one audience with the Englishman, Catherine was just praising Potemkin's surprisingly good mood when she was interrupted by one of her greyhounds barking outside at a child. She reassured the little boy and, turning pointedly to Fawkener, added: 'Dogs that bark don't always bite.'[24]

Potemkin, on the other hand, invited the cowed British bulldog to dinner, where the Englishman was utterly overwhelmed by the Prince's ebullient and entertaining soliloquy – 'strange and full of inconsistency'. Serenissimus 'told me he was Russian and loved his country but he loved England too; that I was an islander and consequently selfish and loved my island only'. He made a Potemkinian offer: why did not Britain have Crete (Candia) in the Mediterranean as its prize from the Ottoman bonanza? This *pied-à-terre* would give Britain control of Egyptian–Levantine trade. And then he went into raptures about his southern lands, the soil, the people, the fleet – 'great projects' whose success depended 'solely on him'. At the end of this performance, the bewildered Fawkener admitted to London that he had not had an opportunity of getting a single word in edgeways, but it left Pitt in no doubt about the seriousness of Russia's commitment to the Black Sea and its refusal to compromise over Ochakov.[25] By early July, England and Prussia realized they would simply have to buckle to Catherine's demands.

Fawkener was further humiliated by the arrival in Petersburg of Robert Adair, sent mischievously (and possibly treasonably) by Charles James Fox as the opposition's unofficial envoy. Simon Vorontsov ensured Adair, aged twenty-eight, a good reception by telling Potemkin that even Georgiana, Duchess of Devonshire, the queen of the *ton*, 'honours him with her friendship'.[26] Adair received a 'great welcome' from Empress and Prince. Before he left, Potemkin gave him a present in Catherine's name – a ring with her portrait.[27]

The Prince, at the height of his dignity, now resembled a noble bear baited by a pack of dogs. Zubov played on Catherine's almost subliminal unease about Potemkin's domineering behaviour by implying that he was becoming a possible threat to her. 'Some secret suspicion hid in the

Empress's heart against this Field-Marshal,'[28] recalled Gavrili Romanovich Derzhavin, the neo-Classical poet and civil servant. Serenissimus muttered that she was surrounded by his enemies. When
Catherine was at Tsarskoe Selo for the summer, Potemkin paid fewer
visits than usual and did not stay long. As an agreement with the Anglo-
Prussians got closer and the Polish Question more urgent, ambassadors
noticed that Catherine seemed to treat him coolly. As so often before,
this coolness gave hope to Potemkin's enemies.

Zubov was not just undermining the Prince with Catherine: first he
managed to turn Suvorov[29] against his former patron by offering favours
that Potemkin had already recommended. So Suvorov fell out with
Potemkin not because of the latter's jealousy but due to the former's
misguided intriguing. Then Zubov told Derzhavin 'in the Empress's
name' not to go to Potemkin for favours: Zubov would provide whatever
he wanted.

Derzhavin had made his name with an 'Ode to Princess Felitsa', which
teasingly described the Procurator-General Viazemsky as 'choleric' and
Potemkin as 'indolent', yet the Prince protected him against Viazemsky
and other enemies over the years.[30] Derzhavin repaid Potemkin's decency
with petty betrayal – and poignant poetry. (His masterpiece, *The Waterfall*, which inspired Pushkin, was a posthumous tribute to Potemkin.)[31]
Zubov offered Derzhavin the post of secretary to the Empress. The poet
accepted the job and moderated praise of Potemkin in his poems.

When he delivered one of these. Potemkin stormed out of his
bedroom, ordered his carriage and rode off 'God knows where' into a
tempest of thunder and lightning outside. Derzhavin called meekly a
few days later and Potemkin, who would have known exactly how Zubov
had turned his protégé, received the poet coolly but without rancour.[32]

The Prince always behaved manically at times of political tension.
He chewed his nails and pursued love affairs with priapic enthusiasm.
Derzhavin and foreigners like Deboli claimed he had gone mad – hinting
that he suffered from the insanity of tertiary syphilis, for which there is
no evidence. One night, Deboli claimed, Potemkin turned up drunk at
a Countess Pushkina's house and caressed her hair. She threatened to
throw him out and he drawled that he had not given up the idea of being
king of Poland.[33] This is an unlikely story. Besides even his enemies
admitted that his seductions had never been more successful. 'Women
crave the attentions of Prince Potemkin', observed his critic, Count
Fyodor Rostopchin, 'like men crave medals.'[34] Serenissimus gave a three-
day fête in one of his houses near Tsarskoe Selo while 'the town talk is
engrossed', Fawkener reported breathlessly to London, 'by his quarrel

with one woman, his apparent inclination for another, [and] his real attachment to a third'.[35]

The trap seemed to be closing on Potemkin. Most histories claim that, when the Prince finally left St Petersburg in late July, he had been ruined by Zubov, rejected by Catherine and defeated by his enemies, and was dying from a broken heart. This could hardly be further from the truth.

In July when the Count was at Peterhof, Zubov thought he had planted enough suspicion in Catherine's mind for his creeping coup to achieve its goal.[36] But who was to replace Potemkin? There was no one else of his military or political stature – with one exception. On 24 June, Count Alexei Orlov-Chesmensky mysteriously arrived. His visits to the capital since 1774 always coincided with attempts to overthrow Potemkin: he liked to boast that, when he came in the door, Potemkin left by the window.[37] But when Orlov-Chesmensky called at Tsarskoe Selo, Catherine let Potemkin know in a note – hardly the behaviour of a empress about to overthrow him.[38] During June and July, Potemkin, in town, wrote to Catherine, in Tsarskoe Selo, about his agonizing hangnail. She was concerned enough to write back, signing her notes 'Adieu Papa'. She enclosed the usual syco-phantic letter from Zubov. Potemkin also sent her a dress as a present.[39] Even Deboli reported that Catherine emphatically ordered Orlov-Chesmensky not to attack 'her great friend'.[40]

Furthermore Potemkin's influence had not disappeared. When Fawk-ener finally suggested that England would agree to Russian terms, Pot-emkin simply accepted the deal himself, without even checking with Catherine. Deboli noted that this irritated Russian ministers – but it hardly suggests that he had lost his power.[41] Then Potemkin delivered a series of victories: on 19 June, he announced that Kutuzov had followed his precise orders to strike at Badadag – and had defeated 20,000 Turks. On 22 June, Gudovich stormed the fortress of Anapa, where – as a bonus – he captured the Chechen hero, Sheikh Mansour who had sought refuge there.* 'This is the key that has opened the door for the big blows,' Potemkin declared to Catherine on 2 July. 'You'll be pleased to see how they will roar in Asia!' That day, maybe to reconcile with Potemkin, the Empress, accompanied by two Zubovs, came into Petersburg from Peterhof to dine with the Prince at the Taurida Palace, where she toasted her consort. So much for the imminent fall of Potemkin.[42]

On 11 July, the Ochakov Crisis ended: the British and Prussians signed

---

* Mansour was despatched to Petersburg, and perished three years later in the dungeons of Schlüsselburg.

the compromise that allowed Catherine to keep Ochakov and the land between the Bug and Dniester – provided that the Turks made peace immediately. If they did not, Russia was free to fight for better terms. That very day, a courier arrived to announce that Repnin, following Potemkin's order to strike across the Danube at enemy concentrations, had won a splendid victory at Manchin on 28 June, destroying the Grand Vizier's army of 80,000 and preventing the two Turkish armies from combining. 'Thank you for the good news, my friend,' Catherine wrote to Potemkin. 'Two holidays in one, my friend, and other wonderful events besides. I'll come to the city to celebrate tomorrow.' The 'Te Deums' were sung before the Empress at the Kazan Cathedral. Catherine threw dinners and balls, attended by the Prince, for Fawkener.[43]

Warsaw and Petersburg now awaited Potemkin's reaction to the May the Third Constitution. The Prince, like a giant if rusty howitzer, was turning slowly towards Poland, but what were his plans? Intrigues and plans swirled around him. Deboli was convinced that Potemkin planned to be king of Poland by creating a 'civil war', meaning either the Confederation or the Cossack invasion.[44] Branicki in Warsaw swaggered from planning his Confederation to patriotic suggestions to increase the size of Poland. Alexandra Branicka wanted Potemkin to be Stanislas-Augustus' heir.[45] Warsaw had been awash for years with pamphlets warning that Potemkin would make Alexandra's children heirs to the throne.[46] There were comical interludes amid the menace. The Prince could not resist teasing the Polish envoy, Deboli, at a party, saying that the Poles liked the Sublime Porte so much they even wore Turkish pantaloons. Deboli was offended by this trouser insult, 'so I responded that we did not need other people's pantaloons because we had our own'.[47]

Potemkin was torn. His duty was to gallop south and negotiate peace with the Turks, but his instinct was to stay in Petersburg, where he remained exposed to Zubov, until he and Catherine had thrashed out what to do about Poland. This once again raised the tension between these two hypersensitive connoisseurs of power, who now became unhappy with each other, ruled by 'little mutual jealousies'.[48] Catherine wanted him to focus on the peace.

When the row blew up, it was about women as well: was she still jealous of Potemkin even though she loved her Blackie or was she simply weary of his parade of debauchery? Potemkin suggested that the feckless Prince Mikhail Golitsyn be appointed one of the new army inspectors, created to wipe out abuses in the military. 'He won't bring credit upon you in the Army,' replied Catherine, but she was most irritated about

Golitsyn's wife. Everyone in Petersburg now knew that Potemkin, bored of the Beautiful Greek, was infatuated by Princess Praskovia Andreevna Golitsyna (*née* Shuvalova), the literary but 'restless' girl who became the Prince's 'last passion'.[49] Catherine told him: 'Let me say that his wife's face, however nice it may be, is not worth the cost of burdening yourself with such a man ... his wife may be charming but there's absolutely nothing to gain by courting her.' Indeed Praskovia's family were protecting her virtue, so Potemkin might well end up with the husband without even getting the wife. Catherine pulled no punches. Both Golitsyns were deceiving him. 'My friend, I am used to telling you the truth. You should also tell it to me.' She begged him to go south and 'conclude peace and after that you'll come back here and amuse yourself as much as you wish ... As for this letter, do tear it to pieces after reading it.'[50] But the Prince kept the most biting letter Catherine ever wrote to him.*

Her paroxysm of anger was, as so often, the letting-off of steam at the end of their argument. She had just signed her second secret rescript to Potemkin of 18 July that settled their debate and meant he could immediately leave for the south. Russian, Polish and Western historians have argued about its meaning for 200 years. Most of the confusion is caused by the problem of reconciling the extraordinary powers it granted Potemkin with the conviction that he was falling from power. The legend claims that the Prince was a broken man, haemorrhaging power, who 'could not bear the thought of disgrace' when 'he learned that Platon Zubov seemed to have absolute power over the Empress's mind'. This is what foreigners were told when they visited Petersburg in the Zubov ascendancy after Potemkin's death.[51] Since it has been accepted that Catherine and Zubov were about to remove him, how could she be giving him vast powers to make peace or war with Turks and Poles? Therefore, they argued, Catherine must have signed a sham just to get rid of him. This was based on hindsight, not on reality.[52]

Not one contemporary in 1791 believed he was about to be dismissed. Though all of them knew that there had been rows, even the hostile foreigners Deboli and British envoy Whitworth reported that Serenissimus was increasing his power, not losing it: 'such is the confidence reposed in him', Whitworth told Grenville, 'he is left in full liberty' to make war or peace with the Turks.[53] As for Zubov's intrigues, 'there is no probability of their succeeding so unaccountable is the predilection of the Empress for him'.[54] Long afterwards, Zubov himself admitted he

---

* It is possible but unlikely that some of Potemkin's letters to 'Praskovia' quoted earlier were addressed to Praskovia Golitsyna, not Praskovia Potemkina.

had 'won a semi-victory', by surviving Potemkin's attempts to dislodge
him, but 'I could not remove him from my path; and it was essential to
remove him because the Empress always met his wishes halfway and
simply feared him as though he were an exacting husband. She loved
only me but she often pointed to Potemkin as an example for me to
follow.' Zubov then revealed his true interest in the Empress's love: 'It is
his fault I am not twice as rich as I am.'[55]

Once one realizes that he was not about to be dismissed at all, it is clear
the rescript was a triumph for Potemkin that more than compensated for
his failure to dislodge Zubov. Once peace with the Porte was signed,
Potemkin was granted massive powers to make war in Poland, to pursue
his plans and even to decide the form of the Polish constitution. The
Prince could negotiate with Potocki on the details, though it was vital
that the Poles be seen to invite the Russians, not vice versa. But 'our own
interests demand that it be carried out as soon as possible so that the
evil ... will not take root.'[56] The rescript implies that Potemkin had
persuaded the Empress that his plans could achieve a submissive neigh-
bour without partition. But Catherine made clear that, if the Prince's
schemes failed, partition was the only alternative.

On his last night in Petersburg, Serenissimus dined at his niece Tatiana's
along with Countess Golovina, who thought him a most disreputable
man. But this time he moved her. He told her again and again that he
would never forget her. He was sure he was going to die soon.[57]

At 4 a.m. on 24 July 1791, Potemkin set off from Tsarskoe Selo. As the
Prince was galloping south at breakneck speed, the Empress sent a note
after him filled with the loving warmth of their old friendship: 'Goodbye
my friend, I kiss you.'[58] They never met again.

33

THE LAST RIDE

His niece wanted to know...
'What news do you bring?'
'I bring you great sorrow
Put on black
Your uncle has died
Lying on a coat in the midst of the steppes.'
Soldiers' marching song, 'The Death of Potemkin'

The ringing of bells, the firing of cannons and the cloud of dust raised by his carriages marked Potemkin's arrival in Mogilev on his way south. Civil servants and nobles from distant corners of the province, and the ladies in their best clothes, waited at the Governor's house.

When his carriage pulled up, the crowd rushed to the bottom of the steps: the Prince of Taurida emerged in a flowing summer dressing gown, covered in dust, and strode through the crowd without glancing at anyone. At dinner that night, Serenissimus invited a noble Polish Patriot, Michel Oginski, to join his entourage and cheerfully treated him to a virtuoso performance, discussing Holland, 'which he knew as if he'd lived his whole life there; England, of which the Government, customs and morals were perfectly known to him', and then music and painting, 'adding that the English knew nothing of either'. When they talked about the art of war, the Prince declared the key to victory was breaking the rules, but studying strategy was not enough: 'You've got to be born with it." This was hardly the reception of a fallen politician and scarcely the behaviour of a broken one.

As Potemkin approached Moldavia, Prince Repnin was already nego-tiating with the Grand Vizier in Galatz. Potemkin cheerfully told Cath-erine that preliminaries had been agreed on 24 July, but on the 31st, when he was only one day away, Repnin signed a truce. Potemkin was said to be furious with jealousy that Repnin had stolen his thunder. But Repnin's reports show that Potemkin was perfectly happy for him to negotiate the preliminaries, though not necessarily sign them. Pot-emkin's rage was political and personal – but hardly based on jealousy. Repnin, whom Catherine called 'worse than an old woman', was the late Panin's nephew, a Freemason of the Martinist sect and part of Paul's

Prussophile Court, yet he had become Potemkin's submissive workhorse. 'The Bible unites them,' Ligne explained – the Martinism of one and the superstition of the other 'fit together marvellously'.[2] No more. Repnin's trick was surely encouraged by letters from the capital, claiming that Zubov would protect him from Potemkin's fury. 'You little Martinist,' Potemkin shouted in one version. 'How dare you!'[3]

Repnin had signed the wrong deal at the wrong time: ignorant of the latest agreement with Fawkener, he had agreed an eight-month armistice, which allowed the Turks an ample breather to rebuild their forces, and a Turkish demand that Russia should not fortify ceded territory. Nor did Repnin realize Potemkin was waiting for news of Ushakov and the fleet: if they succeeded, the terms could be raised. It just happened that Ushakov had defeated the Ottoman Fleet on the very day Repnin had signed the terms; Constantinople was in panic. Catherine too was over the moon when Potemkin informed her about the peace, but both she and Bezborodko immediately denounced Repnin's clumsy mistakes. When Catherine learned of Ushakov's triumph, she was angry.[4] Potemkin could have used Ushakov's victory to force the Turks to fight again and therefore free Russia from the Fawkener deal.[5] This was still possible, but Repnin's concessions made it harder.

Serenissimus rushed down to Nikolaev to inspect his new battleships and Palace and almost flew the 500 versts back to Jassy in thirty hours. He then fell ill, as he often did after months of nervous tension, debilitating debauchery, overwork and exhausting travel. There was plague in Constantinople and an epidemic of fevers across the south. 'I've never seen anything like it,' he told Catherine, who was fretting over his health like old times.[6] Jassy was riddled with 'putrid marsh miasma'.[7] Everyone was falling ill.

Granz Vizier Yusuf-Pasha collected yet another Ottoman army of 150,000 over the Danube. His envoy began the negotiations by testing Potemkin's resolve, asking if there was any chance of keeping the Dniester. The Prince broke off talks. The Vizier apologized and offered to execute his own envoy. Potemkin demanded independence for Moldavia, Russian approval for the appointment of the Hospodars of Wallachia, and the cession of Anapa.[8] He was raising the stakes, daring the Turks to fight again and free him from Fawkener's deal. Then came an ominous omen.

On 13 August 1791, one of his officers, Prince Karl Alexander of Württemberg, Grand Duke Paul's brother-in-law, died of the fever. Potemkin, who had become friendly with Paul's wife, laid on an elaborate royal funeral for her brother. The Prince, already haunted by premonitions of death, was fighting his own sickness. He followed the cortège for miles on foot in the stifling heat and took two glasses of iced water at the burial site. As the hearse passed him in the midst of the funeral, the delirious Potemkin thought it was his carriage and tried to climb into it. For a superstitious man, this was the tolling of the bell. 'God is my witness, I am tormented.' He collapsed and was borne out of Galatz, ordering Repnin to evacuate the army from the unhealthy town.[9]

Potemkin rested in nearby Gusha, where Popov finally persuaded him to take his medicine, probably cinchona, the South American bark, an early form of quinine. He recovered enough to appoint Samoilov, Ribas and Lazhkarev as Russian plenipotentiaries – but Catherine sensed that she could lose her indispensable consort: 'I pray to God that He turns away this misfortune from you and saves me from such a blow,' she wrote to him. She wept for several days. On 29 August, she even prayed for Potemkin's life at the night service at the Nevsky Monastery, to which she donated gold and diamonds. Alexandra Branicka was summoned to attend her uncle. But ten days later: 'I am better,' Potemkin told Catherine, 'I did not hope ever to see you again, dear Matushka.'[10] He headed back to Jassy – but he could not shake off the fever.

'I don't understand how you can move about from one place to another, in such a state of weakness,' Catherine wrote, adding that Zubov was 'very worried and for one day he didn't know how to ease my sorrow.' Even a sick Potemkin must have rolled his eye at that, but until his last days he always sent his regards to the 'tooth' he had failed to extract. For four days, he suffered more fevers and headaches, which improved on 10 September. 'I am in God's power,' Potemkin told the Empress, 'but your business will not suffer until the last minute.'[11]

This was true: he supervised the peace talks, sent the Vizier presents,[12] positioned the army in case the war broke out again and reported that the fleet had returned to Sebastopol. Nor did he cease Polish intrigues. He secretly summoned his Polish allies, General of the Polish Artillery Felix Potocki and Field-Hetman of the Polish crown Seweryn Rzewuski: 'I have the honour to propose a personal interview,' at which he would make known the Empress's 'sincere intentions' and 'specific dispositions'.[13] They set off at once. Throughout the summer, he never neglected his colonization, his shipbuilding or his own entertainment.[14] He wanted harmonious music and vibrant company, writing on 27 August to the French politician and historian Sénac de Meilhan, whose thoughts on the French Revolution and Ancient Greece 'are such amiable things that they merit a discussion in person. Come and see me in Moldavia.'

Musically, Potemkin convalesced by writing hymns: 'And now my soul, fearing and hoping in the abyss of its wickedness, seeks help but cannot find it,' went his 'Canon to the Saviour': 'Do give it your hand, Purest Virgin ...'.[15] But he also was about to hire a new and more accomplished composer. 'I want to send you the first pianist and one of the best composers in Germany,' suggested Andrei Razumovsky, Russian envoy in Vienna, to the Prince. He had already offered the job to the composer, who agreed to come: 'He's not happy with his position here and would be eager to undertake this journey. He's in Bohemia now but is expected back. If Your Highness wishes, I shall hire him for a short time, just to listen to him and keep him for a while.'[16] Potemkin's answer is lost. The composer's name was Mozart.*

Potemkin's condition worsened. All the labyrinthine complexities of the Prince's interests were now reduced to the one relationship that had been constant in his life for twenty years. Catherine and Serenissimus wrote simple love letters to each other again as if neither wished to miss an opportunity to express their deep affection. Fever-ridden Jassy was a 'veritable hospital'. Most patients, including Repnin and Faleev, recovered slowly after four days of shivering delirium[17] but Potemkin, attended by Sashenka Branicka and Sophie de Witte, did not.

Catherine wished to follow his illness and supervise his recovery as if he were in her apartments in the Winter Palace, but the couriers took between seven and twelve days, so her caring, frantic letters were always behind events: when she thought the Prince was better, he was really worse. If the initial letter said he was improving, the second would say he was failing fast. On 16 September, the first letter she received 'made me happy because I saw you were better but the second one amplified my anxiety again because I saw you've permanent fever and headaches for four days. I ask God to give you strength ... Goodbye my friend, Christ bless you.'[18]

Catherine could not hear enough about him: she ordered Popov to send daily reports and asked Branicka, 'Please, Countess, write to me how he is and do your best that he takes as much care as possible against a relapse which is the worst of all in someone already weakened. And I know how careless he is about his health.' Branicka and Popov assumed control of the sickroom while the three doctors, the Frenchman, Massot, and two Russians, could do little.[19] So we follow the agonizing decline through the letters of the two partners – Catherine ever more concerned

---

* Mozart died soon afterwards on 24 November/5 December 1791.

by the day and Potemkin ever weaker, until Popov's reports take over.

When Catherine's letters arrived, Potemkin sobbed as he read them. He thought he was improving even though the 'shooting in the ear torments me'. Even as he sank, he worried about the 8,000 ill soldiers. 'Thank God they don't die,' said Potemkin. The Turkish pleni-potentiaries would arrive in four days: 'I expect lots of trickery but I'll be on my guard.' Potemkin was moved out of Jassy to a country house.[20]

The Prince stopped feasting and ate moderately: starving a fever worked and 'His Highness is better every hour.' Potemkin took the opportunity to arrange the route the Russian army should take in with-drawing from Moldavia, since the passage through Poland was still closed. The negotiations progressed. The world watched carefully: the Austrians had now signed their peace with the Porte at Sistova. The gazettes in Vienna followed the Prince's illness, informed almost daily by couriers. They heard he was better and worse and better. If war came, Potemkin was to command himself, but meanwhile he was demanding some influence over Wallachia and Moldavia. The peace talks would be 'stormy'. The Prince was expected to visit Vienna in the autumn as soon as the peace was signed.

The Prince felt 'tired as a dog' but reassured the Empress via Bezbor-odko: 'I don't spare myself.'[21] Three days later, the fever returned with redoubled strength. The Prince shivered and weakened. Branicka spent day and night beside him.* He refused to take his quinine. 'We persuade His Highness to take it in the Highest name of Your Imperial Majesty in spite of his strong aversion to it,' reported Popov. Serenissimus begged Bezborodko to find him a 'Chinese robe . . . I need it desperately.' Cath-erine rushed to send it down to him, along with a fur coat. The Prince was still dictating notes to Catherine about sickness in the army on the very day that he wrote pathetically: 'I am right out of energy and I don't know when the end will come.'[22]

The Prince was suffering 'incessantly and severely'. By the 25th, the Prince's groaning and weeping were distressing the entourage. Once he realized the fever had taken hold, the Prince seemed to have decided to enjoy his decline. Legend claimed that he 'destroyed himself', and cer-tainly his eating did not help. This feverish 'Sultan' devoured a 'ham, a salted goose and three or four chickens', lubricated with *kvass*, 'all sorts of wines' and spirits. Sterlet and smoked goose were ordered from

---

* The Beautiful Greek was presumably no longer required – she disappeared as his illness worsened. Branicka probably ordered her to entertain the Polish magnates arriv-ing to see the Prince.

Astrakhan and Hamburg. 'He purposely looked for the means to avoid recovering.' When he was soaked with sweat, he poured 'ten bottles of eau-de-Cologne over his head'. He was to die as eccentrically as he had lived.[23] He was too ill to care any more.

Potemkin talked 'hopelessly about life', Popov wrote sorrowfully to Catherine, 'and said goodbye to all, without listening to our reassurances.' The Prince was attended by Bishop Ambrosius and Metropolitan Iona, a Georgian who begged him to eat sensibly and take his medicine. 'I'll scarcely recover,' replied Potemkin. 'But God will decide.' Then he turned to Ambrosius to discuss the meaning of his life and showed that, for all his Russian superstitions, he was also a creature of the Enlightenment: 'You, my confessor, you know that I have never wished evil to anybody. To make all men happy was the one thing I wished for.'* When they heard Potemkin's noble confession, the entire chamber burst into sobs. The priests came out and Dr Massot told them the situation was hopeless. 'Deep despair seized us,' wrote the priest, 'but there was nothing we could do.'[24]

The Prince rallied the next day, 27 September. Nothing made him feel better than a line from the Empress. Her letters arrived with the shaggy fur coat and dressing gown, but they made him think about his past with her and his future. 'Abundant tears always flow from his eyes at every mention of Your Majesty's name.' He managed to write her this note: 'Dear Matushka, life is even harder for me when I don't see you.'[25]

On 30 September, he turned fifty-two. Everyone tried to comfort him but, whenever he remembered Catherine, he 'wept bitterly' because he would never see her again. That day, thousands of versts to the north, the Empress, reading all Popov's reports, wrote to her 'dear friend': 'I am endlessly worried about your illness. For Christ's sake,' she implored, he must take his medicines. 'And after taking it, I beg you to keep yourself from meals and drinks that ruin the medicine's effect.' She was reacting to Popov's reports from ten days before, but, as her letter was leaving Petersburg, Potemkin woke up finding it difficult to breathe, probably a symptom of pneumonia. The fever returned again and he fainted. On 2 October, he woke up feeling better. They tried to persuade him to take the quinine but he refused. And then, desperate to see the steppes, this eternal bedouin yearned to travel again and feel the wind off the Black Sea. 'His Highness wishes that we take him away from here,' Popov told

* Jeremy Bentham, whose utilitarianism measured the success of a ruler by the happiness he gave to his subjects, would have appreciated this: one wonders if Samuel had discussed the idea with the Prince on one of their long carriage rides across the south.

Catherine, 'but I don't know how we can move him. He's so exhausted.'[26]

The entourage discussed what to do, while the Prince wrote his last letter to the Empress in his own hand – a simple, courtly expression of devotion to the woman he loved:

> Matushka, Most Merciful Lady! In my present condition, so tired by illness, I pray to the Most High to keep your precious health and I throw myself down at your holy feet.
>
> Your Imperial Majesty's most faithful and most grateful subject,
> Prince Potemkin of Taurida.
> Oh Matushka, how ill I am!

Then he collapsed, did not recognize anyone and subsided into coma. The doctors struggled to find a pulse for nine hours. His hands and feet were cold as ice.[27]

In Petersburg, Catherine was just reading the letters of the 25th and 27th – 'life is even harder when I don't see you'. She wept. She even examined the handwriting, trying to find some hope. 'I confess I am desperately worried by them but I see that your last three lines are written a little better,' she wrote in her last letter to her friend. 'And your doctors assure me you are better. I pray to God ...'. She also wrote to Branicka: 'Please stay with him ... Goodbye, dear soul. God bless you.'[28]

In the afternoon, Potemkin awoke and commanded that they set out. He believed that if he could reach Nikolaev he would recover. He could not sleep that night, but he was calm. The next morning, he kept asking, 'What time is it? Is everything ready?' It was too foggy, but he insisted. They sat him in an armchair and carried him to the six-seater carriage, where they tried to make him comfortable. He dictated his last letter to tell Catherine he was exhausted. Popov brought it to show him and, at the bottom, he managed to scrawl, 'The only escape is to leave.' But he was not strong enough to sign it.

At 8 a.m. accompanied by doctors, Cossacks and niece, his carriage moved off across the open steppe towards the Bessarabian hills.

EPILOGUE

LIFE AFTER DEATH

They trample heroes? – No! – Their deeds
Shine through the darkness of the ages.
Their graves, like hills in springtime, bloom.
Potemkin's work will be inscribed.
Gavrili Derzhavin, *The Waterfall*

The next day, the body was solemnly returned to Jassy for post-mortem and embalming. The dissection was carried out in his apartments in the Ghika Palace.* Slicing open the soft and majestic belly, Dr Massot and his assistants examined the organs and then extracted them one by one, feeding out the entrails like a hose-pipe.[1] They found the innards were very 'wet', awash with bilious fluid. The liver was swollen. The symptoms suggested a 'bilious attack'. There were the inevitable rumours of poisoning, but there was not the slightest evidence. It is most likely that Potemkin was weakened by his fever, whether typhus or malaria, haemorrhoids, drinking and general exhaustion, but these did not necessarily kill him. His earaches, phlegm and difficulties in breathing mean he probably died of bronchial pneumonia. In any case, the stench of the bile was unbearable. Nothing, not even the embalming process, could cleanse it.[2]

The doctors embalmed the body: Massot sawed a triangular hole in the back of the skull and drained the brains out of it. He then filled the cranium with aromatic grasses and potions to dry and preserve the famous head. The viscera were placed in a box, the heart in a golden urn. The corpse was sewn up again like a sack and then dressed in its finest uniform.

All around it, chaos reigned. Potemkin's generals argued about who was to command the army. Everything – a body, a fortune, the imperial love letters, the war and peace of an empire – awaited the reaction of the Empress.[3] When the news reached St Petersburg just seven days later, the Empress fainted, wept, was bled, suffered from insomnia and went into seclusion. Her secretary recorded her days of

---

* It is now appropriately Iaşi University's School of Medicine, though others say the autopsy was conducted in the Cantacuzino Palace.

'tears and desperation', but she calmed herself by writing a panegyric
to Potemkin's

> excellent heart ... rare understanding and unusual breadth of mind;
> his views were always broadminded and generous; he was extremely
> humane, full of knowledge, exceptionally kind and always full of new
> ideas; nobody had such a gift for finding the right word and making
> witty remarks. His military qualities during this war must have struck
> everyone as he never failed on land or sea. Nobody on earth was less
> led by others ... In a word, he was a statesman in both counsel and
> execution.

But it was their personal relationship she most cherished: 'He was passionately and zealously attached to me, scolding me when he thought I
could have done better ... his most precious quality was courage of heart
and soul which distinguished him from the rest of humanity and which
meant we understood each other perfectly and left the less enlightened
to babble at their leisure ...'. It is a fine and just tribute.

She awoke weeping again the next day. 'How can I replace Potemkin?',
she asked. 'Who would have thought Chernyshev and other men would
outlive him? Yes I am old. He was a real nobleman, an intelligent man,
he did not betray me, he could not be bought.' There were 'tears' and
'tears' again.[4] Catherine mourned like a member of Potemkin's family.
They wrote to one another: consolation by graphomania. 'Our grief is
universal,' she told Popov, 'but I'm so raw I can't even talk about it.'[5] The
nieces, travelling to Jassy for the funeral, felt the same. 'My father is dead
and I am rolling tears of grief,' wrote his 'kitten' Katinka Skavronskaya
to Catherine. 'I became accustomed to rely on him for my happiness ...'.
She had just received a loving letter from him when the news of her
'orphanage' arrived.[6] Varvara Golitsyna, whom Potemkin had loved so
passionately right after Catherine, remembered, 'he was so tender, so
gracious, so kind to us'.[7]

Business had to go on. Indeed Catherine, with the selfishness of monarchs, grumbled about the inconvenience as well as her grief: 'Prince
Potemkin has played me a cruel turn by dying! It is me on whom all the
burden now falls.'[8] The Council met the day the news arrived, and
Bezborodko was despatched to Jassy to finish the peace talks. In Constantinople, the Grand Vizier encouraged Selim III to start the war
again, while the foreign ambassadors rightly told him peace was more
likely now that the future King of Dacia was dead.[9]

542 EPILOGUE

Catherine ordered 'Saint' Mikhail Potemkin to fetch her letters from Jassy and sort out the Prince's labyrinthine finances. But the imperial letters were the holiest relics of Potemkin's legacy. Mikhail Potemkin and Vasily Popov argued over them.[10] The latter insisted on handing them over himself. So Mikhail[11] left without them.*

The murky question of the fortune, however, took twenty years and three emperors to settle and was never unravelled. Since 1783, it seems Potemkin had received a total of 55 million roubles – including 51,352,096 roubles and 94 kopecks from the state to pay his armies, build his fleets and construct his cities, and almost 4 million of his own money. His spending of millions could not be accounted for.† Emperor Paul restarted the investigation, but his successor Alexander, who had danced at Potemkin's ball, gave up the impossible task and the subject was finally closed.[12]

Petersburg talked of nothing but his mythical personal fortune – millions or just debts? 'Although his legacy was considerable, especially the diamonds,' Count Stedingk told Gustavus III, 'one guesses that when all the debts are paid, the seven heirs will not have much left.'[13] Catherine was also interested: she could have left his debts for his heirs, which would have used up the entire fortune, said to be worth seven million roubles, but she understood that Potemkin had used the Treasury as his own bank, while spending his own money for the state – it was impossible to differentiate. 'Nobody knows exactly what the deceased left,' wrote the unprejudiced Bezborodko, arriving in Jassy. 'He owes a lot to the Treasury but the Treasury owes a lot to him.' Furthermore, the Court banker Baron Sutherland died at almost the same time as his patron, exposing a financial scandal which was potentially dangerous to Russia's fragile credit. Potemkin owed Sutherland 762,785 roubles[14] – and a total in Petersburg alone of 2.1 million roubles.[15]

Catherine settled the money with her characteristic generosity, buying the Taurida Palace from his heirs for 935,288 roubles plus his art collection, his glass factory, a million roubles of diamonds and some estates. She paid off the debts herself and left the bulk of the fortune to be

* Mikhail Potemkin died strangely in his carriage on his way home from Jassy. His brother Count Pavel Potemkin was later accused of murdering and robbing a Persian prince when he was viceroy of the Caucasus: he wrote a poem pleading his innocence, then died of a fever. Some said he committed suicide.
† The almost 4 million of his 'private' income sounds much too low considering Catherine regularly bought his palaces for sums like half a million roubles. The sums of State money were much more than the entire annual revenue of the whole Russian Empire, which usually oscillated between forty and forty-four million roubles – though it was rising fast.

divided among seven greedy and now very wealthy heirs, a selection of Engelhardts and Samoilovs. In Smila alone, they each received 14,000 male souls, without even counting the Russian lands, yet they were still arguing over the swag a decade later.[16] Even two centuries later, in Soviet times, the villagers of Chizhova were digging up the churchyard in the quest for Potemkin's lost treasure.

The Empress ordered that social life in Petersburg should cease. There were no Court receptions, no Little Hermitages. 'The Empress doesn't appear.'[17] Some admired her grief: Masson understood that 'it was not the lover she regretted. It was the friend whose genius was assimilated to her own.'[18] Stedingk thought Catherine's *sensibilité* was greater praise of the Prince than any panegyric.[19] The capital was draped in a 'veneer of mourning', but much of it concealed jubilance.[20]

While the lesser nobility and junior officers, whose wives wore his medallion round their necks, mourned a hero, some of the old noble and military establishment celebrated.[21] Rostopchin, who thought Zubov 'a twit', was nonetheless 'charmed' that everyone so quickly forgot the 'fall of the Colossus of Rhodes'.[22] Grand Duke Paul is supposed to have muttered that the Empire now boasted one less thief – but then Potemkin had kept him from his rightful place for almost twenty years. Zubov, 'without being triumphant', was like a man who could finally breathe 'at the end of a long and hard subordination'.[23]

However, three of the most talented men in the Empire, two of them supposedly his mortal enemies, regretted him. When Field-Marshal Rumiantsev-Zadunaisky, natural son of Peter the Great, heard the news, his entourage expected him to celebrate. Instead, he knelt in front of an icon. 'What's so surprising?', he asked his companions. 'The Prince was my rival, even my enemy, but Russia has lost a great man ... immortal for his deeds.'[24] Bezborodko admitted he was 'indebted' to 'a very rare and exquisite man'.[25] Suvorov was sad, saying Potemkin was 'a great man and a man great, great in mind and height: not like that tall French ambassador in London about whom Lord Chancellor Bacon said that "the garret is badly furnished" ', but he was simultaneously 'the image of all earthly vanity'. Suvorov felt the heroic age was finished: Potemkin had used him as his own King Leonidas of Sparta. He twice went to pray at Potemkin's tomb.[26]

In Jassy, Engelhardt asked the peasant–soldiers if they preferred Rumiantsev or Potemkin. They acclaimed Rumiantsev's 'frightening but energetic' record, but the Prince 'was our father, lightened our service, supplied us with all we needed; we'll never have a commander like him again. God make his memory live forever.'[27] In Petersburg, soldiers wept for him.[28] Even malicious Rostopchin admitted that Potemkin's Grenadiers were crying – though he said it was because they had lost 'the privilege of stealing'.[29] Bezborodko heard the soldiers mourning Potemkin. When he quizzed them about the deprivations of Ochakov, they usually replied, 'But it was necessary at the time . . .' and Potemkin had treated them with humanity.[30] But the best tributes are the marching songs about Potemkin which the soldiers sang in the Napoleonic Wars.

> Here rests not famed by war alone
> A man whose soul was greater still . . .
>
> Gavrili Derzhavin, *The Waterfall*

The Prince's outrageous personality aroused such emotions in his lifetime and afterwards that it obscured any objective analysis of his achievements and indeed has distorted them grotesquely. His enemies accused him of laziness, corruption, debauchery, indecision, extravagance, falsification, military incompetence and disinformation on a vast scale. The sybaritism and extravagance are the only ones that are truly justified. Even his enemies always admitted his intelligence, force of personality, spectacular vision, courage, generosity and great achievements. 'It cannot be denied', wrote Catherine's earliest biographer Castera, 'that he had the mind and courage and energy which, with the gradual unfolding of his talents, fitted him for a prime minister.' Ligne believed that, in making Potemkin, Nature had used 'the stuff she would usually have used to create a hundred men.'[31]

As a conqueror and colonizer, he ranks close to his hero Peter the Great, who founded a city and a fleet on the Baltic as Potemkin created cities and a fleet on the Black Sea. Both died at fifty-two. There the similarities end, for Potemkin was as humane and forgiving as Peter was brutal and vengeful. But the Prince can be understood and therefore appreciated only in the light of his unique, almost equal partnership with Catherine: it was an unparalleled marriage of love and politics. At its simplest, it was a tender love affair and a noble friendship, but that is to ignore its colossal achievements. None of the legendary romances of history quite matches its exuberant political success.

The relationship enabled Potemkin to outstrip any other minister–favourite and to behave like a tsar. He flaunted his imperial status because he had no limits, but this made him all the more resented. He behaved eccentrically because he could. But his problems stem from the unique ambiguity of his situation, for, though he had the power of a co-tsar, *he was not one*. He suffered, as all favourites do, from the belief that the monarch was controlled by an 'evil counsellor' – hence his first biography was called *Prince of Darkness*. If he had been a tsar, he would have been judged for his achievements, not his lifestyle: crowned heads could behave as they wished but ersatz emperors are never forgiven for their indulgences. 'The fame of the Empire was increased by his conquests,' says Ségur, 'yet the admiration they excited was for her and the hatred they raised was for him.'[32]

Serenissimus was a dynamic politician but a cautious soldier. He was slowly competent in direct command, but outstanding as supreme strategist and commander-in-chief on land *and* sea: he was one of the first to co-ordinate amphibious operations on different fronts across a vast theatre. He was blamed for the fact that the Russian army was chaotic and corrupt, faults as true today as they were two centuries ago, but he deserves credit for its achievements too. When Bezborodko[33] reached the army in 1791, for example, he was amazed at the order he found there, despite what he had heard. Nor were his adversaries as weak as they became: the Turks several times defeated the Austrians, who were supposedly much more competent than the Russians. Overall, Potemkin has been underestimated by military history: he should be upgraded from the ranks of incompetent commanders to those of the seriously able, though second to contemporary geniuses like Frederick the Great, Suvorov or Napoleon. As Catherine told Grimm, he delivered only victories. Few generals can boast that. In the tolerance and decency he showed to his men, Potemkin was unique in Russian history, even today in the age of the Chechen War. 'No man up to that time,' wrote Wiegel, 'had put his power to less evil ends.'

Thirty years later, the Comte de Langeron, whose prejudiced accounts of Potemkin did as much damage to his reputation as those of Ligne and Helbig, admitted, 'I judged him with great severity, and my resentment influenced my opinions.' Then he judged him justly:

Of course he had all the faults of courtiers, the vulgarities of parvenus, and the absurdities of favourites but they were all grist to the mill of the extent and force of his genius. He had learnt nothing but divined everything. His mind was as big as his body. He knew how to conceive and execute his wonders, and such a man was necessary to Catherine. Conqueror of the Crimea, subduer of the Tartars, transplanter of the Zaporogians to the Kuban and civilizer [of the Cossacks], founder of Kherson, Nikolaev, Sebastopol, establisher of shipyards in three cities,

creator of a fleet, dominator of the Black Sea ... all these marvellous
policies should assure him of recognition.

Alexander Pushkin, who befriended Langeron in Odessa in 1824, agreed
that Potemkin was 'touched by the hand of history ... We owe the
Black sea to him.'[34] Cities, ships, Cossacks, the Black Sea itself, and his
correspondence with Catherine, remain his best memorials.

Derzhavin was moved to compose his epic *The Waterfall* soon after
Potemkin's death. It catches many sides of the Maecenas and Alcibiades
that the poet knew. He uses the waterfall itself – its magnificence, speed,
natural power – to symbolize Potemkin as well the turbulence of life
and its transitory nature. Potemkin was one of imperial Russia's most
remarkable statesmen in a class only with Peter the Great and Catherine
herself. The Duc de Richelieu, that fine judge of character and himself a
statesman, was the foreigner who best understood Serenissimus. 'The
sum of his great qualities', he wrote, 'surpassed all his faults ... Nearly
all his public actions bear the imprint of nobility and grandeur.'[35]

> The dust of Alcibiades! -
> Do worms dare crawl about his head there?
>   Gavrili Derzhavin, *The Waterfall*

The Empress decided that the Prince's funeral should be held in Jassy.
Potemkin had asked Popov to bury him in his village of Chizhova,
but Catherine believed he belonged in one of his cities,[36] Kherson or
Nikolaev.[37] It was strange that she did not bury him in Petersburg, but
perhaps that rationalist child of the Enlightenment did not ascribe great
importance to graves. She was much more interested in the places and
people they shared when he was alive. Besides, she knew that the further
from the capital the body of Potemkin rested, the less Paul could degrade
it after her death.

On 11 October, Potemkin's body was placed in a hall, probably in the
Ghika Palace, for his lying-in-state: the catafalque was enclosed in a
chamber of black velvet, trimmed with silver tassels and held up by silver
cords. The dais was decorated in rich gold brocade. He lay in an open
coffin upholstered with pink velvet, covered by a canopy of rose and
black velvet, supported by ten pillars and surmounted by ostrich feathers.
Potemkin's orders and batons were laid out on velvet cushions and on
two pyramids of white satin which stood on either side of the coffin. His
sword, hat and scarf lay on its lid. Nineteen huge candles flickered, six
officers stood guard. Soldiers and Moldavians cried about 'their lost

protector' and filed past the coffin. In front of this magnificent *mise-en-scène* was a black board inscribed with Potemkin's titles and victories.*

At 8 a.m. on 13 October, the Ekaterinoslav Grenadiers and Dnieper Musketeers lined the streets through which the procession was to pass. The cannons fired salutes and the bells rang dolefully as the coffin was borne out by generals, along with the canopy carried by Life-Guards. A squadron of Hussars and then Cuirassiers led the way. The horses were led by stablemen in rich liveries tied with black crêpe. Then 120 soldiers in long black mantles bore torches, thirty-six officers held candles. Next there were the exotic Turkish costumes of the boyars of Moldavia and the princes of the Caucasus. After the clergy, two generals carried the trappings of power. The miniature diamond-encrusted portrait of Catherine which he always wore was more telling than all the medals and batons.

The black hearse, bearing the coffin, harnessed to eight black-draped horses, led by postillions in long black cloaks and hats, clattered through the streets followed by the Prince's nieces. His Cossacks brought up the rear.

The procession approached the rounded corner bastions of the Golia Monastery and passed through the fortified thirty-metre-high gate-tower. The coffin was carried into the Church of the Ascension, once visited by Peter the Great. The mixture of Byzantine, Classical and Russian architecture in its white pillars and spires was Potemkin's own. Cannons fired a final salute.[38]

The loss of Potemkin left a gap in Catherine's life that could never be filled: after Christmas, she stayed in her room for three days without emerging. She talked about him often. She ordered the 101-gun salute for the Peace of Jassy and held the celebration dinner – but she tearfully and curtly waved away any toasts. 'Her grief was as deep as it was before.' On 30 January 1792, when Samoilov delivered the text of the treaty, she and Potemkin's nephew wept alone.[39] When she came back from Tsarskoe Selo that summer, she told everyone that she was going to live at Potemkin's house, which she named the Taurida after him, and she stayed there frequently. She loved that palace and often walked alone in its gardens, as if she was looking for him.[40] A year later, she wept copiously on his birthday and the anniversary of his death, crying alone in her

* This disappeared a few years after Potemkin's funeral. Two hundred years later in October 1998, the author, assisted by a Rumanian priest and two professors, began to search the Golia church in Jassy and found the board and its beautifully inscribed memorial under a piano behind a pile of prayer books: it was dusty but undamaged.

room all day. She visited the Taurida Palace with her grandsons and Zubov in attendance. 'Everything there used to be charming,' she told Khrapovitsky, 'but now something's not quite right.' In 1793, she kept returning to the Taurida: sometimes she arranged to stay there secretly after dinner. 'No one', wrote Khrapovitsky,[41] 'could replace Potemkin in her eyes,' but she surrounded herself with Potemkin's circle.

Popov, already one of her secretaries, now became the living embodiment of the Prince's political legacy. Indeed, Popov had only to say that Potemkin would not have approved for Catherine to refuse even to contemplate a proposal. Such was the power of a dead man. When she came to the Taurida Palace, Popov fell to his knees and thanked her for deigning to live in the house of his 'creator'. Samoilov became procurator-general on the death of Prince Viazemsky. Ribas founded Odessa at Hadjibey as ordered by Potemkin, but Richelieu, as governor-general of New Russia, made it into one of the most cosmopolitan ports of the world. In 1815, Richelieu became prime minister of France.

Two years after Potemkin's death, the Prince de Ligne recalled him to Catherine as 'my dear and inimitable, lovable and admirable' friend. Ligne himself never recovered from not being given command of an army and even begged Metternich to let him take part in Napoleon's invasion of Russia in 1812 – an unworthy repayment of Catherine's and Potemkin's generosity. He survived to become the aged ornament of the Congress of Vienna and managed his final epigram before expiring at the age of seventy-nine: 'Le Congrès', he said, 'ne marche pas; mais il danse'.[42] The Comte de Ségur adapted to the French Revolution to become Napoleon's grand master of ceremonies, advised the Emperor not to invade Russia in 1812, and then emerged as a peer under the Restoration. Nassau-Siegen tried to persuade Napoleon to let him attack British India but died in 1806 in Prussia.

Francisco de Miranda became 'El Precursor' to the Liberator of South America, after serving as a general in the French Revolutionary armies. In 1806, he landed on the Venezuelan coast with 200 volunteers, then had to withdraw again. But in 1811 Simon Bolivar persuaded him to return as commander-in-chief of the Venezuelan patriot army. An earthquake and military defeats made the indecisive Dictator negotiate with the Spanish. When he tried to flee, Bolivar arrested him and handed him over to the Spanish. That lover of liberty died in 1816 in a Spanish prison – thirty years after meeting Serenissimus. Sir James Harris was created Earl of Malmesbury, and Talleyrand called him the 'shrewdest minister of his time'. Sir Samuel Bentham became inspector-general of Navy Works and was responsible for building the fleet that won Trafalgar.

Jeremy Bentham actually built a Panopticon prison, backed by George III, but the experiment failed. He blamed this on the King.

John Paul Jones was commissioned by Washington and Jefferson to defeat the Algerian pirates of the Barbary Coast, but he died in Paris on 7/18 July 1792 aged just forty-five and was given a state funeral. He became revered as the founder of the US Navy. His grave was lost until 1905, when General Horace Porter discovered Jones well preserved in a lead coffin. In an example of necro-imperialism, President Theodore Roosevelt sent four cruisers to bring Jones home and on 6 January 1913, thousands of miles and 125 years after parting with Potemkin, he was reburied in a marble sarcophagus, based on Napoleon's at Invalides, at the Naval Academy at Annapolis, where he now rests.[43]

Catherine saw Branicka as Potemkin's emotional heir, granting her Potemkin's apartments in the imperial palaces so they could spend time together, but specifying that Sashenka should be served by different servants because the faces of Potemkin's old retainers would break her heart.[44] Catherine promoted Platon Zubov to many of Potemkin's posts, but he proved himself direly inadequate for any position.[45] Many missed Serenissimus when they contemplated the insolent mediocrity of the Zubovs – 'the rabble of the Empire'.[46]

Catherine, encouraged by Potemkin, had almost certainly planned to disinherit the 'unstable' Grand Duke Paul and pass the Crown directly to her grandson Alexander. Without Potemkin, she probably did not have the will to do it.[47] On 5 November 1796, Catherine II rose at the usual time. She withdrew into her privy closet where she was struck down by a massive stroke. So, like George II of England, she was taken ill at a moment that unites kings and commoners. After her valet and maid had broken open the door, they bore her into her bedchamber where Dr Rogerson bled her. She was too heavy to lift on to the bed, so they laid her on a mattress on the floor. Emissaries galloped out to Gatchina to inform Grand Duke Paul: when they arrived, he thought they had come to arrest him. He set off for Petersburg. Some time in the afternoon, it is said, he and Bezborodko destroyed documents that suggested passing over Catherine's son. On 6 November, Catherine died at 9.45 p.m., still on the mattress on the floor.

Paul I reversed as many of the achievements of his mother's reign as possible. He avenged himself on Potemkin by making the Taurida Palace into the Horse-Guards' barracks and the Winter Garden their stables. Potemkin's library was childishly 'exiled' to Kazan, a unique example of bibliographic vengeance. He ordered the renaming of Gregoripol. He brought back the Prussian paradomania of his father, treating Russia like a barracks, and did his best to destroy the tolerant 'army of Potemkin' that he so hated.[48] His brand of despotic inconsistency united against him the same elements that had overthrown Peter III. So Paul's haunting fear of assassination became self-fulfilling. (Platon Zubov was one of his assassins.) Though Potemkin's Cossacks remained as pillars of the Romanov regime, Paul's sons, Alexander I and Nicholas I, enforced the same Prussianized paradomania that remained the face of the monarchy for the rest of its history: the 'knouto-Germanic Empire' is what the anarchist Bakunin called it.[49]

Sophie de Witte married the richest 'kinglet' of Poland, Felix Potocki, whom she hooked in Jassy after Potemkin's death. Sophie embarked on a passionately incestuous affair with her stepson Yuri Potocki, committing 'all the crimes of Sodom and Gomorrah'. When Langeron visited her, she told him, 'You know what I am and whence I come, *eh bien*, I cannot live with just 60,000 ducats of revenue.' Four years after her old husband died in 1805, she threw out the son and built up a fortune while raising her children. Countess Potocka died 'honoured and admired' in 1822.[50]

Sashenka Branicka, on the other hand, retired to her estates and became so rich she could not count it. 'I don't know exactly,' she said, 'but I should have about twenty-eight million.' She lived majestically and almost royally into a different era. The witness of Potemkin's last breath became the 'bearer of his glory'. She kept her lithe, slender figure and fresh complexion into middle age but always wore those long Catherinian dresses, held in at the waist with a single wide buckle. She created a shrine to Potemkin at her estate and was painted with his bust behind her. Alexander I visited her twice and appointed her grand mistress of the Court. Even twenty years after Catherine's death, Wiegel was amazed to observe the grandest noblewomen kissing her hand as if she were a grand duchess, which she seemed to accept 'without the slightest unease or embarrassment'. Swathes of the Polish and Russian aristocracy were descended from her children by the time she died aged eighty-four in 1838, when Victoria was Queen of England.[51]

Potemkin's 'angel', Countess Skavronskaya, was liberated by the death of her melomaniac husband and married an Italian Knight of Malta, Count Giulio Litta, for love.[52] Tatiana, the youngest niece, Mikhail Potemkin's widow, married the much older Prince Nikolai Yusupov, the descendant of a Tartar khan named Yusuf and said to maintain a whole village of serf–whores. Princess Yusupova was unhappily married but, like her uncle, amassed jewels that included the earrings of Marie-Antoinette, the Polar Star diamond and the diadem of Napoleon's sister,

Caroline Murat, Queen of Naples. Felix Yusupov, who killed Rasputin in 1916, was proud of his connection to Serenissimus.[53]

Two great-nieces complement Potemkin's life. Branicka's daughter Elisabeth, known as Lise, married Prince Michael Vorontsov, the son of Potemkin's enemy Simon, who brought him up in England as a dry, phlegmatic milord. He became viceroy of New Russia and the Caucasus like his wife's great-uncle. Lise was said to have inherited the secret certificate of Potemkin's marriage to Catherine and tossed it into the Black Sea – an appropriate home for it. 'Milord' Vorontsov found it impossible to control his flirtatious, exquisitely mannered Princess. She was already involved in a secret affair with one of her Raevsky cousins, when in 1823 she met Alexander Pushkin, who had been exiled to Odessa. Her Potemkin connection was surely part of the attraction to the poet: he knew Potemkin's nieces and noted down the stories they told. He fell in love with Princess Vorontsova. The poet hinted in his poems that they made love on a Black Sea beach. She was believed to be the inspiration for the women in many of his poems, including Tatiana in *Eugene Onegin*. In his poem 'The Talisman' he wrote, 'There where the waves spray, The feet of solitary reefs ... A loving enchantress, Gave me her talisman.' The gift was a ring engraved in Hebrew.

Vorontsov ended the affair by sending Pushkin away. The poet avenged this by writing doggerel that mocked Vorontsov and (probably) by fathering his daughter Sophie, born to Lise nine months after Pushkin's departure. Thus the blood of Potemkin and Pushkin was fused. Pushkin was wearing her 'talisman' when, in 1837, he was killed in a duel.[54]

Skavronskaya's daughter, also Ekaterina, became a European scandal. Known as the 'Naked Angel' because of her fondness for wearing veil-like, transparent dresses and 'le Chat Blanc' – the 'White Pussycat' – for her sensual avidity, she married the heroic general Prince Peter Bagratian. Like her mother, who was Potemkin's 'angel', her face had a seraphic sweetness, her skin was alabaster, her eyes were a startling blue and her hair was a cascade of golden locks. She became Metternich's mistress in Dresden in 1802 and bore him a daughter, Clementine, who was thus related to both Potemkin and the 'Coachman of Europe'. Goethe saw her at Carlsbad and raved about her as she began another affair with Prince Louis of Prussia. After Bagratian's death at the Battle of Borodino, she flaunted herself and dabbled in European politics at the Congress of Vienna in 1814. She competed ruthlessly with the Duchess of Sagan for the favours of Tsar Alexander I: each occupied different wings of the Palais Palm. The Austrian policemen who spied on her bedroom in Vienna reported on her superb 'practical expertise'. The White Pussycat then moved to Paris, where she was famous for her promiscuity, fine carriage and Potemkin diamonds. In 1830, she married an English general and diplomat Lord Howden. Touchingly, when she visited the old Metternich thirty-five yeas later in his exile in Richmond, his daughter remembered that she could barely stop laughing because the old 'Angel' was still ludicrously wearing the see-through dresses that had once enraptured the princes of Europe. She lived until 1857, but her daughter Clementine, who was brought up by the Metternichs, died young.[55]

Finally, Sophia, Samoilov's daughter, married Count Bobrinsky's son, so that the blood of Catherine, the Orlovs and the Potemkins was also fused.[56]

The 1905 Revolution was heralded in Odessa by the mutiny of sailors of the *Battleship Prince Potemkin of Taurida*. This spawned Eisenstein's film: the very name Potemkin, fostered by tsarist autocracy, thus became the symbol of Bolshevism.* The Richelieu Steps in Odessa were renamed the 'Potemkin Steps,' so the statue of the French Duke today looks down the steps named after the 'extraordinary man' he so admired.

The Taurida Palace was to be 'the birthplace, the citadel and the burial ground of Russian democracy'.† On 6 January 1918, the Constituent Assembly, the first truly democratic parliament in Russian history until 1991, met, watched by Lenin and a horde of drunk Red Guards, for the first and last time in the Colonnade Hall where Potemkin had fallen to his knees before Catherine. Lenin left, the Red Guards threw out the parliamentarians and the Taurida was locked up.[57] Today, the Palace houses the Commonwealth of Independent States, so the residence of the man who brought many of these lands into the Russian Empire is now the home of its disintegration.[58]

And of course the phrase 'Potemkin Village' entered the language.

Not all the body of Potemkin arrived in Kherson on 23 November 1791. When great men were embalmed their viscera were buried separately. The resting place of the heart was especially significant. Earlier that year, for example, the heart of Mirabeau had been carried through the streets of Paris at his state funeral in a leaden box covered in flowers.[59]

Potemkin's viscera were said to be buried in the Church of the Ascen-

---

* Indeed George V was so worried that he banned the film from being shown to the schoolboys of Eton: 'It is not good for the boys to witness mutinies, especially naval mutinies.'

† In 1906 the State Duma, Tsar Nicholas II's reluctant concession to the 1905 Revolution, sat in what had been the Winter Garden. After the February Revolution, it housed for a while both the Provisional Government of Russia and the Petrograd Soviet.

LIFE AFTER DEATH   553

sion at the Golia Monastery in Jassy. There was no apparent sign of it in
the church, but through the centuries of the Kingdom of Rumania,
Communism and now democracy a few intellectuals knew that it rests
in a golden box under the carpet and flagstone before the Hospodar of
Moldavia's red-velvet medieval throne. So the brain that had conceived
the Kingdom of Dacia lay beneath the portrait of a bearded Moldavian
Prince, Basil the Wolf, wearing a gold, white and red kaftan and a bonnet
with three feathers.[60]

Potemkin's family had not forgotten the place of the Prince's death in
the hills of Bessarabia, marked by the lance of Cossack Golavaty.[61] Samoilov had a small, square Classical pillar built there in 1792, with the date
and event engraved on its sides: its design and white stone is so similar
to the fountain built at the Nikolaev palace that it must be by the
same architect, Starov himself. Later, in the early nineteenth century,
Potemkin's heirs erected a pyramid ten metres high in dark stone with
steps rising up to it.*

When the body reached Kherson, it was not buried, simply laid in an
unsealed, specially constructed tomb in a crypt[62] in the middle of St
Catherine's Church. The Empress ordered a noble marble monument
to be designed and erected over the tomb, but by the time she died, five
years later, the marble was still not ready. So the Prince, a parvenu
who was somehow royal, remained interred but somehow unburied.[63]
Visitors and locals, including Suvorov, prayed there.

In 1798, Paul heard about these visits and decided to avenge himself
on the body: it irritated him all over again that Potemkin was still
managing to defy tradition and decency seven years after his death. So
he issued a decree on 18 April to Procurator-General Prince Alexander
Kurakin: the body was unburied and, 'finding this obscene, His Majesty
orders that the body be secretly buried in the crypt in the tomb designed
for this and the crypt should be covered up by earth and flattened as if
it had never been there'. For a man of Potemkin's stature to be buried
without trace was bad enough. The Emperor allegedly ordered Kurakin
orally to smash any memorial to Potemkin and to scatter the bones in

* The site was lost and presumably destroyed: no one had recorded seeing this spot
since the early nineteenth century. Unmarked on maps and unknown even to local
academics, it survived only on a 1913 Austrian map, but it seemed unlikely that the
monuments could exist today. Yet they are still there on a country lane on a Bessarabian
hillside, known only by the local peasants who took the author to 'Potemkin's place',
which has survived Russian and Ottoman rule, the Kingdom of Rumania, annexation
by Stalin in 1940, German occupation and its return to Rumania, re-inclusion in the
Soviet Union and the creation of the independent Republic of Moldova.

the nearby Devil's Gorge. Under cover of darkness, the tomb was filled
in and covered up, but no one knew whether the officers had obeyed
Paul's orders. Had the bones been tossed into the Gorge, buried secretly
in a pauper's grave or taken away by Countess Branicka?[64] For a long
time, no one was sure.[65]

In another midnight grave opening, on 4 July 1818, the Archbishop of
Ekaterinoslav, Iov Potemkin, a cousin of Serenissimus, lifted the church
floor, opened the coffin and discovered that the embalmed cadaver was
still there after all. So it turned out that, in this as in so much else, the
despotic whims of Emperor Paul were fudged by his officers. But they
had obeyed him in making it look as if there was nothing there. Iov
Potemkin was said to have placed some artefact from the grave in his
carriage when he left: was this an act of familial and episcopal grave-
robbing? Or was it the urn containing a special part of the body? Was
the Prince still there after the Archbishop's tinkering?[66]

Every nocturnal burrowing sowed more doubts. But that is the trouble
with secrecy, darkness and graves. In 1859 yet another official commission decided to open the grave to prove that the Prince was still there:
when they opened the tomb, they discovered a large crypt, a wooden
coffin inside a lead one and a gold fringe to go round it. Milgov, a local
bureaucrat, tidied up the crypt and closed it again.[67]

Now that everyone was finally sure there was a grave there, it was
decided there should be a grandiose gravestone. But no one could recall
where exactly the tomb had been, so they did not know where to put it.
This sounds like a poor excuse for some more digging by inquisitive
busybodies. In 1873, another commission excavated and found the
wooden coffin containing a skull with the triangular hole in the back
left by Massot's embalming, and tufts of dark-blonde hair, the remnants
of the coiffure that was said to be finest in Russia, as well as three medals,
clothes and gold-braid scraps of uniform. They sealed it up again and
constructed a fitting gravestone approximately above the tomb.[68] Finally,
Potemkin, if it was he, was allowed some peace.

Then came the Revolution: the Bolsheviks gleefully dug up the graveyard of St Catherine's that contained the bodies of officers killed in the
siege of Ochakov. There are yellowed photographs, kept by the local
priest today, that show a macabre revolutionary scene; crowds of peasants in the clothes of 1918 point at the wizened skeletons still with hair,
wearing the braided tailcoats, breeches and boots of Catherine's era –
while in the background we can spot the jackboots and leather coats of
the Chekist secret police.[69]

Twelve years later, in 1930, a young writer named Boris Lavrenev returned to his hometown of Kherson to visit his sick father. He went for a walk through the fortress and saw a sign outside St Catherine's that read 'Kherson's Anti-Religious Museum'. Inside he saw a pyramidal glass case. There was 'a round brown thing' inside it. When he got closer, he saw it was a skull. On the table next to it was written: 'The skull of Catherine II's lover Potemkin'. In the next-door case there was a skeleton, still with shrivelled muscles on the bones. A sign read: 'The Bones of Catherine II's lover Potemkin'. In the third case, there were remains of a green velvet jacket, white satin trousers and rotten stockings and shoes – Potemkin's clothes.

Lavrenev rushed out of the church and sent a telegram to the ministry in charge of protecting art. When he was back in Leningrad, a friend wrote to tell him that the 'museum' was closed. Potemkin was gathered up, put in a new coffin in the vault and bricked up again. 'So in 1930 in Kherson,' wrote Lavrenev, 'Field-Marshal Serenissimus Prince Grigory Alexandrovich Potemkin, who was the exhibit of the Kherson Anti-Religious Museum, was buried for the second time.'[70]

On 11 May 1984, the mystery of Potemkin once again proved irresistible to local bureaucrats: the chief of Kherson's Forensic Medical Department L. G. Boguslavsky opened the tomb and found '31 human bones ... belonging to the skeleton of a man, probably of 185 cm ... of about 52–55 years old' who had probably been dead for about 200 years. But there were apparently some epaulettes in the coffin too, said to belong to a British officer of the time of the Crimean War. The coffin was more modern, but it had a Catholic as well as an Orthodox cross on it. The analysts decided this was undoubtedly Potemkin.

In July 1986, Boguslavsky wrote to Professor Evgeny Anisimov, the distinguished eighteenth-century scholar, who was unconvinced by the evidence: if it was Potemkin, why a Catholic cross on the coffin and why the British epaulettes? Were they concluding that this was Potemkin out of wishful thinking instead of forensic analysis? Quite apart from the fascinating question of the identity of the British officer whose uniform was found there, was it Potemkin or not?

The size, age and dating of the body were right. The old coffins, leaden, gilded or wooden, as well as the medals, any remaining icons and the clothes, all disappeared in the Revolution. The Catholic coffin, which was shorter than the skeleton, was probably supplied in 1930. The English epaulettes are from another grave, the relics of the ignorant Bolshevik pilfering. So, in 1986, the Prince of Taurida was once again buried for, if one counts the viscera of Jassy and all the other excavations, the eighth time – and again forgotten.[71]

St Catherine's Church is now again filled with worshippers. The first thing one sees if one peers from the outside between Starov's Classical pillars is a wooden and iron rail around a solitary flat white marble gravestone, seven foot long and three wide, that lies right in the middle underneath the cupola. Inside, beneath a large gilded crest set on the stone, one reads:

> Field Marshal
> Serenissimus Prince
> Grigory Alexandrovich
> Potemkin of Taurida
> Born 30th September 1739
> Died 5th October 1791.
> Buried here 23rd November 1791

Around the edge of the marble there are seven gilded rosettes, each engraved with his victories and cities.* An old lady is selling candles at the door. Potemkin? 'You must wait for the priest, Father Anatoly,' she says. Father Anatoly, with long straight blond hair, blue eyes and the tranquillity of clergy in provincial towns, represents a new generation of young Orthodox brought up under Communism and he is most pleased to show a foreigner the tomb of Potemkin. No one has opened the tomb for a few years and no foreigner has ever seen it.

Father Anatoly lights six candles, walks to the middle of the floor and opens a concealed wooden trapdoor. The steep steps fall away into darkness. Father Anatoly leads the way and uses the wax to stick the first candle to the wall. This lights up a narrow passageway. As he walks along he fixes other candles to illuminate the way until he reaches a small chamber: it was once lined with icons and contained the silver, lead and wooden coffins of Potemkin, 'all stolen by the Communists'. The simple wooden coffin, with a cross on it, stands on a raised dais in the midst of the vault. The priest sticks the remaining candles around the chamber to light it up. Then he opens the lid of the coffin: there is small black bag inside containing the skull and the numbered bones of Prince Potemkin. That is all.

There is one final mystery: the heart. It was not buried at Golia like the entrails and brains but was placed in a golden urn. But where was it

---

* The top row reads 'Ochakov 1788, Crimea and Kuban 1783, Kherson 1778'. The two in the middle: 'Akkerman 1789' and 'Ekaterinoslav 1787'. At the bottom: 'Bender 1789' and 'Nikolaev 1788'.

taken? Samoilov said it was placed under the throne of St Catherine's in Kherson, but Father Anatoly says there is no trace of it. The likeliest scenario for the heart is that it this was the object removed by Archbishop Iov Potemkin in 1818. Where did he take it – Branicka's estate or Chizhova, where Serenissimus asked to be buried? Today, the villagers of Chizhova still believe the heart of Potemkin was buried there in the family church where he learned to sing and read.

This would be most fitting: the Empire, which Serenissimus did so much to build, is in ruins today and most of Potemkin's conquests are no longer Russian. If his innards are in Rumania and his bones in Ukraine, it seems right that his heart rests in Russia.

> Roar on, roar on, O waterfall!
> Gavrili Derzhavin, *The Waterfall*

LIST OF CHARACTERS

Prince Grigory Potemkin of Taurida, Catherine II's secret husband, statesman, soldier

Catherine II the Great, born Princess Sophia of Zerbst, Empress of Russia 1762–96

Abdul-Hamid I, Ottoman Sultan, 1774–88

Jeremy Bentham, English philosopher and creator of utilitarianism

Samuel Bentham, brother of above, inventor, naval officer, shipbuilder

Alexander Bezborodko, Catherine's secretary, then foreign minister

Ksawery Branicki, Polish courtier married to Potemkin's niece Alexandra Engelhardt

Alexandra Branicka, Potemkin's favourite niece, *née* Engelhardt, married to above

Alexei Bobrinsky, natural son of Catherine and Grigory Orlov

Praskovia Bruce, Catherine's confidant, supposed to be sampler of favourites

Count Cagliostro, Italian charlatan

Zakhar Chernyshev, early admirer of Catherine, courtier, war minister, ally of the Orlovs

Ivan Chernyshev, brother of above, courtier, navy minister

Count Louis Cobenzl, Austrian ambassador to Petersburg

Elisabeth Countess of Craven, aristocratic English adventuress, traveller, writer

Comte de Damas, French aristocrat and officer in Potemkin's army

Ekaterina Dashkova, *née* Vorontsova, Catherine's supporter and irritant

Ekaterina Dolgorukaya, wife of Russian officer, mistress of Potemkin

Elisabeth, daughter of Peter the Great, Empress 1741–61

Mikhail Faleev, entrepreneur, quartermaster, merchant, builder of Nikolaev

Frederick II the Great, King of Prussia 1740–86

Frederick William, nephew of the above, King of Prussia 1786–97

Mikhail Garnovsky, minder of the Duchess of Kingston, Potemkin's *homme d'affaires*

Varvara Golitsyna, *née* Engelhardt, Potemkin's niece who married
   Prince Sergei Golitsyn
Praskovia Golitsyna, married to Prince Mikhail Golitsyn, Potemkin's
   'last mistress'
William Gould, Potemkin's English gardener
Sir James Harris, British envoy to Petersburg, later Earl of Malmesbury
Henry of Prussia, younger brother of Frederick the Great
John Paul Jones, legendary American admiral regarded as founder of
   US Navy
Joseph II, Holy Roman Emperor or Kaiser 1765–90, co-ruler, then ruler
   of Habsburg lands 1780–90
Alexander Khrapovitsky, diarist and Catherine's secretary
Elisabeth Duchess of Kingston, Countess of Bristol, English adventuress
   and bigamist
Alexander Lanskoy, Catherine's favourite 1779–84
Leopold, Holy Roman Emperor, brother of Joseph II and his successor
   1790–2
Prince de Ligne, European aristocrat, Austrian courtier and field-
   marshal
Lewis Littlepage, American from Virginia, Polish courtier and officer
   in Potemkin's flotilla
Alexander (Dmitryev-)Mamonov, Catherine's favourite 1786–9
Maria Theresa, Empress–Queen, ruler of Habsburg lands 1740–80,
   mother of Joseph
Francisco de Miranda, South American revolutionary, later dictator of
   Venezuela
Prince de Nassau-Siegen, European aristocrat and soldier of fortune
Grigory Orlov, leader of Catherine's coup and favourite 1761–72
Alexei Orlov-Chesmensky, 'Scarface', murderer of Peter III and victor
   of Battle of Chesme, brother of above
Nikita Panin, governor of Grand Duke Paul, then Catherine's foreign
   minister
Peter Panin, brother of above, general and subjugator of Pugachev
Grand Duke Paul, Catherine and Peter III's son, Emperor 1796–1801,
   assassinated
Peter III, nephew of Empress Elisabeth; husband of Catherine II,
   Emperor 1761–2
Reginald Pole Carew, English gentleman, traveller and friend of
   Potemkin, later MP
Stanislas Poniatowski, Catherine's second lover, later Stanislas-
   Augustus last King of Poland

Vasily Popov, Potemkin's head of chancellery

Pavel Potemkin, the Prince's cousin, general and viceroy of the Caucasus

Praskovia Potemkina, wife of above and mistress of the Prince

Emelian Pugachev, pretender, Cossack, leader of peasant rebellion 1773–4

Alexei Razumovsky, Cossack chorister who became Elisabeth's favourite

Kirill Razumovsky, brother of above, Hetman of Ukraine until 1764, courtier

José (Osip) de Ribas, Neapolitan adventurer, Potemkin crony and admiral

Duc de Richelieu, officer in Potemkin's army, later builder of Odessa, prime minister of France

Ivan Rimsky-Korsakov, Catherine's favourite 1778–9

Peter Rumiantsev-Zadunaisky, military hero in First Turkish War

Serge Saltykov, Catherine's first lover

Alexander Samoilov, Potemkin's nephew and general, later procurator-general

Ekaterina Samoilova, wife of above and probably Potemkin's mistress

Comte de Ségur, French ambassador to Russia

Selim III, Ottoman Sultan, 1788–1807

Major James George Semple, English conman – 'Prince of Swindlers'

Shagin Giray, Russian ally, descendant of Genghis Khan, and last Khan of the Crimea

Stepan Sheshkovsky, secret policeman – the 'knout-master'

Ivan Shuvalov, Empress Elisabeth's favourite who invited Potemkin to Petersburg

Ekaterina Skavronskaya, 'angel' and 'kitten', née Engelhardt, Potemkin's niece

Alexander Suvorov, military hero, Potemkin's favourite general

Alexander Vassilchikov, Catherine's favourite 1772–4, nicknamed 'Iced Soup'

Alexander Viazemsky, administrator of internal affairs, procurator-general

Simon Vorontsov, Russian ambassador to London

Alexander Vorontsov, brother of above, minister of commerce

Sophie de Witte, slavegirl, courtesan, mistress of Potemkin, then Countess Potocka

Alexander Yermolov, Catherine's favourite 1786

Tatiana Yusupova, née Engelhardt, married to Mikhail Potemkin, then Prince Yusupov

Alexander Zavadovsky, Catherine's favourite 1776–7, courtier, minister

Joshua Zeitlin, Jewish merchant, rabbinical scholar, Potemkin's friend
Semyon Zorich, Catherine's favourite 1777–8, founder of military school
Platon Zubov, Catherine's last favourite 1789–96

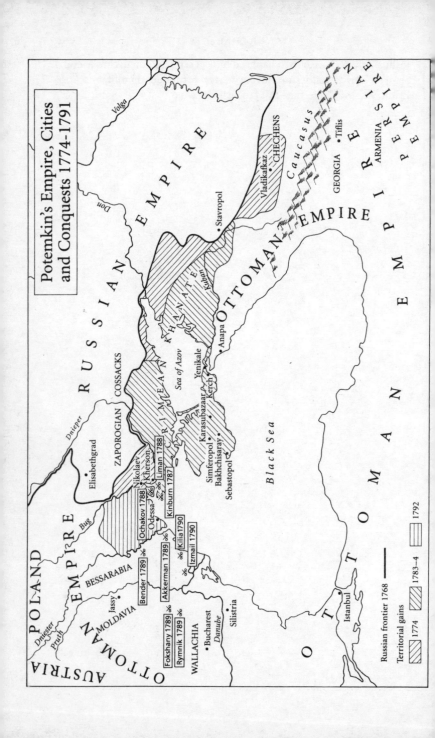

Potemkin's Empire, Cities
and Conquests 1774-1791

POLAND

AUSTRIA

OTTOMAN EMPIRE

BESSARABIA

MOLDAVIA

Jassy

Dniester

Pruth

WALLACHIA

Fokshany 1789

Rymnik 1789

Bucharest

Danube

Silistria

Bender 1789

Akkerman 1789

Izmail 1790

Kilia 1790

Kinburn 1787

Ochakov 1788

Odessa

Liman 1788

Nikolaev

Kherson

Bug

Dnieper

Elisabethgrad

ZAPOROGIAN COSSACKS

RUSSIAN EMPIRE

Volga

Don

Stavropol

CRIMEAN KHANATE

Sea of Azov

Yenikale

Kerch

Karasubazaar

Simferopol

Bakhchisaray

Sebastopol

Black Sea

Kuban

Anapa

OTTOMAN EMPIRE

Caucasus

Vladikafkaz

CHECHENS

GEORGIA

Tiflis

ARMENIA

PERSIAN EMPIRE

Istanbul

OTTOMAN EMPIRE

Russian frontier 1768

Territorial gains

1774   1783–4   1792

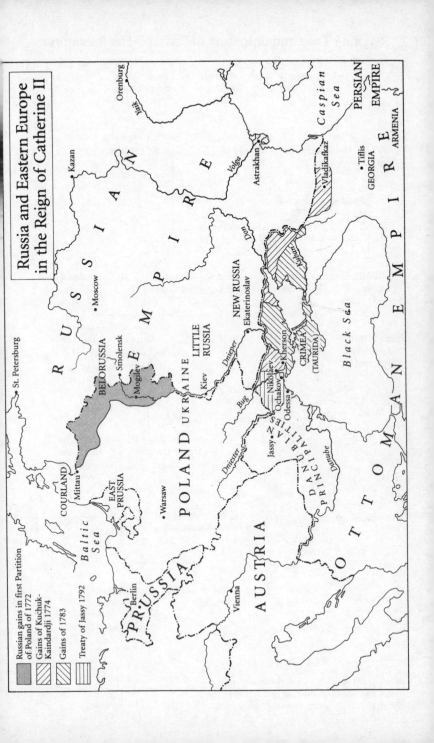

Russia and Eastern Europe in the Reign of Catherine II

St. Petersburg

R U S S I A N

Orenburg

Yaik

Kazan

Moscow

E M P I R E

Volga

Astrakhan

Caspian Sea

PERSIAN EMPIRE

Tiflis

GEORGIA

Vladikafkaz

ARMENIA

Kuban

Don

BELORUSSIA

Smolensk

Mogilev

NEW RUSSIA

Ekaterinoslav

LITTLE RUSSIA

Kiev

Dnieper

CRIMEA (TAURIDA)

Kherson

Black Sea

COURLAND

Mittau

EAST PRUSSIA

Baltic Sea

Bug

Nikolaev

Ochakov

Odessa

O T T O M A N   E M P I R E

U K R A I N E

P O L A N D

Warsaw

Dniester

Jassy

DANUBIAN PRINCIPALITIES

Danube

PRUSSIA

Berlin

AUSTRIA

Vienna

Russian gains in first Partition of Poland of 1772

Gains of Kuchuk-Kaindardji 1774

Gains of 1783

Treaty of Jassy 1792

Reigning Tsars and Emperors of Russia – The Romanovs

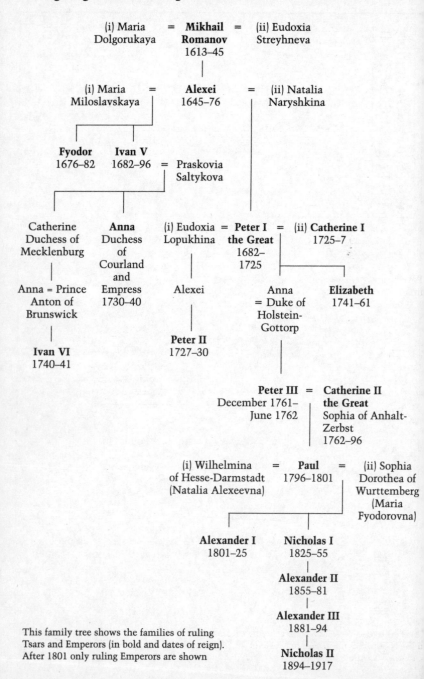

This family tree shows the families of ruling
Tsars and Emperors (in bold and dates of reign).
After 1801 only ruling Emperors are shown

The Wider Family of Prince Potemkin

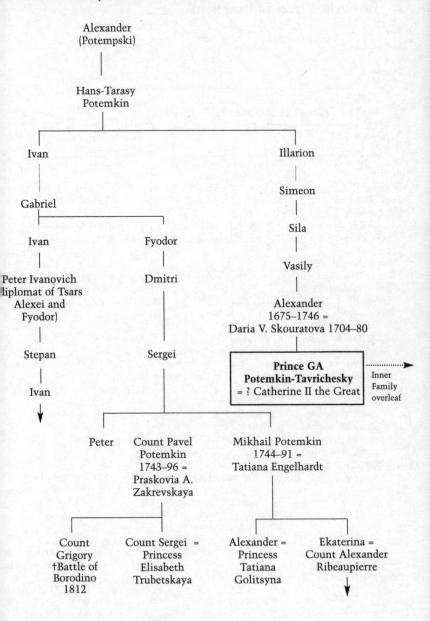

Alexander
(Potempski)

Hans-Tarasy
Potemkin

Ivan   Illarion

Gabriel   Simeon

Ivan   Fyodor   Sila

Peter Ivanovich
(diplomat of Tsars
Alexei and
Fyodor)   Dmitri   Vasily

Alexander
1675–1746 =
Daria V. Skouratova 1704–80

Stepan   Sergei

Ivan

**Prince GA
Potemkin-Tavrichesky**
= ? Catherine II the Great
   ┈┈┈> Inner Family overleaf

Peter   Count Pavel
Potemkin
1743–96 =
Praskovia A.
Zakrevskaya   Mikhail Potemkin
1744–91 =
Tatiana Engelhardt

Count
Grigory
†Battle of
Borodino
1812   Count Sergei =
Princess
Elisabeth
Trubetskaya   Alexander =
Princess
Tatiana
Golitsyna   Ekaterina =
Count Alexander
Ribeaupierre

This family tree shows the main characters featured
in the book and is not meant to be complete
= married   † died

The Inner Family of Prince Potemkin including Favourite Nieces and Nephews

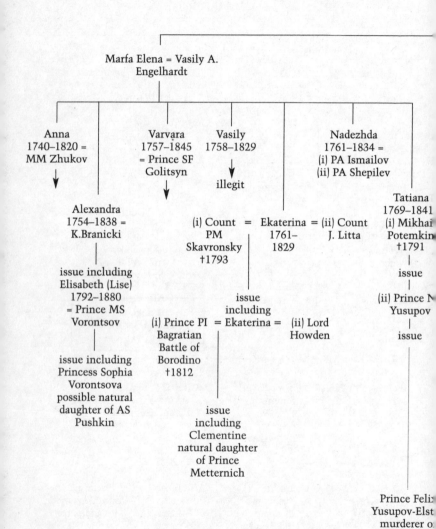

Marfa Elena = Vasily A. Engelhardt

Anna
1740–1820 =
MM Zhukov

Alexandra
1754–1838 =
K.Branicki

issue including
Elisabeth (Lise)
1792–1880
= Prince MS
Vorontsov

issue including
Princess Sophia
Vorontsova
possible natural
daughter of AS
Pushkin

Varvara
1757–1845
= Prince SF
Golitsyn

Vasily
1758–1829

↓

illegit

(i) Count   =   Ekaterina   =   (ii) Count
PM   1761–   J. Litta
Skavronsky   1829
†1793

issue
including

(i) Prince PI   =   Ekaterina   =   (ii) Lord
Bagratian   Howden
Battle of
Borodino
†1812

issue
including
Clementine
natural daughter
of Prince
Metternich

Nadezhda
1761–1834 =
(i) PA Ismailov
(ii) PA Shepilev

Tatiana
1769–1841
(i) Mikhai
Potemkin
†1791

issue

(ii) Prince N
Yusupov

issue

Prince Felix
Yusupov-Elst
murderer o
Rasputin 191

This family tree shows the main characters featured
in the book and is not meant to be complete
= married   † died

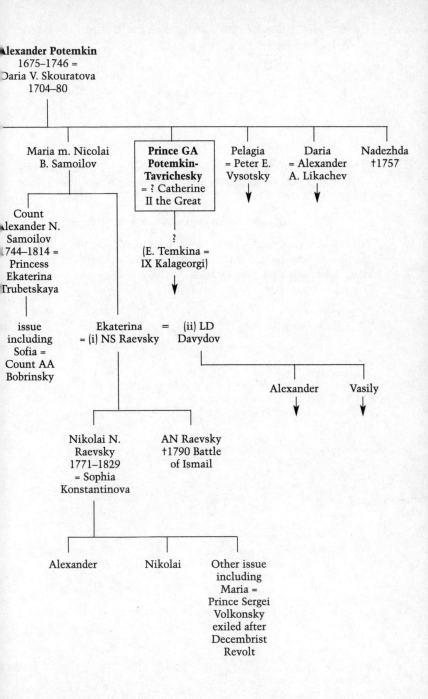

Alexander Potemkin
1675–1746 =
Daria V. Skouratova
1704–80

Maria m. Nicolai
B. Samoilov

**Prince GA
Potemkin-
Tavrichesky**
= ? Catherine
II the Great

Pelagia
= Peter E.
Vysotsky

Daria
= Alexander
A. Likachev

Nadezhda
†1757

Count
Alexander N.
Samoilov
1744–1814 =
Princess
Ekaterina
Trubetskaya

?
(E. Temkina =
IX Kalageorgi)

issue
including
Sofia =
Count AA
Bobrinsky

Ekaterina
= (i) NS Raevsky

= (ii) LD
Davydov

Alexander

Vasily

Nikolai N.
Raevsky
1771–1829
= Sophia
Konstantinova

AN Raevsky
†1790 Battle
of Ismail

Alexander

Nikolai

Other issue
including
Maria =
Prince Sergei
Volkonsky
exiled after
Decembrist
Revolt

NOTES

The full and extremely extensive references for this book, which were included in the hardback edition, are available on the author's website at:

http://www.simonsebagmontefiore.com

To make the paperback a manageable and readable size, the author and publishers have decided not to include them in the paperback. We hope the readers will agree that, for most, the balance of convenience is best served by this policy.

SELECT BIBLIOGRAPHY

In the case of a character about whom such a malicious mythology developed, even during his lifetime, a word on sources is helpful. I have been very fortunate to find much new and unpublished material in the various archives. Of the Russian archives, large amounts were published in the last century in SIRIO and ZOOID, as well as in historical journals such as RA and RS and collections of documents such as Dubrovin's *Bumagi Potemkina* (SBVIM). Then there are the published Vorontsov archives that remain a key source. All contain materials ignored or forgotten. For example, SIRIO contains documents such as Richelieu's 'Voyage en Allemagne' and Catherine's own account of Potemkin's ball, which have been relatively neglected in the West. Overall these are invaluable and usually accurate, though I have checked the originals wherever possible.

V. S. Lopatin's newly published collection of the Catherine–Potemkin correspondence is a massive work of scholarship and research, the fruit of twenty years' labour, and I have used it liberally. This is now indispensable to any student of this epoch. Even these over 1,000 letters are unlikely to be complete and there are more notes between the two of them still be catalogued. Lopatin's collection of letters between Suvorov and Potemkin and his account of their relationship are equally obligatory reading, for his research has successfully reinterpreted their relationship. That said, Lopatin's accounts sometimes lean towards the romantic – he accepts for example that Catherine was the mother of Elisaveta Temkina and gave birth to her in Moscow in 1775; and that Catherine visited Chizhova on her return from Mogilev. His datings of the letters are always sensitive and plausible, but there are occasions, such as the letters referring to Cagliostro, where Western research proves that the timing must be much later. In my awe of, and gratitude for, Lopatin's monumental work, I have humbly corrected these assertions or at least suggested doubt.

The archives – particularly RGADA, RGVIA and AVPRI, all in Moscow, and RGIA, in Petersburg, and AGAD, the Polish State Historical Archive in Warsaw – remain full of unpublished material. In RGADA, for example, I have found a wealth of unpublished letters to and from Potemkin, on questions of state, on his personal finances and on his love life, including many anonymous love letters and letters from Alexandra Branicka. RGVIA, the War Ministry archive, contains the archive of Potemkin's Chancellery and many fascinating state and private documents which I have used here. RGIA contains unpublished letters from Frederick the Great as well as personal accounts. In Warsaw, the huge Deboli archive has been under-used and there is also a wealth of letters from Potemkin to Stanislas-Augustus. Overall, the correspondence in these four archives contain a mass of unpublished material, much of which is used in the book: this includes letters to and from the Emperors Joseph and Leopold; Prince Kaunitz; Frederick the Great; King Gustavus III of Sweden; King Stanislas-Augustus of Poland; Prince Henry of Prussia; Potemkin's nieces Countess Alexandra Branicka and Princess Tatiana Yusupova; his nephews Count Skavronsky and Count Branicki and Potemkin's Polish allies and agents; his art dealers such as Lord Carysfort; visitors like Lady Craven, Reginald Pole Carew and Sénac de Meilhan; Count Simon Vorontsov and other Russian statesmen; the Prince de Ligne; the Comte de Ségur; the Earl of Malmesbury; the Duke of Leeds; Jeremy and Sir Samuel Bentham; the Prince de Nassau-Siegen; John Paul Jones; Lewis Littlepage; Francisco de Miranda; his secret diplomatic agents and Russian ambassadors from Vienna, Paris, Constantinople; his bankers, including Baron Richard Sutherland; and many fascinating jewels such as his shopping-list in Paris. Many of these correspondences, such as those with Stanislas-Augustus and Sutherland, stretch across all these archives.

Sadly, I have been able to use only a fraction of the materials I have found: some such as the huge materials on Potemkin and Poland or Potemkin's military orders belong in other books; some such as those from Ligne and Malmesbury simply add interesting twists to relationships that are already well documented. Some are simply too detailed or obscure to use.

In the local museums in Ukraine and Russia, the archives often contain copies of documents long since sent to the Moscow RGADA or RGVIA, but I was lucky enough to find some rarities there too, like the original invitation to Potemkin's ball in the Odessa State Local Historical Museum, which may be the only one in existence. There is also immense local knowledge of fact and legend that has not been tapped for a century, as well as information on characters, such as M. L. Faleev in Nikolaev, that is not available elsewhere.

In Britain, the PRO contains the unpublished despatches of Fitzherbert and Fawkener, which give a fresh account of Potemkin's last months in Petersburg and which have rarely been used. The British Museum's Bentham archive, though much has been published, still yields many unseen treasures. I found most useful the unpublished archive at Antony in Cornwall of Reginald Pole Carew's diaries of his visits to Russia and his time with Potemkin. In Paris, AAE, the Foreign Ministry Archives at the Quai d'Orsay, contain a wealth of useful documents, many unpublished, as well as the complete account of the Comte de Langeron, which is invaluable. Parts of Langeron have been published in Russia and a full Western publication is being prepared.

The published material on Potemkin divides clearly into the prejudiced and the unprejudiced, or at least the mythical and the documentary. Naturally, I have treated anything connected to Helbig, *The Memoirs of the Life of Prince Potemkin*, Cerenville (both Helbig adaptions) or Saint-Jean (whose very identity is a mystery) as hostile or untrustworthy, while Castera is more useful.

Even when recounting neutral stories, Charles Masson, Saint-Jean, and Helbig must be regarded as 'myth-writers', not historians. But the mythology of Potemkin is important too and tells its own tales, though I try to reassess it wherever possible using documents. Masson hated Emperor Paul and his *Secret Memoirs* were notoriously published in his lifetime, yet he records some Potemkin anecdotes that ring true. Eye-witnesses like Ligne, Ségur, Corberon, Richelieu, Miranda, Damas and Langeron (all foreigners) and Rostopchin, Tsebrikov, Ribeaupierre, Derzhavin, Bezborodko, Vorontsov, Zavadovsky, Wiegel, Engelhardt and Samoilov were prejudiced and subjective, but one senses that they were telling what they *believed* to be the truth. Some are openly malicious, such as Rostopchin and Vorontsov; Dolgoruky is malicious and a fantastist; while others such as Samoilov are supporters. Many fall somewhere in between. Bezborodko for example strikes one as studiously fair. The 'Table Talk', history of the Pugachev Rebellion and Historical Notes of A. S. Pushkin are other underused sources: the poet was captivated by Potemkin, knew his family and circle, and carefully recorded their stories, which I therefore treat as valuable anecdotal history from the people who knew him. Among the foreigners, Ligne's and Langeron's malicious accounts of Potemkin's war record have completely blackened his reputation through all the histories ever since. Yet they are also invaluable, given Langeron's fair tribute to Potemkin later in life. In Ligne's case, unpublished letters in Potemkin's archives give us the chance to put his prejudices in perspective. Richelieu's, Stedingk's and Miranda's much more positive accounts of the same period have often been overlooked, and redress the balance.

In terms of published Western histories, I have used as my reference books the works of Isabel de Madariaga and J. T. Alexander, along with Marc Raeff, David Ransel, Roger Bartlett (*Human Capital*), John LeDonne (*Ruling Russia*), Anthony Cross (on the British in Russia), Lord and Zamoyski (on Poland) and Kinross and Mansel (on Constantinople). Of Potemkin's previous biographers, Brückner is the most important, while Soloveytchik is useful but lacks all references.

ARCHIVES, PERIODICALS AND ABBREVIATIONS USED IN NOTES AND BIBLIOGRAPHY

AAE	Archives des Affairs Etrangères, Quai d'Orsay, Paris, volumes 68–139
AGAD	Archiwum Glowne Akt Dawnych w Warszawie
AGS	Arkhiv Gosudarstvennogo Soveta
AHR	*American History Review*
AKV	Arkhiv Knyaza Vorontsova
AVPRI	Arkhiv Vneshnyey Politiki Rossiyskhoy Imperii
B&F	*Joseph II und Graf Ludwig Cobenzl: Ihr Briefwechsel Fontes Rerum Austriacarum*, ed. A. Beer and J. Fiedler, Vienna 1873
BM	British Museum, London

CASS/CSS	*Canadian American Slavic Studies/Canadian Slavic Studies*
CHOIDR	Chteniya v Imperatorskom Obshchestve Istorii Drevnostyey Rossiyskikh
CMRS	*Cahiers du Monde Russe et Soviétique*
CtG/CII	Catherine the Great/the Second, Empress of Russia
DVS	*Dukh Velikogo Suvorova ili Anekdoty Podlinnyye o Knyaze Italiyskoye. Grafe Alexandre Vasileviche Suvorove-Rymnikskom*, St Petersburg 1808
FtG/FII	Frederick the Great/the Second, King of Prussia
GAOO	Gosudarstvenny Arkhiv Odesskoy Oblasti
GAP/GAPT	Grigory Alexandrovich Potemkin (–Tavrichesky)
GARF	Gosudarstvenny Arkhiv Rossiskoy Federatskii, Moscow
GIM OPI	Gosudarstvenny Istoricheskiy Muzyey Otdel Pismennykh Istochnikov
GPB	Gosudarstvennaya Publishnaya Biblioteka
H	Sir James Harris, 1st Earl of Malmesbury
HZ	*Historische Zeitschrift*
IRLI	Institut Russkoy Literatury Akademii Nauk SSSR
ITUAK	*Izvestiya Tavricheskoy Uchenoy Arkhivoy Komissii*
IV	*Istoricheskiye Vestnik*
IZ	*Istoricheskiy Zapiski*
JB	Jeremy Bentham
JII	Joseph II, Holy Roman Emperor
KD	M. I. Kutuzov, *Dokumenty*, Moscow 1950–6, vols 1–5
KFZ	*Kamer Fureskiy Zhurnal*
L	V. S. Lopatin, ed. *Ekaterina II i G. A. Potemkin, Lichnaya Perepiska 1769–91*, Moscow 1997
MIRF	*Materialy dlya istorii Russkogo flota*
N-S	Charles, Prince de Nassau-Siegen
PRO	Public Record Office, London
PSZ	*Polnoye Sobraniye Zakonov*
RA	*Russkiy Arkhiv 1863–1917*
RGADA	Rossiskiy Gosudarstvenny Arkhiv Drevnikh Aktov, Moscow
RGIA	Rossiskiy Gosudarstvenny Istoricheskiy Arkhiv, St Petersburg
RGVIA	Rossiskiy Gosudarstvenny Voenno-Istoricheskiy Arkhiv, Moscow
RP	Grand Duke Nikolai Mikhailovich, *Russkiye Portrety xxviii i xix stoletiy (Portraits Russes)*, St Petersburg, 1906–13, vols 1–5
RS	*Russkaya Starina 1870–1918*
RV	*Russkiy Vestnik*
SA	Stanislas-Augustus (Poniatowski), King of Poland
SB	(Sir) Samuel Bentham
SBVIM	*Sbornik Voenno-Istoricheskikh Materialov*, St Petersburg, 1893–5

SD   A. V. Suvorov, *Dokumenty*, ed G. P. Mescheryakov, Moscow 1949–53, vols 1–4

SeA   Severny Arkhiv

SEER   *Slavonic and East European Review*

SENA   Senatskiy Arkhiv

SIMPIK KV   *Sbornik Istoricheskikh Materialov po Istorii Kubanskoyo Kazachego Voyska 1737–1901*, ed I. I. Dmitrenko, St Petersburg 1896

SIRIO   *Sbornik Imperatorskogo Russkogo Istoricheskogo Obshchestva*

TGV   *Tavricheskiye Gubernskiye Vedomosti*

VI   *Voprosy Istorii*

VIZ   *Voenno-Istoricheskiy Zhurnal*

ZG   *Zapiski Garnovskogo*

ZOOID   *Zapiski Odesskogo Obshchestva Istorii Drevostye*

PRIMARY

Albrecht, J. F. E., *Panslavin Fürst der Finsternis, und seine geliebte, Prince of Darkness, a satirical tale being the History of Catherine II and Potemkin*, Germanien 1794

Alexeev, G. P., 'Episode from the Life of Prince Potemkin', IV (1889) vol 37

Anonymous, *General Observations Regarding the Present State of the Russian Empire*, London 1787

Anonymous, *Anecdoten zur Lebensgeschichte des Ritters und Reichs-fürstern Potemkin*, Freistadt-am-Rhein 1792

Anonymous, *Authentic Memoirs of the Life and Reign of Catherine II, Empress of all the Russias, collected from authentic manuscripts, translations, etc of the King of Sweden, Right Honourable Lord Mountmorres, Lord Malmesbury, Monsieur de Volney and other indisputable authorities*, 2nd edn, London 1797

Anonymous, *La Cour de la Russie il y a cent ans 1725–1783, extraits des dépêches des ambassadeurs anglais et français*, Berlin 1858

Anonymous, *The Memoirs of the Life of Prince Potemkin, comprehending original anecdotes of Catherine II and of the Russian court, translated from the German*, London 1812 and 1813

Anonymous, 'Songs of the Russian army about Potemkin', ZOOID 9 (1875): 459–6

Antoine, M. (Baron de Saint-Joseph), *Essai Historique sur le commerce et la navigation de la Mer Noire*, Paris 1820

Anspach, Margravine of (Lady Craven), *Journey through the Crimea to Constantinople*, London 1789

Anspach, Margravine of (Lady Craven), *Memoirs*, London 1826

Asseburg, A. F. von der, *Denkwürdigkeiten*, Berlin 1842

Banq, J., Letters to G. A. Potemkin, RGVIA f52

Barbarykin, A. D., Legend about Prince Potemkin-Tavrichesky, RA (1907) 11

Bentham, Jeremy, *Collected Works*, ed Sir J. Bowring, Edinburgh 1838–43

Bentham, Jeremy, *Correspondence of*, London vols 2–4 1968–1981

Bentham, Sir Samuel, Papers, Archives f 33540 BM

Bezborodko, A. A., Letters to G. A. Potemkin, RS (1873)

Bezborodko, A. A., Letters to S. R. Vorontsov, A. R. Vorontsov, P. V. Zavadovsky etc, AKV 13, Moscow 1879 (also ZOOID 11 and SIRIO 29)

Bezborodko, A. A., 'Pisma A. A. Bezborodka k grafu P. A. Rumiantsevu 1777–93', ed P. M. Maykov, *Starina i novizna* (1900) vol 3

Bibikov, A. A., *Zapiski o zhizni i sluzhbe Alexandra Ilicha Bibikova*, Moscow 1865

Bolotov A. T., *Zhizn i priklyucheniya Andreya Bolotova 1738–93*, Leningrad 1931

Branicka, A. V., Letters to G. A. Potemkin, RGADA f 11

Bruce, P. H., *Memoirs*, London 1782

Buckinghamshire, Earl of, *The Despatches and Correspondence of John, 2nd Earl of Buckinghamshire, Ambassador to the Court of Catherine II of Russia 1762–5*, ed A. D. Collyer, London 1900–2

Bulgakov, Ya. I., *Iz bumagy Ya. I. Bulgakova*, RA (1905) 7 pp 337–408

Bulgakov, Ya. I., *Pisma Ya. I. Bulgakova k knyazyu Potemkinu*, RA (1861)

Burke, Edmund, *Collected Works*, London 1826

Casanova, Giacomo, Chevalier de Seingalt, *History of my Life*, trans Williard R. Trask, Baltimore and London 1997

Catherine II

Bumagi Ekateriny 1744–1796, SIRIO 7, 10, 13, 27, 42

Imperatritsa Ekaterina II i knyaz Potemkin-Tavrichesky, podlinnaya ikh perepiska, RS (1876) 16

Pisma imperatritsky ii k Grimmu 1774–1796, SIRIO 23, St Petersburg 1878

Pisma imp. Ekateriny II k gr. P. V. Zavadovskomu 1775–1777, ed I. A. Barskov, *Russkiy istoricheskiy zhurnal* (1918) vols 2, 3, 4

Catherine II: Books

Correspondence of Catherine the Great when Grand Duchess with Sir Charles Hanbury Williams and Letters from Count Poniatowski, ed and trans the Earl of Ilchester and Mrs Langford-Brooke, London 1928

Documents of Catherine the Great, the Correspondence with Voltaire and the Instruction of 1767 in the English Text of 1768, ed W. P. Reddaway, Cambridge 1931

Filosofskaya i politicheskaya perepiska Imperatritsy Ekateriny II s doctorom Zimmermanom 1785–1792, St Petersburg 1803

Joseph II und Katharina von Russland. Ihr briefwechsel, ed Alfred Ritter von Arneth, Vienna 1869

Lettres de Catherine II au prince de Ligne 1780–96, Paris 1924

Memoirs of Catherine the Great, ed D. Maroger, London 1955

Memoirs of Catherine the Great, trans Katherine Antony, New York 1927

Oeuvres complètes de Voltaire, correspondance avec l'Imperatrice de Russie, vol lviii, Paris 1821

Sochineniya imperatritsy Ekateriny II na osnovanii podlinnykh rukopsye c obyasnitelnmi primechaniyami, ed A. N. Pypin, vols 1–12, St Petersburg 1901–7

Catherine II: Miscellaneous Papers

Catherine's charter about the recognition of Potemkin's merits, GAOO f 162

Instruction to our Gentleman of the Bedchamber G. A. Potemkin, RGADA f 18

Letters to:

    V. S. Popov, RGADA f 5

    G. A. Potemkin on Georgia, VI (1983) no 7 (RGVIA f 52)

    A. N. Samoilov, RA (1878) no 10

    O.-M. Stackelberg, RS, vol 3, St Petersburg 1871

Reports and orders to G. A. Potemkin on the south, RGADA f 16

Rescripts to G. A. Potemkin, SIRIO 27, St Petersburg 1880

Rescripts to G. A. Potemkin about the Crimea and development of Kherson, RGADA f 5 d 85

Rescripty G. A. Potemkinu 1791, RA (1874) 2 pp 246–58

Cerenville, J. E., *La Vie de Prince Potemkine, rédigée par un officier français d'après les meilleurs ouvrages allemands et français, qui ont paru sur la Russie à cette époque*, Paris 1808

Chernyshev, G. I., Letters to S. F. Golitsyn during siege of Ismail, RA (1791)

Cook, J., *Voyages and Travels through the Russian Empire*, Edinburgh 1770

Corberon, Marie-Daniel Bourrée, Chevalier de, *Un Diplomate français à la cour de Catherine II 1775–1780, journal intime*, ed L. H. Labande, Paris 1904

Coxe, W., *Travels into Poland, Russia, Sweden and Denmark*, London 1874

Custine, the Marquis de, *Empire of the Tsar: A Journey through Eternal Russia*, New York 1989

Czartoryski, Adam, *Memoirs*, London 1888

Damas d'Antigny, J. E. R., *Mémoires du Comte Roger de Damas*, Paris 1912

Dashkova, E. R., *The Memoirs of Princess Dashkov*, ed and trans Kyril Fitzlyon, London 1958

Deboli, Augustyn, Secret despatches to King Stanislas-Augustus of Poland, AGAD 420–1

Derzhavin, G. R., Letters to V. S. Popov, Reshetilovskiy Archive

Derzhavin, G. R., *Sobraniye sochineniya*, St Petersburg 1864–72

Derzhavin, G. R., *Works*, Moscow 1985

Diderot, Denis, *Mémoires pour Catherine II*, ed P. Vernière, Paris 1966

Diderot, Denis, *Oeuvres complètes*, ed J. Assezat and M. Tourneux, Paris 1875–7

Dimsdale, Baroness Elisabeth, *An English Lady at the Court of Catherine the*

Great: the Journal of Baroness Elisabeth Dimsdale 1781 (ed. Anthony Cross), Cambridge 1989

Dmitrenko, I. I. (ed), SIMPIK KV, St Petersburg 1896

Dolgoruky, Yury Vladimirovich, *Notes (Zapiski)*, RS (1889) no 9, pp 481–517

Dubrovin, N. F. (ed), *Prisoyedineniye Kryma k Rossii (reskripty, pisma, relatsii, doneseniya)*, St Petersburg 1885–9

Economic Descriptions of Russian towns, Nikolaev, Kherson etc, RGADA f 1355

Engelhardt, L. N., *Zapiski 1766–1836*, Moscow 1868 and (ed I. I. Fedyukin) 1997

Erenstrum, John-Albert, Historical Notes, RS (1893)

Esterhazy, Valentin Ladislas, *Nouvelles Lettres du Comte Valentin L. Esterhazy à sa femme 1792–95*, ed Ernest Daudet, Paris 1909

Faleev, M. L., Reports to Potemkin, ZOOID 8, 13

Family information about Prince Potemkin, RS (1872) 5

Frederick II the Great, King of Prussia, Letters to Potemkin, RGIA, St Petersburg ff 1640–1

Frederick II the Great, King of Prussia, *Politische Correspondenz*, Berlin 1879–1939

Garnovsky, M., *Zapiski Mikhaila Garnovskago*, 1786–90, RS (1876) 15, 16, 17

Glinka, S. N., *Novoye sobraniye russkikh anekdotov*, Moscow 1829

Glinka, S. N., *Russkiye chteniya, izdavaemye Sergeem Glinkoyu, otechestvennye istoricheskiy pamyatniki XVIII i XIX stoleiya*, St Petersburg 1845

Glinka, S. N., *Zapiski*, St Petersburg 1895

Goertz, J. E. von der, *Mémoire sur la Russie*, ed W. Stribrny, Wiesbaden 1969

Golovina, V. N., *Zapiski grafini Golovinoy*, ed S. Shumigorsky, St Petersburg 1900; *Souvenirs*, Paris 1910; *Memoirs*, London 1910

Gribovsky, A. M., *Notes on Catherine the Great*, Moscow 1864

Gribovsky A. M., *Vospominaniya i dnevnkik Adriana Moiseevicha Gribovskago*, RA (1899) 1

Guthrie, Maria, *A Tour performed in the years 1795–6 through the Taurida or Crimea*, London 1802

Harris, James, *Diaries and Correspondence of James Harris, 1st Earl of Malmesbury*, London 1844

Helbig, Georg von, *Ein interessanter betirang zur Regierungsgeschichte Katarina der Zweiten*, Leipzig 1804

Helbig, Georg von, Potemkin der Taurier. Anecdoten zur Geschichte seines Lebens und seiner Zeit, *Minerva, ein Journal historischen und politischen Inhalts herausgegeben von J. M. von Archenholtz*, Hamburg 1797–1800

Helbig, Georg von, *Russische Günstlinge*, Berlin 1917

Helbig, Georg von, 'Russkie izbrannye i sluchainye liudi', RS 56 (10) 1887

Hercules II (Herakles, Irakli), King/Tsar of Kartli-Kahetia (Georgia), Letters to Potemkin, RGVIA f 52. VI (1983) no 7

Howard, J., *The State of Prisons in England and Wales with preliminary observations and an account of some foreign prisons and hospitals*, London 1792

Iona (Jonah), Metropolitan, Description of Potemkin's last days,
ZOOID 3

Joseph II, Holy Roman Emperor
Letters to Potemkin, RGVIA f 52
Joseph II, Leopold II und Kaunitz. Ihr Briefwechsel, ed A. Beer, Vienna 1873
Joseph II und Katharina von Russland. Ihr Briefwechsel, ed Alfred Ritter von
Arneth, Vienna 1869
Maria Theresa und Joseph II. Ihre Correspondenz, ed Alfred Ritter von Arneth,
Vienna 1867
*Joseph II und Graf Ludwig Cobenzl. Ihr Briefwechsel, fontes rerum
austriacarum,* ed A. Beer and J. Fiedler, Vienna 1873
Joseph II und Leopold von Toscana. Ihr Briefwechsel 1781 bis 1790 ed. Alfred
Ritter von Arneth, Vienna 1872
Keith, Sir Robert Murray, *Memoirs and Correspondence,* London 1849
Khrapovitsky, A. V., *Dnevnik 1782–93,* St Petersburg 1874 and Moscow 1901
Korsakov, N. I., Letters and reports to Potemkin, RGVIA f 52
Langeron, Alexandre, Comte de, AAE, Quai d'Orsay, Paris
  Des armées russes et turques
  *Détails sur la composition et l'organisation des armées turques et sur la
    manière actuelle des russes de faire la guerre*
  *Journal de campagnes faites au service de Russie par le comte de Langeron:
    résumé de campagnes de 1787, 1788, 1789 des russes contre les turcs en
    Bessarabie, en Moldavie and dans le Kouban*
  Deuxième campagne en Bessarabie et en Moldavie en 1790
  Evénements politique de l'hiver de 1790–1791 en Russie et fêtes de Petersburg
  *Troisième campagne en Moldavie et en Bulgarie 1791 – événements de la
    campagne en 1791 des russies contre les turcs*
Lanskoy, A. D., Letters to Potemkin, RGADA f 11
Leopold II, Holy Roman Emperor, *Letters to Potemkin,* RGVIA f 52
*Leopold II, Franz II und Katharina, ihre correspondenz, nebst eine einleitung
  zur geschichte der politik Leopold II,* ed A. Beer, Leipzig 1874
Ligne, C. J. E., Prince de, *Fragments des mémoires de prince de Ligne,* Paris
  1880
Ligne, C. J. E., Prince de, *Letters and Reflections of the Austrian Field Marshal,*
  ed Baroness de Staël-Holstein, Philadelphia 1809
Ligne, C. J. E., Prince de, Letters to Potemkin, RGVIA f 52 and RGADA 11
Ligne, C. J. E., Prince de, *Les Lettres de Catherine II au prince de Ligne, 1780–
  96,* Brussels/Paris 1924
Ligne, C. J. E., Prince de, *Lettres du prince de Ligne à la marquise de Coigny
  pendant l'année 1787,* ed M. de Lescure, Paris 1886
Ligne, C. J. E., Prince de, *Lettres et pensées,* London 1808
Ligne, C. J. E., Prince de, *Mélanges militaires, littéraires et sentimentaires,*
  Dresden 1795–1811

Ligne, C. J. E., Prince de, *Mémoires et mélanges historiques et littéraires*, Paris 1827–9

Louis XVI and the Comte de Vergennes: correspondence, ed J. Hardman and M. Price, Studies on Voltaire and the Eighteenth Century, Voltaire Foundation, Oxford 1998

Macartney, George, Earl, *An Account of Russia in 1767*, London 1768

Malachowski, S., *Pamietniki Stanislawa hr. Nalecz Malachowskiego wyd. Wincenty hr. Los*, Poznan 1885

Mamonov, A. D. Dmitriyev-, Letters to Potemkin, RGADA f 11 and RGIA

Maria Theresa, Empress–Queen, *Maria Theresias letzte Regierungszeit, 1763–80*, ed Alfred Ritter von Arneth, Vienna 1879

Masson, Charles François Philibert, *Secret Memoirs of the Court of Petersburg*, London 1800

Ministerstvo imperatorskago dvora, kamer-fureskiy tseremonialnyy zhurnal 1762–96, St Petersburg 1853–96

Miranda, Francisco de, *Archivo del General Miranda*, 1785–7, Caracas 1929

Mniszech, Urszula, *Listy pani mniszchowej zony marszalka w. koronnego, in, rocznik towarzystwa historyczno literackiego*, Paris 1866

Murzakevich, N., *Report on Gravestone Monuments of Kherson Fortress Church*, ZOOID 9 (1874)

Niemcewicz, Julian Ursyn, *Pamietniki czasow moich*, Paris 1848

Oginski, Michel, *Mémoires sur la Pologne et les Polonais*, Paris and Geneva 1826

Orlov-Chesmensky, A. G., Letters to Potemkin, RA vol 2, St Petersburg 1876

Orlov-Chesmensky, A. G., Tayna pisma Alexyey Orlova iz Ropshi. ed O. A. Ivanov, *Moskovskiy zhurnal* (1995) nos 9–12, (1996) nos 1–3

Panin, N. I., Letters to P. I. Panin etc, SIRIO 6

Panin, P. I., Letters to N. I. Panin, RA vol 2, 1876

Parelo, Marquis de, Despatches, SIRIO 26 (1879): 306–16

Parkinson, John, *A Tour of Russia, Siberia and the Crimea 1792–1794*, ed William Collier, London 1971

Paul I, Emperor of Russia (Grand Duke Paul Petrovich and Grand Duchess Maria Fyodorovna), Letters to Potemkin, RGADA f 5 and RS (1873) 9, 12

Pishchevich, A. A., *Zhizn A. S. Pishchevicha 1764–1805*, Moscow 1885

Pole Carew, Sir Reginald, Unpublished archives on Russia, CO/r-2; CAD 50; CO/r/3/92, 93, 95, 101, 195, 210

Poniatowski, Prince Stanislas (nephew of King of Poland), *Pamietniki synowca Stanislawa Augusta przekl*, ed Jerzy Lojek, Instytut wydawniczy pax, Warsaw 1979

Popov, V. S., Papers, Reshetilovskiy estate archive, RA (1865 and 1878) (including Popov's reports to Catherine II on Potemkin's death)

Popov, V. S., Papers and letters to various recipients, including Catherine II, Potemkin and A. A. Bezborodko, RGADA f 11, ZOOID 8, RGVIA f 52

G. A. Potemkin-Tavrichesky: Selected Documents

Service record of father A. V. Potemkin, RGADA f 286. Spisok voennym chinam 1-oy poloviny 18go stoletiya SeA vii 1895

Genealogy, *Istochnik* (1995) no 1, (RGADA f 286)

Heraldic Office war record, *Geroldmeysterskaya contora*, book 890, RGADA f 268

Pisma Potemkina, ZOOID Odessa 1844–1956

Accounts details, RGIA ff 468, 1374, 602, 1285, 899, 1640, 1088, 899, 1146

Accounts details, GARF 9

Ekaterina i Potemkin: podlinaya ikh perepiska 1782–91, RS (1876) 16

Personal Papers, RGADA f 11 (various letters from unknown women), RS (April 1875) 12

Papers of the Chancellery of Potemkin, RGVIA f 52

Letters to:

A. A. Bezborodko, RGADA f 11 and ZOOID 8 and RA (1873) no 9 (originals in archive of family of S. V. Kochubey in village of Dikanka, Poltava Region)

A. V. Branicka, RGADA f 11 d 857

Brzojovsky, assessor of Smila, RGVIA f 5

Ya. I. Bulgakov, ZOOID 8, SBVIM vol 8 and RGVIA f 52

Catherine II on Georgia, VI (1983) no 7; general and personal AVPRI, ff 1, 2, 5, RGADA ff 1, 16, 5, RGVIA f 52; on Ismail to Catherine and others RV (1841) vol 8; on Poland, RA (1874) 2

Varvara Engelhardt, in M. I. Semevsky, *Grigory Alexandrovich Potemkin-Tavrichesky*, RS (1875) 3

M. L. Faleev, ZOOID 2, 4, 8

Prince Henry of Prussia, RGADA f 5

S. Lazhkarev and I. S. Barozzi, ZOOID 8, RA (1884) 2

I. V. Loginov, *Istochnik*, (1995) no 6, Moscow

N. V. Repnin, RV (1841) vol 8, ZOOID 8

P. A. Rumiantsev-Zadunaisky, SBVIM vols 4, 6

King Stanislav-Augustus of Poland, 1764–1779, AGAD 172, RGADA ff 5, 11, RGVIA f 52

A. V. Suvorov, RS (May 1875) 13; (1839) 9. AKV 2 (1790); SD vol 2 and KD vol 1 (1791); RA (1877) 10. RGVIA f 52 op 1 d 586; SBVIM vol 4

P. I. Panin, RGADA f 1274, RA (1876) 2

Paul I (Grand Duke Paul Petrovich), RS (1873) 11, 12

V. S. Popov, concerning government and personal affairs, 'Prince G. A. Potemkin-Tavrichesky's own personal papers', Reshetilovskiy archive

Praskovia A. Potemkina 1789–90, RS (June 1875) 13

Various (including reports on town building to Catherine II and officials), ZOOID 2, 4, 8, 10, 11, 12, 13, 15, 1872. Orders to officials on building of Kherson and southern development, ZOOID 11 and ITUAK 3, 8, 10.

RGADA ff 14, 16, and ZOOID 2. Orders of Most Serene Prince G. A. Potemkin-Tavrichesky regarding foundation of Tavrichesky Region 1781–6, M. S. Vorontsov's Family Archive, AKV 13. To provincial governors, GAOO f 150, particularly on Crimea GIM OPI f 197. Also OOIKM dd 651, 7, 652

Various foreign royalty (including Frederick William, Duke of Württemberg; Charles, Prince of Courland; the Prince of Anhalt-Bernburg; Prince of Hesse-Philipstal; Margrave of Anspach), RGADA f 5

Knyaz Grigory Alexandrovich Potemkin-Tavrichesky 1739–91, biograficheskiy ocherk po neizdannym materialam, RS (1875)

Rasporyazheniya svetleyshego knyazya Grigoriya Alexandrovicha Potemkina-Tavricheskogo kasatelno tavricheskoy oblasti s 1781 po 1786, ZOOID 1881

Sobstvennoruchnyye bumagi Knyazya Potemkina, RA (1865)

Proposals and orders concerning the Kremlin Armoury, RGADA f 396

Poetry on foundation of Ekaterinoslav, ed G. Vernadsky, ITUAK (1919) no 56

Contents of Potemkin's library, RGADA f 17 d 262; original at Kazan University

Announcement of fall of Ismail, GAOO f 150

Register of debts, RGADA f 11, ZOOID 8, 9

G. A. Potemkin-Tavrichesky: Books

Lettres d'amour de Catherine II à Potemkine: correspondence inédite, ed Georges Ouvrard, Paris 1934

Ekaterina II i G. A. Potemkin, lichnaya perepiska 1769–1791, ed V. S. Lopatin, Moscow 1997

Perepiska Ekaterina II i G. A. Potemkina v period vtoroy russko-turetskoy voiny (1787–1791): istochnkovedcheskiye issledovaniya, ed O. I. Yeliseva, Moscow 1997

Bumagi Knyaza Grigoriya Alexandrovicha Potemkina-Tavricheskogo, ed N. F. Dubrovin, SBVIM, 1774–88 and 1790–3, St Petersburg 1893 and 1895

Pisma i bumagi A. V. Suvorova, G. A. Potemkina, i P. A. Rumiantseva 1787–1789 kinburn ochakovskaya operatsiya, ed D. F. Maslovsky, SBVIM, St Petersburg 1893

Sbornik istoricheskikh materialov po istorii kubanskogo kazachego voyska, 1737–1801, ed I. I. Dmitrenko, St Petersburg 1896

Radishchev, A. N., *A Journey from St Petersburg to Moscow,* trans Leo Wiener, ed Roderick Page Thaler, Cambridge, Mass. 1958

Ribas, José de, Letters to Potemkin, ZOOID 8, 11

Ribeaupierre, A. I. *Mémoires (Zapiski grafa Ribopera),* RA (1877) vol 1

Richardson, William, *Anecdotes of the Russian Empire,* London 1784 and 1968

Richelieu, Armand du Plessis, Duc de, *Journal de mon voyage en Allemagne,* SIRIO 54 (1886): 111–98

Rostopchin, Fyodor, *La Verité sur l'incendie de Moscou*, Paris 1823

Ruhlière, Claude Carloman de, *A History or Anecdotes of the Revolution in Russia*, London 1797, New York, 1970

Rumiantsev-Zadunaisky, P. A., Letters to Potemkin RGADA f 11 and SBVIM vol 4

Rumiantseva, E. M., *Pisma grafini E. M. Rumiantsevoy k ee muzhu feldmarshalu grafu P. A. Rumiatsevu-Zadunayskomu, 1762–1779*, St Petersburg 1888

Sabatier de Cabre, *Catherine II, her Court and Russia in 1772*, Berlin 1861

Saint-Jean, Sekretär des Fürsten Potemkin, *Lebensbeschreibung des Gregor Alexandrowitsch Potemkin des Tauriers*, Karlsruhe 1888

Samoilov, A. N., *Zhizn i deyaniya generala feldmarshala knyazya Grigoriya Alexandrovicha Potemkina-Tavricheskogo*, RA (1867)

Ségur, Louis Philippe, Comte de, Letters to Potemkin, RGVIA f 52, ZOOID 9

Ségur, Louis Philippe, Comte de, *Mémoires et souvenirs et anecdotes*, Paris, 1859

Ségur, Louis Philippe, Comte de, *Memoirs and Recollections of Count Ségur, ambassador from France to the Courts of Russia and Prussia etc, written by himself*, London 1825–7

Ségur, Louis Philippe, Comte de, *Memoirs of Louis Philippe Comte de Ségur*, ed Eveline Cruikshanks, London 1960

Ségur, Louis Philippe, Comte de, *Memoirs of the Comte de Ségur*, ed Gerard Shelley, New York 1925

Ségur, Louis Philippe, Comte de, *Oeuvres complètes de Monsieur le comte de Ségur, Mémoires et souvenirs et anecdotes*, Paris 1824–6

Shcherbatov, M. M., *On the Corruption of Morals in Russia*, ed and trans A. Lentin, Cambridge 1969

Stanislas II Augustus, King of Poland

Letters to Potemkin, RGADA f 5, AGAD 172, RGVIA f 52

Mémoires du roi Stanislas-Auguste Poniatowski, St Petersburg 1914, Leningrad 1924

Mémoires secrètes et inédites de Stanislas-Auguste, Leipzig 1862

Stedingk, Curt Bogislaus Christophe, Comte de, *Un Ambassadeur de Suède à la cour de Catherine II; feld-maréchal comte de Stedingk; choix de dépêches diplomatique, rapports secrets and lettres particulières de 1790 à 1796*, ed Comtesse de Brevern de la Gardie, Stockholm 1919

Sumarokov, P. I., *Cherty Ekateriny velikoy*, St Petersburg 1819

Sumarokov, P. I., *Travelling through all the Crimea and Bessarabia 1799*, Moscow 1800

Sutherland, Baron Richard, Letters to Potemkin, RGADA f 11, RGVIA f 52

Suvorov, A. V., *Dokumenty*, ed G. P. Meshcheryakov, Moscow 1949–53

Suvorov, A. V., *Pisma*, ed V. S. Lopatin, Moscow 1986

Suvorov, A. V., *Pisma i bumagi A. V. Suvorova, G. A. Potemkina, i P. A. Rumiantseva 1787–1789, kinburn ochakovskaya operatsiya*, D. F. Maslovsky, SBVIM, St Petersburg 1893

Suvorov, A. V., *Pisma i bumagi Suvorova*, ed V. Alekseyev, Petrograd 1916

Thiébault, D., *Mes souvenirs de vingt ans séjour à Berlin*, Paris 1804

Tott, Baron de, *Memoirs of the Turks and the Tartars*, London 1786

Tregubov, N. Y., *Zapiski*, RS (1908) 136 pp 101–2

Tsebrikov, R. M., *Vokrug ochakova 1788 god (dnevnikochevidtsa)*, RA (1895) 84, no 9

Vigée Lebrun, Elisabeth, *Souvenirs*, Paris 1879

Vinsky, G. S., *Moe vremya, Zapiski*, St Petersburg 1914 and Cambridge Partners 1974

Vizin, D. I. von, *Sobraniye sochineniya*, ed G. P. Makogonenko, Moscow/Leningrad 1959

Vorontsov, S. R., Letters to Potemkin, AKV 9

Voltaire, *Oeuvres complètes de Voltaire: correspondance avec l'imperatrice de Russie*, vol lviii, Paris 1821

Wills, Richard, *A Short Account of the Ancient and Modern State of the Crim-Tartary Land*, London 1787

Wiegel (Vigel), F. F., *Zapiski Filipa Filipovich Vigela*, Moscow 1873, 1891 and 1928; *Vospominaniya F. F. Vigela*, Moscow 1864–6 and 1891

Wraxall, N., *A Tour through Some of the Northern Parts of Europe*, London 1776

Wraxall, Sir N. William, *Historical Memoirs of my own Time*, London 1904

Yusupov, Prince Felix, *Lost Splendour*, London 1953

Zavadovsky, P. V., 'Pisma grafa P. V. Zavadovskago k feldmarshalu grafu P. A. Rumiantsevu 1775–1791', ed P. M. Maykov, *Starina i novizna* (1901) vol 4

SECONDARY

Adamczyk, T., *Fürst G. A. Potemkin: Untersuchungen zu seiner Lebensgeschichte*, Emsdetten 1936

Alden, John R, *Stephen Sayre, American Revolutionary Adventurer*, Baton Rouge 1983

Alexander, J. T., *Autocratic Politics in a National Crisis: The Imperial Russian Government and Pugachev's Revolt 1773–1775*, Bloomington 1969

Alexander, J. T., *Catherine the Great: Life and Legend*, Oxford 1989

Alexander, J. T., *Emperor of the Cossacks: Pugachev and the Frontier Jacquerie of 1773–75*, Lawrence 1973

Alexeeva, T. V., *Vladimir Lukich Borovikovskii i russkaia kultura na rubezhe 18–19 vekov*, Moscow 1875

Allen, W. E. D., *A History of the Georgian People*, London 1932

Anderson, M. S., *The Eastern Question 1774–1923*, New York 1966

Anderson, M. S., *Europe in the Eighteenth Century 1713–83*, London 1961

Anderson, M. S., 'Samuel Bentham in Russia 1779–91', *American Slavic and East European Review* (1956) 15 no 2

Anderson, R. C., *Naval Wars in the Levant*, London 1952

Andreevsky, I., *On the Place Where Potemkin's Body was Buried*, ZOOID 5

Anisimov, E. V., *Empress Elisabeth: Her Reign and Her Russia 1741–61*, ed J. T. Alexander, Gulf Freeze, Fla 1995

Anisimov, E. V., *Rossiya v seredine xviii vek; borba za nasledie petra*, Moscow 1986

Anisimov, E. V., *Zhenshchina na rossiyskom prestole*, St Petersburg 1997

Annenkov, I., *History of the Cavalry Guards Regiment 1738–1848*, St Petersburg 1849

Anonymous, *Persons on the staff of Prince Potemkin*, ZOOID 11: 506–8

Anonymous, *Potemkin's household and staff*, RA (1907) 2

Anonymous, 'A Short Biography of Anton Golovaty', *Odessky vestnick*, 31 October 1995

Aragon, L. A. C., Marquis d', *Un Paladin au XVIII siècle. Le Prince Charles de Nassau-Siegen*, Paris 1893

Aretz, Gertrude, *The Empress Catherine*, London 1947

Ascherson, Neal, *Black Sea: The Birthplace of Civilisation and Barbarism*, London 1996

Askenazy, S., *Die letzte polnische Königswahl*, Göttingen 1894

Asprey, Robert B., *Frederick the Great: The Magnificent Enigma*, New York 1986

Ayling, Stanley, *Fox: The Life of Charles James Fox*, London 1991

Baddeley, John F., *The Russian Conquest of the Caucasus*, London 1908

Bain, R. Nisbet, *Peter III: Emperor of Russia*, London 1902

Baron, S. W., *The Russian Jew under Tsar and Soviets*, New York 1964

Barsukov, A. R., *Razskazy iz russkoi istorii xviii veka*, St Petersburg 1885

Barsukov, A. R., *Knyaz Grigory Grigorevich Orlov*, RA (1873) vols 1–2

Bartenev, P. B., 'Biografi generalissimov i general-feld-marshalov Rossiyskoy Imperatorskoy armii', *Voenno-istoricheskiy sbornik*, St Petersburg 1911

Bartenev, P. B., *On Catherine and Potemkin's Marriage: a Book of Notes of the Russki Arkhiv*, RA (1906) no 12

Bartlett, Roger P., *Human Capital: The settlement of foreigners in Russia 1762–1804*, Cambridge 1979

Batalden, Stephen K., *Catherine II's Greek Prelate: Eugenios Voulgaris in Russia 1771–1806*, New York 1982

Baylen, Joseph A. and Woodward, Dorothy, 'Francisco Miranda and Russia: Diplomacy 1787–88', *Historian* xiii (1950)

Beales, Derek, *Joseph II: In the Shadow of Maria Theresa 1741–80*, Cambridge 1987

Begunova, A., *Way through the Centuries*, Moscow 1988

Belan, Yu. Ia., Marchenko, M. I., and Kotov, V. N., *Istoria USSR*, Kiev 1949

Belyakova, Zoia, *The Romanov Legacy: The Palaces of St Petersburg*, London 1994

Bennigsen Broxup, Maria (ed), *The North Caucasus Barrier: the Russian Advance towards the Moslem World*, London 1992

Bentham, M. S., *The Life of Brigadier-General Sir Samuel Bentham*, London 1862

Bilbasov, V. A., *Prisoedineniye Kulyandii k Rossii*, RS (1895) 83

Bilbasov, V. A., *Istoricheskiye Monografia*, St Petersburg 1901

Bilbasov, V. A., *Istoriya Ekateriny II*, Berlin 1900

Blanning, T. C. W., *Joseph II and Enlightened Despotism*, London 1970

Blanning, T. C. W., *Joseph II: Profiles in Power*, London 1994

Blum, K. L., *Ein russischer Staatsmann: Des Grafen Jakob Johann Sievers Denkwürdigkeiten zur Geschichte Russlands*, Lepizig/Heidelberg 1857

Bolotina, N. Y., *Degree thesis on Potemkin's work in the south*, RSUH, Moscow 1991

Bolotina, N. Y., 'Grigory Alexandrovich Potemkin', *Children's Encyclopaedia*, Moscow 1996

Bolotina, N. Y., 'The Private Library of Prince G. A. Potemkin-Tavrichesky', *Kniga issledovaniya i materialy* (1995) no 71

Bolotina, N. Y., *Sebastopol has to be the main fortress: documents on the foundation of the Black Sea fleet*, Istoricheskiy arkhiv (1997) no 2

Bolotina, N. Y., *Ties of Relationship between G. A. Potemkin and the Vorontsov Family: The Vorontsovs – two centuries in Russian History*, Petushki 1996

Bolotina, N. Y., *Ties of Relationship between Prince G. A. Potemkin and the Family of the Princes Golitsyn, Conference of Golitsyn Studies*, Bolshiye vyazemy, Moscow 1997

Bolshoya Sovetskaya Enziklopediya, Moscow 1940

Browning, Reed, *The War of Austrian Succession*, London 1994

Bruess, Gregory I., *Religion, Identity and Empire: A Greek Archbishop in the Russia of Catherine the Great*, New York 1997

Brückner, A. G., *Istoriia Ekateriny vtoroi*, St Petersburg 1885; and *Katharina der zweite*, Berlin 1883

Brückner, A. G., *Potemkin*, St Petersburg 1891

Bugomila, Alexander, *The History of Government of New Russia by G. A. Potemkin*, Ekaterinoslav 1905

Byron, Lord, *Don Juan*, Penguin Classics, London 1977

Castera, Jean-Henri, *The Life of Catherine II, Empress of Russia*, trans William Tooke, London 1798

Cate, Curtis, *War of the Two Emperors: The duel between Napoleon and Alexander, Russia 1812*, New York 1985

Christie, I. R., *The Benthams in Russia*, Oxford/Providence 1993

Christie, I. R., 'Samuel Bentham and the Russian Dnieper Flotilla', SEER (April 1972) 50 no 119

Christie, I. R., 'Samuel Bentham and the Western Colony at Krichev 1784–7', SEER (April 1970) 48 no 111

Clardy, Jesse V., *G. R. Derzhavin: A Political Biography*, Mouton 1967

Coughlan, Robert, *Elisabeth and Catherine, Empresses of All the Russias*, New York 1974

Crankshaw, Edward, *Maria Theresa*, London 1969

Cronin, Vincent, *Catherine, Empress of All the Russias*, London 1978

Cross, Anthony, *By the Banks of the Neva: Chapters from the Lives and Careers of the British in Eighteenth-Century Russia*, Cambridge 1997

Cross, Anthony, *By the Banks of the Thames: Russians in Eighteenth Century Britain*, Newtonville, Mass. 1980

Cross, Anthony, 'The Duchess of Kingston in Russia', *History Today* (1977) 27

Cross, Anthony (ed), *Great Britain and Russia in the Eighteenth Century: Contacts and Comparisons, Proceedings of an International Conference*, Newtonville, Mass. 1979

Cross, Anthony, 'John Rogerson: Physician to Catherine the Great', CSS (1970) 4

Davies, Norman, *Europe: A history*, Oxford 1996

Davis, Curtis Carroll, *The King's Chevalier: A Biography of Lewis Littlepage*, Indianopolis 1961

Demmler, Franz, *Memoirs of the Court of Prussia*, London 1854

Dmitrenko, I. I., ed, *Sbornik istoricheskikh materialov po istorii kazacheskogo voyska 1737–1901* St Petersburg, 1896

Dornberg, John, *Brezhnev*, London 1974

Dostyan, I. S., *Russia and the Balkan Question*, Moscow 1972

Druzhinina, E. I., *Kyuchuk-Kaynardzhiyskiy mir 1774 goda*, Moscow 1955

Druzhinina, E. I., *Severnoye prichernomorye v 1775–1800*, Moscow 1959

Dubnow, S. M., *History of the Jews in Russia and Poland*, Philadelphia 1916–20

Dubrovin, N. F. ed, *Istoriya voyny i vladychestva russkih na Kavkaze*, St Petersburg 1886

Dubrovin, N. F., *Pugachev i ego soobshchniki*, St Petersburg 1884

Duffy, Christopher, *Frederick the Great: A Military Life*, London 1985

Duffy, Christopher, *Russia's Military Way to the West: Origins and Nature of Russian Military Power 1700–1800*, London 1981

Dukes, Paul, *Catherine the Great and the Russian Nobility: A Study Based on the Materials of the Legislative Commission of 1767*, Cambridge 1967

Dulichev, V. P., *Raskazy po istorii Kryma*, Simferopol 1997

Dumas, F. Ribadeau, *Cagliostro*, London 1967

Duran, James A., 'Catherine, Potemkin and Colonization', *Russian Review* (January 1969) 28 no 1

Duran, James A., 'The Reform of Financial Administration in Russia during the Reign of Catherine II', CSS (1970) 4

Dvoichenko-Markov, Demetrius, 'Russia and the First Accredited Diplomat in the Danubian Principalities 1779–1808', *Slavic and East European Studies* (1963) 8

Dyachenko, L. I., *Tavricheski Dvorets*, St Petersburg 1997

Dzhedzhula, K. E., *Rossiya i velikaya Frantzuzskaya burzhuaznaya revolyutsiya kontsa XVIII veka*, Kiev 1972

Ehrman, John, *The Younger Pitt*, vol 2: *The Reluctant Transition*, London 1983

Eighteenth Century Studies in Honor of Donald F. Hyde, New York 1970

Elliott, J. H., *The Count-Duke of Olivares: The Statesman in an Age of Decline*, New Haven/London 1986

Elliott, J. H., and Brockliss, L. W. B., *The World of the Favourite*, New Haven/London 1999

Fadyev, V., *Vospominaniya 1790–1867*, Odessa 1897

Fateyev, A. M., *Potemkin-Tavrichesky*, Prague 1945

Feldman, Dmitri, *Svetleyshiy Knyaz G. A. Potemkin i Rossiskiye Evrei*. Materials of the Seventh International Conference on Jews, Moscow 2000.

Figes, Orlando, *A People's Tragedy: The Russian Revolution 1891–1924*, London 1996

Figes, Orlando, and Kolonitskii, Boris, *Interpreting the Russian Revolution: The Language and Symbols of 1917*, New Haven/London 1999

Fisher, Alan W., *The Crimean Tartars*, Studies in Nationalities of USSR, Stanford 1978

Fisher, Alan W., 'Enlightened Despotism and Islam under Catherine II', *Slavic Review* (1968) 27

Fisher, Alan W., *The Russian Annexation of the Crimea 1772–83*, Cambridge 1970

Fishman, David E., *Russia's First Modern Jews, The Jews of Shklov*, New York London 1996

Foreman, Amanda, *Georgiana, Duchess of Devonshire*, London 1998

Fothergill, Brian, *Sir William Hamilton, Envoy Extraordinary*, London 1969

Fournier-Sarloveze, M., *Artistes oubliés*, Paris 1902

Fox, Frank, 'Negotiating with the Russians: Ambassador Ségur's Mission to St Petersburg 1784–89', *French Historical Studies* (1971) 7

Fraser, David, *Frederick the Great*, London 2000

Fuks, E. B., *Istoria generalissimusa knyazia italikogo graf Suvorova-Rymniksogo*, Moscow 1811

Garrard, J. G. (ed), *The Eighteenth Century in Russia*, Oxford 1973

Gay, Peter, *The Enlightenment: An Interpretation, the Science of Freedom*, London 1969

Ghani, Cyrus, *Iran and the Rise of Reza Shah – Qajar Collapse to Pahlavi Power*, London/New York 1999

Gilbert, O. P., *The Prince de Ligne: A Gay Marshal of the Old Regime*, London 1923

Golder, Frank, *John Paul Jones in Russia*, Garden City, NY 1927

Golitsyn, Prince Emmanuel, *Récit du voyage de Pierre Potemkin: la Russie du XVII siècle dans ses rapports avec l'Europe Occidentale*, Paris 1855

Goncharenko, V. S., and Narozhnaya, V. I., *The Armoury, State Museum Preserve of History and Culture, the Kremlin: A Guide*, Moscow 1995

Gooden, Angelica, *The Sweetness of Light: A Biography of Elisabeth Vigée Lebrun*, London 1997

Goodwin, Frederick K., and Jamison, Kay Redfield, *Manic-Depressive Illness*, Oxford 1990

Grahov, J., *Potemkin's Military Printing House*, ZOOID 4, 1855

Grave, B., *Vosstaniye Pugacheva*, Leningrad 1936

Greenberg, Louis, *The Jews in Russia*, vol 1: *The Struggle for Emancipation*, New Haven 1944

Gribble, Francis, *The Comedy of Catherine the Great*, London 1932

Griffiths, David M., 'The Rise and Fall of the Northern System: Court Politics in the First Half of Catherine's Reign', CSS (1970) pp 547–69

Grigorevich, N., *Kantsler knyaz A. A. Bezborodko v svyazi s sobytiyami ego vremeni*, SIRIO 26 and 29

Grob, G. N. (ed), *Statesmen and Statecraft of the Modern West: Essays in Honor of Dwight E. Lee and H. Donaldson Jordan*, Barr, Mass. 1967

Grundy, Isobel, *Lady Mary Wortley Montagu: Comet of the Enlightenment*, Oxford 1999

Harvey, Robert, *Clive: The Life and Death of a British Emperor*, London 1998

Haupt, G., 'La Russie et les Principautés Danubiennes en 1790: Le Prince Potemkin-Tavrichesky et le Courrier de Moldavie', CMRS (January–March 1966) 7 no 1

Herodotus, *The Histories*, Penguin Classics, London 1954

Horwood, D. D. (ed), *Proceedings of the Consortium on Revolutionary Europe*, Tallahassee 1980

Hosking, Geoffrey, *Russia: People and Empire 1552–1917*, London 1997

Hughes, Lindsey, *Russia in the Age of Peter the Great*, New Haven/London 1998

Iorga, N., *Histories des relations Russo-Roumaines*, Iaşi, 1917

Istoriia SSSR, s drevnyeyshikh vremen do kontsa XVIII v. (various authors), Moscow 1939

Ivanov, P. A., *Fabre's Summer Residence*, ZOOID 22

Ivanov, P. A., *The Management of Jewish Immigration from Abroad to the Novorossisky Region*, Ekaterinoslav archives, ZOOID 17

Jamison, Kay Redfield, *The Unquiet Mind*, London 1996

Jenkins, Michael, *Arakcheev, Grand Vizier of the Russian Empire*, New York 1969

Jones, Robert E., *Provincial Development in Russia: Catherine II and Jakov Sievers*, New Brunswick 1984

Jones, Robert E., 'Urban Planning and the Development of Provincial Towns in Russia 1762–96', in J. G. Garrard (ed), *The Eighteenth Century in Russia*, Oxford 1973

Josselson, Michael, and Josselson, Diana, *The Commander: A Life of Barclay de Tolly*, Oxford 1980

Kabuzan, V. M., *Narodonaseleniye rossii v XVIII-pervoy polovine XIX veka*, Moscow 1976

Karabanov, P. F., *Istoricheskiye rasskazy i anekdoty, zapisannyye so slov imenityh lyudey P. F. Karabanovym*, RS (1872) 5

Karnovich, E. P., *Zamechatchyye bogatstva chastnykh lits v Russii*, Petersburg 1885

Karpova, E. V., *Cultural Monuments, New Discoveries*, Leningrad 1984

Keen, B., and Wasserman, M., *A History of Latin America*, Boston 1998

Keep, John L. H., *Soldiers of the Tsar: Army and Society in Russia 1462–1874*, Oxford 1985

Kelly, Laurence (ed), *Moscow: A Travellers' Companion*, London 1983

Kelly, Laurence (ed), *St Petersburg: A Travellers' Companion*, London 1981

Kinross, Lord, *The Ottoman Centuries: The Rise and Fall of the Turkish Empire*, New York 1979

Klier, John Doyle, *Russia Gathers her Jews: The Origins of the Jewish Question in Russia 1772–1825*, Dekalb, Ill. 1986

Kliuchevsky, V. O., *A Course in Russian History: The Time of Catherine the Great*, trans and ed Marshall S. Shatz, New York 1997

Korolkov, K., *Hundredth Anniversary of the Town of Ekaterinoslav 1781–1887*, Ekaterinoslav, 1887

Korsakov, A. N., 'Stepan Ivanovich Sheshkovsky 1727–94: Biograficheskiy Ocherk', *Storicheskiy vestnik* (1885) 22

Kramer, Gerhard F., and McGrew, Roderick E., 'Potemkin, the Porte and the Road to Tsargrad: The Shumla Negotiations 1789–90', CASS (Winter 1974) 8

Krasnobaev, B. I., *Russian Culture in the Second Part of the Eighteenth Century and at the Start of the Nineteenth*, Moscow 1983

Kruchkov, Y. S., *Istoria Nikolaeva*, Nikolaev 1996

Kukiel, M., *Czartoryski and European Unity 1770–1861*, Princeton Westport, Conn. 1955

Lang, D. M., *The Last Years of the Georgian Monarchy 1658–1832*, New York 1957

Lang, D. M., *A Modern History of Georgia*, London 1962

Lashkov, F. F., *Prince G. A. Potemkin-Tavrichesky as Crimean Builder*, Simferopol 1890

Lavrenev, B. A., 'Potemkin's Second Burial', *Pamyatniki otechestva* (1991) no 2 pp 154–5

Lebedev, P., *Studies of New Russian History from Unpublished Sources*, St Petersburg 1863

LeDonne, John P., *Ruling Russia: Politics and Administration in the Age of Absolutism 1762–96*, Princeton 1984

Lentin, A., *Russia in the Eighteenth Century from Peter the Great to Catherine the Great*, London 1973

Levitats, I., *The Jewish Community in Russia 1722–1844*, New York 1970

Lewis, D. B., Wyndham, *Four Favourites*, London 1948

Lincoln, W. Bruce, *The Romanovs: Autocrats of All the Russias*, New York 1981

Liske, X., 'Zur polnischen Politik Katharina II 1791', HZ (1873) 30

Lockyer, Roger, *Buckingham*, London 1981

Lojek, J., 'Catherine's Armed Intervention in Poland: Origins of the Political Decisions at the Russian Court in 1791 and 1792', CSS (Fall 1970) 4 no 3

Lojek, J., 'The International Crisis of 1791: Poland between the Triple Alliance and Russia', *East Central Europe* (1975) 2 no 1

Longworth, Philip, *The Art of Victory: The Life and Achievements of Field Marshal Suvorov 1729–1800*, New York 1965

Longworth, Philip, *The Cossacks*, London 1969

Longworth, Philip, *The Three Empresses – Catherine I, Anne and Elisabeth of Russia*, London 1972

Lopatin, V. S., *Potemkin i Suvorov*, Moscow 1992

Lord, Robert H., *The Second Partition of Poland*, Cambridge, Mass. 1915

Loudon, J. C., *An Encyclopaedia of Gardening*, London 1822

Louis, Victor and Jennifer, *Complete Guide to the Soviet Union*, New York 1991

Lukowski, Jerzy, *The Partitions of Poland 1772, 1793, 1795*, London 1999

MacConnell, A., *A Russian Philosophe: Alexander Radishchev 1749–1802*, The Hague 1964

MacDonogh, Giles, *Frederick the Great*, London 1999

McGrew, Roderick E., *Paul I of Russia 1754–1801*, Oxford 1992

McKay, Derek, and Scott, H. M., *The Rise of the Great Powers 1648–1815*, London 1983

Mackay, James, *I Have Not Yet Begun to Fight: A Life of John Paul Jones*, Edinburgh/London 1998

McNeill, William H., *Europe's Steppe Frontier 1500–1800*, Chicago 1964

Madariaga, Isabel de, *Britain, Russia and the Armed Neutrality of 1780: Sir James Harris's Mission to St Petersburg during the American Revolution*, New Haven 1962

Madariaga, Isabel de, *Catherine the Great: A Short History*, New Haven/London 1990

Madariaga, Isabel de, *Introduction to G. S. Vinsky, Moe vremya, Zapiski*, Cambridge 1974

Madariaga, Isabel de, *Politics and Culture in Eighteenth-Century Russia: Collected Essays*, London/New York 1998

Madariaga, Isabel de, *Russia in the Age of Catherine the Great*, London 1981

Madariaga, Isabel de, 'The Secret Austro-Russian Treaty of 1781', SEER (1959) 38 pp 114–45

Madariaga, Isabel de, *The Travels of General Francesco de Miranda in Russia*, London 1950

Madariaga, Isabel de, 'The Use of British Secret Service Funds at St Petersburg 1777–1782', SEER (1954) 32 no 79

Mansel, Philip, *Constantinople: City of the World's Desire 1453–1924*, London 1995

Mansel, Philip, *Le Charmeur de l'Europe: Charles-Joseph de Ligne 1735–1814*, Paris 1992

Mansel, Philip, *Louis XVIII*, London 1981

Mansel, Philip, *Pillars of Monarchy*, London 1984

Markova, O. P., *O nevtralnoy sisteme i franko-russkikh otnosheniyakh (Vtoraya polovina xviii v)*, Istoriya SSSR (1970) no 6

Markova, O. P., *O proiskhozhdenii tak nazyvayemogo Grecheskogo Proekta (80e gody XVIII v.)*, Istoriya SSSR (1958) no 4

Maslovsky, D. F., *Zapiski po istorii voiennogo iskusstva v rossii, tsarstvovaniye Ekateriny velikoy 1762–94*, St Petersburg 1894

Massie, Robert, *Peter the Great: His Life and World*, New York 1981

Masters, John, *Casanova*, London 1969

Mavrodin, V. V., *Krestyanskaya voyna v rossiya*, Leningrad 1961, 1966, 1970

Mellikset-Bekov, L., *From the Materials for a History of the Armenians in the South of Russia*, Odessa 1911

Menning, B. W., *G. A. Potemkin and A. I. Chernyshev: Two Dimensions of Reform and the Military Frontier in Imperial Russia* in D. D. Horwood (ed), *Proceedings of the Consortium on Revolutionary Europe*, Tallahassee 1980

Mikhailovich, Grand Duke Nikolai *Russkiye Portrety XVIII i XIX stoletiy*, St Petersburg 1906–9 (republished as *Famous Russians*, St Petersburg 1996)

Mitford, Nancy, *Frederick the Great*, London 1970

Mitford, Nancy, *Madame de Pompadour*, London 1954

Mitford, Nancy, *Voltaire in Love*, London 1957

Mooser, R. Aloys, *Annales de la musique et des musiciens en Russie au XVIII Siècle*, Geneva 1948–51

Morane, P., *Paul I de Russie*, Paris 1907

Morison, Samuel Eliot, *John Paul Jones: A Sailor's Biography*, Boston 1959

Moskvityanin zhurnal, *O privatnoy zhizni Knyazya Potemkina (Potemkinskiy prazdnik)*, (1852) 3, ed M. P. Pogodin, republished Moscow 1991

Moskvityanin zhurnal, *Verbal Chronicle of Catherine's visit to Tula and Potemkin*, (1842) 2

Mourousy, Prince, *Potemkine mystique et conquerant*, Paris 1988

Muftiyzade, I., *Essays on Crimean Tartars' Military Service from 1783–1889*, ITUAK (1889)

Murray, Venetia, *High Society in the Regency Period*, London 1998

Murzakevich, N. N., *The materials for a history of the principal town of a province – Kherson*, ZOOID 11

Nicolson, Harold, *The Congress of Vienna*, London 1948

Nirsha, A. M., *Anton Golovaty*, Odessa State Local Historical Museum

Nolde, B., *La Formation de l'Empire Russe: études, notes et documents*, Paris 1953

Norman, Geraldine, *The Hermitage: The Biography of a Great Museum*, London 1997

Novitsky, G. A., *Istoriya USSR (XVIII vek)*, Moscow 1950

Ogarkov, Vasily V., *Grigory Alexandrovich Potemkin*, St Petersburg 1892

Oldenbourg, Zoë, *Catherine the Great*, London 1965

Orlovsky, I. I., *In the Motherland of His Highness*, Smolensk 1906

Otis, James, *The Life of John Paul Jones, together with Chevalier Jones' own account of the campaign of the Liman*, New York 1900

Palmer, Alan, *Alexander I, Tsar of War and Peace*, London 1974

Palmer, Alan, *Metternich, Councillor of Europe*, London 1972

Palmer, Alan, *Napoleon in Russia*, London 1967

Panchenko, A. M., *Potemkinskie derevni kak kulturlnyy mif, XVIII Vek* (1983) 14

Papmehl, K., 'The Regimental School Established in Siberia by Samuel Bentham', *Canadian Slavonic Papers*, xviii, 1966

Pasteur, Claude, *Le Prince de Ligne: l'enchanteur de l'Europe*, Paris 1957

Petrov, A, *Voyna rossii s turetskiey i polskimi konfederatami*, St Petersburg 1866–74

Petrov, A., *Vtoraya turetskaya voyna v tsarstvovaniye imperatritsy Ekateriny II 1787–91*, St Petersburg 1880

Petrovich, M. B., 'Catherine II and a Fake Peter III in Montenegro', *Slavic Review* (April 1955) 14 no 2

Petrushevsky, A., *Generalissimus Knyazi Suvorov*, St Petersburg 1884

Pevitt, Christine, *The Man Who Would Be King: The Life of Philippe d'Orléans, Regent of France*, London 1997

Pflaum, Rosalynd, *By Influence and Desire: The True Story of Three Extraordinary Women – the Grand Duchess of Courland and her Daughters*, New York 1984

Pikul, V. S., *Favurit: roman-khroniki vremen Ekateriny II, Moscow 1985*

Pilaev, M. I., *Staryy Peterburg*, St Petersburg 1889, Moscow 1997

Pipes, R., 'Catherine II and the Jews', *Soviet Jewish Affairs* 5 no 2

Plumb, J. H., *Sir Robert Walpole*, London 1956

Porphiry, Bishop, *Information about Prince Potemkin's service in the Synod*, Moscow 1882, ZOOID 13

Preedy, George R., *The Life of Rear-Admiral John Paul Jones*, London 1940

Pushkin, A. S., *The Captain's Daughter*, in *The Queen of Spades and Other Stories*, Penguin Classics, London 1958

Pushkin, A. S., *Complete Prose Fiction*, ed Paul Debreczeny, Stanford 1983

Pushkin, A. S., *Istoriya Pugacheva*, in *Polnoye Sobraniye Sochineniya*, vol 12, Moscow/Leningrad, 1937–49

Pushkin, A. S., *Notes on Russian History of the Eighteenth Century*, Istoricheskiye Zametki, Leningrad 1984

Pushkin, A. S., *Polnoye Sobraniye Sochineniya*, Moscow/Leningrad 1937–49

Radzinsky, Edvard, *Rasputin*, London 2000

Raeff, Marc (ed), *Catherine the Great: A Profile*, New York 1972

Raeff, Marc, '*The Style of Russia's Imperial Policy and Prince G. A. Potemkin*', in G. N. Grob (ed), *Statesmen and Statecraft of the Modern West: Essays in Honor of Dwight E. Lee and H. Donaldson Jordan*, Barr, Mass. 1967

Raffel, Burton, *Russian Poetry under the Tsars*, New York 1971

Ragsdale, Hugh (ed), *Imperial Russian Foreign Policy*, Woodrow Wilson Center Series, Cambridge 1993

Rakhamatullin, M. A., *Firm Catherine*, Otechestvennaya Istoriya (1997)

Ransel, David L., 'Nikita Panin's Imperial Council Project and the Struggle of Hierarchy Groups at the Court of Catherine II', CSS (December 1971) 4 no 3

Ransel, David L., *The Politics of Catherinian Russia: The Panin Party*, New Haven 1975

Reid, Anna, *Borderland: A Journey through the History of Ukraine*, London 1997

Rhinelander, Anthony L. H., *Prince Michael Vorontsov, Viceroy to the Tsar*, Montreal 1990

Robb, Graham, *Balzac*, London 1994

Roider, Karl A., *Austria's Eastern Question 1700–1790*, Princeton 1982

Roider, Karl A., 'Kaunitz, Joseph II and the Turkish War', SEER (October 1976) 54 no 4

Rose, Kenneth, *George V*, London 1983

Rotikov, K. K., *Drugoy Peterburg*, St Petersburg 1998

Rulikowski, Edward, *Smila*, Slownik geograficzny krolestwa polskiego i innych krajow, slowianskich (ed Filip Sulimierski, Bronislaw Chlebowski and Wladyslaw Walewski), vol 10, Warsaw 1889

Russkiy Biographicheskiy Slovar (including biographies of Varvara Golitsyna vol 5 1916; Ekaterina Skavronskaya vol 18 1904, I. A. Hannibal vol 4 1914; P. S. and M. S. Potemkin vol 14 1904) vol 1–25, A. A. Polovtsev, St Petersburg 1896–1916

Ruud, Charles A., and Stepanov, Sergei A., *Fontanka 16: The Tsars' Secret Police*, Quebec 1999

Segal, Harold G., *The Literature of Eighteenth-Century Russia*, New York 1967

Semevsky, M. I., *Grigory Alexandrovich Potemkin-Tavrichesky*, RS (1875) 3

Semevsky, M. I., *Vosemnadtsatyy vek, istoricheskiye sbornik*, Russkaya Starina, vols 12–14, St Petersburg 1875

Shahmagonov, N. R., *Hrani Gospod' Potemkina*, Moscow 1991

Shaw, Stanford J., *Between the Old and New: The Ottoman Empire under Selim III 1789–1807*, Cambridge, Mass. 1971

Shilder, N. K., *Imperator Aleksandr I*, St Petersburg 1890–1904

Shilder, N. K. *Imperator Pavel Pervyy*, St Petersburg 1901

Shugorov, M. F., *Prince Potemkin's Tomb*, RA (1867)

Shvidkovsky, Dimitri, *The Empress and the Architect: British Architecture and*

Gardens at the Court of Catherine the Great, New Haven/London 1996

Skalkovsky, A., *Chronological Review of New Russia 1730–1823*, Odessa 1836

Skalkovsky, A., *The History of the New Sech or the Last Zaporogian Kosh*, Odessa 1886

Soldatsky, A., *Secret of the Prince*, ZOOID 9

Soloveytchik, George, *Potemkin: A Picture of Catherine's Russia*, London 1938

Soloveytchik, George, *Potemkin: Soldier, Statesman, Lover and Consort of Catherine of Russia*, New York 1947

Soloviev, S. M., *Istoriya padeniya polshi*, Moscow 1863

Soloviev, S. M., *Istoriya rossii s drevneyshikh vremyon*, Moscow 1959–66

Storch, H. von, *Annalen der Regierung Katharina der Zweyten, Kaiserin von Russland*, Leipzig 1798

Storch, H. von, *Tableau historique et statistique de l'Empire de Russie*, Paris/Basle, 1801

Suny, Ronald Grigor, *The Making of the Georgian Nation*, Bloomington/Indianapolis 1988/1994

Temperley, Harold, *Frederick the Great and Kaiser Joseph*, London 1968

Tillyard, Stella, *Aristocrats*, London 1995

Tiktopulo, Y. A., *The Mirage of Tsargrad: On the Destiny of Catherine's Greek Project*, Rodina 1991

Timoshevsky, G. I., *Mariupol and its Environs*, Mariupol 1892

Tolstoy, A., *Peter the Great*, Moscow 1932

Tolstoy, L., 'Hadji Murat', in *Master and Man and Other Stories*, Penguin Classics, London 1977

Tourneux, M., *Diderot et Catherine II*, Paris 1899

Trowbridge, W. R. H., *Cagliostro: The Splendour and Misery of a Master of Magic*, London 1910

Troyat, Henri, *Catherine the Great*, London 1977

Troyat, Henri, *Pushkin*, Paris 1946, New York 1970

Ustinov, V. I., 'Moguchiy velikoross', (1991) no 12

Vallentin, Antonina, *Mirabeau, Voice of the Revolution*, London 1948

Vassilchikov, A. A., *Semeystvo Razumovskikh*, St Petersburg 1880

Vernadsky, G. V., *History of Russia*, New Haven 1954

Vernadsky, G. V., *Ocherk istorii prava russkogo gosudarstva XVIII–XIX v*, Prague 1924

Vernadsky, G. V., *Russkoye masonstvo v tsarstvovovaniye Ekateriny II*, Petrograd 1917

Vernadsky, G. V., *Imperatritsa Ekaterina II i Zakonodatclnaya Komissiya 1767–68*, Perm 1918

Vinogradov, V. N., *The Century of Catherine II*, Novaya i noveyshaya istoriya no 4, Moscow 1996

Vitale, Serena, *Pushkin's Button: The Story of the Fatal Duel that Killed Russia's Greatest Poet*, London 1999

Vyborny, P. M., *Nikolaev*, Odessa 1973

Waliszewski, K., *Autour d'un trône*, Paris 1894

Waliszewski, K., *The Romance of an Empress: Catherine II of Russia*, New York 1894, Paris 1893

Weidle, Wladimir, *Russia: Absent and Present*, London 1952

Wheatcroft, Andrew, *The Habsburgs*, London 1995

White, T. H., *The Age of Scandal*, London 1950

Wilson, Arthur M., *Diderot*, New York 1972

Yavornitskiy, D. I., *Istoriya goroda Ekaterinoslava*, Dniepropetrovsk 1996

Yeliseeva, O. I., *G. A. Potemkin's Geopolitical Projects, Associates of Catherine the Great*, lecture at conference Moscow, 22/23 September 1997, published Moscow 1997

Yeliseeva, O. I., *Lubenzy moy pitomez: Catherine II and G. A. Potemkin in the Years of the Second Russo-Turkish War*, Otechestvennya Istoriya (1997) 4

Yeliseeva, O. I., *Noble Moscow, from the History of the Political Life of Eighteenth-Century Russia* (including *Red Coat*), Moscow 1997

Zagorovsky, E. A., *Organisation of the Administration in New Russia under Potemkin 1774–91*, Odessa 1913

Zagorovsky, E. A., *Potemkin's Economic Policy in New Russia*, Odessa 1926

Zakalinskaya, E. P., *Votchinye khozyaystva Mogilevskoy gubernii vo vtoroy polovinye XVIII veka*, Mogilev 1958

Zamoyski, Adam, *Holy Madness: Romantics, Patriots and Revolutionaries 1776–1871*, London 1999

Zamoyski, Adam, *The Last King of Poland*, London 1992

Zayev, L., Motherland of Prince Potemkin, IV, St Petersburg 1899

Zheludov, Victor M., '*Favurit russiski* [*Russian favourite*]', '*Pero istorii soyedinilo ikh* [*History's pen has written them*]', '*Serdtse knyazya Potemkina* [*Potemkin's heart*]', '*Zdes rodilsia Potemkin* [*Here Potemkin was born*]' and '*Tsarski kolodets* [*The Tsarina's well*]', all published in *Rayonnay Gazeta* of the Dukhovshchina Region of Smolensk Oblast, 6 May 1996, 14 December 1995, 12 October 1993, 6 August 1992 respectively

Ziegler, Philip, *The Duchess of Dino*, London 1962

Zotov, V., *Cagliostro: His Life and Visit to Russia*, RS (1875)

Zubov, P. A., *Knyaz Platon Alexandrovich Zubov 1767–1822*, RS 16 and 17

Zuev, V., *Travel Notes*, Istoricheskiy i geographicheskiy mesyazeslov, St Petersburg 1782–3

INDEX

Simon Sebag Montefiore

'When history is written this way, one can never have too much'
The Times

THE ROMANOVS
The intimate story of twenty tsars and tsarinas, touched by genius and madness, tainted by remorseless killing and sexual decadence, ruthless empire-building and palace conspiracy.

9780297852667 • £25.00 • Hardback
9781474600279 • £25.00 • Ebook
9781409161035 • £25.00 • Audio

JERUSALEM: THE BIOGRAPHY
The epic 3,000-year history of the city at the centre of the world.
'Utterly compelling from start to finish'
Sunday Times

9781780220253 • £12.99 • Paperback
9780297858645 • £9.99 • Ebook
9781409113799 • £25.00 • Audio

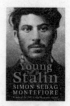

YOUNG STALIN
The dramatic early life of one of history's most dangerous and enigmatic men.
'A masterpiece'
The Times

9780753823798 • £9.99 • Paperback
9780297863847 • £9.99 • Ebook
9780752888927 • £16.99 • Audio

STALIN: THE COURT OF THE RED TSAR
The thrilling biography of Stalin and his entourage in the terrifying decades of his supreme power.
'The most civilised and elegant chronicle of brutality and ruthlessness I have ever read'
Daily Telegraph

9781780228358 • £12.99 • Paperback
9780297863854 • £12.99 • Ebook
9780752884691 • £19.99 • Audio

CATHERINE THE GREAT AND POTEMKIN: THE IMPERIAL LOVE AFFAIR
A sweeping tale of passion, power, conquest and extravagance on a magnificent Russian scale.
'One of the great love stories of history'
Economist

9781780228341 • £14.99 • Paperback
9780297866237 • £14.99 • Ebook